D0208546

NEW TESTAMENT GREEK

Gerald L. Stevens

UNIVERSITY
PRESS OF
AMERICA

Lanham • New York • London

Copyright © 1994 by
University Press of America,® Inc.
4720 Boston Way
Lanham, Maryland 20706

3 Henrietta Street
London WC2E 8LU England

Library of Congress Cataloging-in-Publication Data

Stevens, Gerald L.
New Testament Greek / Gerald L. Stevens.
p.   cm.
Includes bibliographical references and index.
1. Greek language, Biblical—Grammar—Textbooks.   I. Title.
PA817.S73   1994   487'.4—dc20   94-20696 CIP

ISBN 0-8191-9600-2 (cloth : alk. paper)

Second Printing, corrected, October 1995

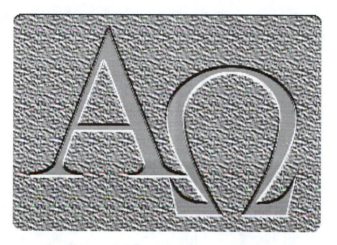

dedicated to my students
past, present, and future

TABLE OF CONTENTS

LIST OF TABLES

xi

xiii

PREFACE
A Better Mousetrap

First, because I thought I could build a better mousetrap. More tables. Generous graphics. And greater point sizes! How can you learn what you cannot *see*? Second, because personal computers have changed the landscape of teaching forever, for those who will access the technology. Desktop publishing was a revolution of the 1980s that now is commonplace—except in education! I wanted to reverse that trend and to contribute an appealing text.

Third, because my students always were hounding me after class for copies of overhead cells used to present lesson material. I always demurred, insisting I wanted to publish at some point. Well, here they are—you can stop hassling me now. OK?

"What To Learn." This text is written as both a beginning and intermediate grammar. A section at the end of each lesson entitled "What To Learn" reduces all discussion to salient points to master. This section is divided into two parts, when applicable, "Beginning" and "Advanced." The first part lists items to learn for first-year Greek students. The items under "Advanced" are for intermediate students. First-year students who want to investigate

What To Learn—LESSON 1 (εἶς)

Beginning
☐ 1. The Greek alphabet, in order, with proper formation and pronunciation
☐ 2. Vowel quantities
☐ 3. Definition of a *diphthong* and the twelve diphthongs
☐ 4. The two Greek *breathing* marks and their effect upon pronunciation
☐ 5. The three Greek *accent* marks and their effect upon pronunciation
☐ 6. The five Greek *punctuation* marks
☐ 7. Transliteration equivalents
☐ 8. Vocabulary words

Advanced
☐ 9. Definitions of *majuscule*, *uncial* and *minuscule* letters
☐ 10. Definition of *scripto continua*
☐ 11. The two ways to indicate quotations in Greek
☐ 12. Definitions of *diaeresis*, *elision*, and *crasis*

further will profit from studying the "Advanced" material. However, discussion in the lesson itself is not divided into beginning and advanced. I have found that many beginning students go ahead and pick up information along the way if they are not told in advance, "Do not learn this." Also, discussion that is broken into beginning and advanced parts is more cumbersome for review later. The strategy is that the beginning student will read through all the material once, check the "What To Learn" section at the end for specific items to work on and reread that information.

This double exposure has pedagogical purpose. However, on a few occasions, the beginning student will be advised to skip over certain material. Translation often incorporates syntactical considerations, usually reserved for intermediate study. However, on occasion, the beginning student is introduced to some syntax, which just seemed imperative for learning what "translation" is all about in the first place.

Structure. Thirty-four total lessons are designed to be thorough in coverage of beginning grammar, but also to be quite adaptable. A few lessons might be ignored without too much disruption of the structure and plan of the book. (Vocabulary still would need to be covered.) Other lessons might be combined by whatever rationale seems appropriate to the professor.

Noun System. The entire noun system is covered by Lesson 15 and all adjectives and numerals by Lesson 17. Great advantage seems to accrue by concentrating on all the nouns early in the study of Greek, rather than parceling out disparate pieces of the noun system over too long a time, leaving the whole unconnected.

Verb System. However, neither is the student left in the dark about Greek verbs the entire time studying nouns. Present active indicative is treated in Lesson 3, and the first principal part has been covered by Lesson 13. Then, Lesson 18 begins a steady charge through the rest of the indicative mood, infinite forms of infinitives and participles, the other moods, and concluding with two lessons on -μι verbs.

Lagniappe. We have a wonderful little word coming from the French heritage of the south Louisiana bayous, "lagniappe" (lan-yap). Lagniappe was a small gift a store owner would give in appreciation to a customer who had made a purchase. Now we use the word to mean any nice "extra" thrown in for fun or interest: gifts, comments, or even stories that illustrate our conversation. I want Greek students to become fascinated by the manuscripts that give us our New Testament and research tools such as textual criticism. So I have thrown in a little lagniappe. The readings, which fall at the end of some chapters after the "What To Learn" section, are not required and are just for fun. Perhaps they will stir the inquisitive to learn more.

Methodology. The approach is traditional.[1] The method is deductive, the content grammatically and exegetically oriented. The text moves from basic verb

---

[1] A lively debate has entered discussions of New Testament Greek. Traditional categories have been challenged. Many individuals are involved in these discussions, but the issues most clearly seem focused in Bruce M. Fanning, *Verbal Aspect in New Testament Greek* (Oxford: Clarendon Press, 1990) and Stanley E. Porter, *Verbal Aspect in the Greek of the New Testament, with Reference to Tense and Mood* (New York: Peter Lang, 1989). A more accessible form of Porter's views is found in Stanley E. Porter, *Idioms of the Greek New Testament*, Biblical Languages: Greek 2 (Sheffield: JSOT Press, 1992). The debate is summarized concisely in Stanley E. Porter and D. A. Carson, eds., *Biblical Greek Language and Linguistics: Open Questions in Current Research*, Journal for the Study of the New Testament Supplement Series 80 (Sheffield: JSOT Press, 1993). Any effort toward understanding the Greek grammar of the New Testament will have to struggle with the issues as they have been formulated in the debates between Fanning and Porter. While this is true, what is *not* clear at the present time is exactly how the dust will settle out from these engaging arguments. Especially

and noun structures to more subtle syntactical nuances in an effort to weave all lessons into a building, harmonious whole. Similarity is used as a pedagogical tool. Vocabulary is organized from frequency lists and carefully worked into sentences for translation.

English to Greek. A number of students who sit down for the first time in a Greek class to learn Greek do not even know English. The procedure has been to present English grammar first at the beginning of a new unit of material and then build a bridge to Greek grammar where similarity can function as a teaching tool.

Diagramming. Diagramming is required of beginning students. The results for understanding Greek are a quantum leap, because students are forced to grapple seriously with English grammar—sometimes for the first time in their educational career. However, diagramming may be moved to the "Advanced" section if desired.

Analyses. Syntax discussion follows the suggested categories and terminology from Brooks and Winbery (*Syntax of New Testament Greek*). Morphological analysis in the main conforms to their material on morphology (*Morphology of New Testament Greek: A Review and Reference Grammar*). The goal was to provide a beginning text in grammar that facilitated a smooth transition to these advanced texts. However, any shortcomings in the grammar are fully my own, to be sure.

The five case system is used. At the same time, in preparation for a later course in syntax, eight functions are covered. Consistently the word "function" is used to refer to ablative, locative, and instrumental uses. These uses, while not labeled cases, are not "brand new" to the student when they hit syntax, e.g., with prepositions.

Biblical Examples. Examples are copious. Almost every single item discussed has at least one example from the New Testament text, many with several. I have worked hard to find my own illustrations in many hours of personal research in standard concordances. I used no concording software, except vocabulary searches in *MacBible*. I have endeavored not to replicate common examples one can cull from other texts, although sometimes the best examples are few and must be repeated.

Exercises. A workbook of exercises is included. Inductive methodology is integrated into this material, so that the student receives the best of both worlds. Sentences are taken from the biblical text. The student translates the Bible from the very beginning, an approach very rewarding and encouraging in beginning Greek.

Vocabulary. Vocabulary is emphasized without apology. I disagree strongly with the idea that vocabulary work past a given frequency is "unproductive."

---

unclear at the moment is how the results methodologically should work their way into introductory grammars. For those who must teach elementary Greek and are curious where to position this effort in the context of the Fanning/Porter debate, I have used the traditional categories and terminology that have been in place for some time. However, at times I have worked in here and there observations which any conversant reader could trace to these new discussions; I have been mildly eclectic in the matter. While the approach is conservative, this seemed the best course for the present.

Vocabulary acquisition is imperative for rapid reading and pure enjoyment of the Greek text. Students *will* learn vocabulary: (1) if they are asked to, and (2) are reading the Greek New Testament regularly. You can parse a form all day long knowing every constituent part meticulously, but if the lexical meaning is not in your head and a dictionary not nearby, you are pretty much dead in the water.

Memorization. Paradigms and tables are given, but short cuts are suggested to reduce the load of memory work. Some modern linguistic research and principles have been worked in without much technical terminology to take advantage of the assistance given in learning another language. The inductive workbook material should help significantly here.

Indexes. Tables and charts include the ubiquitous paradigms, principal parts of verbs, substantive declensions, and so forth. Three vocabularies are included: Greek to English, Greek Vocabulary by Lesson and English to Greek. A full subject index covers even minor elements.

Useful Items. Other useful items that I hope contribute to the value of this text include an Appendix, "On the Art of Translation," which introduces the need for developing a translation theory, and the ideas of formal and functional equivalence. A Glossary of terms provides a useful and handy reference to remind the student of technical terminology introduced in the grammar, and even contains more detail than in the grammar on certain topics. An Annotated Bibliography contains about seventy-five resources covering the topics of texts and textual criticism, lexical aids, grammar and syntax, concordances, wordbooks, semantics and linguistics, and exegesis and interpretation—to launch the student into further study.

I hope all this makes for a very worthwhile addition to the library of the beginning and intermediate Greek student. You still may ask, "So what's new?" Well, as Philip said to Nathanael (John 1:46),

Ἔρχου καὶ ἴδε.

ACKNOWLEDGMENTS

United Bible Societies, 1865 Broadway, New York, NY 10023 for use of selections from *The Greek New Testament*, Fourth Revised Edition, Barbara Aland, Kurt Aland, Johannes Karavidopoulos, Carlo M. Martini, and Bruce M. Metzger, editors. Published by United Bible Societies and Deutsche Bibelgesellschaft, 1966, 1993, in exercises and examples, and the image of page eight of UBS[4] in Table 30.9, p. 359. Used by permission. All rights reserved.

Wm. B. Eerdmans Publishing Co., 255 Jefferson Ave. SE, Grand Rapids, MI 49503 for the use of the clay lamp image heading the "What To Learn" sections, from a photograph by Everett Ferguson in *Backgrounds of Early Christianity*, p. 104, the Milan Archeological Museum. Used by permission. All rights reserved.

Linguist's Software, P. O. Box 580, Edmonds, WA 98020 (206-775-1130; fax 206-771-5911) for the fonts *Hebraica*, *Graeca*, and *SymbolGreek* used in this work. Used by permission. All rights reserved.

Howard Vos, King's College, 150 Lodge Rd., Briarcliffe Manor, NY 10510 for the scanned image of the Greek capital marking chapter beginnings and endings taken from the *Wycliffe Historical Geography of Bible Lands* (Grand Rapids: Moody Press, 1967). Used by permission. All rights reserved.

Foundation Martin Bodmer, Bibliotheca Bodmeriana, 19–21, Route Du Guignard, CH–1223, Cologny-Genève, Switzerland for the lines from $\mathfrak{P}^{66}$ and $\mathfrak{P}^{75}$ used on p. 80 and the images of $\mathfrak{P}^{66}$ and $\mathfrak{P}^{75}$ on pp. 92 and 166 respectively, from *Papyrus Bodmer II, Supplement, Evangile de Jean, chap. 14–21;* Nouvelle édition augmentée et corrigée: avec reproduction photographique complète du manuscrit, chap. 1–21 (Cologny-Genève, Switzerland: Bibliothèque Bodmer, 1962) and from *Papyrus Bodmer XIV–XV: Evangiles de Luc et Jean, Tome II, XV: Jean, chap. 1–15* (Cologny-Genève, Switzerland: Bibliothèque Bodmer, 1961). Used by permission. All rights reserved.

Harvard University Press, 79 Garden Street, Cambridge, Mass. 02138, for the image of Lectionary 59 on p. 7, the Synod Collection of the Moscow State Historical Museum, from William Henry Paine Hatch, *Facsimiles and Descriptions of Minuscule Manuscripts of the New Testament* (Cambridge, Mass.: Harvard University Press, 1951). Used by permission. All rights reserved.

Oxford University Press, Walton Street, Oxford, England OX2 6DP, for the image of Codex Sinaiticus on pp. 7, 194 and 302 from Helen and Kirsopp Lake, *Codex*

Sinaiticus Petropolitanus: The New Testament, The Epistle of Barnabas and the Shepherd of Hermas, Preserved in the Imperial Library of St. Petersburg, Now Reproduced in Facsimile From Photographs by Helen and Kirsopp Lake, with a Description and Introduction to the History of the Codex by Kirsopp Lake (The Clarendon Press, 1911); Alexandrinus on p. 146 from Frederick G. Kenyon, *The Codex Alexandrinus (Royal MS. 1 D v–viii) in Reduced Photographic Facsimile; New Testament and Clementine Epistles* (1909); 𝔓⁴⁶ on p. 286 from Frederic G. Kenyon, *The Chester Beatty Biblical Papyri: Descriptions and Texts of Twelve Manuscripts on Papyrus of the Greek Bible; Fasciculus III Supplement: Pauline Epistles* (1937). By permission of Oxford University Press. All rights reserved.

Cambridge University Library, West Road, Cambridge, England CB3 9DR, for the image of Codex Bezae, p. 80, from *Codex Bezae Cantabrigiensis, Quattuor Euangelia et Actus Apostolorum, Complectens Graece et Latine, Sumptibus Academiae Phototypice Repraesentatus; Tomus Posterior*. (London: Cantabrigiae, 1899). By permission of the Syndics of Cambridge University Library. All rights reserved.

Broadman Press, The Baptist Sunday School Board, 127 Ninth Avenue, North, Nashville, TN 37234 for the composite scanned image of the pen, ink well, and manuscript, p. 233, derived from William Stephens, *The New Testament World in Pictures* (Nashville: Broadman Press, 1987), pp. 144–45. Used by permission. All rights reserved.

Bibliotheca Apostolica Vaticana, 00120 Città del Vaticano, for the image of MS. Vat. gr. 1209 ("Codex Vaticanus") on p. 156. Used by permission. All rights reserved.

The John Rylands University Library, University of Manchester, Oxford Road, Manchester M13 9PP, England, for the image of 𝔓⁵² on p. 244. Reproduced by courtesy of the Director and University Librarian, the John Rylands University Library of Manchester. Used by permission. All rights reserved.

American Academy of Arts and Sciences, Norton's Woods, 136 Irving Street, Cambridge, Mass. 02138, for the image of Ms. 375 on p. 320 from *Dated Greek Minuscule Manuscripts to the Year 1200*. Kirsopp and Silva Lake, eds. Vol. 10: Manuscripts in Florence, Athens, Grottaferrata and the Meteora (Boston, Mass.: The American Academy of Arts and Sciences, 1939). Used by permission. All rights reserved.

Öffentliche Bibliothek der Universität Basel, Schöbeinstrasse 18-20, 4056 Basel, Switzerland, for the image of Greek Gospel MS. 2 on p. 328 from Mscr. A N IV 1, f. 138r. Used by permission. All rights reserved.

This project was done on a Macintosh computer using *Microsoft Word* 5.1 and an Apple LaserWriter Select 360. Some searches utilized Zondervan's *MacBible* 2.1. A few graphics were created in MicroFrontier's *Color It!* 2.3. Scans were taken with Thunderware's Lightning Scan Pro/256 and edited in *ThunderWorks* 2.0.

I am indebted to those whose contributions facilitated this work. These have included James J. Cate, W. Craig Mann, Yajaira L. Rincon, and my colleagues Charles A. Ray, Thomas L. Strong, and William F. Warren, Jr. The Greek Grammar class, Fall 1993, provided invaluable feedback. Helpful observations were received gladly from Carlton L. Winbery and James A. Brooks. Billy K. Smith, academic dean, assisted not only by his continual encouragement, but by granting a teaching load reduction in the final writing stage. Gregory Julius compiled the vocabulary subsets for use in the *Memcards* software. Important assistance also was rendered by Joseph W. Looney and Janis van Meerveld, for which I am grateful.

My wife, Jean, was integral to the success at every stage. Her constant faith, her prayers, and her words of encouragement never will be repaid. Jean also contributed substantially by procuring copyright permissions, proofreading, and assisting in the tedious job of compiling the indexes. That's true love.

My students helped the most. They taught me Greek.

❧

Your communications will be appreciated, corrections especially. Write to: Gerald L. Stevens, NOBTS, 3939 Gentilly Blvd., New Orleans, LA 70126. I also would be happy to hear your comments. Our seminary switchboard is 504-282-4455.

❧

- Apple is a registered service mark; LaserWriter is a registered trademark; and Macintosh is a trademark licensed to Apple Computer, Inc.
- Color It! is a registered trademark of MicroFrontier, Inc.
- Graeca, Hebraica, and SymbolGreek are registered trademarks of Linguist's Software.
- Helvetica and Times are registered trademarks of Linotype AG.
- ITC Zapf Dingbats copyright © International Typeface Corporation 1991. All rights reserved.
- LightningScan, Thunderware, and ThunderWorks are registered trademarks of Thunderware, Inc.
- MacBible is a registered trademark of The Zondervan Corporation.
- Memcards is a registered trademark of Memorization Technology.
- Microsoft and Microsoft Word are registered trademarks of Microsoft Corporation.
- Nadianne Book is a registered trademark of Agfa, a Division of Miles, Inc.

INTRODUCTION
The Language of God's Revelation

 Greeks have been writing for thousands of years. At least five stages in these millenniums can be specified: (1) the earliest stage of "Linear B" back to the 13th century B.C., (2) the stage of "Classical Greek" from the 8th through 4th centuries, Homer to Plato, building on a basically Phoenician alphabet (as did Hebrew), (3) the stage of "Hellenistic Greek," or "koine" usually associated with the conquest of the world by Alexander the Great (336-323 B.C.) which spread Greek culture and language to non-Greek peoples, (4) the Byzantine stage, when Greek manuscripts were being copied in Byzantium until that city fell to the Ottoman Turks in A.D. 1453, and (5) the stage of modern Greek. Those who study the Greek language, especially Classical, are impressed by its power and ability to capture every nuance of meaning in human communication.

Yet until just this century, Biblical scholars were bewildered by New Testament Greek. The rules of grammar and syntax were mysteriously different from the Classical Greek of Homer. The unexplained phenomena of New Testament Greek generated abundant, sometimes fantastic, theories. Favorites included "Hebraisms" and "Holy Ghost Greek." Some thought the unusual Greek of the New Testament was the result of disciples who spoke Aramaic and tried to write in Greek, creating a mutant or "Hebrew" Greek. Others—substituting piety for history—wildly speculated that the Greek of the New Testament represented the "perturbations of inspiration." That is, the New Testament must have been the natural result of almost uncontrollable Spirit ecstasy which threw all grammar and rules of grammar to the four winds. After all, God was not subject to the rules of humans! Some more moderately suggested that New Testament Greek simply was tailor-made, a sort of "God's Greek" created uniquely for the New Testament revelation!

However, at the turn of this century, the scholar Adolf Deissmann revolutionized our understanding of New Testament Greek. Deissmann had devoted his life to a study of the New Testament and knew the Greek of the New Testament as an expert. Yet he also was unable to explain the grammar and syntax with Classical standards. However, Egyptian papyri recently had been discovered in the hot sands of Egypt, written in Greek, which Deissmann became acquainted with by pure serendipity. These Egyptian documents represented a typical ancient Egyptian "trash basket" of old letters, receipts, wills, incantations, and the like. Deissmann was surprised that he could translate these documents. He began to realize that his "training" had been his study of New Testament Greek. Suddenly, New Testament Greek was discovered to be not some specially commissioned "Holy Ghost Greek" but the commonly spoken, or "koine," Greek. The grammar and syntax was that of a non-literary Hellenistic Greek, the Greek of the marketplace, such as in these Egyptian materials. New Testament Greek was the everyday Greek spoken by any commoner in the Hellenistic world, from slave to free. With Deissmann's discovery, the study of New Testament Greek took a quantum leap in understanding and catalyzed the production of the great, magisterial Greek lexicons of this century, thus revolutionizing our study of the New Testament.

However, the implications of this language of the New Testament actually are much more profound than lexicons or "Holy Ghost Greek." Christmas, after all, is the story of humility. God who came in the flesh was found wrapped in swaddling clothes, lying in a feeding trough, worshipped not by emperors but by common shepherds in the field. Yet that's the beauty. His place was common. His language was everyday. His life for every person.

God's language, in the end, is *my* language. And why not? How else could genuine revelation take place?

This Greek language, then, supremely belongs to you. It's the common tongue of anyone of the first century you would have wanted to tell the story. The study of New Testament Greek is worth your devotion. Your challenge is to make this Greek the common language for those who live in your world, those who need to hear the Good News announced within these sacred pages of the New Testament.

LESSON 1 (εἶς)
Writing and Pronouncing Greek

 The ancient Greeks had several dialects. The Dorian Hellenes who invaded Greece around 1100 B.C. distinctively maintained their particular cultural and linguistic traits. Cities such as Sparta and Corinth transmitted Dorian influence to the Greek world. The Doric dialect was heard in the Peloponnesus, Crete, and various Aegean islands, as well as Sicily and southern Italy. Another group of Hellenes, the Ionians, provided the basic Greek alphabet later adopted at Athens.

The greatest influence upon the Greek language was provided by the Hellenes of ancient Attica (Athens). The Attic dialect developed with remarkable beauty and style and became the premier dialect of literary expression. Preciseness and elegance were prominent features. This Attic dialect continued to impact Greek language centuries later. Some phenomena of New Testament Greek are explained as "Attic influence." One might compare praying today with "Thee's" and "Thou's," even though these seventeenth-century English terms are archaic and defunct in contemporary English.

Alexander the Great expanded into a world empire the Macedonian power base his father had welded together from the unwilling Greek city-states (336–323 B.C.). Alexander, who had tutored under the famous Aristotle, loved all things Greek, and promoted the already expanding influence of the Greek language in his cosmopolitan vision for his empire. Greek thus became a second tongue for the world.

However, the use of Greek by non-Greeks altered the language. A continual metamorphosis transformed the ancient native dialects within the new world order of Alexander. The fine nuance of meanings within the sophisticated Attic Greek began to blur. Grammatical principles were "broken" (as English are told not to split infinitives but do all the time). This second-language Greek became the common tongue of all, which we call koine Greek. New Testament Greek basically is this koine Greek, but also includes literary Greek, as well as unusual forms due to Semitic influence.

The Greek Alphabet

The term "alphabet" is borrowed from the first two Greek letter names, "alpha" and "beta." The following table gives the koine letters of the Greek New Testament,

1

the Greek "A, B, C's." (Ancient Greek had a few other letters, such as digamma, Ϝ.)
The letters do not follow the English order exactly. Footnotes are on the next page.

Table 1.1 The Greek Alphabet

Letter		Name	English	Pronunciation
majuscule	*minuscule*	*common*	*transliteration*	*academic*
A	α	alpha	a	*a*lms, *a*lley (short)
B	β	beta	b	*b*etter
Γ	γ	gamma	g, n[1]	*g*ambit
Δ	δ	delta	d	*d*elta
E	ε	epsilon	e	*e*pic
Z	ζ	zeta	z	*z*oo, a*dz*e (internal)[2]
H	η	eta	e[3]	pr*ey*
Θ	θ	theta	th	*th*in
I	ι[4]	iota	i, y[5]	id*i*om, *i*diom (short)
K	κ	kappa	k, c[6]	*k*ayak
Λ	λ	lamba	l	*l*amb
M	μ	mu	m	*m*usic
N	ν	nu	n	*n*uclear
Ξ	ξ	xi	x	he*x*
O	ο	omicron	o[7]	*o*melet
Π	π	pi	p	*p*ie
P	ρ	rho	r	*r*oad
Σ	σ and ς[8]	sigma	s	*s*ignal
T	τ	tau	t	*t*aunt
Υ	υ	upsilon	u, y[9]	*u*se, *u*sher (short)
Φ	φ	phi	ph	*ph*ilosophy
X	χ	chi	ch	*ch*iropractic
Ψ	ψ	psi	ps	li*ps*
Ω	ω	omega	o[10]	*o*mit

Table 1.2 Vowel Quantity

Quantity	Vowels
short	ε, ο
long	η, ω
(diphthongs)	αι, αυ ει, ευ, οι, ου υι, ηυ, ωυ
variable	α, ι, υ

Pronunciation. We do not know exactly how koine Greek was spoken. The Renaissance scholar Erasmus often is credited with devising a system based on Latin for standardizing the pronunciation of Greek. This "academic" system, not really connected to how Aristotle or the Apostle Paul spoke Greek, is that generally used in institutions today, with some elements unclear. Modern Greek is different and will confuse you.

Vowels. Vowels can be short, long or variable (either short or long, simply learned by observation). The short vowels are epsilon (ε), and omicron (ο). The long vowels are eta (η), omega (ω). The variable vowels are α, ι, υ.

---

[1]Some gamma combinations yield an "n" sound: γγ = ng, γκ = nk, γξ = nx, γχ = nch. Thus, ἄγγελος = *angelos* ("angel"); ἐγκαίνια = *enkāinia* ("renewal"); λάρυγξ = *larynx* ("throat"); σπλάγχνα = *splanchna* ("compassion"). See Table 1.6.

[2]When zeta is within a word, its pronunciation is more "voiced" (more resonance in the voice box), hence "dz" for pronunciation. For example, ζάω = *zaō* ("I live"), but σῴζω = *sōidzō* ("I save").

[3]Eta is a long "e." Write with a stroke over the letter. For example, ἐκκλησία = *ekklēsia* ("church").

[4]A small iota called "iota subscript" may be found beneath the three vowels alpha (α), eta (η), and omega (ω), i.e., ᾳ, ῃ, ῳ. For a capitalized vowel, the iota subscript must be written after the vowel. This form is called "iota adscript." Iota subscript is transliterated the main vowel first, with a stroke over it to indicate a long vowel, then an "i" following. For example, λύῃ = *luēi* ("you are being loosed").

[5]Hebrew terms beginning with the consonant *yod* (ʼ) come into Greek as an iota (I). This iota for the *yod* is transliterated two different ways, depending on whether a vowel follows. When a vowel follows, the *yod* is given as "Y." When no vowel follows, the *yod* is given as "I." Thus, יַעֲקֹב comes into Greek as Ἰακώβ = *Yacōb* ("Jacob"), but יִשְׂרָאֵל is Ἰσραήλ = *Israēl* ("Israel"). When the "y" sound then is made into an English word, the equivalent letter used is "J" (e.g., "Jacob"). In the example used above (Ἰακώβ), do not confuse the initial Greek smooth breathing mark (ʼ) with the Hebrew consonant *yod* (ʼ). The Greek mark simply notifies smooth breathing for the initial vowel iota (ι). Smooth breathing marks are discussed later.

[6]Those Greek words coming into English through the Latin use "c" for the kappa (κ). E.g., the word "canon" is from the Latin, *canon*, which is itself from the Greek, κανών, (*kanōn*).

[7]Whether the koine omicron (ο) was pronounced exactly as the koine omega (ω)—as in modern Greek—is argued. We choose to distinguish for clarity.

[8]The sigma form σ is written within a word. The sigma form ς is called "final sigma." This alternate letter form is written at the end of a Greek word. I.e., σεισμός = *seismos* ("earthquake").

[9]Upsilon (υ) normally is transliterated as "y." The "u" is used for diphthongs (double vowels). For example, ὑπό = *hypo* ("under"), in which the upsilon (υ) is transliterated by a "y"; compare *hypodermic*, "under the skin." However, αὐτός = *autos* ("he"); the upsilon (υ) is transliterated by a "u" as part of the initial diphthong αυ-. *Do not confuse Greek pronunciation with English transliteration.* The pronunciation of ὑπό is "hupo," sounded as "hoopah;" (short "o;" some would sound as "hoopō," long "o"). The initial mark over the upsilon (ʽ) is "rough breathing," transliterated by an "h." Rough breathing marks are discussed later.

[10]Omega is long "o;" write with a stroke over the letter. For example, ζάω = *zaō* ("I live").

Table 1.3   Diphthongs

Vowels	Pronunciation
αι	*ai*sle
αυ	*ou*t (some: *au*tumn)
ει	*ei*ght (some: h*ei*ght)[10]
ευ	[ehü] (no equivalent)[11]
οι	*oi*l
ου	gr*ou*p
υι	s*ui*te (notice "w" feel)
ηυ	[äü] (no equivalent)
ωυ	s*ou*l

Diphthongs. An "open" vowel is made by an open mouth when sounded (α, ε, ο, η, ω). "Close" vowels tend to close the mouth when sounded (both υ and ι). *Diphthongs are double vowel units sounded together as one.* The second vowel always is iota (ι) or upsilon (υ), because either of these vowels "close" the sounding of the diphthong unit. *All diphthongs are long* (αι, αυ, ει, ευ, οι, ου, υι, and the rare ηυ and ωυ). The diphthong exception is that *αι and οι are considered short when final* (that is, at the end of the word).

Proper diphthongs. These are the normal diphthongs. In other words, proper diphthongs are pronounced normally, combining open and close vowels into one sound, as expected.

Improper diphthongs. Vowels having iota subscript (ᾳ, ῃ, ῳ) are called "improper diphthongs" because the iota (ι) is not pronounced. This notation distinguishes forms only as *written* language, not as spoken. Yet, iota subscripts still are key for distinguishing inflectional forms, so the *iota subscript must be observed carefully.*

Consonants. By nature consonants are distinguished from vowels in how the air

Table 1.4 Improper Diphthongs

Vowels	Pronunciation
ᾳ	*a*lms (note: same as α)
ῃ	pr*ey* (note: same as η)
ῳ	*o*mit (note: same as ω)

flows during vocalization (interrupted or restricted). You can interrupt—"stop" or "mute"—the flow with the lips ("labials" as pi, π), the tongue at or just behind the teeth ("dentals" as tau, τ) or the tongue at the roof of the mouth ("palatals" as kappa, κ). Or, you can just restrict the air flow, allowing some air to escape during pronunciation, creating a "continuant" or a "fricative" (as in theta, θ). Most Greek consonants are easy to pronounce; they have the equivalent pronunciation of their English counterparts. Some consonants need extra attention for proper pronunciation.

---

[10]Disagreement exists; we choose to distinguish from the cousin diphthong αι.
[11]No English phonetic equivalent exists for the short or long "e" sound diphthongs closed by upsilon (ευ, ηυ). "Feud" actually is f(y)üd, pronounced as "fee-ood." Neither the Greek epsilon (ε) nor the eta (η) is phonetically a "y" ("ee") sound. The combination of letters appears in the English word **leu**kemia, but this English diphthong is a long "oo." Sounds of ευ and ηυ must be approximated in English, as indicated.

Double Consonants. Five consonants require two letters for pronunciation. These are called "double consonants": theta (θ), phi (φ), chi (χ), psi (ψ), and internal zeta (ζ within a word). If xi (ξ) is to be pronounced "xs," it is being treated as a double consonant.

Table 1.5 Double Consonants

θ = th	φ = ph	χ = ch	ψ = ps	ζ = dz

Gamma Combinations. The gamma (γ) consonant modifies its pronunciation in certain combinations. The pronunciation is modified to an "n" (nasal) type sound.

Table 1.6 Gamma Combinations (Gamma Nasals)

Letters	Pronunciation	Example
γγ	si**ng**	ἄγγελος = *angelos* ("angel")
γκ	i**nk**	ἐγκαίνια = *enkainia* ("renewal")
γξ	lary**nx**	λάρυγξ = *larynx* ("throat")
γχ	I**nc**a (*not* soft as in "inch")	σπλάγχνα = *splanchna* ("compassion")

Mispronunciations. Some consonants have different air flow, making rough or smooth sounds, by different positions of tongue with teeth or palate. Notice carefully:
1. Gamma (γ)—always smooth, never rough (as in **g**o, never **g**iant)
2. Zeta (ζ) internal—always rough (as in su**ds**); thus, σῴζω = *sōidzō* ("I save")
3. Theta (θ)—always rough (as in **th**in, never as **th**en)
4. Sigma (σ)—always smooth (as in **s**ing, never as ro**s**e)

Proportions. Concentrate on the relative proportions of Greek letters.[12] Fix in your mind uncials and their corresponding minuscules. Say the letters orally, memorizing form with sound. Point to each letter as you move through the alphabet. The last line illustrates the iota subscript and rough and smooth breathing. The letters are formed first, then the appropriate marks are formed in connection with each letter.

---

[12]A common error is the guide rule's position, two thirds the distance from the base line.

Table 1.7 Formation of the Greek Letters

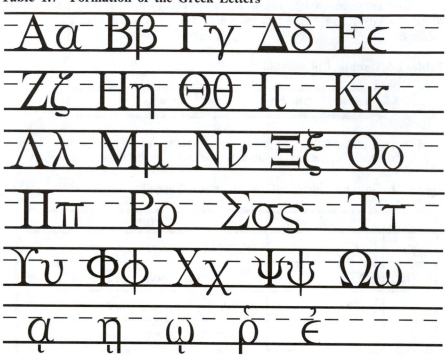

Uncials. Capital letters are "uncials" (also "majuscules"). Ancient uncial writing was a formal style for literary works. Each letter was formed carefully, separated from the next. The style had virtually no word divisions or accents, and no punctuation! This running of letters and words together is called *scripto continua* for "continuous script." Many ancient copies of the New Testament are uncials written in this *scripto continua*, the best coming from the third to sixth centuries. Cursive uncials, letters joined together for more rapid writing, were common in non-literary documents.

Uncial letters are used infrequently in today's edited text.[13] One will find them in four types of situations: (1) as the first letter of proper names, (2) at the beginning of a

---

[13]*The Greek New Testament, Fourth Edition,* Kurt Aland *et al.* eds., in cooperation with the Institute for New Testament Textual Research, Münster/Westphalia (New York: United Bible Societies, 1966, 1968, 1975, 1983, 1993). Abbreviated as UBS[4] hereinafter.

direct quotation, (3) at the beginning of a paragraph, or (4) at the beginning of a sentence understood to be a new thought.

Table 1.8   Greek Uncial and Minuscule Manuscripts

Codex Sinaiticus. Section image of one column of Codex Sinaiticus, a 4th century uncial. This manuscript has four columns, each just a little over 2 inches wide. Sinaiticus is one of our best uncial manuscripts, and the only one having the entire New Testament. The section above shows Luke 2:1–2.

Lectionary 59. Section image of one column of the Greek lectionary 59 (Fol. 81, verso), dated around the 10th century. This manuscript has two columns, each a little over 2.7 inches wide. One can see how the cursive minuscule hand is quite different than the stylized uncial script. The large capital A begins at Rom. 12:1.

Minuscules. Uncial writing eventually deteriorated in the process of time. Literary handwriting then reformed about the ninth century in a transition to a cursive minuscule hand. The term "minuscule" means small-case letters. Manuscript copying took place mostly in Byzantium, capital of the eastern Roman empire until the city fell to the Turks in 1493. The majority of the New Testament manuscripts are these later "Byzantine" type. Thus, our New Testament manuscripts fall fairly well into two major camps: the earlier uncials and the later minuscules.[14]

Formation. Carefully observe the placement of ascenders and descenders. The following table shows you where to begin the first stroke, and then any subsequent

---

[14]Such great uncial manuscripts were not even known when the King James translators worked on an English translation in the seventeenth century. Greek students are encouraged to study textual criticism. For the material in the last three paragraphs above, see Bruce Manning Metzger, *The Text of the New Testament: Its Transmission, Corruption and Restoration,* Third Edition (New York and Oxford: Oxford University Press, 1992).

strokes, if needed. The first stroke is at the "1," a second stroke at the "2," a third stroke, if needed, at the "3."[15]

Table 1.9 Greek Ascenders and Descenders

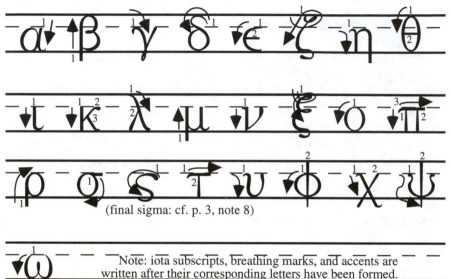

(final sigma: cf. p. 3, note 8)

Note: iota subscripts, breathing marks, and accents are written after their corresponding letters have been formed.

Letter Confusion. Carefully distinguish Greek similarities. Distinguish: psi, ψ, and phi, φ (some Greek fonts render the phi without breaking the stroke, as in φ); nu, ν, and upsilon, υ (pointed versus rounded bottom), and nu, ν, and gamma, γ (baseline descender). Never dot the iota. Also, distinguish from English. Eta (η) is *not* the English "n." Nu (ν) is *not* the English "v." Rho (ρ) is *not* the English "p." Chi (χ) is *not* the English "x." Omega (ω) is *not* the English "w."

Greek Marks

We briefly describe breathing marks, accents, punctuation, and a few other Greek marks. While spelling alone distinguishes most Greek words, some words have

---

[15]The first letter alpha (α) is so similar to its English counterpart ("a") written in a cursive hand that Greek students usually substitute the English letter. This is allowable. However, for the other letters, care is urged to imitate as closely as possible the proper formation of each letter.

exactly the same letters, but different marks. The student cannot ignore these marks long without impeding a thorough grasp of Greek. For example, εἰς, *eis* (pronounced "ace") is the preposition "into," but εἷς, *heis* (pronounced "hace") is the number "one."[16] Again, πότε, *pote*, is the interrogative adverb "when?", but ποτέ, *pote*, is a particle meaning "at the same time." (Notice accents: over omicron or epsilon.)

Breathing. Perhaps you noticed no letter corresponding to the English "h" in the Greek alphabet. This English letter's job is to provide an air flow in connection with sounding other letters. Greek has a similar sound function provided by a certain kind of *breathing mark*, called *rough breathing*. All *beginning* vowels require a breathing mark: either rough breathing with an "h" sound, or smooth breathing, pure vowel, no aspiration. Written above the vowel (the *second* vowel in diphthongs), breathing is *like* an English apostrophe curved inward for rough breathing, outward for smooth. Breathing marks occur to the *side* of the acute and *under* the circumflex. Initial ρ or υ *always* receive *rough* breathing. Initial ῥ is transliterated as "rh," as in ῥῆμα = *rhēma*, "word." Sometimes, however, initial ῥ is given simply as "r," as in ῥαββί = *rabbi*, "rabbi." If the letter is a capital, the breathing mark comes *before* the vowel.

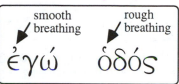

Table 1.10   Breathing Marks

Name	Mark	Example	w/capitals	Diphthongs
smooth breathing	᾿	ἐγώ (*egō*)	Ἰησοῦς (*Yēsous*)	εἰμί (*eimi*)
rough breathing	῾	ὁδός (*hodos*)	Ῥαββί (*Rabbi*)	αἷμα (*haima*)

Accents. Greek accents developed later in the history of the copying of New Testament manuscripts.[17] Originally, accents reflected inflection. Now, accents mark stress. The acute is strong stress, the grave weak, circumflex a modest rise and fall.

---

[16]We would catch the difference immediately by hearing the word, but our path is a written one. To gain the advantage of these type auditory cues, practice all vocabulary by *pronouncing* the words.

[17]Greek accents began to be used by the Greeks about the fourth century B.C., but not systematically until about 200 B.C. Even so, the oldest copies of the Greek New Testament usually do not have accent marks. One of the earliest accented New Testament manuscripts is 𝔓75 (ca. 2nd cent.), which seems to have breathing marks and diaeresis. As New Testament documents continued being copied over the centuries, accents were added, but not fully until the 9th to 11th centuries. Later copyists added the Greek accents to aid in the pronunciation of a Greek language no longer spoken.

Table 1.11 Accent Marks

Name	Mark	Example	w/breathing	Diphthongs
acute	´	λέγω	ἄγω, ἔξ	αἴρω, οὕτως
circumflex	⌢	δοῦλος	ἦν, ὧδε	οἶκος, εἰς
grave	`	τὸ φῶς	ὃν ἂν ἴδῃς	καὶ λέγω

Punctuation.[18] Comma (,) and period (.) are identical to English. The colon (:) and semicolon (;) are both a single dot above the line (·). The Greek question mark is identical to the English semicolon (;)—the only confusion with English punctuation.

Table 1.12 Punctuation Marks

Name	Mark	Example
period	.	ἐδάκρυσεν ὁ Ἰησοῦς. *Jesus wept.* (John 11:35)
comma	,	Λάζαρε, δεῦρο ἔξω. *"Lazarus, come forth."* (John 11:43)
question	;	Ποῦ τεθείκατε αὐτόν; *Where have you laid him?* (John 11:34)
semicolon	·	ἔρχεται εἰς τὸ μνημεῖον· *He comes (came) to the tomb;* (John 11:38)
colon	·	γένωται· ἠγάπησαν (see between John 12:42 and 43 in RSV)

Greek has no quotation mark. Assessing what is a direct quote can be difficult.[19] Direct quotes are indicated two ways in the edited text: (1) a beginning capital letter

---

[18]Remember, the oldest manuscripts are not punctuated. (A few are, such as 𝔓⁶⁶, about A.D. 200). Thus, punctuation in today's edited Greek text is decided by a committee of scholars. Punctuation marks in all translations also are editorial decisions of those translators and committees.
[19]As is the case with the beloved John 3:16, for example.

following a comma, or, (2) by ὅτι recitative ("*hoti* recitative"), the word ὅτι understood as introducing a quote; the word after ὅτι will be capitalized.[20]

Table 1.13   Greek Quotations

Method	Example
capital letter	καὶ λέγει, Οὐκ εἰμί. And he says (said), "I am not." (John 1:21)
ὅτι recitative	ὡμολόγησεν ὅτι Ἐγὼ οὐκ εἰμὶ ὁ Χριστός. *He confessed, "I am not the Messiah."* (John 1:20)

Other Marks: diaeresis, elision, crasis. The two terms "diaeresis" and "elision" relate to diphthong sounds. *Diaeresis* divides a diphthong back into its original two vowels. Over the *second* vowel of the diphthong, diaeresis indicates the two vowels should be pronounced separately, not as a diphthong. The acute or grave accent mark is printed in the middle of the dots of the diaeresis mark.

In English we might write "cannot" as "can't," dropping out some letters. Greek is similar. *Elision* is the dropping of a letter ("eliding"). Often, a vowel at the end of one word will drop when followed by a vowel beginning the next word. A stroke like an apostrophe is used to represent the elided vowel, like the English custom.

Table 1.14   Diaeresis, Elision, and Crasis

Name	Mark	Examples
diaeresis	¨	Μωϋσῆς, Ἡσαΐου, ἀΐδιος (*Mōusēs*) (*Ēsaiou*) (*aidios*)
elision	ʼ	ἐπί αὐτόν = ἐπʼ αὐτόν ἀλλά ἐπί = ἀλλʼ ἐπὶ
crasis	ʼ	καὶ ἐγώ = κἀγώ ("and I") *kai egō = kagō*

---

[20]The word ὅτι (*hoti*) means "that," but when introducing a direct quote is left untranslated.

Crasis is the merging of two words into one for pronunciation, with the loss of one or more letters. The Greek mark indicating crasis is called a *coronis* and is like an apostrophe. Crasis does not affect meaning. The resultant word still is translated as the two originally separate words. The phenomenon of crasis usually involves the conjunction καί ("and"), but the neuter definite article τό also adds two forms.[21]

Transliteration

Table 1.15 Transliteration Equivalents

α	=	a	ε	=	e	κ	=	k
ἀ	=	a	ἐ	=	e	λ	=	l
ἁ	=	ha	ἑ	=	he	μ	=	m
ᾳ	=	āi	ζ	=	z	ν	=	n
β	=	b	η	=	ē	ξ	=	x
γ	=	g	ἠ	=	ē	ο	=	o
γγ	=	ng	ἡ	=	hē	π	=	p
γκ	=	nk				ρ	=	r
γξ	=	nx	ῃ	=	ēi	ῥ	=	rh, r
γχ	=	nch	θ	=	th	σ	=	s
δ	=	d	ι	=	i, y	ς	=	s

τ	=	t
υ	=	y, u
φ	=	ph
χ	=	ch
ψ	=	ps
ω	=	ō
ὠ	=	ō
ὡ	=	hō
ῳ	=	ōi

Transliteration is not recommended for learning Greek. Transliteration too easily becomes a visual crutch. However, sometimes Greek fonts are unavailable so that transliteration becomes necessary. The table above is intended to assist writing Greek words without Greek fonts. Vocabulary is transliterated for the first three lessons. This should help you ease into pronouncing the Greek vocabulary assigned for each lesson in the grammar. However, rapidly learn Greek sounds for Greek letters. *Not every transliteration will provide the proper pronunciation*—use Greek pronunciation for Greek words![22]

---

[21]The following forms: κἀγώ (καὶ ἐγώ), κἀμέ (καὶ ἐμέ), κἀμοί (καὶ ἐμοί), κἀκεῖ (καὶ ἐκεῖ), κἀκεῖθεν (καὶ ἐκεῖθεν), κἀκεῖνος, -η, -ο (καὶ ἐκεῖνος, -η, -ο), κἄν (καὶ ἐν or καὶ ἐάν or καὶ ἄν). The neuter article creates two others: τοὔνομα (τὸ ὄνομα) and τοὐναντίον (τὸ ἐναντίον).
[22]See Table 1.1, note 9.

Exercises

Exercises, including some inductive learning, are provided in the *New Testament Greek Workbook*. This activity reinforces material presented in the text. Since your learning is visual, not spoken, *some memorization is absolutely fundamental.*

Vocabulary

Be certain that software programs you buy for vocabulary review *randomize* the presentation. Avoid commercial audio tapes based on modern Greek pronunciation. This type of pronunciation is different from the academic, so these tapes will confuse you in class. Consult professors before investing in any software or tapes.

Vocabulary 1

Word	*Transliteration*	*Meaning*
εἷς	*heis*	one (numeral)
ἐγώ	*egō*	I
θεός	*theos*	God
καί	*kai*	and, also, even, but

What To Learn—LESSON 1 (εἷς)

Beginning

☐ 1. The Greek alphabet, in order, with proper formation and pronunciation, and an understanding of the use of the final sigma (p. 3, note 8)

☐ 2. Vowel quantities

☐ 3. Definition of a *diphthong* and the twelve diphthongs

☐ 4. The two Greek *breathing* marks and their effect upon pronunciation

☐   5. The three Greek *accent* marks and their effect upon pronunciation

☐   6. The five Greek *punctuation* marks

☐   7. Familiarity with transliteration equivalents

☐   8. Vocabulary words

Advanced

☐   9. Definitions of *majuscule*, *uncial* and *minuscule* letters

☐ 10. Definition of *scripto continua*

☐ 11. The two ways to indicate quotations in Greek

☐ 12. Definitions of *diaeresis*, *elision*, *coronis*, and *crasis*

LESSON 2 (δύο)
Consonants, Syllables, and Accents

Consonants are divided into classes, which helps in the analysis of word formations. Syllable study aids: (1) the effective memorization of vocabulary and (2) working with accents. Accents are important for: (1) distinction between words with the same spelling, (2) determination of inflectional forms, and (3) clues to word formations.

Vocabulary 2

Word	Transliteration	Meaning
δύο	dyo	two (numeral)
ἄνθρωπος	anthrōpos	man
κύριος	kyrios	master, Lord
λόγος	logos	word
ἀκούω	akouō	I hear
βλέπω	blepō	I see
γράφω	graphō	I write
λέγω	legō	I say
λύω	lyō	I loose

Consonant Classes

The Greek consonants can be divided into three classes: liquids, stops, and sibilants. *These three classes must be mastered.* Each class behaves in certain ways to create spelling changes in words. Suffixes added to noun and tense stems ending with these consonants will react so that the spelling changes. Thus, a thorough knowledge of these classes is vital for understanding the morphology of such words. Nouns are affected, but verbs especially need to be mastered in this matter.

15

Liquids. Technically, the *liquid* consonants are just lambda (λ) and rho (ρ). In common usage, however, two other letters often are included as liquids—mu (μ) and nu (ν). In fact,

Table 2.1   Liquid/Nasal Consonants

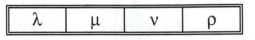

mu (μ) and nu (ν) are *nasals*. However, because letter reactions to nasals are similar to those with lambda (λ) and rho (ρ), the nasals often are included in discussions of "liquid" consonants. Double lambda (λλ) reacts the same as a single lambda (λ).

Stops. Greek has nine consonants which involve a momentary control of the air flow. These consonants are called *stops*, subdivided into "classes" according to where the sound is stopped. "Labials" are the lip-produced sounds (*p*–sounds). "Palatals" (also called "gutturals") are the throat-produced sounds (*k*–sounds). "Dentals" (also called "linguals") are the teeth-produced sounds (*t*–sounds). The stop "orders" are the degrees of air release: "sharp" (smooth), "flat" (middle), and "aspirate" (rough).[1]

Table 2.2   Stop Consonants

Formation	Breathing Pattern			Sound
	sharp	flat	aspirate	
labials	π	β	φ	*p*–sounds
palatals	κ	γ	χ	*k*–sounds
dentals	τ	δ	θ	*t*–sounds

Sibilants. Sibilant consonants have an "s" sound (hissing sound due to air flow over the teeth in their pronunciation). The *sibilants* are four: sigma (σ) and the three consonants psi (ψ), xi (ξ), and zeta (ζ). Sigma (σ)

Table 2.3   Sibilant Consonants

Simple	Complex		
σ	ψ	ξ	ζ

is referred to as the "simple sibilant." The other three letters are called "complex" (or "compound") sibilants because they represent combined consonants (ψ = πσ, βσ, φσ; ξ = κσ, γσ, χσ; ζ = δσ, σδ). The sibilant zeta (ζ) when on the end of a verb represents a class of verbs all to its own.

---

[1]We here are simplifying somewhat complicated terminology. One also may analyze whether the sound includes use of the voice box, that is, "voiced" or "voiceless." See the Glossary on "Stop."

| Syllables |

Divisions. The basic syllable rule is:

♦ *A Greek word has as many syllables as vowels and/or diphthongs.*

Starting from the left, the divisions occur after each vowel or diphthong, except the last vowel or diphthong. The final consonant goes with the last vowel or diphthong. Note well: a single vowel can represent a syllable by itself. The table below gives examples to illustrate syllable divisions. The ability to divide syllables is important for learning vocabulary. A word that cannot be pronounced is that much harder to learn.

Table 2.4 Syllable Divisions

Principle	*Example*	*Division*
simple, single vowel	λόγος	λό-γος
simple, double vowel	θέος	θέ-ος
simple, diphthong	αὐτοῦ	αὐ-τοῦ
two consonants	εὐαγγέλιον	εὐ-αγ-γέ-λι-ον
three consonants	ἄνθρωπος	ἄν-θρω-πος
consonant unit (first)	σχίσμα	σχί-σμα
consonant unit (intern.)	πάσχα	πά-σχα
nasal -μ unit (first)	σμύρνα	σμύρ-να
nasal -μ unit (internal)	ἀριθμός	ἀ-ρι-θμός
nasal -ν unit (first)	πνεῦμα	πνεῦ-μα
nasal -ν unit (internal)	ἔγνωσαν	ἔ-γνω-σαν
compound	ἐκβάλλω (ἐκ + βάλλω)	ἐκ-βάλ-λω

Multiple Consonants. Two consonants together (including doubled consonants) are split. The first consonant closes the syllable before, the second consonant opens the syllable following. Of three consonants together, the first closes the syllable before; the last two open the syllable following. (See Table 2.4.)

Consonant Units. Certain consonant combinations *never* divide. Such indivisible units can be called "consonant units."[2] These are learned by observation as you learn vocabulary. *Any such consonant unit that may begin a word will not divide within a word.* The unit will go with the following vowel or diphthong. (See Table 2.4.)

Liquid Units. As mentioned above, two of the liquids are the "nasals" mu (μ) and nu (ν). Nasals do not divide when *second* in a consonant pair. (See Table 2.4.)

Compound Words. Greek words can be compounded to form new words, especially verbs. Prepositions tacked onto the front of the verb may add direction to the verb's action.[3] Compounds are divided as would be the separate words, that is, one division always is at the point the words are joined together. (See Table 2.4.)

Positions. A Greek word with three or more syllables is called *polysyllabic*. A *disyllabic* word has two syllables. *Monosyllabic* is a one syllable word. The idea of syllable "position" relates only to the final three syllables of a Greek word, regardless of the total number of syllables. The *last three* syllables of a Greek word are called the "antepenult," "penult," and "ultima." Whether a word is polysyllabic, disyllabic, or monosyllabic, the last syllable is the ultima.

Table 2.5   Final Three Syllable Positions

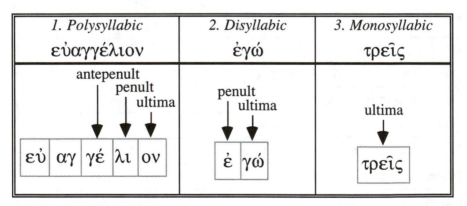

---

[2]The terminology is not fixed. "Clusters," "groups," and other terms are used.

[3]Do not confuse compounds with crasis. In crasis, *the meaning does not alter.* One translates crasis as two individual words. With compounds, a *new* word is created with enhanced meaning (strengthening verbal action). However, whether the "strengthened" meaning in fact applies has to be decided. Overuse watered down the original force of many newly coined compounds.

Quantity. Syllable quantity is the vowel or diphthong quantity in that syllable. A long vowel (η, ω, diphthong) creates a long syllable. A short vowel (ε, o, and αι, οι when final) creates a short syllable. Syllables with α, ι, or υ may be long or short; the length of α, ι, or υ is determined by observation.

Accents

Accents are said to be non-essential to understanding Greek. We disagree. The UBS[4] text *is* accented. The mystery of the unknown intimidates. We prefer to remove the mystery. Further, baseless rumors to the contrary, accents are *not* hard. Master the visuals of the following tables and you are well on your way to conquering Greek accents—and well ahead of the pack of most beginning Greek students.

Accent Positions. Accent positions involve the last three syllables of any word. The acute accent occurs on any of the last *three* syllables, the circumflex only on the last *two* syllables. The grave is found only on the *last* syllable.

Table 2.6 Possible Accent Positions

	Antepenult	*Penult*	*Ultima*
acute	/	/	/
circumflex		⌢	⌢
grave			\

Syllable Quantity and Accents. Syllable quantity—whether long or short—affects accents. Both the acute and grave accents can stand over either long or short syllables. That is, the acute and grave accents are *unrestricted by syllable quantity.* However, in contrast:

♦ *The circumflex accent can stand over long syllables only.*

Accent Sustain. Sustain is the ability of a particular accent's stress to carry the

Table 2.7 Quantity and Accents

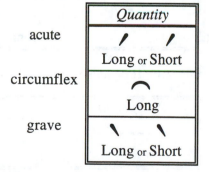

	Quantity	
acute	/	/
	Long or Short	
circumflex	⌢	
	Long	
grave	\	\
	Long or Short	

syllables that follow. The acute can sustain up to three syllables, but *only two adjacent can be long*. The circumflex can sustain up to two syllables, but *the second must be short*. The grave can sustain a maximum of only one long syllable.

Table 2.8 Maximum Accent Sustain

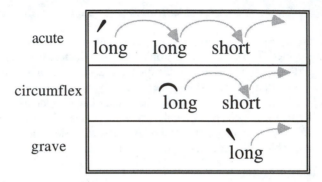

	acute	long long short
circumflex	long short
grave	long

Accent Rules. "Rules" simply describe what is observed after the *lexical* form is known. These rules do not *predict* whether a syllable will be accented (decided by Greeks long ago), only what accent to use *if* the syllable is accented. First, two tables give a visual summary of the crucial accent rules one through six, if that syllable is to be accented. Visually fix these tables in your mind. They will assist you greatly.

Table 2.9 If Syllable Accented—Short Ultima

Antepenult	Penult	Ultima
´	⌢ ´	´ `
	Long Short	Short Short

Table 2.10 If Syllable Accented—Long Ultima

Antepenult	Penult	Ultima
- - - - -	´	´ ⌢ `
(cannot be accented)		Long Long Long

Visualize the following rules by referring to Tables 2.9 and 2.10. Remember that the diphthongs -οι and -αι are short when final (p. 4). Other accent rules concerning "oxytones," "enclitics," and "contract verbs" are presented later.

Table 2.11   Accent Rules

Short ultima rules:
1. The accented antepenult must be acute (κύριος).
2. The accented, *long* penult *must* be circumflex; acute if short (δῶρον; λόγος).
3. The accented ultima is acute, grave if rule 8 (θεός; but Θεὸς ἦν ὁ λόγος).
Long ultima rules:
4. The antepenult *cannot* be accented (κυρίου).
5. The accented penult is acute (δώρου).
6. The accented ultima can be any accent (γραφή; γραφὴ λέγει; γραφῆς).
Circumflex rule:
7. The circumflex accent can stand over long syllables only (δῶρον; αὐτοῦ) Note ἡμῖν—the circumflex accent reveals that the iota, which is a variable vowel that can be either long or short, is declared *long* by the accent.
Grave rule:
8. An acute ultima becomes grave when no punctuation breaks the flow to the next word (πρὸς τὸν θεόν).
Noun rule:
9. Noun accents are "persistent"—in a declension, the accent tends to stay in the syllable of the lexical form, if rules allow: λόγος, λόγου, λόγῳ, λόγον, λόγοι, λόγων, λόγοις, λόγους; but ἄνθρωπος, ἀνθρώπου, ἀνθρώπῳ, ἄνθρωπον, ἄνθρωποι, ἀνθρώπων, ἀνθρώποις, ἀνθρώπους; the long ultimas force the acute back to the penult syllable due to rules 4 and 5.
Verb rule:
10. Verb accents are "recessive"—in a conjugation, the accent tends to move away from the ultima as far as possible, if rules allow: λύω, λύεις, λύει, λύομεν, λύετε, λύουσι, in which the acute *penult* of the disyllabic form (λύω) recedes back to the *antepenult* in the polysyllabic forms of the plurals with their short ultimas, λύομεν, λύετε, λύουσι, as allowed by rule 1.

The first six rules above demonstrate the decisive factor in determining accent:

◆ *The deciding factor for accents is the quantity of the ultima.*

Table 2.12   Accent Determination Procedure

> **1. What is the lexical form?**
> Both *accent* and *position* in the lexical form must be known in advance in order to apply the rules of accent.
> **2. What is the word class?**
> a.   If a *noun*, apply the *persistent* rule of accent in following step three.
> b.   If a *verb*, apply the *recessive* rule of accent in following step three.
> **3. What is the ultima quantity?**
> Keeping in mind possible accent positions (Table 2.6) and the two special rules for circumflex and grave accents:
> a.   If *short*, apply rules one through three.
> b.   If *long*, apply rules four through six.

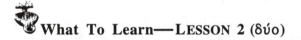

What To Learn—LESSON 2 (δύο)

Beginning

- ☐   1.   The three classes of consonants: *liquids*, *stops*, *sibilants*.
- ☐   2.   Stop subcategories: *labials*, *palatals*, *dentals*, and the table of stops
- ☐   3.   Know the basic syllable rule
- ☐   4.   The last three syllables of any Greek word: *antepenult*, *penult*, *ultima*
- ☐   5.   A syllable quantity's effect upon the three accents, the possible accent positions for each accent, and the deciding factor for all accents
- ☐   6.   Ten rules of accent
- ☐   7.   Vocabulary words

Advanced

- ☐   8.   The twelve examples of syllable division and the rule each illustrates
- ☐   9.   Maximum sustain for any accent

LESSON 3 (ΤΡΕῖΣ)
Present Active Indicative

λύω

 The sophistication of the Greek verb system provides a power to communicate that can reveal beautiful truths within the New Testament. This chapter is a broad overview. You will not retain all the concepts immediately. Do not fret. Continual exposure over time will help this material sink in.

Vocabulary 3

Word	Transliteration	Stem	Meaning
τρεῖς	treis		three (numeral)
ἄγγελος	angelos		angel, messenger
ἀδελφός	adelphos		brother
ἀπόστολος	apostolos		apostle
οἶκος	oikos		house
οὐ, οὐκ, οὐχ [1]	ou, ouk, ouch		not (indicative mood; no accent)
γινώσκω	ginōskō	γνο-	I know
διδάσκω	didaskō	διδακ-	I teach
ἔχω	echō	σεχ-	I have
λαμβάνω	lambanō	λαβ-	I take, receive

[1]Alternates: οὐκ before vowels (οὐκ ἀκούω), but οὐχ before rough breathing (οὐχ ἁμαρτάνω).

23

Analysis

Table 3.1 Principal Parts: Tenses and Voices

Principal Parts	Tenses	Voices		
First Principal Part	*Present*	*active*	middle	passive
	Imperfect	active	middle	passive
Second Principal Part	Future	active	middle	
Third Principal Part	First Aorist	active	middle	
	Second Aorist	active	middle	
Fourth Principal Part	Perfect	active		
	Future Perfect	active		
	Pluperfect	active		
Fifth Principal Part	Perfect		middle	passive
	Future Perfect		middle	passive
	Pluperfect		middle	passive
Sixth Principal Part	First Aorist			passive
	First Future			passive
	Second Aorist			passive
	Second Future			passive

Principal Parts. The Greek verb system is divided on the basis of the six formations of the tense stems. This division is referred to as the "six principal parts" of a verb (see Table 3.1). If one tense "borrows" the tense stem of another to form itself, then that tense is part of the same system due to the common stem. Thus, the "first principal part" is comprised of *two* tenses, present and imperfect, because the imperfect "borrows" the present tense stem to form itself. The present tense is the first tense of two in the "first principal part."[2]

Conjugations. The Greek verb system is divided into two major conjugations. The second conjugation is much less frequent and is not studied until later.

---

[2]The student actually does not "know" a Greek verb just by recalling the lexical definition of its present active indicative form. Not until all six principal parts for that verb are known is mastery obtained. For example, one does not "know" the verb γινώσκω simply by saying "that verb means, 'I know'." One also must know that the future is γνώσομαι, the aorist is ἔγνων, the perfect active is ἔγνωκα, the perfect middle/passive is ἔγνωσμαι, and the aorist passive is ἐγνώσθην. One must know the six principal parts of a verb to recognize all its forms in the New Testament. But you do not have to learn all six principal parts at once! These parts are learned one at a time.

Thematic Verbs (-ω Verbs). The first conjugation of Greek verbs is the "thematic verb." The term comes from the manner of formation using a theme vowel (ε/ο) to join endings to tense stems. The majority of New Testament verbs are of this class. These thematic verbs also are called "-ω verbs," because the first person singular form, active voice ends in -ω.[3]

Non-thematic Verbs (-μι Verbs). The -μι verbs have no thematic vowels. The ending is joined directly to the tense stem.[4]

Components. A Greek verb consists of the following components: tense, voice, mood, person, number, and lexical. We discuss these components, then show structural formation of the present active indicative verb.

Table 3.2 Greek Verb Components—Tense

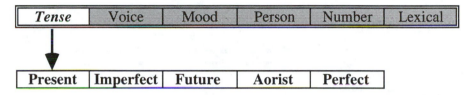

Tense	Voice	Mood	Person	Number	Lexical

Present	Imperfect	Future	Aorist	Perfect

Tense. The tense component reveals the major difference between English and Greek verbs. English tense primarily has only *one* element, but Greek tense has *two.* Think of Greek verbal elements on the analogy of an equation. For English, the verb equation is "tense = time." In Greek, the verb equation is "tense = time + kind." Here "kind" of action refers to *tense aspect.* The following is an *extremely* important equation for the meaning of the Greek verb:

♦ *Greek Tense = Time + Aspect*

Time of Action. The primary function of English tense is to indicate time of action. *The primary function of the Greek tense is to indicate kind of action.* Time is a consideration in only *one* of the four Greek moods.[5] Greek students are lost until they begin to react with the question: "what *kind* of action?" Build the habit of emphasizing the kind-of-action question until this response is close to automatic when confronted with any Greek verb.

---

[3]Technically, in the first person, the -ω form actually is a *resultant* interaction of the actual first person singular ending with the thematic vowel. But this is not important right now.

[4]Hence, the -μι is the first person singular ending itself with no thematic vowel.

[5]Thus, we will deal with *time* of action more fully under discussion of Greek *mood.*

Kind of Action. All verbal action can be boiled down into three fundamental states or realities of experience. Thus, Greek verbs have *three* kinds of action, usually called "aspects":

1. *Durative*—action that happens as a duration in time, either continuous ("the faucet is running") or continual ("the faucet is dripping"). The emphasis is on process. This kind of action sometimes is called the "imperfective aspect."

2. *Undefined*—*either* of two ideas: (1) action that punctuates time at a point, *or* (2) action without defined process or result (= "undefined," as in "the faucet dripped" = once? twice? over and over?). The action is taken as a whole without comment. This kind of action also is called the "aoristic aspect."

3. *Perfective*—action that, whether originally punctiliar or durative in nature, has generated on-going results or consequences ("the faucet is fixed"). "Perfective" hints at the use of the perfect tenses.

Table 3.3 Kinds of Action

Durative	———— or – – – – –
Undefined	●
Perfective	– – ➤ or ●– – ➤

This lesson introduces the present tense. *The present tense is a durative tense.* For all durative tenses such as the present tense, the beginning Greek student is encouraged to use the pattern of translation with the "-ing" form (for the present tense, "am ____ing" as in "I am loosing," instead of the form "I loose"). The reason is to emphasize the *durative* (on-going) nature of the action.[6]

Table 3.4 Greek Verb Components—Voice

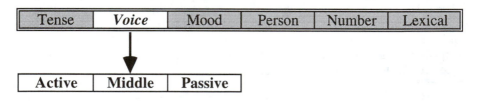

Tense	*Voice*	Mood	Person	Number	Lexical

Active	Middle	Passive

---

[6]The present tense *can* have a punctiliar aspect, but only very rarely. Cf. Acts 9:34, "heals."

Voice. Voice deals with the subject of the verb. The subject of the verb stands in one of three fundamental relationships to the verbal action. These relationships are called "voices": active, middle, and passive. Voice *indicates the relationship of the verb's action to the verb's subject.* English has only *two* voices: active and passive. English has no equivalent to the Greek middle voice. Translating the Greek middle voice, therefore, is a problem, since English has no middle voice counterpart. This subject-to-verb relationship can be described as:

1. Active voice—the verb's subject is *performing* the verb's action ("I am writing to you," 1 John 2:1).

2. Middle voice—the verb's subject is *reflecting* the verb's action, in two ways: (1) the *direct* middle, in which the verb's subject is reflecting directly the action of the verb onto itself ("he hanged himself," Matt. 27:5); (2) the *indirect* middle, in which the subject is acting with self-interest in the action ("Teacher, I *have kept* [i.e., in my own self interest] all these things from my youth up," Mark 10:20). The presence of the Greek middle is difficult to translate because English has no middle voice. However, true middle voice is uncommon in the New Testament.

3. Passive voice—the verb's subject passively *receives* the verb's action ("I am being poured out," Phil. 2:17).

Table 3.5 Greek Voice and Verbal Action

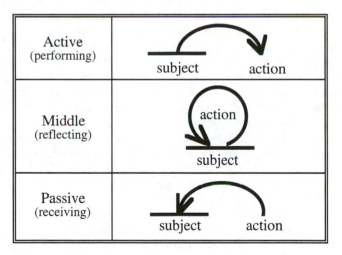

The verb εἰμί ("I am") is introduced in a future lesson. This verb expresses a state of being, not transitive (i.e., "she wrote a book") or intransitive ("he ran")

action. In terms of the current discussion on voice, εἰμί as a state of being verb has no action to relate to a subject, so *εἰμί has no voice component*.

Table 3.6 Greek Verb Components—Mood

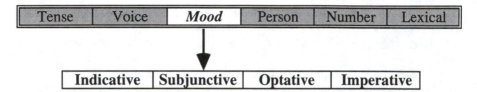

Mood. The mood component can indicate two elements of the Greek verb. One is the degree of reality assigned to the statement of the verb's action by the speaker. The other element is most familiar to English students: the presence of time interest.

<u>Degree of Reality</u>. The term "mood" comes from the Latin *modus*, meaning "manner." Mood is the manner of affirmation by the speaker of the reality of a statement. Is the action considered a real set of events, or is it a wish? Is it a command (that may or may not be executed) or a conditional sentence (condition must be realized before the statement is true)? Such degree of reality assumptions are indicated by mood. Greek has *four* moods, one of reality, three others of potential reality, each with a greater degree of contingency.

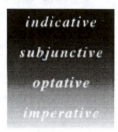

1. *Indicative (reality)*—indicates that the *reality* of the statement is assumed or asserted. Three main types are: (1) common declarative fact statements or assertions, (2) interrogatives, and (3) first class conditional sentences, in which the main condition is assumed true. E.g., "now we *are* children of God," 1 John 3:2; "if they *persecuted* me [which they did]," John 15:20.

2. *Subjunctive (probability)*—indicates *some contingency* bearing upon the statement made. The two main types are *probable reality* statements and the third class conditional sentence (main condition *probably* true). E.g., "*Do not think* [which some probably do] that I came to destroy the law," Matt. 5:17; "If anyone *loves* the world [and some probably do]," 1 John 2:15.

3. *Optative (possibility)*—indicates *greater contingency* about the statement made, a weaker form of the subjunctive. The statement is considered *possible reality*, but remote. Use of the optative mood was fading in New Testament times, so the optative is uncommon in the New Testament (sixty-seven occurrences). The main uses are in fourth class conditional sentences (main condition only remotely

possible) and in wishes, benedictions, and prayers.[7] E.g., "For *how am I able* unless someone guides me?" Acts 8:31; "what *would he wish* to say?" Acts 17:18.

4. *Imperative (command)*—indicates *greatest contingency* bearing upon the statement made, the conventional mood used for commands or entreaties. "*Let* your kingdom *come*," Matt. 6:10; "*Do not be conformed*," Rom. 12:2.

In summary, the four moods depict reality, probability, possibility, and command. All four relate degree of reality from the perspective of the speaker only.

Time of Action. Greek tense also can involve the time element, but only in *one* mood, the indicative.[8] Remember, the indicative is the mood of assumed *reality*, which would include the reality of *time*. So, time of action is not a consideration in the other three moods. *Greek tenses indicate past, present, and future time only in the indicative mood.* Further, since the Greek tense has the added element of kind of action, any of *three* Greek tenses can indicate past time, with distinctions made based on the three *kinds* of action in that past time. Thus, *durative* action in past time would call for the imperfect tense, *undefined* action in past time the aorist tense, and *perfective* action in past time the pluperfect tense.

Table 3.7 Primary and Secondary Tenses

Kind of Action	Time of Action (Indicative Mood)		
	Secondary Tenses (secondary endings)	Primary Tenses (primary endings)	
	Past	Present	Future
durative	Imperfect	Present	---------[9]
undefined ●	Aorist ●	---------[9]	Future ●
perfective - - -▶	Pluperfect - - -▶	Perfect - - -▶	Future Perfect - - -▶

Primary and Secondary Tenses. When time *is* a consideration (indicative mood), tenses can be classified in two ways based on this time element: *primary* and

---

[7]This is a *literary* convention in benedictions and prayers, not an actual doubt of the author.

[8]Following Fanning's analysis for the time being. (See Preface, xvi n. 1, and the Annotated Bibliography under "Grammar and Syntax.")

[9]On *rare* occasion one finds a punctiliar present and a durative future.

secondary. Primary tenses are those tenses in indicative mood of *present and future time* (present, future, present perfect, future perfect). Secondary tenses are those tenses in indicative mood of *past time* (imperfect, aorist, pluperfect). This classification is *very* important. This applies to all thematic verbs, yielding two fundamental rules of the indicative mood:

♦ *Primary tenses take primary endings.*

♦ *Secondary tenses take secondary endings.*

Two sets of endings cover the entire -ω verb indicative system! That's good news.

Use of οὐ. Greek has two words to indicate the negative ("no" or "not"), both οὐ and μή. The usage is distinguished by mood. The negative οὐ is used with the indicative mood. The negative μή is used in the other moods. So the negative οὐ is a tip-off to the mood of the verb. [10]

Table 3.8 Greek Verb Components—Person and Number (Inflection)

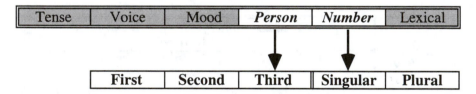

Tense	Voice	Mood	*Person*	*Number*	Lexical

First	Second	Third	Singular	Plural

Person and Number—Inflection (Pronominal Suffixes). Inflection is a predictable system of changes to word endings to indicate grammatical relationships. Greek is highly inflected, as English is not. In English, the one spelling of the verb "go" will do for all persons except third singular ("I go," "you go," but "he go*es*," "we go," "you go," "they go") The inflection "-es" which is added to the end of "go" immediately signals to the English speaking person the third person singular.

Greek has such indicators for *all* persons. For verbs, these changes in the endings represent the person and number of the verbal action's subject. English uses distinct pronouns to indicate the subject: the person speaking ("I", "we"), the person directly addressed ("you," "you"), and the person indirectly addressed ("he, she, it," "they"). These are called first, second, and third person, respectively. Greek has personal pronouns too but does not need them to indicate the verb's subject. The

---

[10]With minor exceptions.

subject is indicated by the verb inflection on the ending. These endings on verbs indicate person and number and are called "pronominal suffixes." The same endings are used for all moods except the imperative. Since middle and passive voice often use the exact same ending, then primary and secondary indicative endings each have two sets, one for active voice, and one for the middle/passive. The table below summarizes our discussion. You will see this particular table each lesson a new set of endings is introduced. For now, memorize just the far left column. Also, do not forget the basic rule of all subjects and verbs, whether English or Greek:[11]

♦ *A verb agrees with its subject in person and number.*

Table 3.9 Greek Primary and Secondary Endings—Indicative Mood

Subject		*Indicative Endings*			
		Primary Tenses		*Secondary Tenses*	
Number	Person	**Active**	Mid/Pass	Active	Mid/Pass
Singular	1st	**-ω**	-μαι	-ν	-μην
	2nd	**-εις**	-σαι (η)	-ς	-σο (ου)
	3rd	**-ει**	-ται	(-εν)	-το
Plural	1st	**-ομεν**	-μεθα	-μεν	-μεθα
	2nd	**-ετε**	-σθε	-τε	-σθε
	3rd	**-ουσι(ν)**	-νται	-ν, -σαν	-ντο

Notes 1 and 2 deal with the particular endings for this introductory lesson on verbs.
1. The thematic vowel, discussed later, is included only in the primary active set. The vowel is not given in the other patterns. The thematic vowel in the primary active is somewhat lost to sight due to interactions. (The vowel is clearly visible only on the first and second persons plural). So the primary active endings are learned *with* the thematic vowel.
2. The primary active, third plural can end with nu (ν), called "movable nu." This letter does not affect meaning but smoothes pronunciation for a following word beginning with a vowel, or when the verb comes at the end of a clause or sentence.

---

[11]With two exceptions: neuter plurals and compound subjects, discussed in Lesson 4 (p. 59).

3.   The primary middle, second person singular changes; when combined with the thematic vowel, the σ drops out, leaving a vowel (ε) and a diphthong (αι). These vowel sounds combine into a resultant improper diphthong, ῃ.

4.   The secondary active, third person singular has no ending. This leaves the thematic vowel epsilon (-ε) exposed alone as the ending. Sometimes a "movable nu" (-ν) is then added to this exposed thematic vowel (when the next word begins with a vowel, or the verb ends the sentence). Compare the use of the alternate forms of the English indefinite article ("a," "an").

5.   The secondary active, third person plural exists in *two* forms. Most verbs take the -ν (a true ending; *not* "movable nu"). Some verbs take the -σαν.

6.   The secondary middle, second person singular changes; when combined with the thematic vowel, the σ drops out (called "intervocalic sigma"), leaving two vowels (ε, ο), which combine into a resultant contract diphthong, -ου.

These primary, active, indicative endings are the endings you will be putting on verbs in the exercises in the *Workbook*, given separately in the table below.

Table 3.10 Primary Active Endings—Indicative Mood

Number	Person	Form	Translation
Singular	1st	-ω	"I"
	2nd	-εις	"you (sg.)"
	3rd	-ει	"he (she, it)"
Plural	1st	-ομεν	"we"
	2nd	-ετε	"you (pl.)"
	3rd	-ουσι(ν)	"they"

Table 3.11 Greek Verb Components—Lexical

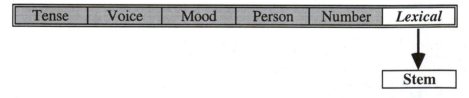

Lexical. The final component of the Greek verb is the lexical, the information found in a Greek dictionary. We must understand roots, verb stems, and tense stems.

Root. In the hierarchy of word formation, including verbs, the first level is the *root*. This is the base for all related word forms. The second level is the *stem*, in which the root forms a trunk for creating related nouns, adjectives, and verbs through noun stems, adjective stems, and verb stems. "Cognates" are all word forms related to the same root, whether noun, adjective, verb, etc.[12]

Verb Stem. A *verb stem* is that particular form in which a word root manifests itself as a verb. Verb stems communicate the fundamental "action," the verbal idea ("know," "teach," "have," "receive," "send"). To illustrate, the word root γνο- can grow into the noun cognate γνῶσις ("knowledge"), the adjective cognate γνωστός ("known"), and the verb cognate γινώσκω ("I know").

Tense stems. The third level of hierarchy is for verbs, because verbs have the additional job of forming separate tenses. The third level, then, is a verb stem's several different tense stems. A *tense stem* is a limb coming off the trunk of a verb stem that through formatives (prefixes, suffixes, infixes) creates a distinct verb tense. One verb stem can have up to six different tense stems. How will one know this basic verb stem?

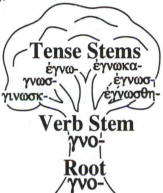

Omega Form. The -ω form of a verb is the typical lexical form of thematic verbs.[13] For quite a number of verbs, dropping the -ω from this lexical form provides the basic *verb stem*. This basic stem is the building block of conjugations. The verb λύω is a good example. However, this procedure is not applicable to all verbs.

Hidden Verb Stems. Dropping the -ω from the lexical form of a verb does not *always* provide the verb stem. The lexical entry is the present tense of the verb. Yet, the present tense is one of the most irregular forming tenses in the entire Greek verb system! The verb stem often is *modified* in forming the present tense stem. As a result, *the present tense spelling represents the present tense stem, not the spelling of the original verb stem.* We call these "hidden" verb stems, a descriptive term, simply because they are not immediately obvious in the verb's first lexical entry.

For example, the verb stem of βαπτίζω is βαπτιδ-, *not* βαπτιζ-. The verb stem of κηρύσσω is κηρυκ-, *not* κηρυσσ-. The verb stem of γινώσκω is γνο-. How will you know? Vocabulary will indicate hidden stems. Also, such stems are pointed out in your lexicons, because the lexicon will give the formations in other tenses,

---

[12]A *cognate accusative*, for example, is a direct object noun whose root is the same as the verb (cf. φυλάσσοντες φυλακὰς in Luke 2:8 and ἐφοβήθησαν φόβον in Luke 2:9).

[13]Later we will add the lexical ending -μαι for "deponents."

indicating the present tense stem is not the verb stem. These "hidden" verb stems are important, so note them carefully to be able to specify conjugations correctly.

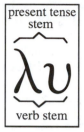

In summary, then, for some verbs, the verb stem *does* give the present tense stem. So λύω has the verb stem λυ-, which also is the present tense stem. This is because λύω belongs to a large class of verbs that does not modify the verb

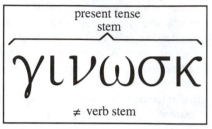

stem to create the present stem. However, for other verbs, the verb stem does *not* give the present tense stem. So γινώσκω has the verb stem γνο-, which is modified significantly in generating the present stem.[14]

Formation

Having overviewed the Greek verb system in an analysis of the verb's component parts (tense, voice, mood, person, number, lexical), we now turn to the procedure for constructing the present tense, a primary verb which takes primary endings, in the active voice and the indicative mood.

Tense Stem. For the thematic verb we will use λύω as our paradigm.[15] We use λύω because this verb is "regular," that is, well-behaved, does not show unexpected forms (because of the stem class). Many thematic verbs are regular verbs like λύω. For these regular verbs, just drop the -ω ending of the dictionary form and you have the present tense stem. The present tense stem of λύω, then, is λυ-.

---

[14]Tense stem formation can be understood on the basis of stem classes. The verbs λύω and γινώσκω belong to different stem classes. The six classes are: (1) present stem identical to verb stem, such as λύω, (2) a -π stem adding -τ for a -πτ present stem, such as κρυπ- to κρύπτω, (3) a stem adding "consonantal iota" creating various reactions, such as βαπτιδ- + ι giving the zeta result in βαπτίζω, (4) a stem adding certain ν forms, generating various reactions, such as βα- adding ν and lengthening the stem vowel to βαίνω, (5) a stem adding -σκ or -ισκ, such as γινώσκω, (6) a verb that uses different verb stems depending on the principal part being created, such as λέγω. These major classes are subdivided, but provide the basic framework for understanding Greek verb formation. The advanced student may consult the discussion on verbs in James A. Brooks and Carlton L. Winbery, *Morphology of New Testament Greek: A Review and Reference Grammar* (Lanham, MD: University Press of America, 1994).

[15]A "paradigm" is a pattern used to illustrate all other words in that class or category. The verb λύω will accompany our journey throughout the thematic verb system as we illustrate verb formation in the six principal parts.

$$\lambda \acute{\upsilon} \varphi = \lambda \upsilon\text{-}$$

present tense stem

Thematic Vowel. The thematic vowel joins the pronominal suffix to the tense stem. This vowel occurs in a pattern ("thematic") according to the voice and number. Take the vowel for the first person plural, for example. We then have:

$$\lambda \upsilon\text{-}o$$

stem + thematic vowel

Table 3.12 Thematic Vowel Pattern

Number	Person	Vowel
Singular	1st	o
	2nd	ε
	3rd	ε
Plural	1st	o
	2nd	ε
	3rd	o

Pronominal Suffix. Finally, one adds the appropriate pronominal suffix according to the subject of the action. However, these endings in their primary active form (-ω, -εις, -ει, -ομεν, -ετε, -ουσι) have undergone change that obscures the thematic vowel in all but -ομεν and -ετε. For clarity, we have chosen the first person *plural*, because this form shows the actual thematic vowel. Our final result is:

$$\lambda \upsilon\text{-}o\text{-}\mu\epsilon\nu$$

stem + thematic vowel + pronominal suffix

Table 3.13 Present Active Indicative—Construction

Stem	Vowel	Ending
λυ-	[o]	-ω
λυ-	[ε]	-εις
λυ-	[ε]	-ει
λυ-	o	-μεν
λυ-	ε	-τε
λυ-	[o]	-ουσι

So the tense stem is the basic building block of any conjugation. One takes the tense stem, adds the thematic vowel, then pronominal suffix. Remember, though, that in the present tense, the actual thematic vowels are hidden in most active forms.

In summary, tense stems indicate *action*. Voice indicates *direction* of the action. Person indicates the *subject* of the action. For our paradigm, λύω, the action is "loose." The present tense is durative, "is loosing." In active voice, the subject is *performing* the loosing action, and, adding a first person plural subject, one has the result, "we are loosing."

Table 3.14 Conjugation—Six Forms (Present Active Indicative—λύω)

Number	Person	Form	Translation
Singular	1st	λύω	"I am loosing"
	2nd	λύεις	"you are loosing"
	3rd	λύει	"he (she, it) is loosing"
Plural	1st	λύομεν	"we are loosing"
	2nd	λύετε	"you (pl.) are loosing"
	3rd	λύουσι(ν)	"they are loosing"

Conjugation. A *conjugation* is that particular pattern of inflection (defined on page 43) for a given tense stem in a given tense, voice, and mood. To "conjugate" a verb means to give the six inflectional forms indicating person and number in a particular tense, voice, and mood for that verb. For λύω, one would give the six forms: λύω, λύεις, λύει, λύομεν, λύετε, λύουσιν.

Location. Distinguish "locate" from "conjugate." To "locate" (or "parse") a verb in the Greek text, you specify an *individual* verb form's six component parts: tense, voice, mood, person, number, lexical form. As our example in this section:

$$\lambda \acute{v} o \mu \epsilon v$$

Table 3.15 Location: Six Components (λύομεν)

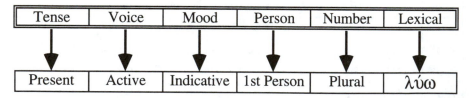

Tense	Voice	Mood	Person	Number	Lexical
Present	Active	Indicative	1st Person	Plural	λύω

Sometimes you will be asked to provide a "full" location. In addition to the regular six component parts, a "full" location also would include the lexical *definition* of the lexical form, as well as a *translation* of the form in question.

Verb Accents

Table 3.16 Verb Accent—Recessive

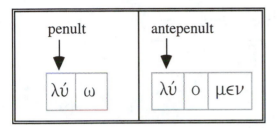

Verb accents are said to be *recessive*. That is, if no accenting rule is violated, the verb's accent will recede from the ultima as far possible. Notice this tendency in the paradigm of λύω. The acute accent opens the paradigm on the tense stem in penult position. However, study the plural forms λύομεν, λύετε, λύουσιν. Accent has receded to the *antepenult* position in these polysyllabic forms. Nothing in the rules of accent prevents the acute from doing so. The ultima is short, which allows the possibility of accenting the antepenult. Therefore, the acute accent *recedes* from the opening penult position of λύω to the antepenult position of the plural forms. Do not make the incorrect assumption that the accent of λύω in the conjugation simply is staying on the vowel upsilon (υ) no matter what form is presented. The accent is on the upsilon in the plural forms because of the *recessive* rule for verbs.

Diagramming

Diagramming a sentence visually helps the student analyze the constituent parts. Diagramming also helps restore the English order of the Greek words for a better conceptual grasp of the word relationships. An *independent clause* is a verb and its subject. A *simple sentence* is one independent clause by itself. *One word* in Greek can be a sentence, since the pronominal suffix at the verb's end is the subject. An independent clause goes on a horizontal line, called the *base line*. The subject is first, the verb second, separated by a vertical stroke breaking the line. For a subject in the verb, put the pertinent English pronoun in parenthesis in the subject position.

Compound subjects and predicates are written on separate, parallel lines angled in a point back to the base line. A dotted (broken) line with the conjunction in the middle connects the compound elements at the point's beginning. A *compound sentence* has two or more independent clauses joined by conjunctions. These clauses are put on separate but parallel base lines, connected by a dotted line at the front, the conjunction in the middle. In the examples, the ὁ is the definite article, which does not have to be translated in every occurrence (p. 56; for diagramming, see p. 60).

Table 3.17 Diagramming Subjects and Verbs

1. λύουσιν. "They are loosing."	*Simple Sentence = Independent Clause* 1. $\underline{\text{(They)} \;\big|\; \text{λύουσιν}}$

2. ὁ θεός καὶ ὁ κύριος λύουσιν.
 	
"God and the Lord are loosing."
	Compound Subject
	
	2. ὁ θεός
	     καὶ ⟩— λύουσιν
	     ὁ κύριος

3. ὁ θεός λύει καὶ διδάσκει. "God is loosing and is teaching."	*Compound Verb* 3. ὁ θεός — λύει / καὶ / διδάσκει

4. ὁ θεός καὶ ὁ κύριος λύουσιν καὶ διδάσκουσιν.
 	
"God and the Lord are loosing and are teaching."
	Compound Subject, Compound Verb
	
	4. ὁ θεός — λύουσιν
	     καὶ — καὶ
	     ὁ κύριος — διδάσκουσιν

5. ὁ θεός λύει καὶ ὁ κύριος διδάσκει.
 	
"God is loosing and the Lord is teaching."
	Compound Sentence
	
	5. ὁ θεός ∣ λύει
	     καὶ
	     ὁ κύριος ∣ διδάσκει

What To Learn—LESSON 3 (τρεῖς)

Beginning

- ☐   1.   The meaning of *principal parts* of a verb
- ☐   2.   Two conjugations of verbs: *thematic* and *non-thematic*
- ☐   3.   Components of a Greek verb: *tense, voice, mood, person, number, lexical*
- ☐   4.   Equation of meaning for a Greek verb
- ☐   5.   Significance of verbal aspect as *durative*
- ☐   6.   Significance of voice as *active*
- ☐   7.   Significance of mood as *indicative*
- ☐   8.   Significance of *primary* and *secondary* tenses
- ☐   9.   Two rules specifying the endings of indicative verbs
- ☐ 10.   *Primary active endings* for indicative mood
- ☐ 11.   Relationship of *root, verb stem, and tense stem*
- ☐ 12.   Function and pattern of the *thematic vowel*
- ☐ 13.   Distinction between *conjugation* and *location*
- ☐ 14.   Paradigm of λύω in the present active indicative
- ☐ 15.   Definitions of *independent clause, compound sentence*
- ☐ 16.   Diagramming independent clauses and compounds
- ☐ 17.   Vocabulary words

Advanced

- ☐ 18.   Illustrate verb accent as *recessive*
- ☐ 19.   Research the six basic verb stem classes and explain

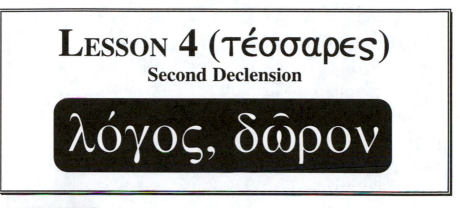

LESSON 4 (τέσσαρες)

Second Declension

λόγος, δῶρον

Greek has three declensions. A particular word belongs to one declension only. Gender varies within a declension. The second declension consists mostly of masculine and neuter nouns. Masculine nouns are more frequent. A few feminine nouns of second declension are treated later.

Vocabulary 4

Word		Meaning
τέσσαρες	numeral	four
γάρ	post-positive conjunction	for
δέ	post-positive conjunction	but, and, now
ὁ, τό	definite article (masculine, neuter)	the
ἄρτος, -ου, ὁ[1]		bread
γάμος, -ου, ὁ		marriage, wedding
δοῦλος, -ου, ὁ		slave, servant
θάνατος, -ου, ὁ		death
κόσμος, -ου, ὁ		world

---

[1] The vocabulary lists will include: (1) the lexical form of the noun (the nominative singular), (2) the ending of the genitive case for these nouns, (3) the appropriate definite article for that gender.

41

νόμος, -ου, ὁ	law
οὐρανός, -οῦ, ὁ (oxytone)	heaven
υἱός, -οῦ, ὁ (oxytone)	son
Χριστός, -οῦ, ὁ (oxytone)	Christ (Messiah, Anointed)
δῶρον, -ου, τό	gift
ἔργον, -ου, τό	work
εὐαγγέλιον, -ου, τό	gospel, good news
ἱερόν, -ου, τό (oxytone)	temple
πρόσωπον, -ου, τό	face, presence
τέκνον, -ου, τό	child
ἄγω	I lead
βαπτίζω (stem: βαπτιδ-)	I baptize
εὑρίσκω (stem: εὑρ-)	I find
κηρύσσω (stem: κηρυκ-)	I preach
πέμπω	I send
πιστεύω	I believe
σῴζω (stem: σῳδ- or σωδ-)[2]	I save

Analysis

English Meaning. A noun designates a person, place or thing. A verb expresses action or a state of being. Meaning is generated by relationships among nouns and verbs. In English, word relationships are indicated by *word order* and *prepositions*, which helps explain why Greek is perceived "harder." For example, note the order:

He   **is saying**   **the words.**
(Subject)   (Predicate)   (Object)

---

[2]The stem of σῴδω varies in ancient sources. Some show iota subscript, as if from σῳδ-, some do not, as if from σωδ-.

Word Order. The primary way of generating meaning in English is word *order*. Observe how the subject, "He," occurs first. The verb "is saying" follows the subject. The direct object, "the words," comes last, after the verb. This positioning of words actually creates the sense of the sentence in English. Notice how changing the word order makes the sentence sound "awkward": "The words is saying he." Thus, an English speaking person even can make some sense out of nonsense simply by word order. Take the following nonsense sentence:

The monwees renabed the knop.

While you have no idea of precise lexical meaning, you still have an intelligible flow of the ideas: subject = "monwees," verbal action = "renabed," direct object = "knop." This flow is not a guess on your part, but meaning you derived in part out of *word order*. The English word order pattern—subject, predicate, object—you applied immediately to the nonsense sentence and squeezed *some* sense from the statement. You probably could do the same with the even greater nonsense sentence:

Eht tneduts deiduts eht nossel.

Prepositions. The second way of indicating relationship in English is through prepositions. Note how further relationships of other sub-groups of words are given through prepositions in the following sentence: "He is saying the words of the gospel to the man." In this sentence, the preposition "of" provides a way of relating the following phrase "the gospel" to the direct object "the words." Further, the preposition "to" alerts the English reader to the indirect object "the man" to be related to the action of the verb, "is saying." Thus, in English, both word order and prepositions provide relationships among words in a sentence.[3]

Greek Meaning. Greek is different. Greek does not depend on word order to provide word relationships for the sense of the sentence. Further, Greek has prepositions, but does not have to use them.

Inflection. The reason is simple. *Greek indicates word relationships with word endings.* These endings are called "inflection." Inflection is a particular change in a word's ending to indicate a particular type of relationship, or function, in the sentence: subject, direct object, indirect object, and so forth. A *declension* is a

---

[3]Inflection occurs in English in a minor way: subjective ("I," "we"), possessive ("my," "mine," "our," "ours"), and objective ("me," "us"). But the *meaning* still fundamentally is communicated through word order and prepositions, not this minor inflection. Some words do not change their form at all in any of the three English cases (cf. "student" as subjective, objective, and possessive).

particular pattern of inflection for a given noun. Greek has three major patterns of inflection for nouns, hence the three declensions. Inflection does not change the basic meaning of the word, just the particular relationship to other words in the sentence. In the figure below is one of many possible configurations in Greek of the example sentence, "He is saying the words of the gospel to the man."

Table 4.1 Inflection as Word Relationships

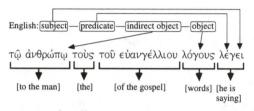

So word order is not essential to meaning in Greek. The subject does not have to be first. The direct object does not have to be after the verb. *Need for word order is made mute by inflection.* The inflection shows relationship to the other words of the sentence, not word order. So you carefully must note word endings to generate sense out of a Greek sentence. Since Greek does not rely on word order, English students heavily conditioned to expect word order to generate sense out of a sentence are caught off-guard initially in their study of Greek. Train yourself immediately to start to think word *endings*, not word order!

Position. While word order is not structurally crucial to meaning in Greek, sometimes position can indicate some meaning, especially *primary position.* The head of the sentence or the clause is called the "primary position," or sometimes

Table 4.2 Primary Position

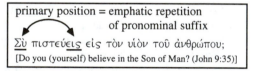

"positive position." A Greek word can be placed in primary position for *emphasis.* A common example occurs with personal pronouns. The Greek verb already has a pronominal suffix. A personal pronoun beginning the clause intensifies the meaning from "you," for example, to "you *yourself*."

Words which never occur first in a clause are called *postpositives.* Words such as γάρ and δέ are examples. (You learn this function as a part of vocabulary or simply by observation.) Postpositives always are positioned as the *second* word

Table 4.3 Postpositive Position

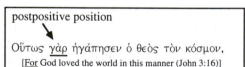

in the Greek clause. However, in English translation, postpositives still are translated first, for this is their regular position in English.

Components. Greek nouns consist of the following components: case, gender, number, lexical form. We discuss these components, then show structural formation of the second declension.

Table 4.4 Greek Noun Components—Case

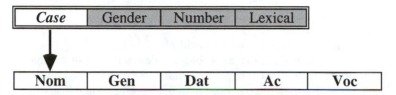

| Nom | Gen | Dat | Ac | Voc |

Table 4.5 Word Relationships—The Greek Cases

Case	Function	Relationship
Nominative	designation, naming	**subject**
Genitive	description, possession	*of*
	separation, origin, source	*of, from, by*
Dative	personal interest	*to, for,* **indirect object**
	location	*in, on, at, by, among*
	means, agency	*by, with*
Accusative	extension	**direct object**
Vocative	direct address	[not connected]

Case. Each type of word relationship in Greek is called a "case." Greek has five cases if one counts distinct forms. Greek has eight cases if one counts distinct functions. We will use a "five case" system, so we will show five distinct forms. At the same time, we will refer to eight distinct functions.[4] The descriptions offered in the table are intended simply to convey a *basic* idea for each case.

---

[4]The student needs to be alerted to the variation of terminology among grammars. Five distinct *forms* and yet eight distinct *functions* caused grammarians to debate the descriptive accuracy of labeling Greek as a "five" or an "eight" case system. A few grammars still refer to Greek as an "eight case" system, under the influence of A. T. Robertson. Most modern grammars refer to Greek as a

New Testament examples are provided in English with the inflected Greek word to illustrate these case functions. You are not expected to remember the details of these examples, but notice word endings. Visualize that case means *function*.

| Nominative |

Nominative ("N"). The nominative is the case of *designation* or naming—usually the subject of the sentence. Other uses would be, for example, as a *predicate nominative,* that is, a nominative following a form of the verb "to be." The masculine singular, second declension ending is -ος.

1. the **κόσμος** is passing away = **world** (1 John 2:17)
2. you call me **διδάσκαλος** and **κύριος**. = **Teacher** and **Lord** (John 13:13)
3. **Παῦλος δοῦλος** of Christ Jesus = **Paul, a servant** (Rom. 1:1)
4. I am the **ἄρτος** of life = **bread** (John 6:35, predicate nominative)

♦ *Genitive and dative cases often require use of a preposition for translation.*

| Genitive |

Genitive ("G"). All genitives *describe*, but some further show possession or ownership, specification or kind. In English, for example, we use an "apostrophe s" for ownership, as in "the student's book." Essentially, the genitive answers the question, "what kind?" The masculine singular ending is -ου (first declension feminine, next lesson, is -ας). A common preposition to use is "of."

1. children **θεοῦ = of God** (John 1:12; possession)
2. body **ἁμαρτίας = of sin** (Rom. 6:6; description)
3. Simon **Ἰωάννου** = (son) **of John** (John 21:15; relationship)

| Ablative |

The *ablative* function is a subcategory of the genitive case. The ablative shows *origin, source, separation, departure*. With passive voice the ablative shows *personal* agency. The form of the ending is the same as the genitive. A common preposition to use is "from." Thus:

1. **αὐτοῦ** at his appearing = **from him** (1 John 2:28; separation)
2. a voice **οὐρανῶν** saying = **from heaven** (Matt. 3:17; source; plural form)
3. I have need **σοῦ** to be baptized = **by you** (Matt. 3:14; personal agency)

"five case" system. The "genitive" case form in a five case system means both "genitive" and "ablative" functions in an eight case system. The "dative" case form in a five case system means "locative," "instrumental," and "dative" functions in the eight case system. However, even in a five case system, neuter nouns illustrate a problem of attempting to use forms to distinguish "cases." For any neuter noun, nominative, vocative, and accusative endings always are the same form—yet we have three distinct functions. Thus, we compromise. We ask the student to learn five case forms in paradigms and yet to recognize eight case *functions* in translation. This saves time later in syntax. All Greek students should take a course in syntax. A good text still is James A. Brooks and Carlton L. Winbery, *Syntax of New Testament Greek* (Lanham, MD: University Press of America, Inc., 1979).

Dative

Dative ("D"). The dative indicates *personal interest*. Often in Greek this is equivalent to the English *indirect object* ("to whom" or "for whom" something is done). The second declension ending for dative masculine singular words is -ῳ. (Be sure to notice the iota subscript.) Common prepositions to use are "to" and "for." Examples are:

1. they were bringing **αὐτῷ** children = **to him** (Mark 10:13; indirect object)
2. I judged this **ἐμαυτῷ** = **for myself** (2 Cor. 2:1; advantage)
3. name **αὐτῷ** John = **his** (John 1:6; possession, with personal interest; literally, "name **to him** [was] John")

Locative

The *locative* function is the first of two subcategories of the dative case. Locative indicates *location* or *position* (the "in" case). Endings are the same as the dative. Examples 2 and 3 use the first declension endings η and α (note iota subscript). Common prepositions to use are "in," "at," "on." Thus:

1. if anyone be **Χριστῷ** = **in Christ** (2 Cor. 5:17; sphere)
2. they placed it **κεφαλῇ** = **on** (his) **head** (John 19:2; place)
3. **μιᾷ** of the week = **on the first** (day) (Luke 24:11; time)

Instrumental

The *instrumental* function is a second subcategory of the dative case. Instrumental use points to *means* or *agency*. The instrumental shows *impersonal* agency when used with the passive voice. The endings are the same as the dative. Examples one and three use first declension endings, four a masculine plural (-οις). Common prepositions to use are "by" and "with."

1. to kill **ῥομφαίᾳ** = **with the sword** (Rev. 6:8; means)
2. **λιμῷ** I am perishing here = **because of famine** (Luke 15:17; cause)
3. **ἐπιθυμίᾳ** I have longed = **with great desire** (Luke 22:15; manner, i.e., circumstances accompanying an action)
4. he eats **αὐτοῖς** = **with them** (Luke 15:2; association)
5. he casts out spirits **λόγῳ** = **with a word** (Matt. 8:16; impersonal agency)

Accusative

Accusative ("Ac"). The accusative is *extension*. Often, this is the *direct object*; yet, think more than just direct object. Concentrate on "extension"—adverbial action which enriches the verbal idea. The accusative case indicates measure, reference, intensity or other *adverbial* quality. This extension of the verb inherently limits the verbal action. A verb can have *two* accusatives, variously called the *double accusative* or the *object complement*. Example one is a masculine plural; two, feminine singular; three, neuter singular; four is a double accusative (both masculine singular).

1. he was teaching the **ὄχλους** = **crowds** (Luke 5:3; object)
2. it fell beside the **ὁδόν** = **road** (Mark 4:4; measure)

3.   to be wise **ἀγαθόν** = (with reference to) **the good** (Rom. 16:19; adverb of
     reference)
4.   David called **κύριον αὐτὸν** = **him Lord** (Luke 20:44, double accusative)

| Vocative |

Vocative ("V"). This is the case of direct address ("Lord,
save us!"). Technically, the vocative is not a case, because the
vocative has no grammatical relationship to the rest of the
sentence. The vocative is infrequent in the New Testament, generally has the same
form as the nominative, and is set off by commas in the edited Greek text. (In other
words, one hardly can miss a vocative, even without memorization.) The end result
is that in the paradigms, the vocative often is not included.

1.   **Κύριε**, come and see. = **Lord** (John 11:34; address)
2.   **υἱὲ** of the devil = **you son** (Acts 13:10; address)
3.   **Ἄνδρες** of Judea = **Men** (Acts 2:14; address)

Table 4.6 Greek Noun Components—Gender

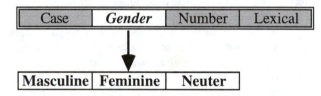

Gender. Greek has three genders—masculine, feminine, and neuter. Greek
gender is a *grammatical* function, *not* sex identification. This is different than in
English and takes some adjustment. Further, Greek gender is not predictable. For
example, "world" is masculine (not neuter). "Road" is feminine (not neuter).

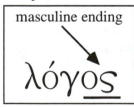

So, how will one know
the gender of a Greek word?
Gender is memorized as a
part of vocabulary work. The
vocabulary will show gender
through the definite article.
Most nouns ending in -ος are

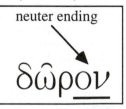

(second declension) masculine. Such nouns will take the masculine definite article,
which is ὁ. *All* nouns ending in -ον are second declension *neuter* nouns and take the
neuter article, τό. *A few second declension nouns ending in -ος are feminine*, as are
ὁδός and ἔρημος, and take the feminine article, ἡ (studied later). The definite article
with such nouns will indicate the feminine gender (as in ἡ ὁδός instead of ὁ ὁδός).

Table 4.7 Greek Noun Components—Number

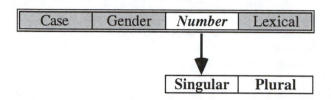

Number. The number of a noun is either singular or plural. The Classical Greek dual number disappeared in koine Greek.

Table 4.8 Greek Noun Components—Lexical

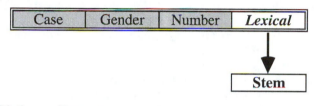

Table 4.9 Dictionary Format

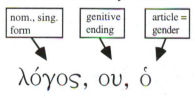

Lexical. The lexical form of the word is the dictionary form, always given as the nominative singular. Remember, the ending of the nominative singular will vary according to the three genders. The genitive singular ending is listed next. This is provided to notify the student of the declension pattern, especially third declension. This declension will generate some confusion with endings. The genitive singular ending in the third declension usually is -ος, exactly the same form as the nominative masculine singular ending of the second declension. One will want to know whether the noun is a regular second declension, meaning the -ος form is a nominative, or a third declension, meaning the -ος form is a genitive. The last item listed in the dictionary entry is the article form to declare gender. Sometimes gender is given with a letter ("m," "n," "f").

Thus, the entry "λόγος, ου, ὁ" indicates that the noun is a regular second declension masculine noun taking the masculine article form ὁ, whose genitive singular form is λόγου. In contrast, the entry "ὁδός, ου, ἡ" indicates that the noun is a second declension noun, whose genitive singular form is ὁδοῦ, but which is *feminine*, because of the feminine article, ἡ. On the other hand, the entry "σῶμα, -ματος, τό" indicates that the noun is a *third* declension neuter noun taking the neuter article τό, whose genitive singular form is σώματος (hence, a third declension -ος form). Vocabulary in this grammar is entered in this typical dictionary pattern.

Stem. The second declension noun stem derives from the nominative singular form (the first dictionary entry). Remove the inflectional ending (-ος from λόγος or -ον from δῶρον), and this provides the base for building the declension.[5] (Third declension stems, studied later, derive from the *second* entry, the genitive form.)

Hidden. Lexical noun forms do not always reflect the base of the declension (similar to the problem in verbs). A "hidden" stem different from the lexical, especially in first and third declensions, will be pointed out in vocabulary.

Formation

Having surveyed the Greek noun system in an analysis of the noun's component parts (case, person, number, lexical), we now turn to the procedure for constructing the second declension. This is a simple process.

Noun Stem. As mentioned before, nouns have three major declensions, first, second, and third. Our second declension study will use four paradigms: λόγος, υἱός, δῶρον, and ἱερόν.

The form λόγος is how the student will find the word listed in the dictionary. So we start with the lexical form. Drop the nominative, masculine singular ending -ος. The stem, then, of the masculine noun λόγος is λογ-.

$$\lambda\acute{o}\gamma o\varsigma = \lambda o\gamma -$$

Inflectional Endings. To this stem one adds the appropriate endings. These endings are given in the table below. The eight functions compress into *only five distinct case forms* in the masculine singular (-ος, -ου, -ῳ, -ον, -ε) and plural (-οι, -ων, -οις, -ους, -οι) and the neuter singular (-ον, -ου, -ῳ, -ον, -ον) and plural (-α, -ων, -οις, -α, -α).

---

[5]The vowel omicron (o) actually is part of the stem (λογο-, δωρο-). Thus, the second declension also is known as the "omicron" declension, for all the noun stems end with the vowel omicron. However, this vowel ending is obscured in some forms due to contraction. *The omicron gets lost in the shuffle.* Learning the vowel as part of *inflection* makes stems *appear* regular, i.e., more "familiar."

Table 4.10 Second Declension Inflections

	Masculine		Neuter	
	Sing.	Plu.	Sing.	Plu.
N	-ος	-οι	-ον	-α
G	-ου	-ων	-ου	-ων
D	-ῳ	-οις	-ῳ	-οις
A	-ον	-ους	-ον	-α
V	-ε	-οι	-ον	-α

In the format of the table, we can refer to the genitive and dative cases as the "interior" cases. Notice the interior cases. Masculine and neuter forms are identical. This neuter replication of the masculine is true across the board in all paradigms of the various substantives (that is, nouns, pronouns, adjectives). Masculine and neuter distinctions occur in nominative and accusative cases only. Learn the masculine paradigm, and you already have learned half of any neuter paradigm! Further still, the other two cases of the neuter, nominative and accusative, duplicate each other. These two observations are important neuter declension inflection patterns to pick up quickly to reduce memorization work.[6]

♦ *Neuter forms replicate masculine forms in the interior cases.*

♦ *Neuter accusative replicates the neuter nominative.*

Continuing our noun formation, to the noun stem add the appropriate case ending, given gender. The gender of our example is masculine, so we will choose among the masculine endings. Take the masculine accusative plural, for example:

$$λογ\text{-}ους$$

stem + ending

Thus, we have:

$$λόγους$$

---

[6]For this reason, frequently, instead of the traditional order of gender in tables (masculine, feminine, neuter) we have swapped neuter and feminine (masculine, neuter, feminine) to illustrate how similar neuter usually is to masculine.

This accusative form would translate as "words," and could function as a direct object in the sentence.[7] For example, λέγει **λόγους** = "He is saying **words**." Notice how the subject is given by verb inflection of a particular conjugation, and the direct object is given by noun inflection of a particular declension. The term λόγους is direct object, *not* because the word follows the verb, but because of the inflection. The order λόγους λέγει would have the same translation.

Neuter nouns are formed similarly. We use δῶρον as our example. Drop the nominative, neuter singular ending -ον. The stem is δωρ-.

$$\delta\hat{\omega}\rho\cancel{ov} = \delta\omega\rho\text{-}$$

The accusative plural ending, *neuter* gender is -α. Add this inflection to the stem:

$$\delta\omega\rho\text{-}\alpha$$

Thus, we have:

$$\delta\hat{\omega}\rho\alpha$$

This accusative would translate as "gifts," and could function as a direct object. For example, πέμπει **δῶρα** = "He is sending **gifts**."

Declension. To "decline" a noun means give the different inflectional forms in singular and plural number for that particular word. For λόγος, one would give the five singular forms: λόγος, λόγου, λόγῳ, λόγον, λόγε, and then the five plural forms: λόγοι, λόγων, λόγοις, λόγους, λόγοι. Similarly for δῶρον, one would give the five singular forms: δῶρον, δώρου, δώρῳ, δῶρον, δῶρον, and then the five plural forms: δῶρα, δώρων, δώροις, δῶρα, δῶρα. The vocative reduplicates the nominative in masculine plural and all neuter forms. The vocative masculine singular is distinct—a rarity. A four row paradigm means the vocative is to be taken to have the same form as the nominative, so only four distinct forms actually need be specified.

---

[7]One would *not* put a neuter ending on a masculine stem or vice versa.

Table 4.11 Second Declension—Masculine and Neuter Paradigms

	λόγος			δῶρον	
Case	Singular	Plural	Case	Singular	Plural
N	λόγος	λόγοι	N	δῶρον	δῶρα
G	λόγου	λόγων	G	δώρου	δώρων
D	λόγῳ	λόγοις	D	δώρῳ	δώροις
A	λόγον	λόγους	A	δῶρον	δῶρα
V	λόγε	λόγοι	V	δῶρον	δῶρα

Table 4.12 Basic Translations

	Singular		Plural	
Case	Form	Translation	Form	Translation
N	λόγος	"a word" (subject)	λόγοι	"words" (subject)
G	λόγου	"of a word"	λόγων	"of words"
		"from a word"		"from words"
D	λόγῳ	"to a word"	λόγοις	"to words"
		"in a word"		"in words"
		"by a word"		"by words"
A	λόγον	"a word" (direct object)	λόγους	"words" (direct object)
V	λόγε	"Word" (address)	λόγοι	"Words" (address)

Several prepositions are possible for some inflectional forms (Table 4.5). Which preposition to use requires attention to the specific context and observations of syntax. These are skills which you will develop over time. Greek prepositions, studied later, further will help clarify the Greek cases.[8]

---

[8]For example, the preposition ἀπό, used with the ablative function only, might clarify the form λόγου as "from a word" (source) and not "of a word" (specification) in a given context.

Using Table 4.12 and the vocabulary at the beginning of this lesson, suggest a translation of the sentence below. Concentrate on the word *endings* to do this. The answer is given in the footnote, but first try yourself. The form ὁ means "the."

δούλοις καὶ ἀνθρώποις λέγει ὁ κύριος λόγους νόμου.[9]

Location. Distinguish "locate" from "decline." To "locate" a noun in the Greek text, you specify that individual noun form's *four component parts*: case, gender, number, lexical form, plus meaning. As our example in this section:

λόγους

Table 4.13 Location: Four Components Plus Meaning (λόγους)

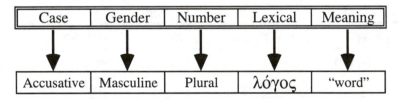

Case	Gender	Number	Lexical	Meaning
Accusative	Masculine	Plural	λόγος	"word"

Table 4.14 Oxytone Paradigms—Masculine and Neuter

	υἱός			ἱερόν	
Case	*Singular*	*Plural*	*Case*	*Singular*	*Plural*
N	υἱός	υἱοί	N	ἱερόν	ἱερά
G	υἱοῦ	υἱῶν	G	ἱεροῦ	ἱερῶν
D	υἱῷ	υἱοῖς	D	ἱερῷ	ἱεροῖς
A	υἱόν	υἱούς	A	ἱερόν	ἱερά
V	υἱέ	υἱοί	V	ἱερόν	ἱερά

---

[9]The translation is: "The Lord is speaking words of law to servants and men."

Oxytones. An oxytone is any noun having an *acute* accent in the *ultima* in the nominative singular form (that is, in the lexical form in the dictionary). The term "oxytone" means "sharp-toned." Vocabulary examples are: the masculine nouns θεός, ἀδελφός, οὐρανός, υἱός, and Χριστός, and the neuter noun ἱερόν. Oxytone nouns paradigms show different *accents*. The key is simple: *the interior cases take circumflex accent on the ultima* ("interiors go circumflex").[10]

The Definite Article

Analysis. Greek has a definite article but *not an indefinite article* (as does English with "a," "an"). Greek is more efficient than English in this regard, for the English indefinite article is, in fact, superfluous.

Anarthrous
λόγος

Anarthrous construction. The term *anarthrous* means, in effect, "without the article." An anarthrous noun does not have a definite article in the construction. An anarthrous Greek noun is understood naturally to be indefinite. The translations in the paradigms in Table 4.12 above include the English indefinite article—because no Greek definite article is present. That is, the above paradigms are anarthrous constructions, so we include "a" or "an" automatically.

Articular
ὁ λόγος

Articular construction. The term *articular* means, in effect, "with the article."[11] An articular noun *does* have the definite article in the construction. Note: the article may not be immediately adjacent! "The" is used in translation.

The basic function of the Greek article is to point. The article points to a noun, but the article can point to an entire group of words, even verbal units such as participles and infinitives. The article can

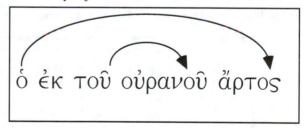

ὁ ἐκ τοῦ οὐρανοῦ ἄρτος

---

[10]Neuter oxytone *nouns* (second declension) actually are quite rare in the New Testament. They are: ἑρπετόν ("reptile"), ἱερόν ("temple"), Ἰλλυρικόν ("Illyricum"), λουτρόν ("bath"), πετεινόν ("bird"), σφυδρόν ("ankle;" variant σφυρόν in א² B² D E Ψ 𝔐), and ᾠόν ("egg"). However, though the noun is rare, *the neuter oxytone noun paradigm is important* because many neuter *adjectives* are oxytone, so the neuter *adjectives* will follow the second declension neuter noun paradigm (ἱερόν).

[11]English terms derive from the Greek ἄρθρον, "article." Articular also is called "arthrous."

be separated by other words from the noun to which the article points, such as in a prepositional phrase (e.g., ὁ ἐκ τοῦ οὐρανοῦ **ἄρτος**; literally, "**the** out of the heaven **bread**" = "the heavenly bread"). To find what the article points to, *carefully note concord* (on "concord," see below).

This quite flexible Greek article actually can be difficult to translate, for the use in Greek goes well beyond the use in English. The article can occur more times in Greek than needs translating into English (e.g., Μακάριοι **οἱ** πτωχοὶ **τῷ** πνεύματι; literally, "blessed (are) **the** poor in **the** spirit" = "the poor in spirit"). Proper names usually take an article, but translating this pointer is not imperative (ὁ Ἰησοῦς = "Jesus," not "the Jesus;" τοῦ θεοῦ = "of God," not "of the God"). Abstract nouns are the same way (ἡ ἀγάπη = "love," not "the love," as in 1 Cor. 13:13).

Inherent articular. Words which have a distinctive character, or a uniqueness in a class, already are distinct inherently. Thus, an anarthrous noun still can be definite, even without the article. For example, ἥλιος without the article still can be translated "the sun," since only one sun in our particular solar system exists. Notice how "sun," "moon," and "stars" all are anarthrous in Luke 21:25 (UBS[4]), but are translated variously with or without English definite articles (cf. RSV and NRSV). Other words to notice without the article yet articular in idea are: θεός, πνεῦμα, κόσμος, and νόμος.[12] Context can be an important factor for determining distinctiveness.

Formation. *The article does not belong to any one declension.* The same article paradigm works in all three declensions. Inflection still has the case significance: ὁ = "the" as pointing to the subject, whereas τοῦ = "of the" or "from the," τῷ = "to the," "by the," or "in the" and τόν = "the" as pointing to the direct object. The plurals mean the same as the singulars, just pointing to plural nouns.

Table 4.15 Definite Article—Masculine (ὁ) and Neuter (τό)

	ὁ		τό		
Case	Sing.	Plural	Sing.	Plural	Meaning
N	ὁ	οἱ	τό	τά	"the"
G	τοῦ	τῶν	τοῦ	τῶν	"of the," etc.
D	τῷ	τοῖς	τῷ	τοῖς	"to the," etc.
A	τόν	τούς	τό	τά	"the"

---

[12]Thus, translating John 1:1 as "the Word was a god" (θεὸς ἦν ὁ λόγος) does not reflect actual Greek grammar.

Gender. The article is declined in all three genders. The article, when present, is the *unfailing indicator of the gender of any noun,* because of concord (see below).

Proclitics. Observe that the nominative masculine forms of the article have no accent. These unaccented forms represent a class of words that are called *proclitics.* A proclitic so "leans upon" the word following as to have no accent of its own. Proclitics simply are to be treated as another syllable prefixed to the following word.

Notes.

1. The first letter always is τ except nominative masculine forms. This provides a similar look to the English definite article with its beginning "t."
2. The endings are very close to the second declension endings, but with a prefixed τ. The four exceptions are: nominative masculine singular and plural (ὁ, not τός; οἱ, not τοί) and the nominative and accusative neuter singular (τό, not τόν for both).
3. The accent follows the *oxytone pattern* ("interiors go circumflex").
4. Nominative forms of the masculine have *rough* breathing.
5. Nominative forms of the masculine have *no accent* (= proclitic).

Concord. Concord is a grammatical principle of "agreement" in the basic components of the noun: case, gender, number. Thus, for example, this concord principle specifies that adjectives must agree in case, gender, and number with the nouns they modify. Adjectives are said to be "in concord" with the nouns they modify when both the noun and the adjective have the same case, gender, and number. The definite article always maintains concord.

Table 4.16 The Principle of Concord

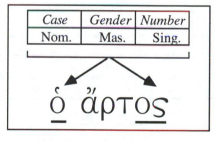

Case	Gender	Number
Nom.	Mas.	Sing.

♦ *The gender of the definite article declares the gender of the noun.*

The principle of concord also is important for understanding that a word can be articular, *even though the article is not immediately adjacent* to the noun or clause pointed to by the article. Our example of an intervening prepositional phrase used earlier again illustrates: ὁ ἐκ τοῦ οὐρανοῦ ἄρτος = "the out of the heaven bread." Concord indicates that ὁ goes with ἄρτος; that is, ἄρτος is in articular construction, even though the article is not immediately adjacent.

Translation. The masculine noun λόγος in articular constructions is illustrated below. Since the vocative is independent syntactically, this case does not have a definite article construction. Notice that the acute ultima of the article goes to grave when no punctuation intervenes—the grave rule of accent. Finally, observe the *oxytone accent pattern of the articles.*

Table 4.17 Masculine Articular Constructions—ὁ λόγος

	Singular	Translation	Plural	Translation
N	ὁ λόγος	"the word"	οἱ λόγοι	"the words"
G	τοῦ λόγου	"of the word"	τῶν λόγων	"of the words"
		"from the word"		"from the words"
D	τῷ λόγῳ	"to the word"	τοῖς λόγοις	"to the words"
		"in the word"		"in the words"
		"by the word"		"by the words"
A	τὸν λόγον	"the word"	τοὺς λόγους	"the words"
V	λόγε	"Word"	λόγοι	"Words"

Table 4.18 Neuter Articular Constructions—τὸ δῶρον

	Singular	Translation	Plural	Translation
N	τὸ δῶρον	"the gift"	τὰ δῶρα	"the gifts"
G	τοῦ δώρου	"of the gift"	τῶν δώρων	"of the gifts"
		"from the gift"		"from the gifts"
D	τῷ δώρῳ	"to the gift"	τοῖς δώροις	"to the gifts"
		"in the gift"		"in the gifts"
		"by the gift"		"by the gifts"
A	τὸ δῶρον	"the gift"	τὰ δῶρα	"the gifts"
V	δῶρον	"Gift"	δῶρα	"Gifts"

The *neuter* articular forms are given also. Close observation will reveal that these neuter forms correspond exactly to the masculine forms in the interiors. This conformity is a neuter pattern already pointed out. Observe further that the nominative and accusative articular forms are alike; thus, the singular for both nominative and accusative is τὸ δῶρον ("the gift," as subject *or* as direct object); the plural form is τὰ δῶρα ("the gifts," as subject *or* as direct object). Once again, also notice how the grave accents conform to the grave accent rule (no intervening punctuation). Finally, observe the oxytone accent pattern.

Neuter Plural. An oddity in Greek is that a *neuter plural can take a singular verb.* The idea of a *collective* plural is present (a noun considered as a class or as a collective identity). Observe: τὰ τέκνα λαμβάνει τὸν ἄρτον, "the children are receiving the bread." Here, τέκνα is nominative *plural*, but λαμβάνει is third person *singular*. The idea "children" is understood in this case as a collective plural.

Table 4.19 Neuter Plural with Singular Verb

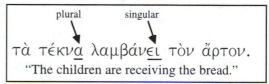

plural   singular

τὰ τέκνα λαμβάνει τὸν ἄρτον.
"The children are receiving the bread."

Compound Subject. Another oddity is the *compound subject,* which always is plural in English, but not in Greek. *The element of the compound subject closest to the verb determines the number of the verb.*[13]

Noun Accents

Persistent Accent. Noun accents are labeled *persistent.* If accenting rules allow, the noun's accent will persist in the syllable of the lexical form. Notice this feature in the paradigm of λόγος. The acute accent persists in the

Table 4.20 Noun Accent—Persistent Example

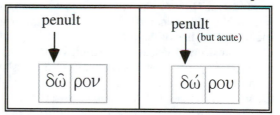

penult	penult (but acute)
δῶ ρον	δώ ρου

---

[13]Thus, observe: κηρύσσει ὁ Ἰησοῦς καὶ οἱ μαθηταὶ = "Jesus and the disciples are preaching." The subject is compound, but the verb is singular because of the singular Ἰησοῦς. Switch the order of the compound subject such that the plural nominative μαθηταί is closest to the verb, and the verb becomes plural: κηρύσσουσιν οἱ μαθηταὶ καὶ ὁ Ἰησοῦς = "the disciples and Jesus are preaching." Though the resultant translation is the same in either example, this second configuration is parallel to standard English usage, while the first is not. For the declension of μαθητής, ὁ, see pp. 95–96.

penult position, because no rules of accent prevent the acute from doing so as one moves through the formation of the paradigm.

Contrast δῶρον. The circumflex changes to acute when the ultima becomes long. This is the problem of the quantity of the ultima. If the ultima is *long*, rules of accent require that an accented penult *must* be acute. The accent of δῶρον on the penult persists in that position as a noun, but must change to acute not to violate the rules concerning long ultimas.

Antepenult Acute. Some masculine and neuter nouns have an acute accent on the antepenult in the lexical form. For such nouns, a long ultima in some inflectional forms pulls this antepenult

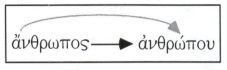

acute back to the penult. Masculine examples would be ἄνθρωπος (cf. ἀνθρώπου, ἀνθρώπῳ, ἀνθρώπων, ἀνθρώποις, ἀνθρώπους), and κύριος (cf. κυρίου, κυρίῳ, κυρίων, κυρίοις, κυρίους). Neuter examples would be εὐαγγέλιον (cf. εὐαγγελίου, εὐαγγελίῳ, εὐαγγελίων, εὐαγγελίοις, εὐαγγελίους), and πρόσωπον (προσώπου, προσώπῳ, προσώπων, προσώποις, προσώπους).[14]

Diagramming

Direct Object. The direct object of the verb (usually accusative) is placed on the horizontal base line following the verb, but separated by a perpendicular stroke which does not break the horizontal. A double accusative (also termed the "object complement") immediately follows the direct object on the horizontal, but separated by a line slanted to the left which does not break the horizontal.

Indirect Object. The indirect object (dative) is placed parallel underneath the verb. A line with a slant to the left is drawn downward to connect the indirect object line to the base line of the verb.

Prepositional Phrase. The genitive and dative cases usually come across as some type of prepositional phrase in English translation. As modifiers, such phrases are placed underneath the word modified on a parallel line, again, joined by a line slanted to the left, as with the indirect object.

Definite Article. The Greek article's function is more complex than the English and is hard to represent by diagramming. The best solution is to position each article on the same line and immediately before whatever is the word of concord.

---

[14]The forms ἄθρωποι and κύριοι have a *final* -οι, which for accent is considered short, though a diphthong; the antepenult acute remains. The -α of the neuter nominative and accusative plural endings is considered short; hence, the antepenult acutes on εὐαγγέλια and πρόσωπα are correct.

Table 4.21 Diagramming Substantives

1. γράφω τοὺς λόγους. "I am writing the words."	*Direct Object and Definite Article* 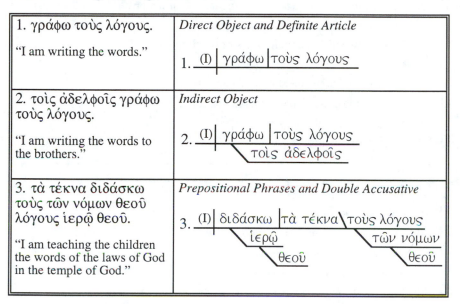
2. τοῖς ἀδελφοῖς γράφω τοὺς λόγους. "I am writing the words to the brothers."	*Indirect Object*
3. τὰ τέκνα διδάσκω τοὺς τῶν νόμων θεοῦ λόγους ἱερῷ θεοῦ. "I am teaching the children the words of the laws of God in the temple of God."	*Prepositional Phrases and Double Accusative*

What To Learn—LESSON 4 (τέσσαρες)

Beginning

☐ 1. The two main ways English generates meaning contrasted with Greek

☐ 2. The definition of *primary position* and of *postpositive* position

☐ 3. Components of a Greek noun: *case, gender, number, lexical*

☐ 4. The basic idea or the essential function of each Greek case and English prepositions associated with each

☐ 5. Significance of Greek gender

☐ 6. Pattern of the lexical entry format for Greek nouns

☐ 7. Second declension masculine and neuter endings

☐ 8. Second declension paradigms λόγος, δῶρον

☐   9. How to locate a noun

☐ 10. Definitions of *anarthrous* and *articular* constructions

☐ 11. Function of the Greek definite article

☐ 12. Masculine and neuter paradigms of the definite article

☐ 13. Meaning of the principle of *concord*

☐ 14. Significance of the neuter plural subject

☐ 15. Reverse the order of the letters in the nonsense statement (p. 43)

☐ 16. Diagramming substantives

☐ 17. Vocabulary words

Advanced

☐ 18. Definition of an *oxytone*

☐ 19. Oxytone rule of accents

☐ 20. Oxytone paradigms: υἱός, ἱερόν

☐ 21. Definition of *proclitic*

☐ 22. Meaning of *persistent accent*

☐ 23. Compound subjects and subject/verb agreement (p. 59, n. 13)

LESSON 5 (πέντε)
First Declension

κapδία, ἀγάπη

Mostly feminine nouns, first declension noun endings basically use a pattern incorporating either -α or -η. Some masculine nouns are found in the first declension, ending in -ας, -ης. In contrast, some feminine nouns ending in -ος are of the second declension. Such nouns will be presented later.

Vocabulary 5

Word		Stem	Meaning
πέντε	numeral		five
ἡ	definite article (feminine)		the
ἀλήθεια, -ας, ἡ		(-ε, -ι, -ρ)	truth
ἁμαρτία, -ας, ἡ		(-ε, -ι, -ρ)	sin
βασιλεία, -ας, ἡ		(-ε, -ι, -ρ)	kingdom
ἐκκλησία, -ας, ἡ		(-ε, -ι, -ρ)	church
ἡμέρα, -ας, ἡ		(-ε, -ι, -ρ)	day
καρδία, -ας, ἡ		(-ε, -ι, -ρ)	heart
χαρά, -ας, ἡ		(-ε, -ι, -ρ)	joy
ὥρα, -ας, ἡ		(-ε, -ι, -ρ)	hour
ἀγάπη, -ης, ἡ		(-η pure)	love

γραφή, -ης, ἡ	(-η pure)	writing, scripture
διδαχή, -ης, ἡ	(-η pure)	teaching
εἰρήνη, -ης, ἡ	(-η pure)	peace
ἐντολή, -ης, ἡ	(-η pure)	commandment
ζωή, -ης, ἡ	(-η pure)	life
παραβολή, -ης, ἡ	(-η pure)	parable
φωνή, -ης, ἡ	(-η pure)	sound, voice
ψυχή, -ης, ἡ	(-η pure)	life, soul, living being
γλῶσσα, -ης, ἡ	(sibilant)	tongue
δόξα, -ης, ἡ	(sibilant)	glory
θάλασσα, -ης, ἡ	(sibilant)	sea

Stem Types

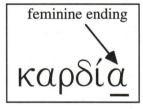

feminine ending

Feminine first declension nouns have three basic stems: (1) -ε, -ι, -ρ, (2) nominatives in -η, and (3) sibilants. All such nouns end in either -α or -η. Inflection patterns by stem type are given below.

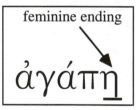

feminine ending

General Observations. These stem classifications are based on morphology alone and do not affect lexical meaning. Regardless of classification:

♦ *In first declension all the plurals are the same.*

Thus, after securing in memory the one plural pattern that applies regardless of stem type, the student should focus on the three simple singular patterns: one builds on the vowel α, another on the vowel η; the third mixes the two. Genitive singular (-ας, -ης) and accusative plural (-ας) *always* are long. The genitive plural *always* is circumflex. The -ε, -ι, -ρ stems are called "α pure." The nominatives in -η stems are called "η pure." The sibilant stems are called "α/η mixed."

Table 5.1 First Declension Inflection Patterns By Stem Type

| Case | Singulars by Stem Type | | | Plurals |
	-ε, -ι, -ρ	Nom. in -η	Sibilant	
N	-α	-η	-α	-αι
G	-ας	-ης	-ης	-ων
D	-ᾳ	-ῃ	-ῃ	-αις
A	-αν	-ην	-αν	-ας

Table 5.2 First Declension—E, -ι, -ρ ("α pure") Stem Paradigms

| | καρδία | | | | ἀλήθεια | |
| | *(long a in N, Ac)* | | | | *(short a in N, Ac)* | |
Case	Singular	Plural		Case	Singular	Plural
N	καρδία	καρδίαι		N	ἀλήθεια	ἀλήθειαι
G	καρδίας	καρδιῶν		G	ἀληθείας	ἀληθειῶν
D	καρδίᾳ	καρδίαις		D	ἀληθείᾳ	ἀληθείαις
A	καρδίαν	καρδίας		A	ἀλήθειαν	ἀληθείας

Type 1: -E, -ι, -ρ Stems ("α pure"). *Notice the -α throughout the singular.* The alpha can be long or short, so a paradigm is given to represent either case. When long (καρδία), the alpha generates acute accents, *except in the genitive plural, which always is circumflex throughout the first declension regardless of accent rules* (καρδιῶν). Final -αι always is short, so the nominative plural is acute. A short alpha allows an acute accent on the antepenult (ἀλήθεια). If the

| | χαρά | |
| | *(oxytone)* | |
Case	Singular	Plural
N	χαρά	χαραί
G	χαρᾶς	χαρῶν
D	χαρᾷ	χαραῖς
A	χαράν	χαράς

nominative singular α is long (καρδία), the accusative singular will be long (καρδίαν). If the nominative singular α is short (ἀλήθεια), the accusative singular will be short (ἀλήθειαν). The oxytone paradigm (χαρά) provides both an alternate example using a -ρ stem and an illustration of the consistency of the oxytone pattern ("interiors go circumflex").

Table 5.3 First Declension—Nominative in -η ("η pure") Paradigms

Case	ἀγάπη (regular) Singular	Plural	Case	γραφή (oxytone) Singular	Plural
N	ἀγάπη	ἀγάπαι	N	γραφή	γραφαί
G	ἀγάπης	ἀγαπῶν	G	γραφῆς	γραφῶν
D	ἀγάπη	ἀγάπαις	D	γραφῇ	γραφαῖς
A	ἀγάπην	ἀγάπας	A	γραφήν	γραφάς

Type 2: Nominative in -η ("η pure"). This class represents stems other than Type 1 or Type 3. Notice the -η throughout the singular. *Any first declension noun whose lexical form ends in -η will retain that η throughout the singular* (= "η pure"). The γραφή paradigm represents oxytone accent.

Type 3: Sibilant Stems ("α/η mixed"). These are stems ending with most sibilants (-σ, -ξ, -ζ). *Notice how the interior singular slips to -η.* The singular starts with -α, as if conforming to Type 1. Then, the genitive and dative take the -η of Type 2, and return to the -α of Type 1 in the accusative. The plural is the same as *all* plurals. No oxytone first declension sibilant *noun* occurs in the New Testament.[1]

Table 5.4 Sibilant Paradigm

Case	δόξα Singular	Plural
N	δόξα	δόξαι
G	δόξης	δοξῶν
D	δόξῃ	δόξαις
A	δόξαν	δόξας

Feminine Article

The feminine definite article follows the γραφή pattern (i.e., nominative in -η; oxytone). The paradigm is given in the table. The proclitics forms are ἡ and αἱ (no

---

[1] Other forms are treated later (-ης, -ας masculines and contracted feminines γῆ, συκῆ, μνᾶ).

accent; but notice the *rough breathing*). Note the first τ- in most forms, reminiscent of the English article "the."

Recall that the one feminine article paradigm is used for *all* feminine nouns coming from *any* declension. The principle of concord, then, helps to locate any noun constructed with this article. In the paradigms that follow, notice the feminine article's concord with various feminine inflections.

Table 5.5 Definite Article—Feminine (ἡ)

	ἡ		
Case	*Sing.*	*Plural*	*Meaning*
N	ἡ	αἱ	"the"
G	τῆς	τῶν	"of the," etc.
D	τῇ	ταῖς	"to the," etc.
A	τήν	τάς	"the"

Table 5.6 Feminine Articular Constructions—ἡ καρδία

	Singular	Translation	Plural	Translation
N	ἡ καρδία	"the heart"	αἱ καρδίαι	"the hearts"
G	τῆς καρδίας	"of the heart" "from the heart"	τῶν καρδιῶν	"of the hearts" "from the hearts"
D	τῇ καρδίᾳ	"to the heart" "in the heart" "by the heart"	ταῖς καρδίαις	"to the hearts" "in the hearts" "by the hearts"
A	τὴν καρδίαν	"the heart"	τὰς καρδίας	"the hearts"

Table 5.7 Feminine Articular Constructions—ἡ ἀγάπη

	Singular	Translation	Plural	Translation
N	ἡ ἀγάπη	"the love"	αἱ ἀγάπαι	"the loves"
G	τῆς ἀγάπης	"of the love" "from the love"	τῶν ἀγαπῶν	"of the loves" "from the loves"
D	τῇ ἀγάπη	"to the love" "in the love" "by the love"	ταῖς ἀγάπαις	"to the loves" "in the loves" "by the loves"
A	τὴν ἀγάπην	"the love"	τὰς ἀγάπας	"the loves"

Table 5.8 Feminine Articular Constructions—ἡ δόξα

	Singular	Translation	Plural	Translation
N	ἡ δόξα	"the glory"	αἱ δόξαι	"the glories"
G	τῆς δόξης	"of the glory"	τῶν δοξῶν	"of the glories"
		"from the glory"		"from the glories"
D	τῇ δόξῃ	"to the glory"	ταῖς δόξαις	"to the glories"
		"in the glory"		"in the glories"
		"by the glory"		"by the glories"
A	τὴν δόξαν	"the glory"	τὰς δόξας	"the glories"

What To Learn—LESSON 5 (πέντε)

Beginning

☐ 1. Paradigms of καρδία, ἀγάπη, and δόξα
☐ 2. The paradigm of the feminine article, ἡ
☐ 3. The principle of concord of the feminine article
☐ 4. Vocabulary words

Advanced

☐ 5. The three stem types of first declension nouns
☐ 6. The meaning of "α pure" and "η pure" first declension nouns
☐ 7. Accenting variations of ἀλήθεια, χαρά, and γραφή

LESSON 6 (ἕξ)
Adjectives and Εἰμί

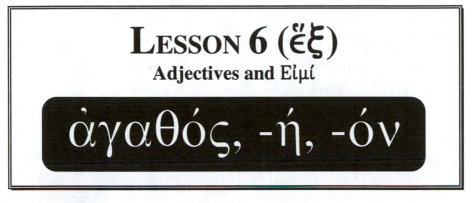

ἀγαθός, -ή, -όν

 Greek adjectives are inflected in concord with the noun modified. Thus, any adjective can be masculine, feminine, or neuter. Eighty-five percent of all New Testament adjectives show second and first declension noun inflection patterns. The key idea with Greek adjectives is that of "position."

Vocabulary 6

Word	Meaning
ἕξ	six (numeral)
εἰμί	I am
ἀγαθός, ἀγαθή, ἀγαθόν[1]	good
ἀγαπητός, ἀγαπητή, ἀγαπητόν	beloved
ἄλλος, ἄλλη, ἄλλο[2]	other, another (same kind)
βασιλικός, βασιλική, βασιλικόν	royal
δίκαιος, δικαία, δίκαιον	righteous, just
ἔσχατος, ἐσχάτη, ἔσχατον	last
ἕτερος, ἑτέρα, ἕτερον	another (different kind)

---

[1]Adjectives are given in all three genders in this introductory lesson. Later they will be abbreviated to the form ἀγαθός, -ή, -όν representing the three genders in their traditional order.

[2]Nominative and accusative singular end in -o, not -ov. This is a pronoun pattern, studied later.

69

ἴδιος, ἰδία, ἴδιον	one's own
καινός, καινή, καινόν	new
κακός, κακή, κακόν	bad
καλός, καλή, καλόν	good
μακάριος, μακαρία, μακάριον	blessed
μικρός, μικρά, μικρόν	small, little
νεκρός, νεκρά, νεκρόν	dead
πιστός, πιστή, πιστόν	faithful

Adjectives

An adjective either modifies a substantive (noun, pronoun, adjective) or substitutes for one. English does not inflect adjectives. That is, the spelling "good" works for any gender, as in "good man," "good woman," "good book."

Concord. Not so in Greek. Greek is inflected. Thus, the principle of concord applies. The student has been introduced to the principle of concord through a study of the Greek article. As does the Greek article, an adjective's ending changes according to the concord of the substantive modified. The spelling ἀγαθός works for second declension masculine nouns in nominative case and singular number, as in ὁ ἀγαθὸς ἄνθρωπος (= "the good man"). Change the *number* and the spelling changes. The plural expression "the good men" would be οἱ ἀγαθοὶ ἄνθρωποι. Likewise, change the *gender* and the

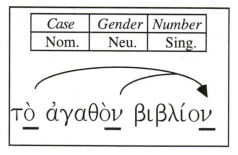

Case	Gender	Number
Nom.	Neu.	Sing.

τὸ ἀγαθὸν βιβλίον

spelling changes too. Thus, "the good book" is τὸ ἀγαθὸν βιβλίον. Further, in the plural, "the good books" is τὰ ἀγαθὰ βιβλία. Observe concord of both article and adjective. Adjectives of three genders are called "three termination adjectives."

Second and First Declension Patterns. Greek adjectives are inflected. Good news: the student actually need memorize no paradigms for these adjectives! This is because many adjectives in the New Testament follow second and first declension inflection patterns precisely. Accents are more regular; even first declension genitive plural is back to normal. Oxytone patterns are dominant.

Only *feminine singular* forms need attention. To distinguish these feminine forms, adjectives can be classed by stem: (1) -ε, -ι, -ρ stems, and (2) all others. The -ε, -ι, -ρ stems create feminine endings with α throughout the singular ("-α pure"). Otherwise, feminine endings have η throughout the singular ("-η pure").

All masculine and neuter second declension adjective endings follow second declension nouns exactly. Only accent distinguishes paradigms. All first declension plurals are all the same. In fact, in any given gender, the *plural forms are the same, save for accent.* Oxytones follow oxytone accent patterns.

Three adjective paradigms can summarize accent and endings: ἀγαθός, δίκαιος, μικρός. These forms are thoroughly redundant once the second and first declension noun paradigms are mastered. The following tables are for comparison purposes.[3]

Table 6.1 Adjectives By Gender: Second and First Declension

	Masculine		Neuter		Feminine	
	Singular	*Plural*	*Singular*	*Plural*	*Singular*	*Plural*
ἀγαθός	ἀγαθός	ἀγαθοί	ἀγαθόν	ἀγαθά	ἀγαθή	ἀγαθαί
	ἀγαθοῦ	ἀγαθῶν	ἀγαθοῦ	ἀγαθῶν	ἀγαθῆς	ἀγαθῶν
	ἀγαθῷ	ἀγαθοῖς	ἀγαθῷ	ἀγαθοῖς	ἀγαθῇ	ἀγαθαῖς
	ἀγαθόν	ἀγαθούς	ἀγαθόν	ἀγαθά	ἀγαθήν	ἀγαθάς
δίκαιος	δίκαιος	δίκαιοι	δίκαιον	δίκαια	δικαία	δίκαιαι*
	δικαίου	δικαίων	δικαίου	δικαίων	δικαίας	δικαίων*
	δικαίῳ	δικαίοις	δικαίῳ	δικαίοις	δικαίᾳ	δικαίαις
	δίκαιον	δικαίους	δίκαιον	δίκαια	δικαίαν	δικαίας
μικρά	μικρός	μικροί	μικρόν	μικρά	μικρά	μικραί
	μικροῦ	μικρῶν	μικροῦ	μικρῶν	μικρᾶς	μικρῶν
	μικρῷ	μικροῖς	μικρῷ	μικροῖς	μικρᾷ	μικραῖς
	μικρόν	μικρούς	μικρόν	μικρά	μικράν	μικράς

---

[3] A masculine oxytone ἀγαθός looks exactly like the second declension υἱός. A neuter oxytone ἀγαθόν looks exactly like the second declension ἱερόν. A feminine oxytone ἀγαθή looks exactly like the first declension γραφή. A masculine, antepenult acute δίκαιος looks exactly like the second declension ἄνθρωπος. A neuter, antepenult acute δίκαιον is exactly like the second declension εὐαγγέλιον. A feminine, penult acute δικαία looks (almost) exactly like the first declension -ε, -ι, -ρ stem καρδία with long α (*nominative plural has *antepenult* acute, not penult—more on the short alpha pattern of ἀλήθεια; genitive plural does *not* have circumflex on the ultima, as do *all* feminine genitive plural nouns). Finally, feminine oxytone μικρά looks exactly like first declension χαρά.

Table 6.2 Adjectives By Accent Pattern: Second and First Declension

	ἀγαθός Singular	ἀγαθός Plural	δίκαιος Singular	δίκαιος Plural	μικρά Singular	μικρά Plural
Masculine	ἀγαθός	ἀγαθοί	δίκαιος	δίκαιοι	μικρός	μικροί
	ἀγαθοῦ	ἀγαθῶν	δικαίου	δικαίων	μικροῦ	μικρῶν
	ἀγαθῷ	ἀγαθοῖς	δικαίῳ	δικαίοις	μικρῷ	μικροῖς
	ἀγαθόν	ἀγαθούς	δίκαιον	δικαίους	μικρόν	μικρούς
Neuter	ἀγαθόν	ἀγαθά	δίκαιον	δίκαια	μικρόν	μικρά
	ἀγαθοῦ	ἀγαθῶν	δικαίου	δικαίων	μικροῦ	μικρῶν
	ἀγαθῷ	ἀγαθοῖς	δικαίῳ	δικαίοις	μικρῷ	μικροῖς
	ἀγαθόν	ἀγαθά	δίκαιον	δίκαια	μικρόν	μικρά
Feminine	ἀγαθή	ἀγαθαί	δικαία	δίκαιαι	μικρά	μικραί
	ἀγαθῆς	ἀγαθῶν	δικαίας	δικαίων	μικρᾶς	μικρῶν
	ἀγαθῇ	ἀγαθαῖς	δικαίᾳ	δικαίαις	μικρᾷ	μικραῖς
	ἀγαθήν	ἀγαθάς	δικαίαν	δικαίας	μικράν	μικράς

Adjective Uses

Adjectives are used three ways: (1) attributive, (2) predicative, (3) substantive. For predicative use, one may need to supply a form of "to be." Construction with the article is the key for distinguishing most attributive and predicative uses:
1. Articular adjectives *always* are attributive.
2. Anarthrous adjectives with *articular* nouns always are predicative.
3. Anarthrous adjectives with anarthrous nouns are ambiguous; the adjective could be attributive *or* predicative—but most often is attributive.

Attributive. Attributive position means the adjective attributes a quality to the noun, limiting the noun's meaning. "The son" might mean any son. Modify "son" with an adjective, "good," and the noun is limited to a smaller class, "the good son." Not all sons qualify anymore. Thus, "the **good** son" could be either ὁ υἱὸς **ὁ ἀγαθός** or **ὁ ἀγαθὸς** υἱός (anarthrous noun).[4] When both noun and adjective are anarthrous, the construction is ambiguous. In such cases, though, always as a general rule, *try an attributive translation first: πᾶν δέδρον ἀγαθὸν = "every good tree" (Matt. 7:17).

---

[4] Nouns *must* have the article if the articular adjective *follows* the noun, called *restrictive attributive* position, implying *emphasis*; e.g., John 10:11, ὁ ποιμὴν ὁ καλός, "the *good* shepherd" (as others are not). Otherwise, the adjective is in simple attributive position, called *ascriptive attributive*.

Predicative. Predicate position means the adjective makes an *assertion* about the noun. Some form of the verb "to be" is present. A statement results: "The son *is* good." English predicate adjectives always follow an explicit form of "to be," but predicate adjectives in Greek do not need an explicit form of "to be." *An anarthrous adjective with an articular noun signals the predicative use.* "The son is good" in Greek could be either ὁ υἱὸς ἀγαθός or ἀγαθὸς ὁ υἱός. Word order does not matter, as long as the *adjective* is *without* the article and the noun *has* the article.

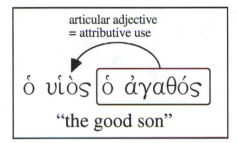

articular adjective
= attributive use

ὁ υἱὸς ὁ ἀγαθός

"the good son"

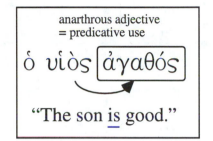

anarthrous adjective
= predicative use

ὁ υἱὸς ἀγαθός

"The son is good."

Table 6.3 Adjective Position: Summary

Position	Formulations	Translation
Attributive (articular)	ὁ ἀγαθὸς υἱός	"the good son" (ascriptive)
	ὁ ἀγαθὸς ὁ υἱός	"the *good* son" (restrictive)
	ὁ υἱὸς ὁ ἀγαθός	"the *good* son" (restrictive)
Predicative (anarthrous)	ἀγαθὸς ὁ υἱός.	"The son *is* good."
	ὁ υἱὸς ἀγαθός.	"The son *is* good."

Substantive. The adjective can substitute for the noun, or any other substantive. When found by itself, the adjective is being used substantively. The construction can be either with or without the article; the key is that no noun is expressed. An example is Matt. 22:14, πολλοὶ γάρ εἰσιν κλητοὶ = "For **many** are called."

Gender and Number. The adjective's gender and number declare the subject addressed. Thus, δίκαιος = "a righteous man," etc. In the plural, δίκαιοι = "righteous men" and so forth. The article makes identification specific: ὁ δίκαιος = "the righteous man," etc.

Table 6.4 Adjective—Substantival Use

Singular		Plural	
Form	*Translation*	*Form*	*Translation*
δίκαιος	"a righteous man"	δίκαιοι	"righteous men"
δικαία	"a righteous woman"	δίκαιαι	"righteous women"
δίκαιον	"a righteous thing"	δίκαια	"righteous things"
ὁ δίκαιος	"the righteous man"	οἱ δίκαιοι	"the righteous men"
ἡ δικαία	"the righteous woman"	αἱ δίκαιαι	"the righteous women"
τὸ δίκαιον	"the righteous thing"	τὰ δίκαια	"the righteous things"

Articular and Plural. An articular plural adjective used substantively can stand alone in translation without adding "ones," "men," "people," etc. Thus, οἱ δίκαιοι can be translated "the righteous." ("The righteous ones" or "the righteous people" would not be wrong—just not demanded.) Often, for example, a term such as οἱ νεκροί is translated simply as "the dead," as in **οἱ νεκροὶ** ἐν Χριστῷ ἀναστήσονται πρῶτον = "**the dead** in Christ will be raised first," 1 Thess. 4:16.

The Verb Εἰμί

Table 6.5 Εἰμί—Present Indicative

Number	Person	Form	Translation
Singular	1st	εἰμί	"I am"
	2nd	εἶ	"you (sg.) are"
	3rd	ἐστί(ν)	"he (she, it) is"
Plural	1st	ἐσμέν	"we are"
	2nd	ἐστέ	"you (pl.) are"
	3rd	εἰσί(ν)	"they are"

Analysis. Εἰμί ("I am") is frequent in the New Testament. This verb belongs to the second conjugation of Greek verbs (-μι verbs) but is introduced for now disregarding issues of -μι verbs. Notice carefully that the paradigm is not labeled "Present, *Active*, Indicative." The verb εἰμί expresses a state of being, not transitive or intransitive action (e.g., "she wrote a book" or "he ran"); thus, εἰμί has no action to relate to a subject, so *εἰμί has no voice component*. Two of the forms (third person, singular and plural) can be found either with or without a nu (-ν) ending. Just treat the εἰμί paradigm as six different vocabulary words to learn. The accent is irregular (always ultima). Some endings actually reveal the more primitive forms of the pronominal suffix, which will be encountered again when -μι verbs are studied.

Enclitic. A word that looses accent by "leaning on" the previous word for accent is called an *enclitic*. The enclitic has no accent of its own. Such words one might suspect would generate exceptions to general accent rules. We introduce enclitic accent rules now because the verb εἰμί is enclitic in all forms but εἶ.

In reviewing the following enclitic accent rules, realize that the final appearance that results from enclitic accent is not all that strange. The enclitic is just an extra syllable being considered for accent. However, another table is provided for the three enclitic results that do seem "odd" in the text—from rules 1, 3, and 4. In these instances, either a word receives *two* accents, or the grave accent fails to show up.

Table 6.6 Enclitic Accent Rules

Acute rules:
1. The acute antepenult adds an acute to the ultima (κύριός ἐστιν).
2. The acute penult:
a. causes a monosyllabic enclitic to loose accent (λόγος μου).
b. allows a disyllabic enclitic to retain accent (λόγος ἐστίν).
3. The acute ultima does not revert to grave (υἱός ἐστιν).
Circumflex rules:
4. The circumflex penult adds an acute to the ultima (δοῦλοί εἰσιν).
5. The circumflex ultima causes enclitics to loose accent (φωνῆς μου; αὐτῶν ἐστιν).
Double enclitic rule:
6. A preceding word itself an enclitic retains accent (μού ἐστιν).
Emphasis rule:
7. The enclitic may retain accent for emphasis or when beginning a clause or sentence (Ἔστιν δὲ ἐν τοῖς Ἱεροσολύμοις).
Compound rule:
8. A word compounded by an enclitic treats the enclitic as a separate word (ὥστε = ὡς + τέ).

Table 6.7 Enclitic Oddities—Double Accents on One Word and No Grave

	Antepenult	*Penult*	*Ultima*
acute	´		´
circumflex		⌢	´
grave			´

Predicate Nominative. The predicate *adjective* is defined as an adjective found in anarthrous construction used with a form of "to be." Now we study predicate *nominatives*. Εἰμί expresses state of being, not action. Εἰμί is thus called a *linking* verb—i.e., εἰμί links two correlated elements in a sentence. One can think of εἰμί along the lines of the "similar to" sign in math (≈). Εἰμί focuses attention grammatically on the subject (nominative case; "A" in the tables). Since εἰμί links *similar* elements, then the second element which is linked by εἰμί has to be another nominative, the *predicate nominative* ("B" in the

Table 6.8 Εἰμί—Linking Verb[5]

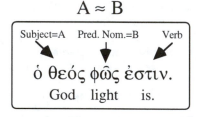

$$A \approx B$$

Subject=A   Pred. Nom.=B   Verb

ὁ θεός φῶς ἐστιν.
God   light   is.

Table 6.9 Εἰμί—Equative Verb[6]

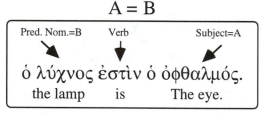

$$A = B$$

Pred. Nom.=B   Verb   Subject=A

ὁ λύχνος ἐστὶν ὁ ὀφθαλμός.
the lamp   is   The eye.

tables). *The predicate nominative tells more about the subject nominative.* The major decision is *which* of the *two* nominatives is the subject of the form of "to be" for the translation. The decision is made by observing a hierarchy of precedence in the three following grammatical categories of words (lowest to highest): nouns, proper names, and pronouns. This hierarchy is simple and is described below.

---

[5] 1 John 1:5.
[6] Adapted from Matt. 6:22, Ὁ λύχνος τοῦ σώματός ἐστιν ὁ ὀφθαλμός.

Table 6.10 Subject Versus Predicate Nominative

Category	Subject
Noun versus Noun	Articular Noun
Proper Name versus Noun	Proper Name
Pronoun in any Combination	Pronoun

The first level involves two nouns. When confronted with two nouns, both of them nominative, *the subject noun has the definite article*. In cases in which *both* nouns have the definite article, εἰμί is like an equals sign; subject nominative and predicate nominative can be interchanged as identical. This is the "equative" or "copulative" function of εἰμί. Generally, the noun positioned before the εἰμί verb is taken as subject ("pre-positioned"). However, proverbial statements poetically reverse this normal order (cf. Matt. 6:22, Table 6.9). Finally, when *neither* noun has the article, *context* must decide.

The second level is proper names versus nouns. Regardless of articles, a proper name takes precedence over another noun and is the subject of an εἰμί construction.

Pronouns, the third level, take the highest precedence. A pronoun is subject in any combination over nouns and proper names. The following examples illustrate, the subject nominative underlined, the predicate nominative in bold.[7]

1. Articular Precedence (two nouns)
   καὶ **θεὸς** ἦν <u>ὁ λόγος</u> = "<u>The Word</u> was [imperfect tense] **God**" (John 1:1)
2. Proper Name Precedence
   <u>Ἰησοῦς</u> ἐστιν **ὁ Χριστὸς** = "<u>Jesus</u> is **the Christ**"(John 20:31)
3. Pronoun Precedence
   A. Over *nouns:*
      <u>Οὗτός</u> ἐστιν **ὁ υἱός** μου = "'<u>This</u> is my **son**'" (Matt. 3:17)
   B. Over *proper names:*
      <u>Οὗτός</u> ἐστιν **Ἰησοῦς** = "'<u>This</u> is **Jesus**'" (Matt. 27:37)
4. Symmetry = decision by context
   A. Both nouns articular
      ὁ δὲ <u>ἀγρός</u> ἐστιν **ὁ κόσμος** = "and <u>the field</u> is **the world**" (Matt. 13:38; an explanation of a parable; subject implied by pre-positioning)
   B. Both substantival adjectives anarthrous
      <u>πολλοὶ</u> γάρ εἰσιν **κλητοὶ** = "For <u>many</u> are **called**" (Matt. 22:14)

---

[7]These principles for deciding the question of the predicate nominative are associated with the name of Ernest Colwell, thus called "Colwell's Rule." Actually, in particular, Colwell's discussion focused on the definitive nature of an anarthrous predicate nominative when positioned prior to the verb. See Ernest C. Colwell, "A Definite Rule For the Use of the Article in the Greek New Testament," *Journal of Biblical Literature* 52 (1933): 12–21. The importance of these observations is dramatically demonstrated in the fallacy of a well-known mistranslation of John 1:1, καὶ **θεὸς** ἦν <u>ὁ λόγος</u>, a mistranslation best elucidated by Colwell's observations.

Diagramming

Adjectives are placed underneath the word or phrase modified. They are joined to the base line by a forward-slanted line (as with the indirect object).[8] Multiple modifiers of the same word are joined on the same slant. Substantival adjectives are diagrammed according to the grammatical function (subject, direct object, etc.) Predicate nominatives and adjectives are placed on the base line to the right of the verbal idea, separated by a back slanting line not breaking the base line.[9]

Table 6.11 Diagramming Adjectives, Predicate Nominative and Adjective

1. πᾶν δένδρον **ἀγαθὸν** καρποὺς **καλοὺς** ποιεῖ
 	
"**every good** tree produces **healthy** fruit" (Matt. 17:7)
	Adjectives
	
	1. δένδρον | ποιεῖ | καρποὺς
	   \πᾶν \καλοὺς
	   \ἀγαθὸν

2. Ἰησοῦς ἐστιν **ὁ Χριστός**. "Jesus is **the Christ**." (John 20:31)	*Predicate Nominative* 2. Ἰησοῦς | ἐστιν \ ὁ Χριστός
3. πολλοὶ γάρ εἰσιν **κλητοὶ** "For many are **called**" (Matt. 22:14)	*Predicate Adjective* γάρ 3. ⌐ πολλοὶ | εἰσιν \ κλητοὶ

---

[8]Some suggest distinguishing *verbal content* by the *nature* of the slant: (1) *back slant* for non-verbal ideas, as adjectives, adverbs, and prepositions, (2) *perpendicular* for partial verbals, as in participles and infinitives, and (3) *forward slant* for full verbals, as with subordinate clauses. Such distinctions can be incorporated if the student finds them helpful.

[9]Some suggest a *double* slanted line further to distinguish predicate adjectives from predicate nominatives. This option may be used, but is ignored in this text as somewhat superfluous.

What To Learn—LESSON 6 (ἕξ)

Beginning

☐ 1. Second and first declension noun patterns applied to adjective declensions

☐ 2. The meaning of adjective *position*

☐ 3. Definition of *attributive* adjective and significance for translation

☐ 4. Definition of *predicate* adjective and significance for translation

☐ 5. The *substantival* use of adjectives and significance for translation

☐ 6. The six forms of the present indicative of εἰμί

☐ 7. The significance of the εἰμί verb and the *predicate nominative*

☐ 8. Diagramming adjectives and predicate nominative (and adjective)

☐ 9. Vocabulary words

Advanced

☐ 10. The two feminine singular adjective stem classes and reasons for them

☐ 11. Definition of an *enclitic* and enclitic rules of accent

☐ 12. Explain "Colwell's Rule" related to identifying the predicate nominative

Vocabulary 3 provides an interesting clue to the breathing at John 8:44 in two Greek manuscripts that do not have breathing marks at this verse, 𝔓⁶⁶ and 𝔓⁷⁵, late second to early third century papyrus manuscripts in the Bodmer collection (cf. pp. 92, 166) . The vocabulary word οὐ ("not") has alternate spellings before the two breathing marks: οὐκ with the kappa is used before smooth breathing (e.g., οὐκ εἰμί.); οὐχ with the chi is used before rough breathing (e.g., οὐχ ἡ γραφή).

Now, one -μι verb, ἵστημι, shows itself spelled the same in two tenses—an odd development of the koine. The perfect tense is normal, e.g., ἕστηκεν. Observe the rough breathing. The only imperfect tense form for this verb in the New Testament is ἔστηκεν, which inexplicably mimics the perfect form. Note carefully the *smooth* breathing. This imperfect form occurs just once, at John 8:44, and scribes did have trouble with this form. Some important manuscripts support the perfect tense. Without breathing marks, though, how could we know this? A neat trick! The verb is preceded by the negative. Now οὐ before the perfect form with rough breathing is οὐχ ἕστηκεν. The negative οὐ before the imperfect form with smooth breathing is οὐκ ἔστηκεν. While uncial letters in the papyri are formed a little differently—e.g., the sigma looks like a capital "C"—you probably can recognize many letters. Note carefully: the spelling of οὐ before the verb demonstrates that 𝔓⁶⁶ has the imperfect tense in mind but 𝔓⁷⁵ the perfect tense, though neither has breathing marks here.

You might also notice: (1) the use of uncial letters and *scripto continua* style; (2) οὐ occurs twice in the line of 𝔓⁷⁵, once as οὐχ and once as οὐκ; (3) iota subscript—a much later convention in writing—is not part of the notation; (4) the scribe of 𝔓⁶⁶ spelled ἀλήθεια as ἀλήθια, a spelling variation ("itacism," confusing like-sounding vowels or diphthongs); (5) the scribe of 𝔓⁶⁶ changed the word order, pulling the second ἀλήθεια before the negative (not shown) after the word ὅτι; and (6) the punctuation mark in 𝔓⁶⁶.

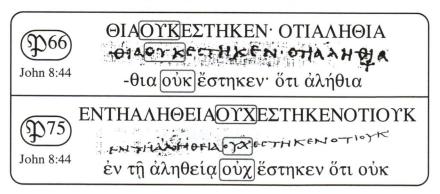

LESSON 7 (ἑπτά)

Contract Verbs and Conjunctions

φιλέω, δηλόω, τιμάω

 Contract verbs are one of two special sub-classes of the thematic verb which requires extra attention. Contract verb stems end in one of three short vowels: ε, ο, α. Conjunctions join sentences or clauses in logical transitions.

Vocabulary 7

Word		Meaning
ἑπτά	numeral	seven
ἀλλά, ἀλλ᾽[1]	adversative coordinate conjunction	but, yet, rather
καὶ . . . καί	construction	both . . . and
ὅτι	subordinate conjunction	because, that
εὐλογέω	-ε contract	I bless
ζητέω	-ε contract	I seek
θεωρέω	-ε contract	I observe
καλέω	-ε contract	I call
λαλέω	-ε contract	I speak
ὁμολογέω	-ε contract	I confess, profess
παρακαλέω	-ε contract (παρά + καλέω)	I comfort

[1] Alternate form: elision before another vowel or diphthong (ἀλλ᾽ ἐκ θεοῦ, John 1:13).

81

περιπατέω	-ε contract (περί + πατέω)	I walk; walk around
ποιέω	-ε contract	I do, make
φιλέω	-ε contract	I love (brotherly)
δηλόω	-o contract	I show
πληρόω	-o contract	I fulfill
σταυρόω	-o contract	I crucify
ἀγαπάω	-α contract	I love
γεννάω	-α contract	I give birth to, beget
ἐρωτάω	-α contract	I ask
ζάω	-α contract	I live
τιμάω	-α contract	I honor

Analysis

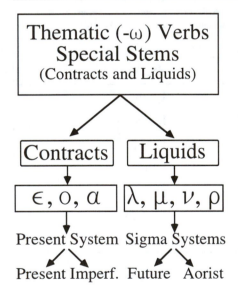

Thematic (-ω) Verbs
Special Stems
(Contracts and Liquids)

Contracts   Liquids

ε, ο, α   λ, μ, ν, ρ

Present System   Sigma Systems

Present Imperf.   Future Aorist

Most thematic verb stems end in consonants. Adding the thematic vowel (ε/ο) has no consequence. However, some stems end in vowels. Adding a thematic vowel generates reactions. This reaction is restricted to the first principal part. Verb formation in other principal parts involves a *consonant* in a suffix or an ending. This consonant *separates* the vowels in question. The offending parties (verb stem vowel and thematic vowel) have no chance to interact. So the contraction of vowels does not take place in the other principal parts. This contract verb subcategory of thematic verbs is one of two special stems that need to be studied. The other subcategory, liquid verbs, will be presented later.

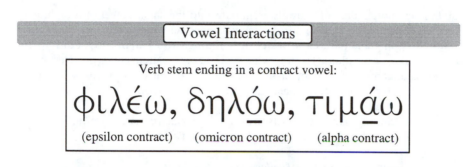

Vowel Interactions

Verb stem ending in a contract vowel:

φιλέω, δηλόω, τιμάω

(epsilon contract)   (omicron contract)   (alpha contract)

Contraction. The combination of the stem vowel and the thematic vowel (or pronominal suffix, as, for example, in the -ω of the first person singular) produces a resultant long sound (long vowel/diphthong). This process is illustrated in the table below. On the top row are the particular vowels to be found in the pertinent pronominal suffixes of the first principal part. On the side column are the contract vowels. The resultant combinations are the intersections of rows and columns. The table does not summarize all vowel contractions, but helps the student visualize what is happening in the first principal part in verb formation.

Table 7.1 Contraction Chart—First Principal Part

Contract Vowels	Pronominal Suffix Vowels						
	ε	ει	η	ῃ	ο	ου	ω
ε	ει	ει	η	ῃ	ου	ου	ω
ο	ου	οι	ω	οι	ου	ου	ω
α	α	ᾳ	α	ᾳ	ω	ω	ω

◆ *A circumflex accent will be a typical feature resulting from contraction.*[2]

We can summarize the table so that memorization is not necessary. Two general remarks are made, followed by six specific observations. For general remarks, first, observe how forms involving ι always survive as ι or iota subscript. Second, with

---

[2]With a few exceptions; e.g., present middle indicative, second person singular, λύῃ (λύεσαι → λύεαι → λύῃ).

diphthongs notice that: (1) vowels assimilate into the same vowel of a diphthong (εει = ει, οου = ου), and (2) different vowels contract with diphthongs, the υ close vowel dropping and the ι close vowel subscripting (αου = ω, αει = ᾳ, εαι = ῃ; but οει = οι is one exception). The following specific observations focus on determining the original contract verb combination for present and imperfect verbs, which have the resultant forms η, ῃ, α, ᾳ, ω, and the diphthongs ει, οι, ου.

Basic Results.

(1)   Forms of α are -α contracts with any "e" sound (αε/αει or αη/αῃ).

(2)   Forms of η are -ε contracts with η or αι (εη/εη or εσαι = εαι = ῃ).

(3)   ω is:

      (i) *any* contract with ω (εω/οω/αω)

      (ii) -α contracts with "o" sounds (αο/αου)

      (iii) -o contracts with η (οη).

Diphthong Results.

(4)   ει is an -ε contract with "e" sounds (εε or εει).

(5)   οι is an -o contract with "e" sounds (οει /οη).

(6)   ου is an -o contract (οε/οου/οο) or an -ε contract (εο/εου).

Lexical Form. The lexical form is the *uncontracted* form, but *this form does not exist in reality*. This is the form, for example, φιλέω ("I love"). This lexical form is *to facilitate identification of the vowel ending* of a contract verb stem. However, in the real world of the actual Greek text, one finds the *contracted* form only, that is, φιλῶ (ε + ω = ω). Again, δηλόω ("I show") in the Greek text is found only as δηλῶ (ο + ω = ω). Likewise, τιμάω ("I honor") is τιμῶ (α + ω = ω).

Lengthening. Contract verbs show contraction in the first principal part *only* (present system containing the present and imperfect tenses). Contract verbs do not contract in the other principal parts.[3] In these other principal parts, contract vowels *lengthen*.[4] The process of lengthening means that the short contract vowels take their corresponding long vowel sound. This process of lengthening is *not* to be referred to as contraction.

Translation. Contract verbs are studied in order to recognize their forms in the New Testament. The student needs to be clear that these forms involve morphology (appearance) only. Translation is not affected at all by the contraction process or by lengthening. The problem simply is one of recognition. So one translates a present contract as any present tense verb.

---

[3]The "principal parts" were introduced in Lesson 3. A review of this material might be helpful.

[4]The term "ablaut" also is used to refer to this lengthening process. Ablaut is a broad term referring to any pattern of vowel changes representing grammatical processes, as in "drink," "drank," "drunk."

Table 7.2 Epsilon Contract—φιλέω

Person	Contraction	Form	Translation
1st	ε + ω = ω	φιλῶ	"I am loving"
2nd	ε + ει = ει	φιλεῖς	"you are loving"
3rd	ε + ει = ει	φιλεῖ	"he (she, it) is loving"
1st	ε + ο = ου	φιλοῦμεν	"we are loving"
2nd	ε + ε = ει	φιλεῖτε	"you (pl.) are loving"
3rd	ε + ου = ου	φιλοῦσι(ν)	"they are loving"

Table 7.3 Omicron Contract—δηλόω

Person	Contraction	Form	Translation
1st	ο + ω = ω	δηλῶ	"I am showing"
2nd	ο + ει = οι	δηλοῖς	"you are showing"
3rd	ο + ει = οι	δηλοῖ	"he (she, it) is showing"
1st	ο + ο = ου	δηλοῦμεν	"we are showing"
2nd	ο + ε = ου	δηλοῦτε	"you (pl.) are showing"
3rd	ο + ου = ου	δηλοῦσι(ν)	"they are showing"

Table 7.4 Alpha Contract—τιμάω

Person	Contraction	Form	Translation
1st	α + ω = ω	τιμῶ	"I am honoring"
2nd	α + ει = ᾳ	τιμᾷς	"you are honoring"
3rd	α + ει = ᾳ	τιμᾷ	"he (she, it) is honoring"
1st	α + ο = ω	τιμῶμεν	"we are honoring"
2nd	α + ε = α	τιμᾶτε	"you (pl.) are honoring"
3rd	α + ου = ω	τιμῶσι(ν)	"they are honoring"

Contract Accents

Accent Rules. First, observe the accent of the two vowels contracting. Ask, "which vowel is accented prior to contraction?" Then know the following rules.

Table 7.5 Contract Accent Rules

> *Stem vowel rule:*
> 1. A stem vowel accent creates a circumflex contract (φιλέεις→φιλεῖς).
> *Thematic vowel rule:*
> 2. A thematic vowel accent creates an acute contract (φιλεόμεθα→φιλούμεθα).
> *Diphthong rule:*
> 3. Final -οι and -αι are considered long in contracts (δηλόει→δηλοῖ).
> *Accented alpha rule:*
> 4. An accented α always is considered long (τιμάετε→τιμᾶτε).

Observations. These rules explain basic contract accents, because, otherwise, regular verb accenting rules apply. A few other observations can be added.

Epsilon contracts. All epsilon contracts accent the stem vowel in the lexical form (penult). Thus, with the stem vowel rule, *all epsilon contracts have circumflex accents throughout the present active indicative.* Resultant contract forms are spelled just as their thematic verb counterparts in all but

Stem Vowel (Circumflex Rule)

φιλέεις➔φιλεῖς

| stem vowel accent | = | circumflex contract |

first and second persons plural (φιλοῦμεν, φιλεῖτε). Otherwise, the circumflex accent alone distinguishes what is a regular verb and what is a contract verb.

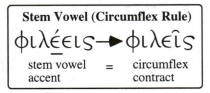

Thematic Vowel (Acute Rule)

φιλεόμεθα➔φιλούμεθα

thematic vowel accent = acute contract

Pronominal suffixes of more than one syllable affect normally circumflex contracts. These suffixes push the accent back to the antepenult (as far back as the accent can recede). This antepenult happens to be the thematic vowel and becomes long in contraction. A long antepenult *must* be acute. An example suffix is -ομεθα (not yet introduced). To be accented, this long antepenult position *must* be acute (φιλεόμεθα = φιλούμεθα).

Omicron contracts. Recall that the diphthongs αι and οι when final are considered short for accenting purposes. This general rule is *not* observed in contracts. A final -οι, if accented, is considered *long* in contracts. Thus, a circumflex occurs over the final οι in δηλοῖ, the third person singular contraction (δηλο + ει = δηλόει = δηλοῖ).

Alpha contracts. Recall that the vowel α is variable and can be long or short. However, in contract syllables that receive accent, alpha always is considered long. Thus, a circumflex occurs over the α in τιμᾶτε (τιμά + ετε = τιμάετε = τιμᾶτε).

Translation

Progressive. Present tense primarily indicates durative action. The "progressive present" focuses on the durative aspect (emphasized in translations). A story line commonly will have this use of the present tense: Ἴδε νῦν ἐν παρρησίᾳ **λαλεῖς** = "Behold, now you **are speaking** plainly," John 16:29.

Simple. The translation is "simple present" because of less durative emphasis. Thus, ταῦτα **λαλῶ** ἐν τῷ κόσμῳ = "these things **I speak** in the world," John 17:13.

Historical. Note the following: "There we were, just minding our own business, when, Bang! like a shot in the dark we heard this noise from the other room, and *he comes out shouting . . .*" See the tense shift? Greek does this too, called "historical present." Refer to John 1:21 in Table 1.13 of Lesson 1, an example of "historical present": Σύ Ἠλίας εἶ; καὶ **λέγει**, Οὐκ εἰμί. = "'Are you Elijah?' And he **said**, 'I am not.'" The historical present is used for dramatic effect, to draw the reader into the story. Mark's Gospel particularly shows use of the historical present, providing a characteristic "vividness;" e.g., observe ἐκβάλλει in Mark 1:12 or λέγει in Mark 2:5. *Proper translation of the Greek historical present is English past tense.*

Aoristic. The aoristic use of the present tense is rare. The present tense usually is durative. A very few cases show, *by context alone*, that a punctiliar sense is meant. An example is Acts 9:34, **ἰᾶταί** σε Ἰησοῦς Χριστός ("Jesus Christ **heals** you"). Another is Acts 16:18, **Παραγγέλλω** σοι ἐν ὀνόματι Ἰησοῦ Χριστοῦ ("**I command** you in the name of Jesus Christ"). The student simply is alerted to this possibility. Commentaries often will point out this rare aspect of the present tense for you.

Conjunctions

You already have learned the conjunctions καί, γάρ, and δέ. This lesson includes ἀλλά and ὅτι. *Conjunctions* join words, phrases, clauses, and sentences. We now focus on clauses. Clauses are classified two ways, as *subordinate* or *coordinate*.

Subordinate Clause. A *subordinate clause* is dependent on a related clause and is joined by a subordinate conjunction as: (1) consecutive, using "that," (2) final, using "in order that," (3) causal, using "because," (4) temporal, using "when," (5) conditional, using "if," (6) comparative, using "as," "just as," and (7) concessive, using "although," "even if." Subordinate clauses have secondary levels in sentences.

The common subordinating conjunction ὅτι has numerous uses. Two involve discourse. Direct discourse is indicated by "ὅτι recitative," covered in Lesson 1, Table 1.13. Review that information now. Indirect discourse will be treated later. Uses of ὅτι as a subordinating conjunction are described below.

Causal ὅτι ("because"). First, ὅτι can be causal: ὅτι provides the cause or basis for the preceding clause or word, translated "because" or "for." Matt. 5:3 illustrates: Μακάριοι οἱ πτωχοὶ τῷ πνεύματι, **ὅτι** αὐτῶν ἐστιν ἡ βασιλεία τῶν οὐρανῶν ("Blessed are the poor in spirit, **for** theirs is the kingdom of heaven."). Again, John 7:29, ἐγὼ οἶδα αὐτόν, **ὅτι** παρ' αὐτοῦ εἰμι, "I know Him, **because** I am from Him."

Explanatory ὅτι ("that").[5] Second, ὅτι can elaborate on the preceding word or clause. An example is Matt. 16:8, Τί διαλογίζεσθε ἐν ἑαυτοῖς . . . **ὅτι** ἄρτους οὐκ ἔχετε; ("Why are you discussing among yourselves . . . **that** you have no bread?"). Another is John 3:19, αὕτη δέ ἐστιν ἡ κρίσις **ὅτι** τὸ φῶς ἐλήλυθεν ("and this is the judgment, **that** light has come"). This use sometimes is called an "object clause."

Substantival ὅτι ("that"). Third, ὅτι can introduce a clause that functions as a substantive, commonly as the subject or direct object of the main verb. An example of a ὅτι clause functioning as the subject is Heb. 7:14, πρόδηλον γὰρ **ὅτι** ἐξ Ἰούδα ἀνατέταλκεν ὁ κύριος ἡμῶν ("For **that** our Lord has arisen out of Judah is clearly obvious."). A frequent direct object use of a ὅτι clause is after verbs of perception (see, hear, think, know, read). An example is Matt. 5:21, Ἠκούσατε **ὅτι** ἐρρέθη ("You have heard **that** it has been said"). Another is 1 John 2:5, γινώσκομεν **ὅτι** ἐν αὐτῷ ἐσμεν ("we know **that** we are in Him").

Coordinate Clause. A *coordinate clause* has equal status with a related clause. Such clauses are joined by coordinate conjunctions in four ways: (1) copulative using "and," (2) adversative using "but," "yet," "rather," "nevertheless," (3) inferential using "therefore," and (4) causal, using "for." In the following discussion, we will focus on copulative and adversative uses of coordinating conjunctions.

Copulatives. A *copulative* expresses equality or similarity of words or clauses. The workhorse conjunction is the copulative καί (used 8947 times!). Καί can join sentence strings (continuity of thought; cf. Gospel of Mark). Greek has no word for "both." However, the series καί . . . καί is translated "both . . . and" (**καὶ** ἐμὲ **καὶ** τὸν πατέρα μου = "**both** me **and** my Father," John 15:24).

---

[5]Also known as "epexegetic." Grammatically, the clauses are in apposition.

Adversatives. The coordinating conjunctions δέ and ἀλλά as *adversatives* express contrast, antitheses, or opposition. Degree of contrast is distinguished: δέ communicates *slight contrast;* ἀλλά communicates *strong contrast.* Thus, δέ can serve as a simple connecting particle; δέ can mark new development in the narrative or argument, translated "and" or "now." In contrast, ἀλλά always is strong and is translated "but," "yet" or "rather." Ἀλλά sets a following clause in strong contrast, even sometimes suggesting antithesis or opposition. How does one know these different uses? *Context* is all important. Learn flexibility in translating the adversatives δέ and ἀλλά by carefully following context. Some examples follow:

1. Ἐγένετο **δὲ** ἐν ταῖς ἡμέραις ἐκείναις = "**Now** it happened in those days" (Luke 2:1; weak connective)

2. Ἀνέβη **δὲ** καὶ Ἰωσὴφ ἀπὸ τῆς Γαλιλαίας = "**And** Joseph went up also from Galilee" (Luke 2:4; weak connective)

3. ἡ **δὲ** Μαριὰμ πάντα συνετήρει τὰ ῥήματα ταῦτα συμβάλλουσα ἐν τῇ καρδίᾳ αὐτῆς. = "**But** Mary treasured up all these words in her heart." (Luke 2:19; slight contrast)

4. καὶ ἀποκριθεῖσα ἡ μήτηρ αὐτοῦ εἶπεν, Οὐχί, **ἀλλὰ** κληθήσεται Ἰωάννης. = "And his mother answering said, 'Absolutely not; **rather** he will be called John!'" (Luke 1:60; strong contrast)

5. ὁ Ἰησοῦς εἶπεν πρὸς αὐτούς, Οὐ χρείαν ἔχουσιν οἱ ὑγιαίνοντες ἰατροῦ **ἀλλὰ** οἱ κακῶς ἔχοντες = "Jesus said to them, 'It is not those are healthy who need a physician, **but** those who are sick.'" (Luke 5:31; antithesis)

6. **ἀλλ'** οὐχὶ ἐρεῖ αὐτῷ = "**yet** will he not say to him?" (Luke 17:8; opposition)

Complex Sentence. In contrast to a compound sentence (two independent clauses), a *complex sentence* combines an independent clause with at least one dependent clause. Subordinating conjunctions indicate complex sentences.

Diagramming

Coordinating conjunctions are put on a short horizontal line just above and beginning the clause they introduce, joined by a short dotted (broken) line down to the base line. Of subordinate clauses, those using ὅτι have been the focus in this lesson. **Subordinate clauses** have their own base lines, distinguished by their two functions: (1) a slanted line to show the subordination—like indirect objects—used for causal ὅτι (under the verb given basis) and explanatory ὅτι (under the substantive or phrase explained), or (2) on a "standard," (i.e., a base line on stilts = Λ̄), used for substantival ὅτι. In the first method, the ὅτι breaks the slanting line; in the second method, the ὅτι breaks the vertical line of the standard.

Table 7.6 Diagramming Conjunctions and Complex Sentences

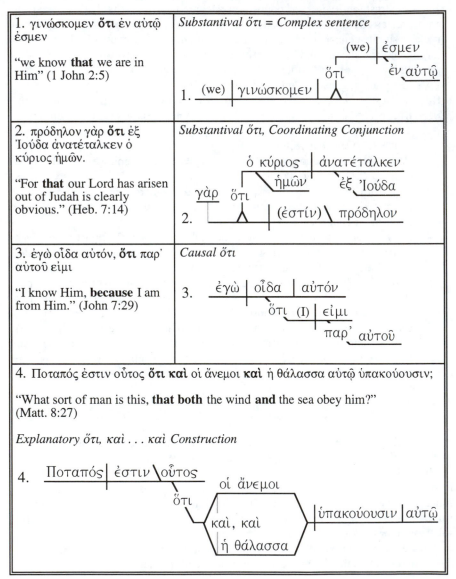

1. γινώσκομεν **ὅτι** ἐν αὐτῷ ἐσμεν

"we know **that** we are in Him" (1 John 2:5)

Substantival ὅτι = Complex sentence

2. πρόδηλον γὰρ **ὅτι** ἐξ Ἰούδα ἀνατέταλκεν ὁ κύριος ἡμῶν.

"For **that** our Lord has arisen out of Judah is clearly obvious." (Heb. 7:14)

Substantival ὅτι, Coordinating Conjunction

3. ἐγὼ οἶδα αὐτόν, **ὅτι** παρ' αὐτοῦ εἰμι

"I know Him, **because** I am from Him." (John 7:29)

Causal ὅτι

4. Ποταπός ἐστιν οὗτος **ὅτι καὶ** οἱ ἄνεμοι **καὶ** ἡ θάλασσα αὐτῷ ὑπακούουσιν;

"What sort of man is this, **that both** the wind **and** the sea obey him?" (Matt. 8:27)

Explanatory ὅτι, καὶ . . . καὶ Construction

🏺 What To Learn—LESSON 7 (ἑπτά)

Beginning

☐ 1. Definition of *contract verb* and what principal part is affected by the contraction process

☐ 2. Determining contract verb type from contraction results

☐ 3. Recognizing person and number in the three contract paradigms

☐ 4. Meaning of *conjunction* and *subordinate* and *coordinate* clauses

☐ 5. Three uses of the subordinating conjunction ὅτι besides discourse

☐ 6. Meaning of *copulative* and *adversative* coordinating conjunctions

☐ 7. The difference between δέ and ἀλλά

☐ 8. Definition of a *complex sentence*

☐ 9. Diagramming conjunctions and complex sentences

☐ 10. Vocabulary words

Advanced

☐ 11. Four basic rules of contract accents

☐ 12. Uses of the Greek present tense: *progressive, simple, historical, aoristic*

☐ 13. Options for translating the adversative δέ

☐ 14. Contract paradigms

 Ancient manuscripts came in two forms, the scroll and the codex. The codex is used today, with leaves as pages folded and sewn together. Two types of material were used in these codexes, papyrus and parchment. Papyrus was paper made from a reed plant grown along the Nile River. Papyrus was fragile, so easily lost. Parchment was made from animal skin and was more durable, but also much more expensive. The Bodmer Library in Cologny, Switzerland, near Geneva, holds one of our oldest, extensive copies of the Gospel of John, papyrus $\mathfrak{P}^{66}$, dated A.D. 200 or earlier.

John 12:29–34

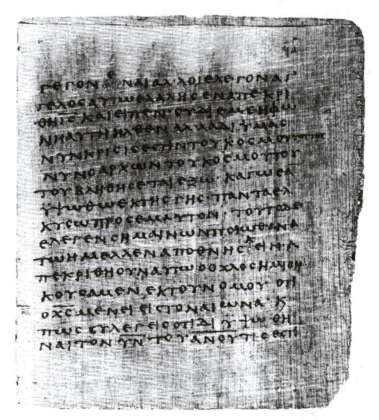

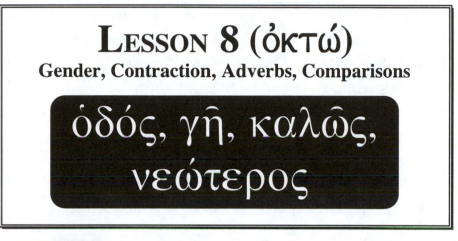

LESSON 8 (ὀκτώ)

Gender, Contraction, Adverbs, Comparisons

ὁδός, γῆ, καλῶς, νεώτερος

A few feminine nouns are found with second declension inflection (stems in -ος). A few masculine nouns are found with first declension inflection (stems in -ας, -ης). These can be confusing for concord. Some nouns contract as verbs do. Adverbs and comparisons are presented.

Vocabulary 8

Word		Meaning
ὀκτώ	numeral	eight
ἤ	comparative conjunction	than, or
ἤ . . . ἤ	construction	either . . . or
μὲν . . . δέ	construction	on the one hand . . . on the other hand[1]
οὐδέ	conjunction (combination: οὐ + δέ)	and not, nor, neither, not even
οὐδὲ . . . οὐδέ	construction	neither . . . nor
οὖν	conjunction	therefore

---

[1] A grammatical construction indicating contrast, but in some cases left *untranslated*.

ὁδός, -ου, ἡ (!)	2nd decl.	way, road
ἔρημος, -ου, ἡ (!)	2nd decl.	wilderness, desert
παρθένος, -ου, ἡ (!)	2nd decl.	virgin
Ἰησοῦς, -οῦ, ὁ		Jesus
Ἰωάννης, -ου, ὁ (!)	1st decl.	John
μαθητής, -οῦ, ὁ (!)	1st decl.	disciple
μεσσίας, -ου, ὁ (!)	1st decl.	messiah
προφήτης, -ου, ὁ (!)	1st decl.	prophet
γῆ, -ῆς, ἡ (contract)	1st decl.	earth, land
συκῆ, -ῆς, ἡ (contract)	1st decl.	fig tree
μνᾶ, -ᾶς, ἡ (contract)	1st decl.	mina (coin)
μόνος, -η, ον	adj.	only, alone
νέος, -α, ον	adj.	new
σοφός, -ή, όν	adj.	wise
ἄνω	adverb	up
δικαίως	adverb	justly
ἐγγύς	adverb	near
ἔξω	adverb	outside
εὐθέως (also, εὐθύς)	adverb	immediately
κακῶς	adverb	badly
καλῶς	adverb	well
νῦν	adverb	now
πάλιν	adverb	again
ταχέως (also, ταχύ)	adverb	quickly, soon

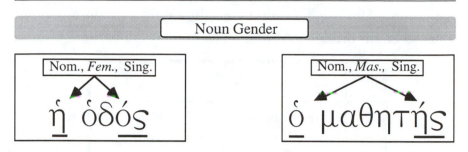

Noun Gender

Nom., *Fem.*, Sing.

ἡ ὁδός

Nom., *Mas.*, Sing.

ὁ μαθητής

Table 8.1 First Declension *Masculine*—ὁ μαθητής

	ὁ μαθητής	
	Singular	*Plural*
N	ὁ μαθητής	οἱ μαθηταί
G	τοῦ μαθητοῦ	τῶν μαθητῶν
D	τῷ μαθητῇ	τοῖς μαθηταῖς
A	τὸν μαθητήν	τοὺς μαθητάς
V	μαθητά	μαθηταί

Table 8.2 First Declension *Masculine*—ὁ μεσσίας[2]

	ὁ μεσσίας	
	Singular	*Plural*
N	ὁ μεσσίας	οἱ μεσσίαι
G	τοῦ μεσσίου	τῶν μεσσιῶν
D	τῷ μεσσίᾳ	τοῖς μεσσίαις
A	τὸν μεσσίαν	τοὺς μεσσίας
V	μεσσία	μεσσίαι

---

[2]Additional patterns for first declension masculines focus on variations in nominative, genitive singular: (1) **-ας/-ου**, as in Ἡσαΐας, Ἡσαΐου, (2) **-ας/-α**, as in σατανᾶς, σατανᾶ, (3) **-ης/-η**, as in Μανασσῆς, Μανασσῆ. These forms are uncommon, the last quite rare.

Table 8.3 Second Declension *Feminine*—ἡ ὁδός

	ἡ ὁδός	
	Singular	*Plural*
N	ἡ ὁδός	αἱ ὁδοί
G	τῆς ὁδοῦ	τῶν ὁδῶν
D	τῇ ὁδῷ	ταῖς ὁδοῖς
A	τὴν ὁδόν	τὰς ὁδούς
V	ὁδέ	ὁδοί

A few first and second declension nouns require special attention to gender. Inspect the articular paradigms above, especially observing concord. Not all second declension nouns are masculine (or neuter), and not all first declension nouns are feminine. Some second declension stems in -ος are *feminine*. The inflection is exactly second declension, but *concord* is feminine. Further, all first declension nouns ending in -ης or -ας are *masculine*, but inflection is first declension (similar to "η pure" and "α pure"). First declension inflection appears regular, except a masculine inflection shows up in the -ου of the genitive singular. A second irregularity is the -α of the vocative singular. Observe concord in the figure below.

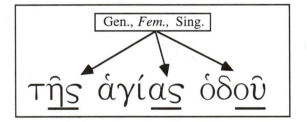

These special cases of concord in the second and first declension are easy to remember. When memorizing the vocabulary, use the phrase, "John the prophet's disciples await Messiah," to sum up the first declension masculines Ἰωάννης, προφήτης, μαθητής, and μεσσίας. Then, use the second phrase, "a way in the wilderness," to catch the second declension feminines ὁδός and ἔρημος. This leaves only παρθένος from this lesson's vocabulary.

In the Greek text, concord confusion can be a problem, especially -ος feminines in the singular. However, remember: *the principle of concord always declares the noun's gender, regardless of the noun's inflection appearance*. Notice carefully the concord of definite article and adjective declaring the gender of the noun in the above illustration.

Noun Contraction

Three "α pure" first declension nouns contract—similar to contraction in verbs. These nouns are found in the New Testament in singular forms only. Solely the look of the declension is affected. Observe the following.

Table 8.4 Noun Contraction—"α pure"

Case	First Declension "α pure" Contraction (Singular) γῆ		συκῆ		μνᾶ	
N	γέ + α =	γῆ	συκέ + α =	συκῆ	μνά + α =	μνᾶ
G	γέ + ας =	γῆς	συκέ + ας =	συκῆς	μνά + ας =	μνᾶς
D	γέ + ᾳ =	γῇ	συκέ + ᾳ =	συκῇ	μνά + ᾳ =	μνᾷ
A	γέ + αν =	γῆν	συκέ + αν =	συκῆν	μνά + αν =	μνᾶν

Adverbs

Analysis. "Adverbs add to the verb." Of course, this statement, while partially true, is an oversimplification. Adverbs have several functions that we will outline briefly below.

Modifiers. Adverbs can modify substantives. For example, "The Jerusalem *above* is free" (Gal. 4:26). Adverbs also can modify other adverbs.

Substantives. As is the case with adjectives, adverbs can be used substantivally. For example, "Behold, *now* is the day of salvation" (2 Cor. 6:2).

Case Clarifiers ("adverbial prepositions"). Case usage can be ambiguous. One can perceive this ambiguity especially in the interior cases in which one form can have several translations depending on the context. Some adverbs over time were used more and more with nouns. Such use was to clarify case (function) connected to the verbal action. These adverbs less and less were constructed with verbs only and moved into a more prepositional function (more with nominal structures than verbal). Such adverbs are called "adverbial prepositions." One example is ἔξω, "outside." Notice Heb. 11:13, Ἰησοῦς . . . **ἔξω** τῆς πύλης ἔπαθεν, "Jesus . . . suffered **outside** the gate." The adverb ἔξω relates πύλης ("gate") in a directional manner back to the verb ἔπαθεν ("he suffered").

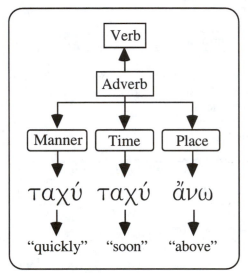

This evolution of prepositional usage actually defines the history of prepositions. In reality, *prepositions are adverbs*—adverbs so fixed in usage with noun type structures for clarifying case as to have lost any vestige of the original verbal composition.[3] Adverbs even can be constructed with prepositions. An article in the construction will be neuter singular. Thus, ἀπὸ τοῦ **νῦν** literally is "from the *now*," but is translated "from the **present**." (Prepositions will be studied later.)

Verbal Qualifiers. The main triad of adverbial use is adding *manner*, *time*, and *place* qualifiers to verbal action. So, adverbs characteristically answer questions such as "when," "where," "how," or "how much," etc. For example, "I am coming" is a simple verbal idea. "I am coming *quickly*" is a verbal idea enhanced by an adverb of manner ("hurriedly") or of time ("soon"); e.g., ἔρχομαι **ταχύ**, "I am coming **soon**," Rev. 22:20.

Formation. The English adverb often is formed by adding the suffix "-ly" to an adjective, as in "quick" to "quick*ly*" (from "he is a quick thinker," to "he thinks quickly."). Similarly, many adverbs in Greek are created from the genitive plural form of the adjective (-ων). A termination of -ως is substituted for the -ων. Thus, καλῶν

Adverbs from Adjectives

-ων ➤ -ως

("good") becomes καλῶς ("well"), κακῶν ("bad") becomes κακῶς ("badly"), and δικαίων ("righteous") becomes δικαίως ("justly"). However, the creation of adverbs is not consistent. Other adverbs were generated from various other cases. For example, ποῦ is a genitive, πάλιν is an accusative, κύκλῳ is locative.[4] Another

---

[3]Rejecting the labeling of some adverbs as "improper prepositions."

[4]Some adverbs even may preserve artifacts of old endings now lost, as the -δον in ὁμοθυμαδόν.

formulation is blending words, which explains other adverb forms, as in κατέναντι.[5] Such case history and other means of formulation are inconsequential from the standpoint of morphology. Once an adverb is memorized as an adverb in vocabulary, the recognition is easy—the adverb is not declined.

Comparisons

English. Comparisons occur in three degrees: positive, comparative, and superlative. Forms may be regular or irregular. *Regular* forms have two patterns in English. The first pattern uses suffixes: "new," "new*er*," "new*est*." The second pattern uses supplementary words ("beautiful," "more beautiful," "most beautiful"). Other English forms are *irregular:* "good," "better," "best."

Greek. Greek comparison is much like English, with one exception—inflection. As usual, Greek shows inflection for case, gender, and number.

Table 8.5 Comparisons—Adjectives

	Comparative "newer"		Superlative "newest"	
	Singular	*Plural*	*Singular*	*Plural*
masculine	νεώτερος	νεώτεροι	νεώτατος	νεώτατοι
	νεωτέρου	νεωτέρων	νεωτάτου	νεωτάτων
	νεωτέρῳ	νεωτέροις	νεωτάτῳ	νεωτάτοις
	νεώτερον	νεωτέρους	νεώτατον	νεωτάτους
neuter	νεώτερον	νεώτερα	νεώτατον	νεώτατα
	νεωτέρου	νεωτέρων	νεωτάτου	νεωτάτων
	νεωτέρῳ	νεωτέροις	νεωτάτῳ	νεωτάτοις
	νεώτερον	νεώτερα	νεώτατον	νεώτατα
feminine	νεωτέρα	νεώτεραι	νεωτάτη	νεώταται
	νεωτέρας	νεωτέρων	νεωτάτης	νεωτάτων
	νεωτέρᾳ	νεωτέραις	νεωτάτῃ	νεωτάταις
	νεωτέραν	νεωτέρας	νεωτάτην	νεωτάτας

[5]Eight occurrences, a favorite of Mark and of Paul, three times each. Cf. Mark 13:3, Rom. 4:17.

Table 8.6 Comparisons—Adjectives vs. Adverbs

Adjective Comparisons			
Comparative	-τερος	-τερα	-τερον
Superlative	-τατος	-τατη	-τατον
Adverb Comparisons			
Comparative	-----	-----	-τερον
Superlative	-----	-----	-τατα

Adjectives. Inflection for adjective comparisons is that of second and first declension adjectives for the most part. Similar to the English suffix ("er," "-est"), masculine Greek forms are -τερος, -τατος, the feminine -τερα, -τατη, and neuter forms -τερον, -τατον.[6]

Adverbs. Comparison of adverbs is easier, for the comparative degree uses the neuter accusative *singular* of the comparative adjective and the superlative degree uses the neuter accusative *plural* of the superlative adjective (usually in a *third* declension form, e.g., ἐγγύς as ἐγγύτερον but the superlative as ἔγγιστα[7]). Remember, an adverb is not declined.

Usage. Use of the superlative form was dying out in New Testament times. The comparative form often did double duty, sometimes used with superlative meaning. Thus, **μικρότερον** ὂν πάντων τῶν σπερμάτων = "**least** of all the seeds" (Mark 4:31). Context is clear that a superlative sense is meant by the comparative form.

Methods of Comparison.[8] Greek uses three methods for comparison. Case usage comes into play. One method uses the ablative function (genitive case). Another method incorporates the accusative case in combination with certain prepositions. The third method is the simple use of the conjunction ἤ.

Table 8.7 Methods of Comparison

Structure	Construction
Ablative	-ου, -ης, -ας, -ων
Accusative	παρά or ὑπέρ
Conjunction	ἤ

Ablative of Comparison. Inherently, comparison implies separation. Source or separation is the ablative function. Thus, a substantive in the genitive provides the

---

[6]A smaller set of comparisons have masculine and feminine -ιων, -ιστος (and -ιστη), and neuter -ιον, -ιστον. These third declension patterns are presented with third declension adjectives.

[7]A third declension neuter ending as explained in the previous note.

[8]The student should take note that a comparison often leaves words unexpressed. The following bracketed words illustrate: "Jesus was making and baptizing more disciples than John [*was making and baptizing disciples*]" (John 4:1). Any process of omission of words, obviously understood but grammatically necessary, is called "ellipsis." Ellipsis is common in adverbial clauses. Notice the ellipsis common to participial constructions: "while taking notes" = "while [I was] taking notes."

standard of the comparison (ablative function). The word "than" necessarily must be supplied in the translation. Notice the ablative function in John 13:16, μείζων **τοῦ κυρίου αὐτοῦ** = "greater ***than*** his master." Notice again 1 Cor. 1:25, σοφώτερον **τῶν ἀνθρώπων** = "wiser ***than*** men." In each example, the ablative function itself declares the comparison idea that generates the need to supply "than" in English.

Accusative of Comparison. The prepositions παρά and ὑπέρ, not yet introduced, can be constructed with the accusative case to generate comparisons. Notice the construction using παρά in Heb. 11:4, Πίστει πλείονα θυσίαν Ἄβελ **παρὰ** Κάϊν προσήνεγκεν = "By faith Abel offered a more acceptable sacrifice **than** Cain." Again, in Heb. 4:11, Ζῶν γὰρ ὁ λόγος τοῦ θεοῦ καὶ ἐνεργὴς καὶ τομώτερος **ὑπὲρ** πᾶσαν μάχαιραν δίστομον = "For the Word of God is living, energetic, and sharper **than** any two-edged sword."[9]

Conjunction ἤ. The third method of setting up a comparison involves use of the conjunction ἤ. The cases of the items compared are the same. In John 4:1, note the underlined words being compared are constructed in the same case (nominative): Ἰησοῦς πλείονας μαθητὰς ποιεῖ καὶ βαπτίζει **ἢ** Ἰωάννης = "Jesus was making and baptizing more disciples **than** John." Another example is Luke 10:14, (dative): πλὴν Τύρῳ καὶ Σιδῶνι ἀνεκτότερον ἔσται ἐν τῇ κρίσει **ἢ** ὑμῖν. = "'However, it will be *more tolerable* for Tyre and Sidon in the judgment **than** for you.'" Entire clauses can be compared, as in Rom. 13:11, νῦν γὰρ ἐγγύτερον ἡμῶν ἡ σωτηρία **ἢ** ὅτε ἐπιστεύσαμεν. = "For now is our salvation *nearer* **than** when we (first) believed."

Proper Names

Table 8.8 Proper Names— Ἰωάννης and Ἰησοῦς

Case	Name	Translation	Name	Translation
N	Ἰωάννης	"John"	Ἰησοῦς	"Jesus"
G	Ἰωάννου	"of John"	Ἰησοῦ	"of Jesus"
D	Ἰωάννῃ	"to John," etc.	Ἰησοῦ	"to Jesus," etc.
A	Ἰωάννην	"John"	Ἰησοῦν	"Jesus"
V	Ἰωάννης	"John"	Ἰησοῦ	"Jesus"

---

[9]The student will not be held responsible for this use until these prepositions are covered in vocabulary. Rom. 8:18 is the only example using πρός (οὐκ ἄξια τὰ παθήματα τοῦ νῦν καιροῦ **πρὸς** τὴν μέλλουσαν δόξαν = "the present sufferings are not worthy **compared with** the coming glory.")

Declension. Proper names are mixed in declension and unpredictable. Those of Semitic background usually are indeclinable. In contrast, Greek and Latin names generally are declined. Two important names, Ἰωάννης ("John") and Ἰησοῦς ("Jesus"), are given above. The noun Ἰωάννης is a masculine first declension. Irregular and unexpected is the dative and vocative -ου of the Ἰησοῦς paradigm.

Genitive of Relationship. Relationship is expressed by the genitive case, called the "genitive of relationship." The genitive case typically expresses possession, called the genitive of possession. The genitive of relationship is an extension of this idea of possession. A proper name in the genitive expresses some familial or other type of relationship (son or daughter, wife, sister, or other relationship, decided by context). Literally, the Greek has "James, of Zebedee," but the translator supplies "son of" for the meaning. The following examples illustrate:

1. Σίμων **Ἰωάννου** = "Simon, *son of* **John**" (John 21:15)
2. Ἰάκωβον τὸν **τοῦ Ζεβαδαίου** = "James, *the son of* **Zebedee**" (Matt. 4:21)
3. Μαρία ἡ **Ἰωσῆτος** = "Mary, *the mother of* **Joses**" (Mark 15:47)
4. τὸν Ἰούδαν **Σίμονος Ἰσκαριώτου** = "Judas, *the son of* **Simon Iscariot**" (John 6:71)
5. Μαρία ἡ **Ἰακώβου** = "Mary, *the mother of* **James**" (Luke 24:10)
6. Μαρία ἡ **τοῦ κλωπᾶ** = "Mary, *the wife of* **Cleopas**" (John 19:25)
7. οἱ **τοῦ Χριστοῦ** = "*the (followers) of* **Christ**" (Gal. 5:24)

Diagramming

Adverbs are diagrammed according to function. If substantival, the adverb will be placed as that substantive's function. A verbal modifier is placed on a slanted line underneath the verbal element. If used as a case clarifier, the adverb is treated like a prepositional phrase coming off the verbal element. Comparisons are on a slanted line generally off the comparative adjective or adverb. Ablative constructions supply "than" in parenthesis on the slant. Accusative constructions place the prepositions παρά or ὑπέρ on the slant. Comparisons using ἤ place the conjunction on the slant.

Table 8.9 Diagramming Adverbs and Comparisons

| 1. ἡ δὲ **ἄνω** Ἰερουσαλὴμ ἐλευθέρα ἐστίν

"Now the Jerusalem **above** is free" (Gal. 4:26) | *Adverb as Substantive (Adjective)*

1. ἡ Ἰερουσαλὴμ \| ἐστίν \ ἐλευθέρα / δὲ / ἄνω |

2. ἰδοὺ **νῦν** ἡμέρα σωτηρίας· "Behold, **now** is the day of salvation" (2 Cor. 6:2)	*Adverb as Substantive (Subject)* 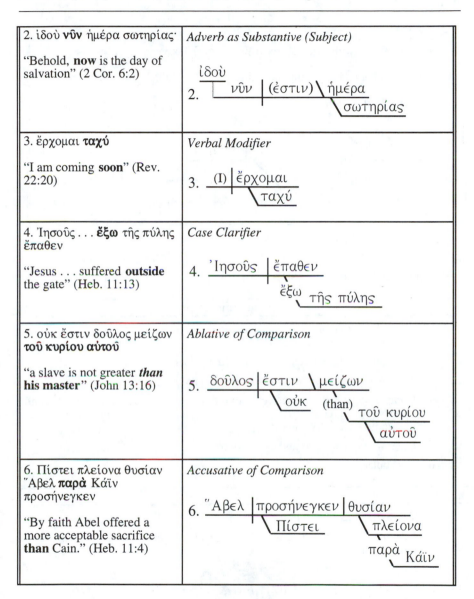
3. ἔρχομαι **ταχύ** "I am coming **soon**" (Rev. 22:20)	*Verbal Modifier*
4. Ἰησοῦς . . . **ἔξω** τῆς πύλης ἔπαθεν "Jesus . . . suffered **outside** the gate" (Heb. 11:13)	*Case Clarifier*
5. οὐκ ἔστιν δοῦλος μείζων **τοῦ κυρίου αὐτοῦ** "a slave is not greater *than his master*" (John 13:16)	*Ablative of Comparison*
6. Πίστει πλείονα θυσίαν Ἄβελ **παρὰ** Κάϊν προσήνεγκεν "By faith Abel offered a more acceptable sacrifice **than** Cain." (Heb. 11:4)	*Accusative of Comparison*

The diagrams within the right-hand column:

2.
```
        ἰδοὺ
2. ___νῦν___|(ἐστιν)\ἡμέρα
                      \σωτηρίας
```

3.
```
3. (I) |ἔρχομαι
          \ταχύ
```

4.
```
4. Ἰησοῦς | ἔπαθεν
           ἔξω\τῆς πύλης
```

5.
```
5. δοῦλος|ἔστιν \μείζων
           \οὐκ  (than)\τοῦ κυρίου
                         \αὐτοῦ
```

6.
```
6. Ἄβελ |προσήνεγκεν|θυσίαν
          \Πίστει      \πλείονα
                    παρὰ\Κάϊν
```

7. Ἰησοῦς πλείονας μαθητὰς ποιεῖ καὶ βαπτίζει **ἢ** Ἰωάννης

"Jesus was making and baptizing more disciples **than** John." (John 4:1)

Comparative Conjunction

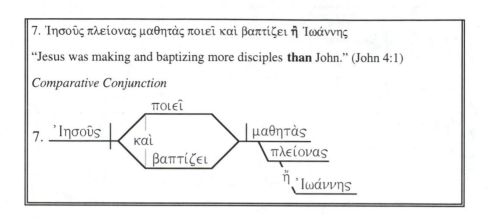

7. Ἰησοῦς | καὶ βαπτίζει ποιεῖ > μαθητὰς πλείονας ἢ Ἰωάννης

What To Learn—LESSON 8 (ὀκτώ)

Beginning

☐ 1. Masculine concord of first declension nouns in -ης/-ας and feminine concord of second declension nouns in -ος

☐ 2. Recognition of contracted "α pure" first declension nouns

☐ 3. Two main uses of adverbs and main formation in -ως

☐ 4. Comparisons: *adjective* comparative degree in -τερος, -τερα, -τερον and superlative degree in -τατος, -τατη, -τατον, and *adverb* comparative degree in -τερον, superlative in -ιστα

☐ 5. Diagramming adverbs and comparisons

☐ 6. Vocabulary

Advanced

☐ 7. Three methods of comparison

☐ 8. Declensions of Ἰωάννης and Ἰησοῦς and the *genitive of relationship* and how to translate

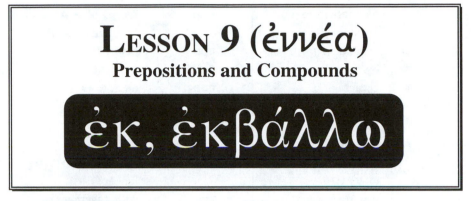

LESSON 9 (ἐννέα)

Prepositions and Compounds

ἐκ, ἐκβάλλω

Prepositions are petrified adverbs. They developed to clarify case usage connected to verbs. Greek cases took on increasingly complex meanings. Prepositions were brought in to help the overloaded case system. Compounds are verbs with prepositions attached, originally to strengthen meaning.

Vocabulary 9

Numeral			through (Ab)
ἐννέα	nine		because of (Ac)
Prepositions		εἰς	**into (Ac)**
ἀνά	**up (Ac)**		to Ac)
	through, in (Ac)		in (Ac)
	each one (Ac)		with respect to (Ac)
ἀντί	**against (Ab)**		resulting in (Ac)
	because of (Ab)		for (Ac)
	for, instead of (Ab)	ἐκ	**out of (Ab)**
ἀπό	**away from (Ab)**		from (Ab)
	from (Ab)		by (Ab)
	by (Ab)		because of (Ab)
	because of (Ab)	ἐν	**in (L)**
διά	**through (G)**		to (D)

	with respect to (D)		for (purpose, Ab)
	among (L)		in regard to (Ac)
	in, at, on (L)	πρό	**before (Ab)**
	by, with (I)		from (Ab)
	because of (I)	πρός	**near, toward (Ac)**
	in, with (I)		at, on (L)
	by (I)		beside (Ac)
ἐπί	**on, upon (G)**		with, to (Ac)
	during (G)		with respect to (Ac)
	to, for (D)		for (Ac)
	with respect to (D)	σύν	**with, together (I)**
	on, at (L)	ὑπέρ	**over, above (Ac)**
	during (L)		for (G)
	in (L)		in behalf of (G)
	because of (I)		concerning (G)
	on, upon (Ac)		than (Ac)
κατά	**down (G)**	ὑπό	**under (Ac)**
	by (G)		by (Ab)

Adverbial Prepositions

	against (Ab)
	as (Ac)
	according to (Ac)

ἅμα	together with
ἄχρι	up to
μετά	**with (G)**
	after (Ac)
ἐγγύς	near
ἔμπροσθεν	before
παρά	**beside (Ac)**
	from (Ab)
ἕνεκεν	for the sake of
	by (Ab)
ἐνώπιον	before
	beside, with (L)
ἔξω	outside
	in (L)
ἐπάνω	above
	with (I)
ἕως	up to
	than (Ac)
μέσον	in the midst of
περί	**around (Ac)**
μέχρι(ς)	until
	for, concerning (G)
ὀπίσω	after, behind
πέραν	beyond

πλήν	except
πλησίον	near
ὑποκάτω	under
χωρίς	without
Compound Verbs	
ἀναβλέπω	I look up (receive sight)

ἀναγινώσκω	I read
εἰσάγω	I lead into
ἐκβάλλω	I throw out
ἐπιγινώσκω	I know fully
καταγινώσκω	I condemn
συνάγω	I gather together

Prepositions

History. Prepositions are old adverbs. Certain old adverbs began to be used so regularly with noun structures that they *lost their adverbial use*. Notice the adverbial function of an English preposition in the construction of English infinitives—always with "to," as in "to say" or "to know." *Proper prepositions* are former adverbs now composed *exclusively with nouns. Adverbial prepositions* have a dual nature: they are old adverbs still showing their original adverbial function, yet sometimes they are composed with nouns. A basic observation illustrating the difference between proper and adverbial prepositions is that adverbial prepositions can be found by themselves modifying a verb. Proper prepositions never are found by themselves—they always are part of a prepositional phrase.

Table 9.1 Proper Prepositions—Functions

	Gen	Abl	Dat	Loc	Ins	Acc
ἀνά						✓
ἀντί		✓				
ἀπό		✓				
διά	✓	✓				✓
εἰς						✓
ἐκ		✓				
ἐν			✓	✓	✓	
ἐπί	✓		✓	✓	✓	✓
κατά	✓	✓				✓
μετά	✓					✓
παρά		✓		✓	✓	✓
περί	✓	✓				✓
πρό		✓				
πρός	✓			✓		✓
σύν					✓	
ὑπέρ	✓					✓
ὑπό		✓				✓

Function. Any prepositional phrase begins with a preposition ("pre-position") and ends with a substantive. In general, prepositional phrases function in two ways: (1) *adjectivally*, modifying a noun or pronoun, as in "the people *in the room*," or (2) *adverbially*, modifying a verb, adverb, or adjective, as in "they walked *on the grass*." Prepositional phrases are important grammatical clarifiers. Such phrases add direction, position, time, cause, agency, means, relation, association, or purpose to the context of the verbal action or related noun structure.

Case. Prepositions were used to clarify case. Conventions of such usage changed over time. Some prepositions became fixed in usage with one case only. Other prepositions developed uses with several cases. Even in just one case, a Greek preposition can have several meanings. As a result, one simply cannot give one "meaning" for a preposition (vocabulary lists provide only root ideas). Greek prepositions can have numerous "meanings." The table that follows (Table 9.2) is intended to illustrate this variety of ways prepositions function. These examples are not exhaustive by any means, but are provided to impress the student with the flexibility of Greek prepositions. We are taking aim now for later study in syntax.

So how should the beginning student approach learning Greek prepositions? First, nail down the root meanings. However, as quickly as possible begin learning other uses. *Always learn any preposition's meaning by case or function.* Use the formula: "[preposition] with the [case/function] means [translation]." For example, "the preposition διά with the genitive means 'through.'" Single out the prepositions used in one case (function) only. These help locate nouns constructed with them.

Table 9.2 Proper Prepositions—Translation Examples

	Usage	*Example*
ἀνά	*up*	ἀναβαίνομεν = "we are going **up**" (Matt. 20:18)
acc.	*through, in*	**ἀνὰ** μέσον τοῦ σίτου = "**in** the midst of the wheat" (position, Matt. 13:25)
acc.	*each one; to the measure of*	**ἀνὰ** μετρητὰς δύο ἢ τρεῖς = "twenty or thirty gallons **each**" (distributive, John 2:6)
ἀντί	*against*	ἀντιλέγει = "he speaks **against**" (John 19:12)
abl.	*because of*	**ἀντὶ** τούτου = "**because of** this" (cause, Eph. 5:31)
abl.	*for, instead of*	**ἀντὶ** τοῦ πατρὸς αὐτοῦ = "**instead of** his father" (relation, Matt. 2:22)
ἀπό	*away from, off*	ἀποχωρεῖτε = "you depart (**from** me)" (Matt. 7:23)
abl.	*away from*	**ἀπὸ** σοῦ = "**away from** you" (separation, Matt. 5:29)
abl.	*from*	**ἀπὸ** Ἰησοῦ Χριστοῦ = "**from** Jesus Christ" (source, Rev. 1:5)
abl.	*by*	**ἀπὸ** τῆς σαρκὸς = "**by** the flesh" (agency, Jude 23)
abl.	*because of*	**ἀπὸ** τῆς εὐλαβείας = "**because of** his reverence" (cause, Heb. 5:7)

διά	*through*	διαγινώσκειν = "to investigate" (Acts 23:15)
gen.	*through*	διὰ τῆς Γαλιλαίας = "**through** Galilee" (adverbial of place, Mark 9:30)
abl.	*through*	διὰ τοῦ εὐαγγελίου = "**through** the gospel" (agency, 2 Tim. 1:10)
abl.	*through*	διὰ πίστεως = "**through** faith" (means, Eph. 2:8)
acc.	*because of*	διὰ τὸ ἔργον αὐτῶν = "**because of** their work" (cause, 1 Thess. 5:13)
εἰς	*into*	εἰσέρχεται = "he enters **into**" (Heb. 9:25)
acc.	*to, unto*	εἰς οὐρανὸν = "**unto** heaven" (adverbial of measure, 1 Pet. 3:22)
acc.	*in*	οὐκ εἰς κενὸν = "not **in** vain" (adverbial of manner, Phil. 2:16)
acc.	*with respect to*	εἰς τὸ ἴδιου σῶμα = "**with respect to** his own body" (adverbial of reference, 1 Cor. 6:18)
acc.	*for*	εἰς ὄλεθρον τῆς σαρκός = "**for** the destruction of his flesh" (purpose, 1 Cor. 6:18)
acc.	*resulting in*	εἰς δικαίωσιν ζωῆς = "**resulting in** the righteousness of life" (result, Rom 5:18)
ἐκ	*out of*	ἐκβαλλει = "he is casting **out**" (Matt. 12:24)
abl.	*out of*	ἐκ γῆς Αἰγύπτοῦ = "**out of** the land of Egypt" (separation, Jude 9)
abl.	*from*	ἐκ τῶν ἡδονῶν ὑμῶν = "**from** your desires" (source, James 4:1)
abl.	*by*	ἐκ θεοῦ = "**by** God" (personal agency, John 1:18)
abl.	*by*	ἐκ τῶν ἔργων μου = "**by** my works" (means, James 2:18)
abl.	*because of*	Ἐκ τούτου = "**because of** this" (cause, John 6:66)
abl.	*on (rare)*	εἰς ἐκ δεξιῶν = "one **on** the right" (position, Matt. 20:21)
ἐν	*in*	ἐνετύλιξεν = "he wrapped [him] **in**" (Luke 23:53)
dat.	*to*	ἐν τοῖς ἀπολλυμένοις = "**to** those who are perishing" (indirect object, 2 Cor. 4:3)
dat.	*with respect to*	ἐν ἀνθρώποις = "**with respect to** men" (adverbial of reference, 1 Cor. 3:21)
loc.	*among*	ἐν τῷ λαῷ = "**among** the people" (place, Acts 6:8)
loc.	*in*	ἐν ἀγρῷ = "**in** the field" (place, Luke 15:25)
loc.	*in, at, on*	ἐν τῇ παρουσίᾳ = "**at** the appearing" (time, 1 Thess. 3:13)

(ἐν)	(in)	
loc.	in	ἐν Χριστῷ = "**in** Christ" (sphere, 2 Cor. 5:17)
ins.	by, with	ἐν πυρὶ = "**with** fire" (means, 1 Cor. 3:13)
ins.	because of	ἐν ἐμοὶ = "**because of** me" (cause, Matt. 26:31)
ins.	in, with	ἐν δυνάμει = "**in** power" (manner, 1 Thess. 1:5)
ins.	by	ἐν τῷ Βεελζεβούλ = "**by** Beelzebul" (personal agency, Matt. 12:24)
ἐπί	**on, upon**	ἐπιβάλλουσιν = "they put **on**" (Mark 11:7)
gen.	during	ἐπ᾽ ἐσχάτου τοῦ χρόνου = "**during** the last time" (adverbial of time, Jude 18)
gen.	on, upon	ἐπὶ τῆς θαλάσσης = "**upon** the sea" (adverbial of place, Mark 6:48)
dat.	to, for	ἐπὶ τοῖς ἀνθρώποις τούτοις = "**to** these men" (indirect object, Acts 5:35)
dat.	with respect to	ἐπὶ Στεφάνῳ = "**concerning** Stephen" (reference, Acts 11:19)
loc.	on, at	ἐπὶ τῷ ποταμῷ = "**at** the river" (place, Rev. 9:14)
loc.	during	ἐπὶ παροργισμῷ ὑμῶν = "**during** your wrath" (time, Eph. 4:26)
loc.	in	ἐπ᾽ ἐλπίδι = "**in** hope" (sphere, Acts 2:26)
ins.	because of	ἐπὶ τῷ λόγῳ = "**because of** the word" (cause, Acts 20:38)
acc.	on, upon	ἐπὶ τοὺς πόδας αὐτῶν = "**upon** their feet" (adverbial of measure, Rev. 11:11)
κατά	**down**	καταβαίνει = "came (comes) **down**" (Rev. 16:21)
gen.	by	**κατὰ** τοῦ θεοῦ = "**by** God" (oath, Matt. 26:63)
abl.	against	**κατὰ** σοῦ = "**against** you" (opposition, Matt. 5:23)
acc.	(distributive)	**κατὰ** τοὺς οἴκους = "house **by** house" (adverbial of measure, Acts 8:3)
acc.	as	**κατὰ** ἄνθρωπον = "**as** a man" (adverbial of reference, Rom. 3:5)
acc.	according to	**κατὰ** τὸν νόμον = "**according to** the law" (adverbial of reference, John 19:7)
μετά	**with**	μεταβεβήκαμεν = "we have crossed over" (1 John 3:14)
gen.	with	**μετὰ** Μαρίας = "**with** Mary" (association, Matt. 2:11)
gen.	with	**μετὰ** τῶν νεφελῶν = "**with** the clouds" (attendant circumstances, Rev. 1:7)
acc.	after	**μετὰ** τὴν θλῖψιν ἐκείνην = "**after** that tribulation" (adverbial of measure, Mark 13:24)

παρά	*beside*	παράγει = "was (is) passing **by**" (Matt. 20:30)
abl.	*from*	**παρὰ** ἀνθρώπων= "**from** men" (source, John 5:41)
abl.	*by*	**παρὰ** Κυρίου = "**by** the Lord" (agency, Luke 1:45)
loc.	*with*	**παρὰ** σοί = "**with** you" (place, Matt. 18:19)
loc.	*beside*	**παρὰ** τῷ σταυρῷ = "**beside** the cross" (place, John 19:25)
loc.	*with*	μωρία **παρὰ** τῷ θεῷ = "foolishness **with** God" (sphere, 1 Cor. 3:19)
ins.	*with*	**παρὰ** τινι Σίμωνι βυρσεῖ = "**with** a certain Simon the Tanner" (association, Acts 9:43)
acc.	*beside*	**παρὰ** τὴν θάλασσαν = "**beside** the sea" (adverbial of measure, Matt. 13:1)
acc.	*than*	**παρὰ** Κάϊν = "**than** Cain" (comparison, Heb. 11:4)
περί	*around*	περιάγετε = "you travel **around**" (Matt. 23:15)
gen.	*for, concerning*	**περὶ** τῆς βασιλείας = "**concerning** the kingdom" (adverbial of reference, Acts 1:3)
gen.	*for*	**περὶ** ὑμῶν = "**for** you" (advantage, 1 Pet. 5:7)
acc.	*around*	**περὶ** τὴν ὀσφὺν αὐτοῦ = "**around** his waist" (adverbial of measure, Matt. 3:4)
acc.	*in regard to*	**περὶ** τὴν πίστιν = "**in regard to** the faith" (adverbial of reference, 1 Tim. 1:19)
πρό	*before*	προάγουσιν = "they go **before**" (Matt. 21:31)
abl.	*before, from*	**πρὸ** καταβολῆς κόσμου = "**before** the foundation of the world" (separation, Eph. 1:4)
abl.	*above*	**πρὸ** πάντων = "**above** all" (rank, James 5:12)
πρός	*near, toward*	προσάγειν = "(they) drew **near to**" (Acts 27:27)
loc.	*at, on*	**πρὸς** τῇ θύρᾳ = "**at** the door" (place, John 18:16)
acc.	*beside*	**πρὸς** τὸν ἄνδρα = "**beside** her husband" (place, Acts 5:10)
acc.	*with, to*	**πρὸς** ἐμαυτὸν = "**with** me" (adverbial of measure, Phile. 13)
acc.	*with respect to*	**πρὸς** ζωὴν καὶ εὐσέβειαν = "**with respect to** life and godliness" (adverbial of reference, 2 Pet. 1:3)
acc.	*for (purpose)*	**πρὸς** εὐσέβειαν = "**for** (the purpose of) godliness" (purpose, 1 Tim. 4:7)
σύν	*with, together*	συνεσθίει = "he eats **with**" (Luke 15:2)
		συνεργεῖ = "work **together**" (Rom. 8:28)
ins.	*with*	**σὺν** τοῖς μαθηταῖς αὐτοῦ = "**with** his disciples" (association, Mark 8:34)

ὑπέρ	over, above	ὑπερνικῶμεν = "we **overwhelmingly** conquer" (Rom. 8:37)
gen.	for	ὑπὲρ δικαίου = "**for** a righteous man" (advantage, Rom. 5:7)
gen.	in behalf of	ὑπὲρ σοῦ = "**in** your **behalf**" (adverbial of reference, Phile. 13)
gen.	concerning	ὑπὲρ τῆς ὑπομονῆς ὑμῶν καὶ πίστεως = "**concerning** your perseverance and faith" (adverbial of reference, 2 Thess. 1:4)
acc.	than	ὑπὲρ τὸν διδάσκαλον = "greater **than** his teacher" (comparison, Matt. 10:24)
ὑπό	under	ὑπομένω = "I endure (abide **under**)" (2 Tim 2:10)
abl.	by	ὑπὸ τοῦ ἀγγέλου = "**by** the angel" (personal agency, Luke 2:21)
abl.	by	ὑπὸ τοῦ νόμου = "**by** the law" (impersonal agency = means, Rom. 3:21)
acc.	under	ὑπὸ νόμον = "**under** law" (adverbial of measure, Rom. 6:14)

Translation. Table 9.2 above illustrates the flexibility of the meaning of Greek prepositions. This flexibility can be frustrating for the beginning Greek student. However, some guidelines can help ease the move into translating prepositions. Three elements factor into the equation of meaning for a Greek preposition. An understanding of these elements is vital to any adequate translation of prepositions.

Elements of Meaning. The translation of any Greek preposition combines three elements toward the resultant

Table 9.3 Greek Preposition Equation

$$\text{meaning} = \text{root} + \text{case} + \text{context}$$

"meaning": (1) root idea, (2) case usage, and (3) context. *First*, one always can begin with the root idea. A basic translation often can follow intuitively from the root idea in the preposition. However, this procedure alone can be dangerous. Root ideas seem to have a narcotic effect on beginning Greek students. The student becomes addicted to the root idea as the only "meaning" and habitually tries to force every occurrence of a given preposition into this translation straight-jacket. So, *second*, move to the noun. Each noun case has a basic idea or function (see Table 4.5). Combining the root idea of the preposition with the root idea of the noun case provides a derivative idea for translation. For example, the ablative root idea is source or separation, but the accusative is extension. Thus, observe how κατά with the ablative means "against," building on that derivative idea of separation. In contrast, κατά with the accusative takes a different sense: either "as" or "according to." We can illustrate these case distinctives concerning κατά with the noun νόμος. Observe in Acts 6:13 how **κατὰ** νόμου (ablative) means "**against** the Law," but, in distinction, in John 18:31 **κατὰ** τὸν νόμον (accusative) means "**according to** the Law."[1] *Third*, the one who pays attention to the immediate context always has an edge in translating prepositions. So remember, prepositional meaning = root + case + context.

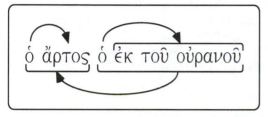

Articular Phrases. A Greek article can point to a prepositional phrase. This phrase can be used as any substantive in attributive position. For example, notice ὁ ἄρτος ὁ ἐκ τοῦ οὐρανοῦ in John 6:50. The second ὁ, in concord with the articular noun ὁ ἄρτος, points to the prepositional phrase ἐκ τοῦ οὐρανοῦ as an adjective modifier of ἄρτος. Compare ὁ ναὸς τοῦ θεοῦ **ὁ ἐν τῷ οὐρανῷ** = "the temple of God **which is in heaven**" (Rev. 11:19). By way of reminder, an adjective can be used substantivally, so an articular prepositional phrase also can be used substantivally.

Table 9.4 Proper Prepositions—Direction

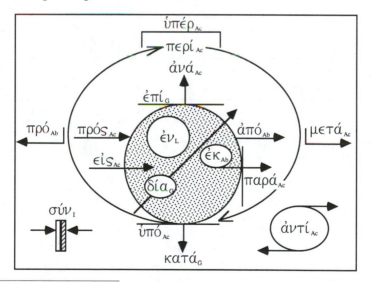

---

[1] Learning these distinctions comes in time, especially in a course in syntax.

Direction. One specific function of proper prepositions is to indicate direction. *Directional usage is case specific.* Adverbial prepositions can be directional too and occasionally can be guessed from proper prepositions. Notice, for example, the πρός in ἔμπροσθεν, the ἐπί and the ἀνά in ἐπάνω, or the ὑπό and the κατά in ὑποκάτω. The diagram of Table 9.4 illustrates the directional idea of the proper prepositions.

Elision. Minor spelling changes occur with prepositions in composition (or compounds). A preposition's final vowel elides before a following vowel.[2] In addition, the sharp stop consonants π and τ alter into their corresponding aspirate forms, φ and θ, before rough breathing (for euphony; see Table 2.2). The student simply needs to recognize such forms as alternate spellings. Inspect Table 9.5.

Table 9.5 Prepositions—Elision and Aspiration

	Smooth	Example	Rough	Example
ἀνά	ἀν᾽	-------	ἀν᾽	-------
ἀντί	ἀντ᾽	-------	ἀνθ᾽	ἀνθ᾽ ὧν (Luke 1:20)
ἀπό	ἀπ᾽	ἀπ᾽ ἐμοῦ (Matt. 7:23)	ἀφ᾽	ἀφ᾽ ὑμῶν (Matt. 21:43)
διά	δι᾽	δι᾽ ἄλλης (Matt. 2:12)	δι᾽	δι᾽ ὑμᾶς (Rom. 2:24)
ἐπί	ἐπ᾽	ἐπ᾽ αὐτόν (Matt. 3:16)	ἐφ᾽	ἐφ᾽ ὅσον (Matt. 9:15)
κατά	κατ᾽	κατ᾽ ὄναρ (Matt. 1:20)	καθ᾽	καθ᾽ ὑμῶν (Matt. 5:11)
μετά	μετ᾽	μετ᾽ αὐτοῦ (Matt. 2:3)	μεθ᾽	Μεθ᾽ ἡμῶν (Matt. 1:23)
παρά	παρ᾽	παρ᾽ αὐτῶν (Matt. 2:4)	παρ᾽	παρ᾽ ἡμέραν (Rom. 14:5)
ὑπό	ὑπ᾽	ὑπ᾽ αὐτοῦ (Matt. 3:6)	ὑφ᾽	ὑφ᾽ ὑμῶν (Acts 4:11)

Compound Verbs

Function. A *compound verb* is a verb with a prefixed preposition. The same phenomenon can be observed in English, as in "downsize," "uplift," or "outrun." In Greek, the verb's meaning may be: (1) strengthened, as in γινώσκω, "I know" to ἐπιγινώσκω, "I know fully," (2) changed, as in γινώσκω, "I know" to ἀναγινώσκω, "I read," (3) directed, as in βάλλω, "I throw" to ἐκβάλλω, "I throw out," or (4)

---

[2]See Table 1.14. Exceptions are inconsequential (περί and πρό; occasionally ὑπό; rarely ἀντί; once ἀνά in Rev. 21:21). Such forms appear "normal"; i.e., the final vowel does not elide (πρὸ ἐμοῦ).

unaffected. (The original compound force was trivialized into insignificance by overuse. So, the verb ἐπιγινώσκω in some contexts may mean no more than "I know.") The repetition of prepositions with the compounded verb was common practice in koine Greek: **ἐκ** τῆς ἐκκλησίας **ἐκ**βάλλει = "he is throwing **out of** the church" (3 John 10). Prepositions commonly repeated are ἀπό, ἐκ, εἰς, ἐν, and ἐπί. However, English translation does not need to repeat the preposition.

Formation. Prepositions are prefixed to verbs in Greek just as in English. The typical form does not alter the spelling of the verb,

$$\dot{\alpha}\pi\acute{o} + \ddot{\alpha}\gamma\omega \longrightarrow \dot{\alpha}\pi\acute{\alpha}\gamma\omega$$

as in ἐκβάλλω. However, verbs with a beginning vowel suffer elision. Elision leaves two separate words in prepositional phrases but only one word in compounds. So, ἀπό plus ἄγω generates the compounded form ἀπάγω. Recognizing the verb ἀπάγω actually is a compounded form using the preposition ἀπό is the key.

Principal Parts. Normally, the *compounded preposition is not reckoned part of the tense stem in the formation of principal parts.* If a prefix is to be added to a tense stem, but the verb is a compound verb, the prefix will go *between* the compound preposition and the stem. As an example, should a principal part require the addition of an ε prefix to the tense stem, this prefix will not go on the front of the preposition of the compounded verb, but between the preposition and the stem. Thus, the verb περιβάλλω, "I put on," in the aorist tense has the prefix ε not before the π of the preposition περί but as περιέβαλον. This principle is mentioned here for reference purposes. The student will be reminded of this principle in discussion of past tense verbs utilizing a prefix, called an "augment."

Diagramming

Use a slanted line for the preposition, then add the noun element on the horizontal line. The prepositional phrase goes under the noun or verbal element modified. Articular phrases include the article with the preposition.

Table 9.6 Diagramming Prepositional Phrases

1. ἐκ τῆς ἐκκλησίας ἐκβάλλει "he is throwing out of the church" (3 John 10)	*Modifying a verbal element* 1. (he) | ἐκβάλλει ἐκ ╲ τῆς ἐκκλησίας

2. ἠνοίγη ὁ ναὸς τοῦ θεοῦ ὁ ἐν τῷ οὐρανῷ	Modifying a noun element (and articular)
"The temple of God which is in heaven was opened" (Rev. 11:19)	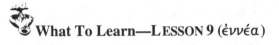

 **What To Learn—LESSON 9 (ἐννέα)**

Beginning
☐ 1. The two main functions of prepositional phrases
☐ 2. The root idea of the proper prepositions
☐ 3. Directional use of the proper prepositions with specific cases or functions
☐ 4. The definition of a *compound verb* and how to recognize forms
☐ 5. The significance for meaning of a *compound verb*
☐ 6. Review *accusative of comparison* (παρά, ὑπέρ, Table 9.2; see Lesson 8)
☐ 7. Diagramming prepositional phrases
☐ 8. Vocabulary words

Advanced
☐ 9. The distinction between *proper prepositions* and *adverbial prepositions*
☐ 10. Three elements that generate the flexible meaning of prepositions
☐ 11. The impact of elision and aspiration on the spelling of prepositions
☐ 12. Significance of compound verbs for the formation of principal parts

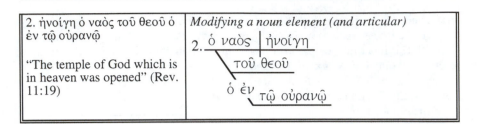

LESSON 10 (δέκα)
Present Middle/Passive Indicative

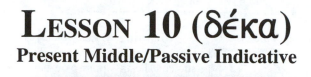

$$\lambda\acute{v}o\mu\alpha\iota$$

Middle and passive voices have identical forms but different meanings. Context alone distinguishes. Deponent verbs have only middle forms but active voice translations. Some verbs take direct objects in cases other than accusative.

Vocabulary 10

Numeral and Conjunctions

δέκα	ten (numeral)
οὔτε	and not (conjunction)
οὔτε . . . οὔτε	neither . . . nor

Nouns, Linking Verb

ἀγρός, -οῦ, ὁ	field
ἄνεμος, -ου, ὁ	wind
ὑπάρχω	I am, exist

Deponent Verbs

ἀποκρίνομαι	I answer
ἀσπάζομαι	I greet
βούλομαι	I wish, am willing
γίνομαι	I am, become, take place (linking verb)

δέχομαι	I receive
ἐργάζομαι	I work, accomplish
ἔρχομαι	I come, go
ἀπέρχομαι	I go away, depart
διέρχομαι	I pass through
εἰσέρχομαι	I enter, come into
ἐξέρχομαι	I come out, go out
παρέρχομαι	I pass away, by
προσέρχομαι	I come to
συνέρχομαι	I come together
λογίζομαι	I account, reckon
πορεύομαι	I go, proceed, travel
ἐκπορεύομαι	I go out
προσεύχομαι	I pray

117

Middle Voice

Table 10.1 Greek Voice

Active (performing)	subject action
Middle (reflecting)	action / subject
Passive (receiving)	subject action

Meaning. Greek voice is used to indicate the relationship of the verbal action to the subject. To this point you have translated only one voice, the active. The active voice presents the subject as doing the verbal action.

We now add the idea of the middle voice to our study. The Greek *middle voice* reflects the verbal action back onto the subject. The subject performs the action on itself or, more commonly, has self-interest in the action.

English has no middle voice. English uses reflexive pronouns instead. For this reason the Greek middle voice is difficult to analyze. We actually have no corresponding English structure equivalent to the Greek middle voice to compare. You will sense this as you work on learning to translate the middle voice. Be patient. The "sixth sense" develops over time. Bear in mind that the following discussion is hamstrung by the absence of a middle voice in English.

Table 10.2 Verb Endings—Indicative Mood

Subject		Indicative Endings			
		Primary Tenses		*Secondary Tenses*	
Num.	Pers.	Active	**Mid/Pass**	Active	Mid/Pass
Sing.	1st	-ω	**-μαι**	-ν	-μην
	2nd	-εις	**-σαι (η)**	-ς	-σο (ου)
	3rd	-ει	**-ται**	(-εν)	-το
Plur.	1st	-ομεν	**-μεθα**	-μεν	-μεθα
	2nd	-ετε	**-σθε**	-τε	-σθε
	3rd	-ουσι(ν)	**-νται**	-ν, σαν	-ντο

Forms. You now add a second set to the base of indicative mood endings. This set is the primary middle/passive and completes the pair of primary tense endings. Using our paradigm verb λύω, the procedure of formation is the same as with the active voice. To the tense stem, λυ-, is added the appropriate thematic vowel, then the middle pronominal suffix. Thus, we have

$$\lambda\upsilon\text{-}o\text{-}\mu\epsilon\theta\alpha$$

stem + thematic vowel + pronominal suffix

Table 10.3 Present Middle Indicative—λύω

Number	Person	Form	Translation
Singular	1st	λύομαι	"I am loosing (*for myself*)"
	2nd	λύῃ[1]	"you are loosing (*for yourself*)"
	3rd	λύεται	"he (she, it) is loosing (*for himself*)"
Plural	1st	λυόμεθα	"we are loosing (*for ourselves*)"
	2nd	λύεσθε	"you are loosing (*for yourselves*)"
	3rd	λύονται	"they are loosing (*for themselves*)"

Translation. The translations in the table are rough approximations, as you will see. The middle voice is hard to analyze. Three uses of the middle are presented, but these uses derive more from classical Greek. The distinctions in koine were breaking down. *Context is crucial to the meaning of any middle form.* Translation does not materialize automatically by the form alone. These uses are not from different forms but are the translator's evaluation of context or an idea inherent in the verb stem.

Direct Middle. Alternately called the "reflexive middle," the reflexive middle by name suggests that the action is reflected directly back onto the subject by the subject. An example is Mark 7:4, ἐὰν μὴ **βαπτίσωνται**[2] οὐκ ἐσθίουσιν = "unless they **wash** *themselves* they do not eat." The *themselves* is not a separate word in the Greek text, but rather the result of the middle voice ending -νται, in this context understood reflexively. Compare 2 Cor. 11:14, used of Satan, μετασχηματίζεται = "he transforms *himself.*"

---

[1]The -σαι ending changes when combined with the thematic vowel; the ("intervocalic") σ drops out, leaving together the vowel ε and diphthong αι. These then combine into an improper diphthong, ῃ.

[2]Aorist tense, subjunctive mood—using a lengthened thematic vowel, o to ω.

Indirect Middle. Also called "intensive middle," the indirect middle lays stress on the subject's participation in the action, usually labeled as "self-interest." This use often is left untranslated. A tactic for the beginning Greek student is to make the self-interest idea parenthetical in translation. This is a work-around, to be sure, but without the equivalent in English, this is about the best we can do. The effect is close to using a reflexive pronoun. Study the use of parentheses in the following attempt at a

Table 10.4 Lexical Distinctions by Voice

Active	Meaning	Middle	Meaning
αἴρω	I take	αἱρέομαι	I choose
ἀποδίδωμι	I give back	ἀποδίδομαι	I sell
ἀπόλλυμι	I destroy	ἀπόλλυμαι	I perish
ἅπτω	I fasten	ἅπτομαι	I touch
ἄρχω	I rule	ἄρχομαι	I begin
γράφω	I write	γράφομαι	I enroll
δανείζω	I lend	δανείζομαι	I borrow
ἵστημι	I place	ἵσταμαι	I stand
λανθάνω	I escape notice	λανθάνομαι	I forget
παύω	I make stop	παύομαι	I cease
πείθω	I persuade	πείθομαι	I obey
φαίνω	I show	φαίνομαι	I appear
φοβέω	I frighten	φοβέομαι	I fear

translation: ἡμέρας **παρατηρεῖσθε** καὶ μῆνας = "you **observe** (*for yourselves*) days and months" (Gal. 4:10). This indirect middle may be the thought expressed in James 4:3, κακῶς **αἰτεῖσθε**[3] = "you **ask** wrongly *for yourselves.*" All in all, translation of the middle voice usually is cumbersome, as if defying words in English. One good example is Rom. 15:7, **προσλαμβάνεσθε**[4] ἀλλήλους = "**receive** (*as this is in your own self interest*) one another."[5]

Reciprocal Middle. In typical form, the *active* voice with the reciprocal pronoun (ἀλλήλους) gives this idea.[6] However, at times, the middle voice too is used. As one example, Matt. 26:4 has συνβουλεύσαντο = "they took counsel *with one another.*"

Lexical Distinctions. Some verbs have different definitions, *depending on voice.* These infrequent verbs should be noted as they occur in vocabulary. The table above, not exhaustive, includes some -μι verbs for later reference. You will pick up these distinctions the more you are exposed to their uses in the New Testament.

---

[3]Can you explain this vocabulary verb's accent? Cf. παρατηρεῖσθε in the previous example.

[4]The mood is imperative (command) which has the same form as the indicative in this instance.

[5]Check several translations. Attempting to render the middle voice seems abandoned by most.

[6]Which is why the *middle* voice of Rom. 15:7 above is so difficult.

Deponents

Deponents are like dodo birds—they did not fly and perhaps they never did. In short, *deponents have active voice without active forms*.[7] The endings of a deponent verb always are middle forms (-μαι, -η, -ται, -μεθε, -σθε, -νται) but the translations are active voice. Thus, ἔρχομαι is *not* "I come (*for myself*)," middle voice, but rather simply the active voice, "I come." The dictionary entry is the middle form, as in the vocabulary for this lesson, which notifies you the verb is a deponent.

Passive Voice

Table 10.5 Present Passive Indicative—λύω

Number	Person	Form	Translation
Singular	1st	λύομαι	"I am being loosed"
	2nd	λύῃ	"you are being loosed"
	3rd	λύεται	"he (she, it) is being loosed"
Plural	1st	λυόμεθα	"we are being loosed"
	2nd	λύεσθε	"you are being loosed"
	3rd	λύονται	"they are being loosed"

Meaning. Passive voice is used when the verb's subject receives the verb's action. The passive voice was a later development in Greek than active and middle. Each language accomplishes the passive idea differently. English uses auxiliary verbs in a complicated maneuver. First, the English construction begins with a form of "to be," as in "is," "are," "was," "were." Next, English throws the verb into a past passive participle ("-ed," "-en," as in "saved" or "written"). In such constructions, English passive forms result in expressions as "is saved" or "was written." Finally, if emphasis is on the *durative* nature of the action, the additional auxiliary verb "being" is used. The expression then becomes "is *being* saved" or "was *being*

---

[7]The term "deponent" is thoroughly unsatisfactory. The term derives from the mistaken notion that some verbs "dropped" their original active voice forms. In fact, some verbs never *had* active voice forms. Yet use of this term "deponent" is too fixed to fight. (I like "dodo verbs" myself.)

written." For the Greek present tense, which is durative, "I am *being* loosed," is the preferred English translation practice for Greek students over "I am loosed."

Forms. Middle and passive endings are exactly the same. The passive never had a distinct set of endings. The passive was a hermit crab, moving into the outer shell of the already existing middle form, relying on context for significance.

Translation. One would think a morphological overlap would create confusion for translation. However, middle voice usage actually was falling off rapidly in New Testament times. Many wrote who lacked the sophistication to maintain true middle nuance in expressions. The passive voice was growing much more dominant.[8]

♦ *Assume a middle/passive form is passive unless context dictates middle.*

Agency. Who did it?—the question of agency—is a key question with passive voice. Three of the four typical uses of the passive address the question of agency.

Table 10.6 Agency and Passive Voice

Agency	Voice	Preposition	Case (func.)	Translation
personal	passive	ὑπό	Gen. (abl.)	"by"
intermediate	passive	διά	Gen. (abl.)	"by," "through"
impersonal	passive	ἐν	Dat. (instr.)	"by," "with"

Personal Agency (ὑπό). Since passive voice focuses on action happening to the subject, the *agency* of that action can be emphasized. Regularly, for personal agency the construction is the preposition ὑπό plus a noun with ablative function: παρακαλούμεθα αὐτοὶ **ὑπὸ τοῦ θεοῦ** = "we ourselves are being comforted **by God**" (2 Cor. 1:4). The use of the preposition ὑπό is not required.

"Divine Passive." Not a true grammatical category, the so-called "divine passive" is routine among New Testament writers. Agency is not explicit, but the reader presumes the passive voice agent is God. Common verbs are "saved" and "raised." Thus, 1 Cor. 15:2, σῴζεσθε = "you are being saved." Again, Luke 7:22, λεπροὶ καθαρίζονται καὶ . . . νεκροὶ ἐγείρονται, πτωχοὶ εὐαγγελίζονται = "lepers are cleansed and . . . the dead are raised, the poor are told the good news." Cf. Matt. 5:5, παρακληθήσονται = "they will be comforted [i.e., by God]."

---

[8]On occasion one can go back and forth whether middle or passive. One example is Paul's question in Rom. 3:9: προεχόμεθα; From προέχω, "I excel," "I am first." If middle, the meaning could be "have an advantage." If passive, the meaning is "am excelled," "put in worse position."

Intermediate Agency (διά). The passive action is executed by a personal agent, but indirectly through another intermediate agency. The construction is the preposition διά plus a noun with ablative function. This is the force of Phile. 22, ἐλπίζω γὰρ ὅτι **διὰ τῶν προσευχῶν ὑμῶν** χαρισθήσομαι ὑμῖν = "For I hope that **through your prayers** I will be given graciously to you." The giver actually is God. Paul anticipated that the prayers of Christians as an intermediate agency would produce this action by God. Compare Rom. 5:9, σωθησόμεθα **δι᾽ αὐτοῦ** ἀπὸ τῆς ὀργῆς = "we shall be saved [by God] **through him** [Christ] from the wrath."

Impersonal Agency (ἐν). The agent as impersonal is established through the preposition ἐν plus a noun with instrumental function: **ἐν πυρὶ** ἀποκαλύπτεται = "will be revealed **by fire**" (1 Cor. 3:13; present tense with future aspect). The use of the preposition ἐν is not required, but the noun will be instrumental in function.

Simple Passive. Emphasis is not on agency, just the action itself. Examples are Πλανᾶσθε = "you are deceived," Matt. 22:29; γαμίζονται = "they are given in marriage," Mark 12:25; κρίνομαι = "I am being judged," Acts 23:6.

Middle Contracts

Table 10.7 Present Middle/Passive Indicative—Contracts

φιλέω	δηλόω	τιμάω
φιλοῦμαι	δηλοῦμαι	τιμῶμαι
φιλῇ	δηλοῖ	τιμᾷ
φιλεῖται	δηλοῦται	τιμᾶται
φιλούμεθα	δηλούμεθα	τιμώμεθα
φιλεῖσθε	δηλοῦσθε	τιμᾶσθε
φιλοῦνται	δηλοῦνται	τιμῶνται

Present middle/passive contracts are regular (Table 7.1). Accent is recessive. However, *penult* acute accents show long ultimas. Final -αι is considered short. The thematic vowel rule is invoked in the first plural. The thematic vowel rule (acute rule) involves a recessive accent pushed back to the antepenult before contraction, which becomes long in contraction, and so *must* be acute (see Table 7.5).

Direct Objects

Table 10.8 Cases for Direct Object

Verb	Direct Object Case	Example
ἀκούω	Genitive	ἀκούουσι τῆς φωνῆς, Acts 9:7
	Accusative	ἀκούουσι τὴν φωνήν, Acts 22:9
ἀπειθέω	Dative	ἀπειθοῦσι τῇ ἀληθείᾳ, Rom. 2:8
ἀποκρίνομαι[9]	Dative	ἀπεκρίθη αὐτοῖς, John 1:26
ἀρέσκω	Dative	πᾶσιν ἀρέσκω, 1 Cor. 10:33
ἄρχω	Genitive	ἄρχειν ἐθνῶν, Rom. 15:12
βοηθέω	Dative	βοήθει μοι, Matt. 15:25
γίνομαι	Nominative (as εἰμί)	ἵνα συνεργοὶ γινώμεθα, 3 John 8
δουλεύω	Dative	δουλεύω σοι, Luke 15:29
ὁμολογέω	Dative	ὁμολογήσει ἐν αὐτῷ, Luke 12:8
	Accusative	ὁμολογῶ δὲ τοῦτο σοι, Acts 24:14
πιστεύω	Dative (or with ἐν)	πιστεύω γὰρ τῷ θεῷ, Acts 27:25
	Accusative (with ἐπί)	πιστεύσομεν ἐπ' αὐτόν, Matt. 27:42
	Accusative (with εἰς)[10]	πιστεύετε εἰς τὸν θεὸν, John 14:1

Accusative is not the only case for direct object.[11] Such verbs are not many, but should be noted so that the grammatical features of a text will not throw the student off guard. Though not accusative, these words are diagrammed as regular direct objects. (Other verbs express state of being, so always take a nominative.) Some verbs can take their direct objects in *more* than one case. The basic case idea may be involved. For example, a *genitive* direct object with ἀκούω may emphasize the *kind* of sound heard (human? animal? etc.), while an *accusative* direct object may emphasize hearing with *comprehension*. However, draw distinctions carefully.[12]

---

[9]Overwhelmingly in the aorist passive forms ἀπεκρίθη and ἀποκριθείς.

[10]Quite characteristic of Johannine style (thirty-six times).

[11]Syntactically, the root idea of another case inherently carries the root idea of the verb.

[12]Appeal to Acts 9:7 and 22:9 as illustrative of the distinction, in the apparent attempt to relieve the tension of two differing descriptions, probably fails for lack of demonstration that the author consistently shows this distinction as a matter of style. In fact, the reverse situation is found in the same contexts; cf. accusative direct object in Acts 9:4 with genitive direct object in Acts 22:7.

Finally, *transitive verbs* inherently, by nature of their verbal action, take direct objects. *Intransitive verbs* do not take direct objects. Some verbs can be used both ways. Some Greek verbs, occurring mostly as intransitive (without direct object), on rare occasion are used transitively (with direct object). When used transitively, these normally intransitive verbs show a direct object case other than the accusative, as βασιλεύω does in Matt. 2:22 or ἐπιθυμέω in 1 Tim. 3:1.

The Verbs γίνομαι and ὑπάρχω

Comparable to εἰμί, two other Greek verbs function as linking verbs. Regularly, these verbs do not take a direct object. Instead, they take the predicate nominative or predicate adjective. These verbs sometimes simply substitute for εἰμί.

The verb γίνομαι is a deponent, so occurs only in middle/passive forms, but is translated with active voice. The most common form is the second aorist, middle, third person, singular, ἐγένετο = "it happened," "it took place," or "it came about." The construction καὶ ἐγένετο = "and it came about that" or "now it happened that," is a form often found in narrative material (cf. Matt. 7:28; Mark 1:9; Luke 1:23).

The verb ὑπάρχω often is used in terms referring to one's possessions in the sense of "that which exists with [= belongs to] me." The form of such an expression usually is a participle, yet to be covered, such as the present active form ὑπάρχων = "being." Use of the verb ὑπάρχω generally represents a somewhat more literary form of hellenistic Greek, that is, above the koine vernacular. A full two-thirds of the sixty New Testament occurrences of the verb ὑπάρχω are in Luke alone (Luke and Acts). Matthew has only three; Mark and John none. Observe the following:

(1) μεῖζον τῶν λαχάνων ἐστὶν καὶ **γίνεται** δένδρον = "it is greater than garden plants and **becomes** a tree" (Matt. 13:32)

(2) **Ἐγίνετο** δὲ πάσῃ ψυχῇ φόβος, πολλά τε τέρατα καὶ σημεῖα διὰ τῶν ἀποστόλων **ἐγίνετο**. = "So great fear **was** upon every person, and many signs and wonders **were taking place** through the apostles." (Acts 2:43); the form is imperfect, middle, but is deponent, as in the present tense[13]

(3) εὐχάριστοι **γίνεσθε** = "Be thankful" (Col. 3:15); the mood is imperative (command; ending is the same as the indicative in this instance)

(4) ἀλλὰ τύπος **γίνου** = "rather, **be** an example" (1 Tim. 4:12); imperative

(5) Μὴ πολλοὶ διδάσκαλοι **γίνεσθε** = "Let not many **become** teachers" (James 3:1); imperative again

---

[13]Notice the *neuter plural* subjects in the second occurrence (τέρατα καὶ σημεῖα) but the third person *singular* verb form (see secondary *middle* forms, Table 12.3); neuter plural subjects take singular verbs.

(6) Ἀργύριον καὶ χρυσίον οὐχ **ὑπάρχει** μοι = "'Silver and gold I **do not have** [does not exist with me]'" (Acts 3:6)

(7) καὶ πάντες ζηλωταὶ τοῦ νόμου **ὑπάρχουσιν** = "and all **are** zealous for the law" (Acts 21:20)

(8) ὃς ἐν μορφῇ θεοῦ **ὑπάρχων** = "who, though **being** in the form of God," (Phil. 2:6; participle taken as concessive, "though")

What To Learn—LESSON 10 (δέκα)

Beginning

☐   1.   The grammatical significance of middle and passive voices

☐   2.   Definition of *deponent* verb and significance for translation

☐   3.   *Primary middle/passive endings* for indicative mood

☐   4.   Paradigm of λύω in the present middle and passive indicative

☐   5.   Awareness of verbs taking other cases for direct object

☐   6.   The linking verbs γίνομαι and ὑπάρχω and similarity to εἰμί

☐   7.   Vocabulary words

Advanced

☐   8.   Translating middle voice and uses: *reflexive, intensive, reciprocal*

☐   9.   Awareness of lexical distinctions between active and middle voice

☐ 10.   Translating passive voice and uses: *personal* and *impersonal* agency

☐ 11.   The meaning of *transitive* and *intransitive* verbs

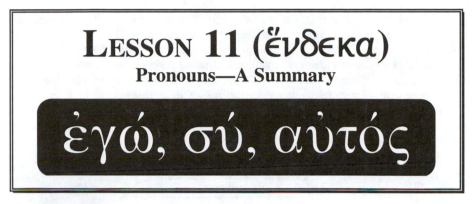

LESSON 11 (ἕνδεκα)
Pronouns—A Summary

ἐγώ, σύ, αὐτός

Greek has twelve categories of pronouns, each described briefly with examples in this reference lesson. Refer to this lesson as directed. You will not learn all these pronouns at once. For now learn the personal (and intensive) pronouns.

Vocabulary 11

Numeral			
ἕνδεκα	eleven (numeral)	ἐγώ (ἡμεῖς)	I (we)
Personal Pronouns (3rd as intensive)		σύ (ὑμεῖς)	you (you—pl.)
		αὐτός, -ή, -ό	he, she, it (self, same)

Analysis

Use. Pronouns are substantives. Pronouns can take the place of nouns: "*They* are working hard." The noun substituted for is called the *antecedent* of the pronoun. The antecedent can be understood in the immediate context or relate to previous sentences. The word *they* used above is understood to refer to some group just mentioned recently in the context.

As substantives, pronouns also can function as adjectives: "*This* disciple is following Jesus." A particular disciple is singled out specifically over others.

Concord. The principle of concord for pronouns involves the antecedent. A pronoun agrees with its antecedent in gender and number. However, pronoun concord is not complete: agreement is only partial (gender and number). *The case of a pronoun is according to grammatical function in the sentence.* For example, ἐκ τοῦ κόσμου **λαλοῦσιν** καὶ ὁ κόσμος **αὐτῶν** ἀκούει = "**They** are speaking from the world, and the world hears **them**" (1 John 4:5). The pronominal suffix provides the *subject* of the sentence in the verb, *they*, the antecedent of the pronoun αὐτῶν. Notice how αὐτῶν is masculine plural in partial agreement with the antecedent. Yet, αὐτῶν is *direct object* as required by the grammatical function with ἀκούει.[1]

In contrast, if used as an *adjective*, a pronoun will maintain *full* concord (that is, including case): ἐσμεν ἐν τῷ κόσμῳ **τούτῳ** = "we are in **this** world" (1 John 4:17). "World" has locative function. The adjective pronoun "this" also has locative function in concord with "world." Further, a pronoun takes the case appropriate in a prepositional phrase: οὐ περὶ **ἐκείνης** λέγω = "not concerning **that** am I saying" (1 John 5:16). The pronoun with περί is genitive.

Paradigms

Table 11.1 Pronouns—Personal, First and Second ("I," "we," "you")

First Person		Second Person	
Singular	*Plural*	*Singular*	*Plural*
(I, me)	*(we, us)*	*(you)*	*(you)*
ἐγώ	ἡμεῖς	σύ	ὑμεῖς
ἐμοῦ (μου)	ἡμῶν	σοῦ (σου)	ὑμῶν
ἐμοί (μοι)	ἡμῖν	σοί (σοι)	ὑμῖν
ἐμέ (με)	ἡμᾶς	σέ (σε)	ὑμᾶς

Table 11.2 Pronouns—Personal, Third ("he," "she," "it," "they")

Third—Masculine		Third—Neuter		Third—Feminine	
Singular	*Plural*	*Singular*	*Plural*	*Singular*	*Plural*
(he, him)	*(they, them)*	*(it)*	*(they, them)*	*(she, her)*	*(they, them)*
αὐτός	αὐτοί	αὐτό	αὐτά	αὐτή	αὐταί
αὐτοῦ	αὐτῶν	αὐτοῦ	αὐτῶν	αὐτῆς	αὐτῶν
αὐτῷ	αὐτοῖς	αὐτῷ	αὐτοῖς	αὐτῇ	αὐταῖς
αὐτόν	αὐτούς	αὐτό	αὐτά	αὐτήν	αὐτάς

---

[1] Remember, genitive is a direct object case for ἀκούω. See Table 10.8.

Personal ("I," "we," "you," "he," "she," "it," "they"). This is the workhorse group. Forms are very close to the adjective ἀγαθός.

Gender. First and second persons can be masculine or feminine in English; similarly, *no gender is indicated in Greek first or second person.* English third person *singular* is gender specific ("he," "she," "it"); *all Greek third person forms are gender specific.* In contrast, the English "they" is not gender specific. Third person forms come from the intensive pronoun.[2]

Emphatic Use (Anarthrous, Nominative). The pronoun already is expressed in the verb; *a personal pronoun constructed with the verb is used for emphasis.* The effect is similar to our English convention of underlining a word. This effect actually cannot be conveyed in English translation.[3] The construction is: (1) anarthrous and (2) nominative. For example:

(1) **ἐγὼ** καὶ ὁ πατὴρ ἕν ἐσμεν = "**I** and the Father are one" (John 10:30)

(2) **σὺ** τίς εἶ; = "who are **you**?" (Rom. 9:20)

(3) καὶ **αὐτός** ἔστιν πρὸ πάντων = "and **he** is before all" (Col. 1:17)[4]

Intensive Use (Third Person). This use is covered as a separate category later. Briefly, we mention here that the third personal pronoun in fact can be used with *any* person of the verb's pronominal suffix; the meaning is "self," if anarthrous. Another distinct use is in articular constructions, with the meaning "same."

Translations. One minor distinction in English forms is between nominative and *oblique*[5] cases ("I/me," "he/him"): "*I* asked *him,* and *he* did that *for me.*" Otherwise, translations follow typical case functions: ἐγώ = "I," ἐμοῦ = "of me," "from me," ἐμοί = "in me," "by me," "to me," ἐμέ = "me," and so forth. Likewise for plurals: ἡμεῖς = "we," ἡμῶν = "of us," "from us," ἡμῖν = "in us," "by us," "to us," ἡμᾶς = "us," and so forth. Enclitic forms (in parentheses in the table) affect accent only.

The third person includes distinct forms for all three genders, as the first and second do not. The declension is close to ἀγαθός, except for the neuter nominative and accusative singular (αὐτό instead of αὐτόν, unlike ἀγαθόν). Translations are "he," "she," "it" in the nominative singular; otherwise, "him" or "her" (oblique cases). All plurals are translated with "they" in the nominative; otherwise, "them."

Genitive of Possession. A common habit was to express possession not with possessive pronouns but with a personal pronoun in the genitive case. (Remember,

---

[2]Actually, Greek never had a definite third personal pronoun. The original use of αὐτός was intensive. What is called the "third personal pronoun" was, in fact, a borrowed intensive pronoun.

[3]However, for beginning students, in homework underline an emphatic personal pronoun.

[4]Realize that only a fine line separates emphatic from intensive meaning with the nominative αὐτός (see intensive use category covered later). Evaluation is subjective—results are very close whether one underlines "he" or translates "himself," as in Col. 1:17 above.

[5]*Oblique* means all other cases besides nominative; sometimes called the "objective" cases.

genitive is the case of specification.) Such constructions properly are translated using English possessive pronouns: "my," "our," "your," "his," "her," "their." So:

(1) καὶ ἔτεκεν τὸν υἱὸν **αὐτῆς** τὸν πρωτότοκον = "and she gave birth to **her** first-born son" (Luke 2:7)

(2) καὶ Ἰωάννην τὸν ἀδελφὸν **αὐτοῦ** = "and John **his** brother" (Mark 1:19)

Intensive ("same," "self"). The *third* personal pronoun has multiple uses. Usually this pronoun means "he," "she," "it," "they," etc. However, though the form is the same, this third personal pronoun also can *intensify* an expression. Two different intensifying effects are achieved, "same" or "self," described below.

"Same" (Articular). The first effect is *equal to the English adjective "same."* The construction is: (1) articular and (2) in

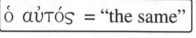

$$\text{ὁ αὐτός} = \text{"the same"}$$

concord with the substantive intensified (i.e., as if an articular adjective, but without person). Notice the articular constructions and concord in these examples:

(1) τὸν **αὐτὸν** λόγον = "the **same** word" (Matt. 26:44)

(2) ὁ γὰρ **αὐτὸς** κύριος = "For the **same** Lord" (Rom. 10:12)

(3) τὸ **αὐτὸ** πνεῦμα = "the **same** spirit" (2 Cor. 4:13)

(4) τῷ **αὐτῷ** λόγῳ = "by the **same** word" (2 Pet. 3:7)

A variation on the adjective theme is use as a substantive:

(1) σὺ δὲ ὁ **αὐτὸς** εἶ = "But you yourself are **the same**" (Heb. 1:12)

(2) καὶ οἱ ἁμαρτωλοὶ τὸ **αὐτὸ** ποιοῦσιν = "even sinners do **the same** (thing)" (Luke 6:33)

(3) τὰ **αὐτὰ** ἐπάθετε = "you suffered **the same** (things)" (1 Thess. 2:14)

"Self" (Anarthrous). Second, αὐτος can be used to *intensify identification, usually of the subject,*[6] *involving the idea "self."*[7] Such

$$\text{αὐτός} = \text{"self"}$$

use appears to be another way of creating a reflexive pronoun. However, this use is not a true reflexive. A true reflexive would include the idea of personal interest. The construction is: (1) anarthrous with (2) only partial concord (i.e., case and number, but not person).[8] Notice anarthrous constructions and partial concord in 3, 4, and 5:

(1) **αὐτοὶ** . . . οὐ θέλουσιν = "they **themselves** are not willing" (Matt. 23:4)

(2) **αὐτὸν** οἶμαι τὸν κόσμον = "I suppose the world **itself**" (John 21:25)

(3) καθὼς **αὐτοὶ** οἴδατε = "just as you **yourselves** know" (Acts 2:22)

(4) στοιχεῖς καὶ **αὐτὸς** = "even you **yourself** walk circumspectly" (Acts 21:24)

---

[6]Logically, then, regularly found in the *nominative* case (αὐτός, -ή, -ό), but not exclusively.

[7]Think of the term *"auto*matic" in English, which we explain as "by it*self.*"

[8]Always *third* person pronoun regardless the antecedent's person—even if intensifying a verb's first or second person subject.

(5) αὐτὸς ἤμην ἐφεστὼς = "I **myself** was standing by" (Acts 22:20)

(6) αὐτὴ ἡ κτίσις = "creation **itself**" (Rom. 8:21)

(7) αὐτό τε τὸ βιβλίον καὶ = "both the book **itself** and" (Heb. 9:19)

(8) ὡς καὶ αὐτὴ ἀπέδωκεν = "as even she **herself** has given" (Rev. 18:6)

A variation expressing the idea of "self" is the redundant construction of αὐτός *with* a personal pronoun, which already emphatically repeats the verb's pronominal suffix. Cf. ἐγώ εἰμι αὐτός = "it is I **myself**" (Luke 24:39) and αὐτοὶ ὑμεῖς μοι μαρτυρεῖτε = "you **yourselves** are my witnesses" (John 3:28).

Table 11.3 Pronouns—Possessive, First Singular ("my")

Masculine		Neuter		Feminine	
Singular	*Plural*	*Singular*	*Plural*	*Singular*	*Plural*
ἐμός	ἐμοί	ἐμόν	ἐμά	ἐμή	ἐμαί
ἐμοῦ	ἐμῶν	ἐμοῦ	ἐμῶν	ἐμῆς	ἐμῶν
ἐμῷ	ἐμοῖς	ἐμῷ	ἐμοῖς	ἐμῇ	ἐμαῖς
ἐμόν	ἐμούς	ἐμόν	ἐμά	ἐμήν	ἐμάς

Table 11.4 Pronouns—Possessive, First Plural ("our")

Masculine		Neuter		Feminine	
Singular	*Plural*	*Singular*	*Plural*	*Singular*	*Plural*
ἡμέτερος	ἡμέτεροι	ἡμέτερον	ἡμέτερα	ἡμετέρα	ἡμέτεραι
ἡμετέρου	ἡμετέρων	ἡμετέρου	ἡμετέρων	ἡμετέρας	ἡμετέρων
ἡμετέρῳ	ἡμετέροις	ἡμετέρῳ	ἡμετέροις	ἡμετέρα	ἡμετέραις
ἡμέτερον	ἡμετέρους	ἡμέτερον	ἡμέτερα	ἡμετέραν	ἡμετέρας

Table 11.5 Pronouns—Possessive, Second Singular ("your")

Masculine		Neuter		Feminine	
Singular	*Plural*	*Singular*	*Plural*	*Singular*	*Plural*
σός	σοί	σόν	σά	σή	σαί
σοῦ	σῶν	σοῦ	σῶν	σῆς	σῶν
σῷ	σοῖς	σῷ	σοῖς	σῇ	σαῖς
σόν	σούς	σόν	σά	σήν	σάς

Table 11.6 Pronouns—Possessive, Second Plural ("your")

| Masculine | | Neuter | | Feminine | |
Singular	Plural	Singular	Plural	Singular	Plural
ὑμέτερος	ὑμέτεροι	ὑμέτερον	ὑμέτερα	ὑμετέρα	ὑμέτεραι
ὑμετέρου	ὑμετέρων	ὑμετέρου	ὑμετέρων	ὑμετέρας	ὑμετέρων
ὑμετέρῳ	ὑμετέροις	ὑμετέρῳ	ὑμετέροις	ὑμετέρᾳ	ὑμετέραις
ὑμέτερον	ὑμετέρους	ὑμέτερον	ὑμέτερα	ὑμετέραν	ὑμετέρας

Table 11.7 Pronouns—Possessive, Third, Using ἴδιος ("his," "her," "their")

| Masculine | | Neuter | | Feminine | |
Singular	Plural	Singular	Plural	Singular	Plural
ἴδιος	ἴδιοι	ἴδιον	ἴδια	ἰδία	ἴδιαι
ἰδίου	ἰδίων	ἰδίου	ἰδίων	ἰδίας	ἰδίων
ἰδίῳ	ἰδίοις	ἰδίῳ	ἰδίοις	ἰδίᾳ	ἰδίαις
ἴδιον	ἰδίους	ἴδιον	ἴδια	ἰδίαν	ἰδίας

Possessive ("my," "our," "your"). These pronouns are uncommon in the New Testament, the third person being absent altogether. Most frequent are inflected forms of ἐμός.[9] One simply could use the personal pronoun in the genitive case instead (e.g., μου, σου, ἡμῶν, ὑμῶν, αὐτοῦ, αὐτῆς, αὐτῶν), the preferred method. However, one also could use the actual possessive pronoun. Such pronouns really function as adjectives: (1) they maintain full concord (*including* case, in distinction from the partial concord of other pronouns), and (2) they always are attributive. Four observations about possessive pronouns apply.

First, *Greek possessive singular pronouns are inflected*, based on concord, as English is not. ("my book," "my books"). So Greek first and second person *singular* possessive pronouns have *plural* inflection—if the noun modified is plural—but not plural meaning. Thus, τὸν **ἐμὸν** οἶκον = "**my** house" (direct object), but also τοὺς **ἐμοὺς** οἴκους = "**my** houses" (direct object).

---

[9]Seventy-six times in the New Testament, over half in John's Gospel (forty-one). Forms of σός twenty-seven times; ἡμέτερος eight times; ὑμέτερος eleven times. Paradigms are provided to demonstrate the regularity of inflection.

Second, *Greek possessive plural pronoun inflections are near replicas*. The only difference is the first letter—ἡμέτερος versus ὑμέτερος (cf. ἡμεῖς and ὑμεῖς).

Third, *Greek possessive pronouns have no third person forms*. Instead, the genitive personal pronoun is used, as noted. However, an alternate method is to use the reflexive pronoun, ἴδιος, with possessive force ("his own," "her own," "their own"). This method makes possession emphatic. For example:

(1) ἀγαπήσας **τοὺς ἰδίους** = "having loved **his own**" (John 13:1)

(2) ἐν **τῷ ἰδίῳ** ὀφθαλμῷ = "in **his own** eye" (Luke 6:41)

(3) ὑπὸ **τῆς ἰδίας** ἐπιθυμία = "by **his own** lust" (James 1:14)

Fourth, English distinguishes possessive pronouns employed as nouns rather than as adjectives.[10] For example: "The choice is *yours*." "The decision was *mine*." "*Ours* were the only votes." Greek does not make this distinction, but possessive constructions can be translated with these alternate English forms as appropriate to the context. Notice 1 Cor. 1:2, **αὐτῶν** καὶ **ἡμῶν** = "**theirs** and **ours**." Again, Matt. 5:3, **αὐτῶν** ἐστιν ἡ βασιλεία τῶν οὐρανῶν = "**theirs** is the kingdom of heaven."

Table 11.8 Pronouns—Reflexive, First ("myself," "ourselves")

| Masculine | | Neuter | | Feminine | |
Singular	Plural	Singular	Plural	Singular	Plural
---------	---------	---------	---------	---------	---------
ἐμαυτοῦ	ἑαυτῶν	---------	---------	ἐμαυτῆς	ἑαυτῶν
ἐμαυτῷ	ἑαυτοῖς	---------	---------	ἐμαυτῇ	ἑαυταῖς
ἐμαυτόν	ἑαυτούς	---------	---------	ἐμαυτήν	ἑαυτάς

Table 11.9 Pronouns—Reflexive, Second ("yourself," "yourselves")

| Masculine | | Neuter | | Feminine | |
Singular	Plural	Singular	Plural	Singular	Plural
---------	---------	---------	---------	---------	---------
σεαυτοῦ	ἑαυτῶν	---------	---------	σεαυτῆς	ἑαυτῶν
σεαυτῷ	ἑαυτοῖς	---------	---------	σεαυτῇ	ἑαυταῖς
σεαυτόν	ἑαυτούς	---------	---------	σεαυτήν	ἑαυτάς

---

[10]The suffix "s" is added, creating "yours," "ours," "hers," and "theirs." However, contrast the first person singular, "mine." The neuter form "its" properly is an adjective, not a pronoun.

Table 11.10 Pronouns—Reflexive, Third ("himself," "themselves," etc.)

| Masculine | | Neuter | | Feminine | |
Singular	Plural	Singular	Plural	Singular	Plural
---------	---------	---------	---------	---------	---------
ἑαυτοῦ	ἑαυτῶν	ἑαυτοῦ	ἑαυτῶν	ἑαυτῆς	ἑαυτῶν
ἑαυτῷ	ἑαυτοῖς	ἑαυτῷ	ἑαυτοῖς	ἑαυτῇ	ἑαυταῖς
ἑαυτόν	ἑαυτούς	ἑαυτό	ἑαυτά	ἑαυτήν	ἑαυτάς

Reflexive ("myself," "yourself," "himself"). The action of the verb is reflected back to the subject. One can see a combination of ἐμέ and σέ with the "oblique cases" of αὐτός, that is, cases excluding the nominative. First and second person have no neuter forms, while the third person *does* have neuter forms. Within each gender, *all plurals, all persons are the same.* A *nominative* reflexive is achieved with an anarthrous, nominative *third personal* pronoun, used emphatically (see John 8:13, example three). Examples are:

(1) ἀφ' **ἑαυτῶν** γινώσκετε = "you can know for **yourselves**" (Luke 21:30)

(2) ἐβουλόμην πρὸς **ἐμαυτὸν** κατέχειν = "I wished to retain for **myself**" (Phile. 13)

(3) Σὺ περὶ **σεαυτοῦ** μαρτυρεῖς· = "You are bearing witness about **yourself**" (John 8:13)

(4) θησαυρίζεις **σεαυτῷ** ὀργὴν = "you are storing up wrath for **yourself**" (Rom. 2:5)

(5) ἁγνίζει **ἑαυτὸν** καθὼς ἐκεῖνος ἁγνός ἐστιν = "he purifies **himself** just as that one is pure" (1 John 3:3)

Reciprocal ("one another"). Only masculine gender and only plural number, these pronouns represent the doubling of the stem of ἄλλος, "other." Just three forms occur in the New Testament, which serve the needs of six functions. Thus, for example:

(1) ἐσμὲν **ἀλλήλων** μέλη = "we are members of one another" (Eph. 4:25)

(2) **ἀλλήλους** προκαλούμενοι, **ἀλλήλοις** φθονοῦντες = "irritating **one another**, envying **one another**" (Gal. 5:26)

Table 11.11 Pronouns— Reciprocal ("one another")

| Masculine | |
Singular	Plural
--------	--------
--------	ἀλλήλων
--------	ἀλλήλοις
--------	ἀλλήλους

Table 11.12 Pronouns—Proximate Demonstrative ("this," "these")

Masculine		Neuter		Feminine	
Singular	*Plural*	*Singular*	*Plural*	*Singular*	*Plural*
οὗτος	οὗτοι	τοῦτο	ταῦτα	αὕτη	αὗται
τούτου	τούτων	τούτου	τούτων	ταύτης	ταύτων
τούτῳ	τούτοις	τούτῳ	τούτοις	ταύτῃ	ταύταις
τοῦτον	τούτους	τοῦτο	ταῦτα	ταύτην	ταύτας

Table 11.13 Pronouns—Remote Demonstrative ("that," "those")

Masculine		Neuter		Feminine	
Singular	*Plural*	*Singular*	*Plural*	*Singular*	*Plural*
ἐκεῖνος	ἐκεῖνοι	ἐκεῖνο	ἐκεῖνα	ἐκείνη	ἐκεῖναι
ἐκείνου	ἐκείνων	ἐκείνου	ἐκείνων	ἐκείνης	ἐκείνων
ἐκείνῳ	ἐκείνοις	ἐκείνῳ	ἐκείνοις	ἐκείνῃ	ἐκείναις
ἐκεῖνον	ἐκείνους	ἐκεῖνο	ἐκεῖνα	ἐκείνην	ἐκείνας

Demonstrative ("this," "these," "that," "those"). The forms are similar to the personal pronoun (third person). The endings of the remote are regular. Two classes are involved; the difference is the idea of relative distance from the speaker. Proximate demonstrative is near the speaker. Remote demonstrative is at some (unspecified) distance. Contrary to the use of most other adjectives, *this pronoun functions adjectivally in the predicate position* (no article). Observe:

(1) **οὗτος** καὶ τὸν πατέρα καὶ τὸν υἱὸν ἔχει = "**this one** has both the Father and the Son" (2 John 9)

(2) τὸ πλοῦτος τῆς δόξης τοῦ μυστηρίου **τούτου** = "the riches of the glory of **this** mystery" (Col. 1:27)

(3) **Ταῦτα** λάλει καὶ παρακάλει καὶ ἔλεγχε = "**These things** speak and exhort and reprove" (Tit. 2:15)

(4) τί ποιήσει τοῖς γεωργοῖς **ἐκείνοις**; = "What will he do to **those** vinegrowers?" (Matt. 21:40)

(5) μετὰ τὰς ἡμέρας **ἐκείνας**, λέγει κύριος = "after **those** days, says the Lord" (Heb. 8:10)

(6) ἀγοράζει τὸν ἀγρὸν **ἐκεῖνον** = "he buys **that** field" (Matt. 13:44)

(7) καὶ ἀπ᾽ **ἐκείνης** τῆς ὥρας ἔλαβεν ὁ μαθητὴς αὐτὴν εἰς τὰ ἴδια = "and from **that** very hour the disciple took her into his own house" (John 19:27)

Table 11.14 Pronouns—Correlative ("such")

Masculine		Neuter		Feminine	
Singular	*Plural*	*Singular*	*Plural*	*Singular*	*Plural*
τοιοῦτος	τοιοῦτοι	τοιοῦτο	τοιαῦτα	τοιαύτη	τοιαῦται
τοιούτου	τοιούτων	τοιούτου	τοιούτων	τοιαύτης	τοιαύτων
τοιούτῳ	τοιούτοις	τοιούτῳ	τοιούτοις	τοιαύτῃ	τοιαύταις
τοιοῦτον	τοιούτους	τοιοῦτο	τοιαῦτα	τοιαύτην	τοιαύτας

Correlative ("such"). The dominant variety of correlative pronoun is τοιοῦτος. Of the others, only ὅσος, -η, -ον ("as much as"), occurs with any frequency—110 times in the New Testament. The pronoun τοσοῦτος ("so much," "so great," "so many") occurs twenty times; οἷος, -α, -ον ("as") is used fifteen times.[11]

The correlative τοιοῦτος *("such")*. A special class of demonstrative pronouns, these are similar to οὗτος, but with a τοι- prefix. Translations are flexible:

(1) Καὶ **τοιαύταις** παραβολαῖς πολλαῖς ἐλάλει αὐτοῖς τὸν λόγον = "And with many **such** parables he was speaking the word to them" (Mark 4:33)

(2) τῶν γὰρ **τοιούτων** ἐστὶν ἡ βασιλεία τοῦ θεοῦ = "for **of such ones** is the kingdom of God" (Luke 18:16, substantive construction)

(3) καὶ οἶδα τὸν **τοιοῦτον** ἄνθρωπον = "and I know **such** a man" (2 Cor. 12:3)

(4) ἡμεῖς οὖν ὀφείλομεν ὑπολαμβάνειν τοὺς **τοιούτους** = "Therefore, we ought to support **such men**" (3 John 8, substantive construction)

The correlative τοσοῦτος *("so much," "so great," "so many")*. This pronoun appears as the prefix τοσ- on the inflections -ουτος, -αυτη, and -ουτον. For example:

(1) παρ᾽ οὐδενὶ **τοσαύτην** πίστιν ἐν τῷ Ἰσραὴλ εὗρον = "**Such great** faith I have not found with anyone in Israel!" (Matt. 8:10)

(2) **Τοσούτῳ** χρόνῳ μεθ᾽ ὑμῶν εἰμι καὶ οὐκ ἔγνωκάς με, Φίλιππε; = "I have been with you for **so** long yet you do not know me, Philip?" (John 14:9)

---

[11]The terms "relative" and "correlative" are not distinct. Classification among grammars and lexicons is inconsistent. Some terms classified as "correlative" just as easily could be placed under the relative pronoun category. Uncommon forms appearing in the New Testament are listed briefly. The pronoun **ὅδε** ("this," "thus") is found only in the forms τῇδε (Luke 10:39), τήνδε (James 4:13), and τάδε (Acts 21:11; Rev. 2:1, 8, 12, 18; 3:1, 7, 14). The pronoun **τηλικοῦτος** ("so great") is found in the forms τηλικούτου (2 Cor. 1:10), τηλικαύτης (Heb. 2:3), τηλικαῦτα (James 3:4), and τηλικοῦτος (Rev. 16:18). The pronoun **τοιόσδε** ("such as this") is found only at 2 Pet. 1:17.

(3) καὶ **τοσούτῳ** μᾶλλον ὅσῳ βλέπετε ἐγγίζουσαν τὴν ἡμέραν = "and **so much** more as you see the day drawing near" (Heb. 10:25)

The correlative οἷος *("as")*. The only New Testament forms are the masculine οἷος, οἷοι, οἷον, οἷους, the neuter οἷον, οἷα, and the feminine οἵα. Examples are:

(1) **οἷος** ὁ χοϊκός, τοιοῦτοι καὶ οἱ χοϊκοί = "**As** is the earthly, such also are those who are earthly" (1 Cor. 15:48)

(2) οὐχ **οἵους** θέλω εὕρω ὑμᾶς = "not **as** I wish will I find you" (2 Cor. 12:20)

(3) καὶ σεισμὸς ἐγένετο μέγας, **οἷος** οὐκ ἐγένετο = "and a great earthquake took place, **such as** had not happened" (Rev. 16:18)

The correlative ὅσος *("as much as")*. Actually, the translation is by context. Several alternatives may be appropriate. Compare the following:

(1) πωλεῖ πάντα **ὅσα** ἔχει = "he sells all **that** he has" (Matt. 13:44)

(2) δώσει αὐτῷ **ὅσων** χρῄζει = "he will give him **as much as** he needs" (Luke 11:8)

(3) **ὅσα** ἐστὶν ἀληθῆ = "**whatever** is true" (Phil. 4:8)

Table 11.15 Pronouns—Relative ("who," "whom," "that")

Masculine		Neuter		Feminine	
Singular	*Plural*	*Singular*	*Plural*	*Singular*	*Plural*
ὅς	οἵ	ὅ	ἅ	ἥ	αἵ
οὗ	ὧν	οὗ	ὧν	ἧς	ὧν
ᾧ	οἷς	ᾧ	οἷς	ᾗ	αἷς
ὅν	οὕς	ὅ	ἅ	ἥν	ἅς

Relative ("who," "whom," "that"). This pronoun sets up relative clauses and looks like the definite article minus the τ but is *accented* with *rough breathing*.[12] The Greek relative pronoun distinguishes number, a distinction lost in translation. (English does not.) A key issue is concord, which involves only gender and number. *Case is governed by the pronoun's function within the relative clause*.[13] Especially note concord issues in the examples.[14]

---

[12]Remember the phrase, "Relatives are rough." Distinguish the enclitic article in example six.

[13]Or by "attraction," the phenomenon in which a word close to the relative pronoun seems to exert more influence on case than the pronoun's actual grammatical function in the clause.

[14]Uncommon forms appearing in the New Testament are listed briefly. The relative ὁποῖος ("as," "such as," "of what kind") occurs five times, as ὁποῖος (Acts 26:29; James 1:24), ὁποῖον (1 Cor. 3:13), ὁποῖοι (Gal. 2:6), and ὁποίαν (1 Thess. 1:9). The relative ἡλίκος ("how great") occurs three times, as ἡλίκον (Col. 2:1; James 3:5) and ἡλίκην (James 3:5). Finally, the relative πηλίκος ("how large") occurs twice, as πηλίκοις (Gal. 6:11) and πηλίκος (Heb. 7:4).

Table 11.16 Pronouns—Relative: Concord Versus Function

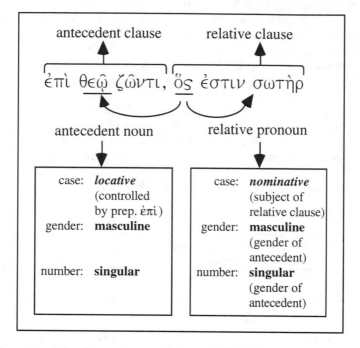

Observe the following relative pronoun examples:

(1) εἷς θεὸς ὁ πατὴρ ἐξ **οὗ** τὰ πάντα . . . καὶ εἷς κύριος Ἰησοῦς Χριστός δι'
    οὗ τὰ πάντα = "one God, the Father, **from whom** are all things . . . and one
    Lord, Jesus Christ, **through whom** are all things" (1 Cor. 8:6)

(2) Γνωρίζω δὲ ὑμῖν, ἀδελφοί, τὸ εὐαγγέλιον **ὃ** εὐηγγελισάμην ὑμῖν, **ὃ** καὶ
    παρελάβετε, ἐν **ᾧ** καὶ ἐστήκατε, δι' **οὗ** καὶ σῴζεσθε = "Now I make
    known to you, brothers, the gospel **which** I proclaimed to you, **which** also
    you received, **in which** also you stand, **through which** also you are being
    saved" (1 Cor. 15:1–2)

(3) **ἅ** ἐστιν σκιὰ = "**which** are a shadow" (Col. 2:17; antecedent in elements
    of 2:16; note: neuter plural subject takes singular verb)

(4) ἐπὶ θεῷ ζῶντι, **ὅς** ἐστιν σωτὴρ = "in the living God, **who** is Savior"
    (1 Tim. 4:10)

(5) τὸ μυστήριον τῶν ἑπτὰ ἀστέρων **οὓς** εἶδες = "the mystery of the seven stars **which** you saw" (Rev. 1:20)

(6) φιάλας χρυσᾶς . . . **αἵ** εἰσιν αἱ προσευχαὶ τῶν ἁγίων = "golden bowls . . . **which** are the prayers of the saints" (Rev. 5:8)

Table 11.17 Pronouns—Interrogative ("who?" "which?" "what?")

Masculine		Feminine		Neuter	
Singular	*Plural*	*Singular*	*Plural*	*Singular*	*Plural*
τίς	τίνες	τίς	τίνες	τί	τίνα
τίνος	τίνων	τίνος	τίνων	τίνος	τίνων
τίνι	τίσι(ν)	τίνι	τίσι(ν)	τίνι	τίσι(ν)
τίνα	τίνας	τίνα	τίνας	τί	τίνα

Interrogative ("who?" "which?" "what?"). Interrogative pronouns have three main varieties of concern for the New Testament reader. These are covered below.[15]

Interrogative ("who?" "which?" "what?"). This principle interrogative pronoun (τίς, τίς, τί) is used to initiate a direct question or to report a question indirectly. The pattern is third declension (masculine and feminine the same) and clones the indefinite pronoun—*except the acute accent throughout*. Examples are:

(1) οἱ βασιλεῖς τῆς γῆς ἀπὸ **τίνων** λαμβάνουσιν = "From **whom** do the kings of the earth receive . . . ?" (Matt. 17:25)

(2) **τί** ἐστιν εὐκοπώτερον; = "**Which** is easier?" (Mark 2:9)

(3) πρὸς **τίνα** ἀπελευσόμεθα; = "to **whom** shall we go?" (John 6:68)

(4) ἐκεῖνοι δὲ οὐκ ἔγνωσαν **τίνα** ἦν = "but they did not understand **what** those things were" (John 10:6)

(5) **τί** ποιοῦμεν; = "**What** are we doing?" (John 11:47)

(6) οὗτοι . . . **τίνες** εἰσὶν; = "**who** are these?" (Rev. 7:13)

Adverbial ("Why?") The form τί at the front of a clause can be used as the question, "why?" The use is adverbial. For example:

(1) **τί** με πειράζετε; = "**why** are you testing me?" (Matt. 22:18)

(2) **τί** ταῦτα διαλογίζεσθε; = "**why** do you discuss these things?" (Mark 2:8)

---

[15]Uncommon forms appearing in the New Testament are listed briefly. The interrogative **ποταπός** ("what sort of?" "what kind?") occurs seven times, as ποταπός (Matt. 8:27; Luke 1:29), ποταποί (Mark 13:1), ποταπαί (Mark 13:1), ποταπή (Luke 7:39), ποταπούς (2 Pet. 3:11), and ποταπήν (1 John 3:1). The interrogative **πότερος** ("which?") occurs once, as πότερον (John 7:17).

Two sub-categories of the interrogative pronoun are the qualitative interrogative and the quantitative interrogative. These are summarized below.

Qualitative Interrogative ("of what type?"). The pronoun ποῖος, ποία, ποῖον—mostly singular in the New Testament—asks, "of what type?" (thirty-three times). Translation as an interrogative ("what?" "which?") can be sufficient. Observe:

(1) Διδάσκαλε, **ποία** ἐντολὴ μεγάλη ἐν τῷ νόμῳ; = "Teacher, **which** commandment is greatest in the law?" (Matt. 22:36)

(2) **ποῖον** οἶκον οἰκοδομήσετέ μοι; = "**What kind** of house will you build for me?" (Acts 7:49)

(3) διὰ **ποίου** νόμου; = "Through **what type** of law?" (Rom. 3:27)

(4) **ποίῳ** δὲ σώματι ἔρχονται; = "And **with what kind** of body do they come?" (1 Cor. 15:35)

(5) **ποία** ἡ ζωὴ ὑμῶν = "**what** your life (will be like)" (James 4:14)

Quantitative Interrogative ("how much?" "how many?" "how great?"). The pronoun πόσος, -η, -ον occurs twenty-seven times in the New Testament. The use can be exclamatory, or reporting indirectly a statement that could be framed as a question. Quite often, this pronoun works in concert with the adverb μᾶλλον. Thus:

(1) εἰ οὖν τὸ φῶς τὸ ἐν σοὶ σκότος ἐστίν, τὸ σκότος **πόσον**. = "If the light in you is darkness, **how great** is that darkness!" (Matt. 22:18)

(2) **πόσων** σπυρίδων πληρώματα κλασμάτων ἤρατε; = "**how many** large baskets full of left-over pieces did you pick up?" (Mark 8:20)

(3) **Πόσον** ὀφείλεις τῷ κυρίῳ μου; = "**How much** do you owe my master?" (Luke 16:5)

(4) **πόσῳ** μᾶλλον τὸ πλήρωμα αὐτῶν = "**how much** more their fullness!" (Rom. 11:12)

Table 11.18 Pronouns—Indefinite ("somebody," "something," "a certain")

Masculine		Feminine		Neuter	
Singular	*Plural*	*Singular*	*Plural*	*Singular*	*Plural*
τις	τινες	τις	τινες	τι	τινα
τινος	τινων	τινος	τινων	τινος	τινων
τινι	τισι(ν)	τινι	τισι(ν)	τινι	τισι(ν)
τινα	τινας	τινα	τινας	τι	τινα

Indefinite ("somebody," "something," "a certain"). These are exact replicas of the interrogative pronoun, but are enclitic (no accent). Enclitic accent rules apply (a possible ultima acute, except genitive plural). Inflection is third declension (masculine = feminine); all interiors are the same, all genders. Observe:

(1) ἄνθρωπός **τις** εἶχεν δύο υἱούς = "**a certain** man had two sons" (Luke 15:11)

(2) ἐν τῷ εἶναι αὐτὸν ἐν τόπῳ **τινὶ** προσευχόμενον = "while he was praying in **a certain** place" (Luke 11:1)

(3) λέγειν **τι** ἢ ἀκούειν **τι** καινότερον = "telling **anything** or hearing **anything** new" (Acts 17:21)

(4) Εἰ δέ **τινες** τῶν κλάδων = "But if **some** of the branches" (Rom. 11:17)

(5) ἀκούομεν γάρ **τινας** περιπατοῦντας ἐν ὑμῖν ἀτάκτως = "For we hear that **some** among you are acting lazy" (2 Thess. 3:11)

Table 11.19 Pronouns—Indefinite Relative ("who," "whoever," "which ones")

| Masculine | | Feminine | | Neuter | |
Singular	*Plural*	*Singular*	*Plural*	*Singular*	*Plural*
ὅστις	οἵτινες	ἥτις	αἵτινες	ὅτι	ἅτινα

Indefinite Relative ("who," "whoever," "which ones"). These combine the relative (ὅς) and indefinite pronoun (τις), both forms inflected. Such pronouns always occur as *subject* of the relative clause, so they are encountered *only in the nominative*. Inflection is third declension. Notice the subject function below:

(1) δέκα παρθένοις, **αἵτινες** λαβοῦσαι τὰς λαμπάδας ἑαυτῶν = "to ten virgins, **who** took their lamps" (Matt. 25:1)

(2) **ἅτινα** ἦν μοι κέρδη = "**whichever things** were gain to me" (Phil. 3:7)

(3) **ὅστις** γάρ ὅλον τὸν νόμον τηρήσῃ = "For **whoever** keeps the whole law" (James 2:10)

Table 11.20 Pronouns—Negative ("no one")

| Masculine | | Neuter | | Feminine | |
Singular	*Plural*	*Singular*	*Plural*	*Singular*	*Plural*
οὐδείς	-------	οὐδέν	-------	οὐδεμία	-------
οὐδενός	-------	οὐδενός	-------	οὐδεμιᾶς	-------
οὐδενί	-------	οὐδενί	-------	οὐδεμιᾷ	-------
οὐδένα	-------	οὐδέν	-------	οὐδεμίαν	-------

Negative ("no one," "anything"). Only singular ("no *one*"), their morphology combines "one" in declined forms (εἷς, μία, ἕν) with the indicative mood negative particle οὐδέ ("not even," or the subjunctive form μηδέ). Often, a negative pronoun can be constructed in any case to function as a substantive. Declension is mixed:

(1) **Μηδεὶς** πειραζόμενος λεγέτω = "Let **no one** say when he is tempted" (James 1:13a; cf. James 1:13b, in example two)

(2) πειράζει δὲ αὐτὸς **οὐδένα** = "and he himself tempts **no one**" (1:13b)

(3) **μηδεμίαν** ἐν **μηδενὶ** διδόντες προσκοπήν = "giving **not even one** cause for offense in **anything**" (2 Cor. 6:3)

(4) παρ' **οὐδενὶ** τοσαύτην πίστιν ἐν τῷ Ἰσραὴλ εὖρον. = "Such great faith I have not found with **anyone** in Israel!" (Matt. 8:10)

Diagramming

Pronouns are diagrammed according to grammatical function. As a noun substitute, the pronoun is situated as subject or predicate nominative or indirect object or direct object or on the horizontal of a prepositional phrase. As an adjective, the pronoun is situated on a slanted line underneath the element modified.

The framing of questions does not change grammatical function. Interrogative pronouns simply invert word order, putting the adverbial or objective interrogative first. "To whom are you going?" grammatically is: "You are going to whom." Not all questions actually have an explicit interrogative ("Are they ministers of Christ?"). Mentally rewrite the question as a simple declarative sentence, and diagram the component elements accordingly. ("They are ministers of Christ.")

Relative pronouns have their own base line, with related elements, operating in three ways: (1) as *subject* of the clause the relative pronoun begins, (2) as *object* of the verb in the pronoun clause, (3) as *object of the preposition* in the clause. The key components are the pronoun and the pronoun's antecedent. Use a dotted line to connect the relative pronoun of one base line unit to the antecedent in the other unit.

Table 11.21 Diagramming Interrogative and Relative Pronouns

1. τί λέγει ἡ γραφή; "**What** does the Scripture say?" (Gal. 4:30)	*Interrogative Pronoun as Object* 1. ἡ γραφή | λέγει | τί

2. τί με περάζετε; "**Why** are you testing me?" (Matt. 22:18)	*Interrogative Pronoun as Adverb* 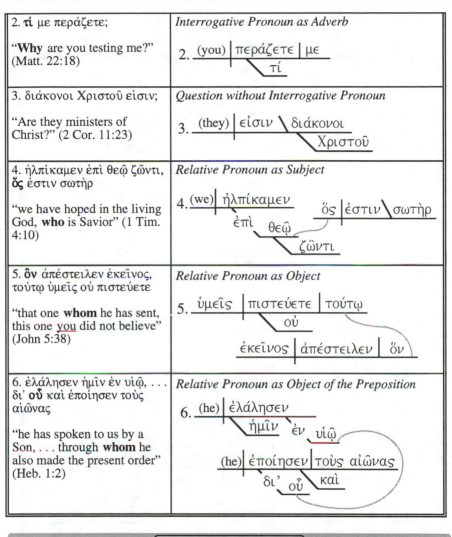
3. διάκονοι Χριστοῦ εἰσιν; "Are they ministers of Christ?" (2 Cor. 11:23)	*Question without Interrogative Pronoun*
4. ἠλπίκαμεν ἐπὶ θεῷ ζῶντι, **ὅς** ἐστιν σωτὴρ "we have hoped in the living God, **who** is Savior" (1 Tim. 4:10)	*Relative Pronoun as Subject*
5. ὃν ἀπέστειλεν ἐκεῖνος, τούτῳ ὑμεῖς οὐ πιστεύετε "that one **whom** he has sent, this one <u>you</u> did not believe" (John 5:38)	*Relative Pronoun as Object*
6. ἐλάλησεν ἡμῖν ἐν υἱῷ, . . . δι' **οὗ** καὶ ἐποίησεν τοὺς αἰῶνας "he has spoken to us by a Son, . . . through **whom** he also made the present order" (Heb. 1:2)	*Relative Pronoun as Object of the Preposition*

Pronoun Summary

Pronouns to learn are listed in a given lesson's vocabulary (itemized in "What to Learn"). When instructed to do so, use this lesson for review. A summary follows.

Table 11.22 Greek Pronouns—A Summary

	Type		English	Greek
1.	Personal		*I, we*	ἐγώ, ἡμεῖς
			you, you (pl.)	σύ, ὑμεῖς
			he, she, it; they	αὐτός, -η, -ο
2.	Intensive		*same, self*	αὐτός, -η, -ο
3.	Possessive		*my*	ἐμός, -η, -ον
			our	ἡμέτερος, -α, -ον
			your	σός, -η, -ον
			your (pl.)	ὑμέτερος, -α, -ον
4.	Reflexive		*myself*	ἐμαυτοῦ, -ης, --
			yourself	σεαυτοῦ, -ης, --
			himself, etc.	ἑαυτοῦ, -ης, -ου
5.	Reciprocal		*of one another*	ἀλλήλων
			to one another	ἀλλήλοις
			one another	ἀλλήλους
6.	Demonstrative:	prx.:	*this, these*	οὗτος, αὕτη, τοῦτο
		rem.:	*that , those*	ἐκεῖνος, -η, -ο
7.	Correlative		*such*	τοιοῦτος, -η, -ο
			so much, so great	τοσοῦτος, -αύτη,
			so many	-οῦτον
			as	οἷος, -α, -ον
			as much as	ὅσος, -η, -ον
8.	Relative		*who, whom, that*	ὅς, ἥ, ὅ
9.	Interrogative		*who? (which? what?)*	τίς, τίς, τί
	qualitative		*what type?*	ποῖος, -α, -ον
	quantitative		*how much?*	πόσος, -η, -ον
10.	Indefinite		*someone (certain one)*	τις, τις, τι
11.	Indefinite Relative		*who, whoever*	ὅστις, ἥτις, ὅτι
12.	Negative		*no one*	οὐδείς, οὐδεμία
			nothing	οὐδέν

What To Learn—LESSON 11 (ἕνδεκα)

☐ 1. The definition of a *pronoun* and the *antecedent*

☐ 2. The uses of a pronoun

☐ 3. Applying the principle of concord to pronouns—noun versus adjective use

☐ 4. Learn *personal* pronouns and their use

☐ 5. Learn *intensive* pronouns and distinguish from the third personal pronoun

☐ 6. Vocabulary words

 Alexandrinus ("A") is a fifth century parchment of the entire Bible given to James I by Cyril Lucar, the Patriarch of Constantinople (actually reaching Britain in 1627). Books besides our canonical ones are included—e.g., 3 and 4 Maccabees in the Old Testament and 1 and 2 Clement in the New Testament, where, unusually, the Catholic Epistles come before the letters of Paul. Determining a manuscript's "text type" is one pursuit of textual criticism. The text type is a common pattern of readings among a group of manuscripts that seems to reveal the stream of tradition from which the manuscript flowed. Alexandrinus is not uniform in its text type: in the Gospels, the inferior "Byzantine"; in the Acts and Pauline letters, "Alexandrian"; however, in Revelation, Alexandrinus is probably our best text.

Rev. 20:7–21:14

LESSON 12 (δώδεκα)
Imperfect Active Indicative

ἔλυον

The first principal part has two tenses, present and imperfect. The imperfect is built on the present stem. Thus, the imperfect is a durative tense. The imperfect, however, is past time. This "historical tense," classified as a secondary tense, calls for a new set of endings, the secondary endings.

Vocabulary 12

Numeral

δώδεκα   twelve (numeral)

Demonstrative Pronouns

οὗτος, αὕτη, τοῦτο   this, these

ἐκεῖνος, -η, -ο   that, those

Correlative Pronoun

τοιοῦτος, -αύτη, -οῦτο   such

Relative Pronoun

ὅς, ἥ, ὅ   who, whom, that

Adverbs

καθώς   as, just as

οὕτως   thus

τότε   then, at that time, next, thereupon

Particles and Conjunctions

πῶς   how? (interrogative)

πώς   somehow, some way

τέ   and, and so, so

τὲ ... τέ (or δέ)   both ... and not only .. but also

ὡς   as, that, how, about, while, when

ἀμήν   truly, amen

ὅτε   when

Nouns and Adjective

δικαιοσύνη   righteousness

ἐξουσία   authority

λαός   people

147

ὄχλος	crowd	ἀποστέλλω	I send, send out
ἅγιος, -α, -ον	holy (adj.)	ἐσθίω	I eat
Verbs		ἤμην	I was
αἰτέω	I ask (-ε contract)	μαρτυρέω	I witness, testify
ἀποθνῄσκω	I die	ὁράω	I see

Analysis

The principal parts of verbs relate to how the tense stem is manipulated to form different tenses. The first principal part has two tenses, present and imperfect. The imperfect belongs to the first principal part because the imperfect tense stem simply clones the present tense stem. To recognize an imperfect tense, then, is a matter involving other verbal components—in this case, a prefix on the front of the tense stem. Further, the endings of the pronominal suffixes also involve a different set. The present tense is durative action in present time. The imperfect is durative action in past time. As past time, the imperfect is a historical, or secondary tense. Primary tenses take primary endings. Secondary tenses take secondary endings. Imperfect

Table 12.1 Principal Parts: Tenses and Voices

Principal Parts	Tenses	Voices		
First Principal Part	Present	active	middle	passive
	Imperfect	active	middle	passive
Second Principal Part	Future	active	middle	
Third Principal Part	First Aorist	active	middle	
	Second Aorist	active	middle	
Fourth Principal Part	Perfect	active		
	Future Perfect	active		
	Pluperfect	active		
Fifth Principal Part	Perfect		middle	passive
	Future Perfect		middle	passive
	Pluperfect		middle	passive
Sixth Principal Part	First Aorist			passive
	First Future			passive
	Second Aorist			passive
	Second Future			passive

Table 12.2 Primary and Secondary Tenses

Kind of Action	Time of Action (Indicative Mood)		
	Secondary Tenses (secondary endings)	Primary Tenses (primary endings)	
	Past	Present	Future
durative	Imperfect	Present	---------
undefined	Aorist	---------	Future
perfective	Pluperfect	Perfect	Future Perfect

tense takes secondary endings. So the imperfect tense will: (1) alter the present stem with a prefix and (2) use different pronominal suffixes.

The secondary active endings follow in Table 12.3. These endings will add the third set of the four sets of indicative mood endings.

Table 12.3 Verb Endings—Indicative Mood

Subject		Indicative Endings			
		Primary Tenses		Secondary Tenses	
Num.	Pers.	Active	Mid/Pass	Active	Mid/Pass
Sing.	1st	-ω	-μαι	-ν	-μην
	2nd	-εις	-σαι (η)	-ς	-σο (ου)
	3rd	-ει	-ται	(-εν)	-το
Plur.	1st	-ομεν	-μεθα	-μεν	-μεθα
	2nd	-ετε	-σθε	-τε	-σθε
	3rd	-ουσι(ν)	-νται	-ν, σαν	-ντο

Formation

The imperfect is built on the present tense stem, but the pronominal suffix endings are different. The principle feature is the past time indicator, the "augment."

Tense Stem. We start with the tense stem. The stem of λύω is λυ-:

$$\lambda\acute{\upsilon}\cancel{\omega} = \lambda\upsilon\text{-}$$

Augment. The main feature of past time verbs is a prefix, called the *augment*, attached to the front of the tense stem to indicate this past time component to the verbal action (*only* in indicative mood). For λυ-, a consonant, we have ἐλυ-:

$$\overset{\text{?}}{\epsilon}\text{-}\lambda\upsilon$$

augment + stem

This augment varies according to whether a vowel or consonant begins the stem. Do not try to memorize augment variations detailed in the table. We may generalize:

♦ *Visible augmentation usually involves some form of* ε, η, ει, *or* ω.

Syllabic Augment (ἐ). A tense stem beginning with a *consonant* adds the prefix ἐ- to the stem. By definition, adding a vowel adds another syllable to the word, hence the name "syllabic" augment. The one deviation is a verb beginning with ρ doubles the ρ, yielding the form ἐρρ-.[1]

Temporal Augment. The vowel forms at first seem more complex, but really fall out into just a few patterns. Some cannot be predicted, but once pointed out several times in the particular verbs they occur easily can be remembered. Typical forms are itemized below.

<u>Short Vowels</u>. Verbs beginning with a *short* vowel (α, ε, ο) augment the stem for past time by *lengthening* that vowel. A long vowel takes longer to pronounce, hence the "temporal" augment. *The basic lengthening pattern is that of contract verbs* (α/η, ε/η, ο/ω; see Table 18.10). An occasional exception is ἐ. At times ἐ arbitrarily seems to "insert" an iota, creating the

Table 12.4 Past Time Augment—Examples

Form	Present	Imperfect
Consonants		
λ- → ἐλ-	λύω	ἔλυον
ρ- → ἐρρ-	ῥίπτω	ἔρριπτον
Vowels		
ἀ- → ἠ-	ἀκούω	ἤκουον
ἐ- → ἠ-	ἐσθίω	ἤσθιον
ἐ- → εἰ-	ἔχω	εἶχον
ὀ- → ὠ-	ὁμολογέω	ὡμολόγουν
ἠ- → ἠ-	ἥκω	ἧκον
ὠ- → ὠ-	ὠφελέω	ὠφέλουν
ἰ- → ῑ-	ἰσχύω	ἴσχυον
ὐ- → ῦ-	ὑμνέω	ὕμνουν
αἰ- → ἠ-	αἰτέω	ᾔτεον
οἰ- → ᾠ-	οἰκοδομέω	ᾠκόδομουν
εἰ- → εἰ-	εἰρηνεύω	εἰρηνεύον
αὐ- → ηὐ-	αὐξάνω	ηὔξανον
εὑ- → ηὑ-	εὑρίσκω	ηὕρισκον
εὐ- → εὐ-	εὐλογέω	εὐλόγουν
εὐα- → εὐη-	εὐαγγελίζω	εὐηγγελίζον
Compounds		
(conson. stem)	ἐνδύω	ἐνέδυνον
(vowel stem)	συνάγω	συνῆγον
elision (con.)	ἀναβαίω	ἀνέβαινον
(vowel stem)	ἀπάγω	ἀπῆγον

diphthong εἰ. (The reason actually is hidden in the history of tense stems.)[2] Simply note and remember this unpredictable "iota insert" for particular verbs.

---

[1]No New Testament example exists in the imperfect. However, this is a regular feature in aorist and perfect tenses. Verbs affected are: ῥαβδίζω, ῥαντίζω, ῥέω, ῥιζόω, ῥίπτω, ῥύομαι, and ῥώννυμι.

[2]Certain primitive consonant stems with syllabic augment for various reasons dropped some consonants leaving two vowels to volatilize (ε + ε = ει, or ε + ι = ει).

Long Vowels. Tense stems beginning with the *long* vowels ἠ and ὠ do not submit to any further lengthening. These tense stems remain unchanged.

Variable Vowels. Tense stems beginning with the variable vowels ι and ὑ lengthen from short to long, to ῑ and ῡ. This effect does not leave a visible sign.

Diphthongs. Two iota diphthongs, αι and οι, transform into improper long diphthongs on a contract lengthening pattern, i.e., ῃ and ῳ. In contrast, the iota diphthong ει remains unchanged. (On *rare* occasion αι and οι remain the same.) The upsilon diphthong αυ shows a contract lengthening pattern, becoming ηυ. The upsilon diphthong ευ, often representing the adverb εὐ ("well") compounded onto tense stems, is inconsistent. On tense stems beginning with a consonant, sometimes ευ lengthens to ηυ. More often ευ remains unchanged. Tense stems beginning with a vowel before the ευ compound will lengthen that vowel.[3]

Compound Verbs. Recall the point in Lesson 9 that normally, *the compounded preposition is not reckoned part of the tense stem in the formation of principal parts.* Thus, an augment attached to the *tense stem* must go *between* the preposition and the stem. Further, recall that prepositions ending in a

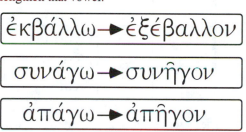

vowel affixed to tense stems that themselves begin with a vowel suffer elision (ἀπό + ἄγω = ἀπάγω). Here, the augment is *after* the elided vowel, that is, still *between* the preposition and the original stem. (Note: rare exceptions *do* occur—ἀνοίγω, ἤνοιγον!) However, *the verb's accent never precedes the augment.* (Observe συνῆγον, ἀπῆγον).

Thematic Vowel. Add the thematic vowel—here, of first person singular:

$$ἐ-λυ-ο$$

augment + stem + thematic vowel

This thematic vowel reacts predictably with contract vowels (α, ε, ο). Review the contract chart, Table 7.1. (Some verbs, however, are exceptions, as is αἰτέω.)

Pronominal suffix. Finally, add the appropriate *secondary* pronominal suffix according to the subject of the verb's action: -ν, -ς, -none, -μεν, -τε, -ν. We arrive at the complete verbal form, "I was loosing":

---

[3]The remaining diphthongs (ου, υι, ηυ, ωυ) are not involved in verbs in the New Testament.

ἐ-λυ-ο-ν

augment + stem + thematic vowel + suffix

Table 12.5 Imperfect Active Indicative—λύω

Number	Person	Form	Translation
Singular	1st	ἔλυον	"I was loosing"
	2nd	ἔλυες	"you were loosing"
	3rd	ἔλυε(ν)	"he (she, it) was loosing"
Plural	1st	ἐλύομεν	"we were loosing"
	2nd	ἐλύετε	"you were loosing"
	3rd	ἔλυον	"they were loosing"

The third person singular, ἔλυεν, actually has *no* ending. What remains is the exposed thematic vowel (and moveable -ν). Third person plural, ἔλυον, represents the -ν option, much more frequent than -σαν (-μι verbs take -σαν; cf. εἰμί below). *Only context distinguishes whether one has first person singular or third person plural.* Accent is recessive. Note carefully the durative nature of the translation.

Table 12.6 Imperfect Active Indicative—Contracts

φιλέω	δηλόω	τιμάω
ἐφίλουν	ἐδήλουν	ἐτίμων
ἐφίλεις	ἐδήλους	ἐτίμας
ἐφίλει	ἐδήλου	ἐτίμα
ἐφιλοῦμεν	ἐδηλοῦμεν	ἐτιμῶμεν
ἐφιλεῖτε	ἐδηλοῦτε	ἐτιμᾶτε
ἐφίλουν	ἐδήλουν	ἐτίμων

Review vowel contraction, Table 7.1. Contract forms of the imperfect, active, indicative are normal. Accent is recessive. However, *penult* acute accents show long ultimas; circumflex accents illustrate the stem vowel accent rule (Table 7.5).

Imperfect of Εἰμί

Table 12.7 Εἰμί—Imperfect Indicative

Number	Person	Form	Translation
Singular	1st	ἤμην	"I was"
	2nd	ἦς	"you (sg.) were"
	3rd	ἦν	"he (she, it) was"
Plural	1st	ἦμεν (ἤμεθα)	"we were"
	2nd	ἦτε	"you (pl.) were"
	3rd	ἦσαν	"they were"

The -μην of the first person singular actually is a middle form. The third person plural takes the -σαν option of the secondary endings. These imperfect forms of εἰμί are not enclitic. (Only the present tense of εἰμί is enclitic.) Remember that the verb εἰμί does not have voice. One does not locate the form ἤμην as "imperfect, middle, indicative," but simply "imperfect, indicative, first person singular," etc.

Translation

The workhorse Greek tense is the aorist. So, *use of other tenses often is intentional.* The translator must strive to recover the author's intent. Listed below are some important nuances for the imperfect tense, *context always the key.*

Progressive Imperfect ("was ___ing"). Emphasis is upon the durative aspect of the tense. Action is conceived as on-going, as with the present, but in past time (adopted in the translations in Table 12.5). For example, καὶ οἱ ἄγγελοι **διηκόνουν** αὐτῷ = "and the angels **were ministering** to him" (Mark 1:13; compound and contract, διακονέω). Progressive use is common, but do not get stuck in a rut here.

Inceptive Imperfect ("began to"). Emphasis is upon the beginning of the action. Time frame is past. For example, καὶ ἀνοίξας τὸ στόμα αὐτοῦ **ἐδίδασκεν** αὐτοὺς = "and opening his mouth, he **began to teach** them" (Matt. 5:2). This inceptive context is clear both explicitly and implicitly. Explicitly, the characteristic expression "opening his mouth" (ἀνοίξας τὸ στόμα αὐτοῦ) shows that this is the beginning of the message Jesus gave (what we call the Sermon on the Mount). Implicitly, the context in verse one helps establish that Jesus is about to teach the crowds that have gathered around him.

Customary Imperfect ("used to"). Habit or custom is the thought. Again, the time frame is past. For example, Καὶ **ἐπορεύοντο** οἱ γονεῖς αὐτοῦ κατ᾽ ἔτος εἰς Ἰερουσαλὴμ τῇ ἑορτῇ τοῦ πάσχα = "And his parents **used to go** each year to Jerusalem at the feast of Passover" (Luke 2:41; deponent, πορεύομαι). The expression κατ᾽ ἔτος, meaning "each year," makes the customary action explicit. Luke's theme in this unit is that those surrounding the infancy of Jesus were pious, law-abiding Jews. Here ἐπορεύοντο carefully is chosen to contribute to this picture. The observant translator should not miss this important Lukan theme.

Conative Imperfect ("tried to"). Attempted action is unsuccessful. Time frame is past. A durative aspect is foremost with a translation "was trying to." Notice Gal. 1:13, ἐδίωκον τὴν ἐκκλησίαν τοῦ θεοῦ καὶ **ἐπόρθουν** αὐτήν = "I was persecuting [progressive imperfect] the church of God and **was trying to destroy** it." Paul did not succeed. Simply translating ἐπόρθουν as "I was destroying" could mislead the reader or introduce an idea actually foreign to Paul's thought.

🐟 What To Learn—LESSON 12 (δώδεκα)

Beginning
☐ 1. The significance of the imperfect tense in the principal parts
☐ 2. The aspect (kind of action) of the imperfect tense
☐ 3. Secondary *active* endings of the indicative mood
☐ 4. Definition and exegetical significance of the *augment*
☐ 5. Position of the augment on compound verbs
☐ 6. Formation of the imperfect tense
☐ 7. Paradigm of λύω in the imperfect active indicative
☐ 8. Paradigm of εἰμί in the imperfect indicative

☐   9.   Learn *demonstrative, correlative,* and *relative* pronouns; carefully review the applicable material in Lesson 11, including diagramming relatives

☐   10.   Vocabulary words

Advanced

☐   11.   Definitions of *syllabic* and *temporal* augments and their formation

☐   12.   Translating the imperfect: *progressive, inceptive, customary, conative*

 With Sinaiticus, Codex Vaticanus ("B") is another of our important fourth-century uncials. The codex is held in the Vatican Library, first mentioned in library records of 1475. Vaticanus has the entire Bible, but parts are missing, including the last of the New Testament (last of Hebrews, the Pastorals, Philemon, Revelation). Vaticanus is the best example of the "Alexandrian" text type (Gospels and Acts). Observe two places in the third column in which a later scribe marked and recorded words omitted by the original scribe (1:4, "of men"; 1:13, "nor of the will of man").

(Vaticanus)

Luke 24:32–53; John 1:1–14

LESSON 13 (δεκατρεῖς)
Imperfect Middle and Conditional Sentences

ἐλυόμην

Imperfect middle and passive are identical. Secondary middle/passive forms are used, which completes the four sets of indicative mood endings for thematic verbs. Present deponents make imperfect deponents. The adjective ὅλος always is attributive. Conditional sentences have four classes.

Vocabulary 13

Numeral

δεκατρεῖς	thirteen (numeral)

Particle, Conjunction, Adjective

ἄν	particle (untranslatable)
εἰ	if
ὅλος, -η, -ον	whole, complete, all, entire

Nouns

καιρός	time, season
οἰκία, -ας, ἡ	house, family, household
ὀφθαλμός	eye
τόπος	place
φόβος	fear

Possessive Pronouns

ἐμός, -η, -ον	my
ἡμέτερος, -α, -ον	our
σός, -η, -ον	your (sg.)
ὑμέτερος, -α, -ον	your (pl.)

Reflexive Pronouns

ἐμαυτοῦ, -ης, --	myself
σεαυτοῦ, -ης, --	yourself
ἑαυτοῦ, -ης, --	himself, herself, itself

Reciprocal Pronouns

ἀλλήλων	of one another, etc.
ἀλλήλοις	to one another, etc.
ἀλλήλους	one another

Adverbs and Negative		Verbs	
ἐκεῖ	there	φοβέομαι	I fear (deponent)
ἔτι	still, yet	ἀκολουθέω	I follow
ὅπου	where	ἀναβαίνω	I go up
μή	not, lest (commonly	ἀνοίγω	I open
	used with moods other	ἄρχω	I rule (active voice)
	than the indicative)	ἄρχομαι	I begin (middle voice)

Analysis

Table 13.1 Verb Endings—Indicative Mood

Subject		Indicative Endings			
		Primary Tenses		*Secondary Tenses*	
Num.	Pers.	Active	Mid/Pass	Active	Mid/Pass
Sing.	1st	-ω	-μαι	-ν	-μην
	2nd	-εις	-σαι (η)	-ς	-σο (ου)
	3rd	-ει	-ται	(-εν)	-το
Plur.	1st	-ομεν	-μεθα	-μεν	-μεθα
	2nd	-ετε	-σθε	-τε	-σθε
	3rd	-ουσι(ν)	-νται	-ν, σαν	-ντο

Table 13.2 Imperfect Middle/Passive Indicative—λύω

Form	Middle Translation	Passive Translation
ἐλυόμην	"I was loosing (for myself)"	"I was being loosed"
ἐλύου	"you were loosing (for yourself)"	"you were being loosed"
ἐλύετο	"he was loosing (for himself)," etc.	"he was being loosed," etc.
ἐλυόμεθα	"we were loosing (for ourselves)"	"we were being loosed"
ἐλύεσθε	"you were loosing (for yourselves)"	"you were being loosed"
ἐλύοντο	"they were loosing (for themselves)"	"they were being loosed"

The second singular is -ου because the ("intervocalic") sigma between the ε thematic vowel and the ο drops out. The ε and ο then contract to ου.

Table 13.3 Imperfect Middle/Passive Indicative—Contracts

φιλέω	δηλόω	τιμάω
ἐφιλούμην	ἐδηλούμην	ἐτιμώμην
ἐφιλοῦ	ἐδηλοῦ	ἐτιμῶ
ἐφιλεῖτο	ἐδηλοῦτο	ἐτιμᾶτο
ἐφιλούμεθα	ἐδηλούμεθα	ἐτιμώμεθα
ἐφιλεῖσθε	ἐδηλοῦσθε	ἐτιμᾶσθε
ἐφιλοῦντο	ἐδηλοῦντο	ἐτιμῶντο

The formation of the imperfect middle is perfectly normal: (1) the tense stem is augmented to indicate past time, and (2) the secondary middle endings are attached with thematic vowels. Contracts are regular (see Table 7.1). Penult acute accents show long ultimas. Circumflex accents show the stem vowel rule (see Table 7.6).

Deponents

Deponent presents make deponent imperfects. Simple enough. If the dictionary form ends in -ομαι, meaning the verb is a deponent, translate the imperfect middle as active voice just as you do the present middle deponent. So the present deponent ἔρχομαι, translated with active voice as "I am coming," as imperfect deponent is ἠρχόμην, also translated with active voice as "I was coming." The endings of a deponent verb in the imperfect tense always are secondary middle forms (-μην, -ου, -το, -μεθα, -σθε, -ντο) but the translations always are active voice.

Position of Ὅλος

Always found in predicate position in the New Testament, the adjective ὅλος is translated as if attributive (articular). So Luke 10:27 has: Ἀγαπήσεις κύριον τὸν θεόν σου ἐξ ὅλης [τῆς] καρδίας σου καὶ ἐν ὅλῃ τῇ ψυχῇ σου καὶ ἐν ὅλῃ τῇ ἰσχύϊ σου καὶ ἐν **ὅλῃ** τῇ διανοίᾳ σου. = "You will love the Lord your God with **all** you heart, and with **all** your being, and with **all** your strength, and with **all** your mind." In other words, ὅλος always is used as a *modifier*, never as a substantive or as a predicate adjective (needing a form of "to be"), even though anarthrous.

Conditional Sentences

Table 13.4 Conditional Sentences—Structure

Class	Condition	Conj.	Protasis	Apodosis
1st TRUE	fulfilled (οὐ in negative)	εἰ + (ἐάν at times)	any indicative	any indicative imperative subjunctive
2nd FALSE	not fulfilled (μή in negative) a. present time	εἰ +	past tense indicative	ἄν + past indicative (ἄν can occur anywhere or at times drop out)
	b. past time	εἰ +	aorist indicative	ἄν + past indicative
		εἰ +	pluperfect indicative	ἄν + past indicative
3rd POSSIBLE	undetermined possible	ἐάν +	subjunctive	future, or any indic. (ἄν)
4th REMOTE	undetermined remote	εἰ +	optative	optative (ἄν)

Analysis. An exegetical wealth of information is available through Greek conditional sentences. Careful attention to the structure and meaning of the four classes of conditional sentences will richly repay the student of the Greek New Testament. The table above will guide our discussion.[1]

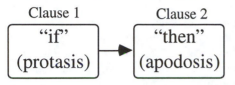

Clause 1   Clause 2

"if" → "then"

(protasis) (apodosis)

Structure. Conditional sentences put forward conditions under which an assertion is presented as true or false. The basic two-clause structure is simple: (1) an "if" clause putting forward the condition, called the *protasis* (πρότασις = "putting forward"), and (2) a "then" clause" giving results, called the *apodosis* (ἀπόδοσις = "giving back"). The "if" clause is a subordinate clause, grammatically dependent. The apodosis ("then" clause) is grammatically independent.

Classes. All conditions exist in two degrees of assumption from the perspective of the speaker: (1) assumed reality = determined, or (2) assumed potentiality = undetermined. *Actual fact is irrelevant to the assumption.* The determined degree takes two forms: (1) assumed true = fulfilled, or (2) assumed false = not fulfilled. The undetermined degree takes two forms: (1) undetermined, but assumed possible, and (2) undetermined, but assumed remote. Four basic conditions result: true, false, possible, remote—which are the four *classes* of conditional sentences.

Grammar. The indicative mood, being the mood of reality, naturally is used to state conditions of assumed reality. Thus, the indicative mood is used for conditional sentences setting forth assumed true (first class = fulfilled) or assumed false (second class = unfulfilled) conditions. The negative is stated with οὐ.[2]

First Class. The first class conditional sentence sets up the protasis using the conjunction εἰ and any indicative mood verb (on rare occasion ἐάν, which is crasis for εἰ ἄν; cf. Luke 19:40; 1 Thess. 3:8). The apodosis likewise uses any indicative mood. The conjunction εἰ ("if") *does not necessarily indicate contingency.* The speaker may assume the assertion to be objectively true. The "if" only sets forth what the speaker is ready to assert. Thus, the εἰ on occasion can be translated as "since," which leaves no doubt for the English reader the speaker's assumption the condition is objectively true. On the other hand, sometimes the condition is assumed true *only for the sake of argument or only what the speaker believes to be true.*[3]

---

[1]The more detailed grammars should be consulted for various other conditional constructions in the New Testament. Enough is presented here to launch the beginning student on the way.

[2]Five exceptions using εἰ μή in Mark 6:5; 1 Cor. 15:2; 2 Cor. 13:5; Gal. 1:7; 1 Tim. 6:3.

[3]Rhetorical analysis is crucial. (Who is the speaker? Who is the audience? What is the situation? What is the rhetoric? Is the speaker being facetious? ironical? satirical? dead serious?)

Second Class. The second class conditional sentence subdivides into assertions the speaker is applying to the present time, or assertions the speaker is applying to past time. Conditions assumed false in present time set up the protasis using the conjunction εἰ and any past tense indicative, but usually the imperfect. If stated in the negative, μή is used.[4] The apodosis normally is set up using the particle of contingency ἄν (non-translatable) and any past tense indicative. The ἄν can occur anywhere in the apodosis, not always first, but sometimes is dropped altogether. Conditions assumed false in *past* time use aorist and pluperfect tenses, and will be discussed as these tenses are introduced.[5] Again, sometimes the condition is assumed false not as a statement of objective reality, but *only for the sake of argument or only what the speaker believes to be false.*

Table 13.5 Conditional Sentences—Components

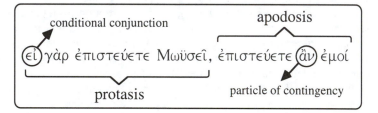

Translation. As usual, *context always is paramount.* English convention calls for insertion of the auxiliary verb "would" in an apodosis using past tense.

First Class (True). Translation is straight-forward. Examples below include both conditions presumed objectively true and those presumed true only for the sake of argument. Present tense constructions are common; imperfects are not. (Aorist and perfect tenses are more common.)

1.   First class, condition assumed objectively true (= "since"):
    A.   protasis = present indicative
        (1)   εἰ ἐκβάλλεις ἡμᾶς = "if you are casting us out" (Matt. 8:31, the demons to Jesus; could use "*since* you are casting us out")
        (2)   εἰ δὲ ἐν πνεύματι θεοῦ ἐγὼ ἐκβάλλω τὰ δαιμόνια = "But if by the Spirit of God I am casting out the demons" (Matt. 12:28, Jesus to the Pharisees opposing him; more forceful is "*since* by the Spirit of God . . . ")

---

[4]With two exceptions, Mark 14:21 and the parallel in Matt. 26:24.
[5]Exceptions include the imperfects in Heb. 11:15 and Matt. 23:30, both contexts past time.

      (3) εἰ γὰρ πιστεύομεν ὅτι Ἰησοῦς ἀπέθανεν καὶ ἀνέστη = "For if we believe that Jesus died and rose again" (1 Thess. 4:14, Paul to Thessalonian believers; better, "For *since* we believe . . .")

  B. protasis = imperfect indicative (uncommon)

      (1) εἰ καὶ μετεμελόμην, βλέπω = "Even if I did regret [sending the letter], I see" (2 Cor. 7:8, Paul to the Corinthian believers)

      (2) (other imperfect tense conditions are perhaps mixed classes)

2. First class, condition assumed true only for argument:

  A. protasis = present indicative

      (1) εἰ ὁ σατανᾶς τὸν σατανᾶν ἐκβάλλει = "if Satan casts out Satan" (Matt. 12:26, Jesus to his Pharisee opponents)

      (2) καὶ εἰ ἐγὼ ἐν Βεελζεβοὺλ ἐκβάλλω τὰ δαιμόνια = "and if I through Beelzebul am casting out the demons" (Matt. 12:27, Jesus continuing the argument against his opponents)

      (3) εἰ περιτομὴν ἔτι κηρύσσω, τί ἔτι διώκομαι; = "If I still preach circumcision, why am I still being persecuted?" (Gal. 5:11, Paul to Galatian believers about gospel misunderstandings)

  B. protasis = imperfect indicative (examples are not clear cut)

Second Class (False). Any past tense indicative is possible. Since we have covered only the imperfect, examples are confined to this tense. As a natural result, then, all the conditions involve *present time* contexts.

3. Second class, condition assumed objectively false:

      (1) εἰ γὰρ ἐπιστεύετε Μωϋσεῖ, ἐπιστεύετε ἂν ἐμοί = "For if you believed Moses, you would believe me" (John 5:46, Jesus to his Jewish opponents)

      (2) εἰ δὲ ἑαυτοὺς διεκρίνομεν, οὐκ ἂν ἐκρινόμεθα = "but if we judged ourselves rightly, we would not be judged" (1 Cor. 11:31, Paul to the Corinthians about taking the Lord's Supper)

      (3) Εἰ γὰρ ἡ πρώτη ἐκείνη ἦν ἄμεμπτος, οὐκ ἂν δευτέρας ἐζητεῖτο τόπος = "For if that first [covenant] were faultless, no occasion would have been sought for a second" (Heb. 8:7, a Christian author exhorting a Christian audience on the supremacy of Christ)

4. Second class, condition assumed false only for argument:

      (1) εἰ μὴ ἦν οὗτος παρὰ θεοῦ, οὐκ ἠδύνατο ποιεῖν οὐδέν = "if this man were not from God, he would not be able to do anything" (John 9:33, the healed blind man responding to his questioners)

      (2) Εἰ μὴ ἦν οὗτος κακὸν ποιῶν, οὐκ ἄν σοι παρεδώκαμεν αὐτόν = "If this man were not an evildoer, we would not have brought him to you" (John 18:30, the Jews to Pilate)

> ### Class Condition
> ### key = protasis mood

Notice the one common denominator for all first and second class sentences—the *indicative mood* in the protasis. The conjunction εἰ can be a false trigger. On rare occasion, one might find a first class conditional sentence using ἐάν. For this reason, *always trigger on the mood of the protasis as the key* to the class conditional sentence, not the conjunction. Conjunctions are *not* fail-safe indicators.

Diagramming

A conditional sentence typically involves two clauses: (1) an independent clause comprising the "then" statement (the apodosis), modified by (2) a subordinate clause comprising the "if" statement (the protasis). The protasis, then, is an adverbial modifier of the verb in the apodosis. Thus, for diagramming, go to the last half of a conditional sentence first. That is, first set up the independent clause of the "then" statement (the apodosis) with a base line. Then, run the "if" statement (the protasis) off the main verb as a subordinate clause, with a slanted line holding the conjunction εἰ running to the horizontal of a subordinate base line. A postpositive, such as γάρ, when present in the protasis, most simply is just placed in line with the conditional conjunction. The particle of contingency, ἄν, when present anywhere in the apodosis, simply should be set in parentheses immediately after the apodosis verb.

Table 13.6 Diagramming Conditional Sentences

1. **εἰ** γὰρ ἐπιστεύετε Μωϋσεῖ, ἐπιστεύετε **ἄν** ἐμοι. "For **if** you believed Moses, you would believe me" (John 5:46)	*Subordinate conditional clause* 1. (you) ἐπιστεύετε (ἄν) ἐμοι εἰ γάρ (you) ἐπιστεύετε Μωϋσεῖ

What To Learn—LESSON 13 (δεκατρεῖς)

- ☐ 1. Secondary middle/passive endings
- ☐ 2. Paradigm of λύω in the imperfect middle/passive indicative

❑ 3. Recognition of contract verbs with secondary middle endings

❑ 4. Significance of deponent imperfects and how to recognize

❑ 5. Significance for translation of the position of ὅλος

❑ 6. Definitions of *protasis* and *apodosis* and grammatical significance

❑ 7. The two degrees of assumption for all conditions from the perspective of the speaker

❑ 8. The four classes of conditional sentences

❑ 9. Definition and structure of first class conditional sentences

❑ 10. Definition and structure of second class conditional sentences (applying to present time)

❑ 11. Translating first and second class conditional sentences

❑ 12. The key to identifying the class conditional sentence

❑ 13. Learn *possessive*, *reflexive*, and *reciprocal* pronouns and carefully review the applicable material in Lesson 11

❑ 14. Vocabulary words

The papyrus $\mathfrak{P}^{75}$, in the Bodmer Library, is dated around A.D. 200, containing the Gospels of Luke and John. The text type is quite similar to that of Vaticanus.

John 3:3–19

LESSON 14 (δεκατέσσαρες)
Third Declension—Stop and Sibilant Stems

ἄρχων, ἄρχοντος

 Third declension inflection patterns are based on stem type, divided here into stop and sibilant stems. The stem is hidden in the genitive singular form. Gender is mixed. One set of endings is crucial later for a major pattern in participles. Some important New Testament words are third declension.

Vocabulary 14

Numeral

δεκατέσσαρες   fourteen

Labial stops (-π, -β, -φ stem)

λίψ, λίβος, ὁ   southwest wind

Palatal stops (-κ, -γ, -χ stem)

γυνή, γυναικός, ἡ   woman
θρίξ, τριχός, ἡ   hair
σάλπιγξ, σάλπιγγος, ἡ   trumpet
σάρξ, σαρκός, ἡ   flesh

Dental stops (-τ, -δ, -θ stem)

ἐλπίς, ἐλπίδος, ἡ   hope
πούς, ποδός, ὁ   foot
χάρις, χάριτος, ἡ   grace, favor

Dental stops (-ητος stem)

πραΰτης, πραΰτητος, ἡ   humility

Dental stops (neuter -ματ stem)

αἷμα, -ατος, τό   blood
γράμμα, -ατος, τό   letter
θέλημα, -ατος, τό   will
ὄνομα, -ατος, τό   name
πνεῦμα, -ατος, τό   spirit, wind
ῥῆμα, -ατος, τό   word
σπέρμα, -ατος, τό   seed (descendants)
στόμα, -ατος, τό   mouth
σῶμα, -ατος, τό   body

Dental stops (-ντ stem)

ἄρχων, -οντος, ὁ   ruler
λέων, -οντος, ὁ   lion
ὀδούς, -οντος, ὁ   tooth

167

Dental stops (-κτ stem)

νύξ, νυκτός, ἡ　　　　night

Dental stops (neuter -τ stem)

οὖς, ὠτός, τό　　　　ear

ὕδωρ, ὕδατος, τό　　water

φῶς, φωτός, τό　　　light

Sibilant (neuter -εσ stem)

γένος, γένους, τό　　race (descendants)

ἔθνος, ἔθνους, τό　　nation, gentile

ἔτος, ἔτους, τό　　　year

μέλος, μέλους, τό　　part, member

μέρος, μέρους, τό　　part (geography)

ὄρος, ὄρους, τό　　　mountain

πλῆθος, -ους, τό　　crowd (multitude)

σκότος, -ους, τό　　darkness

τέλος, τέλους, τό　　end

Stem Types

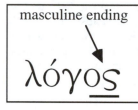

masculine ending

λόγο**ς**

Second declension is called the "-o declension" because all the noun stems technically end in the vowel -o.[1] Further, many nouns of the second declension are masculine. First declension is

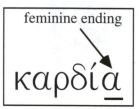

feminine ending

καρδί**α**

called the "-α declension," for most of the nouns stems end in the vowel -α. Most nouns of the first declension are feminine. The two vowels o and α actually function as "theme vowels" (as verbs have), for they help join case suffixes to the noun stem.

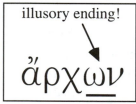

illusory ending!

ἄρχ**ων**

The third declension is called the "consonant declension" because most noun stems end in consonants. (Some third declension stems end in the semivowels ι or υ, which behave as consonants.)[2] However, in contrast to the first and second declension, *third declension has no theme vowel.* Case endings are added directly to the noun stem. Consonant meets consonant, and—*voilà!*—

volatilization, the process whereby certain consonants interact, creating alternate forms. In a typical instance, a consonant will drop, and the left-over vowel will lengthen in what is called *compensatory* lengthening. The upshot is, the nominative singular does *not* provide the noun stem for third declension. The third declension noun stem is illusory, always hidden in the *genitive singular* form.

---

[1]For convenience, we learned the endings in their volatilized forms; the o is obscured at times.

[2]The two close vowels, ι and υ, can act as consonants when they function to approximate the sounds of "y" and "w." The terms *semivowels* or *consonantal iota* and *consonantal upsilon* are used in such cases.

This illusion of the nominative case form in third declension explains the dictionary format for noun entry. In any dictionary, the genitive singular ending is listed after the noun. This is provided to notify the student of the declension pattern, particularly the third declension. Third declension nouns will

Table 14.1 Dictionary Format

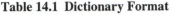

| nom., sing. form | genitive ending | article = gender |

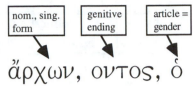

ἄρχων, οντος, ὁ

generate some confusion with endings. The genitive singular ending in the third declension often is -ος, exactly the same form as the nominative singular ending of the second declension. One will want to know whether the noun is a regular second declension, meaning the -ος form is a nominative, or a third declension, meaning the -ος form is a genitive. *Any -ος form in the second dictionary entry indicates a third declension noun.*

Thus, the entry "λόγος, ου, ὁ" indicates that the noun is a regular second declension masculine noun taking the masculine article form ὁ, whose genitive singular form is λόγου. In contrast, the entry "ἄρχων, οντος, ὁ" indicates that the noun is a *third* declension noun taking the masculine article ὁ, whose genitive singular form, however, is ἄρχοντος.

Formation

We now turn to the procedure for constructing the third declension. This consonant declension requires extra attention.

Noun Stem. We start with the lexical form. The form ἄρχων is how the student will find the word listed in the dictionary. However, this nominative form does not provide the stem. We are alerted to this situation by the form of the *second* part of the dictionary entry, -οντος. This genitive ending of -ος signifies a *third* declension noun. *This genitive form provides the stem.* Drop the final -ος from *this* form. The stem, then, of the third declension noun ἄρχων, genitive form ἄρχοντος, is αρχοντ-.

$$ἄρχοντος = ἀρχοντ-$$

Inflectional Endings. To this stem one adds the appropriate third declension endings. Third declension endings are given in the table below. This set will complete all the noun inflection patterns in the New Testament. Congratulations!

Table 14.2 Third Declension Inflection Patterns

Case	Masculine/Feminine		Neuter	
	Singular	*Plural*	*Singular*	*Plural*
N	-ς, --	-ες	----	-α
G	-ος	-ων	-ος	-ων
D	-ι	-σι	-ι	-σι
A	-α, -ν	-ας	----	-α

General Observations. Third declension inflections have distinct characteristics.

(1)   Third declension has a mix of all three genders. Form does not predict gender. *The article must be memorized with the noun to know the gender.*

(2)   Masculine and feminine forms are the same.

(3)   Regardless of gender, all interior patterns are the same.

(4)   The iota does not subscript in dative forms as in vowel declensions.

(5)   Some forms have a "no ending" option (see nominative/accusative). This option can leave a consonant exposed that cannot stand at the end of a Greek word, which drops out.[3] Such a process can generate reactions. These reactions are the reason for unusual nominative/accusative forms.

(6)   The masculine/feminine *accusative* singular has two options, -α and -ν, and is noted for any given word. However, regularly the option is -α.

(7)   Both neuter nominative and accusative singular show no ending. Again, this means exposed consonants may drop.

(8)   The genitive singular ending -ος can be confused with second declension.

(9)   *Nominative singular* and *dative plural* forms will show the most changes. Their sigma forms, -ς and -σι, are most reactive against consonant stems. Sigma volatilization must be known to follow such changes (see below).

(10) Abnormalities in nominative forms (#5, #7, #9) mean noun stems cannot be ascertained in the normal first and second declension pattern of the nominative singular form. Instead, the genitive singular form must be known to produce the third declension stem.

Sigma Volatilization. "Volatilization" is a term applied to all the patterned reactions in word formation surrounding particular letter combinations. Learning sigma volatilization is necessary to work with third declension nouns (see item 9).

---

[3]Have you noticed? Of the consonants, typically only ν, ρ, or ς may end a Greek word!

Review carefully stop and sibilant consonants in Lesson 2 (Tables 2.2 and 2.3). Combined with labials, the simple sibilant (σ) produces the sound of the complex sibilant ψ. Combined with palatals, σ produces the sound of the complex sibilant ξ. Combined with dentals, σ dominates the pronunciation, leaving only σ (i.e., dentals drop before a σ). The following chart summarizes these stop consonant reactions *Learn this table well.* Third declension stems are classified as labial, palatal, and dental stems, *based on the final consonant of the stem,* which determines what happens when a σ type suffix is attached.

Table 14.3 Sigma Volatilization—Stops

	Volatilization Pattern		
Formation	stop consonant	simple sibilant	resultant sibilant
labials	π, β, φ	+ σ	= ψ
palatals	κ, γ, χ	+ σ	= ξ
dentals	τ, δ, θ	+ σ	= σ

Nominative Singular. Continuing with our formation of the third declension noun, to the noun stem add the appropriate case ending, given the gender of the noun. The gender of our example is masculine, so we will choose among the masculine endings. Take the masculine nominative singular, for example, which can have *either* a -ς ending or no ending at all. In the present case, no ending is used:

$$\overset{\text{stem}}{\text{ἀρχοντ-}} \underset{\text{+ \quad ending}}{(\ )}$$

Thus, we have ἄρχοντ. However, τ cannot stand at the end of a Greek word (only ν, ρ, or ς). The τ drops. The form alters to the intermediate form ἄρχον:

$$\text{ἀρχον}\cancel{\tau} = \text{ἀρχον}$$

This form is only intermediate because the loss of the consonant τ generates a secondary reaction. To "compensate" for the loss of the τ, the stem vowel o is lengthened (irregularly) to ω, in a process called *compensatory lengthening*. (The regular lengthened form is ου—as is observed in the dative plural.) This lengthening process is a phenomenon just to be observed and noted:

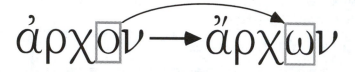

The final form for the nominative singular is ἄρχων. However, the rest of the declension is built on the stem ἀρχοντ- generated from the genitive singular form.

Dative Plural. One other form needs attention, the dative plural. This is -σι:

$$ἀρχοντ\text{-}σι$$
stem   +   ending

The sigma ending of the dative plural, -σι, puts a σ up against the -ντ of the stem. *Any ντ pair always drops before a σ.* Thus, for the dative plural, we have:

$$ἀρχοντσι = ἀρχοσι$$

The stem vowel o then suffers (regular) compensatory lengthening to ου, yielding the final form, ἄρχουσι(ν).

Standard changes are not hard to recognize and explain. Take another example, σάρξ. The gender is feminine, which in third declension has the same endings as the masculine. Take the feminine nominative singular, which can have *either* a -ς ending or no ending at all. In the present case, the -ς is used:

$$\sigma\alpha\rho\kappa\text{-}\varsigma$$

stem   + ending

Thus, we have σαρκς. However, the stem ends in -κ, which classifies this stem as a palatal stem. The -ς ending volatilizes with the κ of the stem, resulting in ξ:

The final form for the nominative singular is σάρξ. In distinction, the rest of the declension is built on the stem σαρκ- generated from the genitive singular form. Perhaps you can explain, then, why the dative plural form is σαρξι(ν).

Stem Formulations. The following material is for the advanced student. However, beginning students should learn the paradigm of ἄρχων. (The inflection is important later for participles.) Also, study the paradigms of the common forms of σάρξ, χάρις, and σῶμα. Then, skip over to the section on "Concord."

Stop Stems. Stop stems react predictably according to stem type and sigma volatilization. The masculine labial stem λιβ- produces the nominative λίψ. The feminine palatal stem σαρκ- produces the nominative σάρξ. The feminine dental stem χαριτ- produces the nominative χάρις, whose accusative opts for the -ν (χάριν).[4] The feminine dental stem ἐλπιδ- produces the nominative ἐλπίς, whose accusative opts for the -α (ἐλπίδα). The only New Testament example of a dental stem in θ is the feminine ὄρνιθ-, producing the nominative ὄρνις.[5]

Dental Subgroups. Dental stems can be subdivided (note vocabulary divisions). Dental stems ending in **-ητος** follow a dental pattern, so the feminine dental stem πραΰτητ- produces the nominative πραΰτης, whose declension is normal.

All dental stems in **-ματ** are neuter. Neuter third declension has no ending for the nominative singular, exposing the final -τ, which must be dropped, producing a -μα noun. So, the stem σωματ- produces the nominative σῶμα.

---

[4]The accusative singular drops the dental τ before the -ν ending (no fixed rule). Twice in the New Testament one finds the alternate form, χάριτα (Acts 24:27; Jude 4).

[5]Only twice in the New Testament (Matt. 23:37; Luke 13:34).

All dental stems in **-ντ** are masculine. Some -ντ stems opt for no ending in the nominative singular, exposing the final -τ, which must be dropped, calling for compensatory lengthening of the stem vowel. So, the masculine dental stem αρχοντ- produces the nominative ἄρχων (irregular lengthening). Other -ντ stems opt for the -ς of the nominative singular, calling for the expulsion of the ντ pair before the σ, which generates lengthening of the stem vowel. So, the masculine dental stem ὀδοντ- produces the nominative ὀδούς (regular lengthening).

Dental stems in **-κτ** are mixed gender. The two-stage reaction involves, first, dropping the dental τ before the sibilant σ. Secondarily, the exposed palatal stop, κ, volatilizes with the σ ending. So, the feminine dental stem νυκτ- produces the nominative νύξ.[6]

Sibilant Stems. "Sibilant stems" here refers to stems ending in the simple sibilant σ. These include genitive stems in -εσ, and the rare -οσ and -ασ. The only sibilant stem of real consequence is the -εσ stem.[7]

All sibilant stems in **-εσ** with nominatives in -ος are neuter. Two interactions are: (1) the *intervocalic sigma*; (sigma between two vowels) often drops, leaving two vowels to contract in standard patterns; (2) *coalescence*, two sigmas together simply coalesce into one sigma. So, the neuter sibilant stem γενεσ- in the genitive singular transforms: γενεσ + ος = γενεσος → γενεος → γένους. Again, the dative plural is γενεσ + σι = γενεσσι → γένεσι(ν). The dative singular creates a diphthong: ε + ι = ει; nominative plural contracts: ε + α = η; genitive plural contracts: ε + ω = ω. However, the nominative singular is in -ος; thus, γένος, also the accusative singular form. With this stem, *all nominative and accusative forms are the same.*

Paradigms. Do not let the multiple number intimidate you. Nail this down:

♦ *Third declension endings never change—some stem forms simply volatilize.*

Remember: (1) feminine endings are exactly the same as masculine endings (see Table 14.5), (2) all interiors are all the same, all genders—with the minor variation of *volatilized* forms in dative plurals, and (3) all neuters have duplicate nominative and accusatives in both singular and plural, repeating the second declension pattern already learned. Vocative is not included, as this case mostly just repeats the nominative. Even on occasions when the vocative is different, this form often looks like a nominative without the -ς, as in ἐλπίς to ἐλπί.

---

[6]The only New Testament -κτ stem—but occurring sixty-one times. Other dental stems in -τ are irregular; e.g., the masculine type ending of φῶς; the noun ὕδωρ adding a -ρ; the noun οὖς with some type of vowel gradation. These are grouped in the vocabulary. No paradigm can summarize them.

[7]The only -οσ stem example in the New Testament is αἰδῶς ("modesty"). The only two -ασ stem examples are κρέας ("meat") and γέρας ("old man").

Table 14.4 Third Declension Stops—Labial and Palatal Paradigms

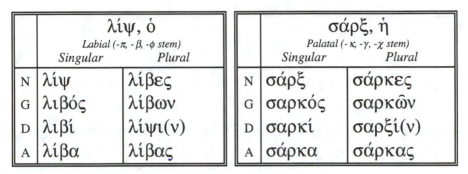

	λίψ, ὁ				σάρξ, ἡ	
	Labial (-π, -β, -φ stem)				*Palatal (- κ, -γ, -χ stem)*	
	Singular	*Plural*			*Singular*	*Plural*
N	λίψ	λίβες		N	σάρξ	σάρκες
G	λιβός	λίβων		G	σαρκός	σαρκῶν
D	λιβί	λίψι(ν)		D	σαρκί	σαρξί(ν)
A	λίβα	λίβας		A	σάρκα	σάρκας

Table 14.5 Third Declension Stops—Dental Paradigms

	χάρις, ἡ				ἐλπίς, ἡ	
	Dental (-τ, - δ, - θ stem, -ν accusative)				*Dental (-τ, - δ, - θ stem, -α accusative)*	
	Singular	*Plural*			*Singular*	*Plural*
N	χάρις	χάριτες		N	ἐλπίς	ἐλπίδες
G	χάριτος	χαρίτων		G	ἐλπίδος	ἐλπίδων
D	χάριτι	χάρισι(ν)		D	ἐλπίδι	ἐλπίσι(ν)
A	χάριν	χάριτας		A	ἐλπίδα	ἐλπίδας

Table 14.6 Third Declension Stops—Dental Subgroup Paradigms

	πραΰτης, ἡ				σῶμα, τό	
	Dental (-ητος stem)				*Dental (neuter -ματ stem)*	
	Singular	*Plural*			*Singular*	*Plural*
N	πραΰτης	πραΰτητες		N	σῶμα	σώματα
G	πραΰτητος	πραυτήτων		G	σώματος	σωμάτων
D	πραΰτητι	πραΰτησι(ν)		D	σώματι	σώμασι(ν)
A	πραΰτητα	πραΰτητας		A	σῶμα	σώματα

Table 14.7 Third Declension Stops—Dental Subgroup Paradigms

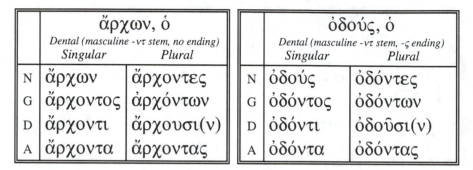

	ἄρχων, ὁ			ὁδούς, ὁ	
	Dental (masculine -ντ stem, no ending)			*Dental (masculine -ντ stem, -ς ending)*	
	Singular	*Plural*		*Singular*	*Plural*
N	ἄρχων	ἄρχοντες	N	ὁδούς	ὁδόντες
G	ἄρχοντος	ἀρχόντων	G	ὁδόντος	ὁδόντων
D	ἄρχοντι	ἄρχουσι(ν)	D	ὁδόντι	ὁδοῦσι(ν)
A	ἄρχοντα	ἄρχοντας	A	ὁδόντα	ὁδόντας

Table 14.8 Third Declension—Dental Subgroup and Sibilant Paradigms

	νύξ, ἡ			γένος, τό	
	Dental (-κτ stem)			*Sibilant (neuter -εσ stem, -ος nominative)*	
	Singular	*Plural*		*Singular*	*Plural*
N	νύξ	νύκτες	N	γένος	γένη (ε + α)
G	νυκτός	νυκτῶν	G	γένους	γενῶν (ε + ω)
D	νυκτί	νύξι(ν)	D	γένει (ε + ι)	γένεσι(ν)
A	νύκτα	νύκτας	A	γένος	γένη (ε + α)

Concord

Numerous rules have been formulated to follow third declension changes. On occasion, however, the changes simply are without explanation. Accents also are unusual. The advanced student should work on the key paradigms. The beginning student should focus on remembering third declension ending patterns. However, in the final analysis, *concord always gives away any information hidden in an unusual third declension form.* The article is your best friend. Locate the article, and you *already* have located any unrecognized third declension noun.

In the following tables, observe how unfamiliar forms are a cinch to locate with articular construction (also true with the neuter article). Whenever grounded by a third declension noun, try taking off in a concord!

Table 14.9 Masculine Articular Constructions—ὁ ὀδούς

	Singular	*Translation*	*Plural*	*Translation*
N	ὁ ὀδούς	"the tooth"	οἱ ὀδόντες	"the teeth"
G	τοῦ ὀδόντος	"of the tooth"	τῶν ὀδόντων	"of the teeth"
		"from the tooth"		"from the teeth"
D	τῷ ὀδόντι	"to the tooth"	τοῖς ὀδοῦσι(ν)	"to the teeth"
		"in the tooth"		"in the teeth"
		"by the tooth"		"by the teeth"
A	τὸν ὀδόντα	"the tooth"	τοὺς ὀδόντας	"the teeth"

Table 14.10 Feminine Articular Constructions—ἡ σάρξ

	Singular	*Translation*	*Plural*	*Translation*
N	ἡ σάρξ	"the flesh"	αἱ σάρκες	"the flesh"
G	τῆς σαρκός	"of the flesh"	τῶν σαρκῶν	"of the flesh"
		"from the flesh"		"from the flesh"
D	τῇ σαρκί	"to the flesh"	ταῖς σαρξί(ν)	"to the flesh"
		"in the flesh"		"in the flesh"
		"by the flesh"		"by the flesh"
A	τὴν σάρκα	"the flesh"	τὰς σάρκας	"the flesh"

What To Learn—LESSON 14 (δεκατέσσαρες)

Beginning

☐   1.   The three noun declension stem types and the distinguishing characteristic of third declension as a consonant declension

☐   2.   How the lexical entry for a noun identifies a third declension stem and how to specify the stem of a third declension noun

☐   3.   General observations on third declension inflections

☐   4.   The pattern of *sigma volatilization* with stops

☐   5.   Why nominative masculine/feminine singular and dative plural forms are most reactant to third declension endings

☐   6.   What type ending generates unusual nominative/accusative forms

☐   7.   Paradigms of common third declension forms: σάρξ, χάρις, σῶμα, ἄρχων

☐   8.   The significance of concord for locating third declension nouns

☐   9.   Vocabulary words

Advanced

☐   10.   The stop paradigms:

        λίψ   =   labial
        σάρξ   =   palatal
        χάρις   =   dental (-ν accusative)
        ἐλπίς   =   dental (-α accusative)

☐   11.   The dental subgroup paradigms:

        σῶμα   =   -ματ neuter
        ἄρχων   =   -ντ masculine (no ending)
        ὀδούς   =   -ντ masculine (-ς ending)
        νύξ   =   -κτ

☐   12.   The sibilant paradigm:

        γένος   =   -εσ neuter (-ος nominative)

LESSON 15 (δεκαπέντε)
Third Declension—Liquid and Vowel Stems

πίστις, πίστεως

Lesson 14 presented third declension inflection patterns based on stem type. Liquid and vowel stem varieties now are presented, which completes the declension. Gender is mixed. Again, these stems are hidden in the genitive singular form. A review of adverb comparisons also is given.

Vocabulary 15

Numeral

δεκαπέντε	fifteen

Liquids (long stem vowel)

αἰών, αἰῶνος, ὁ	age, eternity
μάρτυς, -τυρος, ὁ	witness (martyr)
πῦρ, πυρός, τό	fire
σωτήρ, σωτῆρος, ὁ	savior (redeemer)
χείρ, χειρός, ἡ	hand
Ἕλλην, -ηνος, ὁ	Greek, gentile
ἀμπελών, -ῶνος, ὁ	vineyard
Σίμων, Σίμωνος, ὁ	Simon

Liquids (short stem vowel)

ἀήρ, ἀέρος, ὁ	air
ἀλέκτωρ, -τορος, ὁ	rooster
ἀστήρ, ἀστέρος, ὁ	star

εἰκών, εἰκόνος, ἡ	likeness, image
ἡγεμών, -μόνος, ὁ	governor, ruler
ποιμήν, -μένος, ὁ	shepherd

Liquids (syncopated -ρ stem)

ἀνήρ, ἀνδρός, ὁ	man, husband
θυγάτηρ, -τρός, ἡ	daughter
μήτηρ, μητρός, ἡ	mother
πατήρ, πατρός, ὁ	father

Vowels (-ι stem = feminine)

πίστις, πίστεως, ἡ	faith (trust, belief)
πόλις, πόλεως, ἡ	city, town
κρίσις, κρίσεως, ἡ	judgment
θλῖψις, θλίψεως, ἡ	trouble (distress)
δύναμις, -εως, ἡ	power
ἀνάστασις, -εως, ἡ	resurrection

Vowels (-υ stem)

ἰσχύς, ἰσχύος, ἡ	strength
ἰχθύς, ἰχθύος, ὁ	fish
ὀσφῦς, ὀσφύος, ἡ	waist

Vowels (-ευ stem = masculine)

ἀρχιερεύς, -έως, ὁ   chief priest

βασιλεύς, -έως, ὁ	king
γραμματεύς, -έως, ὁ	scribe (scholar)
ἱερεύς, -έως, ὁ	priest

Vowels (-ου stem = masculine)

νοῦς, νοός, ὁ   mind, thought

Stem Types

The beginning student should overview this material in general. Then, you should focus on the two paradigms of πατήρ (syncopation) and πίστις (iota stems).

Liquid Stems (-ρ and -ν). Strictly speaking, liquid stems are those ending in -λ or -ρ. The liquid category quickly reduces to noun stems ending in -ρ, for only one noun stem in the New Testament ends in -λ.[1] The nasals are μ and ν, but, in fact, no noun stem ends in -μ in the New Testament. So this nasal category also quickly reduces to noun stems ending in -ν. The characteristic feature of both rho and nu stems is that they show *vowel alterations in the stem*—all long, long to short, or dropping out altogether—used to classify them into subgroups.

Long Vowel. The long vowel observed in the nominative form holds throughout the entire inflection. These nouns opt for no ending in the nominative.

Rho Stems. The long vowel -ρ stem paradigm is the masculine σωτήρ, σωτῆρος. A neuter example is πῦρ, πυρός. One minor exception is the feminine χείρ, χειρός, whose dative plural inexplicably degrades the long ει to the short ε (χερσίν). Another exception is the masculine μάρτυς, μάρτυρος. The stem is μαρτυρ-, but inexplicably the final ρ drops before the nominative singular and dative plural endings (μάρτυς, μάρτυσιν).

Nu Stems. *Nasal ν will drop before a sibilant σ.* So, in the sigma form of the dative plural (σι), ν before the sibilant drops. Usually when the nasal ν does this, compensatory lengthening occurs, but the stem vowel does not change in this instance. The long vowel -ν stem paradigm is αἰών, αἰῶνος.

Short Vowel. These stems show a long vowel in the nominative form, but the vowel degrades to a short vowel in all other forms. These nouns opt for no ending in the nominative.

Rho Stems. Short vowel -ρ stems are all masculine. The short vowel -ρ stem paradigm is ἀστήρ, ἀστέρος. Two syncopated categories are subgroups.

---

[1]The Attic noun "salt," ἅλς, ἁλός, τό ("salt") in the textual apparatus at Mark 9:49 (as ἁλί). The form in the next verse, ἅλας (9:50), seems derived from a dental stem variation, ἅλας, -ατος, τό.

Weak Syncopation. The short vowel drops out. This phenomenon is called *syncopation* and occurs as a short vowel is suppressed between two single consonants for pronunciation. "Weak" syncopation describes the suppression of the short vowel in only three forms: genitive and dative singular, and dative plural. However, a syncopated dative plural throws three consonants together (e.g., πατρσι), rendering the ρ unpronounceable. To preserve the pronunciation, Greeks threw in the vowel α, creating the dative plural πατράσιν. The paradigm is πατήρ, πατρός.

Strong Syncopation. The short vowel drops out, but more drastically. "Strong" syncopation describes the suppression of the short vowel in *all* forms but nominative singular. The paradigm is ἀνήρ, ἀνδρός.

Nu Stems. Again, the long vowel of the nominative is short elsewhere. *Nasal ν will drop before a sibilant σ.* So, in the sigma form of the dative plural (σι), ν before the sibilant drops. The short vowel -ν stem paradigm is εἰκών, εἰκόνος.[2]

Vowel Stems (-ι and -υ). The vowels ι and υ on third declension nouns function as *semivowels*, that is, with consonant effect (i.e., sounding as "y" and "w" respectively). The semivowel function includes certain diphthongs (ευ, ου).[3]

Iota Stems. Most are feminine. This actually is an -ε stem that becomes -ι only in the nominative and accusative singular. All others show -ε or ει forms.[4] The accusative singular opts for the -ν. The genitive form is Attic. A striking feature for these feminine nouns is the accusative plural using the same ending as the nominative plural (as in the neuter pattern). The paradigm is πίστις, πίστεως, ἡ.

Upsilon Stems. The -υ stem retains the υ throughout. The old stem had a "w" sound, later vocalized as a consonantal υ. This semivowel did not then undergo any further changes. The accusative opts for the -ν. The paradigm is ἰχθύς, ἰχθύος, ὁ.

Several diphthong stems represent old stems originally ending with a "w" sound, later vocalized with the consonantal υ. The diphthong stem -ευ shows -ευ only before consonants (i.e., the sigmas of the nominative singular, dative plural); otherwise, before vowels, the stem falls to -ε. The genitive form is Attic. All -ευ nouns are masculine. The paradigm is ἱερεύς, ἱερέως, ὁ.

The diphthong stem -ου shows -ου only before consonants; otherwise, before vowels, the stem falls to -ο. The accusative singular opts for -ν. Most are masculine. The most important New Testament example is the paradigm, νοῦς, νοός, ὁ.

---

[2]Two short vowel -ν stem nouns in the New Testament further show strong syncopation, expelling the short vowel altogether in all other forms. These are the masculine ἀρήν, ἀρνός ("lamb"), occurring once in Luke 10:3, and the masculine κύων, κυνός ("dog," consonantal υ), occurring five times (Matt. 7:6; Luke 16:21; Phil. 3:2; 2 Pet. 2:22; Rev. 22:15).

[3]Extremely rare stems include the diphthong -αυ (ναῦς, νεώς) and the -υ stem with -ε before vowels (πῆχυς, πήχεως). Only one iota diphthong pattern occurs (-οι stem), and this in a variant reading in 1 Cor. 2:4, πειθώ, πειθοῦς, ἡ.

[4]Diphthongizing in dative singular (ε + ι = ει), contracting in nominative plural (ε + ε = ει).

Table 15.1 Third Declension Liquids—Long Vowel

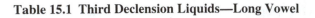

	σωτήρ, ὁ			αἰών, ὁ	
	Liquid (-ρ stem, long vowel)			*Liquid (-ν stem, long vowel)*	
	Singular	*Plural*		*Singular*	*Plural*
N	σωτήρ	σωτῆρες	N	αἰών	αἰῶνες
G	σωτῆρος	σωτήρων	G	αἰῶνος	αἰώνων
D	σωτῆρι	σωτῆρσι(ν)	D	αἰῶνι	αἰῶσι(ν)
A	σωτῆρα	σωτῆρας	A	αἰῶνα	αἰῶνας

Table 15.2 Third Declension Liquids—Short Vowel

	ἀστήρ, ὁ			εἰκών, ἡ	
	Liquid (-ρ stem, short vowel)			*Liquid (-ν stem, short vowel)*	
	Singular	*Plural*		*Singular*	*Plural*
N	ἀστήρ	ἀστέρες	N	εἰκών	εἰκόνες
G	ἀστέρος	ἀστέρων	G	εἰκόνος	εἰκόνων
D	ἀστέρι	ἀστέρσι(ν)	D	εἰκόνι	εἰκόσι(ν)
A	ἀστέρα	ἀστέρας	A	εἰκόνα	εἰκόνας

Table 15.3 Third Declension Liquids—Rho Stem Syncopation

	πατήρ, ὁ			ἀνήρ, ὁ	
	Liquid (-ρ stem, weak syncopation)			*Liquid (-ρ stem, strong syncopation)*	
	Singular	*Plural*		*Singular*	*Plural*
N	πατήρ	πατέρες	N	ἀνήρ	ἄνδρες
G	πατρός	πατέρων	G	ἀνδρός	ἀνδρῶν
D	πατρί	πατράσι(ν)	D	ἀνδρί	ἀνδράσι(ν)
A	πατέρα	πατέρας	A	ἄνδρα	ἄνδρας

Table 15.4 Third Declension Vowels—Iota and Upsilon Stems

	πίστις, ἡ		ἰχθύς, ὁ	
	Vowel (-ι stem, -ε before vowels)		*Vowel (-υ stem, - υ throughout)*	
	Singular	*Plural*	*Singular*	*Plural*
N	πίστις	πίστεις	ἰχθύς	ἰχθύες
G	πίστεως	πίστεων	ἰχθύος	ἰχθύων
D	πίστει	πίστεσι(ν)	ἰχθύι	ἰχθύσι(ν)
A	πίστιν	πίστεις	ἰχθύν	ἰχθύας

Table 15.5 Third Declension Vowels—Diphthongs

	ἱερεύς, ὁ		νοῦς, ὁ	
	Vowel (-ευ diphthong)		*Vowel (-ου diphthong)*	
	Singular	*Plural*	*Singular*	*Plural*
N	ἱερεύς	ἱερεῖς	νοῦς	νόες
G	ἱερέως	ἱερέων	νοός	νοῶν
D	ἱερεῖ	ἱερεῦσι(ν)	νοΐ	νουσί(ν)
A	ἱερέα	ἱερεῖς	νοῦν	νόας

Paradigms. First, observe that the basic inflectional patterns are all the same. Then note that, after learning the nominative singular form as vocabulary, the differences mostly are minor variations in the stems. Further, most accusative singular forms opt for the -α, an ending already familiar from second declension neuter. The only truly unusual forms are in the -ι and -ευ stems: the -εως genitive singular and the -εις nominative and accusative plural (πίστις and ἱερεύς).

Adverb Comparisons

Adjective comparative and superlative degrees build their forms from second and first declension endings, using -τερος and -τατος patterns. The adverb form of comparison is not declined, so has only two forms. The comparative form borrows the neuter accusative *singular* of the comparative adjective. So the comparative of the adverb ἐγγύς is ἐγγύτερον ("nearer"). Another adverb comparative pattern is -τερω, -τατω. So ἄνω becomes ἀνωτέρω ("higher") and ἀνωτάτω ("highest").

What To Learn—LESSON 15 (δεκαπέντε)

Beginning

☐ 1. Paradigms: πατήρ (syncopation), πίστις (iota stem), ἱερεύς (upsilon stem)

☐ 2. Review adverb comparisons

☐ 3. Vocabulary words

Advanced

☐ 4. The liquid, long stem vowel paradigms:
        σωτήρ   = -ρ stem
        αἰών   = -ν stem

☐ 5. The liquid, short stem vowel paradigms:
        ἀστήρ   = -ρ stem
        εἰκών   = -ν stem

☐ 6. The syncopation paradigms:
        πατήρ   = -ρ stem, weak syncopation
        ἀνήρ   = -ρ stem, strong syncopation

☐ 7. The semivowel paradigms:
        πίστις   = -ι stem
        ἰχθύς   = -υ stem

☐ 8. The diphthong paradigms:
        ἱερεύς   = -ευ stem
        νοῦς   = -ου stem

LESSON 16 (δεκαέξ)
Adjectives and Comparisons—Again

πᾶς, πᾶσα, πᾶν

Adjective inflection is similar to noun counterparts. Some follow first and second declension endings (ἀγαθός, δίκαιος). Others show "two-termination," contraction, third declension, and mixed declension patterns. Some adjective comparisons show third declension. Uses of πᾶς are presented.

Vocabulary 16

Numeral

δεκαέξ	sixteen

Two-termination (Second Declen.)

αἰώνιος, -ον	eternal, unending
ἀκαθαρτός, -όν	unclean, defiling
ἁμαρτωλός, -όν	sinful, sinner
ἄπιστος, -ον	unbelieving
διάβολος, -ον	slanderous (Devil)
ἔρημος, -ον	lonely, deserted

Contraction

χρυσοῦς, -ῆ, -οῦν	golden

Third Declension (Sibilant Stem)

ἀληθής, -ές	true, truthful, real
ἀσθενής, -ές	sick, weak
πλήρης, -ές	full, complete

Third Declen. (Short Vowel Stem)

συγγενής, -ές	relative
ὑγιής, -ές	healthy, whole

Third Declen. (Short Vowel Stem)

ἄρσην, -εν	male, man
ἄφρων, -ον	fool, foolish

Third–First Declension Mixed

ταχύς, -εῖα, ὑ	quick, swift
πᾶς, πᾶσα, πᾶν	every, all, whole
μέλας, -αινα, -αν	black, ink

Third/Second–First Mixed

μέγας, μεγάλη, μέγα	large, great
πολύς, πολλή, πολύ	much, many

Comparative Third Declension

κρείσσων, -ον	better, greater
	(also κρείττων)

μείζων, -ον   greater   **Superlative Third Declension**

πλείων, -ον   more than (also   ἐλάχιστος, -η, -ον least, smallest

                   πλέον)   ὕψιστος, -η, -ον   highest

χείρων, -ον   worse

Adjective Forms

This is the final set of adjective paradigms. We cover: (1) two additional second declension variations, "two-termination" and contracts, (2) third declension patterns based on third declension nouns, and (3) hybrid forms of mixed declension.

Two-Termination (second declension). Recall that not all second declension nouns in -ος are masculine. Some feminine nouns have inflection on the pattern of second declension masculine (cf. ὁδός, Table 8.3). So, for some second declension nouns, masculine and feminine have the same endings. Certain adjectives follow a similar pattern. A *two-termination* adjective is a second declension adjective that shows only two sets of endings—using the same inflection for both masculine and feminine forms. The neuter will be standard second declension.

Table 16.1 Two-Termination Adjective—Second Declension

Masculine		Feminine		Neuter	
Singular	*Plural*	*Singular*	*Plural*	*Singular*	*Plural*
ἔρημος	ἔρημοι	ἔρημος	ἔρημοι	ἔρημον	ἔρημα
ἐρήμου	ἐρήμων	ἐρήμου	ἐρήμων	ἐρήμου	ἐρήμων
ἐρήμῳ	ἐρήμοις	ἐρήμῳ	ἐρήμοις	ἐρήμῳ	ἐρήμοις
ἔρημον	ἐρήμους	ἔρημον	ἐρήμους	ἔρημον	ἔρημα

Contraction (second declension). The vowels ε and ο contract with other vowels. Some of the contractions that may be observed are irregular, involving absorption of the vowel. A few adjectives whose stems end in ε or ο and follow the second declension δίκαιος pattern (-ος, -α, -ον) show various forms of contraction in their inflected forms.[1]

---

[1] Only one other adjective in the New Testament fits this category, χαλκοῦς, -ῆ, -οῦν ("made of copper"). Two other adjectives end in a variation with rho (-ρε) and show a pattern similar to χρυσοῦς, only with -ᾶ, -ᾶς, -ᾷ, -ᾶν in the singular. These are σιδηροῦς, -ᾶ, -οῦν ("made of iron"), and ἀργυροῦς, -ᾶ, -οῦν ("made of silver").

Table 16.2 Contract Adjective—Second Declension

| Masculine | | Feminine | | Neuter | |
Singular	Plural	Singular	Plural	Singular	Plural
χρυσοῦς	χρυσοῖ	χρυσῆ	χρυσαῖ	χρυσοῦν	χρυσᾶ
χρυσοῦ	χρυσῶν	χρυσῆς	χρυσῶν	χρυσοῦς	χρυσῶν
χρυσῷ	χρυσοῖς	χρυσῇ	χρυσαῖς	χρυσῷ	χρυσοῖς
χρυσοῦν	χρυσοῦς	χρυσήν	χρυσᾶς	χρυσοῦν	χρυσᾶ

Sibilant Stem. One third declension category is the sibilant stem. The major representative is the neuter -εσ stem with an -ος nominative (γένος, τό; see Table 14.8). A similar pattern can be observed in adjectives, except not neuter gender, so the endings used show different contractions. Since third declension by definition shows the same forms for both masculine and feminine, any third declension adjective of this type could be termed a "two-termination" adjective.

The endings are the typical third declension masculine-feminine patterns. The nominative opts for no ending. The remaining -ες stem undergoes compensatory lengthening to -ης. In other case forms, an intervocalic sigma drops and the remaining vowels contract. Notice the typical third declension phenomena (all interiors are all the same, neuter singular and plurals are the same for nominative and accusative, etc.).

Table 16.3 Sibilant Stem—Third Declension

| Masculine | | Feminine | | Neuter | |
Singular	Plural	Singular	Plural	Singular	Plural
ἀληθής	ἀληθεῖς	ἀληθής	ἀληθεῖς	ἀληθές	ἀληθῆ
ἀληθοῦς	ἀληθῶν	ἀληθοῦς	ἀληθῶν	ἀληθοῦς	ἀληθῶν
ἀληθεῖ	ἀληθέσιν	ἀληθεῖ	ἀληθέσιν	ἀληθεῖ	ἀληθέσιν
ἀληθῆ	ἀληθεῖς	ἀληθῆ	ἀληθεῖς	ἀληθές	ἀληθῆ

Liquid Short Vowel Stem. Another third declension category is the liquid (nasal) -ν, whose long stem vowel in the nominative singular is short elsewhere (εἰκών, εἰκόνος; see Table 15.2). On a similar pattern, one adjective shows an -ην stem going to -εν outside the nominative singular. Another shows an -ων stem going to -ον. The nominative singular opts for no ending. The remaining -εν or -ον stem then undergoes compensatory lengthening to -ην and -ων, respectively. In the dative plural, the typical nasal rule is invoked: *nasal ν drops before the sibilant σ.*

Table 16.4 Liquid Short Vowel Stem—Third Declension

Masculine		Feminine		Neuter	
Singular	*Plural*	*Singular*	*Plural*	*Singular*	*Plural*
ἄφρων	ἄφρονες	ἄφρων	ἄφρονες	ἄφρον	ἄφρονα
ἄφρονος	ἀφρόνων	ἄφρονος	ἀφρόνων	ἄφρονος	ἀφρόνων
ἄφρονι	ἄφροσιν	ἄφρονι	ἄφροσιν	ἄφρονι	ἄφροσιν
ἄφρονα	ἄφρονας	ἄφρονα	ἄφρονας	ἄφρον	ἄφρονα

Mixed Declensions. The final category is an adjective whose forms in the three genders mixes declension patterns. One set mixes third and first declension. Another set mixes third, second, and first.

Third–First Declension. For these adjectives, the masculine and neuter are third declension. Feminine is first declension. Three variations are observed, based on third declension stem varieties.

The -υ/ε stem shows -ε everywhere except the singulars of the nominative and accusative for masculine and neuter, which show -υ. (This stem type was not covered for nouns.)

The -ντ stem opting for -ς in the nominative shows similarity to the noun ὀδούς (Table 14.7). The feminine is like the first declension sibilant δόξα (Table 5.4). The one major example in the New Testament is the very common πᾶς, πᾶσα, πᾶν.

Finally, the -ν stem has only one New Testament example, μέλας. Again, as one might expect, the dative plural shows the typical nasal pattern, in which the nasal ν drops before the sibilant σ.

Table 16.5 Mixed Declension—Third–First Declension (-υ/ε stem)

Masculine		Neuter		Feminine	
Singular	*Plural*	*Singular*	*Plural*	*Singular*	*Plural*
ταχύς	ταχεῖς	ταχύ	ταχέα	ταχεῖα	ταχεῖαι
ταχέως	ταχέων	ταχέως	ταχέων	ταχείας	ταχειῶν
ταχεῖ	ταχέσιν	ταχεῖ	ταχέσιν	ταχείᾳ	ταχείαις
ταχύς	ταχεῖς	ταχεῖαν	ταχέα	ταχύν	ταχείας

Table 16.6 Mixed Declension—Third–First Declension (-ντ stem)

| Masculine | | Neuter | | Feminine | |
Singular	Plural	Singular	Plural	Singular	Plural
πᾶς	πάντες	πᾶν	πάντα	πᾶσα	πᾶσαι
παντός	πάντων	παντός	πάντων	πάσης	πασῶν
παντί	πᾶσιν	παντί	πᾶσιν	πάσῃ	πάσαις
πάντα	πάντας	πᾶν	πάντα	πᾶσαν	πάσας

Table 16.7 Mixed Declension—Third–First Declension (-ν stem)

| Masculine | | Neuter | | Feminine | |
Singular	Plural	Singular	Plural	Singular	Plural
μέλας	μέλανες	μέλαν	μέλανα	μέλαινα	μέλαιναι
μέλανος	μελάνων	μέλανος	μελάνων	μελαίνης	μελαινῶν
μέλανι	μέλασιν	μέλανι	μέλασιν	μελαίνῃ	μελαίναι
μέλανα	μέλανας	μέλαν	μέλανα	μέλαιναν	μελαίνας

Third/Second–First Declension. In this pattern, the masculine and neuter forms are *mostly* second declension. However, the singular forms of the nominative and accusative reveal an *altered* stem. These forms also show third declension endings. In contrast, the feminine is -η pure first declension. Two variations are observed, specifically the following two paradigms and their cognates. Notice the two altered stem forms of μεγαλ- to μεγα- in the first paradigm, and of πολλ- to πολυ- in the second paradigm (nominative and accusative singular).

Table 16.8 Mixed Declension—Third/Second–First Declension (altered stem)

| Masculine | | Neuter | | Feminine | |
Singular	Plural	Singular	Plural	Singular	Plural
μέγας	μεγάλοι	μέγα	μεγάλα	μεγάλη	μεγάλαι
μεγάλου	μεγάλων	μεγάλου	μεγάλων	μεγάλης	μεγάλων
μεγάλῳ	μεγάλοις	μεγάλῳ	μεγάλοις	μεγάλῃ	μεγάλαις
μέγαν	μεγάλους	μέγα	μεγάλα	μεγάλην	μεγάλας

Table 16.9 Mixed Declension—Third/Second–First Declension (altered stem)

Masculine		Neuter		Feminine	
Singular	*Plural*	*Singular*	*Plural*	*Singular*	*Plural*
πολύς	πολλοί	πολύ	πολλά	πολλή	πολλαί
πολλοῦ	πολλῶν	πολλοῦ	πολλῶν	πολλῆς	πολλῶν
πολλῷ	πολλοῖς	πολλῷ	πολλοῖς	πολλῇ	πολλαῖς
πολύν	πολλούς	πολύ	πολλά	πολλήν	πολλάς

Comparisons

Third declension comparative adjectives follow the liquid (nasal) short vowel stem ἄφρων (Table 16.4). Superlative forms are rare. The superlative is included in the following table, *not* as the superlative of πλείων, but as an example only. The suffix -ιστ is distinctive. The endings are -ος, -η, -ον.[2]

Table 16.10 Comparisons—Adjectives (Third Declension)

	Comparative "more than"		Superlative "least, smallest"	
	Sing.	*Plur.*	*Sing.*	*Plur.*
masculine	πλείων	πλείονες	ἐλάχιστος	ἐλάχιστοι
	πλείονος	πλειόνων	ἐλαχίστου	ἐλαχίστων
	πλείονι	πλείοσιν	ἐλαχίστῳ	ἐλαχίστοις
	πλείονα	πλείονας	ἐλάχιστον	ἐλαχίστους
feminine	πλείων	πλείονες	ἐλαχίστη	ἐλάχισται
	πλείονος	πλειόνων	ἐλαχίστης	ἐλαχίστων
	πλείονι	πλείοσιν	ἐλαχίστῃ	ἐλαχίσταις
	πλείονα	πλείονας	ἐλαχίστην	ἐλαχίστας
neuter	πλεῖον	πλείονα	ἐλάχιστον	ἐλάχιστα
	πλείονος	πλειόνων	ἐλαχίστου	ἐλαχίστων
	πλείονι	πλείοσιν	ἐλαχίστῳ	ἐλαχίστοις
	πλεῖον	πλείονα	ἐλάχιστον	ἐλάχιστα

---

[2]One other rare suffix is -τατ, used on ἁγιώτατος, ἀκριβέστατος, and τιμώτατος.

The normal comparative degree of most adjectives is achieved through a first–second inflection using the suffix -τερος, -α, -ον. However, vocabulary in this lesson include some "irregular" adjective comparisons, thus termed because these adjectives follow third declension. Note the corresponding positive degree adjectives with which they are used.

Table 16.11 Irreg. Comparisons

Positive	Comparitive
ἀγαθός	χρείσσων
κακός	χείρων
μέγας	μείζων
πολύς	πλείων

Uses of πᾶς

The πᾶς, πᾶσα, πᾶν adjective is used frequently in the New Testament. The two common uses are the meanings "all" or "the whole," grammatical construction normally distinguishing the two. The following summary statements do not represent hard and fast rules. Context always is your guide, but these are common.

> πᾶς + [article + noun] = "all the _____"

> [article + πᾶς] + noun = "the whole _____"

Articular Constructions. As an anarthrous adjective (predicative), πᾶς with an *articular noun* means "all." Πᾶς as an *articular adjective* (attributive) with an anarthrous noun means "the whole." These uses correspond to English. (Notice the article's position in the two expressions: "*all* the city" versus "*the whole* city.")

(1) πᾶς + [article + noun] = "*all* [the _____]"
     Example: **πᾶσα** ἡ πόλις = "**all** the city" (Acts 13:44)

(2) [article + πᾶς] + noun = "[the *whole*] _____"
     Example: **τὸν πάντα** χρόνον = "**the whole** time" (Acts 20:18)

> πᾶς$_{sg}$ + noun $_{sg}$ = "every _____"

> πάντες$_{pl}$ + noun$_{pl}$ = "all _____"

Anarthrous Constructions. Further, anarthrous construction for both the adjective πᾶς and the noun, *singular* in number, means "every ____." Anarthrous construction for both adjective and noun, *plural* in number, means "all ____."

(3) πᾶς + noun (sg.) = "every ____"
   Example: **πᾶσα** γλῶσσα = "**every** tongue" (Phil 2:11)

(4) πάντες + noun (pl.) = "all ____"
   Example: ὑπὲρ **πάντων** ἀνθρώπων = "for **all** men" (1 Tim. 2:1)

$$\boxed{\pi\hat{\alpha}\varsigma_{sg} = \text{"everyone"}}$$

$$\boxed{\pi\acute{\alpha}\nu\tau\epsilon\varsigma_{pl} = \text{"all men"}}$$

Substantival. Finally, the adjective πᾶς used substantivally (alone, without a noun) means "everyone" in the singular and "all people," "all men," or "all women" in the plural, guided by gender as masculine or feminine and context. The neuter would be ʻeverything" in the singular and "all things" in the plural.

(5) πᾶς = "everyone," "anyone"
   Example: **Πᾶς** οὖν ὅστις ἀκούει = "Therefore **everyone** who hears" (Matt. 7:24)

(6) πάντες = "all (people)"
   Example: **πάντες** γὰρ ἥμαρτον "for **all** have sinned" (Rom. 3:23)
   Example: καθὼς κἀγὼ πάντα **πᾶσιν** ἀρέσκω = "just as I̱ also please **all men** (in) all things" (1 Cor. 10:33)

(7) πᾶν = "everything," "anything"
   Example: **πᾶν** κοινὸν καὶ ἀκάθαρτον = "**anything** common or unclean" (Acts 10:14)

(8) πάντα = "all (things)"
   Example: **πάντα** συνεργεῖ εἰς ἀγαθόν = "(God) works together **all things** for the good" (Rom. 8:28)
   Example: καθὼς κἀγὼ **πάντα** πᾶσιν ἀρέσκω = "just as I̱ also please all men **(in) all things**" (1 Cor. 10:33)

What To Learn—LESSON 16 (δεκαέξ)

Beginning

☐ 1. Adjective paradigms ἔρημος, ἀληθής, πᾶς

☐ 2. Third declension comparative and superlative:

       πλείων   = -ν stem (short vowel stem; cf. ἄφρων)

       ἐλάχιστος = -ιστ suffix (-ος, -η, -ον endings)

☐ 3. Positive and comparative of irregular comparisons

☐ 4. Uses of πᾶς, πᾶσα, πᾶν as "all," "the whole," or "every"

☐ 5. Vocabulary words

Advanced

☐ 6. Additional second declension adjective paradigms:

       ἔρημος   = two-termination (second declension)

       χρυσοῦς = contract (second declension)

☐ 7. Third declension adjective paradigms:

       ἀληθής   = sibilant stem

       ἄφρων   = -ν stem (short vowel stem)

☐ 8. Mixed declension adjective paradigms

       ταχύς   = mixed, third–first (-υ/ε stem)

       πᾶς   = mixed, third–first (-ντ stem)

       μέλας   = mixed, third–first (-ν stem)

       μέγας   = mixed, third/second–first (altered stem)

       πολύς   = mixed, third/second–first (altered stem)

Sinaiticus (א) is one of our best manuscripts, one of the few with a complete text of the New Testament. The Epistle of Barnabas and the Shepherd of Hermes are included, showing the high regard these had in some areas of the church. The quality parchment and calligraphy might indicate an origin as a part of the royal codexes ordered for production after Christianity became the official religion of the Roman Empire (fourth century). The text's discovery by Constantin von Tischendorf at the monastery of St. Catherine on Mount Sinai last century is a famous story. The manuscript went to the Czar of Russia in 1859 but was purchased by the British Museum in 1933. Below is one section of one of the four columns per page.

(Sinaiticus)

Luke 2:1–4b

ЄГЄΝЄΤΟΔЄЄΝΤΝ·
ΗΜЄΡΑΙCЄΚΙΝΑΙ·
ЄΞΗΛΘЄΝΛΟΓΜΑ
ΠΑΡΑΚΑΙCΑΡΟCΑ
ΓΟΥCΤΟΥΑΠΟΓΡΑ
ΦЄCΘЄΠΑCΑΝΤΗΝ
ΟΙΚΟΥΜЄΝΗΝΑΥ
ΤΗΝΑΠΟΓΡΑΦΗ
ЄΓЄΝЄΤΟΠΡΩΤΗ
ΗΓЄΜΟΝЄΥΟΝΤ·
ΤΗCCΥΡΙΑCΚΥΡΗΝΙ
ΟΥΚΑΙЄΠΟΡЄΥΟΝ
ΤΟЄΚΑCΤΟCΑΠΟΙ
ΦЄCΘЄЄΙCΤΗΝЄΑ
ΤΩΝΠΟΛΙΝ
ΑΝЄΒΗΔЄΚΑΙΙΩΝΗ
ΑΠΟΤΗCΓΑΛΙΛΑΙ
ΑCЄΚΠΟΛЄΩCΝΑ
ΖΑΡЄΘЄΙCΤΗΝΙΟΥ
ΔΑΙΑΝЄΙCΤΗΝΠ·
ΛΙΝΔΑΔΗΤΙCΚΑΙ
ΤΑΙΒΗΘΛЄЄΜΔΙΑ
ΤΟЄΙΝΑΙΑΥΤΟΝ·

Lesson 17 (ἑπτά καὶ δέκα)
Numerals

εἶς, μία, ἔν

We wrap up third declension with numerals and some pronouns. The first four cardinals are declined (and over 200). Those above twenty are constructed using καί. The ordinals are declined like ἀγαθός. Grammar is presented about more uses of certain cases, the definite article, negatives, and καί.

Vocabulary 17

Interrogative Pronoun

τίς, τίς, τί	who? which? what?

Indefinite Pronoun

τις, τις, τι	someone (something)

Indefinite Relative Pronoun

ὅστις, ἥτις, ὅτι	who, whoever

Negative Pronoun

οὐδείς, οὐδεμία, οὐδέν	no one

Cardinal Numerals

εἷς, μία, ἔν	one
δύο, (δυσίν)	two
τρεῖς, τρία	three
τέσσαρες, τέσσαρα	four
πέντε	five
ἔξ	six

ἑπτά	seven
ὀκτώ	eight
ἐννέα	nine
δέκα	ten
ἔνδεκα	eleven
δώδεκα	twelve
[δεκατρεῖς]	[thirteen]
δεκατέσσαρες	fourteen
δεκαπέντε	fifteen
[δεκαέξ]	[sixteen]
[ἑπτά καὶ δέκα]	[seventeen]
δεκαοκτώ	eighteen
[ἐννέα καὶ δέκα]	[nineteen]
εἴκοσι	twenty
τριάκοντα	thirty

195

		Ordinal Numerals	
τεσσεράκοντα	forty		
πεντήκοντα	fifty	πρῶτος, -η, -ον	first
ἑξήκοντα	sixty	δεύτερος, -α, -ον	second
ἑβδομήκοντα	seventy	τρίτος, -η, -ον	third
ὀγδοήκοντα	eighty	τέταρτος, -η, -ον	fourth
ἐνενήκοντα	ninety	πέμπτος, -η, -ον	fifth
ἑκατόν	one hundred	ἕκτος, -η, -ον	sixth
διακόσιοι, -αι, -α	two hundred	ἕβδομος, -η, -ον	seventh
τριακόσιοι, -αι, -α	three hundred	ὄγδοος, -η, -ον	eighth
τετρακόσιοι, -αι, -α	four hundred	ἔνατος, -η, -ον	ninth
πεντακόσιοι, -αι, -α	five hundred	δέκατος, -η, -ον	tenth
ἑξακόσιοι, -αι, -α	six hundred	ἑνδέκατος, -η, -ον	eleventh
[ἑπτακόσιοι]	[seven hundred]	δωδέκατος, -η, -ον	twelfth
[ὀκτακόσιοι]	[eight hundred]	τεσσαρεσκαιδέκατος	fourteenth
[ἐνακόσιοι]	[nine hundred]	πεντεκαιδέκατος	fifteenth
χίλιοι, -αι, -α	one thousand	**Adverbials**	
δισχίλιοι, -αι, -α	two thousand	ἅπαξ	once
τρισχίλιοι, -αι, -α	three thousand	δίς	twice
τετρακισχίλιοι (-αι,-α)	four thousand	τρίς	three times
πεντακισχίλιοι (-αι,-α)	five thousand	πεντάκις	five times
ἑπτακισχίλιοι (-αι,-α)	seven thousand	ἑπτάκις	seven times
μύριοι, -αι, -α	ten thousand	ἑβδομηκοντάκις	seventy times

Numerals

Greek numbers are easy to learn: they have been part of vocabulary and their formation is repetitive in nature (☺). Bracketed vocabulary does not occur in the New Testament but shows patterns. Cardinals are the "counting" numbers ("one," "two," "three," etc.). Ordinals are the "ordering" numbers ("first," "second," etc.).

Cardinal Numerals. Only the first four are declined, and those above two hundred. The formulation is logical.

One to Four. The number one is only singular. The numbers two, three, and four are only plural. The number one shows third declension singular in masculine and neuter, first declension singular in feminine. The number two winds up in only two case forms, and those used for all genders. The number three is similar to ἱερεύς in the masculine/feminine plural and σῶμα in the neuter plural. The number four is similar to σωτήρ in the masculine/feminine plural and σῶμα in the neuter plural.

Table 17.1 Numerals—One (Third-First-Third Declension)

εἷς		μία		ἕν	
Masculine		**Feminine**		**Neuter**	
Singular	*Plural*	*Singular*	*Plural*	*Singular*	*Plural*
εἷς	-------	μία	-------	ἕν	-------
ἑνός	-------	μιᾶς	-------	ἑνός	-------
ἑνί	-------	μιᾷ	-------	ἑνί	-------
ἕνα	-------	μίαν	-------	ἕν	-------

Table 17.2 Numerals—Two (Third Declension)

δύο		δύο		δύο	
Masculine		**Feminine**		**Neuter**	
Singular	*Plural*	*Singular*	*Plural*	*Singular*	*Plural*
-------	δύο	-------	δύο	-------	δύο
-------	δύο	-------	δύο	-------	δύο
-------	δυσί	-------	δυσί	-------	δυσί
-------	δύο	-------	δύο	-------	δύο

Table 17.3 Numerals—Three (Third Declension)

τρεῖς		τρεῖς		τρία	
Masculine		**Feminine**		**Neuter**	
Singular	*Plural*	*Singular*	*Plural*	*Singular*	*Plural*
-------	τρεῖς	-------	τρεῖς	-------	τρία
-------	τριῶν	-------	τριῶν	-------	τριῶν
-------	τρισί	-------	τρισί	-------	τρισί
-------	τρεῖς	-------	τρεῖς	-------	τρία

Table 17.4 Numerals—Four (Third Declension)

τέσσαρες Masculine		τέσσαρες Feminine		τέσσαρα Neuter	
Singular	*Plural*	*Singular*	*Plural*	*Singular*	*Plural*
-------	τέσσαρες	-------	τέσσαρες	-------	τέσσαρα
-------	τεσσάρων	-------	τεσσάρων	-------	τεσσάρων
-------	τέσσαρσι	-------	τέσσαρσι	-------	τέσσαρσι
-------	τέσσαρας	-------	τέσσαρας	-------	τέσσαρα

Between Ten and Twenty. The base unit is δέκα. Formulations add to the base. The added numeral can be a prefix, as in ἕνδεκα, or a suffix, as in δεκατρεῖς, or a more pedantic method of combining the units with καί, as in ἑπτά καὶ δέκα. Forms were not fixed by any means. One might encounter δεκαοκτώ or δέκα καὶ ὀκτώ.[1]

Between Twenty and One Hundred. Compound numbers above twenty are formed in similar, minor variations: (1) placing the smaller numeral first and joining the ten interval with καί, as in δύο καὶ εἴκοσι = "twenty-two," (2) placing the ten interval first and joining the smaller number with καί, as in εἴκοσι καὶ δύο, or (3) placing the ten interval first and the smaller number second without καί, as in εἴκοσι δύο.

Over One Hundred. Numbers composed of multiple units over one hundred are played out in Greek units exactly as you would speak them in English. The number two hundred—and each hundred interval above—is declined on the δίκαιος, -α, -ov adjective pattern. Again, the declension is plural only. Observe the following:

(1) ἑκατὸν εἴκοσι = "one hundred twenty" (Acts 1:15)
(2) διακόσιαι ἑβδομήκοντα ἕξ = "two hundred seventy-six" (Acts 27:37)
(3) τετρακοσίιος καὶ πεντήκοντα = "four hundred and fifty" (Acts 13:20)
(4) ἑξακόσιοι ἑξήκοντα ἕξ = "six hundred sixty-six" (Rev. 13:18)
(5) χιλίας διακοσίας ἑξήκοντα = "one thousand two hundred sixty (Rev. 11:3)
(6) χιλιάδες ἑπτά = "seven thousand" (Rev. 11:13)
(7) δώδεκα χιλιάδες = "twelve thousand" (Rev. 7:5)
(8) ἑκατὸν τεσσεράκοντα τέσσαρες χιλιάδες = "one hundred forty-four thousand" (Rev. 7:4)

---

[1]Compare the two variations in Luke 13:4, 11 and 13:16.

Table 17.5 Numerals—200 (διακόσιοι) and intervals (like δίκαιος)

Masculine		Feminine		Neuter	
Singular	*Plural*	*Singular*	*Plural*	*Singular*	*Plural*
-------	διακόσιοι	-------	διακόσιαι	-------	διακόσια
-------	διακοσίων	-------	διακοσίων	-------	διακοσίων
-------	διακοσίοις	-------	διακοσίαις	-------	διακοσίοις
-------	διακοσίους	-------	διακοσίας	-------	διακόσια

Ordinal Numerals. Ordinals follow the pattern of ἀγαθός, -η, -ον, except for δεύτερος. This stem ends in -ρ, so follows that of the adjective δίκαιος, -α, -ον (feminine in -α). So, for example, we have the alternate forms illustrated in κἂν ἐν τῇ **δευτέρᾳ** κἂν ἐν τῇ **τρίτῃ** φυλακῇ ἔλθῃ = "and whether he should come in the **second** or even in the **third** watch" (Luke 12:38). Finally, the articular ordinal grammatically functions as an adjectival substantive. Thus, we have ἐγώ εἰμι ὁ **πρῶτος** καὶ ὁ ἔσχατος = "I am **the first** and the last" (Rev. 1:17).

Table 17.6 Numerals—Ordinals (all as ἀγαθός, except δεύτερος as δίκαιος)

Masculine		Feminine		Neuter	
Singular	*Plural*	*Singular*	*Plural*	*Singular*	*Plural*
πρῶτος	πρῶτοι	πρώτη	πρῶται	πρῶτον	πρῶτα
πρώτου	πρώτων	πρώτης	πρώτων	πρώτου	πρώτων
πρώτῳ	πρώτοις	πρώτῃ	πρώταις	πρώτῳ	πρώτοις
πρῶτον	πρώτους	πρώτην	πρώτας	πρῶτον	πρῶτα

Adverbials. Terms such as "once," "twice," etc. (see vocabulary) are adverbs, hence called *adverbials*. As adverbs, they are not declined. Thus, πρὶν ἢ **δὶς** ἀλέκτορα φωνῆσαι **τρίς** με ἀπαρνήσῃ = "before the rooster crows **twice**, you will deny me **three times**" (Mark 14:30). The distinction between adverbials ("twice") and ordinals ("second") is that adverbials always will be diagrammed underneath the verb ("how many times?"). In distinction, ordinals are adjectives. They either will be placed as a substantive or as a modifier underneath a substantive.

Finally, recognize that the idea "first" is special in and of itself, having many nuances, including priority, rank, status, and so forth. So, in addition to just counting numbers, we encounter the term πρῶτον used as an adverb (not declined) with the varied meanings "first," "in the first place," "above all else," "earlier," "to begin with" and so on. So, for example, we have ζητεῖτε δὲ **πρῶτον** τὴν βασιλείαν [τοῦ θεοῦ] καὶ τὴν δικαιοσύνην αὐτοῦ = "But **above all else**, seek the kingdom and His righteousness" (Matt. 6:33). Again, **πρῶτον** λέγετε, Εἰρήνη τῷ οἴκῳ τούτῳ = "**first** say, 'Peace to this house!'" (Luke 10:5). The adverb πρώτως, "for the first time," is found only at Acts 11:26, χρηματίσαι τε **πρώτως** ἐν Ἀντιοχείᾳ τοὺς μαθητὰς Χριστιανούς = "the disciples **first** were called Christians in Antioch."

Nominative Case

Nominative Absolute. Not all nominatives are subject or predicate. The *nominative absolute* is a nominative with no inherent grammatical relationship to the rest of the sentence. Several scenarios generate this possibility.

Broken Construction. Grammatical change marks a sudden shift. A second nominative occurs, but another nominative in fact is subject of the verb. This second nominative is in apposition to the subject or to some other word. For example: ἐγώ εἰμι, **ὁ λαλῶν** σοι = "I am (he), **the one speaking** to you" (John 4:26).

Letter Openings. The salutation identifies the sender. The name is inscribed using the nominative case, but further self-description might be added. This addition is another nominative (or phrase) in apposition to the sender's name. For example: Παῦλος **δοῦλος** = "Paul, **a servant**" (Rom. 1:1).

Book Titles. This is a publishing form in the first century. The book title is the first word and nominative. For example: Ἀποκάλυψις Ἰωάννου = "**The Revelation** of John" (Rev. 1:1).

Exclamations. Some interjection or exclamation will incorporate a nominative. For example: ἴδε ποταποὶ **λίθοι** καὶ ποταπαὶ **οἰκοδομαί** = "Behold, what manner of **stones** and what wonderful **buildings**!" (Mark 13:1).

Nominative of Appellation. A proper noun is given as nominative, regardless of grammatical use. Thus, ὑμεῖς φωνεῖτέ με **Ὁ διδάσκαλος** καὶ **Ὁ κύριος** = "you call me Teacher and Lord" (John 13:13). One might expect a double accusative.

Genitive Case

The genitive case was growing in significance, eventually swallowing up other functions.[2] Two important uses of the genitive case in the New Testament are the *objective* and *subjective* genitive. The ambiguity of the preposition "of" is the issue.

---

[2]For example, by Byzantine times, the dative case was almost, if not entirely, defunct.

When one says, "the love of God," what is meant? Does this phrase mean the love God has for an individual (subjective genitive), or the love an individual has for God (objective genitive)? These are two different realities!

The key to spotting a subjective or objective genitive is not morphology. The key is a *noun of action*, a noun which inherently carries a verbal idea. Certain nouns of action are easy to spot, because a cognate verb has the same root. Thus, the verb ἀγαπάω has the cognate noun ἀγάπη, the verb φοβέομαι the cognate noun φόβος, and so forth. In distinction, some nouns suggest no verbal idea, as in ἰχθύς or θάλασσα. Other nouns of action tip themselves off by the two endings -μος or -σις (e.g., ἔρημος, κρίσις), for which an associated verb is lurking nearby (ἐρημόομαι and κρίνω)—though this is not an infallible indication. Both subjective and objective genitives *require* that the noun modified be a noun of action.

Subjective Genitive. The subjective genitive *generates* the quality of the noun of action modified. Thus, for example, when Paul wrote τίς ἡμᾶς χωρίσει ἀπὸ τῆς ἀγάπης **τοῦ Χριστοῦ**; ("What will separate us from the love **of Christ**?" Rom. 8:35), he meant the love Christ has for believers. This is the subjective genitive use. That is, the genitive Χριστοῦ is a *subjective* genitive, understood as generating the quality of the modified noun of action, ἀγάπης.

To test for a subjective genitive, one could rewrite the modified noun of action as a verb and make the genitive noun subject of that verb.[3] So, in Rom. 8:35, one could take the noun of action modified (ἀγάπης), rewrite this noun as the corresponding verb (ἀγαπᾷ) and make the genitive noun Χριστοῦ subject of that verb, i.e., Χριστός ἀγαπᾷ ἡμᾶς. This idea is the sense of Paul's statement. The love referenced in τῆς ἀγάπης τοῦ Χριστοῦ is the love Christ has for believers.

Objective Genitive. The objective genitive *receives* the verbal idea of the noun of action modified. Thus, for example, in the expression διὰ τὸν φόβον **τῶν Ἰουδαίων** ("because of fear **of the Jews**," John 7:13), the genitive Ἰουδαίων is an *objective* genitive, understood as receiving the verbal idea of the modified noun of action, φόβον. No one was willing to speak openly about Jesus, for the people feared the Jewish leaders, who were known to oppose Jesus.

A decision as to whether one has a subjective or objective genitive is subjective. The interpreter must decide each case on the basis of context and exegesis. The choice is not always clear. Study 1 John 2:5, ἀληθῶς ἐν τούτῳ ἡ ἀγάπη τοῦ θεοῦ τετελείωται = "truly in this person the

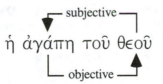

love **of God** has been perfected." Is this subjective or objective genitive?

---

[3]This, in fact, is the idea behind the term "subjective" genitive.

Accusative Case

Do not get stuck in a rut with the idea of direct object for the accusative. Direct object is one use—a major one—but only *one*. Accusative is the case of *extension*.

Adverbial Accusative. The accusative can extend ideas of measure or manner to the verbal idea. A few examples are given here.

Adverbial of Measure. The accusative adds *extent in time* or *extent in space* to refine the precision of the expressed verbal action. Used this way, the accusative inherently answers such questions as "how far?" (in distance) or "how long?" (in time). Use of ὡς or a prepositional phrase can set up this added dimension. The preposition εἰς is king in this regard, but others are used too. The phrases εἰς τὸν αἰῶνα = "forever" or εἰς τοὺς αἰῶνας τῶν αἰώνων = "forever and ever" occur numerous times, used as adverbial of measure. Observe:

(1) ἐληλακότες οὖν **ὡς σταδίους** εἴκοσι πέντε ἢ τριάκοντα = "When they had rowed, therefore, **about** twenty-five or thirty **stadia**" (John 6:19)[4]

(2) ὅς ἐστιν ἐν δεξιᾷ [τοῦ] θεοῦ, πορευθεὶς **εἰς οὐρανόν** = "who is at the right hand of God, having gone **unto heaven**" (1 Pet. 3:22)

(3) Ἕνεκεν σοῦ θανατούμεθα **ὅλην τὴν ἡμέραν** = "For your sake we are being killed **all day long**" (Rom. 8:36)

(4) **τριετίαν νύκτα καὶ ἡμέραν** οὐκ ἐπαυσάμην μετὰ δακρύων νουθετῶν ἕνα ἕκαστον = "**night and day for three years** I did not cease to admonish each one with tears" (Acts 20:31)

Adverbial of Manner. The accusative adds *how* the action takes place. The preposition would be εἰς. Observe:

(1) ὅτι οὐκ **εἰς κενὸν** ἔδραμον = "that I had not run **in vain**" (Phil. 2:16)

(2) ἔφθασεν δὲ ἐπ' αὐτοὺς ἡ ὀργὴ **εἰς τέλος** = "but the wrath has fallen upon them **completely**" (1 Thess. 2:16)

Purpose, Result, Cause. The accusative adds *purpose*, *result*, or *cause* related to the action of the verb. If with a preposition, purpose will have εἰς or πρός, result will have εἰς (always), and cause will have εἰς or διά. Observe:

(1) δικαιοσύνη γὰρ θεοῦ ἐν αὐτῷ ἀποκαλύπτεται ἐκ πίστεως **εἰς πίστιν** = "For in it the righteousness of God is being revealed from faith **for the purpose of faith**" (Rom. 1:17, purpose; the meaning is debated)

(2) οὐ γὰρ ἐλάβετε πνεῦμα δουλείας πάλιν **εἰς φόβον** = "for we have not received a spirit of slavery **resulting in fear**" again" (Rom. 8:15, result)

---

[4] About three or four miles, if a stadion was about two hundred yards (Josephus).

(3) εἰ δὲ Χριστὸς ἐν ὑμῖν, τὸ μὲν σῶμα νεκρὸν **διὰ ἁμαρτίαν**, τὸ δὲ πνεῦμα ζωὴ **διὰ δικαιοσύνην** = "But if Christ is in you, then the body is dead **because of sin**, but the spirit is alive **because of righteousness**" (Rom. 8:10, cause)

Predicate Accusative. The use of εἰς and the accusative following a form of εἰμί is the *predicate accusative*. However, the verb εἰμί is not always explicit.

(1) ὥστε αἱ γλῶσσαι **εἰς σημεῖόν** εἰσιν = "so then tongues are **a sign**" (1 Cor. 14:22)

(2) καὶ ἔσομαι αὐτοῖς **εἰς θεὸν** καὶ αὐτοὶ ἔσονταί μοι **εἰς λαόν** = "I will be **their God** and they will be **my people**" (Heb. 8:10)

Definite Article

The form and function of the Greek definite article have been treated in Lessons 4 and 5. Originally, the article served as a demonstrative pronoun. This definite article is quite dynamic, so here are some other uses. Experience over time helps in determining these uses, whose recognition is driven by context.

Article as Substantive. The Greek article can function as a substantive. The article even shows up sometimes by itself and related to a verb. Gender is important for declaring how to construe this substantive idea. Study the following.

Personal Pronoun. At times the definite article in the nominative can refer to a person or persons previously mentioned. In such cases, "he," "she," or "they" can be used. Observe:

(1) οἱ δὲ πρὸς αὐτὴν εἶπαν, Μαίνῃ. ἡ δὲ διϊσχυρίζετο οὕτως ἔχειν. οἱ δὲ ἔλεγον, Ὁ ἄγγελός ἐστιν αὐτοῦ = "But **they** said to her, 'You are crazy.' But **she** kept on asserting the fact. So **they** began saying 'It is his angel.'" (Acts 12:15, Rhoda and the disciples arguing Peter's miraculous release)

(2) αἱ δὲ προσελθοῦσαι ἐκράτησαν αὐτοῦ τοὺς πόδας = "and **they** came up and seized his feet" (Matt. 28:9, the women at the tomb)

Demonstrative Pronoun. The original function surfaces here. Translation can use "this," "that," if singular, or "these," those," if plural. Thus:

(1) εἰ δέ τις οὐχ ὑπακούει τῷ λόγῳ ἡμῶν διὰ **τῆς** ἐπιστολῆς = "If anyone is not obedient to our instruction through **this** letter" (2 Thess. 3:14)

(2) ὁ δὲ Πέτρος καὶ **οἱ** σὺν αὐτῷ = "Now Peter and **those** with him" (Luke 9:32)

(3) αἱ δὲ οὖσαι ὑπὸ θεοῦ τεταγμέναι εἰσίν = "and **those** [authorities] which exist are established by God" (Rom. 13:1)

(4) καὶ λάμπει πᾶσιν **τοῖς** ἐν τῇ οἰκίᾳ = "and it gives light to all **those** in the house" (Matt. 5:15)

Alternative Pronoun. A literary device using the μέν . . . δέ construction places definite articles before each element as alternative pronouns. These articles are translated "one . . . another" if singular, or "some . . . others" if plural. So:

(1) καὶ **οἱ** μὲν ἐπείθοντο τοῖς λεγομένοις, **οἱ** δὲ ἠπίστουν = "and while **some** were persuaded by the things being spoken, **others** were unbelieving" (Acts 28:24, equivocal Jewish response to Paul in Rome)

(2) καὶ αὐτὸς ἔδωκεν **τοὺς** μὲν ἀποστόλους, **τοὺς** δὲ προφήτας, **τοὺς** δὲ εὐαγγελιστάς, **τοὺς** δὲ ποιμένας καὶ διδασκάλους = "and He Himself gave **some** apostles, **others** prophets, **others** evangelists, **others** pastors and teachers (Eph. 4:11)

Possessive Pronoun. Possession is so obvious as to obviate the need for the possessive pronoun. The article alone is sufficient. Thus:

(1) Οἱ ἄνδρες, ἀγαπᾶτε **τὰς** γυναῖκας = "Husbands, love **your** wives." (Eph. 5:25)

(2) Κύριε, μὴ τοὺς πόδας μου μόνον ἀλλὰ καὶ **τὰς** χεῖρας καὶ **τὴν** κεφαλήν = "Lord, not my feet only but also **my** hands and **my** head" (John 7:44)

Relative Pronoun. An article—or second repeating article—in a modifying phrase functions as a relative pronoun. This use is common. For example:

(1) ὅτι οὐκ ἐστὲ ἐκ τῶν προβάτων **τῶν** ἐμῶν = "because you are not from the sheep **which** are mine" (John 10:26)

(2) ταῖς ἐκκλησίαις τῆς Ἰουδαίας **ταῖς** ἐν Χριστῷ = "to the churches of Judea **which** are in Christ" (Gal. 1:22)

(3) ἐν πίστει **τῇ** ἐν Χριστῷ Ἰησοῦ = "in the faith **which** is in Christ Jesus" (1 Tim. 3:13)

Noun. The article replaces some noun idea within the context of the verbal expression. The neuter plural frequently is used this way. As examples:

(1) **τὰ** ἄνω φρονεῖτε, μὴ **τὰ** ἐπὶ τῆς γῆς = "Concentrate on the **things** above, not the **things** on earth" (Col. 3:2)

(2) Ἐν δὲ **τοῖς** περὶ τὸν τόπον ἐκεῖνον = "Now in the **neighborhood** of that place" (Acts 28:7, context crucial for making sense of the article)

Clarifying Καί. Article position clarifies the relationship of nouns of personal description of the same case conjoined by καί. The nouns are correlated, but their relationships have two possibilities: (1) each noun is a separate person or distinctive aspect, or (2) all nouns are descriptive of, or related to, aspects of the same person. A simple grammatical principle helps spell out the relationship indicated by καί.[5]

---

[5]Called the Granville Sharp Rule, or "Sharp's Rule," first enunciated in 1798 (Granville Sharp, *Remarks on the Uses of the Definitive Article in the Greek Text of the New Testament,* Durham: L. Pennington, 1798, 1802, pp. xxxv–xxxvi). Sharp formulated six rules, but in only one configuration with καί do the nouns apply to the same person, and that only if the first noun alone is articular.

Repeated articles (distinctive aspects). If all nouns before and after the καί are articular, then each noun functions as a separate entity or distinctive aspect (or, extended by symmetry, if *all* nouns constructed with καί are anarthrous). Observe:

(1) ἀπὸ **τῆς** ἐκκλησίας **καὶ τῶν** ἀποστόλων **καὶ τῶν** πρεσβυτέρων = "by **the** church **and the** apostles **and the** elders" (Acts 15:4, three separate groups presented, each with a distinct involvement in the deliberations)

(2) οὗτος καὶ **τὸν** πατέρα **καὶ τὸν** υἱὸν ἔχει = "this one has both **the** Father **and the** Son" (2 John 9, mutual yet distinct operations of Father and Son)

(3) ὑμεῖς γάρ ἐστε ἡ δόξα ἡμῶν **καὶ** ἡ χαρά. = "For <u>you</u> are our glory **and** joy" (1 Thess. 2:20, glory as eschatological aspect, joy as present aspect)

Single article (common aspect). The article used with only the first noun in a καί construction means that all nouns function corporately; together they describe the same person or personal entity. So, for example:

(1) ἀπὸ **τῶν** πρεσβυτέρων **καὶ** ἀρχιερέων **καὶ** γραμματέων = "by **the** elders **and** chief priests **and** scribes" (Luke 9:22, various segments of Jewish leadership conceived together in a common bond of opposition, all acting in concert seeking Jesus' death)

(2) **τοῦ** θεοῦ ἡμῶν **καὶ** σωτῆρος Ἰησοῦ Χριστοῦ = "of our God **and** Savior, Jesus Christ" (2 Pet. 1:1; a famous example, grammar leaving no doubt Jesus is considered God)[6]

Use of Negatives

Greek has two negatives, οὐ and μή. The indicative mood (reality) requires the stronger οὐ for negation. The weaker μή commonly is used for other moods (contingency) to express qualified negation. While μή is the standard form in moods we have yet to cover, two special uses of μή are outlined here.

Emphatic οὐ μή. The double negative is not allowed in English. However, in Greek, the double-barreled οὐ μή represents emphatic negation. This can be expressed variously in English; e.g., "not," "never," "in no way," etc. Observe:

(1) καὶ **οὐ μὴ** ἀπόλωνται εἰς τὸν αἰῶνα = "and they shall **never** perish" (John 10:28, "never" combining οὐ μὴ with the idea εἰς τὸν αἰῶνα)

(2) **οὐ μὴ** φθάσωμεν τοὺς κοιμηθέντας = "**in no way** shall we go before those who have fallen asleep" (1 Thess. 4:15)

(3) καὶ τῶν ἁμαρτιῶν αὐτῶν **οὐ μὴ** μνησθῶ ἔτι = "and I will **not** remember their sins any longer" (Heb. 8:12)

---

[6]Likewise 2 Pet. 2:20 and Tit. 2:13. What about constructions in which καί is absent? It turns out, *any* construction minus καί implies the same person or aspect under Sharp's rules. See Glossary.

(4) καὶ ὁ πιστεύων ἐπ᾽ αὐτῷ **οὐ μὴ** καταισχυνθῇ = "and the one who believes in Him shall **never** be put to shame" (1 Pet. 2:6)

Indicative with Μή. The μή form infrequently can be used with the indicative. Two occasions involve one previously mentioned and the use with questions.

Second Class Conditions. One use has been covered already. For conditional sentences concerning present time, a second class *protasis* stated in the *negative* uses μή. One example given was εἰ **μὴ** ἦν οὗτος παρὰ θεοῦ = "if this man were **not** from God" (John 9:33). The former blind man is arguing with the Jews about the current realities of his experience of healing at the hands of Jesus.

Expected Answers. In English, one can indicate the answer expected by including "do you?" or "will you?" at the end, with or without a negation. (without negation expects a "yes"; negation expects a "no"; i.e., "You will go, won't you?" versus "You would not go, would you?"). In a similar way, the two negative forms in Greek (οὐ, μή) can be used to indicate the type of answer a speaker expects. An *affirmative* answer is anticipated by οὐ (οὐκ, οὐχ, οὐχι) with the indicative mood. A *negative* answer is expected by μή and the indicative. Observe:

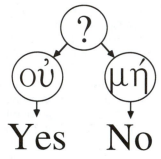

(1) **Οὐκ** εἰμὶ ἐλεύθερος; **οὐκ** εἰμὶ ἀπόστολος; **οὐχὶ** Ἰησοῦν τὸν κύριον ἡμῶν ἑώρακα; **οὐ** τὸ ἔργον μου ὑμεῖς ἐστε ἐν κυρίῳ; = "Am I **not** free? Am I **not** an apostle? Have I **not** seen Jesus our Lord? Are you **not** my work in the Lord?" (1 Cor. 9:1; "Why, yes, most certainly, Paul!")

(2) **μὴ** τῶν βοῶν μέλει τῷ θεῷ; = "God is **not** concerned about oxen, is He?" (1 Cor. 9:9; "No! of course not. Not like He is for humans.")

More Uses of Καί

The flexibility required for translating δέ, treated in Lesson 7, also applies to the coordinating conjunction καί. Here are some additional options for translating καί:

(1) "also" (*adjunctive* use): ὡς **καὶ** ἡμεῖς ἀφήκαμεν τοῖς ὀφειλέταις ἡμῶν = "as we **also** have forgiven our debtors" (Matt. 6:12)

(2) "even" (*ascensive* use): **καὶ** γὰρ τὰ κυνάρια ἐσθίει ἀπὸ τῶν ψιχίων = "Yet **even** the dogs eat from the crumbs" (Matt. 15:27)

(3) "and yet" (*mild adversative*): **καὶ** ἡδέως αὐτοῦ ἤκουεν = "**and yet** he liked to listen to him" (Mark 6:20)

(4) "but" (*adversative*): **καὶ** ἐφοβήθησαν τὸν λαόν = "**but** they feared the people" (Luke 20:19)

Diagramming

A **nominative absolute** is independent. Indicate this independence with a separate base line for the absolute phrase, enclosed within parentheses and placed near the other nominative. More particularly, nominatives can be set in **apposition**, adding more information about another nominative. Nominatives in apposition are indicated by a separate base line followed by an equal sign (=) pointing to the other nominative. (Note: apposition is *not* restricted to nominatives. Apposition can occur with *any* substantive, reflecting that substantive's case, taking a separate base line.)[7]

Table 17.7 Diagramming Nominative Absolutes and Apposition

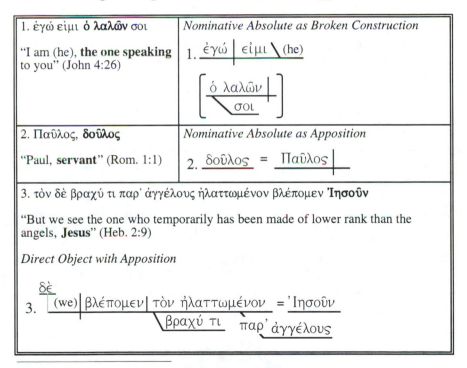

1. ἐγώ εἰμι **ὁ λαλῶν** σοι "I am (he), **the one speaking** to you" (John 4:26)	*Nominative Absolute as Broken Construction*
2. Παῦλος, **δοῦλος** "Paul, **servant**" (Rom. 1:1)	*Nominative Absolute as Apposition*
3. τὸν δὲ βραχύ τι παρ' ἀγγέλους ἠλαττωμένον βλέπομεν **Ἰησοῦν** "But we see the one who temporarily has been made of lower rank than the angels, **Jesus**" (Heb. 2:9) *Direct Object with Apposition*	

---

[7]Also, at the risk of redundancy, we might add that the *nominative of appellation* simply would take the position of the function of that nominative in the sentence (direct object, etc.).

What To Learn—LESSON 17 (ἑπτά καὶ δέκα)

Beginning

☐ 1. The four declined cardinal numerals: εἷς, δύο, τρεῖς, τέσσαρες

☐ 2. Formulation and use of Greek *cardinals*, including the paradigm for διακόσιοι and intervals

☐ 3. Formulation and use of Greek *ordinals*, including the paradigm for πρῶτος

☐ 4. Meaning and use of *adverbials* and the special adverbial use of πρῶτον

☐ 5. Identifying a *nominative absolute* and significance for translation

☐ 6. The various uses of the definite article as a substantive and how to translate

☐ 7. The significance of οὐ μή, μή as the negative in second class conditions, and distinguishing the expected answers to rhetorical questions

☐ 8. Learn *interrogative, indefinite, indefinite relative,* and *negative* pronouns; carefully review applicable material in Lesson 11, including diagramming

☐ 9. Diagramming nominative absolutes and other appositional constructions

☐ 10. Vocabulary words

Advanced

☐ 11. Definition of a *noun of action* and the significance for determining and distinguishing *subjective* and *objective* genitives

☐ 12. Identifying accusatives: *adverbial accusative of measure* and the functions of extent in time or space; *adverbial accusative of manner*; accusative of *purpose, result,* and *cause*; *predicate accusative*

☐ 13. The two basic principles focusing on article position for clarifying the significance of nouns joined by καί (Granville Sharp Rule)

☐ 14. Understanding and developing additional uses of καί

LESSON 18 (δεκαοκτώ)
Future and Liquid Future

λύσω, μενῶ

As a primary tense, the future takes primary endings. The stem adds a suffix, creating the second principal part. The future distinguishes stems, using a different suffix depending on stem type. These special stems are the liquid futures.

Vocabulary 18

Correlative Pronouns

τοσοῦτος, -αύτη, -οῦτον, so much	
οἷος, -α, -ον	as
ὅσος, -η, -ον	as much as

Interrogative Pronouns

ποῖος, -α, -ον	what type?
πόσος, -η, -ον	how much?

Liquid Verbs

αἴρω	I take up, take away
ἀποκτείνω	I kill
ἐγείρω	I raise, raise up
κρίνω	I judge, decide
μένω	I remain

Hidden Stems

ἀγγέλλω	I tell, announce
βάλλω	I throw

πράσσω	I do, practice
δοξάζω	I glorify, honor
ἐγγίζω	I draw near
ἐλπίζω	I hope
κράζω	I shout, cry out

Other Verbs

ἔσομαι	I shall be
θέλω (not liq. fut.)	I wish, desire
καταβαίνω	I go down
μέλλω (not liq. fut.)	I am about to
πίνω (irregular)	I drink
πίπτω (irregular)	I fall
φέρω (irregular)	I bring, carry
φεύγω	I flee, run away
χαίρω (not liq. fut.)	I rejoice

209

Analysis

Principal parts involve how tense stems are fabricated to form the different tenses. We have finished the first principal part—the present and imperfect tenses. The imperfect tense belongs to the first principal part because the imperfect tense stem clones the present stem. Both are durative as a result.

The second principal part involves only one tense, the future. The stem of the future tense employs a suffix on the future stem. This changed stem qualifies as a separate principal part. However, the future tense aspect primarily is punctiliar. (On *some* occasions, context declares that the future is meant with durative aspect.)

The future tense has two formation distinctions. The first is a distinction of voice. The future tense is a primary tense.

Table 18.1 Principal Parts: Tenses and Voices

Principal Parts	Tenses	Voices		
First Principal Part	Present	active	middle	passive
	Imperfect	active	middle	passive
Second Principal Part	Future	active	middle	
Third Principal Part	First Aorist	active	middle	
	Second Aorist	active	middle	
Fourth Principal Part	Perfect	active		
	Future Perfect	active		
	Pluperfect	active		
Fifth Principal Part	Perfect		middle	passive
	Future Perfect		middle	passive
	Pluperfect		middle	passive
Sixth Principal Part	First Aorist			passive
	First Future			passive
	Second Aorist			passive
	Second Future			passive

Table 18.2 Primary and Secondary Tenses

Kind of Action	Time of Action (Indicative Mood)		
	Secondary Tenses *(secondary endings)*	Primary Tenses *(primary endings)*	
	Past	Present	Future
durative	Imperfect	Present	---------
undefined ●	Aorist	---------	Future
perfective - - -▶	Pluperfect	Perfect	Future Perfect

Primary tenses take primary endings. Good news! No new endings to learn for future tense. You already have mastered all four sets for the entire indicative mood. However, note that the second principal part deals with only two voices, active and middle. Why? Because the future *passive* voice is built on *another stem*. So the future passive cannot be covered until that stem structure is introduced. So, the second principal part is future tense, but only active and middle voice.

Second, the future tense has more than one tense suffix because the future tense distinguishes stems. Future stems ending in a liquid consonant (-λ, -μ, -ν, -ρ) take a *different* suffix than the typical future suffix. This different suffix generates some predictable reactions. Such a verb is a *liquid verb*, and creates a secondary future form called the *liquid future*.

Formation

Tense Stem. We start with the tense stem. The future tense stem of λύω is λυ-:

$$\lambda \acute{\upsilon} \cancel{\omega} = \lambda \upsilon \text{-}$$

Tense Suffix. The future adds a -σ suffix to the future stem, altering the stem in the process and creating the second principal part. The main feature of future tense is this suffix, called the *tense suffix*, attached to the end of the tense stem to indicate this future component to the verbal action. For λυ-, we have λυσ-:

$$\lambda \upsilon + \sigma = \lambda \upsilon \sigma \text{-}$$

stem + tense suffix

Stops. Many verbs show a -σ suffix for the future as does λύω, but not stems ending in a stop. A -σ suffix on a stop creates predictable volatilization according to the table presented for third declension nouns in Lesson 14, repeated below.

Table 18.3 Sigma Volatilization—Stops

Formation	Volatilization Pattern		
	stop consonant	simple sibilant	resultant sibilant
labials	π, β, φ	+ σ	= ψ
palatals	κ, γ, χ	+ σ	= ξ
dentals	τ, δ, θ	+ σ	= σ

Thus the future tense stem of ἔχω is ἑξ-, πέμπω is πεμψ-, πείθω ("I persuade") is πεισ-, and so forth. So a stop changes similar to this:

$$\pi \epsilon \mu \pi + \sigma = \pi \epsilon \mu \psi -$$

stem　　　　+　tense suffix

Liquids. Liquid verbs have stems ending in a liquid consonant (-λ, -μ, -ν, -ρ). The future tense suffix for many liquid verbs (especially nasals -μ, -ν) is -εσ, not -σ. With a different suffix, two predictable reactions occur.

Intervocalic Sigma. First of all, a σ between the two vowels ("intervocalic") is expelled. This situation occurs with liquid verbs because the thematic vowel is attached on the other side of the -εσ suffix. The σ now between two vowels (e.g., ε and o) consequently drops.

Vowel Contraction. The second liquid reaction is contraction of the two remaining vowels, the -ε remnant of the tense suffix and the thematic vowel. So, *the liquid future transforms into an -ε contract verb result.* A circumflex accent

> **Thematic (-ω) Verbs Special Stems**
> (Contracts and Liquids)
>
> **Contracts** ‖ **Liquids**
>
> ϵ, o, α ‖ λ, μ, ν, ρ
>
> Present System　Sigma Systems
>
> Present　Imperf.　Future　Aorist

divulges the contraction (see Table 7.5, discussion). *This liquid future looks exactly like a present tense except for this accent.* A liquid stem, then, can change like this:

$$\mu \epsilon \nu + \epsilon \cancel{\sigma} + o = \mu \epsilon \nu o \upsilon -$$

liquid stem + liquid suffix + thematic vowel

Exceptions. Some -λ, -ρ liquid stems form the future in -ησω (not -εσ suffix, but -σ and insert η).[1] Others also show minor stem vowel changes. These include θέλω (θελήσω), μέλλω (μελλήσω), βούλομαι (βουλήσομαι), γίνομαι (γενήσομαι), καταβαίνω (καταβήσομαι), and χαίρω (χαρήσομαι). With exceptions (μέλλω above), -λλ regularly acts as a liquid, taking the -εσ future suffix (see below).

---

[1] The irregular future of λέγω a notable exception: ἐρῶ, ἐρεῖς, ἐρεῖ, ἐροῦμεν, ἐρεῖτε, ἐροῦσιν.

Table 18.4 Hidden Stem Examples

Lexical	Verb Stem	Future Result
βαπτίζω	βαπτιδ-	βαπτισ-
κράζω	κραγ-	κραξ-
κηρύσσω	κηρυκ-	κηρυξ-
πράσσω	πραγ-	πραξ-
ταράσσω	ταραχ-	ταραξ-
ἀγγέλλω	ἀγγελ-	ἀγγελ-(ˆ)
γινώσκω	γνο-	γνωσ-

Hidden Stems. Lexical forms do not always reveal the tense stem (basis of the conjugation) by dropping the -ω. Verbs classes help to understand such "hidden stem" verbs. Not all classes are detailed here, but enough to give the student an idea of what appear to be inexplicable changes that, in fact, can be followed.

Double Sigma. These -σσ present stems in reality end in either -κ or -χ, or occasionally -γ. The consonantal iota added to create the present stem generates a characteristic resultant double sigma present stem. Examples include κηρύσσω (κηρυκ-, κηρύξω), ταράσσω (ταραχ-, ταράξω), and πράσσω (πραγ-, πράξω).

Zeta. The zeta is not part of the verb stem, but a result of creating the present tense stem with a consonantal iota added to a -δ or -γ verb stem. If the verb stem actually ends in -δ, the future suffix added to this -δ stem volatilizes as a dental (drops out, leaving only σ). Examples include βαπτίζω (βαπτιδ-, βαπτίσω), δοξάζω (δοξαδ-, δοξάσω), and σώζω (σωδ-, σώσω).

A zeta variation is the "Attic future." Some dental delta stems add the Attic future suffix -σε, not -σ. The dental delta falls out, then the intervocalic sigma; then the left over -ε contracts. The result is a "liquid" future look with a characteristic circumflex accent. E. g., ἐγγίζω (ἐγγιδσε-, ἐγγιῶ) and ἐλπίζω (ἐλπιδσε-, ἐλπιῶ).

If the verb stem actually ends in -γ, the future suffix added to this -γ stem volatilizes as a palatal (becoming ξ). Examples include κράζω (κραγ-, κράξω) and στηρίζω (στηριγ-, στηρίξω).[2]

---

[2]Some verbs show *both* -δ and -γ forms, as does ἁρπάζω, found as both ἁρπάσω *and* ἁρπάξω.

Double Lambda. These verb stems really end in a *single* lambda. Addition of a consonantal iota going to the present stem generates the double lambda present. This single lambda stem reacts as a true liquid future (adds the suffix -εσ), with a typical circumflex accent. Examples include ἀγγέλλω (ἀγγελ-, ἀγγελῶ), βάλλω (βαλ-, βαλῶ), and ἀποστέλλω (ἀποστελ-, ἀποστελῶ). An exception is μέλλω (μελλήσω).

Sigma Kappa. These verb stems have present tense stems ending in the combination -σκ (or -ισκ). In reality, the ending -σκ has been added to the stem on the way to the present tense. The hidden verb stem ends in either -κ or -χ, which before the -σ of the future suffix volatilizes predictably to -ξ. This is true of a verb such as διδάσκω. Other -σκ stems show individual variations of stem, such as -θαν, a liquid. (We are not covering every reaction here.) In any case, γινώσκω, a reduplicated stem in the present (γι-), really is the verb stem γνο- and a deponent future, γνώσομαι. Or, διδάσκω really is the stem διδακ-, whose future is διδάξω. Again, the verb εὑρίσκω really is the stem εὑρ-, a liquid, to which an added ε goes to the vowel η on the way to the future as εὑρήσω. As a last example, the compound ἀποθνήσκω is really a -θαν stem, which goes to a liquid deponent in the future as ἀποθανοῦμαι.

In summary, hidden stems change differently than expected. The result can be an "unexpected" letter ending the stem in the future. A double sigma present stem, whose real verb stem ends in either -κ, -χ, or -γ, will look similar to this:

$$\text{κηρυκ} + \sigma = \text{κηρυξ-}$$

stem   +   tense suffix

or a zeta stem, whose real verb stem ends in the dental -δ, will look like this:[3]

$$\text{σωδ} + \sigma = \text{σωσ-}$$

stem   +   future suffix

or, with an actual palatal verb stem in -γ, a zeta present stem can look like this:

$$\text{κραγ} + \sigma = \text{κραξ-}$$

stem   +   future suffix

---

[3]The presence of the iota subscript in forms of σῴζω varies in ancient sources. See p. 42, note 2.

A double lambda present stem in fact is a single lambda stem and a liquid future, as:

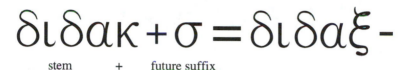

$$\beta\alpha\lambda + \epsilon\not{o} = \beta\alpha\lambda\text{-}(\widehat{})$$

stem   +   liquid future suffix   (epsilon contracts)

A kappa sigma stem in the present really is the simpler -κ verb stem, with future as:

$$\delta\iota\delta\alpha\kappa + \sigma = \delta\iota\delta\alpha\xi\text{-}$$

stem   +   future suffix

Irregular Stems. Some verbs are called "irregular." These verbs have stems that appear to be totally unpredictable from one principal part to the next. In fact, their history is a development borrowing entirely different stems altogether to form various principal parts. In practical terms, such "irregular" forms of the principal parts must be memorized as if individual vocabulary words in their own right—yet always connected to other verb forms. The table illustrates some examples.

Thematic Vowel-Pronominal Suffix. One then adds the thematic vowel and primary endings for active or middle voice. Vowel and ending already have interacted in some active forms, as the -ω ending of first singular, for example. As the final result, the form has this appearance:

Table 18.5 Irregular Verbs

Present	Future
ἔρχομαι	ἐλεύσομαι
λέγω	ἐρῶ
ὁράω	ὄψομαι
πίνω	πίομαι
πίπτω	πεσοῦμαι
φέρω	οἴσω

$$\lambda\upsilon\text{-}\sigma\text{-}o\text{-}\mu\epsilon\nu$$

stem+ tense suffix + thematic vowel + ending

A stop ends up like this:

$$πέμψομεν$$

A liquid stem has the intermediate stage, μενέομεν, which contracts to:

$$μενοῦμεν$$

Here, first observe carefully that the future suffix has been lost. This loss of the typical sign of the future, -σ, can become tricky for locating a verb. Second, how *does* one distinguish from the present active form? Well, often, only your "accenter" knows for sure. Spelling distinctions can be drawn in *some* forms, as first plural, (μένομεν vs. μενοῦμεν) but not in others, save for accent alone. Compare μένω and μενῶ, or μένεις and μενεῖς, and so forth.

$$μένω, \quad μενῶ$$

present tense   future tense

Finally, hidden stems show up in many variations. As just one example, the double sigma present stem in the future ends up as:

$$κηρύξομεν$$

Paradigms. Paradigms summarizing the above discussion are now presented. Observe the use of primary endings with this primary tense. The main features with which to become acquainted in order to recognize the future tense are: (1) a typical -σ suffix, or (2) sigma volatilization,[4] or (3) liquid reactions.

---

[4]With stop stems regularly, but also revealing hidden stems.

Table 18.6 Future Active Indicative—λύω (regular stem)

Number	Person	Form	Translation
Singular	1st	λύσω	"I shall loose"
	2nd	λύσεις	"you will loose"
	3rd	λύσει	"he (she, it) will loose"
Plural	1st	λύσομεν	"we will loose"
	2nd	λύσετε	"you will loose"
	3rd	λύσουσιν	"they will loose"

Table 18.7 Future Active Indicative—πέμπω (stop)

Number	Person	Form	Translation
Singular	1st	πέμψω	"I shall send"
	2nd	πέμψεις	"you will send"
	3rd	πέμψει	"he (she, it) will send"
Plural	1st	πέμψομεν	"we will send"
	2nd	πέμψετε	"you will send"
	3rd	πέμψουσιν	"they will send"

Table 18.8 Future Active Indicative—μένω (liquid)

Number	Person	Form	Translation
Singular	1st	μενῶ	"I shall remain"
	2nd	μενεῖς	"you will remain"
	3rd	μενεῖ	"he (she, it) will remain"
Plural	1st	μενοῦμεν	"we will remain"
	2nd	μενεῖτε	"you will remain"
	3rd	μενοῦσιν	"they will remain"

Table 18.9 Future Active Indicative—κηρύσσω (hidden stem)

Number	Person	Form	Translation
Singular	1st	κηρύξω	"I shall preach"
	2nd	κηρύξεις	"you will preach"
	3rd	κηρύξει	"he (she, it) will preach"
Plural	1st	κηρύξομεν	"we will preach"
	2nd	κηρύξετε	"you will preach"
	3rd	κηρύξουσιν	"they will preach"

Contract Lengthening

♦ *Contract vowels lengthen before the tense suffix or ending of other principal parts.*

Contract verbs show contraction only in the first principal part. In other parts, contract vowels *lengthen* to the corresponding long vowel sound. Accent returns to standard accent for verbs. One exception in the future is καλέω, whose ε does not lengthen. So, one will find καλέσω, καλέσεις, καλέσει, etc. Otherwise:

Table 18.10 Contract Lengthening

Contract	Result
α	η
ε	η
ο	ω

$$\phi\iota\lambda\epsilon + \sigma = \phi\iota\lambda\eta\sigma\text{-}$$

stem   +   tense suffix = contract lengthening

$$\delta\eta\lambda o + \sigma = \delta\eta\lambda\omega\sigma\text{-}$$

stem   +   tense suffix = contract lengthening

$$\tau\iota\mu\alpha + \sigma = \tau\iota\mu\eta\sigma -$$

stem + tense suffix = contract lengthening

Table 18.11 Future Active Indicative—Contracts

φιλέω	δηλόω	τιμάω
φιλήσω	δηλώσω	τιμήσω
φιλήσεις	δηλώσεις	τιμήσεις
φιλήσει	δηλώσει	τιμήσει
φιλήσομεν	δηλώσομεν	τιμήσομεν
φιλήσετε	δηλώσετε	τιμήσετε
φιλήσουσιν	δηλώσουσιν	τιμήσουσιν

Future Middle

Table 18.12 Future Middle Indicative—λύω

Number	Person	Form	Translation
Singular	1st	λύσομαι	"I shall loose"
	2nd	λύση	"you will loose"
	3rd	λύσεται	"he (she, it) will loose"
Plural	1st	λυσόμεθα	"we will loose"
	2nd	λύσεσθε	"you will loose"
	3rd	λύσονται	"they will loose"

Remember, future passive is built on an entirely different stem, covered later. Future middle is regular. The -η (second singular) is contraction after a sigma drops (-εσαι).

Stops show volatilization, as in πέμψομαι, πέμψῃ, πέμψεται, etc. Liquid stems continue their dropping/contraction tricks, as in μενοῦμαι, μενῇ, μενεῖται, etc. Once again, be sure to observe accent.[5] Once a hidden stem is captured in memory, nothing is hidden; thus, κηρύξομαι, κηρύξῃ, κηρύξεται, etc., or διδάξομαι διδάξῃ, διδάξεται, etc. Contraction occurs only in the first principal part (the present and imperfect tenses). In the other principal parts, the reaction is vowel *lengthening,* with primary middle forms then added. So, φιλήσομαι, δηλώσομαι, τιμήσομαι, etc.

Deponent Futures

Some verbs that are not deponent in the present are yet deponent in the future. A *deponent future* is a verb whose present active has regular active forms, but whose future is deponent, showing only middle forms. A future deponent is translated with active voice, though the form is middle. As one might guess, some verbs deponent in the present also are deponent in the future, as χαρίζομαι to χαρίσομαι.

Table 18.13 Deponent Future

Present	Deponent Future
ἀνέχω	ἀνέξομαι
γινώσκω	γνώσομαι
λαμβάνω	λήμψομαι
ὁράω	ὄψομαι
τίκτω	τέξομαι
φεύγω	φεύξομαι

Future of Εἰμί

Table 18.14 Εἰμί—Future Indicative

Number	Person	Form	Translation
Singular	1st	ἔσομαι	"I shall be"
	2nd	ἔσῃ	"you (sg.) will be"
	3rd	ἔσται	"he (she, it) will be"
Plural	1st	ἐσόμεθα	"we shall be"
	2nd	ἔσεσθε	"you (pl.) will be"
	3rd	ἔσονται	"they will be"

---

[5]Learn to cue in on this tip-off: circumflex accent following a liquid probably is a liquid future.

Translation

The workhorse Greek tense is the aorist. So, *use of other tenses usually is quite intentional.* The translator must strive to recover the author's intent. Listed below are some important nuances for the future tense, *context always the key.*

Futuristic (Predictive). The simple statement that action will take place in future time. Notice the string of predictive futures in the following announcement by Jesus about the Holy Spirit in John 16:13, **ὁδηγήσει** ὑμᾶς ἐν τῇ ἀληθείᾳ πάσῃ· οὐ γὰρ **λαλήσει** ἀφ' ἑαυτοῦ, ἀλλ' ὅσα **ἀκούσει λαλήσει**, καὶ τὰ ἐρχόμενα **ἀναγγελεῖ** ὑμῖν = "He **will lead** you into all truth; for He **will not speak** from Himself, but whatsoever He **will hear**, He **will speak**, and the coming things He **will announce** to you."[6]

Imperative. The future can suggest a command, as if in an imperative mood. The form regularly occurs in second person, naturally. Thus, Οὐ **φονεύσεις** = "Do not murder" (literally, "you will not murder," Matt. 5:21). Again, Ἀγαπήσεις τὸν πλησίον σου = "**Love** you neighbor" (Matt. 5:43). However, the context can imply simply polite request or instruction, as in Luke 1:31, καὶ **καλέσεις** τὸ ὄνομα αὐτοῦ Ἰησοῦν = "and you **will call** his name Jesus."

Deliberative (Rhetorical). This nuance occurs in two forms. One variety concerns the question what course of action is now appropriate? The typical example used is Peter's question to Jesus, Κύριε, πρὸς τίνα **ἀπελευσόμεθα**; = "Lord, to whom **shall we go**?" (John 6:68).[7]

This nuance of the future also includes another variety, rhetorical questions. For example, we have Paul's question, ἢ οὐκ οἴδατε ὅτι ἄδικοι θεοῦ βασιλείαν οὐ **κληρονομήσουσιν**; = "or do you not know that the unrighteous **will not inherit** the kingdom of God?" (1 Cor. 6:9). Again, Paul asked, τί γὰρ οἶδας, γύναι, εἰ τὸν ἄνδρα **σώσεις**; = "For what do you know, O wife, whether you **will save** your husband?" (1 Cor. 7:16).

Gnomic. A gnomic statement is a truism or a generally accepted axiom. The statement concerns what always will happen with a given set of circumstances. Observe this use in Rom. 7:3, μοιχαλὶς **χρηματίσει** = "**she will be called** an adulteress."

---

[6]Notice the various types of verb stems and reactions: ὁδηγέω and λαλέω show contract lengthening; ακούω is regular; ἀγγέλλω is a double lambda present, single lambda liquid future.

[7]The verb is irregular, a compound form, from ἀπέρχομαι.

What To Learn—LESSON 18 (δεκαοκτώ)

Beginning

☐ 1. The two formation distinctions of future tense (voice, suffix)

☐ 2. Future tense suffix and reactions with stops

☐ 3. Definition of a *liquid verb*, future tense suffix, resultant interactions

☐ 4. Recognizing future tense for hidden stems and of irregular verbs

☐ 5. Future active/middle indicative paradigms: λύω, πέμπω, μένω

☐ 6. Contract *lengthening* and to what principal parts this process applies

☐ 7. Future active/middle indicative paradigms for contract verbs

☐ 8. Definition of *deponent future*

☐ 9. Future indicative of εἰμί

☐ 10. Learn the additional *correlative* and *interrogative* pronouns and carefully review the applicable material in Lesson 11

☐ 11. Vocabulary words

Advanced

☐ 12. Future tense reactions with hidden stems: -σσ, -ζ, -λλ, -σκ

☐ 13. Translating future tense: futuristic, imperative, deliberative, gnomic uses

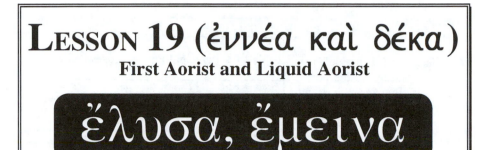

LESSON 19 (ἐννέα καὶ δέκα)

First Aorist and Liquid Aorist

ἔλυσα, ἔμεινα

The aorist is a secondary tense taking secondary endings. The stem is altered with a suffix, creating a new principal part. The aorist distinguishes liquid stems, as does the future, but in a slightly different manner. The aorist is the workhorse tense in Greek. The student should learn this tense well.

Vocabulary 19

Nouns

ἀρχή, ἡ	beginning
δαιμόνιον, τό	demon
διδάσκαλος, ὁ	teacher
θρόνος, ὁ	throne
ἱμάτιον, τό	garment
καρπός, ὁ	fruit
κεφαλή, ἡ	head
πλοῖον, τό	boat
σάββατον, τό	sabbath
σημεῖον, τό	sign, miracle
συναγωγή, ἡ	synagogue

Adjectives

λοιπός, -ή, -όν	remaining, the rest
μέσος, -η, -ον	middle

πονηρός, -ά, -όν	evil
πρεσβύτερος, -α, -ον	elder

Adverbs

ἤδη	now, already
μᾶλλον	more, rather
οὐχί	not (strengthened form)
ὧδε	here

Contract Verbs

δοκέω	I think, seem
ἐπερωτάω	I ask, question
προσκυνέω	I worship
τηρέω	I keep, observe

Other Verbs

ἁμαρτάνω	I sin
ὑπάγω	I go, go away

Analysis

The third principal part involves one tense, the aorist. However, the aorist has two incarnations. Neither meaning nor translation is affected in any way by the different forms. One form is called "first aorist," and the other, based on a different stem, is the "second aorist." English in like manner can distinguish two forms for past tense. Contrast simply adding an -ed suffix, as in "I love" to "I loved," with changing a word's spelling, as in "I write" to "I wrote." The first aorist stem is a past tense formulation in Greek that employs a suffix on the aorist stem similar to the "-ed" suffix for "loved" in English. The aorist aspect is punctiliar— but a better idea is *undefined*.

The first aorist has two formation distinctions. First, a distinction of voice is similar to

Table 19.1 Principal Parts: Tenses and Voices

Principal Parts	Tenses	Voices		
First Principal Part	Present	active	middle	passive
	Imperfect	active	middle	passive
Second Principal Part	Future	active	middle	
Third Principal Part	First Aorist	active	middle	
	Second Aorist	active	middle	
Fourth Principal Part	Perfect	active		
	Future Perfect	active		
	Pluperfect	active		
Fifth Principal Part	Perfect		middle	passive
	Future Perfect		middle	passive
	Pluperfect		middle	passive
Sixth Principal Part	First Aorist			passive
	First Future			passive
	Second Aorist			passive
	Second Future			passive

Table 19.2 Primary and Secondary Tenses

Kind of Action	Time of Action (Indicative Mood)		
	Secondary Tenses (secondary endings)	Primary Tenses (primary endings)	
	Past	Present	Future
durative	Imperfect	Present	---------
undefined ●	Aorist	---------	Future
perfective ---▶	Pluperfect	Perfect	Future Perfect

the future tense. The aorist is a secondary tense and, so, takes secondary endings. Yet, note that this third principal part deals with only two voices, active and middle, as with the future. Why? Because the aorist *passive* voice is built on *another stem*. Aorist passive cannot be covered until the passive stem is introduced. So, the third principal part is aorist tense, but only active and middle voices.

Second, a first aorist stem behaves similarly to a future stem, distinguishing stems ending in a liquid consonant (-λ, -μ, -ν, -ρ). While such verbs take a *different* suffix in the future, they take the same first aorist suffix, -σα. Yet, the σ of the -σα suffix is treated exactly as the future treats the -σ tense suffix. This creates the *liquid aorist*. So, the aorist has two formulations, first aorist and second aorist, but the first aorist can show a liquid form. We concentrate now on first aorist (and liquid) forms.

Formation

The student would do well to reread the formation of the imperfect tense. (Lessons 12 and 13). Formation of the aorist is patterned after the imperfect. Both are secondary, or historical, tenses concerning action in past time. The imperfect is durative action in past time. The aorist is undefined action in past time. The two past time tenses represent two kinds of action in past time.

The past time indicator is the augment, either syllabic or temporal, attached as a prefix on the front of the aorist tense stem. An aorist, like the imperfect, has an augment to indicate past time. Review augments. The pronominal suffix endings are the secondary endings, like the imperfect, because the aorist is a secondary tense. Review secondary endings.

The only distinction between imperfect and first aorist is the tense suffix used for the first aorist. The imperfect simply has the thematic vowel. The first aorist uses a suffix in the place of the imperfect thematic vowel.

Tense Suffix. The first aorist adds a -σα suffix to the aorist stem, altering the stem in the process and creating the third principal part. The main feature of the first aorist tense is this suffix attached to the end of the tense stem to indicate this aoristic component to the verbal action. For λυ-, with the past time indicator of a syllabic augment ἐ-, we have the form ἐλυσα-:

$$\overset{'}{\epsilon} + \lambda\upsilon + \sigma\alpha = \overset{'}{\epsilon}\lambda\upsilon\sigma\alpha-$$

augment + stem + tense suffix

Volatilization. All volatilization patterns of the future tense apply to the first aorist. The σ of the -σα suffix instigates the same reactions for the first aorist as does the -σ of the future suffix. Thus the first aorist tense stem of πέμπω is ἐπεμψα-, πείθω is ἐπεισα-, and so forth. So a stop changes like this:

$$\overset{'}{\epsilon}\pi\epsilon\mu\boxed{\pi+\sigma}\alpha = \overset{'}{\epsilon}\pi\epsilon\mu\boxed{\psi}\alpha-$$

augmented stem + tense suffix

Liquid Stems. You recall that liquid verbs are verbs whose stems end in a liquid consonant (-λ, -μ, -ν, -ρ). The first aorist tense distinguishes itself on a pattern similar to the future. The first aorist tense suffix does not change as in the future, but the first aorist reactions show a similar pattern. The reactions can be twofold. (The second reaction occurs only sporadically.)

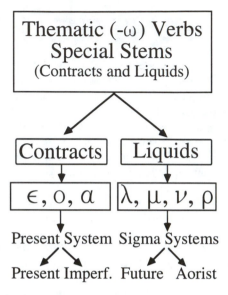

Dropping the Sigma. The principle liquid reaction for first aorists is that the sigma of the tense suffix -σα drops out. This situation always leaves the -α alone as the tense stem suffix for liquid first aorists. The term *asigmatic* first aorist is simply an alternative way of referring to the regular dropping of the σ of the aorist suffix before liquid consonants. A liquid future with its -εσ suffix has a characteristic circumflex accent to divulge the liquid reaction due to left over vowels contracting; a liquid aorist with its normal -σα suffix suffers no contraction after dropping the sigma, so has regular verb accent.

Vowel Lengthening. The second liquid reaction for first aorists is sporadic, observed in a few verbs, but not in all. This second potential reaction is lengthening of the stem vowel, in a process called *compensatory* lengthening. An ε will lengthen to the diphthong ει or some other pattern. This compensatory lengthening is to be observed and noted for any given verb as a part of memorizing principal parts. A liquid first aorist stem change, then, can look like this:

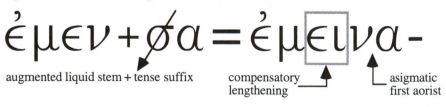

augmented liquid stem + tense suffix   compensatory   asigmatic
                                                lengthening   first aorist

Exceptions. Similar to the future, some liquid stems form the aorist in -ησα-. These include θέλω (ἠθέλησα) and χαίρω (ἐχαίρησα). The verbs βούλομαι and μέλλω have no aorist forms in the New Testament. Two other nasal stem verbs, γίνομαι and καταβαίνω, show only second aorist forms in the New Testament.

Table 19.3 Hidden Stem Examples

Lexical	Verb Stem	Aorist Stem
βαπτίζω	βαπτιδ-	ἐβαπτισα-
κράζω	κραγ-	ἐκραξα-
κηρύσσω	κηρυκ-	ἐκηρυξα-
πράσσω	πραγ-	ἐπραξα-
ταράσσω	ταραχ-	ἐταραξα-
ἀγγέλλω	ἀγγελ-	ἤγγειλα-

Hidden Stems. Hidden stem patterns are similar to future tense. Two differences are the presence of the augment to indicate past time and the alpha that remains after sigma volatilization. So, a **double sigma** present stem, whose real stem ends in either -κ, -χ, or -γ, will look similar to ἐκηρυκ- + -σα = ἐκηρυξα-. A **zeta** stem, whose real stem ends in the dental -δ, will look like ἐσωδ- + -σα = ἐσωσα-. Or, with an actual palatal stem in -γ, a zeta stem can look like ἐκραγ- + -σα = ἐκραξα-. A **double lambda** present stem in fact can be a single lambda stem with a liquid aorist, as ἀπεστειλ- + -σα = ἀπεστειλα-. Finally, a **kappa sigma** stem in the present really is the simpler -κ stem, with a hidden stem aorist as ἐδιδακ- + -σα = ἐδιδαξα-.

Second Aorist. These stems will be treated separately. The idea to remember here is that the key to the distinction between first and second aorist is the stem.

Pronominal Suffix. No thematic vowel is used. The alpha of the tense suffix -σα suffices. One then adds secondary endings for active or middle voice, with one exception. The first person singular does not take the nu (-ν); this leaves the tense suffix -σα alone as the ending for first singular. The third singular already has no ending; the alpha of the -σα tense suffix shows up as the corresponding thematic vowel for third singular, -ε. This creates the ending -σε for third singular. Thus, first singular is -σα, while third singular is -σε(ν). We then have the component parts:

$$ἐ + λυ + σα + ν$$

augment + stem + tense suffix + secondary ending

So a stop ends up like this:

$$\text{ἔπεμψαν}$$

A liquid stem has the intermediate stage, ἔμενσαν, which becomes:

$$\text{ἔμειναν}$$

Here, the sigma of the aorist suffix has been lost (asigmatic). The present active form? Much clearer than in the liquid future, for one always has the augment, and sometimes the stem vowel lengthens, plus the ending is different:

$$\text{μένω, ἔμεινα}$$

present tense   aorist tense

Finally, hidden stems show up in many variations. As just one example, a double sigma present stem in the first aorist becomes:

$$\text{ἐκήρυξαν}$$

Paradigms. Paradigms summarizing the above discussion are now presented. Observe the use of secondary endings with this secondary tense. Remember the two minor observations that the first singular does not have the -ν ending, leaving only the tense suffix exposed. Also, the third singular has no ending but shows a form similar to an exposed thematic vowel.

Table 19.4 First Aorist Active Indicative—λύω (regular stem)

Number	Person	Form	Translation
Singular	1st	ἔλυσα	"I loosed"
	2nd	ἔλυσας	"you loosed"
	3rd	ἔλυσε(ν)	"he (she, it) loosed"
Plural	1st	ἐλύσαμεν	"we loosed"
	2nd	ἐλύσατε	"you loosed"
	3rd	ἔλυσαν	"they loosed"

Table 19.5 First Aorist Active Indicative—πέμπω (stop)

Number	Person	Form	Translation
Singular	1st	ἔπεμψα	"I sent"
	2nd	ἔπεμψας	"you sent"
	3rd	ἔπεμψε(ν)	"he (she, it) sent"
Plural	1st	ἐπέμψαμεν	"we sent"
	2nd	ἐπέμψατε	"you sent"
	3rd	ἔπεμψαν	"they sent"

Table 19.6 First Aorist Active Indicative—μένω (liquid)

Number	Person	Form	Translation
Singular	1st	ἔμεινα	"I remained"
	2nd	ἔμεινας	"you remained"
	3rd	ἔμεινε(ν)	"he (she, it) remained"
Plural	1st	ἐμείναμεν	"we remained"
	2nd	ἐμείνατε	"you remained"
	3rd	ἔμειναν	"they remained"

Table 19.7 First Aorist Active Indicative—κηρύσσω (hidden stem)

Number	Person	Form	Translation
Singular	1st	ἐκήρυξα	"I preached"
	2nd	ἐκήρυξας	"you preached"
	3rd	ἐκήρυξε(ν)	"he (she, it) preached"
Plural	1st	ἐκηρύξαμεν	"we preached"
	2nd	ἐκηρύξατε	"you preached"
	3rd	ἐκήρυξαν	"they preached"

Contract Lengthening

The first aorist tense sign -σα causes contract vowel lengthening. Accent returns to standard accent for verbs. Two exceptions are καλέω and τελέω. So, one will find ἐκάλεσα, ἐκάλεσας, ἐκάλεσεν, etc. and ἐτέλεσα, etc. Otherwise:

$$\text{ἐφιλε} + \text{σα} = \text{ἐφιλησα-}$$

augment + stem   +   tense suffix = contract lengthening

Table 19.8 First Aorist Active Indicative—Contracts

φιλέω	δηλόω	τιμάω
ἐφίλησα	ἐδήλωσα	ἐτίμησα
ἐφίλησας	ἐδήλωσας	ἐτίμησας
ἐφίλησε(ν)	ἐδήλωσε(ν)	ἐτίμησε(ν)
ἐφιλήσαμεν	ἐδηλώσαμεν	ἐτιμήσαμεν
ἐφιλήσατε	ἐδηλώσατε	ἐτιμήσατε
ἐφίλησαν	ἐδήλωσαν	ἐτίμησαν

First Aorist Middle

Table 19.9 First Aorist Middle Indicative—λύω

Number	Person	Form	Translation
Singular	1st	ἐλυσάμην	"I loosed (for myself)"
	2nd	ἐλύσω	"you loosed (for yourself)"
	3rd	ἐλύσατο	"he loosed (for himself)," etc.
Plural	1st	ἐλυσάμεθα	"we loosed (for ourselves)"
	2nd	ἐλύσασθε	"you loosed (for yourselves)"
	3rd	ἐλύσαντο	"they loosed (for themselves)"

Remember, first aorist *passive* is built on an entirely different stem, covered later. First aorist middle is regular, with one explanation. The actual second singular middle ending is -σο (see Table 13.1). With the tense suffix, this becomes -σασο. The second (intervocalic) sigma drops, producing -σαο, which contracts to -σω.

Stops show volatilization, as in ἐπεμψάμην, ἐπέμψω, ἐπέμψατο, etc. Liquid stems continue their dropping/lengthening tricks, as in ἐμεινάμην, ἐμείνω, ἐμείνατο, etc. (All liquid aorists are asigmatic. However, not all liquid aorists undergo compensatory lengthening as does μένω.) Once a hidden stem is captured in memory, nothing is hidden; thus, ἐκηρυξάμην, ἐκηρύξω, ἐκηρύξατο, etc., or ἐδιδαξάμην, ἐδιδάξω, ἐδιδάξατο, etc. Contraction occurs only in the first principal part (the present and imperfect tenses). In the other principal parts, the reaction is vowel *lengthening,* with secondary middle forms then added. So, ἐφιλησάμην, ἐδηλωσάμην, ἐτιμησάμην, etc. (see Table 18.10).

Middle Deponent

A verb may occur in the third principal part only in middle forms. These forms are not true middle voice. The proper translation is active voice. Active forms do

ἐλογισάμην

not exist, but active meaning does. Such an aorist is called a "middle deponent." This term applies only to aorist forms. Thus, any aorist verb whose middle form is deponent is called a "middle deponent." Most present deponents turn out to be middle deponents. For example, λογίζομαι has the aorist middle form, ἐλογισάμην, translated actively as "I reckoned," *not* "I reckoned (for myself)."

Translation

Table 19.10 Kinds of Action

Durative	——— or – – – – –
Undefined	●
Perfective	– – ➤ or ●– – ➤

The workhorse Greek tense is the aorist because of pervasive use in the New Testament. The aspect is undefined, which is suited to summarizing in a generalizing way any past tense report. While aorist aspect is called "punctiliar," this is only partially correct. "Punctiliar" as an idea does not fully capture the aoristic aspect.

A more accurate idea is "undefined." In other words, an author would use aorist as a generic description of past activity, not defining anything particular about the action or its process. This undefined use is common even in English. If asked, "Did you study the lesson?" you answer, "Yes, I studied the lesson." In point of fact, your study activity probably took place over a broad stretch of time, with breaks and other activity interrupting. In reporting your activity of studying, however, you do not bother with these activity details. You just report the action as a whole. Your past tense, "studied," conceives the action in overview of the entire process. Such past tense reporting with undefined overview is the dominant sense of the Greek aorist tense. Listed below are several nuances for the aorist tense, *context always the key.*

Constative (Summary Report).[1] This is a summary report of any past action ("I studied the lesson."). Observe: καθὼς **ἐλάλησεν** πρὸς τοὺς πατέρας ἡμῶν, τῷ Ἀβραὰμ καὶ τῷ σπέρματι αὐτοῦ εἰς τὸν αἰῶνα = "even as he **spoke** to our fathers, to Abraham and to his descendants forever" (Luke 1:55). Summary report could use the auxiliary verb "has, have," perfective in English, *but not when used with the aorist.* A good example is Rom. 3:23, πάντες γὰρ **ἥμαρτον** = "for all **have sinned**." (Beginning students for now should use simple past tense for aorist.)[2]

Table 19.11 Aorist Tense Uses

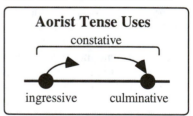

---

[1]Terminology is not fixed because the concept is broad. "Historical," "holistic," "unitary," etc. also are employed. "Summary report" views the action from the speaker's perspective.

[2]I.e., "___ed." Using "has" or "have," as above, is not wrong, but cannot be distinguished from the perfect tense. The example above is second aorist. This context possibly could be a "gnomic" aorist, that is, stating a truism, "all sin," as an empirical observation of general human behavior.

Ingressive (Inceptive). The punctiliar sense comes to the fore, but emphasis is upon the beginning. Helping verbs could include "came," "became," or "began." For example, ὁ λόγος σάρξ **ἐγένετο** = "the Word **became** flesh" (John 1:14).

Culminative. The punctiliar sense comes to the fore, but emphasis is upon the conclusion. This nuance infringes upon the perfect tense. The aorist, however, infers nothing about on-going consequences, as does the perfect. For example, ἐγὼ **ἐβάπτισα** ὑμᾶς ὕδατι = "I̱ **baptized** you with water" (Mark 1:8).

Epistolary. This use is a peculiarity of letter writing conventions. An author in composing a letter, when referring to the work, would not say "I am writing," as is the English style. Instead, the author would anticipate the point of view of the reader at the time of reading the letter and pen "I wrote to you" or "I have written to you," i.e., using the aorist tense. This convention includes other action too, as the sending of an emissary ("I have sent" = "I am sending," as in Col. 4:7–8). This tense shifting on behalf of the reader's perspective is called the "epistolary aorist" and should be translated with English present tense. For example, **ἔγραψα** ὑμῖν, παιδία = "I **am writing** to you, children" (1 John 2:14).

Dramatic. The use is for dramatic effect. Often, this use is found in contexts in which something significant has just taken place. A good example is the conclusion to the prodigal son parable: ὅτι ὁ ἀδελφός σου οὗτος νεκρὸς ἦν καὶ **ἔζησεν** = "because this brother of yours was dead and **is alive**!" (Luke 15:32).[3] The dramatic aorist shows that, given context, a *present* tense could be perfect to translate an aorist tense in the Greek text. Do not become frozen into your past time understanding of the aorist tense.

Prophetic. In prophetic speech, a future event is spoken of *as if already accomplished fact* in the surety of fulfillment. This is a cousin to the dramatic aorist. However, this use is restricted to proclamations. Depending on context, translation

---

[3] The aorist here also probably carries something of an inceptive idea, "is alive (again)."

could use the perfect or future tense. For example, Ἔπεσεν ἔπεσεν Βαβυλὼν ἡ μεγάλη = "**Fallen! Fallen!** is Babylon the Great!" (Rev. 18:2). Again, τῆς χάριτος **ἐξεπέσατε** = "you **will fall** from grace" (Gal. 5:4).

Gnomic. A gnomic statement is a truism generally accepted; this can be made with the aorist tense in Greek. Such a statement inherently is time independent. English translation, therefore, will vary. Rom. 3:23, used earlier, might be a gnomic aorist ("all sin"). Otherwise, James 1:11 shows an entire series of aorist verbs probably used in this gnomic sense, ἀνέτειλεν = "rises," ἐξήρανεν = "dries up," ἐξέπεσεν = "falls off," ἀπώλετο = "perishes."

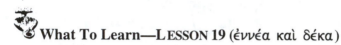 **What To Learn—LESSON 19** (ἐννέα καὶ δέκα)

Beginning

☐   1. The two formation distinctions of the first aorist tense (voice, stem)

☐   2. First aorist tense suffix reactions with stops and liquids

☐   3. First aorist active/middle indicative paradigms: λύω, πέμπω, μένω

☐   4. First aorist active/middle indicative paradigms for contract verbs

☐   5. Significance of the aoristic aspect of the Greek verb

☐   6. Vocabulary words

Advanced

☐   7. First aorist tense reactions with hidden stems: -σσ, -ζ, -λλ, -σκ

☐   8. Translating the aorist tense: constative, ingressive, culminative, epistolary, dramatic, prophetic, gnomic

Second Aorist and Indirect Discourse

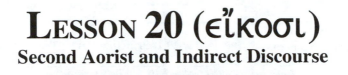

ἔλιπον

The second aorist is a secondary tense taking secondary endings. This aorist stem does not use a tense suffix as does the first aorist but is not a different principal part. Indirect discourse is reported differently in Greek than in English by preserving the tenses of the original statement.

Vocabulary 20

Conjunctions, Adjective, Nouns

διό	wherefore
ὅπως	that (in order that)
δεξιός, -ά, -όν	right (direction)
ἐπαγγελία, ἡ	promise
παιδίον, τό	child
σοφία, ἡ	wisdom
χρόνος, ὁ	time

Verbs

εὐαγγελίζω	I bring good news
λείπω	I leave
πείθω	I persuade

Second Aorist Forms

ἔβαλον (βάλλω)	I threw
ἐγενόμην (γίνομαι)	I became

ἔγνων (γινώσκω)		I knew
εἶδον (ὁράω)		I saw
εἶπον (λέγω)		I said
ἔλαβον (λαμβάνω)		I took, received
ἔλιπον (λείπω)		I left
ἔπεσον (πίπτω)		I fell
ἔπιον (πίνω)		I drank
ἔσχον (ἔχω)		I had
εὗρον (εὑρίσκω)		I found
ἔφαγον (ἐσθίω)		I ate
ἔφυγον (φεύγω)		I fled
ἤγαγον (ἄγω)		I led
ἦλθον (ἔρχομαι)		I came
ἥμαρτον (ἁμαρτάνω)		I sinned
ἤνεγκον (φέρω)		I bore, carried

Analysis

English. Numerous verbs in English are regular. The past tense of "I work" is "I worked." Here, the ending "-ed" is added. Other verbs are irregular. "I write" as past tense is "I wrote," not "I writted." Both forms "I worked" and "I wrote" are past tenses in English, just formed differently.

Greek. The third principal part involves one tense, the aorist. However, the aorist tense has two formation patterns, similar to English verbs that are considered regular or irregular.

Table 20.1 Principal Parts: Tenses and Voices

Principal Parts	Tenses	Voices		
First Principal Part	Present	active	middle	passive
	Imperfect	active	middle	passive
Second Principal Part	Future	active	middle	
Third Principal Part	First Aorist	active	middle	
	Second Aorist	*active*	*middle*	
Fourth Principal Part	Perfect	active		
	Future Perfect	active		
	Pluperfect	active		
Fifth Principal Part	Perfect		middle	passive
	Future Perfect		middle	passive
	Pluperfect		middle	passive
Sixth Principal Part	First Aorist			passive
	First Future			passive
	Second Aorist			passive
	Second Future			passive

Neither meaning nor translation is affected whatsoever by the different forms. One form is called "first aorist," and the other, based on a different stem, is the "second aorist." The second aorist could be considered "irregular." Just as one simply has to learn that "I wrote" is the past tense of "I write" in English, one has to learn second aorist forms as the undefined past tense of certain Greek verbs. These second aorist stems also must be memorized to distinguish second aorist forms from imperfect.

Lexical consultation is essential in determining whether a verb has a first or a second aorist form. This second aorist form is listed as the third principal part of the verb, just as is the first aorist. The form is memorized as part of vocabulary. The second aorist *passive* voice is built on *another stem*, so cannot be covered until that stem structure is introduced.

Formation

Tense Stem. The only distinction between imperfect and second aorist is the tense stem. Second aorist is formed on the aorist stem, the imperfect on the present stem. The difference between present stem and second aorist stem sometimes is just a single letter: observe λείπω, with second aorist stem λιπ-, and βάλλω, with second aorist stem βαλ-. (Perhaps second aorist forms are older than the present stems.)

♦ *Second aorist and imperfect look exactly the same, except for the stem alone.*

Components. Since the second aorist by definition is a secondary tense, then this tense will have a past time *augment* prefixed to the tense stem (as with the imperfect). This *second aorist stem* is quite distinctive. A -σα tense suffix, as found in the first aorist, is *not* used in the second aorist. Instead, a *thematic vowel* and *secondary endings* are used (as with the imperfect). Formation is simpler, since first aorist concerns are not present: no volatilization, no liquid stems, no dropping. The paradigm verb is λείπω, with its second aorist stem, λιπ-. Thus:

$$\overset{\text{'}}{\text{E}}\text{-}\lambda\iota\pi\text{-}\text{O}\text{-}\nu$$

augment + 2 aor. stem + vowel + secondary ending

Notice the replication of the imperfect, save for stem:

$$\overset{\text{''}}{\text{E}}\lambda\epsilon\iota\pi\text{O}\nu, \quad \overset{\text{''}}{\text{E}}\lambda\iota\pi\text{O}\nu$$

imperfect built on present stem   second aorist built on aorist stem

First Aorist Endings. The first aorist pattern (-σα, -σας, -σε, -σαμεν, -σατε, -σαν) sometimes is found on second aorist stems, but minus the sigma (almost in an asigmatic liquid pattern; i.e., -α, -ας, -ε, -αμεν, -ατε, -αν). The two most common forms in the New Testament are εἶπον, second aorist of λέγω, and εἶδον, second aorist of ὁράω. These verbs can be found as εἶπα, εἶπας, εἶπε, etc. and εἶδα, εἶδας, εἶδε, etc. Meaning is not affected.

Mixed Stems. Some verbs exhibit both a first and a second aorist form. These are unpredictable and are noted as one works on principal parts. For example, ἁμαρτάνω has both the first aorist form ἡμάρτησα and the second aorist form ἥμαρτον. *Note well:* φέρω, with second aorist ἤνεγκον, also has the form ἤνεγκα, but this is *not* a first aorist form.[1]

---

[1] This aorist of φέρω, ἐνέγκα, often is incorrectly presented as a "kappa first aorist," but in fact is a *second* aorist, as above, ending in -κ and using first aorist endings (stem ἐνεκ-, reduplicated to ἐνενεκ-, augmented with vowel gradation to ἠνενκ-; ν before palatal assimilates to nasal as ἠνεγκ-).

Table 20.2 Second Aorist Active Indicative—λείπω

Number	Person	Form	Translation
Singular	1st	ἔλιπον	"I left"
	2nd	ἔλιπες	"you left"
	3rd	ἔλιπε(ν)	"he (she, it) left"
Plural	1st	ἐλίπομεν	"we left"
	2nd	ἐλίπετε	"you left"
	3rd	ἔλιπον	"they left"

Table 20.3 Second Aorist Active Indicative—εἶπον (alternate endings)

Second Aorist	1st Aor. Endings	Translation
εἶπον	εἶπα	"I said"
εἶπες	εἶπας	"you said"
εἶπε(ν)	εἶπε(ν)	"he (she, it) said"
εἴπομεν	εἴπαμεν	"we said"
εἴπετε	εἴπατε	"you said"
εἶπον	εἶπαν	"they said"

Table 20.4 Second Aorist Active Indicative—ἁμαρτάνω (mixed stems)

First Aorist	Second Aorist	Translation
ἡμάρτησα	ἥμαρτον	"I sinned"
ἡμάρτησας	ἥμαρτες	"you sinned"
ἡμάρτησε(ν)	ἥμαρτε(ν)	"he (she, it) sinned"
ἡμαρτήσαμεν	ἡμάρτομεν	"we sinned"
ἡμαρτήσατε	ἡμάρτετε	"you sinned"
ἡμάρτησαν	ἥμαρτον	"they sinned"

Second Aorist Middle

Table 20.5 Second Aorist Middle Indicative—λείπω

Number	Person	Form	Translation
Singular	1st	ἐλιπόμην	"I left (for myself)"
	2nd	ἐλίπου	"you left (for yourself)"
	3rd	ἐλίπετο	"he left (for himself)," etc.
Plural	1st	ἐλιπόμεθα	"we left (for ourselves)"
	2nd	ἐλίπεσθε	"you left (for yourselves)"
	3rd	ἐλίποντο	"they left (for themselves)"

Remember, second aorist *passive* is built on a different stem. With the thematic vowel, the second singular ending -σο is -εσο. The sigma becomes an intervocalic sigma and drops, reducing the form to -εο, which contracts to -ου. An important second aorist *deponent* is ἐγενόμην, from γίνομαι (see vocabulary).

Indirect Discourse

Signaled With Ὅτι. The principle method for reporting indirect discourse in Greek is the use of ὅτι with the indicative mood.[2] Remember that direct quotations are indicated this way, called "ὅτι recitative" (Table 1.13). Editors of the UBS[4] provide their estimation of what should be considered a direct quote against indirect discourse by setting off the direct quote with a comma followed by a capital letter, or by using ὅτι followed by a capital letter. The ὅτι is left untranslated, and the material following put within quotation marks. Otherwise, the ὅτι is understood to introduce indirect discourse and is translated normally as "that." Numerous verbs can introduce indirect discourse. Verbs of saying, reporting, proclaiming, thinking, showing, hoping, marveling, and so forth can be involved.

Tense Structure. In moving from the original direct discourse to the indirect discourse report, *Greek always preserves the tense of the original statement.* This

---

[2]The other method, using infinitives, will be covered in a later lesson.

would be straightforward enough, except that such a procedure violates English idiom. English convention for reporting indirect discourse is to modify the verbs of the original direct statement into past tenses. Present tense direct statements convert to preterit, and preterit tense direct statements convert to pluperfect. Notice below.

Table 20.6 English Indirect Discourse—Tense Conversion

Direct Discourse	English Tense Conversion	Indirect Discourse
"I go."	Present Tense → Past tense	He said that he **went**.
"I went."	Past Tense → Pluperfect	He said that he **had gone**.

Such idioms often require adjustments to the Greek tense for English sense. Three basic structures for Greek indirect discourse are given below with suggestions on how to translate them, but also be ready to allow for exceptions in certain cases.

Present Tense Preserved. The Greek indirect discourse preserves the present tense of the original statement. The context involves a supposition generally held, or something considered generally known, etc. In this context, the English translation also can use present tense. For example, οἴδαμεν ὅτι ἁμαρτωλῶν ὁ θεὸς οὐκ ἀκούει = "we know that God does not **hear** sinners" (John 9:31).

Present and Past Tenses Converted. English idiom regularly converts tenses moving from direct to indirect discourse. Thus, often when translating tenses of Greek verbs within indirect discourse, the English translator must supply the correct past tense for proper English idiom. The following two situations are encountered.

Greek Present to English Past. The Greek indirect discourse preserves the present tense of the original statement. However, the translator should supply the appropriate preterit form for proper English translation. For example, ἐκεῖνοι δὲ ἔδοξαν ὅτι περὶ τῆς κοιμήσεως τοῦ ὕπνου **λέγει** = "but they supposed that he **was speaking** about actual sleep" (John 11:13). Observe carefully the present tense of the Greek indirect report in λέγει, which preserves the tense of the projected direct discourse ("He *is speaking* about actual sleep."). However, proper English idiom requires conversion into a preterit form for the English indirect discourse statement.

Greek Past to English Pluperfect. The Greek indirect discourse preserves the past tense of the original statement. However, the translator should supply the appropriate pluperfect tense for proper English translation. For example, ἔγνωσαν γὰρ ὅτι πρὸς αὐτοὺς τὴν παραβολὴν **εἶπεν** = "for they began to understand that he **had spoken** the parable against them" (Mark 12:12).[3] Observe carefully the past

---

[3] The second aorist ἔγνωσαν is taken as ingressive. Notice the optional -σαν ending of the third plural form.

tense of the Greek indirect report in εἶπεν, which preserves the tense of the projected direct discourse ("He *spoke* the parable against us!"). However, proper English idiom requires conversion into a pluperfect form for the English indirect discourse statement.

Table 20.7 Greek to English Indirect Discourse—Tense Conversion

Greek Indirect Discourse	Greek to English Tense	English Translation
ἐκεῖνοι δὲ ἔδοξαν <u>ὅτι</u> περὶ τῆς κοιμήσεως τοῦ ὕπνου **λέγει**	Present Tense → Past tense	"but they supposed <u>that</u> he **was speaking** about actual sleep" (John 11:13)
ἔγνωσαν γὰρ <u>ὅτι</u> πρὸς αὐτοὺς τὴν παραβολὴν **εἶπεν**	Past Tense → Pluperfect	"for they began to understand <u>that</u> he **had spoken** the parable against them" (Mark 12:12)

Principal Parts

The key to long term mastery of the Greek verb system is assembling each verb within a system of principal parts. Knowing principal parts, one can recognize any derivative form encountered in the New Testament. Begin now building verbs of your vocabulary into card sets of principal parts. Add forms as the parts are covered in the grammar. Remembering the principal parts requires time and concentration. However, your reward for reading and translating the New Testament is guaranteed.

Table 20.8 Principal Parts—Learning the Greek Verb System

First	Second	Third	Fourth	Fifth	Sixth
λύω	λύσω	ἔλυσα	λέλυκα	λέλυμαι	ἐλύθην
λείπω	λείψω	ἔλιπον	λέλοιπα	λέλειμμαι	ἐλήφθην

Diagramming

Discourse grammatically functions as a direct object. The ὅτι discourse clause is a subordinate substantival clause (Lesson 7), so the discourse is placed on a standard (⌐). Place the introductory ὅτι on the leg of the standard. For direct discourse, the ὅτι is in parentheses, if present. When ὅτι is not present, a comma followed by an uncial letter is a signal of direct discourse, and this discourse clause following the comma is placed on a standard, with the ὅτι presumed.

Table 20.9 Diagramming Discourse

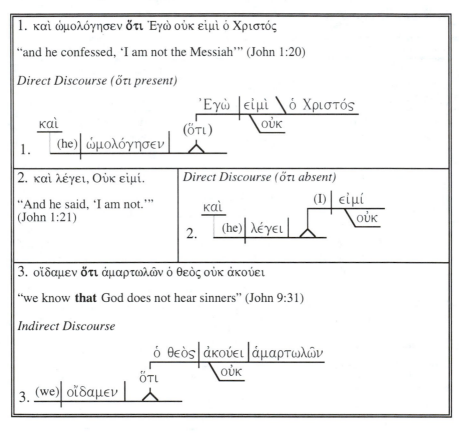

1. καὶ ὡμολόγησεν **ὅτι** Ἐγὼ οὐκ εἰμὶ ὁ Χριστός "and he confessed, 'I am not the Messiah'" (John 1:20) *Direct Discourse (ὅτι present)*

2. καὶ λέγει, Οὐκ εἰμί.

"And he said, 'I am not.'" (John 1:21)

Direct Discourse (ὅτι absent)

3. οἴδαμεν **ὅτι** ἁμαρτωλῶν ὁ θεὸς οὐκ ἀκούει

"we know **that** God does not hear sinners" (John 9:31)

Indirect Discourse

What To Learn—LESSON 20 (εἴκοσι)

Beginning

☐   1.   The significance of the second aorist as an aorist stem

☐   2.   Formation of the second aorist as a secondary tense

☐   3.   The distinction between imperfect and second aorist verbs

☐   4.   Second aorist active and middle indicative paradigms of λείπω

☐   5.   Recognizing ὅτι of indirect discourse, English idiom for reporting tenses of indirect discourse, and three tense patterns for translating indirect discourse

☐   6.   Building the principal parts of the Greek verb system using review cards

☐   7.   Diagramming discourse

☐   8.   Vocabulary words

Advanced

☐   9.   Recognizing asigmatic first aorist endings used on second aorist stems and purpose for the εἶπον/εἶπα paradigm

☐ 10.   Recognizing multiple use of first and second aorist stems for the same verb and the purpose for the ἡμάρτησα/ἥμαρτον paradigm

 The papyrus 𝔓52 is our oldest copy of a portion of the New Testament, a fragment of the Gospel of John, dated around A.D. 100–150. This early date means that 𝔓52 has the distinction of being only fifty to one hundred years removed from the original. This document is held in the John Rylands Library in Manchester.

Generally, the "recto" is the right-hand page of a book, or the front side of a leaf; the "verso" is the left-hand side of a book, or the reverse side of a leaf.[4] The recto of 𝔓52 is the image on the left, and the verso is the image on the right. The recto of 𝔓52 contains John 18:31–33. The verso of 𝔓52 contains John 18:37–38. Further, marks are not common on these early papyri. However, note diaeresis over the iota in line two recto (reading as: ΟΥΔΕΝΑΪΝΑΟΛ = ουδενα ἰνα ο λ[ογος]).

John 18:31–38

---

[4]Papyri designations are different. Papyri are made of strips of reed, one side laid horizontally, the other laid vertically. The horizontal strips, whether the front or back of a page, make the "recto"; the vertical strips, whether front or back, make the "verso." By folding leaves, if the *front* of the first page is horizontal, the *back* of the last page is horizontal (like a bulletin). Thus, with papyri, recto and verso does not have to do with front or back, but with designating horizontal or vertical strips.

LESSON 21 (εἷς καὶ εἴκοσι)
The Passive System—Aorist and Future

ἐλύθην, λυθήσομαι

 The passive system involves an entire scheme for only one voice involving two tenses, aorist and future. In this system, the future is so similar as to need only brief mention and providing paradigms. The system has two configurations.

Vocabulary 21

Adverb and Conjunctions

οὐκέτι	no longer
ἄρα	so, then, as a result
ὥστε	so that, therefore

Nouns and Adjectives

γενεά, ἡ	generation
θηρίον, τό	beast
ναός, ὁ	temple
σωτηρία, ἡ	salvation
τιμή, -ης, ἡ	honor, price
φυλακή, ἡ	guard, prison, watch
χρεία, ἡ	need
ἅπας, -ασα, -αν	all
ἰσχυρός, -ά, -άν	strong
ὅμοιος, -α, -ον	like

τυφλός, -ή, -όν	blind

Verbs

ἀπαγγέλλω	I announce, report
ἀπολύω	I release
δέω	I bind
διώκω	I pursue, persecute
θαυμάζω	I marvel, wonder
θεραπεύω	I heal
καθίζω	I seat, sit
κατοικέω	I inhabit, dwell
κρατέω	I grasp, seize
παραλαμβάνω	I take, receive
προσφέρω	I bring to, offer
σπείρω	I sow
φανερόω	I make manifest

245

Analysis

The sixth principal part has two tenses, the aorist and the future. The aorist passive voice forms itself on a different stem than aorist middle, unlike other passives which simply clone the middle. Oddly enough, future passive borrows this aorist passive stem, thereby becoming part of a unique passive system.

The sixth principal part has a double set. Dropping a suffix consonant, θ, creates a "strong" (or "second") form for both aorist and future. Forms of aorist and future that include the theta are part of the *first passive* system. Forms of aorist and future that drop the theta are part of the *second passive* system. Thus, the first passive system includes the forms of the first aorist passive and the first future passive. The second passive system includes the

Table 21.1 Principal Parts: Tenses and Voices

Principal Parts	Tenses	Voices		
First Principal Part	Present	active	middle	passive
	Imperfect	active	middle	passive
Second Principal Part	Future	active	middle	
Third Principal Part	First Aorist	active	middle	
	Second Aorist	active	middle	
Fourth Principal Part	Perfect	active		
	Future Perfect	active		
	Pluperfect	active		
Fifth Principal Part	Perfect		middle	passive
	Future Perfect		middle	passive
	Pluperfect		middle	passive
Sixth Principal Part	*First Aorist*			passive
	First Future			passive
	Second Aorist			passive
	Second Future			passive

Table 21.2 Primary and Secondary Tenses

Kind of Action	Secondary Tenses (secondary endings)	Primary Tenses (primary endings)	
	Past	Present	Future
durative	Imperfect	Present	---------
undefined	Aorist	---------	Future
perfective	Pluperfect	Perfect	Future Perfect

forms of the second aorist passive and second future passive. The two sets differentiate themselves by the presence or absence of a single letter. Easy enough.

First Passive System

First Aorist Passive. The aorist passive is a past tense, so one will augment to indicate past time (syllabic or temporal). Logically, one would think to add -σα as the first aorist tense suffix. However, in the first aorist *passive* system, this first aorist tense suffix is not used.

Passive Suffix. The aorist passive stem is quite distinctive even without the -σα suffix. The aorist passive suffix is -θη (-θε outside the indicative). So:

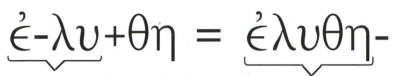

augment + aorist passive stem + passive suffix = aorist passive result

Theta Volatilization. Theta volatilization is a predictable pattern of changes, similar to the predictable patterns of sigma volatilization. For **stops**, resulting combinations are as expected, that is, *aspiration* (labials and palatals) or *dropping* (dentals). However: (1) labial φ plus θ yields φ, creating a true second passive form, and (2) palatal χ plus θ yields χθ. Of the **liquids**, the nasals (μ and ν) usually react, whereas the true liquids (λ and ρ) usually do not. However, any might insert a vowel (either ε or η), as in -ληθ , -μηθ, -νηθ, -ρεθ. Nu drops on occasion. In summary, of the four consonants λ, μ, ν, ρ, three (λ, ρ, and μ) *always are retained in some form.*[1]

Table 21.3 Theta Volatilization—Stops

Formation	Stops	Suffix	Result
labials	π, β, [φ]	+ θ	= φθ [θ drops]
palatals	κ, γ, χ	+ θ	= χθ
dentals	τ, δ, θ	+ θ	= σθ

Table 21.4 Theta Volatilization—Liquids

Liquid	Suffix	Result
λ	+ θ	= λθ or ληθ
ρ	+ θ	= ρθ or ρεθ
μ	+ θ	= μηθ
ν	+ θ	= θ or νθ or νηθ

A few examples are provided to show the general patterns.

---

[1] Really, all lambda (λ) stem liquids are *second* passives, dropping the theta, except βάλλω. Also a nasal -μ aorist passive in the New Testament does not exist (νέμω has no aorist passive).

Stops react similar to the following:

$$\overset{'}{\epsilon}\pi\epsilon\mu\boxed{\pi}\theta\eta = \overset{'}{\epsilon}\pi\epsilon\mu\boxed{\phi\theta}\eta\text{-}$$

augment + stem + passive suffix

$$\sigma\upsilon\nu\eta\boxed{\gamma\theta}\eta = \sigma\upsilon\nu\eta\boxed{\chi\theta}\eta\text{-}$$

augment + stem + passive
(συνάγω) suffix

$$\overset{'}{\epsilon}\pi\epsilon\iota\boxed{\theta\theta}\eta = \overset{'}{\epsilon}\pi\epsilon\iota\boxed{\sigma\theta}\eta\text{-}$$

augment + stem + passive suffix
(πείθω)

Liquids inserting a vowel look similar to the following:

$$\overset{'}{\epsilon}\beta\alpha\lambda\theta\eta = \overset{'}{\epsilon}\beta\lambda\eta\theta\eta\text{-}$$

augment + stem + passive   (vowel
(βάλλω) suffix   gradation)

$$\overset{'}{\epsilon}\rho\rho\theta\eta = \overset{'}{\epsilon}\rho\rho\epsilon\theta\eta\text{-}$$

augment + stem + passive
(λέγω) suffix

$$\overset{'}{\epsilon}\gamma\epsilon\nu\theta\eta = \overset{'}{\epsilon}\gamma\epsilon\nu\eta\theta\eta\text{-}$$

augment + stem + passive suffix
(γίνομαι)

Pronominal Suffix. No thematic vowel is used. The η of the passive suffix -θη suffices as theme vowel in function. An exception: *active endings are used for the aorist passive voice* (-ν, -ς, --, -μεν, -τε, -σαν). This anomaly generates zero confusion, because the -θη passive suffix sitting on the end of the tense stem is so distinctive you can pounce on the location almost any time without thinking.[2] Thus:

$$ἐ\text{-}λυ\text{-}θη\text{-}ν$$

augment + stem + passive suffix + secondary *active*
ending

So a stop stem like πέμπω ends up like this:

$$ἐπέμφθην$$

and a liquid stem such as γίνομαι inserting a vowel becomes:

$$ἐγενήθην$$

In all the first aorist verbs you encounter, observe the invariable appearance of the -θη passive suffix on the end of the tense stem, a dead giveaway to all *first* aorist, passive, indicative forms. One then has left only to explain the minor mutations that are generated by theta volatilization.

Translation of the first aorist passive will represent the standard ideas embodied in the passive voice. A review of the material in Lesson 10 on passive voice, especially the material concerning *agency*, would be advised. Expressing agency is a primary reason for using passive voice. Paradigms follow.

Table 21.5 Greek Voice

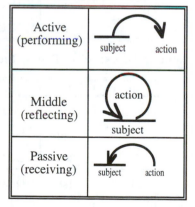

Active (performing)	subject → action
Middle (reflecting)	action / subject
Passive (receiving)	subject ← action

---

[2]The only "gotch ya" are the very few -ε contract verbs already with a θ in the stem that lengthen the contract vowel in future forms, such as ἀκολυθέω, ἀκολυθήσω ("I will follow").

Table 21.6 First Aorist Passive Indicative—λύω

Number	Person	Form	Translation
Singular	1st	ἐλύθην	"I was loosed"
	2nd	ἐλύθης	"you were loosed"
	3rd	ἐλύθη	"he (she, it) was loosed"
Plural	1st	ἐλύθημεν	"we were loosed"
	2nd	ἐλύθητε	"you were loosed"
	3rd	ἐλύθησαν	"they were loosed"

Table 21.7 First Aorist Passive Indicative—πέμπω (stop)

Number	Person	Form	Translation
Singular	1st	ἐπέμφθην	"I was sent"
	2nd	ἐπέμφθης	"you were sent"
	3rd	ἐπέμφθη	"he (she, it) was sent"
Plural	1st	ἐπέμφθημεν	"we were sent"
	2nd	ἐπέμφθητε	"you were sent"
	3rd	ἐπέμφθησαν	"they were sent"

Table 21.8 First Aorist Passive Indicative—βάλλω (liquid, vowel insert)

Number	Person	Form	Translation
Singular	1st	ἐβλήθην	"I was thrown"
	2nd	ἐβλήθης	"you were thrown"
	3rd	ἐβλήθη	"he (she, it) was thrown"
Plural	1st	ἐβλήθημεν	"we were thrown"
	2nd	ἐβλήθητε	"you were thrown"
	3rd	ἐβλήθησαν	"they were thrown"

Table 21.9 First Future Passive Indicative—λύω

Number	Person	Form	Translation
Singular	1st	λυθήσομαι	"I will be loosed"
	2nd	λυθήσῃ	"you will be loosed"
	3rd	λυθήσεται	"he (she, it) will be loosed"
Plural	1st	λυθησόμεθα	"we will be loosed"
	2nd	λυθήσεσθε	"you will be loosed"
	3rd	λυθήσονται	"they will be loosed"

Table 21.10 First Future Passive Indicative—πέμπω (stop)

Number	Person	Form	Translation
Singular	1st	πεμφθήσομαι	"I will be sent"
	2nd	πεμφθήσῃ	"you will be sent"
	3rd	πεμφθήσεται	"he (she, it) will be sent"
Plural	1st	πεμφθησόμεθα	"we will be sent"
	2nd	πεμφθήσεσθε	"you will be sent"
	3rd	πεμφθήσονται	"they will be sent"

Table 21.11 First Future Passive Indicative—βάλλω (liquid, vowel insert)

Number	Person	Form	Translation
Singular	1st	βληθήσομαι	"I will be thrown"
	2nd	βληθήσῃ	"you will be thrown"
	3rd	βληθήσεται	"he (she, it) will be thrown"
Plural	1st	βληθησόμεθα	"we will be thrown"
	2nd	βληθήσεσθε	"you will be thrown"
	3rd	βληθήσονται	"they will be thrown"

First Future Passive. The first future passive borrows the aorist passive stem, adding only sigma (-θησ) and using the thematic vowel with middle endings. Observe carefully: (1) *no augment* (= primary tense), and (2) second singular drops the sigma, then contracts the remaining vowels (-θησεσαι to -θησεαι to -θησῃ).

Contract Lengthening. Contract vowels lengthen in the principal parts outside of the first. In the sixth principal part, the first aorist passive sign of the -θη causes contract vowel lengthening. Accent returns to standard accent for verbs. Even καλέω lengthens as it does not in the active voice of both aorist and future forms. However, one exception in the aorist passive is τελέω, which does not lengthen the ε, but does insert a sigma. So, one will find ἐτελέσθην, ἐτελέσθης, ἐτελέσθη, etc., and τελεσθήσομαι, τελεσθήσῃ, τελεσθήσεται, etc. The future passive contract forms are similar to the aorist passive. However, the future passive: (1) does not have an augment, (2) uses a thematic vowel, and (3) takes middle endings. Thus:

$$ἐφιλε + θη = ἐφιλ\overset{\nearrow}{η}θη-$$

augmented aorist stem + passive suffix = contract lengthening

$$φιλε + θησ = φιλ\overset{\nearrow}{η}θησ-$$

future stem + future passive suffix = contract lengthening

Table 21.12 First Aorist Passive Indicative—Contracts

φιλέω	δηλόω	τιμάω
ἐφιλήθην	ἐδηλώθην	ἐτιμήθην
ἐφιλήθης	ἐδηλώθης	ἐτιμήθης
ἐφιλήθη	ἐδηλώθη	ἐτιμήθη
ἐφιλήθημεν	ἐδηλώθημεν	ἐτιμήθημεν
ἐφιλήθητε	ἐδηλώθητε	ἐτιμήθητε
ἐφιλήθησαν	ἐδηλώθησαν	ἐτιμήθησαν

Table 21.13 First Future Passive Indicative—Contracts

φιλέω	δηλόω	τιμάω
φιληθήσομαι	δηλωθήσομαι	τιμηθήσομαι
φιληθήσῃ	δηλωθήσῃ	τιμηθήσῃ
φιληθήσεται	δηλωθήσεται	τιμηθήσεται
φιληθησόμεθα	δηλωθησόμεθα	τιμηθησόμεθα
φιληθήσεσθε	δηλωθήσεσθε	τιμηθήσεσθε
φιληθήσονται	δηλωθήσονται	τιμηθήσονται

Second Passive System

Dropping the θ of the first passive suffix creates the second passive system. First or second passive involves form only, not translation. Whether a verb will have a first or a second passive form cannot be predicted but is determined by a lexicon. However, a second aorist passive always means a second future passive—the aorist passive serves as the basis for the future passive stem. The second aorist passive verb is unconnected to the second aorist active or middle. A verb can have either, both, or neither. Second passive forms are infrequent in the New Testament, but a few common verbs have second passives (e.g., ἀποστέλλω, γράφω, and χαίρω).

Second Aorist Passive. An augmented passive stem is used, but θ is dropped. Endings remain an exception—secondary *active* forms. These resultant endings are not that much a problem, since not too many second aorist passive forms actually occur. The third singular of the second passive should be distinguished from the first passive by the preceding theta in the first passive.[3] A labial -φ stem drops the θ of the passive suffix automatically (a stop reaction), so γράφω can be our paradigm:

$$ἐγραφθη = ἐγραφη\text{-}$$

augment + stem + passive suffix   remaining vowel

---

[3]The second singular of the first future passive always has the iota subscript.

Table 21.14 Second Aorist Passive Indicative—γράφω

Number	Person	Form	Translation
Singular	1st	ἐγράφην	"I was written"
	2nd	ἐγράφης	"you were written"
	3rd	ἐγράφη	"he (she, it) was written"
Plural	1st	ἐγράφημεν	"we were written"
	2nd	ἐγράφητε	"you were written"
	3rd	ἐγράφησαν	"they were written"

Second Future Passive. Second aorist passive makes a second future passive. Primary tenses have no augment. Thematic vowel with primary middle endings are used. One must know contract verb stems to distinguish the contract future middle from the second future passive (see Table 18.11 with that discussion). So:

$$\gamma\rho\alpha\phi\theta\eta\sigma = \gamma\rho\alpha\phi\eta\sigma\text{-}$$

stem   +   future passive suffix

Table 21.15 Second Future Passive Indicative—γράφω

Number	Person	Form	Translation
Singular	1st	γραφήσομαι	"I shall be written"
	2nd	γραφήσῃ	"you will be written"
	3rd	γραφήσεται	"he (she, it) will be written"
Plural	1st	γραφησόμεθα	"we will be written"
	2nd	γραφήσεσθε	"you will be written"
	3rd	γραφήσονται	"they will be written"

Passive Deponent

Table 21.16 Deponent Terminology

Tense	Voice	Meaning	Description	Example	Translation
Present	Mid./Pass.	*Active*	"Deponent"	βούλομαι (βούλομαι)	*I wish*
Imperfect	Mid./Pass.	*Active*	"Deponent"	ἐβουλόμην (βούλομαι)	*I was wishing*
Future	Middle	*Active*	"Deponent Future"	γνώσομαι (γινώσκω)	*I will know*
Aorist	Middle	*Active*	"Middle Deponent"	ἐγενόμην (γίνομαι)	*I became*
Aorist	Passive	*Active*	"Passive Deponent"	ἐγενήθην (γίνομαι)	*I became*

Table 21.17 Deponent Aorists

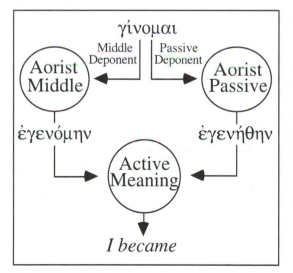

Terminology can become confusing at this point. Lingo for deponents is unsatisfactory in the first place. Just as well might be "dodo verbs." A quick review of terms helps to address "passive deponent."

Table 21.16 summarizes deponent terminology. The simple term "deponent" is the first principal part found only in middle forms. A "deponent future" is the second principal part found only in middle forms, singled out because the present active form exists. A "middle deponent" is the third principal part found only in middle forms. A "passive deponent" is the sixth principal part found only in passive forms. Since "middle deponent" and "passive deponent" both are translated actively, *the result is exactly the same for either form.* The common denominator for all middle/passive deponents in any principal part is an active voice translation. "Dodo verbs" sometimes catch beginning students off guard in attempting middle or passive ideas that do not fly.

Table 21.18 The Passive System—A Quick Summary

Tense	*First Passive*	*Second Passive*
Aorist	-θη (ἐ . . . θη . . .) ἐλύθην	-η (ἐ . . . η . . .) ἐγράφην
Future	-θησ (. . . θησ . . .) λυθήσομαι	-ησ (. . . ησ . . .) γραφήσομαι

Principal Parts

You have learned the first three principal parts. Now add the sixth principal part to your card set of Greek verbs. You will have to research in a lexicon to make sure whether the verb is part of the first passive or second passive system.

Table 21.19 Principal Parts—Learning the Greek Verb System

First	*Second*	*Third*	*Fourth*	*Fifth*	*Sixth*
λύω	λύσω	ἔλυσα	λέλυκα	λέλυμαι	ἐλυθην
λείπω	λείψω	ἔλιπον	λέλοιπα	λέλειμμαι	ἐλήφθην

🏺 What To Learn—LESSON 21 (εἷς καὶ εἴκοσι)

Beginning

☐ 1. The significance of the two passive systems of the sixth principal part

☐ 2. Formation of the first aorist and first future passive

☐ 3. Meaning of the passive voice, including the ideas of agency (Lesson 10)

☐ 4. First passive paradigms, aorist and future: λύω, πέμπω, βάλλω

☐ 5. Recognition of contract verbs in the first passive system

☐ 6. Second passive paradigms, aorist and future: γράφω

☐ 7. Add the sixth principal part to verb cards

☐ 8. Vocabulary words

Advanced

☐ 9. Theta volatilization patterns

☐ 10. Deponent terminology: "deponent," "deponent future," "middle deponent," "passive deponent," and impact on translation

Codex Bezae ("D") contains the Gospels, some of 3 John, and Acts. Greek is on the left side and Latin on the right. The date is argued at about the fifth century. The French Reformer Théodore de Bèze (Beza, 1519–1605) got the manuscript from the monastery of St. Irenaeus at Lyon. Cambridge University Library received the uncial in 1581. The codex, poorly done, has many misspellings and errors. Addition of material is common. Below is a portion of a leaf from Codex Bezae beginning at Luke 6:3b (. . . Οὐδὲ τοῦτο ἀνέγνωτε . . .) and going to 6:9a (. . . εἶπεν δὲ ὁ Ἰησοῦς πρὸς αὐτούς, Ἐπερωτῶ . . .).[4] Remarkable here is a saying of Jesus, found in no other manuscript, so unique to Codex Bezae, after 6:4: "On that same day, as he saw a certain man working on the Sabbath, he said to him, 'Man, if you realize what you are doing, you are fortunate, but if you do not know, you are accursed and a transgressor of the law'" (middle of line seven through line eleven). This saying between Luke 6:4 and Luke 6:6 displaces 6:5 to a position after 6:10.

(Codex Bezae)

Luke 6:3b–9a

---

[4]Notice the insertion of πότε between οὐδέ and ἀνέγνωτε in the first line, a misspelling of τότε ("then"); also note the spelling of the verb ἐπερωτῶ as ἐπερωτήσω in the last word of the last line.

LESSON 22 (δύο καὶ εἴκοσι)
Perfect Active and Future Perfect

λέλυκα, γέγραφα

The perfect tense can be quite meaningful exegetically. This important tense is used with special significance by an author. Two principal parts are generated by the perfect active and perfect middle/passive formulations. As in the passive system, dropping a letter yields "first" and "second" perfects.

Vocabulary 22

Interjection

οὐαί	woe! alas!

Nouns and Adjectives

ἄξιος, -α, -ον	worthy
ἐπιθυμία, -ας, ἡ	desire, passion
θύρα, -ας, ἡ	door
ἱκανός, -ή, -όν	sufficient, able, worthy
πρόβατον, -ου, τό	sheep

Adverbs and Verbs

σήμερον	today
πάντοτε	always
ἅπτομαι	I touch
δικαιόω	I justify
ἑτοιμάζω	I prepare

εὐχαριστέω	I give thanks
κλαίω	I weep
πάσχω	I suffer
φωνέω	I call

Second Perfect Forms

ἀκήκοα (ἀκούω)	I have heard
γέγονα (γίνομαι)	I have become
γέγραφα (γράφω)	I have written
ἐλήλυθα (ἔρχομαι)	I have gone
εἴληφα (λαμβάνω)	I have received
οἶδα (none)	I know
πέπονθα (πάσχω)	I have suffered
πέποιθα (πείθω)	I have persuaded
πέπομφα (πέμπω)	I have sent
πέφευγα (φεύγω)	I have fled

259

Analysis

Completing the series of six principal parts of the Greek verb system are those providing the forms of the perfect tense. Perfect forms are classified by voice into two principal parts. The fourth principal part sets up the perfect active voice, and the fifth principal part provides the perfect middle/passive voices.

The fourth principal part shows a double set. Dropping a suffix consonant, κ, creates a "strong" (or "second") perfect. Forms that include kappa are part of the *first perfect* system. Forms that drop the kappa are part of the *second perfect* system. The two active voice sets of the fourth principal part differentiate themselves by the presence or absence of a single letter. Easy enough. This lesson will cover the perfect and future perfect forms of this fourth

Table 22.1 Principal Parts: Tenses and Voices

Principal Parts	Tenses	Voices		
First Principal Part	Present	active	middle	passive
	Imperfect	active	middle	passive
Second Principal Part	Future	active	middle	
Third Principal Part	First Aorist	active	middle	
	Second Aorist	active	middle	
Fourth Principal Part	*Perfect*	*active*		
	Future Perfect	*active*		
	Pluperfect	active		
Fifth Principal Part	Perfect		middle	passive
	Future Perfect		middle	passive
	Pluperfect		middle	passive
Sixth Principal Part	First Aorist			passive
	First Future			passive
	Second Aorist			passive
	Second Future			passive

Table 22.2 Primary and Secondary Tenses

Kind of Action	← Time of Action → (Indicative Mood)		
	Secondary Tenses *(secondary endings)*	Primary Tenses *(primary endings)*	
	Past	Present	Future
durative	Imperfect	Present	---------
undefined ●	Aorist	---------	Future
perfective - - ▶	Pluperfect	Perfect	Future Perfect

principal part. The pluperfect, though formulated on this principal part, is a secondary tense and so is culled out for coverage in a separate lesson.

Perfect Active System

The perfect tense is a primary tense, requiring no augment. The perfect stem is doubly altered with *both* a prefix and a suffix. The prefix is reduplication. The suffix is a -κα pattern parallel to the first aorist -σα pattern. The aorist suffix parallel means that the perfect, while a primary tense, takes *secondary* endings, in the pattern of the first aorist. The usual perfect third plural (-σι) is different, however.

Reduplication. The signature of the perfect system is a reduplication prefix. The process breaks down into what letter or combination begins the tense stem. The key for the student is to be able to *recognize* a reduplicated stem, thus perfect tense. Reduplication takes two forms, consonant or augment.

Consonant Reduplication. The basic consonant pattern is repetition. An ε vowel acts to join the reduplicated consonant to the tense stem.

Single Consonant. Except stems beginning with rho (ρ), a single consonant is repeated, always inserting the vowel ε. Thus, λύω, beginning with a single consonant λ, repeats the λ, inserting ε, which creates the perfect form λελυ-.

Stop with Lambda/Rho. The single consonant process also applies to a stop followed by λ or ρ. Notice γράφω, which reduplicates as the perfect stem γεγραφ-, or the verb βλέπω, which reduplicates as βεβλεπ-. Exceptions are chi (χ) stems followed by rho (ρ), such as χρίω. These chi stems show smooth patterns, as κέχρικα (see below).

Table 22.3 Perfect Reduplication—Types

Type	Letters	Example	Perfect
Consonant	Single	λύω	λελυ-
	Stop + λ	βλέπω	βεβλεπ-
	Stop + ρ	γράφω	γεγραφ-
	Aspirated	φιλέω	πεφιλε-
	Stops	χαλάω	κεχαλα-
		θύω	τεθυ-
Augment	Vowels	ἀγαπάω	ἠγαπα-
	Iota insert	λαμβάνω	εἴληφ-
	Preserved Vowel	ὁράω	ἑόρα- ἑώρα-
	Sibilant	ξηραίνω	ἐξηραν-
	Pairs	σταυρόω	ἐσταυρο-
	Triplets	σφραγίζω	ἐσφραγιδ-
	Rho	ῥέω	ἐρρυη-
	Attic	ἀκούω	ἀκηκο-
	None	οἶδα	οἶδα

Rough to Smooth Stop. Outside the special case of a stop followed by λ or ρ above, stop consonants require knowledge of Table 2.2, especially classification as sharp and aspirate. If the single consonant is an aspirated (rough) stop (φ, χ, θ), the repeated consonant takes the form of the corresponding sharp (smooth) stop (φ→π = πεφ-, χ→κ = κεχ-, θ→τ = τεθ-). So we have φιλέω with the perfect stem πεφιλε-.

Augment Reduplication. The other process of reduplication uses a vowel as an augment. The vowel usually is ε, η, or ω, similar to the past time augment. A few verbs, of course, will show exceptions, reduplicating with a consonant (e.g., the verbs θνήσκω, μιμνήσκω, πίπτω, and περιτέμνω). Some common types of augment reduplication are detailed below.

Vowels. As mentioned, stems beginning with a vowel *lengthen* that vowel as an augment. Thus, ἀγαπάω reduplicates as a vowel augment, lengthening the α to η, becoming the form ἠγαπα-. Again, ὁμολογέω reduplicates as ὡμολογε-.

Complex Sibilants. The complex sibilants are ζ, ξ, ψ (see Table 2.3). Tense stems beginning with a complex sibilant reduplicate with an epsilon (ε) vowel augment. Thus, we have ξηραίνω ("I dry up") with the perfect stem ἐξηραν-.[1]

Multiple Consonants. Consonants occurring together as pairs (e.g., στ-) or even as triplets (e.g., σφρ-) reduplicate with an epsilon (ε) as the augment. So, σταυρόω reduplicates into the perfect stem ἐσταυρο-, and σφραγίζω ("I seal") reduplicates into ἐσφραγιδ-. The exceptions are stops followed by λ or ρ (outlined above).

Rho Stems. Stems beginning with rho (ρ) *usually* are augmented and doubled to ἐρρ-. However, to be sure exactly what a particular rho stem does, consult a lexicon.

Variations. Minor variations are generated through elements of root history. **"Iota insert"** relates to some ε verbs "inserting" an iota. Examples include εἶπον to εἴρηκα, ἐργάζομαι to the perfect passive εἴγασμαι, and λαμβάνω to the (second) perfect form εἴληφα. **Preserved stem vowel** relates to the verb ὁράω having two perfect forms, both forms augmenting with ε, but preserving or lengthening the stem vowel too, as ἑόρακα and ἑώρακα. **"Attic reduplication"** is syllable doubling with an additional lengthening of the internal vowel. So ἀκούω becomes the second perfect ἀκήκοα. The verb ἐγείρω goes to the passive ἐγήγερμαι. The verb ἔρχομαι goes the second perfect form ἐλήλυθα. Finally, the old second perfect οἶδα has no reduplication and has lost perfective force, meaning simply "I know."

Compound Verbs. As with past time augments, reduplication is prefixed to the tense stem, *not* before the preposition. Thus, we go from ἀναβαίνω to ἀναβέβηκα.

Suffix. The perfect active suffix is -κα. *Secondary* active endings are used—an exception—and first singular has no ending. Third plural can be -ν, but more often is -σι(ν), a primary ending. Thus, the pattern is -κα, -κας, -κε, -καμεν, -κατε, -κασι (less commonly, -καν), i.e., close to the first aorist pattern. Some verbs insert η or ω before the suffix (μένω, μεμένηκα; πίπτω, πέπτωκα). *Dentals will drop before the κ of the -κα suffix.* So, ἐλπίζω, stem ἐλπιδ-, drops the δ to ἤλπικα. Thus:

$$\underbrace{λε\text{-}λυ}_{\text{reduplicated stem}} + \underbrace{κα}_{+\ \text{perfect suffix}} = \underbrace{λελυκα\text{-}}_{=\qquad\text{perfect resultant form}}$$

Stop reduplication is illustrated by θύω, and augment reduplication (along with a dental stem reaction) is illustrated by ἐλπίζω in the following:

---

[1] No example with the complex sibilant ψ occurs in the New Testament.

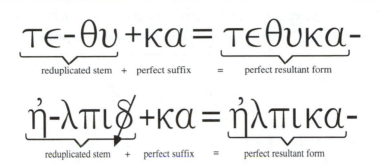

$$\underbrace{\text{ΤΕ-θυ}}_{\text{reduplicated stem}} + \underbrace{\text{κα}}_{\text{perfect suffix}} = \underbrace{\text{ΤΕθυκα-}}_{\text{perfect resultant form}}$$

$$\underbrace{\text{ἠ-λπιϕ}}_{\text{reduplicated stem}} + \underbrace{\text{κα}}_{\text{perfect suffix}} = \underbrace{\text{ἠλπικα-}}_{\text{perfect resultant form}}$$

Second Perfect Active. Recall the sixth principal part's passive system with both first and second passive configurations. Similarly, the perfect system also has a first ("weak") and a second ("strong") perfect form. In the aorist passive system, the θ of the -θη suffix dropped out. Similarly, in the perfect active system, the κ of the -κα suffix falls out. The vowel α is all that remains of the perfect active tense suffix (i.e., -α, -ας, -ε, -αμεν, -ατε, -ασι). Table 22.4 is not intended as an exhaustive list but illustrative of the second perfect form losing the κ of the tense suffix. The paradigm word for the second perfect active will be the same as for the second aorist passive, γράφω.

Table 22.4 Second Perfects

Present	Second Perf.
ἀκούω	ἀκήκοα
γίνομαι	γέγονα
γράφω	γέγραφα
ἔρχομαι	ἐλήλυθα
λαμβάνω	εἴληφα
πάσχω	πέπονθα
πείθω	πέποιθα
πέμπω	πέπομφα
φεύγω	πέφευγα

Table 22.5 Perfect Active Indicative—λύω (consonant reduplication)

Number	Person	Form	Translation
Singular	1st	λέλυκα	"I have loosed"
	2nd	λέλυκας	"you have loosed"
	3rd	λέλυκε(ν)	"he (she, it) has loosed"
Plural	1st	λελύκαμεν	"we have loosed"
	2nd	λελύκατε	"you have loosed"
	3rd	λελύκασι	"they have loosed"

Table 22.6 Perfect Active Indicative—θύω (aspirated stop reduplication)

Number	Person	Form	Translation
Singular	1st	τέθυκα	"I have sacrificed"
	2nd	τέθυκας	"you have sacrificed"
	3rd	τέθυκε(ν)	"he (she, it) has sacrificed"
Plural	1st	τεθύκαμεν	"we have sacrificed"
	2nd	τεθύκατε	"you have sacrificed"
	3rd	τεθύκασι	"they have sacrificed"

Table 22.7 Perfect Active Indicative—ἐλπίζω (augment and dental)

Number	Person	Form	Translation
Singular	1st	ἤλπικα	"I have hoped"
	2nd	ἤλπικας	"you have hoped"
	3rd	ἤλπικεν	"he (she, it) has hoped"
Plural	1st	ἠλπίκαμεν	"we have hoped"
	2nd	ἠλπίκατε	"you have hoped"
	3rd	ἠλπίκασι	"they have hoped"

Table 22.8 Second Perfect Active Indicative—γράφω

Number	Person	Form	Translation
Singular	1st	γέγραφα	"I have written"
	2nd	γέγραφας	"you have written"
	3rd	γέγραφε(ν)	"he (she, it) has written"
Plural	1st	γεγράφαμεν	"we have written"
	2nd	γεγράφατε	"you have written"
	3rd	γεγράφασι	"they have written"

Contract Lengthening. The first perfect active tense sign of the -κα will cause contract vowels to lengthen. Accent returns to standard accent for verbs. Exceptions for perfect active contracts are κοπιάω (κεκοπίακα), πιπράσκω (πέπρακα), ὁράω (ἑόρακα and ἑώρακα), and τελέω (τετέλεκα). So, for example, with τελέω one will find τετέλεκα, τετέλεκας, τετέλεκε(ν), τετελέκαμεν, τετελέκατε, τετελέκασι. Otherwise:

contract lengthening (πεφιλεκα-)

Table 22.9 Perfect Active Indicative—Contracts

φιλέω	δηλόω	τιμάω
πεφίληκα	δεδήλωκα	τετίμηκα
πεφίληκας	δεδήλωκας	τετίμηκας
πεφίληκε(ν)	δεδήλωκε(ν)	τετίμηκε(ν)
πεφιλήκαμεν	δεδηλώκαμεν	τετιμήκαμεν
πεφιλήκατε	δεδηλώκατε	τετιμήκατε
πεφιλήκασι	δεδηλώκασι	τετιμήκασι

Future Perfect Active

The future perfect is part of the perfect active system. The tense is a primary tense. A true future perfect uses: reduplication, perfect active stem, tense suffix -σ, thematic vowel, and primary active endings. If λύω existed in the New Testament as a true future perfect, the forms would be λελύσω, λελύσεις, λελύσει, etc. However, the student need not learn any paradigms. First, the New Testament has only seven occurrences of the future perfect. Second, of these seven, six occurrences are formed using *participles*, not yet covered. Construction includes a form of εἰμί, which is called a *periphrastic* construction (treated with participles). The only true future perfect in the New Testament is a form of the old second perfect οἶδα in Heb. 8:11, which inserts η before the future suffix as εἰδήσουσιν.

Translation

English. Perfect tense in English is action that is completed relative to a fixed point of reference in time. The helping verbs "have," "has," or "had" are used to establish the tense. Such action can be described as "completed action."

Table 22.10 Kinds of Action

Durative	———— or ———————
Undefined	●
Perfective	——▶ or ●——▶

Greek. The Greek perfect tense is quite distinct from this English usage. In Greek, the focus is on the *continuing effects* of a completed action. To illustrate, a potter makes a vase, fires the clay in an oven, glazes the result, and sets the finished product on his mantel. His visitors see the work displayed and exclaim, "What a beautiful vase you *have made*." The past work of the potter's hands is completed and shows on-going consequences into the present time on his mantel. But if a visitor knocks the vase off the mantel, shattering the artwork, the potter exclaims, "You *have broken* the vase I made." The bumbling action of the visitor is completed and likewise has on-going consequences into the present. The completed action in origin could have been durative (making the vase) or punctiliar (knocking the vase off the mantel), but the perfective aspect emphasizes the *consequences* of the action.

Table 22.11 Perfective Aspect—Effects

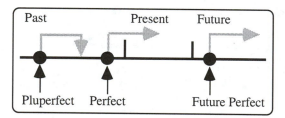

Tense	Action	Effects
Pluperfect	completed	completed
Perfect	completed	continuing
Future Perfect	future	continuing

When completed action has *completed effects*, past perfect tense, i.e., pluperfect, is used. On-going consequences went on for a time, but came to an end at some point in the past. The helping verb incorporated is "had." Completed action with *continuing effects* calls for the perfect tense. On-going results still pertain in present time. The helping verb is "have, has." Future completed action with *future continuing effects* calls for the future perfect tense. The helping verbs would be a combination of "shall" or "will" with "have." *Avoid perfect and aorist confusion:* restrict use of the auxiliary verb "have, has" to the perfect tense for now.

Intensive. Continuing effects are emphasized. The existing state is the point. A present tense translation can be just perfect (☺). Thus, Paul described the present state of believers in Christ, δι' οὗ καὶ τὴν προσαγωγὴν **ἐσχήκαμεν** [τῇ πίστει] εἰς τὴν χάριν ταύτην ἐν ᾗ **ἑστήκαμεν** = "through whom also we **have** access [by faith] into this grace in which we **stand**" (Rom. 5:2).

Completed (consummative). The completed action which generated the continuing effects is emphasized. The past is the point. A translation using the auxiliary verb "has, have" is usual. Thus, ἀπεκρίθη ὁ Πιλᾶτος, Ὃ **γέγραφα, γέγραφα.** = "Pilate answered, 'What I **have written, I have written.**'" (John 19:22). Simple past tense, encroaching on aorist meaning, also might could be used. For the past tense idea, take John 6:32, οὐ Μωϋσῆς **δέδωκεν** ὑμῖν τὸν ἄρτον ἐκ τοῦ οὐρανοῦ = "it is not Moses who **gave** you the heavenly bread" (δίδωμι, "I give," a -μι verb not yet covered). Context is important in this regard. Notice the explicit aorist form in the previous verse, John 6:31, Ἄρτον ἐκ τοῦ οὐρανοῦ **ἔδωκεν** αὐτοῖς φαγεῖν = "He **gave** them bread from heaven to eat."

Iterative. Action is completed, basically, but inherent to the context is an idea of repetition over an interval of time. The past is the point. Use of "has, have" is usual. Sometimes the translator may wish to draw out the implication of repetition by inserting "repeatedly" or some similar phrase into the verbal idea. In the following example, the first instance of the perfect tense is iterative, the second, completed: ταῦτα **λελάληκα** ὑμῖν ἵνα ἐν ἐμοὶ εἰρήνην ἔχητε· ἐν τῷ κόσμῳ θλῖψιν ἔχετε, ἀλλὰ θαρσεῖτε, ἐγὼ **νενίκηκα** τὸν κόσμον. = "These things I **have spoken** [i.e., repeatedly] to you in order that in me you might have peace; in the world you have tribulation, but take courage, I **have conquered** the world." (John 16:33).

Dramatic. Vivid narration or dramatic declaration to involve the reader or listener is the technique. The historical present and dramatic aorist do similarly. The existing state is the point, as with the intensive. Jesus' proclamation in Matt. 3:2 seems to have more force and meaning translated this way: Μετανοεῖτε, **ἤγγικεν** γὰρ ἡ βασιλεία τῶν οὐρανῶν. = "Repent, for the kingdom of heaven **draws near!**"

Aoristic. Has the perfective aspect washed out completely? Translation would become aoristic, if so. The category is dubious, but some include this use. A possible example is ἄγγελος αὐτῷ **λελάληκεν** = "an angel **spoke** to him" (John 12:29).

Future Perfect. Heb. 8:11 is the only example in the New Testament: ὅτι πάντες **εἰδήσουσίν** με ἀπὸ μικροῦ ἕως μεγάλου αὐτῶν = "because all **will know** me, from the least to the greatest of them." However, in this case, notice the simple *future* translation. The verb οἶδα, covered previously, is an exception, whose perfective force washed out and became simply the present tense verb, "I know." Future perfect otherwise would be translated "they will have known" in the pattern "will have ___ed."

Principal Parts

Add the fourth principal part to your Greek verb cards. Research in a lexicon to make sure whether the verb is a first perfect or second perfect system.

Table 22.12 Principal Parts—Learning the Greek Verb System

First	Second	Third	Fourth	Fifth	Sixth
λύω	λύσω	ἔλυσα	λέλυκα	λέλυμαι	ἐλυθην
λείπω	λείψω	ἔλιπον	λέλοιπα	λέλειμμαι	ἐλήφθην

What To Learn—LESSON 22 (δύο καὶ εἴκοσι)

Beginning

☐ 1. Significance of the two perfect systems of the fourth principal part

☐ 2. Formation of the first perfect active

☐ 3. Perfect reduplication patterns

☐ 4. First perfect active paradigms: λύω, θύω, ἐλπίζω

☐ 5. Second perfect active paradigm: γράφω

☐ 6. Recognition of contract verbs in the first perfect system

☐ 7. Add the fourth principal part to verb cards

☐ 8. Vocabulary words

Advanced

☐ 9. The rare future perfect tense as part of the first perfect system

☐ 10. Significance of the perfective aspect and how to translate: *intensive, completed, iterative, dramatic, aoristic*

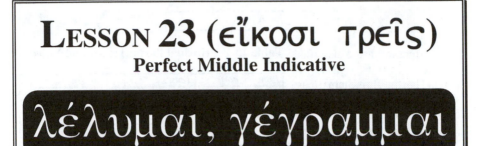

LESSON 23 (εἴκοσι τρεῖς)
Perfect Middle Indicative

λέλυμαι, γέγραμμαι

The perfect middle is the fifth principal part of the Greek verb. The fifth principal part is distinctive for the lack of a thematic vowel. Endings are attached directly to the stem. For consonant tense stems, the consonants of stem and ending collide, resulting in volatilization and spelling changes.

Vocabulary 23

Adverb and Conjunction

ἄρτι	now, just now
ὥσπερ	just as, even as

Nouns and Adjective

διάβολος, ὁ	Devil (adj.: slanderous)
λίθος, ὁ	stone
μαρτυρία, ἡ	testimony, witness
μνημεῖον, τό	tomb, monument
ὀργή, -ῆς, ἡ	wrath
περιτομή, -ῆς, ἡ	circumcision
ὀλίγος, -η, -ον	little, few

Verbs

ἀσθενέω	I am weak
βλασφημέω	I blaspheme
διακονέω	I serve

ἐπιστρέφω	I turn to, return
μετανοέω	I repent
μισέω	I hate
οἰκοδομέω	I build
παραγίνομαι	I come, arrive
περισσεύω	I abound, am rich
πλανάω	I deceive, lead astray
ὑποστρέφω	I return

Perfect Middle (consonant stems)

γέγραμμαι (γράφω)	I have written
ἤγγελμαι (ἀγγέλλω)	I have announced
ἦργμαι (ἄρχω)	I have ruled
ἦρμαι (αἴρω)	I have raised up
κέκριμαι (κρίνω)	I have judged
πέπεισμαι (πείθω)	I have persuaded

269

Analysis

Perfect forms are classified by voice into two principal parts. The fourth principal part sets up the perfect active voice and the fifth principal part the perfect middle/passive voices. This lesson will cover forms of the fifth principal part. The pluperfect, though formulated on the fourth and fifth principal parts, is a *secondary* tense and so is culled out for coverage in a separate lesson.

Reduplication is used as a prefix, just as with the fourth principal part. However, several differences are noted. First, no tense suffix is used. Second, *primary* middle/passive endings are attached. Third, the hitch is, *no thematic vowel is used.* This means consonant collision for consonant ending tense stems, and volatilization occurs. Stem changes must be learned that

Table 23.1 Principal Parts: Tenses and Voices

Principal Parts	Tenses	Voices		
First Principal Part	Present	active	middle	passive
	Imperfect	active	middle	passive
Second Principal Part	Future	active	middle	
Third Principal Part	First Aorist	active	middle	
	Second Aorist	active	middle	
Fourth Principal Part	Perfect	active		
	Future Perfect	active		
	Pluperfect	active		
Fifth Principal Part	Perfect		middle	passive
	Future Perfect		middle	passive
	Pluperfect		middle	passive
Sixth Principal Part	First Aorist			passive
	First Future			passive
	Second Aorist			passive
	Second Future			passive

Table 23.2 Primary and Secondary Tenses

Kind of Action	Time of Action (Indicative Mood)		
	Secondary Tenses *(secondary endings)*	Primary Tenses *(primary endings)*	
	Past	Present	Future
durative	Imperfect	Present	---------
undefined ●	Aorist	---------	Future
perfective - - -→	Pluperfect	Perfect	Future Perfect

take into account juxtaposition of consonant endings of tense stems and consonant beginnings of pronominal suffixes. Fourth, as for the endings themselves, the main oddity is that -νται, third person plural, is not used with *consonant* stem verbs. *Third person plural of consonant stem perfect middle verbs is formed periphrastically.* The periphrastic formation will be covered in the lessons on participles.

Perfect Middle System

Formation. The perfect tense is a primary tense, requiring no past time augment. Reduplication has the same features as for the fourth principal part, that is, divided into consonant reduplication and vowel augmentation. No suffix such as the -κα scheme of the fourth principal part is used. The passive form duplicates the middle form, so context alone determines which voice is used.

Pronominal Suffix. No thematic vowel is used. Certain phonetic changes result.

<u>Vowel Stems</u>. Lack of a thematic vowel creates no problems in vowel stems, such as verbs ending in -η, -ι, -υ, -ω, and diphthongs. Thus:

$$\underbrace{\lambda\epsilon\text{-}\lambda\upsilon}_{\text{reduplicated stem}} \quad = \quad \underbrace{\lambda\epsilon\lambda\upsilon\text{-}}_{\text{perfect middle result}}$$

Pronominal suffixes are attached directly to this perfect middle resultant stem. A minor variation is that the *second singular no longer contracts* into the derivative form -η, instead remaining as -σαι. So:

$$\lambda\epsilon\lambda\upsilon + \sigma\alpha\iota = \lambda\acute{\epsilon}\lambda\upsilon\sigma\alpha\iota$$

perfect middle result   +   ending   =   no thematic vowel

Table 23.3 Perfect Middle/Passive Volatilization

Tense Stem Ending						
Stops			Liquids			
Labial	Palatal	Dental	True Liquid		Nasal	Suffix
π, β, φ	κ, γ, χ	τ, δ, θ	λ	ρ	ν	Letter
μμ	γμ	σμ	-----	-----	μμ[1]	μ
ψ	ξ	σ	-----	-----	-----	σ
ππ	κτ	στ	-----	-----	-----	τ
φθ	χθ	σθ	λθ	ρθ	νθ	σθ

---

[1] The nasal ν reacts variously. Often verbs ending with -ν drop the ν in perfect and aorist passive indicative forms (e.g., κέκρικα, κέκριμαι, ἐκρίθην). In contrast, others show -σμαι in the perfect middle (μιαίνω, μεμίασμαι). On the other hand, notice the -μμ reaction in: (1) some perfect middles, as μαραίνω, μεμάραμμαι, (2) compound formation, as ἐν-μένω = ἐμμένω, (3) in middle/passive participles (suffix -μεν), as μεμιαμμένοις (from μιαίνω).

Consonant Stems. With *consonant* tense stems phonetic changes take place. The tense stem consonants break down, as usual, into stops and liquids. The beginning consonants of the pronominal suffixes involved are μ, σ, τ, σθ.[2] Consult Table 23.3. (Dash means no reaction; letters remain the same.)

As an example, up against the -μαι of the first person singular, the verb γράφω takes this form as a perfect middle:

$$\gamma\acute{\epsilon}\gamma\rho\alpha\boxed{\phi\mu}\alpha\iota = \gamma\acute{\epsilon}\gamma\rho\alpha\boxed{\mu\mu}\alpha\iota$$

Against the -σαι of the second person singular, γράφω is γέγραφσαι, which becomes γέγραψαι. The third person singular, γεγραφται, becomes γέγραπται. Finally, the second person plural, γέγραφσθε, becomes γέγραφθε.

Letter Insert. We have encountered before various verbs that insert a letter before a suffix. Before the pronominal suffix of the perfect middle, a few verbs insert either an η or a σ. One verb inserting η is βάλλω, which becomes the perfect middle βέβληται (the α is lost by vowel gradation). A verb inserting σ is γινώσκω, which becomes the prefect middle ἔγνωσμαι.

Third Plural. *For consonant stems only,* the third plural does *not* use the -νται suffix, but, instead, is formed periphrastically. The student will learn this formation with participles. The perfect middle, third plural of γράφω would use the perfect middle participle, γεγραμμένοι, with the third plural of εἰμί in the present tense, εἰσί, creating the form εἰσὶ γεγραμμένοι = "they have written (for themselves)."

Table 23.4 Perfect Middle/Passive Indicative—λύω (vowel stem)

Form	Middle Translation	Passive Translation
λέλυμαι	"I have loosed (for myself)"	"I have been loosed"
λέλυσαι	"you have loosed (for yourself)"	"you have been loosed"
λέλυται	"he has loosed (for himself)," etc.	"he has been loosed," etc.
λελύμεθα	"we have loosed (for ourselves)"	"we have been loosed"
λέλυσθε	"you have loosed (for yourselves)"	"you have been loosed"
λέλυνται	"they have loosed (for themselves)"	"they have been loosed"

[2]The third plural form (-νται) does not occur; instead, a periphrastic construction is used.

Table 23.5 Perfect Middle/Passive Indicative—Stop Volatilization

γράφω	ἄρχω	πείθω
γέγραμμαι	ἦργμαι	πέπεισμαι
γέγραψαι	ἦρξαι	πέπεισαι
γέγραπται	ἦρκται	πέπεισται
γεγράμμεθα	ἤργμεθα	πεπείσμεθα
γέγραφθε	ἦρχθε	πέπεισθε
(εἰσὶ γεγραμμένοι)	(εἰσὶ ἠργμένοι)	(εἰσὶ πεπεισμένοι)

Table 23.6 Perfect Middle/Passive Indicative—Liquids and Letter Insert

ἀγγέλλω	αἴρω	γινώσκω
ἤγγελμαι	ἦρμαι	ἔγνωσμαι
ἤγγελσαι	ἦρσαι	ἔγνωσσαι
ἤγγελται	ἦρται	ἔγνωσται
ἠγγέλμεθα	ἤρμεθα	ἐγνώσμεθα
ἤγγελσθε	ἦρθε	ἔγνωσθε
(εἰσὶ ἠγγελμένοι)	(εἰσὶ ἠρμένοι)	(εἰσὶ ἐγνωσμένοι)

Second Perfect Middle? The active voice generates a second perfect form by dropping the κ of the -κα active suffix. Perfect middle has no suffix. By default of the formation pattern, the perfect middle has no second perfect middle form.

Contract Lengthening. Contracts lengthen before the suffix or ending of other principal parts. Normally this is the tense suffix, but in the perfect middle this is the personal ending. Accent returns to standard accent for verbs. One contract exception is δέω (δέδεμαι, δέδεσαι, δέδεται, δεδέμεθα, δέδεσθε, δέδενται). Otherwise:

πεφίλημαι

contract lengthening

Table 23.7 Perfect Middle Indicative—Contracts

φιλέω	δηλόω	τιμάω
πεφίλημαι	δεδήλωμαι	τετίμημαι
πεφίλησαι	δεδήλωσαι	τετίμησαι
πεφίληται	δεδήλωται	τετίμηται
πεφιλήμεθα	δεδηλώμεθα	τετιμήμεθα
πεφίλησθε	δεδήλωσθε	τετίμησθε
πεφίληνται	δεδήλωνται	τετίμηνται

Future Perfect Middle

The future perfect middle/passive does not occur in the New Testament except in periphrastic formations. The six instances are ἔσομαι πεποιθώς (Heb. 2:13), ἔσται δεδεμένον (Matt. 16:19), ἔσται λελυμένον (Matt. 16:19), ἔσται δεδεμένα (Matt. 18:18), ἔσται λελυμένα (Matt. 18:18), and ἔσονται διαμεμερισμένοι (Luke 12:52). The translation for such passive voices would be "shall have been ____ed."

Translation

Recognition. Perfect middle in thematic verbs is easy to spot in reduplicated stems. The reduplication points to the perfective aspect. Then, no thematic vowel with middle endings cinches the location. On the other hand, vowel augments are harder, especially for short verbs, such as ἄγω, which loose the dictionary "look" totally in the perfect middle. So ἄγω is ἦγμαι. ("Agō puts ēg on mai face.") Familiarity with principal parts is key for recognition.

Meaning. One's translation of the perfect middle/passive will represent the typical ideas in these voices. The middle may be said to reflect the verbal action. The subject may be

Table 23.8 Greek Voice

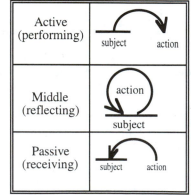

Active (performing)	subject → action
Middle (reflecting)	action ↻ subject
Passive (receiving)	subject ← action

reflecting the action upon himself (*direct middle*). The subject may be participating with self-interest in the action (*indirect middle*). Or, the subject may participate in the action as part of a group (*reciprocal middle*). However, remember that middle voice use was fading out in New Testament times. *Assume middle/passive forms are passive unless context dictates otherwise* (cf. examples #1, #7). Passive voice means the subject receives the action. Passive voice expresses *agency*. (Review Lesson 10).

Examples.

(1) Μὴ καὶ ὑμεῖς **πεπλάνησθε**; = "You **have** not also **been deceived**, have you?" (John 7:47)

(2) ὃ **ἐπήγγελται** δυνατός ἐστιν καὶ ποιῆσαι = "that which He **had promised** He also was able to do" (Rom. 4:21; ἀπαγγέλλομαι)

(3) ὅτι **δέδεκται** ἡ Σαμάρεια τὸν λόγον τοῦ θεοῦ = "that Samaria **had received** the word of God" (Acts 8:14; δέχομαι)

(4) **δέδεσαι** γυναικί; μὴ ζήτει λύσιν· **λέλυσαι** ἀπὸ γυναικός; μὴ ζήτει γυναῖκα. = "**Are you bound** to a wife? Do not seek to be loosed. **Have you been loosed** from a wife? Do not seek a wife." (1 Cor. 7:27; δέω, λύω)

(5) καὶ ὅτι ἐτάφη, καὶ ὅτι **ἐγήγερται** τῇ ἡμέρᾳ τῇ τρίτῃ = "and that he was buried, and that he **was raised** the third day" (1 Cor. 15:4; ἐγείρω)

(6) θεῷ δὲ **πεφανερώμεθα** = "but we **have been manifested** unto God" (2 Cor. 5:11; φανερόω)

(7) καὶ **ἐκλέλησθε** τῆς παρακλήσεως = "but you **have forgotten** the exhortation" (Heb. 12:5; ἐκλανθάνω, voices distinguished; see Table 10.4)

(8) οὗ γὰρ **εἰσιν** δύο ἢ τρεῖς **συνηγμένοι** εἰς τὸ ἐμὸν ὄνομα = "For where two or three **are gathered together** in My name" (Matt. 18:20; συνάγω; consonant stem, third plural formed periphrastically)

Principal Parts

Add the fifth principal part to your Greek verb cards. Research in a lexicon to make sure of the configuration. Compare the expected pattern of ν + μ = μμ in πλατύνω as the perfect middle πεπλάτυμμαι. Other liquids, however, seem to drop the liquid consonant, as does κρίνω, with the perfect middle form κέκριμαι.

Table 23.9 Principal Parts—Learning the Greek Verb System

First	Second	Third	Fourth	*Fifth*	Sixth
λύω	λύσω	ἔλυσα	λέλυκα	λέλυμαι	ἐλύθην
λείπω	λείψω	ἔλιπον	λέλοιπα	λέλειμμαι	ἐλήφθην

What To Learn—LESSON 23 (εἴκοσι τρεῖς)

Beginning

☐   1.   Formation of the perfect middle system

☐   2.   Perfect middle paradigm: λύω

☐   3.   Recognition of contract verbs in the perfect middle system

☐   4.   Recognition of stops and liquids in the perfect middle system

☐   5.   Why perfect middle has no *second* perfect middle forms

☐   6.   Translating the perfect middle/passive and use of passive voice as agency (see Lesson 10)

☐   7.   Add the fifth principal part to verb cards

☐   8.   Vocabulary words

Advanced

☐   9.   Perfect middle/passive consonant stem volatilization chart

☐   10.   Formulation of the *third person plural* of *consonant* stems (periphrastic)

☐   11.   Perfect middle *stop* paradigms: γράφω, ἄρχω, πείθω

☐   12.   Perfect middle *liquid* stem paradigms: ἀγγέλλω, αἴρω

☐   13.   Perfect middle *letter insert* paradigm: γινώσκω

☐   14.   Formulation of the *future perfect middle*

LESSON 24 (εἴκοσι τέσσαρες)
Pluperfect Indicative

ἐλελύκειν

The pluperfect uses fourth and fifth principal parts, but is a *secondary* tense. Past time theoretically has an augment, but an augment often is missing. Forms still are distinct. Aspect focuses on the finished results of a past action.

Vocabulary 24

Nouns and Adjectives

βιβλίον, τό	book
διαθήκη, -ης, ἡ	covenant
προσευχή, -ῆς, ἡ	prayer
δυνατός, -ή, -όν	powerful, able
πτωχός, -ή, -όν	poor

Verbs

ὀφείλω	I owe, ought
πειράζω	I test, tempt, attempt
ὑποτάσσω	I put in subjection

Pluperfect Active

ἐγεγόνειν (γίνομαι)	I had become
εἰρήκειν (εἶπον)	I had said
ἐκβεβλήκειν (ἐκβάλλω)	I had thrown out

ἐληλύθειν (ἔρχομαι)	I had come
ἑωράκειν (ὁράω)	I had seen
ᾔδειν (οἶδα)	I knew (defective)
ᾐεγνώκειν (γινώσκω)	I had known
κεκρίκειν (κρίνω)	I had judged
μεμενήκειν (μένω)	I had remained
πεπιστεύκειν (πιστεύω)	I had believed
πεποιήκειν (ποιέω)	I had made

Pluperfect Middle/Passive

ἐβεβλήμην (βάλλω)	I had thrown
ἐπεγεγράμμην (ἐπιγράφω)	I had written on
λελύμην (λύω)	I had loosed

277

| Analysis |

Augment. The pluperfect is formulated on the fourth and fifth principal parts, as are both the perfect and future perfect. A secondary tense theoretically has an augment. For pluperfect, occasionally an augment is found in typical patterns of past time augment. Yet, often, one finds the augment dropped. The active voice -κει suffix or the reduplicated stem's *secondary* middle/passive form suffice for identifying the pluperfect tense.

Reduplication. For both consonant and vowel varieties, reduplication is standard. Verbs already learned are the same.

Tense Suffix. Active voice tense suffix is -κει, instead of the perfect's -κα. A distinction between the first ("weak") and second ("strong") forms applies to the pluperfect active just as to the perfect active in the

Table 24.1 Principal Parts: Tenses and Voices

Principal Parts	Tenses	Voices		
First Principal Part	Present	active	middle	passive
	Imperfect	active	middle	passive
Second Principal Part	Future	active	middle	
Third Principal Part	First Aorist	active	middle	
	Second Aorist	active	middle	
Fourth Principal Part	Perfect	active		
	Future Perfect	active		
	Pluperfect	*active*		
Fifth Principal Part	Perfect		middle	passive
	Future Perfect		middle	passive
	Pluperfect		*middle*	*passive*
Sixth Principal Part	First Aorist			passive
	First Future			passive
	Second Aorist			passive
	Second Future			passive

Table 24.2 Primary and Secondary Tenses

Kind of Action	Time of Action (Indicative Mood)		
	Secondary Tenses *(secondary endings)*	Primary Tenses *(primary endings)*	
	Past	Present	Future
durative	Imperfect	Present	---------
undefined	Aorist	---------	Future
perfective	Pluperfect	Perfect	Future Perfect

fourth principal part. In fact, if a verb exists as a second perfect active, that verb by default exists as a second pluperfect active as well—that is, if the form even occurs in the New Testament. Dropping the κ in the -κει tense suffix makes a second pluperfect, on the precise pattern as dropping the κ in the -κα perfect active suffix.

Consonant stems ending in stops before the -κει suffix would act as in perfect active, if enough were present to count in the pluperfect. Liquids and nasals would do similarly. Inserting a letter before the -κει tense suffix shows up in the forms of λέγω (εἶπον) as the pluperfect active εἰρήκειν, ἐκβάλλω as ἐκβεβλήκειν, and μένω as μεμενήκειν. (Note: augments and reduplication go *between* compounds.)

Pronominal Suffix. The pluperfect is a secondary tense. Endings, then, are exactly those of past time verbs, as with aorist and imperfect.

Active Voice. The first pluperfect active voice is given by the fourth principal part, but using a -κει tense suffix. Endings are *secondary* active, but -σαν in third plural. So, first pluperfect active endings look like the imperfect, except for this -σαν option. The pronominal pattern with the tense suffix becomes: -κειν, -κεις, -κει, -κειμεν, -κειτε, -κεισαν (i.e., quite distinctive). Second pluperfects, dropping the κ of the -κει suffix, show only the diphthong -ει before the pronominal suffix in the pattern: -ειν, -εις, -ει, -ειμεν, -ειτε, -εισαν.

Middle/Passive Voice. The middle/passive voice is based on the fifth principal part, distinguished by no thematic vowel. The pluperfect, however, uses *secondary* middle endings (-μην, -σο, -το, -μεθα, -σθε, -ντο). Still, any spelling changes would conform to the perfect middle passive volatilization chart of Table 23.3. In reality, the only New Testament verb involved is ἐπιγράφω ("I write on"), which takes the pluperfect middle/passive form ἐπεγεγράμμην. Inserting a letter before the pronominal suffix is the verb βάλλω, in the pluperfect middle/passive form ἐβεβλήμην.

Periphrastic Forms. The pluperfect shows periphrastic formation as does the perfect. The only distinction is generated by the pluperfect's nature as a *secondary* tense. Correspondingly, the forms of εἰμί used are the *imperfect* forms (ἤμην, ἦς, ἦν, ἦμεν, ἦτε, ἦσαν). The participial form is perfect active or middle. The construction, then, would be similar to ἤμην λελυκώς for the active voice, or ἤμην λελυμένος for the middle/passive voice, only also following gender inflections. For all the fuss, the periphrastic formulation is totally redundant. *Resultant meaning translates the same as if the verb were a simple pluperfect indicative.* The student is not responsible for this formulation until participles are covered.

The above discussion is summarized below. First, the reduplicated perfective stem with secondary tense past time augment and pluperfect tense suffix becomes:

$$ \underbrace{ἐλελυ}_{\substack{\text{augmented,} \\ \text{reduplicated stem}}} + \underbrace{κει}_{\text{+ pluperfect suffix}} = \underbrace{ἐλελυκει\text{-}}_{\text{pluperfect active stem}} $$

to which one attaches the secondary active endings, as in:

$$ \underbrace{ἐλελυκει + ν = ἐλελύκειν}_{\text{pluperfect active stem + secondary ending}} $$

Typically, however, the augment is allowed to drop; the tense suffix is distinctive, so dropping the augment generates no confusion with the perfect active. Thus:

$$ἐλελύκειν = λελύκειν$$

The *second* pluperfect form drops the κ of the tense suffix, -κει, e.g., ἔρχομαι:

$$\underbrace{ἐληλυθ}_{\substack{\text{augmented,} \\ \text{reduplicated stem}}} + \underbrace{κει}_{\substack{\text{2nd pluperfect} \\ \text{suffix}}} = \underbrace{ἐληλυθει\text{-}}_{\text{2nd pluperfect active}}$$

To this second pluperfect form are attached the secondary active endings:

$$ἐληλυθει + ν = ἐληλύθειν$$

pluperfect active stem + secondary ending

The pluperfect middle/passive voices use the fifth principal part, augmented for past time. In addition, the *secondary* middle forms are used, in distinction from the perfect's primary middle endings.[1] So:

$$\underbrace{ἐλελυ}_{\substack{\text{augmented,} \\ \text{reduplicated stem}}} + \underbrace{μην}_{\substack{\text{+ secondary} \\ \text{middle suffix}}} = ἐλελύμην$$

Typically, the augment drops, yet the secondary ending is still distinctive:

$$ἐλελύμην = λελύμην$$

Exception. With paradigms, remember the augment often drops. One form *not* translated as a pluperfect is ᾔδειν, the pluperfect of οἶδα. Thus, οἶδα translates with present meaning as "I know," and ᾔδειν translates as imperfect, "I knew."

---

[1]No *second* pluperfect middle exists for the same reason no *second* perfect middle exists: no tense suffix is used in the first place from which a letter could drop out; see p. 273.

Table 24.3 First Pluperfect Active Indicative—λύω

Number	Person	Form	Translation
Singular	1st	ἐλελύκειν	"I had loosed"
	2nd	ἐλελύκεις	"you had loosed"
	3rd	ἐλελύκει	"he (she, it) had loosed"
Plural	1st	ἐλελύκειμεν	"we had loosed"
	2nd	ἐλελύκειτε	"you had loosed"
	3rd	ἐλελύκεισαν	"they had loosed"

Table 24.4 Second Pluperfect Active Indicative—ἔρχομαι

Number	Person	Form	Translation
Singular	1st	ἐληλύθειν	"I had come"
	2nd	ἐληλύθεις	"you had come"
	3rd	ἐληλύθει	"he (she, it) had come"
Plural	1st	ἐληλύθειμεν	"we had come"
	2nd	ἐληλύθειτε	"you had come"
	3rd	ἐληλύθεισαν	"they had come"

Table 24.5 Pluperfect Middle/Passive Indicative—λύω

Form	Middle Translation	Passive Translation
ἐλελύμην	"I had loosed (for myself)"	"I had been loosed"
ἐλέλυσο	"you had loosed (for yourself)"	"you had been loosed"
ἐλέλυτο	"he had loosed (for himself)," etc.	"he had been loosed," etc.
ἐλελύμεθα	"we had loosed (for ourselves)"	"we had been loosed"
ἐλέλυσθε	"you had loosed (for yourselves)"	"you had been loosed"
ἐλέλυντο	"they had loosed (for themselves)"	"they had been loosed"

The following paradigms for οἶδα and ᾔδειν are given to clarify their roles as simple present and imperfect in translation. The literal forms are second perfect and second pluperfect, respectively.

Table 24.6 Second Perfect as Present Tense—οἶδα

Number	Person	Form	Translation
Singular	1st	οἶδα	"I know"
	2nd	οἶδας	"you know"
	3rd	οἶδε(ν)	"he (she, it) knows"
Plural	1st	οἴδαμεν	"we know"
	2nd	οἴδατε	"you know"
	3rd	οἴδασι(ν)	"they know"

Table 24.7 Second Pluperfect as Imperfect Tense—ᾔδειν

Number	Person	Form	Translation
Singular	1st	ᾔδειν	"I was knowing"
	2nd	ᾔδεις	"you were knowing"
	3rd	ᾔδει	"he (she, it) was knowing"
Plural	1st	ᾔδειμεν	"we were knowing"
	2nd	ᾔδειτε	"you were knowing"
	3rd	ᾔδεισαν	"they were knowing"

Contract Lengthening. For the pluperfect middle, the ending itself generates the contract lengthening (the fifth principal part uses no tense suffix). Accent returns to standard accent for verbs. Actual pluperfect contracts are few. Of these one can include ποιέω, οἰκοδομέω, and θεμελιόω (and a few -μι verbs). Middle/passive forms would be similar, only minus the -κει tense suffix; i.e., ἐπεφιλήμην, ἐδεδηλώμην, and ἐτετιμήμην. Exceptions are the pluperfect active of ὁράω, ἑωράκειν, and pluperfect middle/passive of περιδέω ("I wrap"), περιεδεδέμην. So:

ἐπεφιλήκειν

contract lengthening

Table 24.8 Pluperfect Active Indicative—Contracts

φιλέω	δηλόω	τιμάω
ἐπεφιλήκειν	ἐδεδηλώκειν	ἐτετιμήκειν
ἐπεφιλήκεις	ἐδεδηλώκεις	ἐτετιμήκεις
ἐπεφιλήκει	ἐδεδηλώκει	ἐτετιμήκει
ἐπεφιλήκειμεν	ἐδεδηλώκειμεν	ἐτετιμήκειμεν
ἐπεφιλήκειτε	ἐδεδηλώκειτε	ἐτετιμήκειτε
ἐπεφιλήκεισαν	ἐδεδηλώκεισαν	ἐτετιμήκεισαν

Translation

The perfective idea works in all three time frames of past, present, and future. This aspect calls attention to the condition of the effects of the action. Completed action with *completed effects* calls for the past perfect tense, that is, the pluperfect. In this tense, the on-going consequences went on for a time, but came to an end at some point in the past. The two main uses of this pluperfect tense are similar to uses of the perfect.

Intensive. Translation of the pluperfect can emphasize the continuing effects, as with the perfect tense. The

Table 24.9 Perfective Aspect—Effects

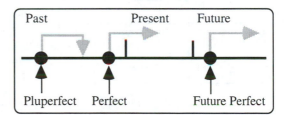

Tense	Action	Effects
Pluperfect	completed	completed
Perfect	completed	continuing
Future Perfect	future	continuing

on-going state which existed for a time is the point. Simple English past tense is used in this case. On occasion, the translation incorporates "was/were ___ing" to pull out the on-going emphasis. For example, καὶ σκοτία ἤδη **ἐγεγόνει** καὶ οὔπω **ἐληλύθει** πρὸς αὐτοὺς ὁ Ἰησοῦς = "and it already **was becoming** dark, but Jesus not yet **had come** to them" (John 6:17; the first is intensive, the other completed).

Completed (consummative). Again, as with the perfect, the completed action generating the continuing effects is emphasized. Use of the helping verb "had" is normal in this application. For example, καὶ ἤγαγον αὐτὸν ἕως ὀφρύος τοῦ ὄρους ἐφ' οὗ ἡ πόλις **ᾠκοδόμητο** αὐτῶν = "and they brought him to the leading edge of the hill upon which their city **had been built**" (Luke 4:29).

Conditional Sentences

Table 24.10 Conditional Sentences

Class	Condition	Conj.	Protasis	Apodosis
1st TRUE	fulfilled (οὐ in negative)	εἰ + (ἐάν at times)	any indicative	any indicative imperative subjunctive
2nd FALSE	not fulfilled (μή in negative) a. present time	εἰ +	past tense indicative	ἄν + past indicative (ἄν can occur anywhere or at times drop out)
	b. past time	εἰ +	aorist indicative	ἄν + past indicative
		εἰ +	pluperfect indicative	ἄν + past indicative
3rd POSSIBLE	undetermined possible	ἐάν +	subjunctive	future, or any indic. (ἄν)
4th REMOTE	undetermined remote	εἰ +	optative	optative (ἄν)

Second class conditions assume the condition is *not* fulfilled. The verb structure can set up the false condition (protasis) in either of two time frames, present or past. Conditions assumed false in *present* time usually use the imperfect tense. Conditions assumed false in *past* time use both aorist and pluperfect tenses. Examples in Lesson 13 presented only conditions assumed false in *present* time (imperfect). The following examples illustrate second class conditional sentences assumed false in *past* time, which set up the protasis in aorist or pluperfect tenses. Remember, the key to class condition is *the mood of the protasis*, not the conjunction. Notice all first and second class conditions require *indicative* mood.

1. Second class, condition assumed objectively false, past time:

    (a) εἰ γὰρ **ἔγνωσαν**, οὐκ ἂν τὸν κύριον τῆς δόξης ἐσταύρωσαν = "for if they **had known**, they would not have crucified the Lord of glory" (1 Cor. 2:8)

    (b) εἰ δὲ **ἐγνώκειτε** τί ἐστιν, Ἔλεος θέλω καὶ οὐ θυσίαν, οὐκ ἂν κατεδικάσατε τοὺς ἀναιτίους. = "But if you **had known** what this means—'I desire mercy and not sacrifice'—you would not have condemned the innocent." (Matt. 12:7)

2. Second class, condition assumed false only for argument, past time:
   (a) εἰ μὴ **ἦλθον** καὶ **ἐλάλησα** αὐτοῖς, ἁμαρτίαν οὐκ εἴχοσαν = "If I **had not come** and **spoken** to them, they would not have sin." (John 15:22)
   (b) Ἀπολελύσθαι ἐδύνατο ὁ ἄνθρωπος οὗτος εἰ μὴ **ἐπεκέκλητο** Καίσαρα. = "This man could have been released, **had** he not **appealed** to the Emperor." (Acts 26:32)

What To Learn—LESSON 24 (εἴκοσι τέσσαρες)

Beginning

☐ 1. Formation of the pluperfect system, including augment, secondary endings

☐ 2. *First* and *second* pluperfect active voice tense suffixes: -κει and -ει

☐ 3. *First* pluperfect active indicative paradigm: λύω

☐ 4. *Second* pluperfect active indicative paradigm: ἔρχομαι

☐ 5. Pluperfect middle/passive indicative paradigm: λύω

☐ 6. Why no *second* pluperfect middle exists

☐ 7. οἶδα with present meaning, ᾔδειν as imperfect

☐ 8. Recognition of contract verbs in the pluperfect system

☐ 9. Recognizing, translating second class conditional sentences with past time conditions

☐ 10. Complete the fifth principal part on verb cards

☐ 11. Vocabulary words

Advanced

☐ 12. Possible volatilization patterns and letter inserts as in perfect tense

☐ 13. Periphrastic construction and significance for translation

☐ 14. Pluperfect aspect and translating the pluperfect: *intensive* and *completed*

The papyrus $\mathfrak{P}^{46}$ is our oldest copy of the Pauline correspondence, dated about A.D. 200, but without the Pastoral Epistles. The eighty-six surviving leaves are kept in two places: the Chester Beatty Library at Dublin and the University of Michigan Library at Ann Arbor. In $\mathfrak{P}^{46}$ Hebrews follows Romans; thus, the Eastern Church regarded Paul the author of Hebrews. The discovery of $\mathfrak{P}^{46}$ (published 1930s) played into the question of the ending of Romans. The image below shows $\mathfrak{P}^{46}$ at Rom. 15:33, followed by the doxology of Rom. 16:25–27, then Rom. 16:1.[2]

Rom. 15:33; 16:25–27; 16:1

---

[2]The "doxology" (Rom. 16:25–27) occurs in different places in the manuscripts: (1) in the old uncials after chapter sixteen, (2) in many minuscules after chapter fourteen, and (3) in $\mathfrak{P}^{46}$ after chapter fifteen—the only witness to this placement. Various placements of the doxology suggest that Romans could have circulated in as many as three different editions—ending with chapter fourteen, fifteen, or sixteen. In an article in 1962, T. W. Manson gave statement to an older theory that Romans 16 was not part of the original letter. Manson voiced the opinion that Paul later composed chapter sixteen and attached this chapter to a copy of Romans sent to Ephesus. The papyrus $\mathfrak{P}^{46}$ seemed to support this theory, because the placement of the doxology in $\mathfrak{P}^{46}$ after chapter fifteen suggested an ancestor having only Romans 1–15. However, for a revised evaluation of the significance of $\mathfrak{P}^{46}$ for the ending of Romans, consult recent critical commentaries.

LESSON 25 (εἴκοσι πέντε)
Infinitives

λύειν, λῦσαι

Infinitives are specialized verbal forms that go beyond indicative considerations of time (past, present, future) or finite limitations of subject (I, you, he, we, you, they). So an infinitive is a verbal divorced from time and infinite regarding subject. Infinitives have both verb and noun heritage.

Vocabulary 25

Conjunction, Adverb, Particles

πρίν (or πρὶν ἤ)	before
ὁμοίως	likewise
γέ (enclitic)	indeed (really, even)
ναί	yes (truly, indeed)

Nouns and Adjectives

ἀρνίον, τό	lamb
διακονία, -ας, ἡ	service, ministry
διάκονος, ὁ, ἡ	servant (administrator)
ἥλιος, ὁ	sun
οἶνος, ὁ	wine
ποτήριον, τό	cup
ὑπομονή, -ῆς, ἡ	steadfastness, patient endurance
φυλή, -ῆς, ἡ	tribe

ἀληθινός, -ή, -όν	true
ἐχθρός, -ά, -όν	hating

Verbs

ἀγοράζω	I buy
ἀρνέομαι	I deny
δύναμαι	I am able
εἶναι	to be (present tense)
ἔσεσθαι	to be (future tense)
καθαρίζω	I cleanse
φαίνω	I shine, appear
φυλάσσω	I guard, keep

Impersonal Verbs

δεῖ	it is necessary, must
ἔξεστι(ν)	it is lawful

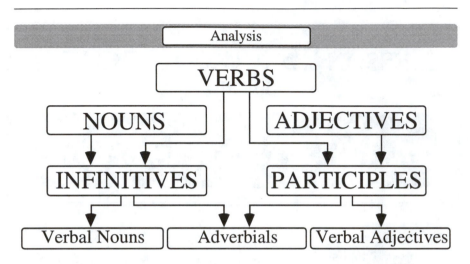

Analysis

Character. Infinitives have tense stems with tense and voice, but not mood, person, and number (no subject, so no conjugation). Infinitives are hybrids—verbal structures with substantive function—that is, acting as verbal nouns or as adverbials.

Forms. Infinitives have their own set of endings that are not to be confused with noun or verb endings. Infinitive

Table 25.1 Infinitive Endings—Resultant

Active			Mid./Pas.	Pas.
-ειν	-σαι	-ναι	-σθαι	-ναι

accent is not "irregular," since rules for finite verbs do not apply. The accent is learned by observation for each form. Infinitive endings have four non-volatilized forms: -εν, -ναι, -αι, -σθαι. These volatilize to the resultant endings -ειν, -ναι, -σαι, -σθαι. Not all paradigm forms occur in the New Testament, but they help to illustrate infinitive formulations. Observe that -ειν and -σαι are always active, -σθαι always middle or passive, and -ναι varies as perfect active or aorist passive.

Table 25.2 Infinitive Paradigms—λύω (Second Aorist: λείπω and γράφω)

	Present	Second Aorist	First Aorist	Perfect
Active	λύειν	λιπεῖν	λῦσαι	λελυκέναι
Middle	λύεσθαι	λιπέσθαι	λύσασθαι	λελύσθαι
Passive	λύεσθαι	γραφῆναι	λυθῆναι	λελύσθαι

Consonant/vowel reactions already learned help explain various infinitive forms in the New Testament. Such formulations need not be memorized, only recognized.[1]

[1]*Present Tense.* Uncontracted active voice accent is penult acute. Uncontracted middle voice accent is antepenult acute. Active Voice. The ending is -εν. The theme vowel is ε. Thus, (1) ε + εν = -ειν, creating a spurious diphthong (result of contraction), the present *active* infinitive ending, as in λύειν; (2) contracts: ε + ειν = -εῖν, as in φιλεῖν; ο + ειν = -οῦν, as in δηλοῦν; α + ειν = -ᾶν, no iota subscript because ει is a spurious diphthong, as in τιμᾶν. Middle/Passive Voice. The ending is -σθαι. The theme vowel is ε. So, (1) ε + σθαι = -εσθαι, the present *middle/passive* infinitive ending, as in λύεσθαι; (2) contracts: ε + εσθαι = -εῖσθαι, as in φιλεῖσθαι; ο + εσθαι = -οῦσθαι, as in δηλοῦσθαι; α + εσθαι = -ᾶσθαι, as in τιμᾶσθαι.

Future Tense. Rarely encountered; the future infinitive has the future tense suffix -σ, but this coalesces with another sigma in the εἰμί form. Two forms, εἰσελεύσεσθαι from εἰσέρχομαι and ἔσεσθαι from εἰμί; five occurrences (Heb. 3:18 and Acts 11:28; 23:30; 24:15; 27:10, respectively).

First Aorist Tense. Infinitives do not express a time component, as in the equation for a Greek verb in indicative mood. So aorist infinitives have no augment. Active Voice. The ending is -αι. The active voice tense suffix is -σα. Thus, (1) σα + αι = -σαι, the two alphas coalesce, the first aorist *active* infinitive ending, as in λῦσαι (perfect mid. ind., second plural has reduplication, different accent, λέλυσαι); (2) contracts: ε + σαι = -ῆσαι, as in φιλῆσαι; ο + σαι = -ῶσαι, as in δηλῶσαι; α + σαι = -ῆσαι, as in τιμῆσαι; (3) stops: π, β, φ + σαι = -ψαι, the labial stem, as in πέμψαι; κ, γ, χ + σαι = -ξαι, palatal stem, as in ἀνοῖξαι (ἀνοίγω); τ, δ, θ + σαι = -σαι, dental stem, as in (4) liquids: λ, ρ + σαι = -λαι or -ραι, the liquid aorist stem, as in ἀπαγγεῖλαι (ἀπαγγέλλω); ν, μ + σαι = -ναι or -μαι, nasal stem, as in μεῖναι. Middle Voice. The ending is -σθαι. The middle voice tense suffix is -σα. So, (1) σα + σθαι = -σασθαι, the first aorist *middle* infinitive ending, as in λύσασθαι; (2) contracts: ε + σασθαι = -ήσασθαι, as in ἀρνήσασθαι (ἀρνέομαι); ο + σασθαι = -ώσασθαι, as in μισθώσασθαι (μισθόω); α + σασθαι = -ήσασθαι, as in καταχρήσασθαι (καταχράομαι); (3) stops: π, β, φ + σασθαι = -ψασθαι, the labial stem, as in μεταπέμψασθαι (μεταπέμπω); κ, γ, χ + σασθαι = -ξασθαι, palatal stem, as in ἀνατάξασθαι (ἀνατάσσω); τ, δ, θ + σασθαι = -σασθαι, dental stem, as in ψεύσασθαι (ψεύδομαι); (4) liquids: ρ + σασθαι = -ρασθαι, the liquid aorist stem, as in κείρασθαι (κείρω). First Passive Voice. The ending used is -ναι. The first passive suffix is -θη. So, (1) θη + ναι = -θῆναι, the first aorist *passive* infinitive ending, as in λυθῆναι; (2) contracts: ε + θηναι = -ηθῆναι, as in διακονηθῆναι (διακονέω); ο + θηναι = -ωθῆναι, as in σταυρωθῆναι; α + θηναι = -ηθῆναι, as in γεννηθῆναι (γεννάω); (3) stops: π, β, φ + θηναι = -φθῆναι, the labial stem, as in προπεμφθῆναι (προπέμπω); κ, γ, χ + θηναι = -χθῆναι, palatal stem, as in διορυχθῆναι (διορύσσω); τ, δ, θ + θηναι = -σθῆναι, dental stem, as in βαπτισθῆναι; (4) liquids: ν + θηναι = -θῆναι or -νθῆναι, the liquid (nasal) stems, as in κριθῆναι or πληθυνθῆναι (πληθύνω).

Second Aorist Tense. No augment. The stem is second aorist. Active and middle voice are the same as present tense, save for stem and accent. Active Voice. The ending is -ειν (resultant active ending). Accent is ultima circumflex. Thus, βαλεῖν (cf. βάλλειν). Middle Voice. The ending is -εσθαι (thematic vowel). Accent is penult acute. Thus, γενέσθαι (cf. γίνεσθαι). Second Passive Voice. The ending is -ναι with -η suffix (dropping θ). So η + ναι = -ῆναι, as in χαρῆναι (χαίρω).

Perfect Tense. Infrequent (under fifty times). Shows reduplication. Active Voice. Tense suffix is -κε. The ending is -ναι, as in λελυκέναι. Other patterns are recognizable (e.g., contract lengthening, πεπληρωκέναι, from πληρόω). The second perfect active, dropping the κ of the -κε suffix, is rare. But, γεγονέναι (γίνομαι). Middle/Passive Voice. The perfect middle/passive stem is used. The ending is -σθαι. Thus, ἀπολελύσθαι (ἀπολύω). Contracts lengthen, so πεφανερῶσθαι (φανερόω). Perfect middle infinitive stems ending in a stop are quite rare.

General Remarks

The student will observe that no translations have been indicated for any of the infinitive forms. The *use* of an infinitive in a particular syntactical structure and context generates the meaning. The infinitive combines the use of a verb and a noun. Some general remarks on this heritage follow, then each use is outlined.

Verb Characteristics. The infinitive shows some components of the finite verb in the indicative mood—particularly, tense and voice. However, the infinitive is without person and number (not limited by a subject), and without mood.

Aspect. The tense aspect is the main verbal feature of the infinitive. Time of action is *not* a component (except as related to main verb). Thus, one could say the present infinitive is durative, the aorist infinitive is undefined, and the perfect infinitive is perfective. Yet, the translation for each tense can be the same. The typical English infinitive form "to _____" on occasion can be used for an infinitive translation in any tense. So λύειν, λυεῖν, or λελυκέναι could be "to loose." Notice that the tense aspect does not come across with such a translation. Again, the form "___ing" sometimes can be used for an English infinitive form. So λύειν, λυεῖν, or λελυκέναι might be "loosing" in English. Again, tense distinction would be lost.

Trying to bring out the infinitive aspect generally is unsuccessful. The results usually are awkward ("over-translating"). One has to *explain* the aspect of a Greek infinitive rather than trying to communicate this in a translation. Observe:

(1) *Durative:* Ἀπὸ τότε ἤρξατο ὁ Ἰησοῦς **κηρύσσειν** καὶ **λέγειν** = "From that time on, Jesus began **to preach** and **to say**" (Matt. 4:17, present active infinitives). Notice the thought of the *activity* of Jesus' ministry.

(2) *Undefined:* οὐ γάρ ἐστιν καλὸν **λαβεῖν** τὸν ἄρτον τῶν τέκνων καὶ τοῖς κυναρίοις **βαλεῖν** = "for it is not good **to take** bread from the children and **throw** it to the dogs (Mark 7:27, second aorist active infinitives). Notice that the actions are conceived as punctiliar.

(3) *Perfective:* κρεῖττον γὰρ ἦν αὐτοῖς μὴ **ἐπεγνωκέναι** τὴν ὁδὸν τῆς δικαιοσύνης ἢ ἐπιγνοῦσιν ὑποστρέψαι ἐκ τῆς παραδοθείσης αὐτοῖς ἁγίας ἐντολῆς. = "For it would be far better for them not **to have known** the way of righteousness than knowing, to turn aside (future active infinitive) from the holy commandment which has been delivered to them." (2 Pet. 2:21, perfect active infinitive). Here, perfective aspect comes across.

"Subject" Relationship. An infinitive has no subject. However, an infinitive does have an *accusative of general reference*. That which produces the infinitive action still can be related to the infinitive grammatically by a substantive in the

accusative case. This substantive is making general reference to the infinitive action in an adverbial manner, and is translated as a "subject." Rom. 6:6 illustrates (see below): τοῦ μηκέτι δουλεύειν **ἡμᾶς** τῇ ἁμαρτίᾳ = "that **we** might no longer be slaves to sin." Here, ἡμᾶς is accusative, not nominative, and functions as an accusative of general reference, translated as "we."[2] The literal idea would be "to serve with reference to us." English sense is more smooth treating ἡμᾶς as subject.

Table 25.3 Accusative of General Reference

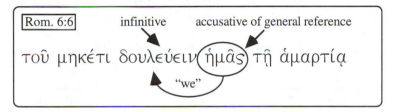

Rom. 6:6   infinitive   accusative of general reference

τοῦ μηκέτι δουλεύειν ἡμᾶς τῇ ἁμαρτίᾳ

"we"

Infinitive Phrase. The infinitive can be part of an entire infinitive phrase. In such a phrase, the infinitive can take its own direct object ("he is not able **to save** *himself*," Mark 15:31). The infinitive can take an indirect object ("I still have many things **to say** *to you*," John 16:12). The infinitive can be modified by an adverb ("but we encourage you, brothers, **to abound** (even) *more*," 1 Thess. 4:10). The infinitive can be modified by a prepositional phrase ("**to go** *through the eye of a needle* is easier for a camel," Matt. 19:24).

Negative (μή). The negative for the indicative mood is οὐ. The infinitive, however, does not have mood. An infinitive, therefore, takes the negative μή.

Noun Characteristics. The noun heritage of an infinitive comes out in case relationships. Also, the noun heritage is observed as the infinitive is modified by adjectives or itself modifies other words.

Case Relationships. The infinitive has case function without case inflection. Infinitives appear as if indeclinable neuter nouns and can be found in constructions with articles and prepositions. When articular, the infinitive is found with the neuter singular article (τό, τοῦ, τῷ), depending on function; e.g., τοῦ λέγειν. The infinitive also is found constructed with prepositions; e.g., εἰς τὸ λέγειν. Meanings are specialized and have to be learned for each particular construction.

Modifying Relationships. As a substantive, an infinitive can be modified by adjectives ("I have *much* **to say** and **to condemn** concerning you," John 8:26).

---

[2]Some opt for the label "subject accusative." If such a label leads the student to think the infinitive grammatically is limited by a subject, and is no longer infinite, the label is unhelpful.

Similarly, an infinitive itself can modify other words ("I have *authority* **to crucify** you," John 19:10).

Adverbial Infinitive

The uses of the infinitive divide on the basis of its dual background into the adverbial infinitive use and the verbal noun use. In the adverbial infinitive use, the verbal heritage is dominant. The infinitive modifies the main verb or makes an additional assertion related to the main verb. Common adverbial uses are outlined.

Table 25.4 Adverbial Infinitive—Use, Constructions, Idea

Adverbial Use	*Constructions*	*Idea*
purpose or result	infinitive τοῦ + infinitive εἰς τό + infinitive ὥστε + infinitive	"to," "so that," "in order to" or "as a result"
purpose	πρὸς τό + infinitive ὡς + infinitive	"to," "so that," "in order to"
cause	διὰ τό + infinitive	"because"
time: antecedent	πρὸ τοῦ + infinitive πρίν + infinitive πρὶν ἤ + infinitive	"before"
simultaneous	ἐν τῷ + infinitive	"while"
subsequent	μετὰ τό + infinitive	"after"
future (Acts 8:40)	ἕως τοῦ + infinitive	"until"

Purpose. The *infinitive of purpose* states the purpose expressed in the action of the main verb. Six constructions are found:

(1) *anarthrous infinitive*, e.g., ἤλθομεν **προσκυνῆσαι** αὐτῷ = "we have come **to worship** him" (Matt. 2:2)

(2) *articular infinitive* [τοῦ + infinitive], e.g., μετέβη ἐκεῖθεν <u>τοῦ</u> **διδάσκειν** καὶ **κηρύσσειν** ἐν ταῖς πόλεσιν αὐτῶν = "he departed from there **to teach** and **to preach** in their cities" (Matt. 11:1)

(3) *preposition* [εἰς τό + infinitive], e.g., ἀλλὰ μεταμορφοῦσθε τῇ ἀνακαινώσει τοῦ νοός, <u>εἰς τὸ</u> **δοκιμάζειν** ὑμᾶς τί τὸ θέλημα τοῦ θεοῦ = "be transformed by the renewing of your mind, *that* you **might approve** what the will of God is" (Rom. 12:2)

(4) *preposition* [πρὸς τό + infinitive], e.g., ἐνδύσασθε τὴν πανοπλίαν τοῦ θεοῦ <u>πρὸς τὸ</u> **δύνασθαι** ὑμᾶς **στῆναι** πρὸς τὰς μεθοδείας τοῦ διαβόλου = "put on the full armor of God, *that* you **be able to stand** against the tricks of the devil" (Eph. 6:11)

(5) *particle* [ὡς + infinitive], e.g., εἰσῆλθον εἰς κώμην Σαμαριτῶν, <u>ὡς</u> **ἑτοιμάσαι** αὐτῷ = "they entered a village of the Samaritans *in order to* **prepare** for him" (Luke 9:52)

(6) *conjunction* [ὥστε + infinitive], e.g., ἀποθανόντες ἐν ᾧ κατειχόμεθα, <u>ὥστε</u> **δουλεύειν** ἡμᾶς ἐν καινότητι πνεύματος = "having died to that by which we were held fast, *so that* we might **serve** in newness of the Spirit" (Rom. 7:6)

Result. The *infinitive of result* states the result of the action in the main verb. Distinction from infinitive of purpose can be unclear. Four constructions are found:

(1) *anarthrous infinitive*, e.g., ὥστε καὶ ἐπὶ τοὺς ἀσθενοῦντας ἀποφέρεσθαι ἀπὸ τοῦ χρωτὸς αὐτοῦ σουδάρια ἢ σιμικίνθια καὶ **ἀπαλλάσσεσθαι** ἀπ᾽ αὐτῶν τὰς νόσους, τά τε πνεύματα τὰ πονηρὰ **ἐκπορεύεσθαι**. = "so that cloths and aprons he had touched were carried to the sick, and *as a result* they **were cured** from their diseases and the evil spirits **went out**" (Acts 19:12)

(2) *articular infinitive* [τοῦ + infinitive], e.g., ἐκάκωσεν τοὺς πατέρας [ἡμῶν] <u>τοῦ</u> **ποιεῖν** τὰ βρέφη ἔκθετα αὐτῶν = "he mistreated [our] fathers, *as a result*, they exposed their infants" (Acts 7:19)

(3) *preposition* [εἰς τό + infinitive], e.g., <u>εἰς τὸ</u> **εἶναι** αὐτοὺς ἀναπολογήτους = "*with the result that* they **are** without excuse" (Rom. 1:20); again, τὴν ἀγάπην τῆς ἀληθείας οὐκ ἐδέξαντο <u>εἰς τὸ</u> **σωθῆναι** αὐτούς = "they did not receive the love of the truth *with the result that* they **be saved**" (2 Thess. 2:10)

(4) *conjunction* [ὥστε + infinitive], e.g., ἐθεράπευσεν αὐτόν, <u>ὥστε</u> τὸν κωφὸν **λαλεῖν** καὶ **βλέπειν** = "he healed him, <u>so that</u> the dumb man **spoke** and **saw**" (Matt. 12:22); again, ὁ δὲ Ἰησοῦς οὐκέτι οὐδὲν ἀπεκρίθη, <u>ὥστε</u> **θαυμάζειν** τὸν Πιλᾶτον. = "Jesus no longer answered anything, so that Pilate **marveled**." (Mark 15:5)

Cause. The *infinitive of cause* answers the question "why?" The translation uses "because." Regularly, the construction is [διὰ τό + infinitive], e.g., <u>διὰ τὸ</u> **εἶναι** αὐτὸν ἐξ οἴκου καὶ πατριᾶς Δαυίδ = "<u>because</u> he **was** of the house and lineage of

David" (Luke 2:4). Again, ἦν γὰρ ἐξ ἱκανῶν χρόνων θέλων ἰδεῖν αὐτὸν διὰ τὸ ἀκούειν περὶ αὐτοῦ = "for he had been wanting to see him for a long time, because he **had heard** about him" (Luke 23:8).

Time. The *infinitive of time* clarifies the time frame of the main verb. The action can be (1) antecedent, (2) simultaneous, (3) subsequent, or (4) future to this verb.

(1) *antecedent* ("before")

prepositional phrase [πρὸ τοῦ + infinitive], e.g., οἶδεν γὰρ ὁ πατὴρ ὑμῶν ὧν χρείαν ἔχετε πρὸ τοῦ ὑμᾶς **αἰτῆσαι** αὐτόν = "for your Father knows the need which you have before you **ask** Him" (Matt. 6:8)

conjunction [πρίν + infinitive], e.g., πρὶν **ἐλθεῖν** ἡμέραν κυρίου τὴν μεγάλην καὶ ἐπιφανῆ = "before the great and glorious Day of the Lord **comes** " (Acts 2:20)

conjunction [πρὶν ἤ + infinitive], e.g., πρὶν ἤ **συνελθεῖν** αὐτοὺς εὑρέθη ἐν γαστρὶ ἔχουσα ἐκ πνεύματος ἁγίου = "before they **came together** she was found with child by the Holy Spirit" (Matt. 1:18)

(2) *simultaneous* ("while") [ἐν τῷ + infinitive], e.g., καὶ ἐγένετο ἐν τῷ **προσεύχεσθαι** αὐτὸν = "and it happened while he **was praying**" (Luke 9:29)

(3) *subsequent* ("after") [μετὰ τό + infinitive], e.g., εἰπὼν ὅτι Μετὰ τὸ **γενέσθαι** με ἐκεῖ δεῖ με καὶ Ῥώμην ἰδεῖν = "saying, 'After I **have been** there, I must see Rome also.'" (Acts 19:21)

(4) *future* ("until") [ἕως τοῦ + infinitive], e.g., εὐηγγελίζετο τὰς πόλεις πάσας ἕως τοῦ **ἐλθεῖν** αὐτὸν εἰς Καισάρειαν = "he continued preaching the good news to all the cities until he **came** to Caesarea" (Acts 8:40).[3]

Verbal Noun

In this infinitive use, the noun heritage is dominant. Any typical substantive function could be expected for a verbal noun. However, three main uses are found.

Subject. The *subject infinitive* functions as subject of the main verb. Thus, Μακάριόν ἐστιν μᾶλλον **διδόναι** ἢ λαμβάνειν. = "**To give** is more blessed than to receive." (Acts 20:35; -μι verb, δίδωμι, "I give").

Direct Object. The *direct object infinitive* functions as direct object of the main verb. Three main uses are found.

Direct Object. As a typical direct object, the infinitive has case function. These cases often are the accusative and genitive. Observe: ὁ Πιλᾶτος ἐζήτει **ἀπολῦσαι** αὐτόν = "Pilate was seeking **to release** him" (John 19:12).

---

[3]The only example of this construction in the New Testament.

Indirect Discourse. This category is a subdivision of the direct object use. The entire indirect discourse statement is represented by an infinitive acting as direct object of the main verb. Distinguish the indirect discourse form in Lesson 20 (ὅτι with the indicative mood). For example, ὁ λέγων ἐν αὐτῷ **μένειν** = "the one who says **he abides** in him" (1 John 2:6). Compare Matt. 22:23; Luke 24:23; Rom. 2:22.

Table 25.5 Paradigm—δύναμαι

Number	Person	Form	Translation
Singular	1st	δύναμαι	"I am able"
	2nd	δύνασαι (or δύνῃ)	"you are able"
	3rd	δύναται	"he (she, it) is able"
Plural	1st	δυνάμεθα	"we are able"
	2nd	δύνασθε	"you are able"
	3rd	δύνανται	"they are able"

Complementary. The *complementary infinitive* serves verbs that require an infinitive form to complete the verbal idea or verbs taking an infinitive in certain constructions. Examples include δεῖ, δύναμαι, ἔξεστι(ν), and μέλλω. The deponent -μι verb δύναμαι is common enough in the New Testament that the paradigm is given now (Table 25.5). Other verbs that can take an infinitive are ἄρχομαι (the middle form "I begin"), βούλομαι ("I want," "wish"), δέομαι ("I beg," "request"), θέλω ("I wish," "will"), ὀφείλω (as "I ought"), and πειράζω (as "I try," "attempt"). Observe:

(1) ἄρχομαι, e.g., ἤρξαντο **λυπεῖσθαι** καὶ **λέγειν** = "they began **to be grieved** and **to say**" (Mark 14:19)

(2) βούλομαι, e.g., με ἐβούλοντο **ἀπολῦσαι** = "they were willing **to release** me" (Acts 28:18)

(3) δεῖ, e.g., δεῖ γὰρ **γενέσθαι**, ἀλλ᾽ οὔπω ἐστὶν τὸ τέλος = "for (these things) must **be**, but the end is not yet" (Matt. 24:6)

(4) δέομαι, e.g., διὸ δέομαι μακροθύμως **ἀκοῦσαί** μου = "therefore I beg you **to hear** me patiently" (Acts 26:3)

(5) δύναμαι, e.g., ἑαυτὸν οὐ δύναται **σῶσαι** = "he is not able **to save** himself" (Mark 15:31)

(6) ἔξεστι(ν), e.g., εἰ ἔξεστιν τῷ σαββάτῳ ἀγαθοποιῆσαι ἢ κακοποιῆσαι, ψυχὴν σῶσαι ἢ ἀπολέσαι; = "which is lawful on the sabbath, **to do good**, or **to do harm**, **to save** a life, or **to destroy**?" (Luke 6:9)

(7) θέλω, e.g., τί πάλιν θέλετε ἀκούειν; μὴ καὶ ὑμεῖς θέλετε αὐτοῦ μαθηταὶ γενέσθαι; = "Why do you want **to hear** again? You do not want **to become** his disciples, do you?" (John 9:27)

(8) μέλλω, e.g., μέλλει γὰρ Ἡρῴδης ζητεῖν τὸ παιδίον τοῦ ἀπολέσαι αὐτό = "for Herod is going **to seek** the child to destroy him" (Matt. 2:13); again, μηδὲν φοβοῦ ἃ μέλλεις πάσχειν = "do not fear the things you are going **to suffer**" (Rev. 2:10)

(9) ὀφείλω, e.g., ὃ ὠφείλομεν ποιῆσαι πεποιήκαμεν = "we have done that which we ought **to have done**" (Luke 17:10)

(10) πειράζω, e.g., ἐπείραζεν κολλᾶσθαι τοῖς μαθηταῖς = "he was trying **to associate** with the disciples" (Acts 9:26); also, ὃς καὶ τὸ ἱερὸν ἐπείρασεν βεβηλῶσαι = "who even was trying **to desecrate** the temple" (Acts 24:6)

Modifier. The *modifying infinitive* functions to modify nouns or adjectives. Notice how infinitives modify the nominal direct objects in οὐκ οἶδας ὅτι ἐξουσίαν ἔχω ἀπολῦσαί σε καὶ ἐξουσίαν ἔχω σταυρῶσαί σε; "Do you not know that I have authority **to release** you and I have authority **to crucify** you?" (John 19:10). Again, observe infinitive modification of the adjective in ὃς οὐκ εἰμὶ ἱκανὸς καλεῖσθαι ἀπόστολος = "who am not worthy **to be called** an apostle" (1 Cor. 15:9).

Finally, as modifiers, infinitives can operate: (1) in apposition to nouns or (2) *epexegetically* to verbs (explanatory).[4] Note: (1) τοῦτο in τοῦτο γάρ ἐστιν θέλημα τοῦ θεοῦ, ὁ ἁγιασμὸς ὑμῶν, ἀπέχεσθαι ὑμᾶς ἀπὸ τῆς πορνείας = "For this is the will of God, your sanctification, *that* you **abstain** from fornication" (1 Thess. 4:3); (2) Κύριε, δίδαξον ἡμᾶς προσεύχεσθαι = "Lord, teach us **to pray**" (Luke 11:1).

The Verb Εἰμί

Pres. Inf.	Fut. Inf.
εἶναι	ἔσεσθαι

The verb εἰμί occurs in only two principal parts, first and second, consisting of the three tenses present, imperfect, and future. The imperfect tense does not have an infinitive form. So εἰμί occurs as an infinitive only in the present and future tenses. Further, εἰμί does not have voice, so does not express voice in the infinitive forms. The present infinitive is εἶναι. The future infinitive is ἔσεσθαι. These infinitive forms of εἰμί are listed as vocabulary.

---

[4]"Epexegetical" terminology is used inconsistently, some applying to nouns or verbs, others only to verbs. An "epexegetical" infinitive seems to be equivalent to an infinitive of purpose or result.

Infinitive Location

To locate an infinitive, specify tense, voice, "infinitive," then the lexical form and lexical meaning. Notice that the word "infinitive" replaces the mood component of the indicative verb. Mood is related to finite verbs only. Infinitives and participles are infinite, so have no mood component. Also, since the infinitive is not inflected, the location cannot acknowledge the infinitive's noun heritage. The meaning of the particular form λύειν already has been provided in your translation.

Table 25.6 Infinitive Location: Five Components—λύειν

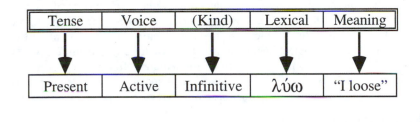

Tense	Voice	(Kind)	Lexical	Meaning
Present	Active	Infinitive	λύω	"I loose"

Impersonal Verbs

Two verbs are classified as impersonal verbs: δεῖ and ἔξεστι(ν). Both forms are (impersonal) third person singular ("it"), and both take a complementary infinitive (an infinitive is required to finish the verbal idea). Thus, δεῖ often is translated "it is necessary (to)," and ἔξεστι(ν) often is translated "it is lawful (to)." For example, **δεῖ** περιτέμνειν αὐτοὺς παραγγέλλειν τε τηρεῖν τὸν νόμον Μωϋσέως = "**it is necessary** to circumcise them and to command them to keep the Law of Moses" (Acts 15:5). However, an "it is" style might be improved at times with a more direct approach. The required complementary infinitive suggests the subject. Substitute the infinitive phrase for "it." For example, ὥστε **ἔξεστιν** τοῖς σάββασιν καλῶς ποιεῖν = "thus, to do good on the Sabbath is lawful" (Matt. 12:12).

On quite a number of occasions, the import of the presence of δεῖ is simply the idea "must." Observe: (1) δεῖξαι τοῖς δούλοις αὐτοῦ ἃ **δεῖ** γενέσθαι = "to show to his servants things which **must** take place" (Rev. 1:1); (2) **Δεῖ** ὑμᾶς γεννηθῆναι ἄνωθεν = "you **must** be born again (from above)" (John 3:7); (3) **Δεῖ** τὸν υἱὸν τοῦ ἀνθρώπου πολλὰ παθεῖν = "the Son of man **must** suffer many things" (Luke 9:22). Finally, the imperfect form, ἔδει, means "it was necessary" or "had (to)."

Diagramming

Infinitives go on a standard whose horizontal is broken by *two* lines before the infinitive. The accusative of general reference has subject position, but is placed in brackets to acknowledge the lack of true English parallel for the function.

Adverbial Infinitives. The adverbial infinitive is placed either on an inverted standard ($\curlyvee$) or on an upright standard ($\curlywedge$) situated on the horizontal of a slanted line. Purpose, result, cause, and time infinitives are placed coming down from the main verb, with conjunctions and prepositions on the support arm, as usual. Keep articles with their respective infinitives.

Verbal Nouns. The infinitive verbal noun is placed on an upright standard ($\curlywedge$) with normal substantive function (subject, direct object, modifier). Infinitive indirect discourse is a direct object, so the introductory infinitive is placed on a standard after the direct object line, with the ὅτι clause following the infinitive on its own standard. Complementary infinitives immediately follow the verb served. Modifiers are placed below the element modified. Apposition is handled normally— an "equals" sign (=) pointing to another base line, but with infinitive construction.

Table 25.7 Diagramming Infinitives

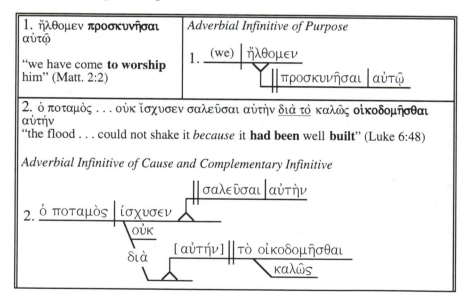

1. ἤλθομεν **προσκυνῆσαι** αὐτῷ "we have come **to worship** him" (Matt. 2:2)	*Adverbial Infinitive of Purpose*

2. ὁ ποταμὸς . . . οὐκ ἴσχυσεν σαλεῦσαι αὐτὴν <u>διὰ τὸ</u> καλῶς **οἰκοδομῆσθαι** αὐτήν
"the flood . . . could not shake it *because* it **had been** well **built**" (Luke 6:48)

Adverbial Infinitive of Cause and Complementary Infinitive

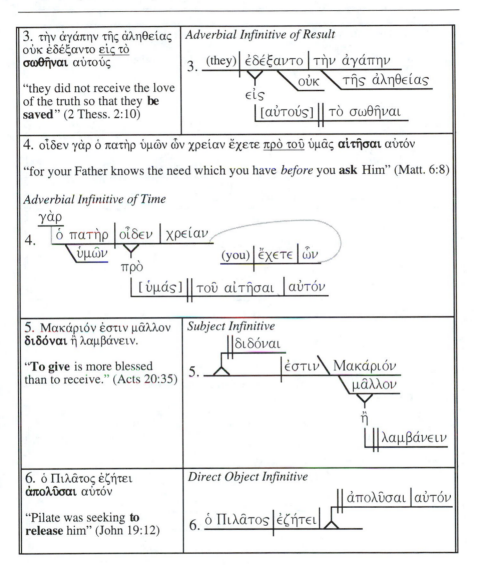

3. τὴν ἀγάπην τῆς ἀληθείας οὐκ ἐδέξαντο εἰς τὸ **σωθῆναι** αὐτούς

"they did not receive the love of the truth so that they **be saved**" (2 Thess. 2:10)

Adverbial Infinitive of Result

3.

---

4. οἶδεν γὰρ ὁ πατὴρ ὑμῶν ὧν χρείαν ἔχετε πρὸ τοῦ ὑμᾶς **αἰτῆσαι** αὐτόν

"for your Father knows the need which you have *before* you **ask** Him" (Matt. 6:8)

Adverbial Infinitive of Time

4.

---

5. Μακάριόν ἐστιν μᾶλλον **διδόναι** ἢ λαμβάνειν.

"**To give** is more blessed than to receive." (Acts 20:35)

Subject Infinitive

5.

---

6. ὁ Πιλᾶτος ἐζήτει **ἀπολῦσαι** αὐτόν

"Pilate was seeking **to release** him" (John 19:12)

Direct Object Infinitive

6.

7. καὶ ἐγένετο ὡσεὶ νεκρός, ὥστε τοὺς πολλοὺς **λέγειν** <u>ὅτι</u> ἀπέθανεν

"and he became so much as a corpse that the majority **declared** <u>that</u> he was dead" (Mark 9:26)

Indirect Discourse Infinitive

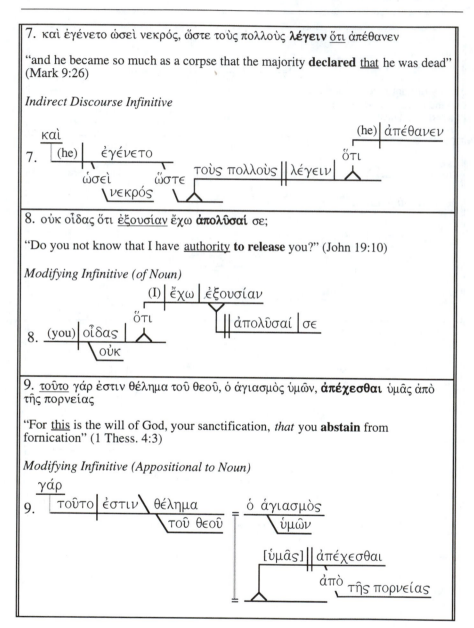

8. οὐκ οἶδας ὅτι <u>ἐξουσίαν</u> ἔχω **ἀπολῦσαί** σε;

"Do you not know that I have <u>authority</u> **to release** you?" (John 19:10)

Modifying Infinitive (of Noun)

9. <u>τοῦτο</u> γάρ ἐστιν θέλημα τοῦ θεοῦ, ὁ ἁγιασμὸς ὑμῶν, **ἀπέχεσθαι** ὑμᾶς ἀπὸ τῆς πορνείας

"For <u>this</u> is the will of God, your sanctification, *that* you **abstain** from fornication" (1 Thess. 4:3)

Modifying Infinitive (Appositional to Noun)

| 10. Κύριε, δίδαξον ἡμᾶς προσεύχεσθαι

"Lord, <u>teach</u> us **to pray**" (Luke 11:1) | *Modifying Infinitive (Epexegetical to Verb)*
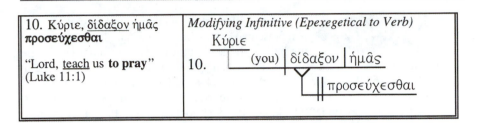 |

 **What To Learn—LESSON 25 (εἴκοσι πέντε)**

Beginning

- ☐ 1. Infinitive paradigms: λύω, λείπω, γράφω
- ☐ 2. Verb and noun characteristics of infinitives, difficulty of translating tense aspect, phenomenon of case relationships without case inflection
- ☐ 3. Meaning of the *accusative of general reference*
- ☐ 4. The paradigm for δύναμαι
- ☐ 5. Translation of impersonal verbs such as δεῖ and ἔξεστιν(ν)
- ☐ 6. Diagramming infinitives
- ☐ 7. Vocabulary words

Advanced

- ☐ 8. Adverbial infinitive uses: purpose, result, cause, time—with constructions
- ☐ 9. Nominal infinitive uses: subject, direct object (indirect discourse, *complementary*), and modifier (appositional, epexegetical)

 The problem of the ending of the Gospel of Mark is represented in this image of Sinaiticus (showing the top half of the leaf). In this ancient, important codex, Mark ends at 16:8 with the word ΓΑΡ (γάρ). Typical text decoration as is found at the end of each book is drawn. Then, the usual closing notation is given in the words εὐαγγέλιον κατὰ μᾶρκον. Finally, as is the normal procedure at the end of a book, the rest of that column is left blank, and the next book begins at the top of the next column. Here, the next column begins the Gospel of Luke. Also, observe the two column headings, ΜΑΡΚΟΝ (Μᾶρκον) and ΚΑΤΑΛΟΥΚΑΝ (Κατὰ Λουκᾶν).

Sinaiticus

Ending of Mark

LESSON 26 (εἴκοσι ἕξ)

Present Active Participle

λύων, λύουσα, λῦον

Participles are specialized verbal forms that go beyond indicative considerations of time (past, present, future) or finite limitations of subject (I, you, he, we, you, they). So a participle is a verbal divorced from time and infinite regarding subject. Participles have both verb and adjective heritage.

Vocabulary 26

Conjunction, Particle, Adverbs

εἴτε	whether
ποτέ	at some time, once, ever
οὔπω	not yet
πόθεν	from where? where?

Adjective and Nouns

φίλος, -η, -ον	loving (noun = "friend")
γνῶσις, -εως, ἡ	knowledge (wisdom)
θυσία, -ας, ἡ	sacrifice
κρίμα, -ατος, τό	judgment
μισθός, -οῦ, ὁ	wages, reward
μυστήριον, τό	mystery
παράκλησις, -εως, ἡ	exhortation, consolation
παρρησία, -ας, ἡ	boldness (confidence)

συνείδησις, -εως, ἡ   conscience

Verbs

γαμέω	I marry
ἐλεάω (ἐλεέω)	I show mercy
ἐνδύω	I put on, clothe
ἐπικαλέω	I call, name
ἐπικαλοῦμαι	I appeal (middle)
ἐπιτιμάω	I rebuke, warn
ἡγέομαι	I am chief (think, regard)
παραγγέλλω	I command, charge
προσκαλέομαι	I summon
σκανδαλίζω	I cause to stumble

Present Active Participles

λύων, λύουσα, λῦον	loosing (λύω)
ὤν, οὖσα, ὄν	being (εἰμί)

303

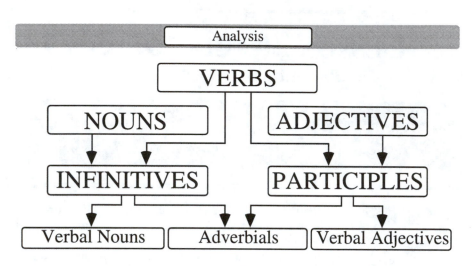

Character. Participles, like infinitives, are infinite. Participles have tense stems with tense and voice, but not mood, person, or number. Yet, unlike infinitives, participles *are* inflected, showing case, gender, and number—their adjectival background. Participles are hybrids—verbal structures with adjectival function—that is, operating as verbal adjectives or as adverbials.

Participles are timeless. Past tense has no augment. Time of action for a participle is related to the main verb. Past participles often occur before the action of the main verb, present participles simultaneous to the main verb, and future participles after the main verb—but not always. This

Table 26.1 Participle Heritage

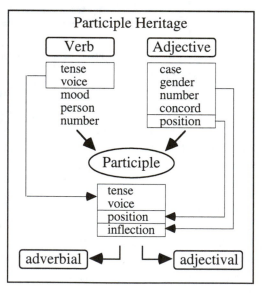

generalization does not really grasp the significance of a participle in context. Context determines the time, and the translator determines the context.

Form. Present active participles are verbals with noun and adjective endings. Masculine and neuter gender use corresponding third declension endings. Feminine gender uses first declension endings. The inflection of a present active participle is very familiar. The participial suffix, -ντ, is very distinctive in most forms, but phonetic changes obscure this suffix in some. Participle accent is not "irregular," since rules for finite verbs do not apply. Accent follows that of nouns and adjectives. Once the accent of the nominative masculine singular in a tense and voice is known, one can observe that: (1) general rules of accent are followed, (2) accent is persistent, (3) the genitive feminine plural of active voice (and aorist passive) has the typical circumflex on the ultima, as in first declension nouns. In formation, the thematic vowel, o, and participial suffix, -ντ, are added to the present stem:

$$\lambda \upsilon + o + \nu\tau = \lambda \upsilon o \nu\tau\text{-}$$

present stem,   +   participial   =   present active
thematic vowel   suffix   participle stem

Inflection by gender is added. Masculine follows ἄρχων (Table 14.7).[1] Feminine follows δόξα (Table 5.4), but feminine forms react with the participial stem, based on the primitive feminine endings, winding up as -ουσ.[2] Recall that neuter third declension has no nominative/accusative singular ending. In the participle, no ending leaves exposed the -οντ. The τ drops. The o, however, does not lengthen.

Table 26.2 Present Active Participle—λύω

	Masculine (ἄρχων)		Neuter (3rd Decl.)		Feminine (δόξα)	
	Singular	*Plural*	*Singular*	*Plural*	*Singular*	*Plural*
Nom	λύων	λύοντες	λῦον	λύοντα	λύουσα	λύουσαι
Gen	λύοντος	λυόντων	λύοντος	λυόντων	λυούσης	λυουσῶν
Dat	λύοντι	λύουσιν	λύοντι	λύουσιν	λυούσῃ	λυούσαις
Acc	λύοντα	λύοντας	λῦον	λύοντα	λύουσαν	λυούσας

[1]In which, as with ἄρχων, the nominative singular form becomes -ων, and the dative plural form becomes -ουσι(ν), because -οντ → -ον → -ων and because -οντσι → -οσι → -ουσι.
[2]Involving consonantal iota, -οντι → -ονσ → -οσ → -ουσ.

Contract verbs show contraction with these resultant endings in typical patterns.[3] Such formulations need not be memorized, only recognized. As examples, the three genders are divided among the three contract paradigms.

Table 26.3 Present Active Participle—Contract Examples

φιλέω (masculine)		δηλόω (neuter)		τιμάω (feminine)	
Singular	*Plural*	*Singular*	*Plural*	*Singular*	*Plural*
φιλῶν	φιλοῦντες	δηλοῦν	δηλοῦντα	τιμῶσα	τιμῶσαι
φιλοῦντος	φιλούντων	δηλοῦντος	δηλούντων	τιμώσης	τιμώσων
φιλοῦντι	φιλοῦσιν	δηλοῦντι	δηλοῦσιν	τιμώσῃ	τιμώσαις
φιλοῦντα	φιλοῦντας	δηλοῦν	δηλοῦντα	τιμῶσαν	τιμώσας

The Verb Εἰμί

Table 26.4 Present Participle—εἰμί

	Masculine (ἄρχων)		Neuter (3rd Decl.)		Feminine (δόξα)	
	Singular	*Plural*	*Singular*	*Plural*	*Singular*	*Plural*
Nom	ὤν	ὄντες	ὄν	ὄντα	οὖσα	οὖσαι
Gen	ὄντος	ὄντων	ὄντος	ὄντων	οὔσης	ουσῶν
Dat	ὄντι	οὖσιν	ὄντι	οὖσιν	οὔσῃ	οὔσαις
Acc	ὄντα	ὄντας	ὄν	ὄντα	οὖσαν	οὔσας

Remember that εἰμί does not have voice. The genitive feminine plural accent follows the noun rule. If this inflection, save for accent, appears to be none other than the present active resultant endings by their lonesome—bingo!

---

[3]For -ε contracts: ε + ω = ω, ε + ο = ου, ε + ου = ου, so φιλῶν, φιλοῦντος, etc. For -ο contracts: ο + ω = ω, ο + ο = ου, ο + ου = ου, so δηλῶν, δηλοῦντος, etc. For -α contracts: α + ω = ω, α + ο = ω, α + ου = ω, so τιμῶν, τιμῶντος, etc.

General Remarks

The participle is a powerful grammatical structure rich in meaning. Translation flexibility makes the participle the premier verbal form in New Testament Greek.

Observe that no translations have been indicated for any of the participle forms. The *use* of a participle in a particular syntactical structure and context generates the meaning. The participle combines the use of a verb and an adjective. Some general remarks on this heritage follow, then a procedure for translation is offered.

Verb Characteristics. The participle shows some components of the finite verb in the indicative mood—particularly, tense and voice. However, the participle is without person and number (not limited by a subject), and without mood.

Aspect. Participles as infinite are timeless. Time of action is *not* a component, except as related to the main verb. Tense *aspect* is the main verbal feature of the participle. Thus, the present participle is durative, the aorist participle is undefined, and the perfect participle is perfective. Yet, the translation for each tense can be the same. The typical English participial form "___ing" sometimes can be used for any tense of a Greek participle. However, tense distinction is obscured. Tense aspect is easier to express for participles than infinitives and generally should be observed.

Participial Phrase. The participle can be part of an entire participial phrase. The participle can take its own direct object ("and **after taking** *food*," Acts 9:19). The participle can take an indirect object ("**while he was saying** these things *to them*," Matt. 9:18). The participle can be modified by an adverb ("**proclaiming** the kingdom of God and **teaching** about the Lord Jesus Christ with all boldness and *without hindrance*," Acts 28:31). The participle can be modified by a prepositional phrase ("**while he was teaching** *in the synagogue at Capernaum*," John 6:59).

Negative (μή). The participle does not have mood. A participle, therefore, takes the negative μή. Rarely, one sees the negative οὐ (seventeen times). For example, οὐ βλέπων = "not seeing" (Luke 6:42; cf. 2 Cor. 12:1; Gal. 4:27; Col. 2:19; Heb. 11:1).

Adjective Characteristics. The adjective heritage of a participle comes out in adjective position and inflection showing concord. Also, the adjective heritage is observed as the participle is modified by adjectives or itself modifies other words, or even functions substantively, as subject, direct object, etc.

Case Relationships. The participle has case function *and* case inflection (unlike the infinitive, which has no inflection). Concord declares the substantive with which the participle is construed. Careful observation of concord is important.

Modifying Relationships. As a substantive, a participle can be modified by adjectives ("*everyone* who **believes**," Rom. 10:11). Similarly, a participle itself can modify other words ("the time of the **appearing** star," Matt. 2:7).

Translation Procedure. The use of the participle divides on the basis of the dual background into the verbal adjective and the adverbial participle.[4] Here are some practical steps for translation. Remember: "Participles are verbal adjectives."

Table 26.5 Participle Translation Flow Chart

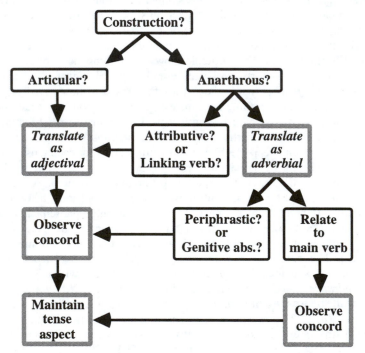

Step 1: Construction. First, study the construction: is this participle *articular or anarthrous*? This method is not foolproof, but it is fast.[5]

Articular Participle. The articular participle *always* is adjectival. Common uses of the adjective apply: (1) *attributive*, so modifying another word; (2) *substantive*— that is, as subject, object, etc.; (3) *predicative*, used with a linking verb as a predicate adjective. ("Participles are verbal *adjectives*.") All these uses, of course, would show appropriate concord (cf. Step 2). So, the articular participle is a verbal adjective and

---

[4]Distinctions of "adverbial" or "adjectival" functions are somewhat arbitrary, since, in reality, participles retain both functions simultaneously. Yet, this analysis seems to offer a decent beginning.

[5]The main exceptions are covered in the procedure.

is translated in the proper adjectival role, finished off by bringing out tense aspect (cf. Step 3). Your translation is finished in short order!

Anarthrous Participle. An anarthrous participle often is adverbial. Yet, before moving on to treat the participle as adverbial, eliminate two possibilities. First, is the anarthrous participle still attributive, performing a modifying role to a noun, etc.? Close inspection of concord and context usually will answer this question. Second, is a linking verb in the neighborhood? If so, the anarthrous participle might very well function as a predicate adjective, similar to an anarthrous adjective said to be in *predicate* position. In short, these two uses of the anarthrous participle are adjectival. If the anarthrous participle does not seem to answer these preliminary questions, though, most likely you have an adverbial participle—but note two special cases. You *may* have a periphrastic or a genitive absolute construction (discussion later). Otherwise, an adverbial translation should work. A key idea must be remembered.

Remember: participles do not show time! Any time element of an adverbial participle derives from the *main verb* (the verb the participle modifies).[6] So, one must *find the main verb*. ("Participles are *verbal* adjectives.") Then, you as translator must *construe* the participle's time as: (1) *antecedent*, happening before the action of the main verb, (2) *simultaneous*, happening with the action of the main verb, or (3) *subsequent*, happening after the action of the main verb. (See later discussion).

Table 26.6 Anarthrous Participle—Concord

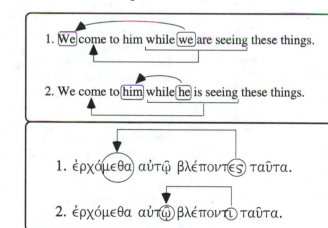

---

[6]The participle action will be: (1) necessary to finish stating the action of the main verb (called "supplementary" or "complementary," as in "he began *saying*"), or (2) unnecessary to the action of the main verb (called "circumstantial" or "adverbial"). "Adverbial" used above is a catch-all phrase.

Step 2: Concord. Concord declares the participle's substantive relationship. The concord declares whether to translate, for example, "we come to him **while *we* are seeing** these things" or "we come to him **while *he* is seeing** these things." For a main verb with first person plural, a "we" option would be declared by a nominative plural participle in concord with this verb's subject and number. A "he" option would be declared by a participle with masculine singular inflection (case given by the substantive case). In Greek: (1) ἐρχόμεθα αὐτῷ **βλέποντες** ταῦτα. (2) ἐρχόμεθα αὐτῷ **βλέποντι** ταῦτα (see Table 26.5).

Step 3: Tense Aspect. Finally, strive to maintain the participle's tense aspect, if possible, in translation. Tense communicates *aspect*, the key verbal component of a participle. The present tense participle is *durative*. As could be inferred from the remarks above about construing the time of an adverbial participle, time is not indicated in a participle's present tense. However, durative kind of action is.

The procedure outlined above is rather mechanical, but at least gives you a good jump start for translating participles. Over time, you will achieve more nuance and sophistication. We now provide examples of adjectival and adverbial participles.

Adjectival Participle

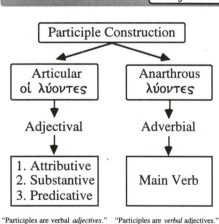

"Participles are verbal *adjectives*."   "Participles are *verbal* adjectives."

An adjectival participle functions as: (1) attributive, (2) substantive, (3) predicative. These uses are outlined.

Attributive. First, we give a small disclaimer about attributive participles. Some *anarthrous* participles are used attributively. However, even with these constructions, participle concord with a noun nearby can suggest a modifying function to an observant student. Some examples are: (1) γυνὴ **ἔχουσα** = "a woman **who had**," Matt. 26:7, (2) ὕδωρ **ζῶν** = "**living** water," John 4:10, (3) **ἀποθνῄσκοντες** ἄνθρωποι = "**mortal** men," Heb. 7:8, (4) εἰς ἐλπίδα **ζῶσαν** = "unto a **living** hope," 1 Pet. 1:3. Again, such anarthrous, attributive participles are not the rule; plus, concord is helpful.

On the other hand, *all* articular participles by definition are attributive, that is, function as adjectives. They will relate to some noun, pronoun, or adjective in the context, indicated by concord, or act as a substantive (see below). The translation is flexible. For example, ὁ πιστεύων could be "he who believes," the man who believes," "the one who believes," "the man believing," or "the one believing" and typically would be subject of the sentence (nominative). As a modifier, the adjectival participle τῷ λύοντι could be "the loosing" or "which is loosing" (the noun modified here assumed to be dative). Thus:

(1) Observe nominative feminine singular concord in καὶ ἐπληρώθη ἡ γραφὴ ἡ **λέγουσα** = "and the scripture was fulfilled **which says**" (James 2:23).

(2) Observe accusative feminine singular concord in ἐργάζεσθε μὴ τὴν βρῶσιν τὴν ἀπολλυμένην ἀλλὰ τὴν βρῶσιν **τὴν μένουσαν** εἰς ζωὴν αἰώνιον = "Do not work for the food which perishes but for the food **which abides** unto eternal life" (John 6:27).

(3) Observe masculine genitive plural concord in Ὃς δ' ἂν σκανδαλίσῃ ἕνα τῶν μικρῶν τούτων **τῶν πιστευόντων** εἰς ἐμέ = "But whoever causes to stumble one of the least of these **who believe** in me" (Matt. 18:6).

One caveat for recognizing articular participles is to remember that the article may not be right *next* to the participle. For example, a prepositional phrase can separate an article from its participle: **τοῖς** ἀπὸ τῶν ἐθνῶν **ἐπιστρέφουσιν** ἐπὶ τὸν θεόν = "**those** from among the Gentiles **who are turning** unto to God" (Acts 15:19). Again, οὗτός ἐστιν ὁ ἄρτος ὁ ἐκ τοῦ οὐρανοῦ **καταβαίνων** = "this is the bread **coming down** from heaven" (John 6:50).

Substantive. As with adjectives, adjectival participles can be used with substantive function, i.e., grammatically equivalent to a noun. Notice the following:

(1) *Subject:* ἄφεσιν ἁμαρτιῶν λαβεῖν διὰ τοῦ ὀνόματος αὐτοῦ πάντα **τὸν πιστεύοντα** εἰς αὐτόν = "all **those who believe** in him receive forgiveness of sins through his name" (Acts 10:43)

(2) *Indirect Object:* ὁ πατὴρ ὑμῶν ὁ ἐν τοῖς οὐρανοῖς δώσει ἀγαθὰ **τοῖς αἰτοῦσιν** αὐτόν = "your Father in heaven will give good gifts **to those who ask** Him" (Matt. 7:11)

(3) *Direct Object:* ἵνα **τὰ λείποντα** ἐπιδιορθώσῃ = "in order that you might set straight **the things that are remaining**" (Titus 1:5)

(4) *Predicate Nominative:* articular (usually) with linking verbs, so nominative case, e.g., ὀλίγοι εἰσὶν **οἱ εὑρίσκοντες** αὐτήν = "few are **the ones who find** it" (Matt. 7:14)

Predicative. This is the second disclaimer about spotting adjectival participles through the article. Adjectives can function as predicate adjectives when following a linking verb (predicative function), which is a different function from a predicate nominative ("Study is *the good*." vs. "Study is *good*."). Predicate use applies to participles when the participle is: (1) with a linking verb, (2) nominative, (3) *anarthrous* (if *articular*, then a predicate nominative, *substantival* use, #4 above).

For the linking verb εἰμί, observe ὅς ἦν παραλελυμένος = "who <u>was</u> **paralyzed**" (Acts 9:33, perfect passive). Again, ⁺Ἦν δὲ θυμομαχῶν Τυρίοις καὶ Σιδωνίοις = "now he <u>was</u> **angry** with Tyre and Sidon" (Acts 12:20). Or, οὗ ἡ οἰκία ἦν συνομοροῦσα τῇ συναγωγῇ = "whose house <u>was</u> **adjacent** to the synagogue" (Acts 18:7). Finally, ὅτι κατεγνωσμένος ἦν = "because he <u>was</u> **condemned**" (Gal. 2:11, perfect passive). For the linking verb γίνομαι, observe καὶ τὰ ἱμάτια αὐτοῦ ἐγένετο στίλβοντα λευκὰ λίαν = "and his garments <u>became</u> **brilliant**, exceedingly white" (Mark 9:3). Notice carefully that predicate use *requires* the participle to complete the verbal idea.

Summarizing, you can spot the adjectival use of a participle by observing the articular status of the participle, with but two exceptions. First, a few *anarthrous* constructions function attributively (but concord often helps anyway). Second, predicate adjectives with linking verbs are anarthrous. Otherwise, adjectival participles clearly are revealed by the definite article.

Adverbial Participle

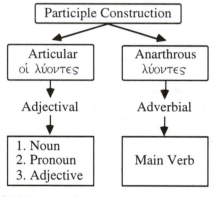

"Participles are verbal *adjectives*."   "Participles are *verbal* adjectives."

Participles as adverbial can modify verbs in several ways. The construction *always* is anarthrous. The distinction from the predicative use (above) is that the adverbial participle phrase is *not required* to complete the verbal idea. Like a dependent clause, the adverbial participle almost always can drop out without crippling the verbal idea.[7]

The adverbial use of the participle is the dominant function of participles in the New Testament. Translation depends not so much on the grammatical form of the participle as on the participle's relationship to the main verb and to the overall context. In short, the adverbial participle must be *interpreted* to be translated. A few uses are outlined briefly.

Temporal. A participle is timeless (infinite). Adverbial participles must be related to the main verb if they are to have any time significance at all. Generally, present participles are treated as simultaneous to the main verb, but not always.

---

[7]One exception, the complementary (supplementary) participle for verbs requiring an infinite to complete the verbal expression.

Context is paramount. The procedure is to set up the participial phrase as a temporal relative clause connected to the main verb. The following table summarizes a few of the main translation options for such temporal clauses, given the tense of the main verb (frequently present or aorist) and the translator's decision as to the three possible time frames of relationship (antecedent, simultaneous, subsequent).

Table 26.7 Participle as Temporal Clause[8]

Participle	Main Verb–*Past*			Main Verb–*Present*		
	Ant.	Simul.	Sub.	Ant.	Simul.	Sub.
Present	*whereas although* ___*ing*	*while as when* ___*ing*	*to* ___ ___*ing*	*whereas although* ___*ing*	*while as when* ___*ing*	*to* ___ ___*ing*
Aorist	*after when* __ *and* __ ___*ing*	__ *and* __ ___*ing*		*after when* ___*ing*	__ *and* __ ___*ing*	

Generally, antecedent action uses "after" or "when" (but can use "whereas" or "although" if set up as a concessive clause). Simultaneous action uses "while" or "as." Subsequent action applies only to present participles, as an infinitive or gerund phrase ("to ____" or "____ing"). (Aorist tense is included for comparison.)

Observe this translation: τυφλὸς **ὢν** ἄρτι βλέπω = "*whereas* I **was** blind, now I see." The participle ὤν is present tense. However, only the tense *aspect* is concerned (durative). The translator has *interpreted* the action of this adverbial participle to be antecedent to the main verb (observe ἄρτι). So, the translator has used a concessive clause, then the English tense for antecedent action, preterit ("was"), even though the participle is present tense. The timeless participle is given time by the main verb. So a present participle still can be "was."

Another twist would be τυφλὸς **ὢν** ἔτι βλέπω = "*while* **I am** blind, yet I see." The idea would be a play on words about seeing as insight, not physical sight. The participle here would be interpreted as *simultaneous* to the main verb ("am").

---

[8]The expression "__ and __" means treating the participle as a finite verb connected to the main verb by the conjunction "and." Also, while an unqualified "___ing" English form can be used to translate a Greek participle, this form can obscure the tense aspect and should be used with discretion.

Observe: ἐκήρυσσον **πορευόμενοι** = "*while* **they were advancing**, they were preaching" (deponent middle). The translator has *interpreted* the participle's action as simultaneous to that of the main verb. Since the main verb is *past* tense, the simultaneous action is translated past tense as well ("*were* advancing"), even though the participle is present tense. Again, participles are timeless, except for the main verb. Note these examples:

(1) Antecedent: **ἀκούοντες** ὅσα ἐποίει <u>ἦλθον</u> πρὸς αὐτόν = "*after* **they heard** whatsoever things he was doing, <u>they came</u> to him" (Mark 3:8); the "they" of the participle translation derives by concord with the subject of the main verb, ἦλθον. Or, ὥστε τὸν ὄχλον θαυμάσαι **βλέποντας** κωφοὺς λαλοῦντας = "so that the crowd <u>marveled</u> *when* **they saw** the dumb speaking" (Matt. 15:31); here ὄχλον is an accusative of general reference for the aorist infinitive of result, θαυμάσαι, providing the accusative case for the concord of the related adverbial participle, βλέποντας.

(2) Simultaneous: <u>προσῆλθον</u> αὐτῷ **διδάσκοντι** οἱ ἀρχιερεῖς καὶ οἱ πρεσβύτεροι τοῦ λαοῦ = "the chief priests and elders of the people <u>came</u> to him *as* **he was teaching**" (Matt. 21:23); observe here how the concord declares what substantive to construe with the participle's action.

(3) Subsequent: Note the phrase καὶ <u>ἦλθεν</u> **ζητῶν** καρπὸν ἐν αὐτῇ = "and <u>he came</u> **looking** for fruit on it" (Luke 13:6).

Purpose. The purpose of the main verb is specified. Translation will use "so that," "in order to," "for the purpose of." The infinitive and gerund translations "to ___" or "___ing" also can be used. Thus, καὶ <u>ἦλθεν</u> **ζητῶν** καρπὸν ἐν αὐτῇ = "and <u>he came</u> **looking** for fruit on it" (Luke 13:6).

Cause. The cause behind the main verb's action is specified. The relative clause is set up with "because," "since," or "for." Thus, <u>Εὐχαριστῶ</u> τῷ θεῷ μου πάντοτε μνείαν σου ποιούμενος ἐπὶ τῶν προσευχῶν μου, **ἀκούων** σου τὴν ἀγάπην καὶ τὴν πίστιν = "<u>I give thanks</u> to my God always making mention of you when I pray, *because* **I hear** of your love and your faith" (Phile. 5). The following causal participle at the same time introduces a direct quote: πολλοὶ ἐπίστευσαν εἰς αὐτὸν τῶν Σαμαριτῶν διὰ τὸν λόγον τῆς γυναικὸς **μαρτυρούσης** <u>ὅτι</u> Εἶπέν μοι πάντα ἃ ἐποίησα = "Many of the Samaritans believed in him because of the word of the woman, *for* she **testified**, 'He told me all the things that I have done'" (John 4:39).

Condition. The protasis of a conditional sentence is specified, translated by "if." The conjunction εἰ is not required. Thus, ἐξ ὧν **διατηροῦντες** ἑαυτοὺς εὖ πράξετε = "from which, *if* **you keep** yourselves, you will do well" (Acts 15:29). The context may involve εἴτε. For example, διὸ καὶ φιλοτιμούμεθα, <u>εἴτε</u> **ἐνδημοῦντες** <u>εἴτε</u> **ἐκδημοῦντες**, εὐάρεστοι αὐτῷ εἶναι. = "Therefore, we desire, <u>whether</u> **living at home** or <u>whether</u> **living away**, to be pleasing to God." (2 Cor. 5:9).

Concession. The circumstances almost hindering the action of the main verb are specified, translated by "although" or "whereas." Thus, τυφλὸς **ὢν** ἄρτι βλέπω = "*whereas* **I was** blind, now I see" (John 9:25, antecedent time also indicated).

Instrumental. The means or agency accomplishing the main verb's action is indicated, typically using "by" or "through." Thus, σταυρώσαντες δὲ αὐτὸν διεμερίσαντο τὰ ἱμάτια αὐτοῦ **βάλλοντες** κλῆρον = "and after they crucified him, they divided his garments among themselves *by* **casting** lots" (Matt. 27:35).

Complementary. The main verb either requires an infinite form to complete the action or takes a complement in certain constructions.[9] Translation will incorporate "that," "to ___," or "___ing." Thus, οὐ παύομαι **εὐχαριστῶν** ὑπὲρ ὑμῶν = "I do not cease **giving thanks** for you" (Eph. 1:16). A subcategory is introduction of indirect discourse. Thus, οἱ δοῦλοι αὐτοῦ ὑπήντησαν αὐτῷ **λέγοντες** ὅτι ὁ παῖς αὐτοῦ ζῇ = "his servants met him **reporting** that his son was alive" (John 4:51).

Circumstantial. Additional action that circumstantially accompanies the action of the main verb is specified. Options are "___ing," or as an adverb, "___ly," or transforming the participial action into that of a finite verb joined to the main verb with "and." Thus, ἤρξαντο ἅπαν τὸ πλῆθος τῶν μαθητῶν **χαίροντες** αἰνεῖν τὸν θεὸν φωνῇ μεγάλῃ = "the entire multitude of the disciples began to praise God **joyfully** with a great voice" (Luke 19:37; cf. Acts 5:41). A typical "___ and ___" form is that used to introduce direct discourse. Commonly, ἀποκρίνομαι is used, as in ὁ δὲ Πιλᾶτος ἀπεκρίθη αὐτοῖς **λέγων** = "and Pilate answered them *and* **said**" (Mark 15:9). Differently, προσῆλθον αὐτῷ διδάσκοντι οἱ ἀρχιερεῖς καὶ οἱ πρεσβύτεροι τοῦ λαοῦ **λέγοντες**, Ἐν ποίᾳ ἐξουσίᾳ ταῦτα ποιεῖς; = "And the chief priests and the elders of the people came to him as he was teaching *and* said, 'By what sort of authority are you doing these things?'" (Matt. 21:23).

Periphrasis

Analysis. *Periphrasis* can be thought of as "phrasing around," a roundabout way of saying something. One tendency of koine Greek was an overemphasis for effect.[10] A periphrastic construction uses *two* verbal forms—a form of a linking verb and a participle—when one finite verb would have sufficed. The tenses of the linking verb used with the present participle are the present, imperfect, and future. These yield the present, imperfect, and future periphrastic tenses, respectively. The idea behind periphrasis may be an emphasis on the *durative* aspect of the tense.

---

[9]A function parallel to that of the complementary infinitive. Common are verbs of appearing, beginning, being, ceasing, continuing, and showing.

[10]Notice overemphasis for effect in the colloquial expression "most unique."

Table 26.8 Periphrastic Tenses—Present Participle

Linking Verb		Participle		Periphrastic Tense
present tense	+	present participle	=	present periphrastic
imperfect tense	+	present participle	=	imperfect periphrastic
future tense	+	present participle	=	future periphrastic

Examples. Take Luke 11:14: ἦν ἐκβάλλων δαιμόνιον = "he **was casting out** a demon," roundabout phrasing for the indicative ἐξέβαλλον (so Mark 6:13, δαιμόνια πολλὰ ἐξέβαλλον = "he was casting out many demons"). Notice a customary imperfect idea in ἐγὼ ἤμην φυλακίζων καὶ δέρων κατὰ τὰς συναγωγὰς τοὺς πιστεύοντας ἐπὶ σέ = "in each synagogue I **used to imprison** and **beat** those who believed in you" (Acts 22:19). Imperfect (ἐφυλάκιζον, ἔδερον) would have sufficed. The linking verb is not always adjacent: οἱ ἄνδρες οὓς ἔθεσθε ἐν τῇ φυλακῇ **εἰσὶν** ἐν τῷ ἱερῷ **ἑστῶτες** καὶ **διδάσκοντες** τὸν λαόν = "the men whom you put in prison **are standing** in the temple and **teaching** the people" (Acts 5:25). Neither does the linking verb invariably precede the participle (cf. Gal. 1:23). For a future tense, observe καὶ οἱ ἀστέρες **ἔσονται** ἐκ τοῦ οὐρανοῦ **πίπτοντες** = "and the stars **will fall** from heaven" (Mark 13:25). For γίνομαι, note Μὴ **γίνεσθε** ἑτεροζυγοῦντες = "**do** not **be bound together**" (2 Cor. 6:14, imperative mood).

Translation. Grammatically, the periphrastic construction can be understood as a complementary participle. The participle completes the verbal idea begun in the linking verb, which would be the most common use of the complementary participle in the New Testament. Syntactically, the construction is predicative (because of the use of a linking verb). The adjectival focus as a predicate adjective would be in view. Either way, translate a periphrastic construction straight ahead: (1) give the linking verb first, (2) followed by the participle (usually an "___ing" form).

Genitive Absolute

Analysis. Here is the one exception of an anarthrous participle that is *not* related to the main verb. The *genitive absolute* is an abrupt shift of construction that is signaled by a participle in the genitive case. The "absolute" means absolutely no syntactical connection to the rest of the sentence. A tip-off to one very common genitive absolute construction is an abrupt change of subject. A participial clause starts off with "they," for example, but the finite verb's subject is "he," i.e., totally different. Such a participial clause is independent of the main verb and its subject.

While the clause adds information, the clause is non-essential to the action of the main verb. While other adverbial participles are said to be non-essential to the action of the main verb, they are not grammatically *independent* of the main verb.

Translation. As the name suggests, the grammatical construction is easy to spot: both the participle and the noun construed with the participle will be genitive. To translate: (1) treat the genitive noun as having a "subject" relationship to the participle,[11] and (2) give a temporal or other adverbial translation to the participle. For example, **λυόντων** δὲ <u>αὐτῶν</u> τὸν πῶλον εἶπαν οἱ κύριοι αὐτοῦ πρὸς αὐτούς = "*while* <u>they</u> **were untying** the colt, his owners said to them" (Luke 19:33). Notice carefully: (1) the abrupt subject shift from "they" to "his owners," (2) the clause is non-essential, and (3) the clause is grammatically *independent* of the main verb.

Table 26.9 Genitive Absolute

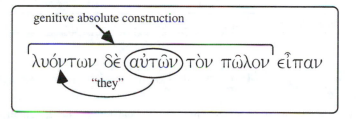

A linking verb also can be found in genitive absolute construction: Καὶ **ὄντος** <u>αὐτοῦ</u> ἐν Βηθανίᾳ ἐν τῇ οἰκίᾳ Σίμωνος τοῦ λεπροῦ **κατακειμένου** <u>αὐτοῦ</u> ἦλθεν γυνὴ = "And *while* <u>he</u> **was** in Bethany at the home of Simon the leper, *as* <u>he</u> **was reclining** [eating], a woman came" (Mark 14:3). This example actually stacks up two genitive absolute constructions back to back. More directly, the story line is "a woman came." These genitive constructions with their different subject are grammatically independent of the main verb, "came," even though adding some information to the basic action expressed in this verb.

Identification. In identifying a genitive absolute, do not get carried away with just tagging a genitive participle. Not all genitive participles are genitive absolutes. For example, ὁ Φίλιππος ἤκουσεν αὐτοῦ **ἀναγινώσκοντος** = "Philip heard him **reading**" (Acts 8:30). This participle is part of a temporal participial phrase (or perhaps complementary) connected to the direct object of ἀκούω (which takes a *genitive* direct object). The adverbial function of the participle is *not* grammatically independent of the main verb.

---

[11]Notice the similarity of function to the accusative of general reference for the infinitive.

Adverbial Summary

Table 26.10 Adverbial Participle—Translation Summary

Temporal	*after, when, while, as, to ___, ___ing*
Purpose	*so that, in order to, for the purpose of, to ___, ___ing*
Cause	*because, since, for*
Condition	*whether, if*
Concession	*whereas, although*
Instrumental	*by, through*
Complementary	*to ___, ___ing*
Circumstantial	*___ing, ___ly, ___ and ___*

Participle Location

To locate a participle, specify tense, voice, "participle," case, gender, number. Then specify the lexical form and lexical meaning. The word "participle" replaces the mood component of the indicative verb, instead identifying the kind of verbal as infinite. Notice this procedure first identifies the participle's verbal components, then finishes off with the adjectival components. The location, then, acknowledges the participle's dual heritage.

Table 26.11 Participle Location: Six Components—λύοντες

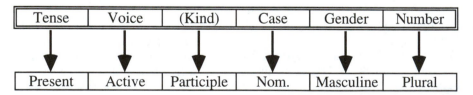

Tense	Voice	(Kind)	Case	Gender	Number
Present	Active	Participle	Nom.	Masculine	Plural

One then would finish the location by identifying the lexical form as λύω, then the lexical meaning as "I loose." The meaning of the particular form λύοντες already has been provided in your translation.

What To Learn—LESSON 26 (εἴκοσι ἕξ)

- ☐ 1. Participle paradigms: λύω; contracts φιλέω, δηλόω, τιμάω; and εἰμί
- ☐ 2. Verb and adjective characteristics of participles
- ☐ 3. Translation procedure: know the five questions and their application
- ☐ 4. Adjectival participle uses: attributive, substantive, predicative
- ☐ 5. Adverbial participle uses: temporal, purpose, cause, condition, concession, instrumental, complementary, circumstantial
- ☐ 6. The meaning of *periphrasis* and how to translate
- ☐ 7. The meaning of *genitive absolute* and how to translate
- ☐ 8. Vocabulary words

The great majority of our Greek New Testament manuscripts are minuscules, which represent the later period in the history of the handwritten text. A reform of handwriting about the ninth century began using small letters in a cursive script. Sometimes words still were written continuously and broken at the end of one line to the beginning of the next. Accents were used. The text type usually is Byzantine. Ms. 375 below, from the Athens National Library, is about the eleventh century.

Ms. 375

Matt. 1:1–6

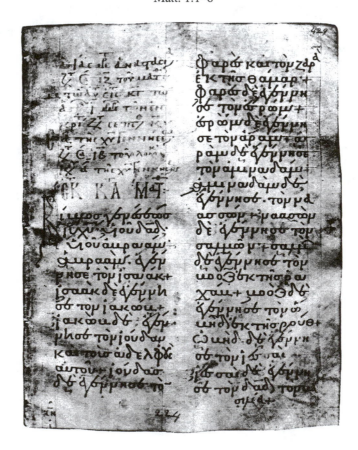

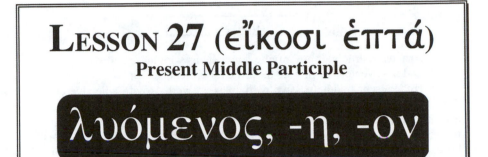

LESSON 27 (εἴκοσι ἑπτά)

Present Middle Participle

λυόμενος, -η, -ον

A participle's verbal components are tense and voice. Tense relates to: (1) tense aspect and (2) the participle's time as a function of the main verb. This lesson focuses on the voice component. Diagramming participles also is presented.

Vocabulary 27

Adverb

ἐκεῖθεν	from there

Adjectives and Nouns

καθαρός, -ά, -όν	clean, pure
πλούσιος, -α, -ον	rich
πνευματικός, -ή, -όν	spiritual
ἀδελφή, -ῆς, ἡ	sister
ἀδικία, -ας, ἡ	unrighteousness
ἔλεος, -ους, τό	mercy, pity
ἑορτή, -ῆς, ἡ	feast
κώμη, -ης, ἡ	village
μάχαιρα, -ης, ἡ	sword
πάσχα, τό (indeclinable)	Passover
σταυρός, -οῦ, ὁ	cross
χήρα, -ας, ἡ	widow
χώρα, -ας, ἡ	country (district)

Verbs

ἁγιάζω	I sanctify
ἀποκαλύπτω	I reveal
βαστάζω	I bear, carry
γνωρίζω	I make known
ἰάομαι	I heal
καταργέω	I abolish, destroy
κελεύω	I order
λυπέω	I grieve
νικάω	I conquer
προφητεύω	I prophesy
τελέω	I complete, fulfill
φρονέω	I think

Present Middle/Passive Participle

λυόμενος, -η, -ον	being loosed (λύω)

Analysis

Character. Participles are infinite, tense stems with tense and voice only. The middle and passive voice forms are the same for present participles.

Form. Present middle/passive participles are verbals with adjective endings. The inflection of the adjective ἀγαθός is followed exactly except for the oxytone accent. Thus, the present middle participle inflection is quite familiar. The middle participial suffix, -μεν, is very distinctive in all forms. Participle accent is not "irregular," since rules for finite verbs do not apply. Nominative masculine singular accent is antepenult acute. Then observe that: (1) general rules of accent are followed, (2) accent is persistent, (3) the genitive feminine plural does *not* have the typical circumflex on the ultima, as in first declension nouns. In formation, the thematic vowel, ο, and participial suffix, -μεν, are added to the present stem:

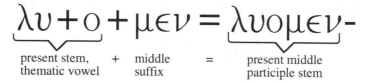

$$\underbrace{\lambda \upsilon + \text{o}}_{\text{}} + \mu \epsilon \nu = \underbrace{\lambda \upsilon \text{o} \mu \epsilon \nu\text{-}}_{\text{}}$$

| present stem, thematic vowel | + | middle suffix | = | present middle participle stem |

Inflection by gender is added. Observe the ἀγαθός pattern and distinctive suffix.

Table 27.1 Present Middle/Passive Participle—λύω

	Masculine (ἀγαθός)		Neuter (ἀγαθός)		Feminine (ἀγαθός)	
	Singular	*Plural*	*Singular*	*Plural*	*Singular*	*Plural*
Nom	λυόμενος	λυόμενοι	λυόμενον	λυόμενα	λυομένη	λυόμεναι
Gen	λυομένου	λυομένων	λυομένου	λυομένων	λυομένης	λυομένων
Dat	λυομένῳ	λυομένοις	λυομένῳ	λυομένοις	λυομένη	λυομέναις
Acc	λυόμενον	λυομένους	λυόμενον	λυόμενα	λυομένην	λυομένας

Contracts. Contract verbs show typical contraction with the resultant endings.[1] As examples, the three genders are divided among the three contract paradigms.

---

[1]For -ε contracts: ε + ο = ου, so φιλούμενος etc. For -ο contracts: ο + ο = ου, so δηλούμενος, etc. For -α contracts: α + ο = ω, so τιμώμενος, etc.

Table 27.2 Present Middle/Passive Participle—Contract Examples

φιλέω (masculine)		δηλόω (neuter)		τιμάω (feminine)	
Singular	*Plural*	*Singular*	*Plural*	*Singular*	*Plural*
φιλούμενος	φιλούμενοι	δηλούμενον	δηλούμενα	τιμωμένη	τιμώμεναι
φιλουμένου	φιλουμένων	δηλουμένου	δηλουμένων	τιμωμένης	τιμωμένων
φιλουμένῳ	φιλουμένοις	δηλουμένῳ	δηλουμένοις	τιμωμένῃ	τιμωμέναις
φιλούμενον	φιλουμένους	δηλούμενον	δηλούμενα	τιμωμένην	τιμωμένας

Infinite Voice

Table 27.3 Articular Participles—Approximate Meanings

Active	*Middle*	*Passive*
ὁ λύων	ὁ λυόμενος	ὁ λυόμενος
he who looses	he who looses (for himself)	he who is being loosed
the man who looses	the man who looses (for himself)	the man who is being loosed
the one who looses	the one who looses (for himself)	the one who is being loosed
the man loosing	the man loosing (for himself)	the man being loosed
the one loosing	the one loosing (for himself)	the one being loosed
οἱ λύοντες	οἱ λυόμενοι	οἱ λυόμενοι
those who loose	those who loose (for themselves)	those who are being loosed
the men who loose	the men who loose (for themselves)	the men who are being loosed
the ones who loose	the ones who loose (for themselves)	the ones who are being loosed
the men loosing	the men loosing (for themselves)	the men being loosed
the ones loosing	the ones loosing (for themselves)	the ones being loosed

Analysis. Voice relates the verb's action to the verb's subject. However, both infinitives and participles are infinite, that is, not limited by a subject. Thus, to speak of the voice of an infinite form is to speak in a relative manner. For an infinitive, voice is related to the substantive with which the infinitive's action is construed, an accusative of general reference, for example. In other cases, this substantive is the subject of the finite verb with which the infinitive is associated. For participles, voice is related to the substantive with which the participle's action is construed, which often is the subject of the main verb. For the genitive absolute, voice relates to the genitive noun in the construction. (See Table 27.3 for generic translations.)

Deponents. Verbs deponent in indicative forms also are deponent in participial forms. For example, the deponent verb πορεύομαι has the present middle participle forms by gender of πορευόμενος, πορευομένη, and πορευόμενον. Though middle in form, these participle forms are translated actively simply as "proceeding," *not* as "proceeding (for himself, herself, itself)" or as "is being proceeded."

Periphrasis. Periphrastic formation can use middle/passive voice. For example:

(1)   present periphrastic: καὶ γὰρ εἴπερ **εἰσὶν λεγόμενοι** θεοὶ = "for even if there **are so-called** gods" (1 Cor. 8:5)

(2)   imperfect periphrastic: ὃς καὶ αὐτὸς **ἦν προσδεχόμενος** τὴν βασιλείαν τοῦ θεοῦ = "who himself also **was waiting for** the kingdom of God" (Mark 15:43)

(3)   future periphrastic: **ἔσται** ὁ υἱὸς τοῦ ἀνθρώπου **καθήμενος** ἐκ δεξιῶν τῆς δυνάμεως τοῦ θεοῦ = "the Son of Man **will be seated** at the right hand of the power of God" (Luke 22:69)

Dative Case

Dative is the case of personal interest (Table 4.5). Indirect object is a frequent use, but not the only one of personal interest. Location function specifies location: *in, on, at, by, among*. Instrumental function expresses means or agency: *by, with*.

Personal Interest. Observe personal interest as dative of: (1) *advantage or disadvantage* ("for," "against"), a special use of indirect object: εὔθυμοι δὲ γενόμενοι πάντες καὶ **αὐτοὶ** προσελάβοντο τροφῆς. = "All then were encouraged and took food **for themselves**." (Acts 27:36); also, ἡ δὲ Ἡρῳδιὰς ἐνεῖχεν **αὐτῷ** καὶ ἤθελεν αὐτὸν ἀποκτεῖναι = "Now Herodias had a grudge **against him**, and wanted to kill him" (Mark 6:19); (2) *possession* ("his," "her," etc.): Τί ὄνομά **σοι**; καὶ λέγει αὐτῷ, Λεγιὼν ὄνομά **μοι** = "'What is **your** name?' And he said to him, '**My** name is Legion" (Mark 5:9); (3) *reference* ("with reference to," "concerning," "about"): καὶ εὑρέθη **μοι** ἡ ἐντολὴ ἡ εἰς ζωὴν αὕτη εἰς θάνατον = "and the very commandment meant for life was found **for me** to result in death" (Rom. 7:10).

Locative. Note locative function as locative of: (1) *place:* πᾶσιν τοῖς οὖσιν **ἐν Ῥώμῃ** = "to all those who are **in Rome**" (Rom. 1:7); (2) a point in *time:* ὅτι ταῦτα ἐποίει **ἐν σαββάτῳ** = "because he was doing these things **on the Sabbath**" (John 5:16); and (3) *sphere:* ὁ μὴ ἀγαπῶν μένει **ἐν τῷ θανάτῳ** = "the one who does not love remains **in death**" (1 John 3:14).

Instrumental. Note instrumental function as instrumental of: (1) original *cause* ("because"): Πάντες ὑμεῖς σκανδαλισθήσεσθε **ἐν ἐμοὶ** ἐν τῇ νυκτὶ ταύτῃ = "All of you will be offended **because of me** on this very night" (Matt. 26:31); (2) intermediary, impersonal *means* ("by means of," "with," "by"): ὅτι **ἐν πυρὶ** ἀποκαλύπτεται = "because it will be revealed **with fire**" (1 Cor. 3:13); (3) *manner*, as accompanying circumstance ("in," "with"): λέγοντες **φωνῇ μεγάλῃ** = "saying **with a loud voice**" (Rev. 5:12); (4) time as an interval of *measure:* **ἱκανῷ χρόνῳ** ταῖς μαγείαις ἐξεστακέναι αὐτούς = **for a long time** he had astonished them with his magical arts" (Acts 8:11); and (5) *association* ("with"): λέγων αὐτοῖς, Συγχάρητέ **μοι** = "saying to them, 'Rejoice **with me!**'" (Luke 15:6).

Diagramming

Participles are placed on a verbal base line according to function. The genitive noun of a genitive absolute construction has subject position, but in brackets.

Verbal Adjectives. Adjectival participles are connected by a slanted line underneath the substantive modified or in any noun position if substantival. If part of a participial phrase, the phrase is situated on a verbal standard (⟋) in any noun position. Apposition is handled normally: an "equals" sign (=) pointing to another base line, but with participial construction.

Adverbial Participles. The adverbial participle is situated on the horizontal of a slanted line coming off the main verb, as are adverbs. However, in periphrastic constructions, keep linking verbs with their respective participles as one verbal unit. Likewise, keep complementary participles on the same base line immediately after the verb served. If the complementary participle is part of a participial phrase, place the whole unit on a standard immediately following the verb served. Participle indirect discourse is a direct object, so the introductory participle is placed with a direct object line, then the ὅτι clause following as direct object on its own standard. Absolute constructions are placed in brackets, as usual.

Table 27.4 Diagramming Participles

| 1. ἠκρίβωσεν παρ' αὐτῶν τὸν χρόνον **τοῦ φαινομένου** ἀστέρος

"he ascertained from them the time **of the appearing** star" (Matt. 2:7) | *Adjectival Participle as Attributive*

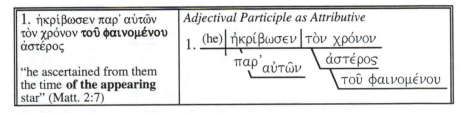 |

2. δώσει ἀγαθὰ **τοῖς αἰτοῦσιν** αὐτόν "He will give good gifts **to those who ask** Him" (Matt. 7:11)	*Adjectival Participle as Substantive* 2. (He) | δώσει | ἀγαθὰ τοῖς αἰτοῦσιν | αὐτόν
3. ὀλίγοι εἰσὶν **οἱ εὑρίσκοντες** αὐτήν "few are **the ones who find** it" (Matt. 7:14)	*Adjectival Participle as Predicate Nominative* οἱ εὑρίσκοντες | αὐτήν 3. ὀλίγοι | εἰσὶν
4. τὰ ἱμάτια αὐτοῦ <u>ἐγένετο</u> **στίλβοντα** "his garments <u>became</u> **brilliant**" (Mark. 9:3)	*Adjectival Participle as Predicative* 4. τὰ ἱμάτια | ἐγένετο \ στίλβοντα αὐτοῦ
5. <u>προσῆλθον</u> αὐτῷ **διδάσκοντι** οἱ ἀρχιερεῖς καὶ οἱ πρεσβύτεροι τοῦ λαοῦ "the chief priests and the elders of the people <u>came</u> to him *as* **he was teaching**" (Matt. 21:23)	*Adverbial Participle as Temporal* οἱ ἀρχιερεῖς 5. καὶ προσῆλθον οἱ πρεσβύτεροι αὐτῷ διδάσκοντι τοῦ λαοῦ

6. οὐ <u>παύομαι</u> **εὐχαριστῶν** ὑπὲρ ὑμῶν
 	
"<u>I do</u> not <u>cease</u> **giving thanks** for you" (Eph. 1:16)
	Adverbial Participle as Complementary
	
	εὐχαριστῶν
	    ὑπὲρ ὑμῶν
	6. (I) | παύομαι
	    οὐ

7. οἱ δοῦλοι αὐτοῦ ὑπήντησαν αὐτῷ **λέγοντες** <u>ὅτι</u> ὁ παῖς αὐτοῦ ζῇ
 	
"his servants met him **reporting** that his son was alive" (John 4:51)
	Adverbial Participle as Indirect Discourse
	
	7. οἱ δοῦλοι | ὑπήντησαν | αὐτῷ
	    αὐτοῦ
	           ὁ παῖς | ζῇ
	           ὅτι αὐτοῦ
	    λέγοντες

8. οἱ ἀστέρες **ἔσονται** ἐκ τοῦ οὐρανοῦ **πίπτοντες** "the stars **will fall** from heaven" (Mark 13:25)	*Adverbial Participle as Periphrasis* 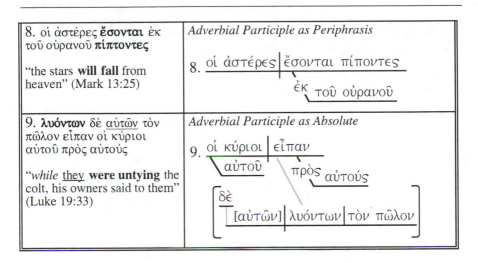
9. **λυόντων** δὲ <u>αὐτῶν</u> τὸν πῶλον εἶπαν οἱ κύριοι αὐτοῦ πρὸς αὐτούς "*while* <u>they</u> **were untying** the colt, his owners said to them" (Luke 19:33)	*Adverbial Participle as Absolute*

What To Learn—LESSON 27 (εἴκοσι ἑπτά)

Beginning

☐ 1. Present middle/passive participle paradigm: λυόμενος, λυομένη, λυόμενον

☐ 2. Recognition of contract verbs as present middle/passive participles

☐ 3. Voice and infinite verbal forms (infinitives and participles), approximate translations, deponent participles, and middle periphrastic constructions

☐ 4. Diagramming participles

☐ 5. Vocabulary words

Advanced

☐ 6. Dative case use as personal interest—*advantage/disadvantage*, *possession*, *reference*; locative function—*place*, *time*, *sphere*; instrumental function—*cause*, *means*, *manner*, *measure*, *association*

 The Greek New Testament first was published by the Dutch scholar Erasmus on the new Gutenberg press in 1516. The project was rushed, based on only six Greek manuscripts and having many errors.[2] Yet, Erasmus's text became the basis for others that followed, such as the Beza text used by the King James translators. Notice corrections for the printer in Erasmus's own hand at the bottom of the image.

Greek Gospel MS. 2

Luke 6:20–30

---

[2]Erasmus competed with another effort under the direction of cardinal Ximenes of Spain. Erasmus used what few manuscripts he could find in Basel: one for the Gospels and one for the Acts and Epistles, each no earlier than the twelfth century. The one Revelation manuscript was defective, missing the last few verses; Erasmus had to translate backwards from the Latin Vulgate, inventing a Greek text here found nowhere else! (See Metzger, *The Text of the New Testament*, pp. 99–100.)

LESSON 28 (ΕΙΚΟΣΙ ΟΚΤΩ)

Aorist and Future Participles

λύσας, λιπών, λυθείς

Aorist participles usually represent action prior to the main verb, but not always. Their essence is to communicate punctiliar force, or in some cases just undefined action. Future participles are uncommon, but they are not hard to recognize.

Vocabulary 28

Conjunction

μήποτε   lest, otherwise

Nouns

δένδρον, -ου, τό   tree

νεφέλη, -ης, ἡ   cloud

πορνεία, -ας, ἡ   fornication

First Aorist Participles

λύσας, -σασα, -σαν   having loosed

λυσάμενος, -η, -ον   having loosed

(for myself, etc.)

Second Aorist Participles

λιπών, -οῦσα, -όν   having left

λιπόμενος, -η, -ον   having left (for

myself, etc.)

Aorist Passive Participles

λυθείς, -θεῖσα, -θέν   having been

loosed

γραφείς, -εῖσα, -έν   having been

written

First Aorist

Active. Infinite, the aorist participle has no augment. First aorist active participles are verbals with noun endings. The aorist stem plus tense suffix -σα is the base to which the participial indicator, -ντ, is added. Masculine and neuter use third declension endings exactly as present active, except the nominative singular forms

329

and masculine dative plural.[1] Accent is penult acute. Feminine follows δόξα (Table 5.4), but primitive feminine forms react with the stem, winding up as -σασ.[2] Thus:

$$\underbrace{\lambda \upsilon + \sigma \alpha}_{} + \nu \tau = \underbrace{\lambda \upsilon \sigma \alpha \nu \tau}_{}\text{-}$$

stem, aorist suffix + participial suffix = first aorist active participle stem

But the feminine becomes:

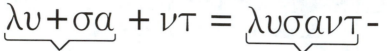

$$\lambda \upsilon \sigma \alpha \nu \tau \iota = \lambda \upsilon \sigma \alpha \nu \sigma = \lambda \upsilon \sigma \alpha \sigma \text{-}$$

Inflection by gender is added, endings generally looking similar to present active.

Table 28.1 First Aorist Active Participle—λύω

Masculine		Neuter		Feminine	
Singular	*Plural*	*Singular*	*Plural*	*Singular*	*Plural*
λύσας	λύσαντες	λῦσαν	λύσαντα	λύσασα	λύσασαι
λύσαντος	λυσάντων	λύσαντος	λυσάντων	λυσάσης	λυσασῶν
λύσαντι	λύσασι(ν)	λύσαντι	λύσασι(ν)	λυσάσῃ	λυσάσαις
λύσαντα	λύσαντας	λῦσαν	λύσαντα	λύσασαν	λυσάσας

Various reactions take on familiar patterns. Contracts lengthen. Thus, φιλήσας, δηλώσας, τιμήσας (with a few exceptions, as in καλέω, καλέσας). Stems with stops are as expected. Thus, the labial πέμπω is πέμψας. Palatal κηρύσσω (κηρυκ-) is κηρύξας. Dental πείθω is πείσας. Liquid ἐγείρω becomes ἐγείρας, and κρίνω becomes κρίνας.

Middle. Forms are as expected. Stem is λυσα-. Voice indicator is -μεν. Endings are like ἀγαθός, without oxytone accent. Accent is antepenult acute. Thus:

---

[1]In which the nominative singular form becomes -σας because σαντς → -σας (ντ dropping before σ, then compensatory lengthening, but lengthening invisible); neuter singular form becomes -σαν, because -σαντ → -σαν (τ cannot stand at the end of a word); the dative plural form becomes -σασι(ν), because σαντσι → -σασι (again, ντ drops before the σ).

[2]Involving consonantal iota, -σαντι →-σανσ → -σασ (τι going to σ).

$$\underbrace{\lambda\upsilon + \sigma\alpha}_{} + \underbrace{\mu\epsilon\nu}_{} = \underbrace{\lambda\upsilon\sigma\alpha\mu\epsilon\nu\text{-}}_{}$$

stem, aorist suffix + voice suffix   =   first aorist middle participle stem

Table 28.2 First Aorist Middle Participle—λύω

Masculine		Neuter		Feminine	
Singular	*Plural*	*Singular*	*Plural*	*Singular*	*Plural*
λυσάμενος	λυσάμενοι	λυσάμενον	λυσάμενα	λυσαμένη	λυσάμεναι
λυσαμένου	λυσαμένων	λυσαμένου	λυσαμένων	λυσαμένης	λυσαμένων
λυσαμένῳ	λυσαμένοις	λυσαμένῳ	λυσαμένοις	λυσαμένῃ	λυσαμέναις
λυσάμενον	λυσαμένους	λυσάμενον	λυσάμενα	λυσαμένην	λυσαμένας

Reaction patterns are the same as with active voice, since the aorist tense suffix continues as part of the formation. For example, the contract ποιέω is ποιησάμενος. The labial περιβλέπω is περιβλεψάμενος. The liquid κείρω is κειράμενος, and so forth.

Passive. The stem is aorist passive. The passive suffix is the original -θε, not the lengthened form -θη of the indicative mood. Otherwise, formation is as with active. Accent is ultima acute. Thus:

$$\underbrace{\lambda\upsilon + \theta\epsilon}_{} = \underbrace{\lambda\upsilon\theta\epsilon\text{-}}_{}$$

stem, passive suffix = first aorist passive participle stem

The nominative singular of masculine and neuter, as well as the masculine dative plural react (for the usual reasons).[3] Again, the feminine forms react too, winding up as -θεῖσα (also for the usual reasons).[4]

---

[3]The nominative singular form becomes -θείς because -θεντς → -θες → -θεις (ντ dropping before σ, then compensatory lengthening); neuter singular form becomes -θέν, because -θεντ → -θεν (τ cannot stand at the end of a word); the dative plural form becomes -θεῖσι(ν), because -θεντσι → -θεσι → -θεισι (again, ντ drops before the σ; stem undergoes compensatory lengthening).

[4]Involving consonantal iota, -θεντι → -θενσ → -θεσ → -θεισ (τι going to σ, then ν dropping before the σ, and compensatory lengthening).

Table 28.3 First Aorist Passive Participle—λύω

Masculine		Neuter		Feminine	
Singular	*Plural*	*Singular*	*Plural*	*Singular*	*Plural*
λυθείς	λυθέντες	λυθέν	λυθέντα	λυθεῖσα	λυθεῖσαι
λυθέντος	λυθέντων	λυθέντος	λυθέντων	λυθείσης	λυθεισῶν
λυθέντι	λυθεῖσι(ν)	λυθέντι	λυθεῖσι(ν)	λυθείσῃ	λυθείσαις
λυθέντα	λυθέντας	λυθέν	λυθέντα	λυθεῖσαν	λυθείσας

Various reactions take on familiar patterns. Contracts lengthen. Thus, φιληθείς, δηλωθείς, τιμηθείς. Stems with stops are as expected. Thus, the labial πέμπω is πεμφθείς. Palatal κηρύσσω (κηρυκ-) is κηρυχθείς. Liquid ἐγείρω becomes ἐγερθείς. Somewhat frequent in the gospels is the verb ἀποκρίνομαι as the aorist passive (deponent), ἀποκριθείς, which drops the ν before the θ. The letter insert variety would include εὑρίσκω, which becomes εὑρεθείς, inserting the ε.

Second Aorist

Active. In a familiar pattern, the second aorist active participle is a duplicate of the present active, except for stem and accent. The accent is ultima acute.

Table 28.4 Second Aorist Active Participle—λείπω

Masculine (ἄρχων)		Neuter (3rd Decl.)		Feminine (δόξα)	
Singular	*Plural*	*Singular*	*Plural*	*Singular*	*Plural*
λιπών	λιπόντες	λιπόν	λιπόντα	λιποῦσα	λιποῦσαι
λιπόντος	λιπόντων	λιπόντος	λιπόντων	λιπούσης	λιπουσῶν
λιπόντι	λιποῦσιν	λιπόντι	λιποῦσιν	λιπούσῃ	λιπούσαις
λιπόντα	λιπόντας	λιπόν	λιπόντα	λιποῦσαν	λιπούσας

Middle. The second aorist middle participle is a carbon copy of the present middle, except stem. Even the accent is antepenult acute.

Table 28.5 Second Aorist Middle Participle—λείπω

Masculine (ἀγαθός)		Neuter (ἀγαθός)		Feminine (ἀγαθός)	
Singular	Plural	Singular	Plural	Singular	Plural
λιπόμενος	λιπόμενοι	λιπόμενον	λιπόμενα	λιπομένη	λιπόμεναι
λιπομένου	λιπομένων	λιπομένου	λιπομένων	λιπομένης	λιπομένων
λιπομένῳ	λιπομένοις	λιπομένῳ	λιπομένοις	λιπομένῃ	λιπομέναις
λιπόμενον	λιπομένους	λιπόμενον	λιπόμενα	λιπομένην	λιπομένας

Passive. The second aorist passive participle is very similar to the first aorist passive. The second passive system, as expected, drops the θ of the -θε passive participle suffix. Resultant endings are then -είς, -εῖσα, -έν. Participial suffix is -ντ.

Table 28.6 Second Aorist Passive Participle—γράφω

Masculine		Neuter		Feminine	
Singular	Plural	Singular	Plural	Singular	Plural
γραφείς	γραφέντες	γραφέν	γραφέντα	γραφεῖσα	γραφεῖσαι
γραφέντος	γραφέντων	γραφέντος	γραφέντων	γραφείσης	γραφεισῶν
γραφέντι	γραφεῖσι(ν)	γραφέντι	γραφεῖσι(ν)	γραφείσῃ	γραφείσαις
γραφέντα	γραφέντας	γραφέν	γραφέντα	γραφεῖσαν	γραφείσας

Translations

General. The form λύσας, means "having loosed," λυσάμενος, "having loosed (for myself)," λυθείς, "having been loosed." These are approximations, of course, and depend upon use, as in present participles. For articular forms, see Table 28.7.

Time. The aorist participle is timeless, just as the present participle. The tense communicates undefined action. Time frame relates to the main verb, as with the present participle. The present participle has *three* frames of reference—antecedent, simultaneous, subsequent—but the aorist participle traditionally has been understood as having only *two* frames: antecedent and simultaneous.[5] (See Table 28.8.)

---

[5] Any proposed subsequent time frame can be explained as either antecedent or simultaneous; however, this traditional conclusion has been challenged recently; see Porter in the Bibliography.

Table 28.7 Articular Aorist Participles—Approximate Meanings

Active	Middle	Passive
ὁ λύσας	ὁ λυσάμενος	ὁ λυθείς
he who loosed the man who loosed the one who loosed	he who loosed (for himself) the man who loosed (etc.) the one who loosed (etc.)	he who has (had) been loosed, was loosed the man who has (had) been loosed, was loosed the one who has (had) been loosed, was loosed
οἱ λύσαντες	οἱ λυσάμενοι	οἱ λυθέντες
those who loosed the men who loosed the ones who loosed	those who loosed (for themselves) the men who loosed (etc.) the ones who loosed (etc.)	those who had been loosed, were loosed the men who had been loosed, were loosed the ones who had been loosed, were loosed

Table 28.8 Aorist Participle as Temporal Clause

Participle	Main Verb–*Past*			Main Verb–*Present*		
	Ant.	Simul.	Sub.	Ant.	Simul.	Sub.
Present	*whereas* *although* ___*ing*	*while* *as* *when* ___*ing*	*to* ___ ___*ing*	*whereas* *although* ___*ing*	*while* *as* *when* ___*ing*	*to* ___ ___*ing*
Aorist	*after* *when* __ *and* __ ___*ing*	__ *and* __ ___*ing*	✕	*after* *when* ___*ing*	__ *and* __ ___*ing*	✕

Many adjectival and adverbial uses outlined for present participles apply just as well to aorist participles. The following are offered as examples.

Adjectival. Common functions are: (1) attributive and (2) substantive. A few attributive cases are anarthrous. Otherwise, most instances are articular.

(1)   Attributive.

Articular: τίς γὰρ μείζων ἐστίν, ὁ χρυσὸς ἢ ὁ ναὸς **ὁ ἁγιάσας** τὸν χρυσόν; = "for which is greater, the gold or the temple **which sanctified** the gold?" (Matt. 23:17). Again, ἐλαλοῦμεν **ταῖς συνελθούσαις** γυναιξίν = "we began speaking to the women **who had gathered together**" (Acts 16:13). Note separation from the article in ἀγγέλους τε **τοὺς** μὴ **τηρήσαντας** τὴν ἑαυτῶν ἀρχὴν ἀλλὰ **ἀπολιπόντας** τὸ ἴδιον οἰκητήριον = "and angels **who did** not **keep** their own beginning but **left** their own habitation" (Jude 6).

Anarthrous: ὅμοιός ἐστιν ἀνθρώπῳ **οἰκοδομήσαντι** οἰκίαν = "he is like a man **who built** a house" (Luke 6:49), but notice the concord helping out. Or again, ἐστὲ ἐπιστολὴ Χριστοῦ **διακονηθεῖσα** ὑφ᾽ ἡμῶν = "you are a letter of Christ **having been cared for** by us" (2 Cor. 3:3); note concord.

(2)   Substantive.

Subject: ὁ **εὑρὼν** τὴν ψυχὴν αὐτοῦ ἀπολέσει αὐτήν = "**the one who finds** his life will lose it" (Matt. 10:39). Another is τὸ γὰρ ἐν αὐτῇ **γεννηθὲν** ἐκ πνεύματός ἐστιν ἁγίου = "for that which has been begotten in her is of the Holy Spirit" (Matt. 1:20). Also, ὁ δὲ **ἀκούσας** καὶ μὴ **ποιήσας** ὅμοιός ἐστιν ἀνθρώπῳ οἰκοδομήσαντι οἰκίαν ἐπὶ τὴν γῆν χωρὶς θεμελίου = "but **the one who has heard** and **has** not **acted** is like a man who built a house upon the ground without a foundation" (Luke 6:49).

Indirect Object: μὴ ἐρεῖ τὸ πλάσμα **τῷ πλάσαντι**, Τί με ἐποίησας οὕτως; = "That which is molded will not say **to the one who molded**, 'Why did you make me this way?' will it?" (Rom. 9:20)

Direct Object: ἤδη κέκρικα ὡς παρὼν **τὸν** οὕτως τοῦτο **κατεργασάμενον** = "already as though present I have judged **the one who** so **has done** this" (1 Cor. 5:3). Again, κύριος ἅπαξ λαὸν ἐκ γῆς Αἰγύπτου **σώσας** τὸ δεύτερον **τοὺς** μὴ **πιστεύσαντας** ἀπώλεσεν = "the Lord once after saving a people from the land of Egypt, again destroyed **those who disbelieved**" (Jude 5)

Predicate Nominative: οὗτοί εἰσιν οἱ **ἀκούσαντες** = "these are the ones who heard" (Luke 8:14)

Adverbial. Common functions are: (1) temporal, (2) cause, (3) condition, (4) concession, (5) instrumental, (6) complementary, (7) circumstantial. The genitive absolute construction appears also.

(1)   Temporal: διὸ καὶ ἀναντιρρήτως ἦλθον **μεταπεμφθείς** = "therefore I came without objection *when* **I was sent for**" (Acts 10:29). Again, observe ἡ δὲ

ἁμαρτία **ἀποτελεσθεῖσα** ἀποκύει θάνατον = "and sin *after* **it has been consummated**, brings forth death" (James 1:15).

(2) *Cause:* ὑπόμνησιν **λαβὼν** τῆς ἐν σοὶ ἀνυποκρίτου πίστεως = "*because* **I remember** the sincere faith which is in you" (2 Tim 1:5). Again, τῇ δεξιᾷ οὖν τοῦ θεοῦ **ὑψωθεὶς** τήν τε ἐπαγγελίαν τοῦ πνεύματος τοῦ ἁγίου **λαβὼν** παρὰ τοῦ πατρὸς ἐξέχεεν τοῦτο ὃ ὑμεῖς [καὶ] βλέπετε καὶ ἀκούετε. = "Therefore, *because* **he has been exalted** to the right hand of God and **has received** the promise of the Holy Spirit from the Father, he has poured out this which you [both] see and hear." (Acts 2:33).

(3) *Condition:* πῶς ἡμεῖς ἐκφευξόμεθα τηλικαύτης **ἀμελήσαντες** σωτηρίας; = "how shall we escape *if* **we neglect** so great a salvation?" (Heb. 2:3)

(4) *Concession:* διότι **γνόντες** τὸν θεὸν οὐχ ὡς θεὸν ἐδόξασαν = "for *though* **they knew** God, they did not glorify as God" (Rom. 1:21). Again, καίπερ μετὰ δακρύων **ἐκζητήσας** αὐτήν = "although with tears **he sought** it" (Heb. 12:17). Finally, ὃν οὐκ **ἰδόντες** ἀγαπᾶτε = "whom, *though* **you have** not **seen** him, you love" (1 Pet. 1:8).

(5) *Instrumental:* ἀλλὰ ἑαυτὸν ἐκένωσεν μορφὴν δούλου **λαβών** = "he emptied himself *by* **taking** the form of a servant" (Phil. 2:7)

(6) *Complementary:* Ἐθεώρουν τὸν Σατανᾶν ὡς ἀστραπὴν ἐκ τοῦ οὐρανοῦ **πεσόντα** = "<u>I was seeing</u> Satan **fall** as lightning from heaven" (Luke 10:18)

(7) *Circumstantial:* πάλιν **ἀπελθὼν** προσηύξατο τὸν αὐτὸν λόγον εἰπών = "again **he went away** *and* prayed, saying the same thing" (Mark 14:39)

For the genitive absolute, compare Ἀναχωρησάντων δὲ <u>αὐτῶν</u> ἰδοὺ ἄγγελος κυρίου φαίνεται = "Now *after* <u>they</u> **had departed**, behold, an angel of the Lord appeared" (Matt. 2:13). We repeat the caution that not all genitives are genitive absolutes. For example, τοῦ **ὁρισθέντος** υἱοῦ θεοῦ ἐν δυνάμει = "**who was designated** Son of God in power" (Rom. 1:4). Articular construction is a key here.

Future Participles

Active. The future participle occurs just thirteen times in the New Testament. Spotting the characteristic -σ tense suffix or letter reactions is all that is required to catch them. Active voice accent is penult acute. Hypothetically, λύω would be:

$$\underbrace{\lambda\upsilon + \sigma}_{} + o\nu\tau = \underbrace{\lambda\upsilon\sigma o\nu\tau}_{}-$$

stem, future suffix + participial suffix = future active participle stem

Middle. Future middle would use the middle voice participial indicator, -μεν. Accent is antepenult acute. Hypothetically, λύω would be:

$$\underbrace{λυ + σ}_{} + ομεν = \underbrace{λυσομεν}_{}-$$

stem, future suffix + middle participial suffix = future middle participle stem

Passive. As expected, the sixth principal part is used, the aorist passive stem, but with the passive suffix, -θη, instead of the aorist passive participial suffix, -θε. The middle/passive voice indicator, -μεν, would be incorporated, finished off with standard adjectival endings. Then, hypothetically, λύω would be:

$$\underbrace{λυ + θησ}_{} + ομεν = \underbrace{λυθησομεν}_{}-$$

stem, future passive suffix + middle suffix   =   future passive participle stem

Translation. Future participles could represent durative or punctiliar action. As active, one has "loosing" or "will loose"; middle voice is "loosing (for myself)" or "will loose (for myself)"; passive voice is "be loosing" or "will be loosing."

Examples. *Active and middle.* Future active and middle participles include: (1) contracts, as in κακόω as κακώσων (1 Pet. 3:13, substantive) and ποιέω as ποιήσων (Acts 24:17, purpose), (2) stops, as in the palatal ἄγω as ἄξων (Acts 22:5, purpose) and the dental σῴζω as σώσων (Matt. 27:49, purpose), (3) liquids, as in the nasal κατακρίνω as κατακρινῶν (Rom. 8:34, substantive), (4) letter insert, as in γίνομαι as γενησόμενον (attributive), and εἰμί as ἐσόμενον (Luke 22:49, substantive). *Passive.* Future passive, in fact, has only one example, the contract λαλέω, in the form λαληθησομένων (Heb. 3:5, attributive).

 **What To Learn—LESSON 28 (εἴκοσι ὀκτώ)**

Beginning
☐ 1. First aorist participle paradigms: λύσας, λυσάμενος, λυθείς
☐ 2. Recognition of reactions for first aorist participles: contracts, stops, liquids
☐ 3. Second aorist participle paradigms: λιπών, λιπόμενος, γραφείς

❑   4. Translating aorist participles: approximate meanings, temporal clauses, uses as adjectival and adverbial

❑   5. Vocabulary words

Advanced

❑   6. The problem of analyzing a subsequent time frame for aorist participles (p. 333, n. 5)

❑   7. Recognizing future participles

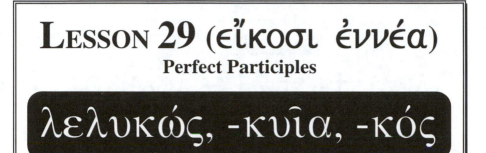

LESSON 29 (εἴκοσι ἐννέα)
Perfect Participles

λελυκώς, -κυῖα, -κός

Perfect participles sing their own song. The active voice formation is different—a new participial suffix. Two special periphrastic formations are: (1) future perfect participles and (2) *consonant stem* perfect middle/passive *indicatives*.

Vocabulary 29

Conjunction

διότι	because, for

Nouns and Adjectives

ἀκοή, -ῆς, ἡ	hearing, report
ἀσθένεια, -ας, ἡ	weakness
ἐπιστολή, -ῆς, ἡ	letter
συνέδριον, -ου, τό	Sanhedrin (Council)
ἐκλεκτός, -ή, -όν	chosen, elect

Verbs

ἀδικέω	I wrong, do wrong
ἀναιρέω	I take up, kill

δουλεύω	I serve
καταλείπω	I leave
μανθάνω	I learn
ὀμνύω	I swear, take oath
προσέχω	I attend to, heed

Perfect Participles

λελυκώς, -κυῖα, -κός	having loosed
λελυμένος, -η, -ον	having loosed
(for myself, etc.),	having been loosed

Perfect Participle

First Active. Some of the first perfect active participle formation is explainable. The perfect active stem is reduplicated. The tense suffix is -κ. However, a different

339

participial indicator is used, generating some reactions—some inexplicable, including inexplicable endings.[1] Accent is ultima acute. Feminine follows καρδία ("α pure," Table 5.2), but primitive feminine forms react with the stem, inexplicably winding up as -κυι.[2] Thus, for masculine and neuter:

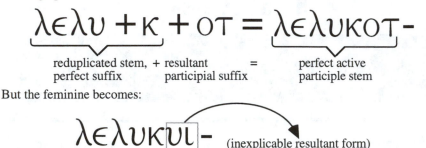

$$\underbrace{\lambda \epsilon \lambda \upsilon + \kappa}_{} + o\tau = \underbrace{\lambda \epsilon \lambda \upsilon \kappa o\tau}_{} -$$

reduplicated stem, + resultant   =   perfect active
perfect suffix   participial suffix   participle stem

But the feminine becomes:

λελυκ⍁υι⍁ -   (inexplicable resultant form)

Inflection by gender is added, endings generally looking similar to present active.

Table 29.1 First Perfect Active Participle—λύω

Masculine		Neuter		Feminine	
Singular	*Plural*	*Singular*	*Plural*	*Singular*	*Plural*
λελυκώς	λελυκότες	λελυκός	λελυκότα	λελυκυῖα	λελυκυῖαι
λελυκότος	λελυκότων	λελυκότος	λελυκότων	λελυκυίας	λελυκυιῶν
λελυκότι	λελυκόσι(ν)	λελυκότι	λελυκόσι(ν)	λελυκυίᾳ	λελυκυίαις
λελυκότα	λελυκότας	λελυκός	λελυκότα	λελυκυῖαν	λελυκυίας

Contracts lengthen: πεφιληκώς, δεδηλωκώς, τετιμηκώς (with a few exceptions, as in δέω, δεδεκώς and ὁράω, ἑωρακώς). No stems with stops are encountered, except a few dentals. One is ἐλπίζω, which is ἠλπικώς. Examples of the letter insert variety include: ἔχω, ἐσχηκώς; compounds of μένω, as in ὑπομένω, ὑπομεμενηκώς; βάλλω, βεβληκώς; and εἶπον (λέγω), εἰρηκώς.

---

[1]Involving the archaic letter digamma, which dropped before vowels. The masculine suffix becomes -κοτ, in which the nominative singular form becomes -κως, because κοτς → -κος → -κως (τ dropping before σ, then compensatory lengthening). Neuter nominative singular form becomes -κος, because -κοτς → -κος (τ dropping before σ, but *no* compensatory lengthening; this sigma ending for the neuter is inexplicable). The dative plural form becomes -κοσι(ν), because κοτσι → -κοσι (again, τ drops before the σ; however, the short vowel does *not* lengthen).

[2]Perhaps somehow involving digamma, consonantal iota, and simply dropping the -οτ.

Second Active. This system is similar to the first perfect active, but the -κ of the suffix is dropped, as expected. Our perfect tense sign is lost as a result. The most common verb is the old second perfect, οἶδα, but this verb has lost perfective force!

Table 29.2 Second Perfect Active Participle—οἶδα

Masculine		Neuter		Feminine	
Singular	*Plural*	*Singular*	*Plural*	*Singular*	*Plural*
εἰδώς	εἰδότες	εἰδός	εἰδότα	εἰδυῖα	εἰδυῖαι
εἰδότος	εἰδότων	εἰδότος	εἰδότων	εἰδυίας	εἰδυιῶν
εἰδότι	εἰδόσι(ν)	εἰδότι	εἰδόσι(ν)	εἰδυίᾳ	εἰδυίαις
εἰδότα	εἰδότας	εἰδός	εἰδότα	εἰδυῖαν	εἰδυίας

Middle/Passive. Forms are the fifth principal part pattern (suffix with no thematic vowel). The stem is λελυ-. The voice indicator is -μεν. Endings are like ἀγαθός, without oxytone accent. Accent is penult acute. Thus:

$$\underbrace{\lambda\epsilon\lambda\upsilon}+\mu\epsilon\nu=\underbrace{\lambda\epsilon\lambda\upsilon\mu\epsilon\nu\text{-}}$$

reduplicated stem + voice suffix   =   perfect middle participle stem

Table 29.3 Perfect Middle/Passive Participle—λύω

Masculine		Neuter		Feminine	
Singular	*Plural*	*Singular*	*Plural*	*Singular*	*Plural*
λελυμένος	λελυμένοι	λελυμένον	λελυμένα	λελυμένη	λελυμέναι
λελυμένου	λελυμένων	λελυμένου	λελυμένων	λελυμένης	λελυμένων
λελυμένῳ	λελυμένοις	λελυμένῳ	λελυμένοις	λελυμένη	λελυμέναις
λελυμένον	λελυμένους	λελυμένον	λελυμένα	λελυμένην	λελυμένας

Contracts lengthen: πεφιλημένος, δεδηλωμένος, τετιμημένος (with exceptions, as in δεδεμένος). For stops, the labial καταλείπω is καταλελειμμένος and γράφω is γεγραμμένος. The palatal διώκω is δεδιωγμένος and συνάγω is συνηγμένος. The dental ἑτοιμάζω is ἡτοιμασμένος. Liquid/nasal classes include κρίνω, κεκριμένος;

ἀποστέλλω, ἀπεσταλμένος; σπείρω, ἐσπαρμένος. A letter insert example would be περιβάλλω, as περιβεβλημένος.

Future Perfect

Active. Conventionally, the formation could have been λελύσω. Practically, the future perfect active is formed periphrastically (εἰμί as future indicative with a perfect active participle; e.g., ἔσομαι λελυκώς). Translation is "I shall have loosed." (See Lesson 22.)

Middle/Passive. The formation could have been λελύσομαι. Yet, construction always is periphrastic (εἰμί as future indicative with a perfect middle participle; e.g., ἔσομαι λελυμένος). Translation is "I shall have been loosed." (See Lesson 23.) Well-known is Matt. 16:19, ἔσται δεδεμένον = "shall have been bound in heaven" and ἔσται λελυμένον ἐν τοῖς οὐρανοῖς = "shall have been loosed in heaven."

Table 29.4 Future Perfect Participle—Periphrastic

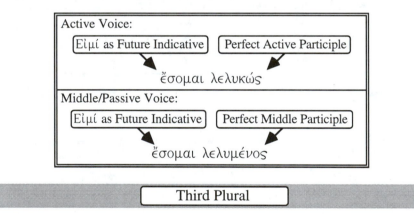

Third Plural

Consonant Stems. Recall that the perfect middle *indicative*, third plural of *consonant* stems is formed periphrastically (εἰμί as present indicative with a perfect middle participle). Thus, οὗ γὰρ **εἰσιν** δύο ἢ τρεῖς **συνηγμένοι** εἰς τὸ ἐμὸν ὄνομα = "For where two or three **are gathered together** in my name" (Matt. 18:20). Or, οἱ δὲ νῦν οὐρανοὶ καὶ ἡ γῆ τῷ αὐτῷ λόγῳ **τεθησαυρισμένοι εἰσίν** πυρί = "but the current heavens and the earth **are being stored up** by His word for fire" (2 Pet. 3:7).

Middle Indicative. Bear in mind that *any* form of the perfect middle indicative can be found in periphrastic construction. As examples:

(1) *First plural:* ἐν ᾧ θελήματι **ἡγιασμένοι ἐσμὲν** = "by which will [God's] we have been sanctified" (Heb. 10:10).

(2) *Second plural:* χάριτί **ἐστε σεσῳσμένοι** = "by grace you have been saved" (Eph. 2:5)

(3) *Third singular:* καὶ ἐπυνθάνετο τίς εἴη καὶ τί **ἐστιν πεποιηκώς** = "and he began inquiring who he was and what **he had done**" (Acts 21:33)

The point here is simply that *third plural* of *consonant* stems in the indicative mood *always* is periphrastic. (See Tables 23.5 and 23.6.)

Translations

Table 29.5 Articular Perfect Participles—Approximate Meanings

Active	Middle	Passive
ὁ λελυκώς	ὁ λελυμένος	ὁ λελυμένος
he who has loosed the man who has loosed the one who has loosed	he who has loosed (for himself) the man who has loosed (etc.) the one who has loosed (etc.)	he who has been loosed the man who has been loosed the one who has been loosed
οἱ λελυκότες	οἱ λελυμένοι	οἱ λελυμένοι
those who are loosed the men who are loosed the ones who are loosed	those who are loosed (for themselves) the men who are loosed (etc.) the ones who are loosed (etc.)	those who have been loosed the men who have been loosed the ones who have been loosed

General. The form λελυκώς, means "having loosed," λελυμένος, "having loosed (for myself)," "having been loosed." Notice the difficulty is distinguishing from the aorist participle in this form. These approximations, of course, depend upon use, as in present participles. Articular forms are given in Table 29.5.

Time. The perfect participle is timeless, as are all participles. This tense is used to communicate perfective action. However, when a temporal element does seem to be present, the use either will be antecedent or simultaneous. A relative clause using "while" or "after" can be used but is not imperative for translation (see examples).

Adjectival. Familiar adjectival and adverbial uses apply. Adjective functions are: (1) attributive, (2) substantive, and (3) predicative. A few attributive cases are anarthrous, and the predicative is anarthrous. Otherwise, all instances are articular.

(1) Attributive.

Articular: (1) οὐδεὶς τῶν ἀνδρῶν ἐκείνων **τῶν κεκλημένων** = "none of those men **who were invited**" (Luke 14:24)

(2) οἱ δὲ διάκονοι ᾔδεισαν **οἱ ἠντληκότες** τὸ ὕδωρ = "but the servants **who had drawn** the water knew" (John 2:9)

(3) οἶδα γὰρ ὅτι Ἰησοῦν **τὸν ἐσταυρωμένον** ζητεῖτε = "For I know that you are seeking Jesus **who has been crucified**" (Matt. 28:5)

(4) ἀνοικοδομήσω τὴν σκηνὴν Δαυὶδ **τὴν πεπτωκυῖαν** = "I will rebuild the tabernacle of David **which has fallen**" (Acts 15:16)

Anarthrous: (1) Ὁμοία ἐστὶν ἡ βασιλεία τῶν οὐρανῶν θησαυρῷ **κεκρυμμένῳ** ἐν τῷ ἀγρῷ = "the kingdom of heaven is like a treasure **having been hidden** in the field" (Matt. 13:44; note concord)

(2) παραλυτικὸν ἐπὶ κλίνης **βεβλημένον** = "a paralytic **who was lying** on a bed" (Matt. 9:2)

(3) Πῶς οὗτος γράμματα οἶδεν μὴ **μεμαθηκώς**; = "How does this one, **untrained**, have education?" (John 7:15)

(4) ἀνήχθημεν ἐν πλοίῳ **παρακεχειμακότι** ἐν τῇ νήσῳ = "we set sail on a ship **which had wintered** on the island" (Acts 28:11)

(2) Substantive.

Subject: ἐξῆλθεν **ὁ τεθνηκὼς** = "**he who had died** came out" (John 11:44). Again, τὴν ἐπαγγελίαν λάβωσιν **οἱ κεκλημένοι** = "**those who have been called** might receive the promise" (Heb. 9:15).

Indirect Object: Εἴπατε **τοῖς κεκλημένοις** = "tell **those who have been invited**" (Matt. 22:4). Again, **τοῖς** δὲ **γεγαμηκόσιν** παραγγέλλω = "**to the married** I give instruction" (1 Cor. 7:10).

Direct Object: ἐξῆλθον δὲ ἰδεῖν **τὸ γεγονὸς** = "they came out to see **what had happened**" (Luke 8:35; contrast Mark 5:14, below). Introducing direct discourse: καὶ ἐμνήσθη ὁ Πέτρος τοῦ ῥήματος Ἰησοῦ **εἰρηκότος** ὅτι Πρὶν ἀλέκτορα φωνῆσαι τρὶς ἀπαρνήσῃ με = "and Peter remembered the word that Jesus **had said**, 'Before the rooster crows three times, you will deny me'" (Matt. 26:75).

Predicate Nominative: ἦλθον ἰδεῖν τί ἐστιν **τὸ γεγονός** = "they came to see what it was that **had happened**" (Mark 5:14). Again, ὑμεῖς δέ ἐστε **οἱ διαμεμενηκότες** μετ᾽ ἐμοῦ = "but <u>you</u> are **the ones who have remained** with me" (Luke 22:28). Or, Οὗτοί εἰσιν **οἱ ἐρχόμενοι** ἐκ τῆς θλίψεως τῆς μεγάλης = "these are **the ones who have come** out of the great tribulation" (Rev. 7:14).

(2) Predicative.

(1) ὃς **ἦν** **παραλελυμένος** = "who was **paralyzed**" (Luke 5:18)

(2) ὅτι οὗτος ὁ υἱός μου νεκρὸς ἦν καὶ ἀνέζησεν, **ἦν** **ἀπολωλὼς** καὶ εὑρέθη = "Because this my son was dead is alive again, he was **lost** and has been found!" (Luke 15:24)

(3) οὐδὲν γάρ ἐστιν **κεκαλυμμένον** ὃ οὐκ ἀποκαλυφθήσεται = "nothing is **hidden** which will not be revealed" (Matt. 10:26)

Adverbial. The following perfect participle examples include: (1) temporal, (2) cause, (3) condition, (4) concession, (5) instrumental, and (6) complementary. The genitive absolute construction also is illustrated.

(1) Temporal.

Antecedent: (1) εἱστήκεισαν δὲ οἱ δοῦλοι καὶ οἱ ὑπηρέται ἀνθρακιὰν **πεποιηκότες** = "and the servants and the officers were standing (around), **having made** a charcoal fire" (John 18:18)

(2) ἔδοξε κἀμοὶ **παρηκολουθηκότι** ἄνωθεν πᾶσιν ἀκριβῶς καθεξῆς σοι γράψαι = "it seemed fitting to me also, **having researched** from the beginning everything accurately, to write to you in proper order" (Luke 1:3)

(3) **ἐληλακότες** οὖν ὡς σταδίους εἴκοσι πέντε ἢ τριάκοντα θεωροῦσιν τὸν Ἰησοῦν = "therefore *after* **they had rowed** about twenty five or thirty stadia, they saw Jesus" (John 6:19)

Simultaneous: εἶδον ἤδη αὐτὸν **τεθνηκότα** = "when he saw that he **was dead** already"(John 19:33)

(2) Cause.

General: (1) ἡ δὲ γυνὴ φοβηθεῖσα καὶ τρέμουσα, **εἰδυῖα** ὃ γέγονεν αὐτῇ, ἦλθεν = "so the woman came with fear and trembling, *because* **she knew** what had happened to her" (Mark 5:33)

(2) ὁ οὖν Ἰησοῦς **κεκοπιακὼς** ἐκ τῆς ὁδοιπορίας ἐκαθέζετο = "therefore, Jesus, *because* **he was weary** from the journey, was sitting" (John 4:6)

(3) ἐδέξαντο αὐτὸν οἱ Γαλιλαῖοι, πάντα **ἑωρακότες** ὅσα ἐποίησεν ἐν Ἱεροσολύμοις ἐν τῇ ἑορτῇ = "The Galileans received him *because* **they had seen** all the things he accomplished in Jerusalem during the feast" (John 4:45)

(4) Τὰς ψυχὰς ὑμῶν **ἡγνικότες** = "*Since* **you have purified** your souls" (1 Pet. 1:22)

Supposition. Using ὡς in the construction: ὡς ἰδίᾳ δυνάμει ἢ εὐσεβείᾳ **πεποιηκόσιν** τοῦ περιπατεῖν αὐτόν = "<u>as if</u> by our own power or godliness **we had made** him to walk" (Acts 3:12). Again, καὶ ἐν μέσῳ τῶν πρεσβυτέρων ἀρνίον ἑστηκὸς <u>ὡς</u> **ἐσφαγμένον** = "and in the midst of the elders a lamb standing <u>as if</u> slain" (Rev. 5:6).

(3) *Condition.*

Observe: <u>κἂν</u> ἁμαρτίας **ᾖ πεποιηκώς**, ἀφεθήσεται αὐτῷ = "<u>and if</u> he has committed sins, they will be forgiven him" (James 5:15, the mood here is subjunctive).

(4) *Concession.*

(1) **ἀνεῳγμένων** δὲ τῶν ὀφθαλμῶν αὐτοῦ οὐδὲν ἔβλεπεν = "*though* his eyes **were open**, he could see nothing" (Acts 9:8).

(2) <u>καίπερ</u> **ἐξεληλυθότας** ἐκ τῆς ὀσφύος Ἀβραάμ = "<u>even though</u> **these have descended** from Abraham" (Heb. 7:5).

(3) Τοσαῦτα δὲ αὐτοῦ σημεῖα **πεποιηκότος** ἔμπροσθεν αὐτῶν οὐκ ἐπίστευον εἰς αὐτόν = "But *though* **he had performed** so many signs before them, they were not believing in him" (John 12:37).

(5) *Instrumental (Modal).*

The *modal* use, cousin to the instrumental, indicates the mode of the action taking place. (Sometimes these two are hard to distinguish.) The modal use is illustrated in Ἰδοὺ ὁ βασιλεύς σου ἔρχεταί σοι, πραῢς καὶ **ἐπιβεβηκὼς** ἐπὶ ὄνον = "Behold, your king comes to you, humble and **mounted** on a donkey" (Matt. 21:5).

(6) *Complementary.*

General: εἶδον ἤδη αὐτὸν **τεθνηκότα** = "*when* <u>he saw</u> that he **was dead** already"(John 19:33). Again, καὶ ἐλθὸν <u>εὑρίσκει</u> **σεσαρωμένον** καὶ **κεκοσμημένον** = "and when he comes <u>he finds</u> it **having been swept clean** and **put in order**" (Luke 11:25).

Indirect Discourse: πᾶν πνεῦμα ὃ <u>ὁμολογεῖ</u> Ἰησοῦν Χριστὸν ἐν σαρκὶ **ἐληλυθότα** = "every spirit which <u>confesses</u> Jesus Christ **has come** in the flesh" (1 John 4:2)

(7) *Genitive Absolute.*

Observe **Συνηγμένων** δὲ <u>τῶν Φαρισαίων</u> ἐπηρώτησεν αὐτοὺς ὁ Ἰησοῦς = "Now <u>the Pharisees</u> **having gathered together**, Jesus questioned them" (Matt. 22:41). Also, ἔρχεται ὁ Ἰησοῦς <u>τῶν θυρῶν</u> **κεκλεισμένων** = "Jesus came, <u>the doors</u> **having been shut**" (John 20:26; cf. 20:19).

Final Observation

Imperfect/Pluperfect Participles? Have you noticed the absence of imperfect or pluperfect participles? These tenses are unnecessary in participles. Their function is covered in relative time with *past* tense verbs. A present participle and past tense verb gives an imperfect idea. Thus, ὑπέστρεψαν εἰς Ἰερουσαλὴμ **ἀναζητοῦντες** αὐτόν = "they returned to Jerusalem and *were* **looking for** him" (Luke 2:45, if circumstantial; if purpose, "to look for"). Likewise, a perfect participle with a past tense verb yields a pluperfect idea. Thus, οἱ δὲ διάκονοι ᾔδεισαν **οἱ ἠντληκότες** τὸ ὕδωρ = "but the servants **who had** drawn the water knew" (John 2:9).

Periphrastic Results. Periphrastic constructions also illustrate. With εἰμί as imperfect, notice the resultant *imperfect* force with the present participle:

(1) Καὶ **ἦσαν** οἱ μαθηταὶ Ἰωάννου καὶ οἱ Φαρισαῖοι **νηστεύοντες** = "And the disciples of John and the Pharisees **were fasting**" (Mark 2:18)

(2) καὶ ὡς **ἀτενίζοντες ἦσαν** εἰς τὸν οὐρανὸν = "and as they **were gazing** into heaven" (Acts 1:10)

Notice the resultant *pluperfect* force with the perfect participle:

(1) ὃ **ἦν λελατομημένον** ἐκ πέτρας = "which **had been hewn** out of rock" (Mark 15:46)

(2) καὶ **ἦν** αὐτῷ **κεχρηματισμένον** = "and it **had been revealed** to him" (Luke 2:26)

(3) Καὶ ἦλθεν εἰς Ναζαρά, οὗ **ἦν τεθραμμένος** = "and he came to Nazareth where he **had been brought up**" (Acts 4:16)

(4) **ἦσαν** γὰρ **προεωρακότες** Τρόφιμον τὸν Ἐφέσιον ἐν τῇ πόλει σὺν αὐτῷ = "for they **earlier had seen** Trophimus the Ephesian in the city with him" (Acts 21:29)

 **What To Learn—LESSON 29** (εἴκοσι ἐννέα)

Beginning

☐ 1. Perfect participle paradigms:
Active: λελυκώς and εἰδώς (οἶδα)
Mid./Pass.: λελυμένος, -η, -ον

☐ 2. Translating perfect participles: approximate meanings, temporal clauses, uses as adjectival and adverbial

❏   3. Vocabulary words

Advanced

❏   4. Recognition of two perfect periphrastic formations:
    (1) future perfect as ἔσομαι λελυκώς
    (2) perfect middle indicative, third person plural of consonant stems (as an example, εἰσιν συνηγμένοι)

❏   5. Explaining the absence of forms for imperfect or pluperfect participles

LESSON 30 (τριάκοντα)
Subjunctive Mood

λύω, λύωμαι

The subjunctive is timeless, a mood of contingency with future orientation. Tense communicates aspect, not time, as with infinitives and participles. Morphology is simple, a lengthened thematic vowel—but translation is by context, not form. English almost has no distinct forms for the subjunctive.

Vocabulary 30

Adverb, Conjunctions, Negatives

οὗ	where
ἐάν	if, when, although
ἵνα	in order that (so that, that)
ὅταν	whenever
μηδέ	but not, nor, not even
μηδείς, μηδεμία, μηδέν	no one
μήτε	and not (neither, nor)

Adjective and Nouns

λευκός, -ή, -όν	white

μετάνοια, -ας, ἡ	repentance	
παῖς, παιδός, ὁ, ἡ	boy, girl, child,	
		servant
παρουσία, -ας, ἡ	presence (coming)	
κοινωνία, -ας, ἡ	fellowship	

Verbs

θεάομαι	I behold
ἥκω	I come, have come
πάρειμι	I am present (have arrived)

Analysis

English. Take the simple indicative statement, "He *comes*." Observe our English conventions: (1) subjunctive as condition: "*Should* he *come*, then . . . ," or,

349

(2) the subjunctive as wish: "Oh, that he *would come!*" Notice in the first case dropping the "s" off the verb to create the subjunctive, or, in the second, using an auxiliary verb ("should" or "would") to set up a subjunctive idea. These are the two basic English formulations of the subjunctive, each with an element of *contingency*.

Greek. Subjunctive is one of the three moods of potentiality in Greek outside the indicative mood of reality. The statement indicates *probable* reality. Some element of

| Tense | Voice | *Mood* | Person | Number | Lexical |

↓

| Indicative | Subjunctive | Optative | Imperative |

contingency bears upon the statement made. The two major uses of the subjunctive mood are for probable reality statements and third class conditional sentences. The most common tense used with the subjunctive is the aorist.

No time element is communicated in the subjunctive mood, regardless of tense, just as with infinite verb forms. If time were a consideration, the author would have used the indicative mood. Tense communicates verbal aspect. Present subjunctive is durative, aorist subjunctive undefined, and perfect subjunctive perfective. However, verbal aspect does not always come across into English. Since (1) time is not a factor and (2) aspect is not always translatable, then the translation of an aorist subjunctive and a present subjunctive can wind up exactly the same in English.

indicative

subjunctive

optative

imperative

Forms. Only primary endings are needed (time is not a factor). Aorist does not have an augment (time is not a factor). The thematic vowel is lengthened, the o to ω, and the epsilon configurations to η or ῃ. Regardless of tense, all the resultant endings come out the same, except present tense of contract verbs. The table presents these endings. The appropriate stem for each principal part is used. Some comments follow.

Table 30.1 Subjunctive Endings

Number	Person	Active	Mid./Pass.
Singular	1st	-ω	-ωμαι
	2nd	-ῃς	-ῃ
	3rd	-ῃ	-ηται
Plural	1st	-ωμεν	-ώμεθα
	2nd	-ητε	-ησθε
	3rd	-ωσι(ν)	-ωνται

Aorist. The first aorist stem uses the tense suffix -σ, not the indicative -σα. For these, contracts lengthen, stops volatilize, liquids drop the sigma—all as usual. The first aorist passive has the suffix -θε, but the ε is swallowed up in contraction, leaving a circumflex accent. Again, contracts lengthen, stops volatilize, liquids drop. Second aorist copies the present tense except for stem. Second passives drop the θ.

Perfect. The perfect subjunctive is rare (about twenty times in various forms). Half of these are the verb οἶδα as first or second person (εἰδῶ, εἰδῶμεν and εἰδῇς, εἰδῆτε). The other half are periphrastic formulations. In active voice, the subjunctive mood comes from the εἰμί verb as present subjunctive, the perfect active from the perfect active participle. The only two occurrences are ἵνα μὴ **πεποιθότες ὦμεν** ἐφ᾽ ἑαυτοῖς = "in order that **we should** not **trust** in ourselves" (2 Cor. 1:9) and κἂν ἁμαρτίας **ᾖ πεποιηκώς** = "and if **he has committed** sins" (James 5:15). Middle and passive perfect subjunctives would be a similar formulation, the participles being middle or passive voice (e.g., ὦμεν λελυμένοι).[1]

Table 30.2 Active and Middle Subjunctive

Active Subjunctive			Middle Subjunctive		
Present	*2nd Aorist*	*1st Aorist*	*Present*	*2nd Aorist*	*1st Aorist*
λύω	λίπω	λύσω	λύωμαι	λίπωμαι	λύσωμαι
λύῃς	λίπῃς	λύσῃς	λύῃ	λίπῃ	λύσῃ
λύῃ	λίπῃ	λύσῃ	λύηται	λίπηται	λύσηται
λύωμεν	λίπωμεν	λύσωμεν	λυώμεθα	λιπώμεθα	λυσώμεθα
λύητε	λίπητε	λύσητε	λύησθε	λίπησθε	λύσησθε
λύωσι(ν)	λίπωσι(ν)	λύσωσι(ν)	λύωνται	λίπωνται	λύσωνται

Similarities. Some of these forms are morphological clones within these tables, or with other forms of the indicative mood. These result from the particular nature of various contraction patterns. Only context can help to say which location is appropriate and, therefore, how to translate. Even then, not every context is clear, and translation is left to a judgment call on the part of the translator. Notice how λύω could be present active *indicative*, first person singular, *or* present active

Table 30.3 Passive Subjunctive

Passive Subjunctive		
Present	*1st Aorist*	*2nd Aorist*
λύωμαι	λυθῶ	γραφῶ
λύῃ	λυθῇς	γραφῇς
λύηται	λυθῇ	γραφῇ
λυώμεθα	λυθῶμεν	γραφῶμεν
λύησθε	λυθῆτε	γραφῆτε
λύωνται	λυθῶσι(ν)	γραφῶσι(ν)

subjunctive, first person singular. Again, λύῃ could be present middle/passive

---

[1]Luke 14:8; John 3:27; 6:65; 16:24; 17:19, 23; 1 Cor. 1:10; 2 Cor. 9:3; Phil. 1:10–11.

indicative, second person singular, *or* present active subjunctive, third person singular, *or* present middle/passive subjunctive, second person singular. Some aorist forms are the same among themselves or with future tense (λύσω, λύσῃ). Similarity also applies to indicative and subjunctive contract forms. Observe the following.

Table 30.4 Present Active Contracts—Indicative versus Subjunctive

φιλέω		δηλόω		τιμάω	
Indicative	*Subjunctive*	*Indicative*	*Subjunctive*	*Indicative*	*Subjunctive*
φιλῶ	**φιλῶ**	**δηλῶ**	**δηλῶ**	τιμῶ	τιμῶ
φιλεῖς	φιλῇς	δηλοῖς	δηλοῖς	τιμᾷς	τιμᾷς
φιλεῖ	φιλῇ	δηλοῖ	δηλοῖ	τιμᾷ	τιμᾷ
φιλοῦμεν	φιλῶμεν	δηλοῦμεν	δηλῶμεν	τιμῶμεν	τιμῶμεν
φιλεῖτε	φιλῆτε	δηλοῦτε	δηλῶτε	τιμᾶτε	τιμᾶτε
φιλοῦσι(ν)	φιλῶσι(ν)	δηλοῦσι(ν)	δηλῶσι(ν)	τιμῶσι(ν)	τιμῶσι(ν)

Table 30.5 Present Middle Contracts—Indicative versus Subjunctive

φιλέω		δηλόω		τιμάω	
Indicative	*Subjunctive*	*Indicative*	*Subjunctive*	*Indicative*	*Subjunctive*
φιλοῦμαι	φιλῶμαι	δηλοῦμαι	δηλῶμαι	τιμῶμαι	τιμῶμαι
φιλῇ	**φιλῇ**	**δηλοῖ**	**δηλοῖ**	τιμᾷ	τιμᾷ
φιλεῖται	φιλῆται	δηλοῦται	δηλῶται	τιμᾶται	τιμᾶται
φιλούμεθα	φιλώμεθα	δηλούμεθα	δηλώμεθα	τιμώμεθα	τιμώμεθα
φιλεῖσθε	φιλῆσθε	δηλοῦσθε	δηλῶσθε	τιμᾶσθε	τιμᾶσθε
φιλοῦνται	φιλῶνται	δηλοῦνται	δηλῶνται	τιμῶνται	τιμῶνται

So, the typical subjunctive signal is a lengthened thematic vowel:

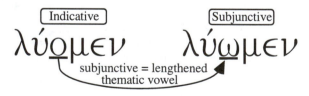

While this pattern is fairly obvious with most forms involving the omega, the other forms based upon the eta require more attention. The contract verbs offer the most difficulty for location with similarity to the indicative, especially the alpha contracts.

Negative. The negative used outside the indicative mood is μή. Thus, for the subjunctive mood, the negative μή will be found, or some combination with μή (see vocabulary). The double negative οὐ μή is emphatic (see Table 30.8).

Subjunctive of Εἰμί

Table 30.6 Εἰμί—Present Subjunctive

Number	Person	Form	Translation
Singular	1st	ὦ	"I might be"
	2nd	ᾖς	"you might be"
	3rd	ᾖ	"he might be" (etc.)
Plural	1st	ὦμεν	"we might be"
	2nd	ᾖτε	"you (pl.) might be"
	3rd	ὦσι(ν)	"they might be"

Translations in the table, of course, are only approximations. Context and use of the subjunctive really determine the translation. With such brief forms, pay attention to the details. Confusion can occur with relative pronouns (cf. ᾧ, ᾗ, and ἧς), imperfect indicative (cf. ἦς, ἦτε), conjunctions (ἤ), particles (ἦ), and interjections (ὦ).

Translations

General. The form λύω, as subjunctive, can mean "I might loose," and λύωμαι, "I might loose (for myself)," or "I might be loosed." The form λίπω can mean "I might leave," and λίπωμαι "I might leave (for myself)," and γραφῶ "I might be written" (as second passive; cf. present active). The form λύσω can mean "I might loose," and λύσωμαι "I might loose (for myself)," and λυθῶ "I might be loosed."

Aspect. All sound the same? Exactly! Time is *not* a factor in the subjunctive, and aspect is difficult to bring across into English. Since the fundamental idea of the subjunctive mood is *contingency*, the procedure generally can be to use an auxiliary verb implying contingency in English, such as "might," "should," or "would."

Future. Inherently, subjunctive is related to the future. Probability exists only as future possibility. However, future is used for what *will* take place, subjunctive for what *may* take place. Observe the subjunctive following a string of futures: Τίς ἐξ ὑμῶν ἕξει φίλον καὶ πορεύσεται πρὸς αὐτὸν μεσονυκτίου καὶ **εἴπῃ** αὐτῷ = "Who among you will have a friend and will go to him in the middle of the night and **will say** to him" (Luke 11:5).

Independent Clauses. Subjunctives traditionally are subdivided by their use in independent or dependent clauses. Uses in independent clauses are presented first.

Hortatory ("Let us"). First person plural is the key. The mood is subjunctive in an independent clause. The speaker is exhorting others to join in a course of action. Translator includes "let us" in the translation to convey the sense. Thus, Ἀγαπητοί, **ἀγαπῶμεν** ἀλλήλους = "Beloved, *let us* love one another" (1 John 4:7).

Prohibition ("Do not"). Aorist tense with μή is the key. Do not *initiate* an action may be the idea resulting from the aorist aspect.[2] The mood is subjunctive, the negative μή, and usually second person is used in an independent clause. One could use "do not ever." Notice this string of aorists: τὰς ἐντολὰς οἶδας· Μὴ **φονεύσῃς**, Μὴ **μοιχεύσῃς**, Μὴ **κλέψῃς**, Μὴ **ψευδομαρτυρήσῃς**, Μὴ **ἀποστερήσῃς** = "You know the commandments: 'Do not murder,' 'Do not commit adultery,' 'Do not steal,' 'Do not bear false witness,' 'Do not defraud'" (Mark 10:19).

Deliberative ("Shall we?"). Interrogation is the key. Interrogative adverbs or pronouns such as "where?" (πόθεν) "when?" (πότε) or "what?" (τί) often appear, and a question mark finishes the expression in an independent clause. Tense and person varies. The speaker questions what is desirable or possible, uncertain of the proper course of action or what might take place. Or the question simply might be rhetorical, which may involve a sense of simple futurity. Thus, with the interrogative pronoun, εἶπεν τῇ μητρὶ αὐτῆς, Τί **αἰτήσωμαι**; = "she said to her mother, 'What shall I ask?'" (Mark 6:24). With the interrogative adverb, Πόθεν **ἀγοράσωμεν** ἄρτους; = "Where shall we buy bread?" (John 6:5). For what might take place in the future, ὅτι εἰ ἐν τῷ ὑγρῷ ξύλῳ ταῦτα ποιοῦσιν, ἐν τῷ ξηρῷ τί **γένηται**; = "If in the green wood they do these things, what will it be in the dry?" (Luke 23:31).

Emphatic Negation ("Never!"). Use of οὐ μή is the key. This double negative with the subjunctive is used for emphatic denial in an independent clause. "Never," "surely not," etc. can be used in translation. Thus, καὶ **οὐ μὴ γνῷς** ποίαν ὥραν ἥξω ἐπὶ σέ = "and **you will** *never* **know** what hour I will come upon you" (Rev. 3:3).[3]

Dependent Clauses. Purpose and result clauses below are the main use of the subjunctive in dependent clauses. However, numerous other uses of the subjunctive

---

[2]Linguistic studies indicate that the idea of "not initiating an action" has been overemphasized.

[3]Notice the close tie of subjunctive mood (γνῷς = aor. act. subj., in context given as "will know") and future tense (ἥξω = fut. act. ind. of ἥκω).

fall into various categories of dependent clauses, but not every one catalogued here. Those that are provided are intended to illustrate the flexible use of the subjunctive. The common denominator in all uses is an element of contingency.

Purpose ("So that"). Use of ἵνα or ὅπως[4] is the key. A dependent purpose clause is introduced by ἵνα, ὅπως, or a relative pronoun. In the negative, either ἵνα μή, ὅπως μή, μήποτε, μή πως, or μή is used, meaning "lest." So, Τὸ θυγάτριόν μου ἐσχάτως ἔχει, ἵνα ἐλθὼν **ἐπιθῇς** τὰς χεῖρας αὐτῇ ἵνα **σωθῇ** καὶ **ζήσῃ** = "My little girl is near death; come, so that you **might lay** hands on her that **she be made well** and **live**!" (Mark 5:23). Then, ὅπως ᾖ σου ἡ ἐλεημοσύνη ἐν τῷ κρυπτῷ = "that your alms **might be** in secret" (Matt. 6:4). In the negative, ὅπως μὴ **καυχήσηται** πᾶσα σὰρξ ἐνώπιον τοῦ θεοῦ = "lest any flesh **should boast** before God" (1 Cor. 1:29).

Result ("As a result"). Use of ἵνα is the key. A dependent result clause is introduced by ἵνα or by ἵνα μή in the negative.[5] Thus, ὁ θερίζων μισθὸν λαμβάνει καὶ συνάγει καρπὸν εἰς ζωὴν αἰώνιον, ἵνα ὁ σπείρων ὁμοῦ **χαίρῃ** καὶ ὁ θερίζων = "The one who reaps is receiving a reward and gathering together fruit unto eternal life, as a result the one sowing and the one reaping **rejoice** together." (John 4:36). In the negative, οὐδένα ὑμῶν ἐβάπτισα εἰ μὴ Κρίσπον καὶ Γάϊον, ἵνα μή τις **εἴπῃ** ὅτι εἰς τὸ ἐμὸν ὄνομα ἐβαπτίσθητε = "I baptized not one of you, except Crispus and Gaius, so as a result no one **could say** that you were baptized in my name!" (1 Cor. 1:14–15).

Relative Pronoun ("who"). The relative pronoun with the subjunctive can be used in a third class conditional sentence or to express practical result. Thus, ὃς δ' ἂν **βλασφημήσῃ** εἰς τὸ πνεῦμα τὸ ἅγιον = "but whoever **blasphemes** against the Holy Spirit" (Mark 3:29).

Comparison ("as"). In stating comparisons, an element of contingency could be present. Thus, ἵνα ἡ ἡμέρα ὑμᾶς ὡς κλέπτης **καταλάβῃ** = "that the day **might overtake** you as a thief" (1 Thess. 5:4). Again, ἦτε γὰρ ὡς πρόβατα πλανώμενοι = "for **you were** as sheep being led astray" (1 Pet. 2:25).

Temporal ("when," "until"). Clauses that are introduced by ὅταν, ἕως, ἄχρι, and μέχρι(ς) have a time element that involves contingency. Thus, Καὶ ὅταν **προσεύχησθε** = "And whenever **you pray**" (Matt. 6:5). Observe two similar constructions in the following: (1) οἱ λοιποὶ τῶν νεκρῶν οὐκ ἔζησαν ἄχρι **τελεσθῇ** τὰ χίλια ἔτη = "The rest of the dead did not come to life until the thousand years **were completed**" (Rev. 20:5), and the variation (2) Καὶ ὅταν **τελεσθῇ** τὰ χίλια ἔτη = "And when the thousand years **is completed**" (Rev. 20:7). Finally, ἀμὴν γὰρ λέγω

---

[4]Vocabulary 20; ὅπως varies in use from indefinite relative ("that," "in order that") to an indirect interrogative ("how"). This term occasionally is used with the future indicative, but mostly ὅπως is used with the subjunctive. The majority of occurrences are in Matthew and Luke-Acts.

[5]Purpose or result distinctions can be ambiguous.

ὑμῖν, ἕως ἂν **παρέλθῃ** ὁ οὐρανὸς καὶ ἡ γῆ = "for truly I tell you, <u>until</u> heaven and earth **pass away**" (Matt. 5:18).

Concession ("even if," "although"). Concession can be stated with subjunctive mood, because of the contingency inherent in certain expressions. Thus, ἀλλὰ <u>καὶ ἐὰν</u> ἡμεῖς ἢ ἄγγελος ἐξ οὐρανοῦ **εὐαγγελίζηται** [ὑμῖν] παρ᾽ ὃ εὐηγγελισάμεθα ὑμῖν = "but <u>even if</u> we ourselves or an angel from heaven **should preach** [to you] a gospel contradicting the gospel we preached to you" (Gal. 1:8). Again, ἡμεῖς δὲ ὡς ἀδόκιμοι **ὦμεν** = "although we <u>ourselves</u> **might be** disapproved" (2 Cor. 13:7).

Substantive. A dependent clause can be substantival (subject, predicate nominative, object, appositive). The expression is similar to a purpose clause, but functions substantivally. Thus, as direct object, παρεκάλεσαν <u>ὅπως</u> **μεταβῇ** ἀπὸ τῶν ὁρίων αὐτῶν = "they pleaded <u>that</u> **he might depart** from their region" (Matt. 8:34). Or, appositively, ἐμοὶ δὲ εἰς ἐλάχιστόν ἐστιν <u>ἵνα</u> ὑφ᾽ ὑμῶν **ἀνακριθῶ** = "but to me it is the smallest thing, <u>that</u> **I should be examined** by you" (1 Cor. 4:3).

Conditional Sentences

Table 30.7 Conditional Sentences

Class	Condition	Conj.	Protasis	Apodosis
1st TRUE	fulfilled (οὐ in negative)	εἰ + (ἐάν at times)	any indicative	any indicative imperative subjunctive
2nd FALSE	not fulfilled (μή in negative) a. present time	εἰ +	past tense indicative	ἄν + past indicative (ἄν can occur anywhere or at times drop out)
	b. past time	εἰ +	aorist indicative	ἄν + past indicative
		εἰ +	pluperfect indicative	ἄν + past indicative
3rd POSSIBLE	undetermined possible	ἐάν +	subjunctive	future, or any indic. (ἄν)
4th REMOTE	undetermined remote	εἰ +	optative	optative (ἄν)

The key to class condition is *the mood of the protasis*, not the type of conjunction. First and second class require indicative mood. Third class requires the subjunctive mood, as this class assumes that the condition is *undetermined*, but possible. Hence, the mood of contingency, subjunctive, is appropriate. Typically the conjunction used is ἐάν and the tense of the apodosis is future. On occasion, one will find the conjunction as εἰ (e.g., Luke 9:13). While the apodosis tense often is future, in fact, any tense in the indicative mood can be found in the apodosis. The examples illustrate third class conditional sentences.

(1) πῶς <u>ἐὰν</u> **εἴπω** ὑμῖν τὰ ἐπουράνια πιστεύσετε; = "<u>if</u> **I tell** you heavenly things, how will you believe?" (John 3:12)

(2) <u>ἐὰν</u> ἄλλος **ἔλθῃ** ἐν τῷ ὀνόματι τῷ ἰδίῳ, ἐκεῖνον λήμψεσθε = "<u>if</u> another **should come** in his own name, you will receive that one" (John 5:43)

(3) ὅτι ἐὰν **ὁμολογήσῃς** ἐν τῷ στόματί σου κύριον Ἰησοῦν, καὶ **πιστεύσῃς** ἐν τῇ καρδίᾳ σου ὅτι ὁ θεὸς αὐτὸν ἤγειρεν ἐκ νεκρῶν, σωθήσῃ = "that if **you confess** with your mouth the Lord Jesus, and **believe** in your heart that God has raised him from the dead, you will be saved" (Rom. 10:9)

(4) Ἐὰν **εἴπωμεν** ὅτι κοινωνίαν ἔχομεν μετ' αὐτοῦ καὶ ἐν τῷ σκότει **περιπατῶμεν**, ψευδόμεθα = "If **we say** that we have fellowship with Him and **are walking** in darkness, we deceive ourselves" (1 John 1:6)

(5) ἐὰν **ὁμολογῶμεν** τὰς ἁμαρτίας ἡμῶν, πιστός ἐστιν καὶ δίκαιος ἵνα ἀφῇ ἡμῖν τὰς ἁμαρτίας = "If **we confess** our sins, He is faithful and just to forgive us our sins" (1 John 1:9)

(6) εἰ μήτι πορευθέντες ἡμεῖς **ἀγοράσωμεν** εἰς πάντα τὸν λαὸν τοῦτον βρώματα = "unless we ourselves go and **buy** food for all these people" (Luke 9:13)

Subjunctive Summary

Table 30.8 Subjunctive Mood—Translation Summary

Independent Clauses	
Hortatory (key: 1st per. plu.)	*Let us*
Prohibition (key: aorist with μή)	*Do not*
Deliberative (key: interrogation)	*Shall we?*
Emphatic Negation (key: οὐ μή)	*never!*
Dependent Clauses	
Purpose (key: ἵνα or ὅπως)	*so that*
Result (key: ἵνα)	*as a result*
Relative Pronoun (key: ὅς, etc.)	*whoever, etc.*
Comparison (key: ὡς)	*as*
Temporal (key: ὅταν, ἕως, ἄχρι, μέχρι)	*when, until*
Concession (key: ἐάν)	*even if, although*
Substantive	[subject, object, etc.]

A word of caution needs to be given on these subjunctive uses. For example, notice the first person plural subjunctives in 1 John 2:28: ἵνα ἐὰν φανερωθῇ σχῶμεν[6] ("we might have") παρρησίαν καὶ μὴ αἰσχυνθῶμεν ("we might not be ashamed") ἀπ᾿ αὐτοῦ ἐν τῇ παρουσίᾳ αὐτοῦ. Here, the subjunctive communicates contingency, but the first plural is not hortatory. A first person plural subjunctive does not *guarantee* that the use has to be hortatory ("Let us"). That subjunctive *might* be hortatory. Context will tell. Again, ἐάν might be found in the subjunctive construction, but does not *have* to be translated concessively with "although." One could have a third class conditional sentence with the idea "if." So observe context.

Greek New Testament

Congratulations! You are at a most significant fork in the road in your journey into Greek. *Workbook* exercises to this point have been composed of New Testament selections. This introduces you to the New Testament immediately. While many students find such a procedure motivating and rewarding at the beginning of their Greek studies, you also are at a disadvantage. You have no running context to assist in the work of translation.

Translating 1 John. Now, however, with this lesson, you begin the systematic translation of 1 John in addition to a few sentences illustrating new grammar and vocabulary. The great advantage to you in working in 1 John is context. You become familiar with the author's language and thought and can move more quickly through a passage. While the 1 John verses for each lesson are provided in the *Workbook*, be sure to consult your *Greek New Testament* and become familiar with the layout for each passage.

UBS[4] Page Layout. Table 30.9 provides a brief, introductory explanation of the page layout of the *Greek New Testament*, using page eight (Matt. 3:16–4:6) as an example. You may want to turn to this page in your own copy of the *Greek New Testament* to see more clearly the material explained.[7]

Do not be intimidated by the many symbols and abbreviations in the edited text or in the material at the bottom of each page. Learn by exploring! Every symbol is explained clearly in the introductory matter in your *Greek New Testament* or in the indexes at the end. While you will not be held responsible for these details, no

---

[6]From ἔχω, an irregular verb (stem σεχ-; see Vocabulary 3, p. 23); subjunctive is σχῶ.

[7]A note on the format of book titles is given. Gospel titles are headed with the preposition κατά, used with the accusative, meaning "according to." For example, ΚΑΤΑ ΜΑΘΘΑΙΟΝ is "According to Matthew." Again, letters to particular churches are headed with the preposition πρός, used with the accusative, meaning "with respect to," or simply "to." For example, ΠΡΟΣ ΡΩΜΑΝΙΟΥΣ is "To the Romans." Finally, a sequence of numbered letters—e.g., 1 John, 2 John, 3 John—is represented in the edited text in the uncial letters A, B, or Γ following the book title, using a standard system of representing Greek numbers with Greek letters. For example, 1 John is ΙΩΑΝΝΟΥ A.

reason exists for not beginning now your facility with the *Greek New Testament*. Observe the textual apparatus. Ask your teacher about details of interest to you as time permits. You will begin learning about textual criticism and the significance of a universally used edited text.

Table 30.9 The UBS[4] Text—Page Layout Description

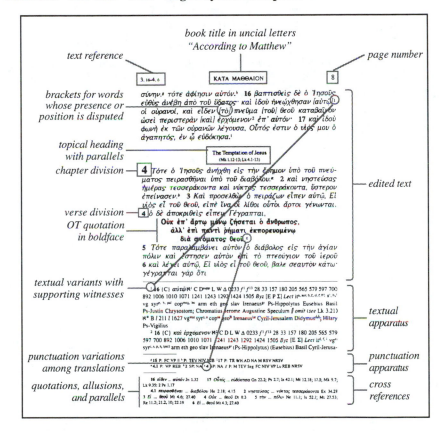

As one interesting example, observe the material related to 1 John 5:7–8 (UBS[4], 819). This particular text is the famous "Comma Johanneum." Contrast the reading in the King James with any modern translation. Discover why the difference and the fascinating story behind this passage's inclusion in the King James translation—one small part of the history of the printed Greek New Testament text.

What To Learn—LESSON 30 (τριάκοντα)

☐ 1. Subjunctive paradigms
      active: λύω, λίπω, λύσω
      mid./pass.: λύωμαι, λίπωμαι, λύσωμαι, λυθῶ, γραφῶ
      copulative: εἰμί as subjunctive (ὦ, ᾖς, ᾖ, etc.)

☐ 2. Contract verbs: indicative versus subjunctive

☐ 3. Subjunctive mood use and translation: hortatory, prohibition, deliberative, emphatic negation, purpose, result, other dependent clauses

☐ 4. Third class conditional sentences: structure, significance, and translation

☐ 5. Familiarity with the UBS[4] page layout

☐ 6. Vocabulary words

LESSON 31 (εἷς καὶ τριάκοντα)
Imperative Mood

λῦε, λύου

The imperative is timeless, a mood of command. Tense communicates aspect, not time, as with infinitives, participles, and subjunctive mood. A fairly distinct set of endings is used. Translation is by context, not form.

Vocabulary 31

Adjective and Noun

ἐλεύθερος, -α, -ον   free

ζῷον, -ου, τό   living creature

Verbs

ἀνάγω   I lead up (middle: I set sail)

αὐξάνω   I cause to grow

γρηγορέω   I watch

Present Imperative

λῦε, λύου

   loose!, loose (for yourself)! be loosed!

Aorist Imperative

λῦσον, λῦσαι, λύθητι

   loose!, loose (for yourself)!, be loosed!

λίπε, λιποῦ, γράφηθι

   leave!, leave (for yourself)!, be written!

ἴδε   lo! behold!

ἰδού   lo! behold!

Present Imperative of εἰμί

ἴσθι   be!

Analysis

English. The command "Go!" actually does not express the second person; the form really is, "You go!" Observe how commands exist only in second person in English. English, then, offers no equivalent for the Greek third person command.

Greek. The imperative is the mood of command. This mood has the least potential of reality (any parent working with children knows this).

Tense	Voice	*Mood*	Person	Number	Lexical

Indicative	Subjunctive	Optative	Imperative

No time element is communicated in the imperative mood, regardless of tense, as with infinite forms. If time were a factor, indicative mood typically would show up. Tense communicates verbal aspect. Present imperative is durative, the aorist imperative undefined, and the perfect imperative perfective. However, verbal aspect does not always come across into English. Since (1) time is not a factor and (2) aspect is not always translatable, an aorist imperative and a present imperative can wind up exactly the same in English.

indicative

subjunctive

optative

imperative

Forms. Imperative mood has its own set of endings.[1] The aorist does not have an augment (time is not a factor). The thematic vowel is ε. The table presents the endings. Active second singular has three options. The appropriate stem for each principal part is used. Some resultant imperative forms turn out exactly as their indicative counterparts. When so, observe that these are always the second person forms. For these, location depends upon context alone (most cases fairly obvious, a few not quite so).

Table 31.1 Imperative Endings

Number	Person	Active	Mid./Pass.
Singular	1st	-------	-------
	2nd	--, ς, θι	-σο
	3rd	-τω	-σθω
Plural	1st	-------	-------
	2nd	-τε	-σθε
	3rd	-τωσαν	-σθωσαν

Present. The present active uses the present stem, thematic vowel ε, and active imperative endings. Second singular opts for no ending, leaving the ε exposed. Second plural looks exactly as the indicative counterpart. All active contracts behave exactly as expected. All active contract second plurals look exactly as their indicative counterparts.

Middle/passive imperative is similar, using middle/passive imperative endings. Second singular volatilizes (the intervocalic sigma drops: εσο → εο → ου). Second

---

[1]Completely true for third person forms. In second person, only the singular shows some distinctiveness (no ending or -θι options). All other second person forms are similar to various indicative endings. The ending -ς (active, 2ps) corresponds to the -ς of secondary active; -τε (active, 2pp) corresponds to the -τε of primary active; -σο (middle, 2ps) corresponds to the -σο of secondary middle; -σθε (middle, 2pp) corresponds to the -σθε of primary middle.

plural looks like the indicative counterpart. All middle contracts behave as expected. Second singulars drop an intervocalic sigma for double contraction results.[2] Middle contract second plurals look exactly as their indicative counterparts.[3]

Table 31.2 Active and Middle Imperative

Active Imperative			Middle Imperative		
Present	*2nd Aorist*	*1st Aorist*	*Present*	*2nd Aorist*	*1st Aorist*
-------	-------	-------	-------	-------	-------
λῦε	λίπε	λῦσον	λύου	λιποῦ	λῦσαι
λυέτω	λιπέτω	λυσάτω	λυέσθω	λιπέσθω	λυσάσθω
-------	-------	-------	-------	-------	-------
λύετε	λίπετε	λύσατε	λύεσθε	λίπεσθε	λύσασθε
λυέτωσαν	λιπέτωσαν	λυσάτωσαν	λυέσθωσαν	λιπέσθωσαν	λυσάσθωσαν

Aorist. The first aorist active stem uses the tense suffix -σα. For these active forms, contract verbs lengthen, stops volatilize, and liquids drop the sigma—as usual. Active voice uses active imperative endings, but the second singular result, -σον, is unexplained. Middle voice uses middle imperative endings, but the second singular result, -σαι, is unexplained. The first aorist passive stem has the suffix -θη.

Table 31.3 Passive Imperative

Passive Imperative		
Present	*1st Aorist*	*2nd Aorist*
-------	-------	-------
λύου	λύθητι	γράφηθι
λυέσθω	λυθήτω	γραφήτω
-------	-------	-------
λύεσθε	λύθητε	γράφητε
λυέσθωσαν	λυθήτωσαν	γραφήτωσαν

This suffix is so distinctive that the *active* endings do not confuse the location. However, the second singular form, -θηθι, undergoes "deaspiration" for pronunciation purposes, becoming -θητι. Again, for these middle forms, contracts lengthen, stops volatilize, liquids drop the sigma.

---

[2] The -ε contract: εεσο → εεο → εου → οῦ; -ο contract: οεσο → οεο → οου → οῦ; -α contract: αεσο → αεο → αου → ῶ.

[3] To visualize these various resultant endings for both active and middle voices of the present tense contract verb, consult Paradigms, "Omega Verb Contraction—Present Tense."

Second aorist copies the present tense except for stem (and accent of middle second singular). Second passive drops the θ. For this very reason, the second singular does not need to deaspirate, as in the first passive, and remains -ηθι.

Perfect. The perfect imperative is quite rare (less than five times, depending on location). An active might be ἴστε, from οἶδα (Eph. 5:5; Heb. 12:17; James 1:19). Middle includes πεφίμωσο, from φιμόω (Mark 4:39) and ἔρρωσθε, from ῥώννυμι (Acts 15:29). Luke 12:35, ἔστωσαν . . . περιζωσμέναι, might be periphrastic.

Similarities. Notice: (1) λύετε, present active *indicative*, second person plural, *or* present active *imperative*, second plural; (2) λύεσθε, present middle/passive *indicative*, second person plural, *or* present middle/passive *imperative*, second plural. Other forms also are similar. The first aorist middle imperative λῦσαι (second singular) also could be a first aorist active infinitive. (An optative form will be λύσαι.) Thus, the pattern in imperative forms shows one distinct second person form, but problems of recognition in other second person forms, especially plurals:

λῦε, λύου λύετε, λύεσθε
present imperative, second singular   present imperative, second plural

Finally, *hear* the difference between active and middle voice: the sharp dental, τ, in the active voice, and the corresponding aspirated form, σθ, in the middle.

Negative. The negative used outside the indicative mood is μή. Thus, for the imperative mood, the negative μή will be found, or some combination with μή. The double negative οὐ μή is emphatic.

Imperative of Εἰμί

Table 31.4 Εἰμί—Present Imperative

Number	Person	Form	Translation
Singular	1st	------	------
	2nd	ἴσθι	"you be"
	3rd	ἔστω (ἤτω)	"he must," (etc.)
Plural	1st	------	------
	2nd	ἔστε	"you (pl.) be"
	3rd	ἔστωσαν	"they must"

Translations in the table, of course, are only approximations. Context and use of the imperative really determine the translation. The second plural looks exactly as the indicative, but notice: *not* enclitic (contrast ἐστέ, which in composition is ἐστε).

Translations

The imperative is straight forward in translation. However, remember that *third* person command has no exact equivalent in English. The typical format is to use the helping verb, "let" ("let him," "let them," etc.). Grammatically, this is a work around, because the subject is transformed into a direct object. Some suggest trying the format using "must" ("he must," "they must," etc.), which preserves the subject nature of the Greek expression. Greek even has the functional equivalent of the *first* person command. This is the *hortatory subjunctive* ("let us") encountered in the last lesson. The following are some particular uses of the imperative mood.

Command. Thus, ἀλλὰ μᾶλλον **δουλευέτωσαν** = "but **they must serve** all the more" (1 Tim 6:2). Again, πάντοτε **χαίρετε** = "**rejoice** always" (1 Thess. 5:16). Observe the series in this soldier's summary: καὶ λέγω τούτῳ, **Πορεύθητι**, καὶ πορεύεται, καὶ ἄλλῳ, Ἔρχου, καὶ ἔρχεται, καὶ τῷ δούλῳ μου, **Ποίησον** τοῦτο, καὶ ποιεῖ = "and I say to this one, '**Go**!' and he goes, and to another, '**Come**!' and he comes, and to my servant, '**Do** this!' and he does it" (Matt. 8:9).

Prohibition. An action already is in progress. To forbid the on-going activity, a durative tense is used with the imperative force of command—the present imperative with μή. If the action were not yet begun, only anticipated, a punctiliar tense would be called for in an ingressive sense to forbid beginning the action—the aorist subjunctive with μή. These distinctions on the use of prohibitions potentially can be helpful for exegesis.[4] Thus, Ἀγαπητοί, μὴ παντὶ πνεύματι **πιστεύετε**, ἀλλὰ **δοκιμάζετε** τὰ πνεύματα εἰ ἐκ τοῦ θεοῦ ἐστιν = "Beloved, **stop believing** every spirit; rather, **examine** the spirits, *to see* if they are from God" (1 John 4:1).

Entreaty. The force of command is diluted to that of request. Inferior rank is implied on the part of the supplicant. "Please" might be appropriate in translation. Thus, Κύριε, **σῶσον**, ἀπολλύμεθα = "Lord, *please* **save** us—we are perishing!" (Matt. 8:25).

Permission. One expresses consent to another person's request, or to an implied request. Thus, ἀσθενεῖ τις ἐν ὑμῖν; **προσκαλεσάσθω** τοὺς πρεσβυτέρους τῆς

---

[4]However, do not go overboard. Newer studies based on different linguistic models warn that this typical understanding of the present imperative (stop action in progress) versus aorist subjunctive (do not start) may not hold. E.g., a present imperative may just express a generalized maxim.

ἐκκλησίας, καὶ **προσευξάσθωσαν** ἐπ᾽ αὐτόν = "Is any among you sick? He **may call upon** the elders of the church, and **they may pray** over him" (James 5:14). Notice Paul's indignant irony, illegally detained in jail, to the civic authorities who have abused their powers: ἀλλὰ ἐλθόντες αὐτοὶ ἡμᾶς **ἐξαγαγέτωσαν** = "but they may come and themselves **lead** us **out**!" (Acts 16:37).

Ἰδού and Ἴδε

Two aorist imperative forms encountered often in the New Testament are ἰδού and ἴδε. Each of these forms is a dramatic, literary device to heighten interest. The form ἰδού (εἰδόμην) is a particle calling attention, and means "Lo!" or "Behold!" The other form, ἴδε (εἶδον), has a similar function, used as an interjection, also meaning "Lo!" or "Behold!" Notice the following examples:

    (1) **ἰδού** ἄγγελος κυρίου κατ᾽ ὄναρ ἐφάνη αὐτῷ = "**lo**, an angel of the Lord appeared to him in a dream" (Matt. 1:20)

    (2) **ἰδού** μάγοι ἀπὸ ἀνατολῶν παρεγένοντο εἰς Ἱεροσόλυμα = "**behold**, magi from the east arrived in Jerusalem" (Matt. 2:1)

    (3) **Ἴδε** ὁ ἀμνὸς τοῦ θεοῦ. = "**Behold**, the Lamb of God!" (John 1:36)

    (4) **ἴδε** οὖν χρηστότητα καὶ ἀποτομίαν θεοῦ = "Therefore, **behold** the kindness and severity of God" (Rom. 11:22).

What To Learn—LESSON 31 (εἷς καὶ τριάκοντα)

  ❑ 1. Imperative paradigms
          active: λῦε, λίπε, λῦσον
        mid./pass.: λύου, λίπου, λύσαι, λύθητι, γράφηθι
        copulative: εἰμί as imperative (ἴσθι, ἔστω, ἔστε, ἔστεσαν)

  ❑ 2. Imperative mood use and translation: command, prohibition, entreaty, permission

  ❑ 3. Meaning and use of ἰδού and ἴδε

  ❑ 4. Vocabulary words

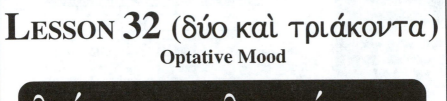

λύοιμι, λυοίμην

The optative is timeless, a mood of wish, formally used in benedictions, for example. Tense communicates aspect, not time, as with any verbal element outside the indicative mood. Once again, then, translation is by context, not form.

Vocabulary 32

Adjective and Nouns

περισσός, -ή, -όν   abundant, more

θυσιαστήριον, -ου, τό altar

σκεῦος, -ους, τό   vessel, goods

Verbs

κατηγορέω   I accuse

κεῖμαι   I lie, am appointed

περιβάλλω   I clothe, put around

Present Optative

λύοιμι, λυοίμην

may I loose!, may I loose (for myself)!
   may I be loosed!

Aorist Optative

λύσαιμι, λυσαίμην, λυθείην
   may I loose!, may I loose (for myself)!,
      may I be loosed!

λίποιμι, λιποίμην
   may I leave!, may I leave (for myself)!

Present Optative of εἰμί

εἴη   may he (she, it) be!

Analysis

Background. The Latin verb *opto* means "I wish." The English designation *optative* derives from this Latin root. The optative mood is a weaker form of the subjunctive, but in degree, a stronger potentiality than the imperative.

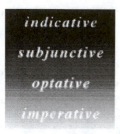

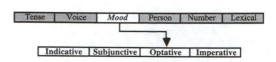

The optative is the mood of wish. Conventional use included prayers and benedictions. For this reason, the optative shows up in these formal settings on a regular basis in the New Testament. However, the optative mood in all occurs just sixty-eight times in the Greek text, so optative forms, in reality, are not encountered that often translating the New Testament.

No time element is expressed in the optative mood, regardless of the tense—always the case outside the indicative. Tense conveys aspect. Present optative is durative, aorist optative undefined. (Perfect optative does not occur.) However, since: (1) time is not a factor and (2) aspect is not always translatable, an aorist optative and a present optative can wind up exactly the same in English.

Table 32.1 Optative Endings

Number	Person	Active	Mid./Pass.
Singular	1st	-ιμι	-ίμην
	2nd	-ις	-ιο
	3rd	-ι	-ιτο
Plural	1st	-ιμεν	-ίμεθα
	2nd	-ιτε	-ισθε
	3rd	-ιεν	-ιντο

Forms. While the subjunctive uses only primary endings, the optative uses only secondary endings.[1] Key to the optative is the mood indicator, an iota: either -ι or -ιε (-ιη in aorist passive). Table 32.1 presents endings *with* this mood indicator.

Table 32.2 Active and Middle Optative

Active			Middle		
Present	*2nd Aorist*	*1st Aorist*	*Present*	*2nd Aorist*	*1st Aorist*
λύοιμι	λίποιμι	λύσαιμι	λυοίμην	λιποίμην	λυσαίμην
λύοις	λίποις	λύσαις	λύοιο	λίποιο	λύσαιο
λύοι	λίποι	λύσαι	λύοιτο	λίποιτο	λύσαιτο
λύοιμεν	λίποιμεν	λύσαιμεν	λυοίμεθα	λιποίμεθα	λυσαίμεθα
λύοιτε	λίποιτε	λύσαιτε	λύοισθε	λίποισθε	λύσαισθε
λύοιεν	λίποιεν	λύσαιεν	λύοιντο	λίποιντο	λύσαιντο

---

[1] One exception, the first singular of all actives, using -μι, familiar to the student through εἰμί.

In Table 32.2, observe how the middle second singular form always reacts. The ending -σο always sets up an intervocalic sigma (e.g., -οισο → -οιο, or -σαισο → -σαιο). Also, you may notice that in the optative mood, final αι and οι are considered *long*, an exception to standard accent rules. The tense stem for each principal part is used to establish the forms.

Present. The thematic vowel is ο for the present tense. This creates the resultant endings -οιμι, -οις, -οι, etc.

Table 32.3 Passive Optative

Passive		
Present	*1st Aorist*	*2nd Aorist*
λυοίμην	λυθείην	-------
λύοιο	λυθείης	-------
λύοιτο	λυθείη	-------
λυοίμεθα	λυθείημεν	-------
λύοισθε	λυθείητε	-------
λύοιντο	λυθείησαν	-------

However, only eight thematic verb examples appear in the New Testament, seven in active voice and one in the middle/passive. No contracted forms of the thematic verb appear at all.

Aorist. The aorist optative is more frequent in the New Testament than the present optative. The aorist does not have an augment (time is not a factor). The first aorist active tense suffix -σα is used, creating the endings -σαιμι, -σαις, -σαι, etc. (The third plural on occasion can show -σειαν instead of -σαιεν.) The middle is -σαίμην, -σαιο, -σαιτο, etc. Contracts lengthen, stops volatilize, and liquids drop the sigma.

First Passive. The first aorist passive uses the suffix -θε, an *alternate* mood sign -ιη, and *active* secondary endings. First person takes the -ν ending, third person the -σαν. The resultant endings are -θείην, -θείης, -θείη, etc. Before this passive suffix, contracts lengthen and stops volatilize, as usual.

Second Aorist. The second aorist optative in active and middle voices copies the present tense, only using the second aorist stem. No second aorist passive optative exists in the New Testament.

Thus, the overall pattern in the forms of the optative mood always shows an iota mood indicator with secondary endings, with the one exception of the active first singular, -μι, which is a primary ending:

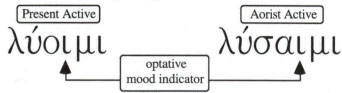

Optative of Εἰμί

Optative is rare enough that only one form of εἰμί is represented in the New Testament. One can see the mood indicator, -ιη, and the secondary endings in the forms: εἴην, εἴης, εἴη, εἴημεν, εἴητε, εἴησαν. However, only the third singular form εἴη ("may he be," "it might be," etc.) actually appears, and that just twelve times.[2]

Μὴ Γένοιτο

Seventeen of the sixty-eight optatives in the New Testament are in the form γένοιτο, usually as the negative, μὴ γένοιτο. All but three of these are in Paul's letters, so quite clearly, this was a characteristic style of Pauline rhetoric.[3] In the negative, the expression might be translated something like "May it never be!"[4]

Translations

The four Greek moods depict reality, probability, possibility, and command. All moods besides the indicative are moods of *potentiality*, with varying degrees of contingency behind them. Subjunctive treats the potential as objectively possible. Optative treats the potential as only subjectively possible. Optative is a diluted subjunctive, a move from assertion to wish. The five forms of the eight present tense optative appearances in the New Testament of the thematic verb are:

(1) καθ᾽ ἡμέραν ἀνακρίνοντες τὰς γραφὰς εἰ **ἔχοι** ταῦτα οὕτως = "daily investigating the scriptures *to see* if these things **might be** so" (Acts 17:11, from ἔχω; again in Acts 25:16)

(2) οὓς ἔδει ἐπὶ σοῦ παρεῖναι καὶ κατηγορεῖν εἴ τι **ἔχοιεν** πρὸς ἐμέ = "who ought to have been present before you and to make accusation, if **they might have** anything against me" (Luke 24:19)

(3) ἐνένευον δὲ τῷ πατρὶ αὐτοῦ τὸ τί ἂν **θέλοι** καλεῖσθαι αὐτό = "and they signaled to his father as to what **he wished** to name him" (Luke 1:62; from θέλω; again in Acts 17:18; 1 Pet. 3:17)

---

[2]Except for John 13:24, all in Luke-Acts: Luke 1:29; 3:15; 8:9; 9:46; 15:26; 18:36; 22:23; Acts 8:20; 10:17; 20:16; 21:33.

[3]Luke 1:38; 20:16; Acts 5:24; Rom. 3:4, 6, 31; 6:2, 15; 7:7, 13; 9:4; 11:1, 11; 1 Cor. 6:15; Gal. 2:17; 3:21; 6:14.

[4]Occasionally one might see, "God forbid!" Such a translation is not recommended, being too close to slang.

(4) ἀλλ᾽ εἰ καὶ **πάσχοιτε** διὰ δικαιοσύνην, μακάριοι. = "But even if **you should suffer** for the sake of righteousness, you are blessed!" (1 Pet. 3:14, from πάσχω)

(5) ἔλεγον εἰ **βούλοιτο** πορεύεσθαι εἰς Ἱεροσόλυμα κἀκεῖ κρίνεσθαι περὶ τούτων = "I was asking if **he was willing** to go to Jerusalem to be judged there concerning these matters" (Acts 25:20, from βούλομαι)

Voluntative. This is the basic use. A prayer or wish is expressed. Thus, Αὐτὸς δὲ ὁ θεὸς τῆς εἰρήνης **ἁγιάσαι** ὑμᾶς ὁλοτελεῖς = "Now **may** the God of peace Himself **sanctify** you completely" (1 Thess. 5:23).

Futuristic. The key is the particle ἄν with the idea of what might happen in the future if a condition were fulfilled. Observe example three above (Luke 1:62). Again, τί ἂν **γένοιτο** τοῦτο = "what **might happen** because of this" (Acts 5:24).

Deliberative. This is a report using an indirect question. Someone either asked a direct question or reflected on a question that now is being reported indirectly using the contingency of the optative. Thus, ἡ δὲ ἐπὶ τῷ λόγῳ διεταράχθη καὶ διελογίζετο ποταπὸς **εἴη** ὁ ἀσπασμὸς οὗτος = "But she was disturbed by this word and kept on wondering what sort of greeting this **might be**" (Luke 1:29).

Conditional Sentences

Table 32.4 Conditional Sentences

Class	Condition	Conj.	Protasis	Apodosis
1st TRUE	fulfilled (οὐ in negative)	εἰ + (ἐάν at times)	any indicative	any indicative imperative subjunctive
2nd FALSE	not fulfilled (μή in negative) a. present time	εἰ +	past tense indicative	ἄν + past indicative (ἄν can occur anywhere or at times drop out)
	b. past time	εἰ +	aorist indicative	ἄν + past indicative
		εἰ +	pluperfect indicative	ἄν + past indicative
3rd POSSIBLE	undetermined possible	ἐάν +	subjunctive	future, or any indic. (ἄν)
4th REMOTE	undetermined remote	εἰ +	optative	optative (ἄν)

With this lesson on the optative mood, we complete the series of the four major classes of conditional sentences in Greek. The key to class condition is *the mood of the protasis*, not the type of conjunction. The fourth class conditional sentence assumes that the condition is *undetermined*, but *remote*, so uses the optative mood (only subjectively possible). The conjunction is εἰ. The particle of contingency in the apodosis is ἄν, which is not translated. Curiously, no complete example of the fourth class conditional sentence exists in the New Testament. That is, never do we find both protasis and apodosis of a fourth class conditional sentence actually expressed. Ellipsis leaves the form incomplete but the thought still clear.

One can see the fragmentary nature of the fourth class condition in example four above (1 Pet. 3:14). Another example would be ἔσπευδεν γὰρ <u>εἰ</u> δυνατὸν **εἴη** αὐτῷ τὴν ἡμέραν τῆς πεντηκοστῆς γενέσθαι εἰς Ἱεροσόλυμα = "for he was making haste, <u>if</u> **it might be** possible for him to be in Jerusalem on the day of Pentecost" (Acts 20:16).

What To Learn—LESSON 32 (δύο καὶ τριάκοντα)

☐   1.   Optative paradigms
            active: λύοιμι, λίποιμι, λύσαιμι
            mid./pass.:   λυοίμην, λιποίμην, λυσαίμην, λυθείην

☐   2.   Sign of the optative mood

☐   3.   The copulative εἰμί as the optative εἴη

☐   4.   Use of μὴ γένοιτο as Pauline style

☐   5.   Optative mood use and translation: voluntative, futuristic, deliberative

☐   6.   Fourth class conditional sentences: structure, significance, translation

☐   7.   Vocabulary words

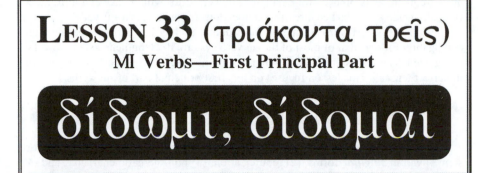

LESSON 33 (τριάκοντα τρεῖς)
MI Verbs—First Principal Part

δίδωμι, δίδομαι

Two major conjugations of Greek verbs divide into -ω verbs and -μι verbs, based on the ending of the present active first person singular. A theme vowel is characteristic of -ω verbs. The -μι verb characteristically does not have a theme vowel. The real difference is in the first principal part.

Vocabulary 33

Ω Verbs (Thematic)

κοπιάω	I toil
μιμνήσκομαι	I remember
χαρίζομαι	I give, grant, pardon, forgive

MI Verbs (Non-thematic)

(number indicates appearances in NT)

ἀπόλλυμι (91)	I destroy (active)

	I perish (middle)
δείκνυμι (33)	I show
δίδωμι (415)	I give, grant, allow
τίθημι (100)	I put, place, lay
φημί (66)	I say
ἵστημι (154)	I place, set, cause to stand (transitive)
	I stand (intransitive)

Analysis

MI verbs are older than -ω verbs. Some endings are the more primitive form as a result, such as the first person singular, -μι. They began losing out to the growing dominance of -ω verbs. Thirty-one different -μι verbs appear in the New Testament. Adding compound forms, their number is 109. However, a few of these actually are quite frequent, as is δίδωμι, for example. The verb εἰμί, which has been introduced right alongside -ω verbs because of its tremendous frequency, is a -μι verb.

Much of the -μι verb formation the student already has learned, because the conjugation follows that of most of the -ω verb system, if a lengthened stem vowel is recognized. The only significant difference is in the first principal part of present and imperfect tenses.[1] This lesson focuses on this first principal part of -μι verbs.

Present Tense

Indicative. *Active.* Four features are to be observed: (1) lengthening a short stem vowel in *singular* forms, (2) reduplication, (3) non-thematic character, and (4) primary resultant endings. These are outlined briefly.

Lengthening. The present active indicative -μι verb lengthens the short stem vowel in *singular* forms. The lexical form, δίδωμι, being a singular form, includes this lengthened stem vowel. So the tense stem of δίδωμι, minus the reduplication, is

$$\delta o - = \delta \omega -$$

lengthened stem vowel

δο-. For τίθημι the stem is θε-. The stem of ἵστημι is στα-. The verb ἀφίημι is a compound using the preposition ἀπό which elides the vowel and changes to ἀφ- before rough breathing. The stem of ἀφίημι, really just ἵημι, is only one letter, ἑ-.

Reduplication. A second feature of -μι verbs is reduplication in the present system for about half of them.[2] The student has encountered reduplication in the fourth and fifth principal parts of the -ω verb (perfect system). There, reduplication repeated the beginning consonant of the tense stem and used the vowel ε, as in λελύω. The pattern in the present system of -μι verbs is similar, only the vowel is ι:

$$\delta\iota + \delta\omega = \delta\iota\delta\omega -$$

reduplicated, lengthened stem

For the verb τίθημι, the duplicated stem θιθη- deaspirates to the form τιθη- for pronunciation. For ἵστημι, the duplicated stem σιστη- drops the initial σ before the vowel, and picks up rough breathing as a result, becoming ἵστη. The verb ἀφίημι, stem ἑ-, duplicates with just the duplication vowel ι as ἱη-.

---

[1] Second aorist is not distinctive, because some -ω verbs show non-thematic second aorists too.

[2] Almost half of the -μι verbs are not reduplicated. Further, some -ω verbs *also* reduplicate the present stem. For example, γίνωσκω (γιγνώσκω, but γ before ν drops), μιμνῄσκομαι, πίπτω, and τίκτω (which swaps the letters, τκ → κτ, called "metathesis").

Non-thematic. The third and distinguishing feature is that -μι verbs do not use a theme vowel.[3] Pronominal suffixes are joined directly to the lengthened, reduplicated stem.

Endings. MI verb endings are regular. To see this, two points are made. First, remember that the pattern learned for -ω verbs (-ω, -εις, -ει, etc.) is a *resultant* pattern with reactions *already* worked in. Second, realize that the -μι verb pattern *also* is learned as a *resultant* pattern. (Original primitive endings were -μι, -σι, -τι, -μεν, -τε, -ντι.)

Thus, we have:

Table 33.1 Primary Active Endings—MI Verbs

Number	Person	Ending
Singular	1st	-μι
	2nd	-ς
	3rd	-σι
Plural	1st	-μεν
	2nd	-τε
	3rd	-ασι

$$\delta\iota\delta\omega + \mu\iota = \delta\acute{\iota}\delta\omega\mu\iota$$

"athematic" =
no thematic vowel

Middle/Passive. Basically similar to the active voice, the indicative middle and passive formation has two distinctions. First the short stem vowel is *not* lengthened. Second, primary middle endings are used (and the second singular does not react).

$$\underbrace{\delta\iota + \delta o}_{\text{reduplicated stem}} = \delta\iota\delta o\text{-}$$

To this stem, the primary middle/passive endings are added:

$$\delta\iota\delta o + \mu\alpha\iota = \delta\acute{\iota}\delta o\mu\alpha\iota$$

"athematic" =
no thematic vowel

Subjunctive. All subjunctives take the endings of Table 30.1. For -μι verbs, short vowel stems contract with these long subjunctive endings. Whatever the exact

---

[3]Except: (1) *future* tense, with a thematic vowel in *resultant* primary endings, (2) *subjunctive* mood, which includes a long thematic vowel in *resultant* subjunctive endings, and (3) present active imperative, second singular.

nature of the contraction, the result is a long syllable with a circumflex accent (except for the antepenult acute in the middle first plural). This, with a reduplicated stem, is the form of the present subjunctive. Thus, the active voice results for δίδωμι are διδῶ, διδῷς, διδῷ, διδῶμεν, διδῶτε, διδῶσι(ν).[4] Middle voice results are διδῶμαι, διδῷ, διδῶται, διδώμεθα, διδῶσθε, διδῶνται.

Imperative. All imperatives take the endings of Table 31.1. For -μι verbs, short vowel stems contract with one form, the active second singular, which opts for no ending, leaving the thematic vowel ε exposed to contract with the stem vowel (e.g., ο + ε = ου or ε + ε = ει).[5] This, with the reduplicated stem, is the form of the present imperative. The active voice imperative forms for δίδωμι are δίδου, διδότω, δίδοτε, διδότωσαν. Middle forms are δίδοσο, διδόσθω, δίδοσθε, διδόσθωσαν.

Optative. Only two -μι verbs have present optatives in the New Testament. The verb εἰμί has the form εἴη, and δύναμαι has the forms δυναίμην and δύναιντο.

Imperfect Tense

The imperfect tense occurs only in the indicative mood. Thus, the imperfect of -μι verbs has to do with only two forms, the active and middle/passive indicative.

Active. Five features are to be observed: (1) lengthening a short stem vowel in the *singular* forms, (2) reduplication, (3) augment, (4) non-thematic character, and (5) secondary endings. These are outlined briefly.

Lengthening. Imperfect active indicative of -μι verbs lengthens short stem vowels in *singular* forms (as in present tense). Pattern varies. For δίδωμι, lengthening is -ου. For τίθημι, however, note the variation: τιθη-, τιθει-, τιθει-. Such

$$\delta o\text{-} = \delta o\upsilon\text{-}$$

lengthened stem vowel

patterns do not need to be memorized, only recognized as representing some type of lengthening process in singular forms.

Reduplication. The reduplication pattern is the same as the present tense—the imperfect being built on the same principal part—so the imperfect reduplication theme vowel is ι. Thus, we have the result:

$$\underbrace{\delta\iota + \delta o\upsilon}_{} = \delta\iota\delta o\upsilon\text{-}$$

reduplicated, lengthened stem

---

[4]Second and third singular can have the alternate results διδοῖς and διδοῖ, respectively.
[5]This form alone appropriates the thematic vowel. The others are non-thematic.

Augment. A secondary tense is augmented. Patterns of syllabic and temporal augment of the -ω verb apply to the -μι verb also (see Table 12.4).

$$\overset{\text{'}}{\varepsilon}\text{-διδου}$$
⌞— augmented stem

Non-thematic. A fourth feature of this conjugation's imperfect tense is that -μι verbs often do not incorporate a theme vowel ("athematic"). As with the present tense, pronominal suffixes are joined directly to the reduplicated stem.

Endings. The -μι verb secondary endings are regular. Most of the time, the third plural takes the -σαν option. On occasion, the third plural takes the -ν option, lengthening the stem vowel when doing so (e.g., -ουν or -ην). Thus, we have:

$$\overset{\text{'}}{\varepsilon}\text{διδου} + \nu = \overset{\text{'}}{\varepsilon}\text{δίδουν}$$

"athematic" = ▲
no thematic vowel ⌐⌙

Middle. Basically similar to the active voice, the indicative middle formation has two distinctions. First the short stem vowel is *not* lengthened. Second, secondary middle endings are used (and the second singular does not react). The final result for the secondary middle in the -μι verb, then, is:

$$\overset{\text{'}}{\varepsilon}\text{διδόμην}$$
↗
secondary middle ending

Table 33.2 Present of δίδωμι

Indicative		Subjunctive		Imperative	
Active	*Mid./Pass.*	*Active*	*Mid./Pass.*	*Active*	*Mid./Pass.*
δίδωμι	δίδομαι	διδῶ	διδῶμαι	-------	-------
δίδως	δίδοσαι	διδῷς	διδῷ	δίδου	δίδοσο
δίδωσι(ν)	δίδοται	διδῷ	διδῷται	διδότω	διδόσθω
δίδομεν	διδόμεθα	διδῶμεν	διδώμεθα	-------	-------
δίδοτε	δίδοσθε	διδῶτε	διδῶσθε	δίδοτε	δίδοσθε
διδόασι(ν)	δίδονται	διδῶσι(ν)	διδῶνται	διδότωσαν	διδόσθωσαν

Tables 33.2 and 33.3 summarize this discussion. Our paradigm is δίδωμι. The formation is regular, and δίδωμι also happens to be a -μι verb frequently encountered in the New Testament. However, be advised that some of these forms of δίδωμι in the tables do not actually appear in the New Testament. They have been included to help illustrate formation patterns. Remember that not every single variation is indicated. For example, the second and third person singular of the present active subjunctive can have two alternate forms, διδοῖς and διδοῖ, respectively. Again, the imperfect active indicative, third person plural can opt for the -ν. If so, the stem vowel is lengthened in the process (i.e., ἐδίδουν).

Table 33.3 Imperfect of δίδωμι

Indicative	
Active	*Mid./Pass.*
ἐδίδουν	ἐδιδόμην
ἐδίδους	ἐδίδοσο
ἐδίδου	ἐδίδοτο
ἐδίδομεν	ἐδιδόμεθα
ἐδίδοτε	ἐδίδοσθε
ἐδίδοσαν	ἐδίδοντο

Finally, be aware that a few verbs actually are found in *both* the -μι and the -ω conjugation. Such verbs that can be found in either conjugation are learned by observing vocabulary. Examples are ἀπόλλυμι (ἀπολλύω) and δείκνυμι (δεικνύω).

What To Learn—LESSON 33 (τριάκοντα τρεῖς)

☐ 1. Background of -μι verbs and where different from -ω verbs
☐ 2. Four key formation features of present active indicative of -μι verbs
☐ 3. Two distinctions of present middle/passive indicative formation
☐ 4. Five key formation features of imperfect active indicative of -μι verbs
☐ 5. Two distinctions of imperfect middle/passive indicative formation
☐ 6. Primary active endings of -μι verbs and present and imperfect paradigms:
        present indicative: δίδωμι   δίδομαι
        present subjunctive: διδῶ   διδῶμαι
        present imperative: δίδου   δίδοσο
        imperfect indicative: ἐδίδουν   ἐδιδόμην
☐ 7. Vocabulary words

LESSON 34 (τριάκοντα τέσσαρες)
MI Verbs—Other Principal Parts

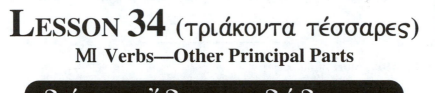

δώσω, ἔδωκα, δέδωκα,
δέδομαι, ἐδόθην

The second major conjugation of the Greek verb system, the -μι verb, is not distinguished from the -ω conjugation outside the first principal part. In the other principal parts, the -μι verb is conjugated as is the -ω verb, with minor variations.

Vocabulary 34

Ω Verbs

κωλύω	I forbid, hinder
πεινάω	I hunger
τελειόω	I fulfill, finish, make complete, make perfect

Δίδωμι Compounds

ἀποδίδωμι (48)	I give back, pay (act.), I sell (mid.)
παραδίδωμι (119)	I hand over, betray

Ἵημι Compounds

ἀφίημι (146)	I permit, forgive
συνίημι (26)	I understand

Ἵστημι Compounds

ἀνίστημι (108)	I cause to arise (trans.), arise (intrans.)
παρίστημι (41)	I present, offer (trans.) am present, stand by (intrans.)

Τίθημι Compounds

ἐπιτίθημι (39)	I lay upon
κάθημαι (91)	I sit down

General analyses applying to the -ω verb conjugation apply as well to -μι verbs outside the first principal part. Only a few additional explanations need be offered. Not all table forms occur in the New Testament but are given to illustrate the tense.

379

♦ *Notice with -μι verbs how short stems are either aorist or future.*

Future

Table 34.1 Future of δίδωμι

Future Indicative		
Active	*Middle*	*Passive*
δώσω	δώσομαι	δοθήσομαι
δώσεις	δώσῃ	δοθήσῃ
δώσει	δώσεται	δοθήσεται
δώσομεν	δωσόμεθα	δοθησόμεθα
δώσετε	δώσεσθε	δοθήσεσθε
δώσουσι(ν)	δώσονται	δοθήσονται

The middle indicative, second person singular volatilizes. Also, remember that the future passive is built on the sixth principal part, the aorist passive stem. The stem vowel is not lengthened in the passive voice (cf. aorist tense).

Aorist

Table 34.2 Aorist Active and Middle of δίδωμι

Aorist Indicative		Aorist Subjunctive		Aorist Imperative	
Active	*Middle*	*Active*	*Middle*	*Active*	*Middle*
ἔδωκα	ἐδόμην	δῶ (δώσω)	δῶμαι	-------	-------
ἔδωκας	ἔδου	δῷς (δώσῃς)	δῷ	δός	δοῦ
ἔδωκε(ν)	ἔδοτο	δῷ (δώσῃ)	δῶται	δότω	δόσθω
ἐδώκαμεν	ἐδόμεθα	δῶμεν (etc.)	δώμεθα	-------	-------
ἐδώκατε	ἔδοσθε	δῶτε (δώσητε)	δῶσθε	δότε	δόσθε
ἔδωκαν	ἔδοντο	δῶσι(ν) (etc.)	δῶνται	δότωσαν	δόσθωσαν

Three verbs (δίδωμι, τίθημι, ἵημι compounds) are called "kappa aorist." The -σα pattern is replaced by -κα, -κας, -κε, -καμεν, -κατε, -καν. The middle indicative, second singular reacts (οσο → οο → ου). Subjunctive and imperative moods are *second* aorist. On occasion one finds the -σ present in the stem, as in the subjunctive of δίδωμι, a first aorist configuration. The passive is built on the aorist passive stem (short stem vowel; cf. future).[1]

Table 34.3 Aorist Passive of δίδωμι

Aorist Passive		
Indicative	*Subjunctive*	*Imperative*
ἐδόθην	δοθῶ	-------
ἐδόθης	δοθῇς	δόθητι
ἐδόθη	δοθῇ	δοθήτω
ἐδόθημεν	δοθῶμεν	-------
ἐδόθητε	δοθῆτε	δόθητε
ἐδόθησαν	δοθῶσι	δοθήτωσαν

Perfect

The perfect active and middle/passive indicative of the -μι verb is regular. The forms for the perfect subjunctive and imperative are not included here because these forms are quite rare, as noted already in discussion of these two moods. For the subjunctive, a -μι verb example is the middle/passive periphrastic construction ᾖ δεδομένον (John 3:27; 6:65). For the imperative, the form ἴσθι probably is the active imperative of εἰμί where it occurs in the New Testament (Matt. 2:13; 5:25; 5:34; Luke 19:17; 1 Tim. 4:15).

Table 34.4 Perfect of δίδωμι

Perfect Indicative	
Active	*Mid./Pass.*
δέδωκα	δέδομαι
δέδωκας	δέδοσαι
δέδωκε(ν)	δέδοται
δεδώκαμεν	δεδόμεθα
δεδώκατε	δέδοσθε
δέδωκαν	δέδονται

Participles

Participles are regular. Reactions take on familiar patterns. However, the stem must be remembered. Thus, δείκνυμι (stem: δεικ-) is δειχθείς in the aorist passive. The verb τίθημι (stem: θε-) ends up like naked endings in the aorist active: θείς, θεῖσα, θέν! As aorist passive, τίθημι is: τεθείς, τεθεῖσα, τεθέν. Here, the opening τε- *is* the stem, only deaspirated to blend with the following θ of the ending.

---

[1]Only two New Testament second aorist -μι optatives: δῴη (δίδωμι) and ὀναίμην (ὀνίνημι).

For the rare perfect, ἵστημι is found in the first perfect active form ἑστηκώς, along with compounded forms (e.g., παρεστηκώς). A second perfect also is found for ἵστημι, in the forms ἑστώς, ἑστῶσα, ἑστός, all of which have contracted and taken on other reactions. This second perfect form shows up in compounded forms also (e.g., παρεστώς). A compounded form of δίδωμι, παραδίδωμι, is found in the form παραδεδωκώς. The verb τίθημι has the perfect participle form τεθεικώς.

Table 34.5 Present Active Participle—δίδωμι

Masculine (ἄρχων)		Neuter (3rd Decl.)		Feminine (δόξα)	
Singular	*Plural*	*Singular*	*Plural*	*Singular*	*Plural*
διδούς	διδόντες	διδόν	διδόντα	διδοῦσα	διδοῦσαι
διδόντος	διδόντων	διδόντος	διδόντων	διδούσης	διδουσῶν
διδόντι	διδοῦσιν	διδόντι	διδοῦσιν	διδούσῃ	διδούσαις
διδόντα	διδόντας	διδόν	διδόντα	διδοῦσαν	διδούσας

Table 34.6 Present Middle/Passive Participle—δίδωμι

Masculine (ἀγαθός)		Neuter (ἀγαθός)		Feminine (ἀγαθός)	
Singular	*Plural*	*Singular*	*Plural*	*Singular*	*Plural*
διδόμενος	διδόμενοι	διδόμενον	διδόμενα	διδομένη	διδόμεναι
διδομένου	διδομένων	διδομένου	διδομένων	διδομένης	διδομένων
διδομένῳ	διδομένοις	διδομένῳ	διδομένοις	διδομένῃ	διδομέναις
διδόμενον	διδομένους	διδόμενον	διδόμενα	διδομένην	διδομένας

Table 34.7 Aorist Active Participle—δίδωμι

Masculine (ἄρχων)		Neuter (3rd Decl.)		Feminine (δόξα)	
Singular	*Plural*	*Singular*	*Plural*	*Singular*	*Plural*
δούς	δόντες	δόν	δόντα	δοῦσα	δοῦσαι
δόντος	δόντων	δόντος	δόντων	δούσης	δουσῶν
δόντι	δούσιν	δόντι	δούσιν	δούσῃ	δούσαις
δόντα	δόντας	δόν	δόντα	δοῦσαν	δούσας

Table 34.8 Aorist Middle Participle—δίδωμι

Masculine (ἀγαθός)		Neuter (ἀγαθός)		Feminine (ἀγαθός)	
Singular	*Plural*	*Singular*	*Plural*	*Singular*	*Plural*
δόμενος	δόμενοι	δόμενον	δόμενα	δομένη	δόμεναι
δομένου	δομένων	δομένου	δομένων	δομένης	δομένων
δομένῳ	δομένοις	δομένῳ	δομένοις	δομένῃ	δομέναις
δόμενον	δομένους	δόμενον	δόμενα	δομένην	δομένας

Table 34.9 Aorist Passive Participle—δίδωμι

Masculine		Neuter		Feminine	
Singular	*Plural*	*Singular*	*Plural*	*Singular*	*Plural*
δοθείς	δοθέντες	δοθέν	δοθέντα	δοθεῖσα	δοθεῖσαι
δοθέντος	δοθέντων	δοθέντος	δοθέντων	δοθείσης	δοθεισῶν
δοθέντι	δοθεῖσι(ν)	δοθέντι	δοθεῖσι(ν)	δοθείσῃ	δοθείσαις
δοθέντα	δοθέντας	δοθέν	δοθέντα	δοθεῖσαν	δοθείσας

Table 34.10 Perfect Active Participle—δίδωμι

Masculine		Neuter		Feminine	
Singular	*Plural*	*Singular*	*Plural*	*Singular*	*Plural*
δεδωκώς	δεδωκότες	δεδωκός	δεδωκότα	δεδωκυῖα	δεδωκυῖαι
δεδωκότος	δεδωκότων	δεδωκότος	δεδωκότων	δεδωκυίας	δεδωκυιῶν
δεδωκότι	δεδωκόσι(ν)	δεδωκότι	δεδωκόσι(ν)	δεδωκυίᾳ	δεδωκυίαις
δεδωκότα	δεδωκότας	δεδωκός	δεδωκότα	δεδωκυῖαν	δεδωκυίας

Table 34.11 Perfect Middle/Passive Participle—δίδωμι

Masculine		Neuter		Feminine	
Singular	*Plural*	*Singular*	*Plural*	*Singular*	*Plural*
δεδομένος	δεδομένοι	δεδομένον	δεδομένα	δεδομένη	δεδομέναι
δεδομένου	δεδομένων	δεδομένου	δεδομένων	δεδομένης	δεδομένων
δεδομένῳ	δεδομένοις	δεδομένῳ	δεδομένοις	δεδομένῃ	δεδομέναις
δεδομένον	δεδομένους	δεδομένον	δεδομένα	δεδομένην	δεδομένας

Infinitives

Active   Mid./Pass.

-ναι	-σθαι

Present. The active voice infinitive ending is -ναι, and middle/passive is -σθαι. Thus, διδόναι and δίδοσθαι are the present active and middle infinitives, respectively. The verb εἰμί has the infinitive form εἶναι. This verb also has one of the rare future infinitives in the New Testament, in the form ἔσεσθαι.

Aorist. The aorist active infinitive can be found in παραστῆσαι, from παρίστημι. Then, δείκνυμι has the aorist active infinitive δεῖξαι. Also, one will find ἀπολέσαι from ἀπόλλυμι. Second aorist forms are seen in δοῦναι (δίδωμι), θεῖναι (τίθημι), and στῆναι (ἵστημι). The aorist middle infinitive shows up in compounds of τίθημι, in ἀποθέσθαι and καταθέσθαι. The aorist passive infinitive, which has an *active* ending, shows up in the forms δοθῆναι, τεθῆναι, and σταθῆναι.

Perfect. The perfect infinitive is rare. The compound ἐξίστημι has the perfect active infinitive ἐξεστακέναι. The second perfect form ἑστάναι comes from ἵστημι.

Τίθημι and Ἵστημι

The three most common -μι verbs in the New Testament are δίδωμι, τίθημι, and ἵστημι. The verb δίδωμι has been used as a paradigm to illustrate -μι verbs in general. While not all the forms of δίδωμι in the tables occur, those that do have been covered. Because of their use, especially including compound forms, the two verbs τίθημι and ἵστημι are outlined here in addition to δίδωμι in the two common appearances as present or aorist tense. Hopefully, these additional tables will be found helpful by the student.

Table 34.12 Present of τίθημι

Present Indicative		Present Subjunctive		Present Imperative	
Active	*Mid./Pass.*	*Active*	*Mid./Pass.*	*Active*	*Mid./Pass.*
τίθημι	τίθεμαι	τιθῶ	τιθῶμαι	-------	-------
τίθης	τίθεσαι	τιθῇς	τιθῇ	τίθει	τίθεσο
τίθησι(ν)	τίθεται	τιθῇ	τιθῆται	τιθέτω	τιθέσθω
τίθεμεν	τιθέμεθα	τιθῶμεν	τιθώμεθα	-------	-------
τίθετε	τίθεσθε	τιθῆτε	τιθῆσθε	τίθετε	τίθεσθε
τιθέασι(ν)	τίθενται	τιθῶσι(ν)	τιθῶνται	τιθέτωσαν	τιθέσθωσαν

Table 34.13 Present of ἵστημι

Present Indicative		Present Subjunctive		Present Imperative	
Active	*Mid./Pass.*	*Active*	*Mid./Pass.*	*Active*	*Mid./Pass.*
ἵστημι	ἵσταμαι	ἱστῶ	ἱστῶμαι	-------	-------
ἵστης	ἵστασαι	ἱστῇς	ἱστῇ	ἵστη	ἵστασο
ἵστησι(ν)	ἵσταται	ἱστῇ	ἱστῆται	ἱστάτω	ἱστάσθω
ἵσταμεν	ἱστάμεθα	ἱστῶμεν	ἱστώμεθα	-------	-------
ἵστατε	ἵστασθε	ἱστῆτε	ἱστῆσθε	ἵστάτε	ἵστασθε
ἱστᾶσι(ν)	ἵστανται	ἱστῶσι(ν)	ἱστῶνται	ἱστότωσαν	ἱστάσθωσαν

Table 34.14 Imperfect of τίθημι

Indicative	
Active	*Mid./Pass.*
ἐτίθην	ἐτιθέμην
ἐτίθεις	ἐτίθεσο
ἐτίθει	ἐτίθετο
ἐτίθεμεν	ἐτιθέμεθα
ἐτίθετε	ἐτίθεσθε
ἐτίθεσαν	ἐτίθεντο

Table 34.15 Imperfect of ἵστημι

Indicative	
Active	*Mid./Pass.*
ἵστην	ἱστάμην
ἵστης	ἵστασο
ἵστη	ἵστατο
ἵσταμεν	ἱστάμεθα
ἵστατε	ἵστασθε
ἵστασαν	ἵσταντο

Table 34.16 Aorist Active and Middle of τίθημι

Aorist Indicative		Aorist Subjunctive		Aorist Imperative	
Active	*Middle*	*Active*	*Middle*	*Active*	*Middle*
ἔθηκα	ἐθέμην	θῶ	θῶμαι	-------	-------
ἔθηκας	ἔθου	θῇς	θῇ	θές	θοῦ
ἔθηκε(ν)	ἔθετο	θῇ	θῆται	θέτω	θέσθω
ἐθήκαμεν	ἐθέμεθα	θῶμεν	θώμεθα	-------	-------
ἐθήκατε	ἔθεσθε	θῆτε	θῆσθε	θέτε	θέσθε
ἔθηκαν	ἔθεντο	θῶσι(ν)	θῶνται	θέτωσαν	θέσθωσαν

Table 34.17 Aorist Active and Middle of ἵστημι

Aorist Indicative		Aorist Subjunctive		Aorist Imperative	
Active	*Middle*	*Active*	*Middle*	*Active*	*Middle*
ἔστην	ἐστάμην	στῶ	στῶμαι	-------	-------
ἔστης	ἔστασο	στῇς	στῇ	στῆθι	στάσο
ἔστη	ἔστατο	στῇ	στῆται	στήτω	στάσθω
ἔστημεν	ἐστάμεθα	στῶμεν	στώμεθα	-------	-------
ἔστητε	ἔστασθε	στῆτε	στῆσθε	στῆτε	στάσθε
ἔστησαν	ἔσταντο	στῶσι(ν)	στῶνται	στήτωσαν	στάσθωσαν

Table 34.18 Aorist Passive of τίθημι

Aorist Passive		
Indicative	*Subjunctive*	*Imperative*
ἐτέθην	τεθῶ	-------
ἐτέθης	τεθῇς	τέθητι
ἐτέθη	τεθῇ	τεθήτω
ἐτέθημεν	τεθῶμεν	-------
ἐτέθητε	τεθῆτε	τέθητε
ἐτέθησαν	τεθῶσι	τεθήτωσαν

Table 34.19 Aorist Passive of ἵστημι

Aorist Passive		
Indicative	*Subjunctive*	*Imperative*
ἐστάθην	σταθῶ	-------
ἐστάθης	σταθῇς	στάθητι
ἐστάθη	σταθῇ	σταθήτω
ἐστάθημεν	σταθῶμεν	-------
ἐστάθητε	σταθῆτε	στάθητε
ἐστάθησαν	σταθῶσι	σταθήτωσαν

Table 34.20 Participle Forms for τίθημι and ἵστημι

	Active			Middle/Passive
	Masculine	*Feminine*	*Neuter*	*Mas., Fem., Neu.*
Present	τιθείς	τιθεῖσα	τιθέν	τιθέμενος, -η, -ον
	ἱστάς	ἱστᾶσα	ἱσταν	ἱστάμενος, -η, -ον
Aorist	θείς	θεῖσα	θέν	θέμενος, -η, -ον
	στάς	στᾶσα	στάν	στάμενος, -η, -ον
1st Perf.	ἑστηκώς	ἑστηκῶσα	ἑστηκός	ἑστάμενος, -η, -ον
2nd Perf.	ἑστώς	ἑστῶσα	ἑστός	---------

Non-thematic Aorists

The verb ἵστημι is a part of a small class of verbs called "non-thematic second aorists." Two others are ἀναβαίνω and γινώσκω. Though part of the -ω conjugation, these two verbs *do not use a thematic vowel for the aorist active indicative*, just as ἵστημι in the -μι conjugation. In terms of the stem, the present stem of βαίνω is the result of reaction with a consonantal iota added to βα-. For γινώσκω, an original vowel stem γνο- added -σκ, lengthened, and reduplicated similar to a -μι verb to form γιγνώσκω. Then, the second gamma dropped out before the nu as γινώσκω.

Table 34.21 Non-thematic Second Aorists

Active Indicative	
ἀναβαίνω	*γινώσκω*
ἀνέβην	ἔγνων
ἀνέβης	ἔγνως
ἀνέβη	ἔγνω
ἀνέβημεν	ἔγνωμεν
ἀνέβητε	ἔγνωτε
ἀνέβησαν	ἔγνωσαν

In creating the aorist forms, the original verb stem βα- was lengthened to create the second aorist stem βη-. This stem was augmented for past time, but no thematic vowel was used, hence, ἐ-βη-ν = ἔβην. As a compound, the form becomes ἀνέβην. For γινώσκω, the stem γνο-, when lengthened and augmented, created the second aorist form ἔ-γνω-ν. Again, no thematic vowel was used for this second aorist form, though an -ω verb.

Due to their frequency (including compound forms), these two -ω verbs are given in the second aorist active indicative. In these forms, observe how such verbs are similar to the -μι verb ἵστημι.

Principal Parts

Table 34.22 Principal Parts—δίδωμι, τίθημι, ἵστημι

First	*Second*	*Third*	*Fourth*	*Fifth*	*Sixth*
δίδωμι	δώσω	ἔδωκα	δέδωκα	δέδομαι	ἐδόθην
τίθημι	θήσω	ἔθηκα	τέθεικα	τέθειμαι	ἐτέθην
ἵστημι	στήσω	ἔστησα (ἔστην)	ἕστηκα	ἕσταμαι	ἐστάθην

What To Learn—LESSON 34 (τριάκοντα τέσσαρες)

☐   1. Basic formation patterns of the -μι verbs in the other principal parts, and as participles and infinitives

☐   2. Recognizing stems and forms of δίδωμι, τίθημι, ἵστημι

☐   3. Significance of a "non-thematic" second aorist and three examples

☐   4. Vocabulary words

APPENDIX: On The Art of Translation

Translation

All of life is a translation procedure. In the doctor's office, your physician tries to reduce to terms you can understand just exactly what those tests revealed. The intelligence officer converts the nonsense on his computer screen into the knowledge of his enemy's recent instructions to troop commanders. And the code on the can in the supermarket becomes dollars and cents on the cashier's register.

To "translate" is to "carry across." A message in a source language is carried across into a receptor language; however, the question is whether the message retains equivalent meaning in the process. The problem is, language is more than the sum of its parts. Many students begin Greek with a preconceived notion of how to translate: (1) Take an individual element encountered in the text. (2) Go to the dictionary. (3) Look up that element. (4) Write down the meaning. (5) Go to the next element. (6) Repeat steps one through five. However, this procedure shows a basic ignorance to one of the most fundamental features of any language.

Idioms and Other Complications

One cannot just stack up dictionary definitions on top of one another for each individual element and come up with a resultant, correct meaning of an expression. The problem is the "idiom." Every language has peculiarities of expression, called idioms, that can be understood only through a thorough exposure to the use of a language in the native context. Idioms put words together that transcend what the dictionary says about each individual component. When it comes to idioms, two plus two does *not* equal four. Mechanically noting each element's denotation is far removed from the reality of the idiom's actual expressed thought. "Break a leg!" you say to your sister about to make her stage debut. But what do you *mean*? That is the issue of idioms. Further, a source language can have an idiom with no equivalent in the receptor language.

Besides the complication of idiomatic expressions, individual word meanings can be difficult. Even among peoples using what is supposed to be the same language, meanings of the *same* word are not equivalent. I was on the tennis court having finished a match with a new South African friend, and we were trying to establish the time of another match. We were having trouble finding an open date,

389

and time was pressing on other things to do, so my friend said, "Well, I'll just give you a tinkle, then, all right?" I did not know what to say. I had this comical picture of a dog at a fire hydrant. Seeing my amusement, my friend pressed on until we discovered together that what he meant was that he would call me on the telephone later to arrange another match. "Give you a tinkle" for "I'll call you?" We had a good laugh together as I explained my comic strip image. If two English speaking persons can have trouble with the use of a word, imagine the greater degree of complication trying to bring over a word alien to the receptor language. Just how many different ways can Paul use the word σάρξ ("flesh") after all?

Words also change in meaning over time. The venerable King James verb "prevent" at 1 Thess. 4:15 was clear to those in England in the 1600s. However, that word now confuses contemporary American readers, for the meaning has changed. Modern translations use "precede," a long way from today's "prevent." Who can read Chaucer's *Canterbury Tales* and not be lost after three lines? You need to think through what language *is* in order to grasp the task at hand in translation. Language is a living, dynamic entity that grows and develops and changes over time, a *spoken* reality before ever committed to pen and paper. Words already are an abstraction of thought. Words change as thoughts change. We always will need a new translation.

A Problem of English, Not Greek

First, you must know the source language. That is what you are doing now in studying New Testament Greek. However, the neglected side of the translation equation is that you also must have facility in the receptor language. Students have trouble learning Greek because they, in fact, have only a superficial understanding of their own English language. I advise all Greek students to put a high school English grammar right next to their Greek grammar for handy quick reference. If the word "predicate nominative" flies right over your head, you are going to be lost until you learn the basic grammatical terminology. (I could have said, "bone up on" for "learn," but just try getting that out of strict dictionary definitions!)

Translation Theory

♦ *Good translation always is the proper balance of freedom and restraint.*

On one side is the mechanically literal. On the other side is the totally free form. Somewhere in between the two is a good translation. The interlinear is the naively mechanical. The paraphrase is the free form. Neither one is *translation*. One wants to be faithful to the author's original intent. Yet, one also wants the contemporary reader to understand what they read. These are the two strong poles in the process of translation whose forces must be balanced carefully. The more literal one becomes, the more obscure is the language! You actually defeat your purpose of translation. On the other hand, the more free one is, the greater the jeopardy of cutting oneself loose from the author's actual meaning. In our attempts to "modernize" we may destroy historical and cultural accuracy. Either method is too extreme really to help.

Trying to avoid these literal/free extremes are the theories "formal equivalence" and "functional equivalence." Formal equivalence emphasizes more the source language, tending to the literal; functional equivalence emphasizes more the receptor language, tending to the dynamic. Either method's emphasis has tradeoffs, but neither method focuses on simple denotations. The functional equivalence model attempts to provide word groups in the source language with a functionally equivalent word group in the receptor language faithfully and accurately reflecting the author's exact thought, if not exact words, in clear, readable form. One has to estimate the proper balance of literal and free in this process. Below are a number of translations as they might be placed on a continuum of translation theory.

formal		functional			free
KJV	RSV	NIV	GNB	Phillips	LB
NASB		NAB	JB	CEV	
		NRSV	NEB		

Beginning students in seeking to be faithful to God's Word can be too hung up on word for word mechanical translation, as if in so doing they have preserved that Word. However, such a procedure in fact is the opposite of genuine *translation*—the thought becomes even *more* obscure and incomprehensible. They bury the Word!

Translation Procedure

One does not become a translator overnight, nor does knowing the Greek alphabet qualify you as a Bible translator. One has to begin to become familiar with the Greek idiom. This takes years. But you have to start somewhere. Here's how you can do your work and begin the process now. First, *know the goal*. You are taking across meaning from first-century Greek to twentieth-century English such that the English reader will know not only exactly what the author said, but what he meant. Second, *be aware of the problems of languages and develop a methodology that addresses these problems.* Then move through this simple procedure outlined below.

A. Know the source language.
1. Start with the dictionary, but do not stop there.
2. Set out the basic grammatical elements: subject, verb, object.
3. Clarify unusual constructions that do not make sense with the dictionary alone. These are probably idioms that must be researched and understood. Consult lexicons, dictionaries, commentaries, Bible handbooks and other resources that put the first-century history, culture, and thought before you. Facility with Biblical backgrounds accumulates over time, and you must work at it all the time.
4. Be aware of the context before and after. Understand how this verse moves out of the previous verse and into the subsequent verse, the logic, the structure. Know your author. Know the literary setting.
5. Allow for rhetorical expressions and other literary techniques that affect word usage.

B. Know the receptor language.
1. Equip yourself with knowledge of English structures that correspond with the Greek structures you encounter.
2. Lay out a tentative translation based on dictionary analysis where the meaning remains clear by doing so.
3. Seek to establish the dynamic equivalent in English of Greek idioms.
4. Reread the entire sentence to see if it makes sense. If something does not "sound right," it probably is not. An idiom has not been dealt with properly, or some other weakness in understanding the Greek probably needs to be strengthened and clarified. Perhaps the verb tense was located incorrectly. Perhaps a noun was confused with a similarly looking adjective, and so forth.
5. Finish your translation, smoothing out form and striving for clear, readable English. Remove the wooden stilts of your literal beginning without introducing your own concepts or some other alien thought. Find your own sense of balance. Develop the art of translation.

Finally, you probably should read an article written years ago by J. B. Phillips, entitled, "The Problems of Making A Contemporary Translation."[1] Phillips pointed out the problems of translation as he reacted to the then recent publication of the *New English Bible*. While his comments were penned years ago, his insights are timeless and worth your time.

---

[1]This article first appeared in *The Churchman*, June 1961, but was reprinted in *The Bible Translator*, Vol. 16 (Jan. 1965): 25–32.

GLOSSARY

Ablaut—any pattern of vowel changes representing grammatical processes.

Accidence—study focusing on word inflections, sometimes used synonymously with morphology.

Accusative of General Reference—a substantive in accusative case grammatically related to an infinitive; specifies that which produces the infinitive action, and, so, functions like a "subject."

Active Voice—the subject of the verb performs the verbal action. ("I hit.")

Adverbial Prepositions—old adverbs with dual nature; still acting as adverbs, they also had prepositional function, i. e., were used mainly with noun structures; can be found by themselves (modifying a verb). Cf. *Proper Preposition*.

Adverbials—with numbers, those numbering terms used as adverbs, such as "once," "twice," and diagrammed under the verb.

Adverbial Use—with infinitives and participles, that use in which the verbal heritage is dominant and the grammatical function is to modify or make an additional assertion related to the main verb.

Adversative—coordinating conjunctions showing contrast, antithesis, or opposition.

Alpha Privative—the letter alpha prefixed to a word to negate the meaning, similar to the Latin prefix "un-," as in "unlike" (νόμος = "law"; ἄνομος = "lawless"). Cf. *Workbook*, Lesson 6, note 9.

Alpha Pure ("α pure")—first declension stem with α throughout the singular.

Anarthrous—construction without the definite article.

Antecedent—the word, phrase, or clause to which a pronoun refers.

Antepenult—the third syllable from the end of a Greek word.

Apodosis—the "then" clause of a conditional sentence that specifies the results of the condition; functions and diagrams as an independent clause.

Apposition—placement side by side or in close proximity of two grammatical elements with equal syntactical relation to other parts of the sentence; acts as explanatory material. Cf. *Epexegetic*.

Ascriptive Attributive—an articular adjective in simple attributive position, i.e., normally situated before the anarthrous noun modified.

Aspect—alternate term for kind of action in the equation of meaning of Greek verbs.

Aspiration—the degree of air allowed to flow around the tongue when using the mouth cavity for pronunciation, creating a rough sound; with stops, the consonants φ, χ, and θ are aspirated.

Attic Future—a dental delta tense stem that forms the future with the suffix -σε, forcing the dental consonant to drop; the sigma becomes intervocalic and drops; the remaining vowels contract.

Attic Reduplication—a perfect reduplication pattern that doubles the opening syllable and simultaneously lengthens the internal vowel (ἀκούω to the second perfect form ἀκήκοα).

Attributive Position—the adjective attributes a quality to the noun, which limits the noun's meaning.

Augmentation—adding a vowel prefix to tense stems beginning with a consonant or lengthening the opening vowel of a tense stem to indicate past time.

Base Line—in diagramming, the basic horizontal line upon which any verbal is placed, including subordinate, relative, infinitive, and participial clauses.

Byzantine—Constantinople, capital of the Eastern Roman Empire—later renamed Byzantium—fell to the Turks in A.D. 1453. Greek manuscripts produced in the scriptoriums there, today called Byzantine, went with Christians fleeing West, affecting the transmission of the New Testament.

393

Cardinal Numerals—the counting numbers ("one," "two," "three").

Closed Vowels—the mouth is relatively closed as they are pronounced. Cf. *Open Vowels*.

Coalescence—two of the same letters merge into one in word formation (e. g., $\sigma + \sigma = \sigma$).

Cognates—all words related to the same root, whether noun, adjective, or verb.

Colwell's Rule—clarifies which of two nominatives is subject and which is predicate.

Compensatory Lengthening—compensating for the loss of letters by lengthening a remaining vowel.

Complex Sentence—an independent clause with at least one dependent clause; subordinating conjunctions indicate complex sentences.

Complex Sibilant—the "s" sounding consonants ψ, ξ, and ζ.

Compound Predicate—two verbal structures joined by a conjunction.

Compound Sentence—two or more independent clauses joined by conjunctions.

Compound Subject—two subjects joined by a conjunction.

Compound Verb—verb modified by adding a prepositional prefix.

Conjugation—variously used to refer to: (1) an entire group of verbs with similar inflected forms, or (2) a presentation of all inflected forms of a verb, or (3) the individual pattern of inflection for a given tense stem in a given tense, voice, and mood.

Conjunctions—function words that join words, phrases, clauses, and sentences.

Consonant Declension—the third declension, as all stems end either in consonants or ι and υ acting as semivowels (*consonantal iota* with "y" sound, *consonantal upsilon* with "w" sound).

Consonantal Iota—when the vowel iota functions as a semivowel, that is, as a consonant with "y" sound; affects pronunciation and word formation.

Consonantal Upsilon—when the vowel upsilon functions as a semivowel, that is, as a consonant with "w" sound; affects pronunciation and word formation.

Contract Verbs—verbs whose stems end in one of the three vowels ε, o, or α, which contract with pronominal suffix vowels in the first principal part, or lengthen in other principal parts.

Contraction—the reaction of certain vowels in word formation resulting in a long vowel or diphthong; contract verbs are a special category in verb formation.

Coordinate Clause—a clause with parallel grammatical status to a related clause, joined by a coordinate conjunction.

Coordinate Conjunction—connects two identically constructed grammatical elements.

Copulative—expresses equality or similarity of words or clauses; one function of εἰμί; cf. *Equative*.

Deaspiration—altering a rough stop (ϕ, χ, θ) to its corresponding smooth stop (π, κ, τ) for pronunciation purposes (e. g., the imperative ending -θηθι to -θητι).

Declension—a word group involving nouns, pronouns and adjectives with a similar inflection pattern; Greek has three basic patterns: first, second, and third declensions.

Degrees—relates to making comparisons in three modes: positive, comparative, and superlative ("new," "newer," "newest").

Denotation—the explicit dictionary meaning of a word or grammatical element.

Dependent Clause—See *Subordinate Clause*.

Deponent Future—a verb having present active forms, but a deponent future tense.

Deponent—a verb whose form occurs only as middle or passive, but is not translated with middle or passive voice; rather, the deponent, though middle in form, always translates with active voice.

Digamma—an archaic letter of the Greek alphabet, written as Ϝ, pronounced similarly to the English "w." Irregularities of word formation seem to be traceable to the sounding of this vowel.

Direct Discourse—direct quotation.

Direct Middle—the verb's subject directly reflects the verbal action back onto itself.

Disyllabic—a word having just two syllables.

Divine Passive—the reader is to presume the agent of the passive voice is God.

Double Accusative—a verb having two accusative direct objects; also called "object complement."

Edited Text—used to refer to the *Greek New Testament*. We have no original manuscripts, and no two copies agree exactly. What to print as the Greek text must be decided at every point of significant variation by a team of editors using the scientific principles of textual criticism.

Elision—dropping of a vowel before another vowel or diphthong.

Ellipsis—omission of words obviously understood, but grammatically necessary.

Enclitic—a word that loses its accent, leaning on the previous word for accent.

Epexegetic—additional explanatory material.

Equative—possessing equal status or function, as εἰμί can act as an equative verb; cf. *Copulative*.

Erasmus—Renaissance scholar credited with standardizing the pronunciation of koine Greek using Latin; also produced the first published Greek New Testament, coming off the new Gutenberg printing press in 1516. Erasmus's text was the basis for other published Greek New Testaments, including the Beza text used by the King James translators for the 1611 Authorized Version.

Eta Pure ("η pure")—first declension stem with η throughout the singular.

First Class—conditional sentence category; condition is assumed true; the mood used is indicative.

Fourth Class—conditional sentence category; condition is assumed undetermined, but remote; the mood used is optative.

Genitive Absolute—a participle in the genitive case with no syntactical relationship to the rest of the sentence; an abrupt change of subject from participle to main verb is typical; the participle adds information, but is independent of the main verb and its subject; a genitive noun is treated as "subject" of the participle.

Gradation—changes which vowels undergo in the process of word formation.

Idiom—meaning which transcends the denotation of individual grammatical elements, the linguistic expressions of a given language that lie closest to the heart of a particular culture and time.

Improper Diphthongs—vowels containing iota subscript; the iota might seem to create a diphthong sound, but does not, because the iota actually is not pronounced.

Independent Clause—a verb and its related subject.

Indirect Discourse—indirect quotation; grammatically functions as direct object of the main verb.

Indirect Middle—the verb's subject acts with self-interest in the action.

Infinite—verbal forms not limited by a subject, such as infinitives and participles.

Inflection—patterns of changes in word endings that indicate word relationships.

Interjection—a part of speech composed of exclamatory words that can stand alone in the sentence.

Intervocalic Sigma—a sigma between two vowels; the construction can volatilize, the sigma dropping, the remaining two vowels contracting.

Intransitive Verb—does not require a direct object for completion. ("He ran.")

Kappa Aorist—are -μι verbs that substitute a -κα pattern for the aorist suffix (δίδωμι, τίθημι, ἵημι).

Lectionary—Christian worship developed a system of readings (called "lections") from the Gospels and Epistles, apparently following the pattern of synagogue worship, which used readings from the Law and the Prophets each Sabbath. The Christian readings were coordinated with Sundays and the Christian calendar. A book containing these Scripture lections is called a lectionary. Lectionary study contributes to a knowledge of the history of the New Testament text.

Lengthening—changing a short vowel to a corresponding long vowel or diphthong.

Lexical Form—the form of the initial entry of a word in a Greek dictionary; for verbs, the present active indicative, first person singular form; for nouns, the nominative singular form.

Liquid Aorist—a liquid verb that forms the aorist active indicative by dropping the sigma of the -σα aorist suffix before the liquid consonant that ends the tense stem; only the alpha of the suffix remains; a further reaction can be the occasional compensatory lengthening of a stem vowel.

Liquid Future—a liquid verb that forms the future active indicative with the suffix -εσ, creating an intervocalic sigma that drops, resulting in contraction of the remaining vowels.

Liquid Verb—a verb whose tense stem ends in a liquid consonant.

Liquid—a continuant consonant (sounding as long as air is allowed to flow) pronounced with a breathing pattern through the mouth cavity, but no interruption of air flow, as with stops; generates a class of reactions in word formation; typically includes nasals.

Location—specifying an individual word's component grammatical parts.

Main Verb—a finite verb, usually; a descriptive term in connection with adverbial participles, whose relationship usually is to a finite verb nearby.

Majuscule—close in meaning to the term uncial (a handwriting style using large letters, similar to our capital letters, all run together) but really refers just to capital letters themselves.

Middle Deponent—a verb that occurs in the third principal part (aorist) in middle forms only, but has active translation.

Middle Voice—the subject reflects the verbal action upon itself. ("I hit myself.")

Minuscule—a reform in handwriting beginning about the ninth century using small case letters in a cursive (connected together) style.

Monosyllabic—a word having just one syllable.

Morphology—study of phonology (pronunciation, phonetic change, and accent) and word formation (inflection, derivation, and compounds); the form of a word. Cf. *Accidence*.

Moveable ν—addition of the letter ν to a pronominal suffix to smooth pronunciation for the following word beginning with a vowel, or when the verb comes at the end of a clause or sentence.

Nasal—a continuant consonant (sounding as long as air is allowed to flow) produced with a breathing pattern through the nose, but creating no friction (noise), in contrast to liquids, sibilants, and stops; generates a class of reactions in word formation.

Nominative Absolute—a nominative with no inherent grammatical relationship to the sentence.

Non-thematic Second Aorists—a small class of verbs, including -ω verbs ἀναβαινω and γινώσκω and the -μι verb ἵστημι, that do not use a thematic vowel in the second aorist active indicative.

Non-thematic—joining the pronominal suffix directly to the tense stem without a thematic vowel.

Oblique—all other cases besides the nominative; sometimes called "objective" cases, as they function as objects of prepositions or direct/indirect objects of verbs, whereas the nominative does not.

Open Vowels—the mouth is relatively open as the vowels are pronounced. The degree of openness often is illustrated in the "vowel pyramid," but any graphic is an attempt to schematize the position of tongue and jaw. Positions of the tongue up and down are noted as high, medium, and low. Positions of the tongue front to back are known as

high	ι		υ
medium	η		ω
low	ε	α	ο
	front	center	back

front, central, and back. The seven vowel pronunciations combine these two tongue positions: three vowels are low (front = ε, central = α, and back = ο), two vowels are medium (front = η and back = ω), and two vowels are high (front = ι and back = υ). Of these, alpha is the most open when pronounced, iota and upsilon the least open (cf. *Closed Vowels*).

Ordinal Numerals—ordering numbers indicating sequence ("first," "second"); used as adjectives.

Ὅτι Recitative—used to refer to the occurrence of ὅτι understood to be introducing a direct quote; the ὅτι is left untranslated.

Oxytone—any noun having an acute accent in the ultima of the lexical form.

Paradigm—a pattern used to illustrate all other words in that class or category.

Passive Voice—the subject of the verb receives the verbal action. ("I was hit.")

Penult—the second syllable from the end of a Greek word.

Perfect—in Greek, a tense expressing on-going *present* consequences.

Periphrasis—a construction using two verbal forms, a participle and a linking verb, when one finite verb would have sufficed; "phrasing around," a roundabout way of saying something; represents typical koine tendency toward overemphasis.

Persistent Accent—in noun declensions, the tendency of the accent to remain in the syllable of the lexical form, in as much as rules allow.

Pluperfect—in English, the tense expressing past action completed prior to a specified time, formed with a past participle and auxiliary verbs: "had written"; in Greek, on-going *past* consequences.

Polysyllabic—a word having three or more syllables.

Postpositives—words that never occur first in a clause.

Potentiality—the potential reality of a statement, with degrees of contingency.

Predicate Adjective—an adjective in predicate position (anarthrous construction).

Predicate Nominative—a nominative noun in predicate position (anarthrous).

Predicative Position—an anarthrous adjective used to make an assertion about a related noun, which requires a form of "to be," whether implicit or explicit.

Preterit—the simple past tense in English: "wrote."

Primary Position—the head of a sentence or clause; also called "positive position."

Proclitics—a word having no accent of its own that leans to the following word.

Pronominal Suffixes—endings attached to tense stems that give person and number of the subject.

Proper Prepositions—former adverbs now composed exclusively with nouns; never by themselves; always part of a prepositional phrase. Cf. *Adverbial Preposition*.

Protasis—the "if" clause of a conditional sentence that puts forth the condition; functions and diagrams as a dependent clause.

Recessive Accent—in verb conjugations, the tendency of the accent to move as far away from the ultima as rules allow.

Reciprocal Middle—the subject participates in the middle action as part of a group.

Reduplication—creation of a tense stem prefix by repeating an opening consonant and inserting a vowel, or by augmenting an opening vowel.

Relative Clause—a subordinate (dependent) clause introduced by a relative pronoun.

Restrictive Attributive—an articular adjective positioned after an articular noun to add emphatic force (ὁ ποιμὴν ὁ καλός = "the *good* shepherd," John 10:11). Cf. *Ascriptive Attributive*.

Scripto Continua—style of writing in ancient manuscripts of the New Testament; all letters are formed as uncials, with no word divisions and no punctuation.

Second Aorist—an alternate form of the aorist tense stem that does not affect meaning; also called "strong" aorist (The form probably is older than first aorist, having survived the developmental tendency to alter aorist stems with a tense suffix, which generated a "weak" or "first" aorist.)

Second Class—conditional sentence category; condition is assumed false; mood used is indicative.

Second Passive—an alternate passive form that drops the theta of the passive suffix.

Second Perfect—an alternate perfect active form that drops the kappa of the perfect active tense suffix; also called "strong" perfect.

Second Pluperfect—an alternate pluperfect active form that drops the kappa of the pluperfect active tense suffix; also called "strong" pluperfect.

Sharp's Rule—actually six rules, together clarifying the significance of personal nouns joined by καί, grammatical observations—under specific parameters—that reveal whether these nouns are thought of as distinct entities or as the same person or aspect. As formulated by Granville Sharp in 1798, the nouns must be: (1) of personal description and (2) of the same case. I have taken liberty to condense Sharp's rules into the following format ("A" = article, "N" = noun, "Same" = applying to the same person or aspect, "Distinct" = applying to distinct persons or aspects):

SAME:
1. $[A_1 N_1]$ **καί** N_2
2. $[A_1 N_1] [A_2 N_2]$ (exception: a string of dependent genitives)
3. $[A_1 N_1] N_2$

DISTINCT:
4. When the nouns do not relate to personal description
5. N_1 **καί** N_2 (exception: construction involving the numeral εἷς)
6. $[A_1 N_1]$ **καί** $[A_2 N_2]$

Once studied, these six rules can be reduced even further: (1) any construction with καί absent relates to the same person or aspect (#2–3); (2) any *symmetrical* construction with καί—*all* nouns articular or *all* nouns anarthrous—relates to the distinct persons or aspects (#5–6); and (3) only one construction with καί relates to the same person, and this construction is asymmetrical; only the first noun has the article (#1). Rule #1 traditionally is the preeminent one for exegesis.

Sigma Volatilization—a pattern of interaction between the sibilant σ and the stop consonants.

Simple Sentence—an independent clause by itself.

Spurious Diphthong—when ει results from combinations other than ε + ι, and ου results from combinations other than ο + υ, or compensatory lengthening has taken place.

Stop—a consonant pronounced with a breathing pattern through the mouth cavity, creating air friction, hence a noise, as with liquids, but further complicated by the use of the tongue to stop the air flow momentarily, both at various points and with varying degrees of release.

Two major questions about stop sounds are *where* and *how*. First, answering the question *where* provides two sets of terms: (1) those related to the **physiology of production**, the use of the vocal chords ("voiced/voiceless"), and (2) those related to the **place of obstruction**, controlling the air flow ("stops"). The stop consonants created with the vocal chords ("voiced") are β, γ, δ. The stop consonants created without the vocal chords ("voiceless") are both sets of π, κ, τ and φ, χ, θ. Further, these stops subdivide into three stop *classes* of where air flow is obstructed: (1) at the <u>throat</u> ("palatal/guttural"), (2) behind the <u>teeth</u> ("dental/lingual"), or (3) with the <u>lips</u> ("labial").

Second, answering the question *how* provides a third set of terms related to stop consonant sounding. The direction and degree of air flow can be controlled. This dimension relates to how noisy the sound is. Noise is created by the friction of moving air. The air can be moved through two main passage ways, the nose or the

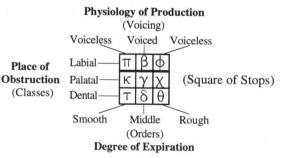

mouth. Air forced through the nasal cavity escapes without friction (***nasals*** μ and ν). Air forced through the mouth cavity escapes with only slight friction, hence a little noise (***liquids*** λ and ρ, and σ). However, air moved through the mouth cavity also can add further sophistication to sound production through the manipulation of tongue or lips. Air can be manipulated both through specific placement (labial, palatal, dental) and through degree of air allowed to flow in that placement. How the obstruction of the air is removed creates **degrees of expiration** of the air—the three stop *orders*. The flow may be released: (1) completely, with less noise, by smoothly and sharply releasing the blocked air ("sharp/smooth")—π, κ, τ, (2) somewhat, with some noise, by more openly releasing the blocked air ("flat/middle")—β, γ, δ, or (3) barely, with greater noise, by fully aspirating the sound with an open release ("aspirate/rough")—φ, χ, θ. The crux of the matter relates to the voiceless stops—the smooth (sharp) π, κ, τ, and the rough (aspirate) φ, χ, θ—on either side of the voiced. Note how these often interrelate in Greek.

      Finally, a *continuant* is a consonant whose sound quality does not change as long as air is allowed to flow (voiced = μ, ν, λ; voiceless = σ, φ, χ, θ). A *fricative* is a consonant forced through a constricted passage. Technically, the aspirates φ, χ, θ are not stops, but fricative continuants. The rough breathing is a fricative continuant, which explains some volatilizations.

Subordinate Clause—a clause that cannot stand by itself as a sentence, and grammatically acts as a noun, adjective, or adverb. Also called a dependent clause.

Subordinate Conjunction—conjunction that introduces a dependent clause; quite common is ὅτι.

Substantive—any word functioning as a noun or noun equivalent.

Syllabic Augment—augmentation of a tense stem that begins with a consonant by adding a vowel, thereby adding another syllable to the word.

Syncopation—suppressing a short vowel between two single consonants for pronunciation; "weak syncopation" means the suppression occurs in only three forms (genitive and dative singular, dative plural); "strong syncopation" means the suppression occurs in *all* forms except for the nominative singular.

Syntax—word arrangements in a given context that carry meaning across through particular use in a sentence—in contrast to morphology (or, accidence), which studies word formation by noting inflection and other rudimentary elements of grammar.

Temporal Augment—augmentation of a tense stem beginning with a vowel by lengthening that vowel, theoretically thereby adding time to the pronunciation.

Textual Criticism—the study of differing copies of manuscripts to determine the most likely original reading, but also, in New Testament textual criticism, to write a history of those manuscripts.

Third Class—conditional sentence category; condition is assumed undetermined, but possible; mood used is subjunctive.

Transitive Verb—verbal action that takes a direct object inherently by nature. ("She wrote a book.")

Two Termination—adjectives with just two inflections for the three genders.

Ultima—the last syllable on the end of a Greek word.

Uncial—a handwriting style using all large letters, similar to our capital letters.

Volatilization—a descriptive term applied to the patterned reactions in word formation surrounding particular letter combinations; the most common are those involving sigma, stops, theta, elision, and contraction.

ANNOTATED BIBLIOGRAPHY[1]

Texts and Textual Criticism

Aland, Kurt, and Barbara Aland. *The Text of the New Testament.* Rev. ed. Grand Rapids: Wm. B. Eerdmans Publishing Co., 1989. Contains a large amount of technical language and assumes a rather substantial amount of knowledge on the part of the reader. While not as usable as an introductory text as Metzger's, this volume provides an excellent overview of the manuscript witnesses to the New Testament text. The analysis of the history of the transmission of the text is concise and insightful, while the review of the history of modern textual criticism leans toward European continental contributions, thereby downplaying the British and North American contributions.

Fee, Gordon D. "The Textual Criticism of the New Testament." In *Biblical Criticism: Historical, Literary, and Textual* by R. K. Harrison *et al.* Grand Rapids: Zondervan Publishing House, 1978, pp. 127-55. A concise summary.

Greenlee, Harold. *Introduction to New Testament Textual Criticism, Revised Edition.* Grand Rapids: Zondervan Publishing House, 1993. A good introduction.

The Greek New Testament, Fourth Edition. Kurt Aland, *et al.* eds., in cooperation with the Institute for New Testament Textual Research, Münster/Westphalia. New York: United Bible Societies, 1966, 1968, 1975, 1983, 1993. The standard Greek text in use in schools and colleges around the world, based upon modern principles of textual criticism.

Kenyon, Frederic G. *The Text of the Greek Bible.* 3d ed., rev. by A. W. Adams. London: Gerald Duckworth & Co., 1975.

Metzger, Bruce M. *Manuscripts of the Greek Bible: An Introduction to Paleography.* New York/Oxford: Oxford University Press, 1981; corrected edition 1991. A study of the process of hand copying of manuscripts, including habits of the scribes and the difficult conditions under which they worked. This volume will enlighten the student on the reasons behind variant readings. [GLS]

_____. *The Text of the New Testament: Its Transmission, Corruption, and Restoration.* 3d ed. New York/Oxford: Oxford University Press, 1992. An established standard text in the field, Metzger's work is the best introductory text available at present. The content is comprehensive, the style is readable, and the organization is logical. Unfortunately, the revision for the third edition was comprised solely in the addition of an appendix noting more recent developments. Had the appendix been woven into the text, the result would have been more useful. Highly recommended for studying textual criticism.

---

[1] This section has been included at the recommendation of my colleague, William F. Warren, Jr., Th.D., who contributed most of the annotations. The last stage in beginning Greek is to learn about the resources available for study. We usually devote some lecture time toward the end of the grammar course for reviewing in more detail the type of material mentioned in these annotations.

_____. *A Textual Commentary on the Greek New Testament.* United Bible Societies, 1971. Brief but very helpful discussions of the issues of significant textual variants in the Greek New Testament based upon the work of the committee of scholars responsible for the UBS text.

Novum Testamentum Graece. 27th ed. Kurt Aland *et al.* eds. Stuttgart: Deutsche Bibelstiftung, 1898, 1993. Essentially the same text as the UBS text, but the textual apparatus is much more detailed in places.

Vaganay, Léon. *An Introduction to New Testament Textual Criticism.* Second edition, revised and updated by Christian-Bernard Amphoux. Translated by Jenny Heimerdinger. English edition amplified and updated by Christian-Bernard Amphoux and Jenny Heimerdinger. Cambridge, New York, Port Chester, Melbourne, Sydney: Cambridge University Press, 1991. An update of an older 1934 work by Vaganay filling a useful niche: the non-technical, general introduction that assumes no prior knowledge on the reader's part. The rejection of the *textus receptus* (the "received text" tradition) is rather strong, the Western text rather highly evaluated, and the emphasis is more on text history than the original text—but still a useful work. [GLS]

Lexical Aids

Abbott-Smith, G. *A Manual Greek Lexicon of the New Testament.* 3d ed. Edinburgh: T. & T. Clark, 1937.

Alsop, John R. *An Index to the Bauer-Arndt-Gingrich Greek Lexicon.* Grand Rapids: Zondervan Publishing House, 1968.

Bauer, Walter, William F. Arndt, F. Wilbur Gingrich, and Frederick W. Danker. *A Greek-English Lexicon of the New Testament and Other Early Christian Literature.* Chicago/London: University of Chicago Press, 1979. This lexicon is the standard in the field of New Testament Greek studies. Words are discussed based upon usage through history with citations pointing to primary sources for further study. The historical research within this volume makes it not only a lexicon but also a beginning historical dictionary on New Testament Greek.

Carson, D. A. *Greek Accents: A Student's Manual.* Grand Rapids: Baker Book House, 1985. A concise summary of the rules guiding Greek accents. [GLS]

Clapp, Philip S., Barbara and Timothy Friberg. *Analytical Concordance of the Greek New Testament; Volume 1: Analytical Focus, Volume 2: Grammatical Focus.* Baker's Greek New Testament Library, Edited by Barbara Friberg and Timothy Friberg. Grand Rapids: Baker Book House, 1991. The University of Minnesota morphologically tagged Greek New Testament is used to provide grammatical forms broken down into seven analytical divisions, then subdivided alphabetically by the grammatical tags, preceding word, and canonical order. Exhaustive work, but the tag system takes time to learn. [GLS]

Kubo, Sakae. *A Reader's Greek-English Lexicon of the New Testament and A Beginner's Guide for the Translation of New Testament Greek.* Andrews University Monographs, Volume IV. Grand Rapids: Zondervan Publishing House, Regency Reference Library 1971, 1975. Kubo's work is organized following the text of the New Testament: book by book, verse by verse. He provides enough vocabulary so that most students will be able to translate virtually all of the New Testament with only the aid of this book. What he does not do is show the nuances of words for study purposes.

Liddell, H. G. and R. Scott. *A Greek-English Lexicon: A New Edition Revised and Augmented Throughout with Supplement.* 9th ed. London: Oxford University Press, 1925–1940; Supplement, 1968.

Louw, Johannes P., Eugene A. Nida, Rondal B. Smith, Karen A. Munson, eds. *Greek-English Lexicon of the New Testament Based on Semantic Domains, Second Edition.* 2 Vols. New York: United Bible Societies, 1988.1989. Whereas the Bauer-Arndt-Gingrich work supplies a diachronic (through history) study of Greek words, Louw and Nida offer a synchronic approach, ranges of meaning within a given time period. This two volume set is unique and extremely valuable because it delineates the differences and similarities among words with like meaning and range of usage. The words are located under topics that serve to group the vocabulary according to areas of life and thought, then the meanings of the words within the New Testament time period are given.

Metzger, Bruce M. *Lexical Aids for Students of New Testament Greek.* New Edition. Princeton, NJ: Theological Book Agency, distributors, 1974. This work can serve as an excellent guide for learning the vocabulary of the Greek New Testament as well as reviewing some aspects of grammar. The vocabulary is arranged in frequency lists that contain words that occur ten times or more in the *Greek New Testament.*

Moulton, Harold K., ed. *The Analytical Greek Lexicon Revised.* Grand Rapids: Zondervan Publishing House, 1978.

Moulton, James H. and G. Milligan. *The Vocabulary of the Greek Testament, Illustrated from the Papyri and Other Non-Literary Sources.* 2d ed. London/Grand Rapids: Hodder and Stoughton/Eerdmans Publishing Company, 1957, 1963.

Mounce, William D. *Analytical Lexicon to the Greek New Testament.* Grand Rapids: Zondervan Publishing House, 1993.

Perscherbacher, Wesley J., ed. *The New Analytical Greek Lexicon.* Peabody, Mass.: Hendrickson Publishers, Inc., 1990.

Rienecker, Fritz. *A Linguistic Key to the Greek Testament.* Edited by Cleon L. Rogers, Jr. Grand Rapids: Zondervan/Regency Reference Library, 1976, 1980. This volume follows the New Testament text, offering locations for many of the verbs and definitions for selected other words. Comments from numerous commentaries have been culled and presented when most pertinent. While not offering as much vocabulary help as Kubo, many students will find this work more than sufficient as an aid to reading the Greek New Testament.

Thayer, Joseph H. *A Greek-English Lexicon of the New Testament: A Dictionary Numerically Coded to Strong's Exhaustive Concordance.* Grand Rapids: Baker Book House, 1977.

Trenchard, Warren C. *The Student's Complete Vocabulary Guide to the Greek New Testament: Complete Frequency Lists, Cognate Groupings & Principal Parts.* Grand Rapids: Zondervan Publishing House, 1992. Trenchard has built upon Metzger's ideas, including vocabulary listings down to the *hapax legomena.* At present this volume seems the better of the two.

Zerwick, Max and Mary Grosvenor. *A Grammatical Analysis of the Greek New Testament.* 2 vols. Rome: Biblical Institute Press, 1974, 1979.

Grammar and Syntax

Beekman, John and John Callow. *Translating the Word of God.* Zondervan Publishing House, 1974.

Belcher, Richard P. *Diagramming the Greek New Testament.* Columbia, SC: Richbarry Press, 1985. Emphasis is upon grammatical elements, offering some syntactical observations. The approach overviews English structure first—very helpful to beginning Greek students. Since very few books on diagramming Greek are available, obtain this one, if still in print. [GLS]

Blass, Friedrich, Albert Debrunner and Robert. W. Funk. *A Greek Grammar of the New Testament and Other Early Christian Literature*. Chicago/London: University of Chicago Press, 1961. While comprehensive, this grammar functions best as a reference grammar due to the scanty explanations and assumption of rather extensive prior knowledge. As a reference volume, it stands near the work of Robertson and that of Moulton, Howard, and Turner.

Brooks, James A. and Carlton L. Winbery. *Syntax of New Testament Greek*. Lanham, MD: University Press of America, 1979. As an introductory work to Greek syntax, this small text is both understandable and well organized. The lack of explanation is at times frustrating, but by and large it is the best introduction available currently.

_____. *Morphology of New Testament Greek: A Review and Reference Grammar*. University Press of America, 1994. While adaptable as an introductory grammar text, this volume is most useful as a reference work or intermediate/advanced grammar text. The logical and comprehensive presentation of the material is especially useful when difficult grammatical constructions are encountered and demand explanation.

Burton, Ernest D. *Syntax of the Moods and Tenses in New Testament Greek*. 3d ed. Edinburgh: T. & T. Clark, 1898.

Dana, H. E. and Julius R. Mantey. *A Manual Grammar of the New Testament*. Toronto: Macmillan Co. 1927, 1955.

Fanning, Bruce M. *Verbal Aspect in New Testament Greek*. Oxford: Clarendon Press, 1990. Is time a component of the Greek verb? Are time considerations inherent to the indicative mood? Yes, Fanning would reply. Agreeing with Porter that verbal aspect is subjective and simply that which is presented by the speaker, not objective reality about the action, Fanning against Porter would insist that the Greek verb form *does* have other semantic weight, including temporal considerations. Fanning has applied the Vendler–Kenny taxonomy of verbs to the New Testament, yielding results somewhat akin to what older Greek grammarians labeled *Aktionsart*. Fanning's study is a serious investigation for the advanced Greek student only. [GLS]

Funk, Robert W. *A Beginning-Intermediate Grammar of Hellenistic Greek*. 3 vols. 2d ed. Missoula: Scholars Press, 1977.

Harris, Murray J. "Appendix: Prepositions and Theology in the Greek New Testament." In *The New International Dictionary of New Testament Theology*. Ed. by Colin Brown. Grand Rapids: Zondervan Publishing House, 1978, 3:1171–1215. A balanced and enlightening discussion in the important area of the exegesis of Greek prepositions.

Hewett, James Allen. *New Testament Greek: A Beginning and Intermediate Grammar*. Peabody, Mass.: Hendrickson Publishers, 1986. The organization yields a good review for brushing up on Greek grammar. [GLS]

Machen, J. G. *New Testament Greek for Beginners*. New York: Macmillan Co., 1944. The standard old grammar, still useful for a concise presentation. [GLS]

McLean, John A. *A Handbook for Grammatical Diagramming Based on Philippians*. Vancouver, WA: The Gramcord Institute, 1993. With Belcher's, one of the few books on diagramming Greek (others are out of print). This is a workbook format, with more heavy emphasis on syntax than Belcher's guide. The Philippians text is used as the basis for analysis. The coverage is full, but the layout is cramped and occasionally confusing; yet, the work is very useful. [GLS]

Moule, C. F. D. *An Idiom-Book of New Testament Greek*. 2d ed. London/New York: Cambridge University Press, 1959. Helpful analysis of features of New Testament Greek not always covered in beginning grammar. [GLS]

Moulton, James H., W. F. Howard, and Nigel Turner. *A Grammar of New Testament Greek.* 4 vols. Edinburgh: T. & T. Clark, 1929-1976. Although somewhat dated, this set offers one of the two best comprehensive studies of koine Greek available. The fourth volume on style by Turner is especially helpful as it delineates the style of each of the New Testament writers. When grammatical questions cannot be answered by consulting the basic grammar works, this work and that by Robertson rarely fail to produce reliable results.

Mounce, William D. *Basics of Biblical Greek.* Grand Rapids: Zondervan Publishing House, Academic and Professional Books, 1993. A non-standard approach; may appeal to some. [GLS]

_____. *The Morphology of Biblical Greek.* Grand Rapids: Zondervan Publishing House, 1993. Intricate referencing system, but generally useful. [GLS]

Porter, Stanley E. *Verbal Aspect in the Greek of the New Testament, with Reference to Tense and Mood.* Studies in Biblical Greek, 1. New York: Peter Lang, 1989. The other side of the Fanning and Porter debate. Using a model based on systemic linguistics, Porter argues that Greek verb forms convey aspect only: the perfective aspect comes through the aorist; the imperfective aspect comes through the present and imperfect; and the stative aspect comes through the perfect and pluperfect. Time is a part of the larger matrix of context, discourse, etc. Fanning is charged with semantic ambiguity, having an analysis too arbitrary to be methodologically helpful. Porter's study is a serious investigation for the advanced Greek student. [GLS]

_____. *Idioms of the Greek New Testament.* Biblical Languages: Greek, 2. Sheffield: JSOT Press, 1992. A more accessible form of Porter's linguistic arguments not so heavily freighted with the linguistic terminology of *Verbal Aspect.* Useful as an intermediate Greek resource with very helpful analyses of prepositions, participles, and so forth. [GLS]

Porter, Stanley E. and D. A. Carson, eds. *Biblical Greek Language and Linguistics: Open Questions in Current Research.* Journal for the Study of the New Testament Supplement Series, 80. Sheffield: JSOT Press, 1993. A short volume providing an introduction to the Fanning/Porter debate. Requires patience with technical terms used in semantics and linguistics. [GLS]

Robertson, Archibald T. *A Grammar of the Greek New Testament in the Light of Historical Research.* 4th ed. Nashville/London: Broadman Press/Hodder and Stoughton, 1923. This is the single most exhaustive grammar available, covering the history of modern research on koine Greek, Greek grammar, and syntax. As a reference grammar, Robertson's work continues to be respected and consulted. One could hardly go wrong in obtaining a copy of this standard.

Smyth, Herbert Weir. *Greek Grammar.* Rev. ed. Cambridge: Harvard University Press, 1963. This is the classic standard Greek grammar and a veritable lodestone of morphological analyses that helps illuminate obscurities in koine Greek even though dealing with classical Greek. [GLS]

Zerwick, Max. *Biblical Greek Illustrated by Examples.* Rome: Biblical Institute Press, 1963.

Concordances

Aland, Kurt. ed. *Vollständige Konkordanz zum griechischen Neuen Testament.* 2 vols. Berlin: Walter de Gruyter, 1975, 1976.

Bachmann, Horst and H. Slaby, eds. *Computer-Concordance of the Greek New Testament According to Nestle-Aland, 26th Edition, and of the Greek New Testament, 3d Edition.* Berlin/New York: Walter de Gruter, 1980. The advantages of this concordance include: it is based upon the UBS/Nestle-Aland text; it is comprehensive in word coverage; it includes a substantial amount of context surrounding text with each entry, thus reducing the need to guess about the context; and it is lemma based in the sense of listing all forms under the lexical form, eliminating the need to look several places for stem-changed forms. Currently this seems to be the best concordance on the market.

Kohlenberger, John R., III. *The Greek-English Concordance of the New Testament.* Grand Rapids: Zondervan Publishing House, 1991.

Moulton, William F. and A. S. Geden. *A Concordance to the Greek Testament According to the Texts of Westcott and Hort, Tischendorf and the English Revisers.* 5th ed. rev. by H. K. Moulton, with a supplement. Edinburgh: T. & T. Clark, 1978. An economical alternative to Bachmann and Slaby, this volume is quite serviceable but suffers because it does not follow the UBS/N-A text.

Schmoller, Alfred. *Handkonkordanz zum griechischen Neuen Testament.* 15th ed. Stuttgart: Württembergesche Bibelanstalt, 1973. This edition is brief, but very useful in pulling together a basic understanding of the use of various Greek words. Good, useful resource for sermon preparation and other study.

Strong, James. *The Exhaustive Concordance of the Bible.* New York/Cincinnati: Hunt Eaton/ Cranston Curts, 1894; regularly reprinted by other publishers. The Greek/Hebrew word numbering system has worked its way into numerous products, including computer software. Some grammatical analyses are not correct; the material should be used with discretion. Mars software programs dependent upon the Strong analysis only. [GLS]

Wigram, George V. *The Englishman's Greek Concordance Numerically Coded to Strong's Exhaustive Concordance.* Grand Rapids: Baker Book House, 1979.

Young, R. *Analytical Concordance to the Bible.* 8th ed. London/New York: Lutterworth Press/Funk and Wagnalls, 1939; regularly reprinted by others.

Wordbooks

Balz, Horst and Gerhard Schneider, eds. *Exegetical Dictionary of the New Testament.* 3 vols. Grand Rapids: Wm. B. Eerdmans Publishing Co., 1990–93.

Brown, Colin, ed. *The New International Dictionary of New Testament Theology.* 3 vols. Grand Rapids/Exeter: Zondervan Publishing House and Paternoster Press, 1975–1978. Built upon an earlier German work, these volumes offer a comprehensive historical study of the words used in the Greek New Testament. For the pastor/teacher, this set is ideal. The words are located according to their most common English meanings, then studied based upon the Greek forms. Classical, Old Testament esp. LXX, and New Testament usages are presented. The fourth volume is an index that aids greatly in locating a specific Greek word that one wishes to study.

Kittel, Gerhard and Gerhard Friedrich, eds. *Theological Dictionary of the New Testament.* 10 vols. Trans. by Geoffrey W. Bromiley. Grand Rapids/London: Wm. B. Eerdmans Publishing Company/SCM Press, 1964–1976; one vol. abridged, 1985. The recognized standard for New Testament word studies, this ten volume set includes a wealth of information from virtually all of the major historical sources, including classical authors, Old Testament usages, other Jewish usages, and New Testament usages. While invaluable for serious research, these volumes can lead one astray due to anachronistic tendencies especially prevalent in the earlier volumes.

Richardson, Alan, ed. *A Theological Word Book of the Bible.* London/New York: SCM Press/Macmillan Company, 1950, 1951.

Robertson, Archibald T. *Word Pictures in the New Testament.* 6 vols. New York/London: Harper & Brothers, 1930–1933.

Semantics and Linguistics

Barr, James. *The Semantics of Biblical Language*. London/New York: Oxford University Press, 1961.

Black, David A. *Linguistics For Students of New Testament Greek: A Survey of Basic Concepts and Applications*. Foreword by Moisés Silva Grand Rapids: Baker Book House, 1988. Black provides an understandable introductory text that will serve the Greek student well for understanding how to utilize Greek studies responsibly.

Caird, G. B. *The Language and Imagery of the Bible*. London/Philadelphia: Gerald Duckworth & Co., Ltd./Westminster Press, 1980.

Cotterell, Peter and Max Turner. *Linguistics and Biblical Interpretation*. Downers Grove, IL: InterVarsity Press, 1989. As with Black, this volume also can serve as an excellent primer for entrance into the field of linguistics as related to research in the Greek New Testament. Some knowledge of the field of linguistics is desirable in order to avoid wrong uses of word studies, translation methodologies, etc.

Louw, Johannes P. *Semantics of New Testament Greek*. Chico/Philadelphia: Scholars Press/Fortress Press, 1982.

Nida, Eugene A. and C. R. Taber. *The Theory and Practice of Translation*. 2d ed. Leiden: E. J. Brill, 1982.

Exegesis and Interpretation

Black, David Allen, ed. *Linguistics and New Testament Interpretation: Essays on Discourse Analysis*. Nashville: Broadman Press, 1992. Translating sentences is not enough for exegesis. Discourse analysis, a branch of linguistics, is overviewed by way of the principles behind this new research, then results are applied to specific New Testament texts. Lacks consistency, as these are individual essays, but demonstrates possibilities for new vistas of interpretation. [GLS]

_____. *Using New Testament Greek in Ministry: A Practical Guide for Students and Pastors*. Grand Rapids: Baker Book House Company, 1993. Black attempts to bridge the gap between the initial foray into Greek in seminary and the decline in use of Greek for sermon and teaching preparation after graduation. A reference library is suggested, principles for building interpretation are given, and a text is used as a model. Good practical insights. [GLS]

Carson, D. A. *New Testament Commentary Survey, Fourth Edition*. Grand Rapids: Baker Book House Company, 1993. Surveys resources for study, but particularly commentaries, providing Carson's evaluation of usefulness and approach. Fifty sets of commentaries and over 700 books renders this guide immensely helpful for New Testament study. As long as the student does not overestimate Carson's own opinions, this little volume can be used with great profit. [GLS]

Countryman, Louis William. *The New Testament in Greek: A Short Course for Exegetes* Grand Rapids: Wm. B. Eerdmans Publishing Co., 1993.

Fee, Gordon D. *How To Read The Bible For All Its Worth*. Grand Rapids: Zondervan, Acadamie Books, 1993. A popular book that presents genre analysis as a part of the approach to exegesis. Well-written and usable. Beginning students find this text very helpful in getting started on the road to interpretation. [GLS]

_____. *New Testament Exegesis: A Handbook for Students and Pastors*. Philadelphia: The Westminster Press, 1983. This work is geared to Greek students and provides a step-by-step guide for exegeting a New Testament passage, including analyzing the Greek text. Some work of this type should be studied so that the student can realize the goal of Greek studies: the use of Greek in order to understand better the Biblical text.

Hayes, John H. and Carl R. Holladay. *Biblical Exegesis: A Beginner's Handbook, Revised Edition.* Atlanta: John Knox Press, 1987. A short, concise explanation of some modern exegetical methodologies, with good bibliographies. [GLS]

Klein, William W., Craig L. Blomberg, and Robert L. Hubbard, Jr. Kermit A. Ecklebarger, consulting ed. *Introduction to Biblical Interpretation.* Dallas: Word Publishing, 1993. A longer text, but worth the reading for putting together the entire hermeneutical process from text to sermon or Bible study. [GLS]

Tate, W. Randolph. *Biblical Interpretation: An Integrated Approach.* Peabody, Mass.: Hendrickson Publishers, 1991. An excellent text that is short yet comprehensive. Terminology may be technical, but all is explained. [GLS]

Paradigms

Nouns

Case Endings

Case endings can be inspected from two perspectives. One perspective is the final ending in its already volatilized form (with a lengthened vowel, etc.). The other perspective is the actual ending prior to any reactions, which requires a number of explanations, since what you see is not what you get. However, the advantage in the second angle is to see how the case endings actually are the same in a number of instances across declensions. While the second perspective is not emphasized in this grammar, the endings are provided here.

Actual Case Endings

		First/Second			Third	
		Mas.	Fem.	Neu.	M/F	Neu.
Sing.	N	-ς	–	-ν	-ς	–
	G	-ο[1]	-ς	-υ	-ος	
	D		-ι[2]		-ι	
	A		-ν		-α, -ν	–
Plu.	N		-ι	-α	-ες	-α
	G		-ων		-ων	
	D		-ις		-σι (ν)	
	A	-νς[3]	-ς	-α	-ας	-α

---

[1]Contraction of this ending with the omicron stem vowel produces -ου.

[2]The stem vowel lengthens; the iota becomes a subscript.

[3]This nu before the sigma drops; the second declension -ο then lengthens to -ους; the first declension -α remains -ας.

409

Resultant Case Endings

Second Declension			
Mas./Fem.[4]		*Neuter*	
Sing.	Plu.	Sing.	Plu.
-ος	-οι	-ον	-α
-ου	-ων	-ου	-ων
-ῳ	-οις	-ῳ	-οις
-ον	-ους	-ον	-α

First Declension						Third Declension[5]					
Singular						*Mas./Fem.*		*Neuter*[6]			
Feminine			Masculine[7]		*Plu.*	Sing.	Plu.	Sing.	Plu.	Sing.	Plu.
-α	-η	-α	-ης	-ας	-αι	-ς, --	-ες	–	-α	-ος	-η
-ας	-ης	-ης	-ου	-ου	-ων	-ος	-ων	-ος	-ων	-ους	-ων
-ᾳ	-η	-η	-η	-ᾳ	-αις	-ι	-σι(ν)	-ι	-σι(ν)	-ει	-σι(ν)
-αν	-ην	-αν	-ην	-αν	-ας	-α, -ν	-ας	–	-α	-ος	-η

The Definite Article

Masculine		*Neuter*		*Feminine*	
ὁ	οἱ	τό	τά	ἡ	αἱ
τοῦ	τῶν	τοῦ	τῶν	τῆς	τῶν
τῷ	τοῖς	τῷ	τοῖς	τῇ	ταῖς
τόν	τούς	τό	τά	τήν	τάς

---

[4]The feminine paradigm is ἡ ὁδός; Table 8.3, *NTG*, 96.

[5]Two forms often volatilize, obscuring the ending: (1) nominative singular, (2) dative plural.

[6]The second set of endings is the odd sibilant form of the neuter -εσ stem with -ος nominative. Table 14.8, *NTG*, 176.

[7]The paradigms are ὁ μαθητής and ὁ μεσσίας, Tables 8.1 and 8.2, *NTG*, 95.

Noun Paradigms

4.11 (2D Mas.)		*4.11 (2D Neu.)*		*4.14 (2D Mas. Oxy.)*		*4.14 (2D Neu. Oxy.)*	
λόγος	λόγοι	δῶρον	δῶρα	υἱός	υἱοί	ἱερόν	ἱερά
λόγου	λόγων	δώρου	δώρων	υἱοῦ	υἱῶν	ἱεροῦ	ἱερῶν
λόγῳ	λόγοις	δώρῳ	δώροις	υἱῷ	υἱοῖς	ἱερῷ	ἱεροῖς
λόγον	λόγους	δῶρον	δῶρα	υἱόν	υἱούς	ἱερόν	ἱερά

8.3 (2D Fem.)		*5.2 (1D "α pure")*		*5.2 (1D Antepenult)*		*5.2 (1D "α pure" Oxy.)*	
ὁδός	ὁδοί	καρδία	καρδίαι	ἀλήθεια	ἀλήθειαι	χαρά	χαραί
ὁδοῦ	ὁδῶν	καρδίας	καρδιῶν	ἀληθείας	ἀληθειῶν	χαρᾶς	χαρῶν
ὁδῷ	ὁδοῖς	καρδίᾳ	καρδίαις	ἀληθείᾳ	ἀληθείαις	χαρᾷ	χαραῖς
ὁδόν	ὁδούς	καρδίαν	καρδίας	ἀλήθειαν	ἀληθείας	χαράν	χαράς

5.3 (1D "η pure")		*5.3 (1D "η pure" Oxy.)*		*5.4 (1D Sibilant)*		*8.1 (1D Mas., -ης nom.)*	
ἀγάπη	ἀγάπαι	γραφή	γραφαί	δόξα	δόξαι	μαθητής	μαθηταί
ἀγάπης	ἀγαπῶν	γραφῆς	γραφῶν	δόξης	δοξῶν	μαθητοῦ	μαθητῶν
ἀγάπῃ	ἀγάπαις	γραφῇ	γραφαῖς	δόξῃ	δόξαις	μαθητῇ	μαθηταῖς
ἀγάπην	ἀγάπας	γραφήν	γραφάς	δόξαν	δόξας	μαθητήν	μαθητάς

8.2 (1D Mas., -ας n.)		*8.4 (1D "α pure" cntr.)*		*8.4 (1D "α pure" cntr.)*		*8.4 (1D "α pure" cntr.)*	
μεσσίας	μεσσίαι	γῆ	-------	συκῆ	-------	μνᾶ	-------
μεσσίου	μεσσιῶν	γῆς	-------	συκῆς	-------	μνᾶς	-------
μεσσίᾳ	μεσσίαις	γῇ	-------	συκῇ	-------	μνᾷ	-------
μεσσίαν	μεσσίας	γῆν	-------	συκῆν	-------	μνᾶν	-------

8.8 (1D Proper Name)		*8.8 (Irreg. Prop. Name)*		*14.4 (3D Labial)*		*14.4 (3D Palatal)*	
Ἰωάννης	-------	Ἰησοῦς	-------	λίψ	λίβες	σάρξ	σάρκες
Ἰωάννου	-------	Ἰησοῦ	-------	λιβός	λίβων	σαρκός	σαρκῶν
Ἰωάννῃ	-------	Ἰησοῦ	-------	λιβί	λίψι(ν)	σαρκί	σαρξί(ν)
Ἰωάννην	-------	Ἰησοῦν	-------	λίβα	λίβας	σάρκα	σάρκας

14.5 (3D Den. -ν acc.)		*14.5 (3D Den. -α acc.)*		*14.6 (3D Dn. -ητος st.)*		*14.6 (3D Den. -ματ st.)*	
χάρις	χάριτες	ἐλπίς	ἐλπίδες	πραΰτης	πραΰτητες	σῶμα	σώματα
χάριτος	χαρίτων	ἐλπίδος	ἐλπίδων	πραΰτητος	πραυτήτων	σώματος	σωμάτων
χάριτι	χάρισι(ν)	ἐλπίδι	ἐλπίσι(ν)	πραΰτητι	πραΰτησιν	σώματι	σώμασιν
χάριν	χάριτας	ἐλπίδα	ἐλπίδας	πραΰτητα	πραΰτητας	σῶμα	σώματα

14.7 (3D Den. -ντ st.)[8]		*14.7 (3D Den. -ντ st.)*		*14.8 (3D Den. -κτ st.)*		*14.8 (3D Sib. -ος nom.)*	
ἄρχων	ἄρχοντες	ὀδούς	ὀδόντες	νύξ	νύκτες	γένος	γένη
ἄρχοντος	ἀρχόντων	ὀδόντος	ὀδόντων	νυκτός	νυκτῶν	γένους	γενῶν
ἄρχοντι	ἄρχουσιν	ὀδόντι	ὀδοῦσιν	νυκτί	νύξι(ν)	γένει	γένεσιν
ἄρχοντα	ἄρχοντας	ὀδόντα	ὀδόντας	νύκτα	νύκτας	γένος	γένη

---

[8] The -ντ stem has two variations, one with no ending in the nominative singular, the other, -ς.

15.1 (3D Liq. long, η)		15.1 (3D Liq. long, ω)		15.2 (3D Liq. η→ε)		15.2 (3D Liq. ω→ο)	
σωτήρ	σωτῆρες	αἰών	αἰῶνες	ἀστήρ	ἀστέρες	εἰκών	εἰκόνες
σωτῆρος	σωτήρων	αἰῶνος	αἰώνων	ἀστέρος	ἀστέρων	εἰκόνος	εἰκόνων
σωτῆρι	σωτῆρσιν	αἰῶνι	αἰῶσιν	ἀστέρι	ἀστέρσιν	εἰκόνι	εἰκόσιν
σωτῆρα	σωτῆρας	αἰῶνα	αἰῶνας	ἀστέρα	ἀστέρας	εἰκόνα	εἰκόνας
15.3 (3D Weak Syn.)		15.3 (3D Strong Syn.)		15.4 (3D Vowel - ι st.)		15.4 (3D Vowel - υ st.)	
πατήρ	πατέρες	ἀνήρ	ἄνδρες	πίστις	πίστεις	ἰχθύς	ἰχθύες
πατρός	πατέρων	ἀνδρός	ἀνδρῶν	πίστεως	πίστεων	ἰχθύος	ἰχθύων
πατρί	πατράσιν	ἀνδρί	ἀνδράσιν	πίστει	πίστεσιν	ἰχθύι	ἰχθύσιν
πατέρα	πατέρας	ἄνδρα	ἄνδρας	πίστιν	πίστεις	ἰχθύν	ἰχθύας
15.5 (3D Dipht. -ευ st.)		15.5 (3D Dipht. -ου st.)					
ἱερεύς	ἱερεῖς	νοῦς	νόες				
ἱερέως	ἱερέων	νοός	νοῶν				
ἱερεῖ	ἱερεῦσιν	νοΐ	νουσίν				
ἱερέα	ἱερεῖς	νοῦν	νόας				

Adjectives

6.1 (2D Mas. Oxy.)		(2D Neu. Oxy.)		(1D "η pure" Oxy.)	
ἀγαθός	ἀγαθοί	ἀγαθόν	ἀγαθά	ἀγαθή	ἀγαθαί
ἀγαθοῦ	ἀγαθῶν	ἀγαθοῦ	ἀγαθῶν	ἀγαθῆς	ἀγαθῶν
ἀγαθῷ	ἀγαθοῖς	ἀγαθῷ	ἀγαθοῖς	ἀγαθῇ	ἀγαθαῖς
ἀγαθόν	ἀγαθούς	ἀγαθόν	ἀγαθά	ἀγαθήν	ἀγαθάς
6.1 (2D Antep. Acute)		(2D Antepenult Acute)		(1D "α pure")	
δίκαιος	δίκαιοι	δίκαιον	δίκαια	δικαία	δίκαιαι
δικαίου	δικαίων	δικαίου	δικαίων	δικαίας	δικαίων
δικαίῳ	δικαίοις	δικαίῳ	δικαίοις	δικαίᾳ	δικαίαις
δίκαιον	δικαίους	δίκαιον	δίκαια	δικαίαν	δικαίας
6.1 (2D Mas. Oxy.)		(2D Neu. Oxy.)		(1D "α pure" Oxy.)	
μικρός	μικροί	μικρόν	μικρά	μικρά	μικραί
μικροῦ	μικρῶν	μικροῦ	μικρῶν	μικρᾶς	μικρῶν
μικρῷ	μικροῖς	μικρῷ	μικροῖς	μικρᾷ	μικραῖς
μικρόν	μικρούς	μικρόν	μικρά	μικράν	μικράς

16.2 (2D Contr., M)		(N)		(F)	
χρυσοῦς	χρυσοῖ	χρυσοῦν	χρυσᾶ	χρυσῆ	χρυσαῖ
χρυσοῦ	χρυσῶν	χρυσοῦς	χρυσῶν	χρυσῆς	χρυσῶν
χρυσῷ	χρυσοῖς	χρυσῷ	χρυσοῖς	χρυσῇ	χρυσαῖς
χρυσοῦν	χρυσοῦς	χρυσοῦν	χρυσᾶ	χρυσήν	χρυσᾶς

16.1 (2D 2-trm., M/F)		(N)	
ἔρημος	ἔρημοι	ἔρημον	ἔρημα
ἐρήμου	ἐρήμων	ἐρήμου	ἐρήμων
ἐρήμῳ	ἐρήμοις	ἐρήμῳ	ἐρήμοις
ἔρημον	ἐρήμους	ἔρημον	ἔρημα

16.3 (3D 2-trm., M/F)[9]		(N)	
ἀληθής	ἀληθεῖς	ἀληθές	ἀληθῆ
ἀληθοῦς	ἀληθῶν	ἀληθοῦς	ἀληθῶν
ἀληθεῖ	ἀληθέσιν	ἀληθεῖ	ἀληθέσιν
ἀληθῆ	ἀληθεῖς	ἀληθές	ἀληθῆ

16.4 (3D Liq., M/F)[10]		(N)	
ἄφρων	ἄφρονες	ἄφρον	ἄφρονα
ἄφρονος	ἀφρόνων	ἄφρονος	ἀφρόνων
αφρονι	ἄφροσιν	αφρονι	ἄφροσιν
ἄφρονα	ἄφρονας	ἄφρον	ἄφρονα

16.5 (Mix1: 3-3-1, M)		(N)		(F)	
ταχύς	ταχεῖς	ταχύ	ταχέα	ταχεῖα	ταχεῖαι
ταχέως	ταχέων	ταχέως	ταχέων	ταχείας	ταχειῶν
ταχεῖ	ταχέσιν	ταχεῖ	ταχέσιν	ταχείᾳ	ταχείαις
ταχύς	ταχεῖς	ταχεῖαν	ταχέα	ταχύν	ταχείας

16.6 (Mix2: 3-3-1, M)		(N)		(F)	
πᾶς	πάντες	πᾶν	πάντα	πᾶσα	πᾶσαι
παντός	πάντων	παντός	πάντων	πάσης	πασῶν
παντί	πᾶσιν	παντί	πᾶσιν	πάσῃ	πάσαις
πάντα	πάντας	πᾶν	πάντα	πᾶσαν	πάσας

16.7 (Mix3: 3-3-1, M)		(N)		(F)	
μέλας	μέλανες	μέλαν	μέλανα	μέλαινα	μέλαιναι
μέλανος	μελάνων	μέλανος	μελάνων	μελαίνης	μελαινῶν
μέλανι	μέλασιν	μέλανι	μέλασιν	μελαίνῃ	μελαίναις
μέλανα	μέλανας	μέλαν	μέλανα	μέλαιναν	μελαίνας

[9]Following the third declension sibilant pattern of γένος, a neuter -ες stem with -ος nominative.
[10]Short vowel stem; long vowel only in masculine/feminine nominative singular (η→ε, ω→ο).

16.8 (Mix4: 3-2-1, M)		(N)		(F)	
μέγας	μεγάλοι	μέγα	μεγάλα	μεγάλη	μεγάλαι
μεγάλου	μεγάλων	μεγάλου	μεγάλων	μεγάλης	μεγάλων
μεγάλῳ	μεγάλοις	μεγάλῳ	μεγάλοις	μεγάλῃ	μεγάλαις
μέγαν	μεγάλους	μέγα	μεγάλα	μεγάλην	μεγάλας
16.9 (Mix5: 3-2-1, M)		(N)		(F)	
πολύς	πολλοί	πολύ	πολλά	πολλή	πολλαί
πολλοῦ	πολλῶν	πολλοῦ	πολλῶν	πολλῆς	πολλῶν
πολλῷ	πολλοῖς	πολλῷ	πολλοῖς	πολλῇ	πολλαῖς
πολύν	πολλούς	πολύ	πολλά	πολλήν	πολλάς

Comparisons

8.5 (Comparative, M)		(N)		(F)	
-τερος	-τεροι	-τερον	-τερα	-τερα	-τεραι
-τερου	-τερων	-τερου	-τερων	-τερας	-τερων
-τερῳ	-τεροις	-τερῳ	-τεροις	-τερᾳ	-τεραις
-τερον	-τερους	-τερον	-τερα	-τεραν	-τερας
8.5 (Superlative, M)		(N)		(F)	
-τατος	-τατοι	-τατον	-τατα	-τατα	-ταται
-τατου	-τατων	-τατου	-τατων	-τατας	-τατων
-τατῳ	-τατοις	-τατῳ	-τατοις	-τατᾳ	-ταταις
-τατον	-τατους	-τατον	-τατα	-ταταν	-τατας
16.10 (Comp., M, F)		(N)			
-ιων	-ιονες	-ιον	-ιονα		
-ιονος	-ιονων	-ιονος	-ιονων		
-ιονι	-ιοσι	-ιονι	-ιοσι		
-ιονα	-ιονας	-ιον	-ιονα		
16.10 (Superla., M)		(N)		(F)	
-ιστος	-ιστοι	-ιστον	-ιστα	-ιστη	-ισται
-ιστου	-ιστων	-ιστου	-ιστων	-ιστης	-ιστων
-ιστῳ	-ιστοις	-ιστῳ	-ιστοις	-ιστῃ	-ισταις
-ιστον	-ιστους	-ιστον	-ιστα	-ιστην	-ιστας

Numerals

Cardinals

17.1 "one" (M)		(N)		(F)	
εἷς	-------	ἕν	-------	μία	-------
ἑνός	-------	ἑνός	-------	μιᾶς	-------
ἑνί	-------	ἑνί	-------	μιᾷ	-------
ἕνα	-------	ἕν	-------	μίαν	-------

17.2 "two" (M/F/N)	
-------	δύο
-------	δύο
-------	δυσί
-------	δύο

17.3 "three" (M/F)		(N)
-------	τρεῖς	-------	τρία
-------	τριῶν	-------	τριῶν
-------	τρισί	-------	τρισί
-------	τρεῖς	-------	τρία

17.4 "four" (M/F)		(N)
-------	τέσσαρες	-------	τέσσαρα
-------	τεσσάρων	-------	τεσσάρων
-------	τέσσαρσι	-------	τέσσαρσι
-------	τέσσαρας	-------	τέσσαρα

17.5 "two hundred" (M)		(N)		(F)	
-------	διακόσιοι	-------	διακόσια	-------	διακόσιαι
-------	διακοσίων	-------	διακοσίων	-------	διακοσίων
-------	διακοσίοις	-------	διακοσίοις	-------	διακοσίαις
-------	διακοσίους	-------	διακόσια	-------	διακοσίας

Ordinals

17.6 "first" (M)		(N)		(F)	
πρῶτος	πρῶτοι	πρῶτον	πρῶτα	πρώτη	πρῶται
πρώτου	πρώτων	πρώτου	πρώτων	πρώτης	πρώτων
πρώτῳ	πρώτοις	πρώτῳ	πρώτοις	πρώτῃ	πρώταις
πρῶτον	πρώτους	πρῶτον	πρῶτα	πρώτην	πρώτας

Pronouns

11.1 "I," "we"

ἐγώ	ἡμεῖς
ἐμοῦ	ἡμῶν
ἐμοί	ἡμῖν
ἐμέ	ἡμᾶς

11.1 "you," "you"

σύ	ὑμεῖς
σοῦ	ὑμῶν
σοί	ὑμῖν
σέ	ὑμᾶς

11.2 "he," "they"   *"it," "they"*   *"she," "they"*

αὐτός	αὐτοί	αὐτό	αὐτά	αὐτή	αὐταί
αὐτοῦ	αὐτῶν	αὐτοῦ	αὐτῶν	αὐτῆς	αὐτῶν
αὐτῷ	αὐτοῖς	αὐτῷ	αὐτοῖς	αὐτῇ	αὐταῖς
αὐτόν	αὐτούς	αὐτό	αὐτά	αὐτήν	αὐτάς

11.3 "my" (M)   *(N)*   *(F)*

ἐμός	ἐμοί	ἐμόν	ἐμά	ἐμή	ἐμαί
ἐμοῦ	ἐμῶν	ἐμοῦ	ἐμῶν	ἐμῆς	ἐμῶν
ἐμῷ	ἐμοῖς	ἐμῷ	ἐμοῖς	ἐμῇ	ἐμαῖς
ἐμόν	ἐμούς	ἐμόν	ἐμά	ἐμήν	ἐμάς

11.4 "our" (M)   *(N)*   *(F)*

ἡμέτερος	ἡμέτεροι	ἡμέτερον	ἡμέτερα	ἡμετέρα	ἡμέτεραι
ἡμετέρου	ἡμετέρων	ἡμετέρου	ἡμετέρων	ἡμετέρας	ἡμετέρων
ἡμετέρῳ	ἡμετέροις	ἡμετέρῳ	ἡμετέροις	ἡμετέρα	ἡμετέραις
ἡμέτερον	ἡμετέρους	ἡμέτερον	ἡμέτερα	ἡμετέραν	ἡμετέρας

11.5 "your" sg. (M)   *(N)*   *(F)*

σός	σοί	σόν	σά	σή	σαί
σοῦ	σῶν	σοῦ	σῶν	σῆς	σῶν
σῷ	σοῖς	σῷ	σοῖς	σῇ	σαῖς
σόν	σούς	σόν	σά	σήν	σάς

11.6 "your" pl. (M)   *(N)*   *(F)*

ὑμέτερος	ὑμέτεροι	ὑμέτερον	ὑμέτερα	ὑμετέρα	ὑμέτεραι
ὑμετέρου	ὑμετέρων	ὑμέτερου	ὑμετέρων	ὑμετέρας	ὑμετέρων
ὑμετέρῳ	ὑμετέροις	ὑμετέρῳ	ὑμετέροις	ὑμετέρα	ὑμετέραις
ὑμέτερον	ὑμετέρους	ὑμέτερον	ὑμέτερα	ὑμετέραν	ὑμετέρας

11.7 *"his," "their"*		*"own" "their"* (N)		*"her," "their"*	
ἴδιος	ἴδιοι	ἴδιον	ἴδια	ἰδία	ἴδιαι
ἰδίου	ἰδίων	ἰδίου	ἰδίων	ἰδίας	ἰδίων
ἰδίῳ	ἰδίοις	ἰδίῳ	ἰδίοις	ἰδίᾳ	ἰδίαις
ἴδιον	ἰδίους	ἴδιον	ἴδια	ἰδίαν	ἰδίας

11.8 *"myself," "-slvs."*		(N)		(F)	
---------	---------	---------	---------	---------	---------
ἐμαυτοῦ	ἑαυτῶν	---------	---------	ἐμαυτῆς	ἑαυτῶν
ἐμαυτῷ	ἑαυτοῖς	---------	---------	ἐμαυτῇ	ἑαυταῖς
ἐμαυτόν	ἑαυτούς	---------	---------	ἐμαυτήν	ἑαυτάς

11.9 *"yourself," "-selves"*				(F)	
---------	---------	---------	---------	---------	---------
σεαυτοῦ	ἑαυτῶν	---------	---------	σεαυτῆς	ἑαυτῶν
σεαυτῷ	ἑαυτοῖς	---------	---------	σεαυτῇ	ἑαυταῖς
σεαυτόν	ἑαυτούς	---------	---------	σεαυτήν	ἑαυτάς

11.10 *"himself," etc.*		*"itself," "themslvs."*		*"herself," "themslvs."*	
---------	---------	---------	---------	---------	---------
ἑαυτοῦ	ἑαυτῶν	ἑαυτοῦ	ἑαυτῶν	ἑαυτῆς	ἑαυτῶν
ἑαυτῷ	ἑαυτοῖς	ἑαυτῷ	ἑαυτοῖς	ἑαυτῇ	ἑαυταῖς
ἑαυτόν	ἑαυτούς	ἑαυτό	ἑαυτά	ἑαυτήν	ἑαυτάς

11.11 *"one another"*					
---------	---------				
---------	ἀλλήλων				
---------	ἀλλήλοις				
---------	ἀλλήλους				

11.12 *"this," "these"*		(N)		(F)	
οὗτος	οὗτοι	τοῦτο	ταῦτα	αὕτη	αὗται
τούτου	τούτων	τούτου	τούτων	ταύτης	ταύτων
τούτῳ	τούτοις	τούτῳ	τούτοις	ταύτῃ	ταύταις
τοῦτον	τούτους	τοῦτο	ταῦτα	ταύτην	ταύτας

11.13 *"that," "those"*		(N)		(F)	
ἐκεῖνος	ἐκεῖνοι	ἐκεῖνο	ἐκεῖνα	ἐκείνη	ἐκεῖναι
ἐκείνου	ἐκείνων	ἐκείνου	ἐκείνων	ἐκείνης	ἐκείνων
ἐκείνῳ	ἐκείνοις	ἐκείνῳ	ἐκείνοις	ἐκείνῃ	ἐκείναις
ἐκεῖνον	ἐκείνους	ἐκεῖνο	ἐκεῖνα	ἐκείνην	ἐκείνας

11.14 "such" (M)		(N)		(F)	
τοιοῦτος	τοιοῦτοι	τοιοῦτο	τοιοαῦτα	τοιαύτη	τοιαῦται
τοιούτου	τοιούτων	τοιούτου	τοιούτων	τοιαύτης	τοιαύτων
τοιούτῳ	τοιούτοις	τοιούτῳ	τοιούτοις	τοιαύτῃ	τοιαύταις
τοιοῦτον	τοιούτους	τοιοῦτο	τοιαῦτα	τοιαύτην	τοιαύτας

11.15 "who," "whom"		(N)		(F)	
ὅς	οἵ	ὅ	ἅ	ἥ	αἵ
οὗ	ὧν	οὗ	ὧν	ἧς	ὧν
ᾧ	οἷς	ᾧ	οἷς	ᾗ	αἷς
ὅν	οὕς	ὅ	ἅ	ἥν	ἅς

11.17 "who?" (M/F)		"what?" (N)	
τίς	τίνες	τί	τίνα
τίνος	τίνων	τίνος	τίνων
τίνι	τίσι(ν)	τίνι	τίσι(ν)
τίνα	τίνας	τί	τίνα

11.18 "someone" (M/F)		"something" (N)	
τις	τινες	τι	τινα
τινος	τινων	τινος	τινων
τινι	τισι(ν)	τινι	τισι(ν)
τινα	τινας	τι	τινα

11.19 "whoever" (M)		"which ones" (N)		"whoever" (F)	
ὅστις	οἵτινες	ὅτι	ἅτινα	ἥτις	αἵτινες
-------	-------	-------	-------	-------	-------
-------	-------	-------	-------	-------	-------
-------	-------	-------	-------	-------	-------

11.20 "no one" (M)		"anything" (N)		"no one" (F)	
οὐδείς	-------	οὐδέν	-------	οὐδεμία	-------
οὐδενός	-------	οὐδενός	-------	οὐδεμιᾶς	-------
οὐδενί	-------	οὐδενί	-------	οὐδεμιᾷ	-------
οὐδένα	-------	οὐδέν	-------	οὐδεμίαν	-------

Omega Verbs

Omega Verb Tense Components—Indicative Mood

Tense	Prefix	Stem	Suffix	Vowel	Ending	Paradigm
Present		Present		ο/ε	Prim. Act.	λύω
M/P		Present		ο/ε	Prim. M/P	λύομαι
Future		Future	σ	ο/ε	Prim. Act.	λύσω
Mid.		Future	σ	ο/ε	Prim. M/P	λύσομαι
Liquid		Future	εσ	ο/ε	Prim. Act.	μενῶ
1st Pas.		Aor. Pas.	θησ	ο/ε	Prim. M/P	λυθησομαι
2nd Pas.		Aor. Pas.	ησ	ο/ε	Prim. M/P	γραφήσομαι
Imperfect	ἐ	Present		ο/ε	Sec. Act.	ἔλυον
M/P	ἐ	Present		ο/ε	Sec. M/P	ἐλύομην
2nd Aorist	ἐ	Aorist		ο/ε	Sec. Act.	ἔλιπον
Mid.	ἐ	Aorist		ο/ε	Sec. Mid.	ἐλίπομην
2nd Pas.	ἐ	Aor. Pas.	η		Sec. Act.	ἐγράφην
1st Aorist	ἐ	Aorist	σα		Sec. Act.	ἔλυσα
Mid.	ἐ	Aorist	σα		Sec. Mid.	ἐλύσαμην
Liquid	ἐ	Aorist	α		Sec. Act.	ἔμεινα
1st Pas.	ἐ	Aor. Pas.	θη		Sec. Act.	ἐλύθην
1st Perfect	λε	Perf. Act.	κα		Sec. Act.	λέλυκα
M/P	λε	Perf. M/P			Prim. M/P	λέλυμαι
(2nd Perf.)	λε	Perf. Act.	α		Sec. Act.	γέγραφα
Fut. Perfect[11]	λε	Perf. Act.	σ	ο/ε	Prim. Act.	λελύσω
1st Pluperf.	ἐλε	Perf. Act.	κει		Sec. Act.	ἐλελύκειν
M/P	ἐλε	Perf. M/P			Sec. M/P	ἐλελύμην
(2nd Pluprf.)	ἐλε	Perf. Act.	ει		Sec. Act.	ἐληλύθειν

---

[11]Except for Heb. 8:11, all forms in the New Testament are periphrastic.

Omega Verb Endings

The primary active indicative endings are set out in their already volatilized form. The primary middle indicative, second singular, -σαι, can volatilize to -η. Likewise, the secondary middle indicative, second singular, -σο, becomes -ου or -ω. The secondary active indicative, third singular has no ending, exposing the thematic vowel and taking a movable -ν (-εν). The secondary active third plural has two options, but most of the time the -ν option is taken. The verb γινώσκω takes the -σαν.

The active subjunctive, built on the primary active indicative, is shown with the thematic vowel in volatilized form. The middle subjunctive endings in composition would show the mood sign of the lengthened thematic vowel (-ωμαι, -η, -ηται, etc.).

The active imperative has three options for the second singular: --, -ς, -θι. Which option a verb will take has to be learned by observation. If the option for no ending is taken (--), the result will simply expose the -ε thematic vowel (e.g., λῦε). The aorist passive suffix, -θη, will opt for the -θι ending; however, -θηθι then "deaspirates" to -θητι (λύθητι). Neither the aorist active nor middle second singular (λῦσον, λῦσαι) can be explained. The middle imperative, second singular, -σο, can volatilize, dropping the sigma and contracting to -ου (e.g., λύου).

The optative uses the thematic vowel -ο throughout the singular and plural, so the forms appear with the diphthong -οι (-οιμι, -οις, -οι, etc.; -οιμην, -οιο, -οιτο, etc.); middle second singular drops the sigma (-οιο); the third plural is -οιεν. Aorist active and middle has a -σαι pattern (-σαιμι, -σαις, -σαι, etc.; -σαιμην, -σαιο, -σαιτο, etc.). Aorist passive uses the unlengthened passive suffix (-θε) with the alternate mood sign -ιη (-θειην, -θειης, -θειη, etc.).

	Active	Mid./Pass.
Indicative—Primary		
	-ω	-μαι
	-εις	-σαι (η)
	-ει	-ται
	-ομεν	-μεθα
	-ετε	-σθε
	-ουσι	-νται
Indicative—Secondary		
	-ν	-μην
	-ς	-σο (-ου, -ω)
	-- (-εν)	-το
	-μεν	-μεθα
	-τε	-σθε
	-ν, -σαν	-ντο
Subjunctive		
	-ω	-μαι
	-ης	-η
	-η	-ται
	-ωμεν	-μεθα
	-ητε	-σθε
	-ωσι	-νται
Imperative		
	----	----
	--, -ς, -θι	-σο (-ου)
	-τω	-σθω
	----	----
	-τε	-σθε
	-τωσαν	-σθωσαν
Optative		
	-ιμι	-ιμην
	-ις	-ιο
	-ι	-ιτο
	-ιμεν	-ιμεθα
	-ιτε	-ισθε
	-ιεν	-ιντο

Omega Verb Conjugation—Present, Imperfect, Second Aorist

PRESENT		IMPERFECT		SECOND AORIST		
Active	*M/P*	*Active*	*M/P*	*Active*	*Middle*	*Passive*[12]
Indicative		**Indicative**		**Indicative**		
λύω	λύομαι	ἔλυον	ἐλυόμην	ἔλιπον	ἐλιπόμην	ἐγράφην
λύεις	λύῃ	ἔλυες	ἐλύου	ἔλιπες	ἐλίπου	ἐγράφης
λύει	λύεται	ἔλυε	ἐλύετο	ἔλιπε	ἐλίπετο	ἐγράφη
λύομεν	λυόμεθα	ἐλύομεν	ἐλυόμεθα	ἐλίπομεν	ἐλιπόμεθα	ἐγράφημεν
λύετε	λύεσθε	ἐλύετε	ἐλύεσθε	ἐλίπετε	ἐλίπεσθε	ἐγράφητε
λύουσι	λύονται	ἔλυον	ἐλύοντο	ἔλιπον	ἐλίποντο	ἐγράφησαν
Subjunctive				**Subjunctive**		
λύω	λύωμαι			λίπω	λίπωμαι	γραφῶ
λύῃς	λύῃ			λίπῃς	λίπῃ	γραφῇς
λύῃ	λύηται			λίπῃ	λίπηται	γραφῇ
λύωμεν	λυώμεθα			λίπωμεν	λιπώμεθα	γραφῶμεν
λύητε	λύησθε			λίπητε	λίπησθε	γραφῆτε
λύωσι	λύωνται			λίπωσι	λίπωνται	γραφῶσι
Imperative				**Imperative**		
-------	-------			-------	-------	-------
λῦε	λύου			λίπε	λιποῦ	γράφηθι
λυέτω	λυέσθω			λιπέτω	λιπέσθω	γραφήτω
-------	-------			-------	-------	-------
λύετε	λύεσθε			λίπετε	λίπεσθε	γράφητε
λυέτωσαν	λυέσθωσαν			λιπέτωσαν	λιπέσθωσαν	γραφήτωσαν
Optative				**Optative**		
λύοιμι	λυοίμην			λίποιμι	λιποίμην	
λύοις	λύοιο			λίποις	λίποιο	
λύοι	λύοιτο			λίποι	λίποιτο	
λύοιμεν	λυοίμεθα			λίποιμεν	λιποίμεθα	
λύοιτε	λύοισθε			λίποιτε	λίποισθε	
λύοιεν	λύοιντο			λίποιεν	λίποιντο	
Infinitive				**Infinitive**		
λύειν	λύεσθαι			λιπεῖν	λιπέσθαι	γραφῆναι
Participle				**Participle**		
λύων[13]	λυόμενος			λιπών	λιπόμενος	γραφείς
λύουσα	λυομένη			λιποῦσα	λιπομένη	γραφεῖσα
λῦον	λυόμενον			λιπόν	λιπόμενον	γραφέν

[12]Second aorist passive is built on the second passive system, dropping the θ of the -θη passive suffix and using secondary *active* forms. *NTG*, 253. A labial -φ stem drops the θ of the passive suffix automatically (a stop reaction), so γράφω is a good second aorist passive paradigm. Compare infinitive and participle forms. Second aorist passive actually is not common in the New Testament.

[13]The pattern is not clear from this nominative form. Most other masculine (and neuter) forms show the participial suffix, -οντ, and third declension endings (cf. λύοντος).

Omega Verb Conjugation—First Aorist, Future[14]

FIRST AORIST			FUTURE			
Active	*Middle*	*Passive*	*Active*	*Middle*	*1st Passive*[15]	*2nd Passive*
Indicative			**Indicative**			
ἔλυσα	ἐλυσάμην	ἐλύθην	λύσω	λύσομαι	λυθήσομαι	γραφήσομαι
ἔλυσας	ἐλύσω	ἐλύθης	λύσεις	λύσῃ	λυθήσῃ	γραφήσῃ
ἔλυσε	ἐλύσατο	ἐλύθη	λύσει	λύσεται	λυθήσεται	γραφήσεται
ἐλύσαμεν	ἐλυσάμεθα	ἐλύθημεν	λύσομεν	λυσόμεθα	λυθησόμεθα	γραφησόμεθα
ἐλύσατε	ἐλύσασθε	ἐλύθητε	λύσετε	λύσεσθε	λυθήσεσθε	γραφήσεσθε
ἔλυσαν	ἐλύσαντο	ἐλύθησαν	λύσουσι	λύσονται	λυθήσονται	γραφήσονται
Subjunctive[16]						
λύσω	λύσωμαι	λυθῶ				
λύσῃς	λύσῃ	λυθῇς				
λύσῃ	λύσηται	λυθῇ				
λύσωμεν	λυσώμεθα	λυθῶμεν				
λύσητε	λύσησθε	λυθῆτε				
λύσωσι	λύσωνται	λυθῶσι				
Imperative						
-------	-------	-------				
λῦσον	λῦσαι	λύθητι				
λυσάτω	λυσάσθω	λυθήτω				
-------	-------	-------				
λύσατε	λύσασθε	λύθητε				
λυσάτωσαν	λυσάσθωσαν	λυθήτωσαν				
Optative						
λύσαιμι	λυσαίμην	λυθείην				
λύσαις	λύσαιο	λυθείης				
λύσαι	λύσαιτο	λυθείη				
λύσαιμεν	λυσαίμεθα	λυθείημεν				
λύσαιτε	λύσαισθε	λυθείητε				
λύσαιεν	λύσαιντο	λυθείησαν				
Infinitive			**Infinitive**			
λῦσαι	λύσασθαι	λυθῆναι	λύσειν	λύσεσθαι	λύσεσθαι	γραφήσεσθαι
Participle			**Participle**			
λύσας	λυσάμενος	λυθείς	λύσων	λυσόμενος	λυθησόμενος	γραφησόμενος
λύσασα	λυσαμένη	λυθεῖσα	λύσουσα	λυσομένη	λυθησομένη	γραφησομένη
λύσαν	λυσάμενον	λυθέν	λύσον	λυσόμενον	λυθησόμενον	γραφησόμενον

[14]Future tense occurs only in the indicative mood and the infinite forms (infinitive, participle).

[15]Built on the first aorist passive, using the -θη suffix. The second future passive drops the θ of the -θη suffix (as does the second aorist passive).

[16]Active and middle use a -σ tense suffix, not -σα. Passive uses -θε, but the ε is swallowed up in contraction.

Omega Verb Conjugation—Perfect and Pluperfect[17]

| | PERFECT | | | PLUPERFECT | |
1st Active	2nd Active[18]	M/P	1st Active	2nd Active	M/P
Indicative	**Indicative**		**Indicative**	**Indicative**	
λέλυκα	γέγραφα	λέλυμαι	ἐλελύκειν	ἐληλύθειν[19]	ἐλελύμην
λέλυκας	γέγραφας	λέλυσαι	ἐλελύκεις	ἐληλύθεις	ἐλέλυσο
λέλυκε	γέγραφε	λέλυται	ἐλελύκει	ἐληλύθει	ἐλέλυτο
λελύκαμεν	γεγράφαμεν	λελύμεθα	ἐλελύκειμεν	ἐληλύθειμεν	ἐλελύμεθα
λελύκατε	γεγράφατε	λέλυσθε	ἐλελύκειτε	ἐληλύθειτε	ἐλέλυσθε
λελύκασι	γεγράφασι	λέλυνται	ἐλελύκεισαν	ἐληλύθεισαν	ἐλέλυντο
Subjunctive[20]					
ὦ λελυκώς		ὦ λελυμένος			
ᾖς λελυκώς		ᾖς λελυμένος			
ᾖ λελυκώς		ᾖ λελυμένος			
ὦμεν λελυκότες		ὦμεν λελυμένοι			
ἦτε λελυκότες		ἦτε λελυμένοι			
ὦσι λελυκοτες		ὦσι λελυμένοι			
Imperative					
-------		-------			
λέλυκε		λέλυσο			
λελυκέτω		λελύσθω			
-------		-------			
λελύκετε		λέλυσθε			
λελυκέτωσαν		λελύσθωσαν			
Infinitive					
λελυκέναι	γεγονέναι[21]	λελύσθαι			
Participle					
λελυκώς	εἰδώς[22]	λελύμενος			
λελυκυῖα	εἰδυῖα	λελυμένη			
λελυκός	εἰδός	λελυμένον			

---

[17]One other tense, future perfect active, would be λελύσω, etc., but only one instance is found (Heb. 8:11; see *NTG*, 265). The middle/passive does occur periphrastically (e.g., ἔσται λελυμένον, Matt. 16:19; see *NTG*, 274). As to mood, no perfect optative forms occur in the New Testament.

[18]The κ of the -κα suffix drops. A second perfect *middle* does not exist, because no -κα tense suffix is used in the fifth principal part. (Endings are attached directly to the stem, with volatilization, as in γέγραμμαι, γέγραψαι, γέγραπται, etc. See *NTG*, 272–3.) The second pluperfect drops the κ of the -κει suffix. Again, a second pluperfect *middle* also does not exist, likewise by default.

[19]From ἔρχομαι.

[20]Rare in the New Testament, half involving the verb οἶδα as εἰδῶ, εἰδῶμεν, εἰδῆς, εἰδῆτε; the rest are periphrastic (*NTG*, 350–51). The imperative also can be periphrastic (*NTG*, 362).

[21]From γίνομαι.

[22]From οἶδα.

Omega Verb Contraction—Present Tense[23]

PRESENT ACTIVE	ε	ο	α	PRESENT MIDDLE/PASSIVE	ε	ο	α
Indicative				**Indicative**			
-ω	-ῶ	-ῶ	-ῶ	-ομαι	-οῦμαι	-οῦμαι	-ῶμαι
-εις	-εῖς	-οῖς	-ᾷς	-η	-ῇ	-οῖ	-ᾷ
-ει	-εῖ	-οῖ	-ᾷ	-εται	-εῖται	-οῦται	-ᾶται
-ομεν	-οῦμεν	-οῦμεν	-ῶμεν	-ομεθα	-ούμεθα	-ούμεθα	-ώμεθα
-ετε	-εῖτε	-οῦτε	-ᾶτε	-εσθε	-εῖσθε	-οῦσθε	-ᾶσθε
-ουσι	-οῦσι	-οῦσι	-ῶσι	-ονται	-οῦνται	-οῦνται	-ῶνται
Subjunctive				**Subjunctive**			
-ω	-ῶ	-ῶ	-ῶ	-ωμαι	-ῶμαι	-ῶμαι	-ῶμαι
-ης	-ῇς	-οῖς	-ᾷς	-η	-ῇ	-οῖ	-ᾷ
-η	-ῇ	-οῖ	-ᾷ	-ηται	-ῆται	-ῶται	-ᾶται
-ωμεν	-ῶμεν	-ῶμεν	-ῶμεν	-ωμεθα	-ώμεθα	-ώμεθα	-ώμεθα
-ητε	-ῆτε	-ῶτε	-ᾶτε	-ησθε	-ῆσθε	-ῶσθε	-ᾶσθε
-ωσι	-ῶσι	-ῶσι	-ῶσι	-ωνται	-ῶνται	-ῶνται	-ῶνται
Imperative				**Imperative**			
-------	-------	-------	-------	-------	-------	-------	-------
-ε	-ει	-ου	-α	-ου	-οῦ	-οῦ	-ῶ
-έτω	-είτω	-ούτω	-άτω	-έσθω	-είσθω	-ούσθω	-άσθω
-------	-------	-------	-------	-------	-------	-------	-------
-ετε	-εῖτε	-οῦτε	-ᾶτε	-εσθε	-εῖσθε	-οῦσθε	-ᾶσθε
-έτωσαν	-είτωσαν	-ούτωσαν	-άτωσαν	-έσθωσαν	-είσθωσαν	ούσθωσσ'ν	-άσθωσαν
Infinitive				**Infinitive**			
-ειν	-εῖν	-οῦν	-ᾶν	-εσθαι	-εῖσθαι	-οῦ͜σθαι	-ᾶσθαι
Participle				**Participle**			
-οντ-	-οῦντ-[24]	-οῦντ-	-ῶντ-	-ομεν-	-ουμεν-	-ουμεν-	-ωμεν-
-ουσ-	-οῦσ-	-οῦσ-	-ῶσ-[25]	-ομεν-	-ουμεν-	-ουμεν-	-ωμεν-
-οντ-	-οῦντ-[26]	-οῦντ-	-ῶντ-	-ομεν-	-ουμεν-	-ουμεν-	-ωμεν-

---

[23]Contract vowels *lengthen* outside the first principal part of present and imperfect tenses.

[24]For all contracts, the nominative masculine singular is -ῶν. The dative masculine plural is -οῦσιν for -ε and -ο contracts, -ῶσιν for -α contracts. The genitive masculine plural is acute (-ούντων or -ώντων).

[25]Long ultimas generate an acute accent (e.g., -ώσης).

[26]With no ending in nominative/accusative neuter singular, the τ drops, leaving -οῦν for -ε and -ο contracts, -ῶν for -α contracts. The dative neuter plural is -οῦσιν for -ε and -ο contracts, -ῶσιν for -α contracts. The genitive neuter plural is acute (-ούντων or -ώντων).

Omega Verb Contraction—Imperfect Tense

IMPERFECT ACTIVE				IMPERFECT MIDDLE/PASSIVE			
	ε	ο	α		ε	ο	α
Indicative				**Indicative**			
-ον	-ουν	-ουν	-ων	-ομην	-ούμην	-ούμην	-ώμην
-ες	-εις	-ους	-ας	-ου	-οῦ	-οῦ	-ῶ
-ε	-ει	-ου	-α	-ετο	-εῖτο	-οῦτο	-ᾶτο
-ομεν	-οῦμεν	-οῦμεν	-ῶμεν	-ομεθα	-ούμεθα	-ούμεθα	-ώμεθα
-ετε	-εῖτε	-οῦτε	-ᾶτε	-εσθε	-εῖσθε	-οῦσθε	-ᾶσθε
-ον	-ουν	-ουν	-ων	-οντο	-οῦντο	-οῦντο	-ῶντο

Omega Verb Conjugation—Liquid Future

	LIQUID FUTURE		
Active	*Middle*	*1st Passive*	*2nd Passive*[27]
Indicative			
μενῶ	μενοῦμαι	βληθήσομαι [28]	φανήσομαι
μενεῖς	μενῇ	βληθήσῃ	φανήσῃ
μενεῖ	μενεῖται	βληθήσεται	φανήσεται
μενοῦμεν	μενούμεθα	βληθησόμεθα	φανησόμεθα
μενεῖτε	μενεῖσθε	βληθήσεσθε	φανήσεσθε
μενοῦσι	μενοῦνται	βληθήσονται	φανήσονται
Infinitive			
μενεῖν	μενεῖσθαι	βληθῆσεσθαι	φανήσεσθαι
Participle			
μενῶν	μενούμενος	βληθησόμενος	φανησόμενος
μενοῦσα	μενουμένη	βληθησομένη	φανησομένη
μενοῦν	μενούμενον	βληθησόμενον	φανησόμενον

---

[27]A second aorist passive makes a second future passive. However, such a future form is uncommon in the New Testament.

[28]The α of the stem βάλ- (βάλλω) is lost by vowel gradation. Stems react variously: here, an η is inserted before the -θη suffix; see notes with the liquid aorist table.

Omega Verb Conjugation—Liquid Aorist

	LIQUID AORIST		
Active	Middle	1st Passive[29]	2nd Passive
Indicative			
ἔμεινα	ἐμεινάμην	ἐβλήθην	ἐστάλην
ἔμεινας	ἐμείνω	ἐβλήθης	ἐστάλης
ἔμεινε	ἐμείνατο	ἐβλήθη	ἐστάλη
ἐμείναμεν	ἐμεινάμεθα	ἐβλήθημεν	ἐστάλημεν
ἐμείνατε	ἐμείνασθε	ἐβλήθητε	ἐστάλητε
ἔμειναν	ἐμείναντο	ἐβλήθησαν	ἐστάλησαν
Subjunctive			
μείνω	μείνωμαι	βληθῶ	σταλῶ
μείνῃς	μείνῃ	βληθῇς	σταλῇς
μείνῃ	μείνηται	βληθῇ	σταλῇ
μείνωμεν	μεινώμεθα	βληθῶμεν	σταλῶμεν
μείνητε	μείνησθε	βληθῆτε	σταλῆτε
μείνωσι	μείνωνται	βληθῶσι	σταλῶσι
Imperative			
-------	-------	-------	-------
μεῖνον	μεῖναι	βλήθητι	στάλητι
μεινάτω	μεινάσθω	βληθήτω	σταλήτω
-------	-------	-------	-------
μείνατε	μείνασθε	βλήθητε	στάλητε
μεινάντων	μεινάσθων	βληθέντων	σταλέντων
Optative			
μείναιμι	μειναίμην	βληθείην	σταλείην
μείναις	μείναιο	βληθείης	σταλείης
μείναι	μείναιτο	βληθείη	σταλείη
μείναιμεν	μειναίμεθα	βληθείημεν	σταλείημεν
μείναιτε	μείναισθε	βληθείητε	σταλείητε
μείναιεν	μείναιντο	βληθείησαν	σταλείησαν
Infinitive			
μεῖναι	μείνασθαι	βληθῆναι	σταλῆναι
Participle			
μείνας	μεινάμενος	βληθείς	σταλείς
μείνασα	μειναμένη	βληθεῖσα	σταλεῖσα
μεῖναν	μεινάμενον	βληθέν	σταλέν

---

[29]An η is inserted before the -θη; other stems retain the liquid before θ (e.g., ἠγγέλθην, ἀγγέλλω); others drop the liquid (e.g., ἐκλίθην, κλίνω); others show a second passive (ἐστάλην, στέλλω). Some, as φαίνω, show *both* a first and a second passive (cf. ἐφάνθην *or* ἐφάνην). We use στέλλω to illustrate a second passive; a common compound is ἀποστέλλω (ἀπεστάλην).

MI Verbs

MI Verb Endings

The key difference is in the primary active indicative of the *present tense*, which uses more primitive verb endings. Outside this first principal part, endings revert to the omega verb pattern and also can show a thematic pattern (e.g., future tense = δώσω, δώσεις, δώσει, etc.). Secondary active indicative is normal. The third singular's no ending exposes the stem vowel in its lengthened form (ἐδίδου). The third plural usually takes the -σαν ending. On occasion, though, -μι verbs can show the -ν option in this third plural, and a lengthened stem vowel (e.g., ἐδίδουν). Middle indicative second singulars do *not* volatilize in the present tense, but *do* in the future and aorist (δίδοσαι, ἐδίδοσο vs. δώσῃ or ἔδου). Three verbs are "kappa aorists": δίδωμι, τίθημι, and ἵημι.

The subjunctive mood *is* thematic, *using the typical lengthened thematic vowel* (ω/η), then contracting with the stem vowel. So, subjunctive results depend upon the stem vowel. For -ο stems, already lengthened to -ω in the singular, the result is always some form of ω in singular and plural. Both ε and α stems (τίθημι, ἵστημι) would result in -ῶ, -ῇς, -ῇ, -ῶμεν, -ῆτε, -ῶσι and -ῶμαι, -ῇ, -ῆται, -ώμεθα, -ῆσθε, -ῶνται; however, in fact, only δύναμαι actually occurs in the New Testament (δύνηται, δύνωνται). Second aorist also would contract in similar patterns. Both the subjunctive and the imperative almost always are *second* aorist in the aorist systems of -μι verbs.

The *only* New Testament optative forms are: (1) Pres. Act. = εἴη (εἰμί); Mid. = δυναίμην, δύναιντο (δύναμαι); (2) Sec. Aor. Act. = δῴη (δίδωμι; mood indicator is -ιη); Mid. = ὀναίμην (ὀνίνημι).

Active		Mid./Pass.
Indicative—Primary		
-μι	(-ω)	-μαι
-ς	(-εις)	-σαι (-η)
-σι	(-ει)	-ται
-μεν	(-ομεν)	-μεθα
-τε	(-ετε)	-σθε
-ασι	(-ουσι)	-νται
Indicative—Secondary		
-ν		-μην
-ς		-σο (-ου)
–		-το
-μεν		-μεθα
-τε		-σθε
-ν, -σαν		-ντο
Subjunctive		
-ῶ		-ῶμαι
-ῇς	(-ῇς)	-ῇ (-ῇ)
-ῷ	(-ῇ)	-ῷται (-ῆται)
-ῶμεν		-ώμεθα
-ῶτε	(-ῆτε)	-ῶσθε (-ῆσθε)
-ῶσι		-ῶνται
Imperative		
----		----
--, -ς, -θι		-σο (-ου)
-τω		-σθω
----		----
-τε		-σθε
-τωσαν		-σθωσαν
Optative		
-ιμι		-ιμην
-ις		-ιο
-ι		-ιτο
-ιμεν		-ιμεθα
-ιτε		-ισθε
-ιεν		-ιντο

δίδωμι—Present, Imperfect, Second Aorist[30]

PRESENT		IMPERFECT		SECOND AORIST	
Active	*M/P*	*Active*	*M/P*	*Active*	*Middle*
Indicative		**Indicative**		**Indicative**	
δίδωμι	δίδομαι	ἐδίδουν	ἐδιδόμην		ἐδόμην
δίδως	δίδοσαι	ἐδίδους	ἐδίδοσο		ἔδου
δίδωσι	δίδοται	ἐδίδου	ἐδίδοτο		ἔδοτο
δίδομεν	διδόμεθα	ἐδίδομεν	ἐδιδόμεθα		ἐδόμεθα
δίδοτε	δίδοσθε	ἐδίδοτε	ἐδίδοσθε		ἔδοσθε
διδόασι	δίδονται	ἐδίδοσαν	ἐδίδοντο		ἔδοντο
Subjunctive		(or ἐδίδουν)		**Subjunctive**	
διδῶ				δῶ	
διδῷς				δῷς	
διδῷ				δῷ	
διδῶμεν				δῶμεν	
διδῶτε				δῶτε	
διδῶσι				δῶσι	
Imperative				**Imperative**	
-------				-------	
δίδου				δός	
διδότω				δότω	
-------				-------	
δίδοτε				δότε	
διδότωσαν				δότωσαν	
				Optative	
				δῴην	
				δῴης	
				δῴη	
				δῴημεν	
				δῴητε	
				δῴησαν	
Infinitive				**Infinitive**	
διδόναι	δίδοσθαι			δοῦναι	
Participle				**Participle**	
διδούς	διδόμενος			δούς	
-------	-------			-------	
διδόν	διδόμενον			-------	

---

[30]Whereas the -ω verb tables use only one verb, λύω, as a paradigm, the -μι verb tables are given to important individual -μι verbs appearing in the New Testament. An attempt was made, therefore, to include a particular -μι verb conjugation only when at least one form of that conjugation appears in the New Testament text, including compounds. For more thorough paradigm forms, consult Lessons 33 and 34.

δίδωμι—First Aorist,[31] Future

FIRST AORIST			FUTURE		
Active	*Middle*	*Passive*	*Active*	*Middle*	*Passive*
Indicative			**Indicative**		
ἔδωκα[32]		ἐδόθην	δώσω	δώσομαι	δοθήσομαι
ἔδωκας		ἐδόθης	δώσεις	δώσῃ	δοθήσῃ
ἔδωκε		ἐδόθη	δώσει	δώσεται	δοθήσεται
ἐδώκαμεν		ἐδόθημεν	δώσομεν	δωσόμεθα	δοθησόμεθα
ἐδώκατε		ἐδόθητε	δώσετε	δώσεσθε	δοθήσεσθε
ἔδωκαν		ἐδόθησαν	δώσουσι	δώσονται	δοθήσονται
Subjunctive					
δώσω		δοθῶ			
δώσῃς		δοθῇς			
δώσῃ		δοθῇ			
δωσώμεν		δοθῶμεν			
δώσητε		δοθῆτε			
δωσώσι		δοθῶσι			
Infinitive					
		δοθῆναι			
Participle			**Participle**		
		δοθείς	δώσων		
		δοθεῖσα	-------		
		δοθέν	-------		

---

[31]**First aorist** *imperative* -μι verbs are rare. For active voice, cf. κίχρημι, "I lend" (Luke 11:5; the pattern is ----, χρῆσον, χρησάτω, ----, χρήσατε, χρησάτωσαν). For middle voice, cf. ζώννυμι, "I fasten my belt," "dress" (Acts 12:8; the pattern is ----, ζῶσαι, ζωσάσθω, ----, ζώσασθε, ζωσάσθωσαν). **First aorist** *infinitives* are rare. Cf. ἐνδείκνυμι (Rom. 9:22; as ἐνδείξασθαι). **First aorist** *participle* forms are rare. Cf. περιζώννυμι (Luke 17:8; Eph. 6:14; the pattern is περιζωσάμενος, -μένη, -μενον).

[32]A "kappa aorist," as are τίθημι and ἵημι and compounds (*NTG*, 379).

δίδωμι—Perfect and Pluperfect[33]

PERFECT		PLUPERFECT
Active	*M/P*	*Active*
Indicative	**Indicative**	**Indicative**
δέδωκα	δέδομαι	ἐδεδώκειν
δέδωκας	δέδοσαι	ἐδεδώκεις
δέδωκε	δέδοται	ἐδεδώκει
δεδώκαμεν	δεδόμεθα	εδεδώκειμεν
δεδώκατε	δέδοσθε	ἐδεδώκειτε
δέδωκαν	δέδονται	ἐδεδώκεισαν
Subjunctive		
	ὦ δεδομένος	
	ἦς δεδομένος	
	ᾖ δεδομένος	
	ὦμεν δεδομένοι	
	ἦτε δεδομένοι	
	ὦσι δεδομένοι	
Participle		
δεδωκώς	δεδομένος	
-------	δεδομένη	
-------	δεδομένον	

---

[33]**Perfect** *imperative* -μι verbs, of course, are rare. For the middle voice, cf. ῥώννυμι, "I am healthy" (some give as deponent, ῥώννυμαι); as imperative, "Farewell!" (cf. Acts 15:29; the pattern is ----, ἔρρωσο, ἐρρώσθω, ----, ἔρρωσθε, ἐρρώσθωσαν). One possible periphrastic form in the New Testament is ἔστωσαν . . . περιζωσμέναι (Luke 12:35). **Pluperfect** *indicative* could be periphrastic, as in ἦν δεδομένον (John 19:11).

τίθημι—Present, Imperfect, Second Aorist

PRESENT		IMPERFECT		SECOND AORIST	
Active	*M/P*	*Active*	*M/P*	*Active*	*Middle*
Indicative		**Indicative**		**Indicative**	
τίθημι	τίθεμαι	ἐτίθην	ἐτιθέμην		ἐθέμην
τίθης	τίθεσαι	ἐτίθεις	ἐτίθεσο		ἔθου
τίθησι	τίθεται	ἐτίθει	ἐτίθετο		ἔθετο
τίθεμεν	τιθέμεθα	ἐτίθεμεν	ἐτιθέμεθα		ἐθέμεθα
τίθετε	τίθεσθε	ἐτίθετε	ἐτίθεσθε		ἔθεσθε
τιθέασι	τίθενται	ἐτίθεσαν	ἐτίθεμην		ἔθεντο
Subjunctive		(or ἐτίθουν)		**Subjunctive**	
τιθῶ				θῶ	θῶμαι [34]
τιθῇς				θῇς	θῇ
τιθῇ				θῇ	θῆται
τιθῶμεν				θῶμεν	θώμεθα
τιθῆτε				θῆτε	θῆσθε
τιθῶσι				θῶσι	θῶνται
Imperative				**Imperative**	
-------	-------			-------	-------
τίθει	τίθεσο			θές	θέσο
τιθέτω	τιθέσθο			θέτω	θέσθω
-------	-------			-------	-------
τίθετε	τίθεσθε			θέτε	θέσθε
τιθέτωσαν	τιθέσθωσαν			θέτωσαν	θέσθωσαν
Infinitive				**Infinitive**	
τιθέναι	τίθεσθαι			θεῖναι	θέσθαι [35]
Participle				**Participle**	
τιθείς	τιθέμενος			θείς	θέμενος
-------	τιθεμένη			-------	-------
-------	τιθέμενον			-------	-------

---

[34] Only one second aorist middle subjunctive -μι verb form in the New Testament, from ἀποτίθημι, as ἀποθώμεθα (Rom. 13:12).

[35] Compounds of τίθημι (ἀποθέσθαι, Eph. 4:22; καταθέσθαι, Acts 24:27; 25:9).

τίθημι—First Aorist, Future

FIRST AORIST			FUTURE		
Active	*Middle*	*Passive*	*Active*	*Middle*	*1st Passive*
Indicative			**Indicative**		
ἔθηκα		ἐτέθην	θήσω	θήσομαι	τεθήσομαι
ἔθηκας		ἐτέθης	θήσεις	θήσῃ	τεθήσῃ
ἔθηκε		ἐτέθη	θήσει	θήσοται	τεθήσεται
ἐθήκαμεν		ἐτέθημεν	θήσομεν	θησόμεθα	τεθησόμεθα
ἐθήκατε		ἐτέθητε	θήσετε	θήσεσθε	τεθήσεσθε
ἔθηκαν		ἐτέθησαν	θήσουσι	θήσονται	τεθήσονται
Subjunctive					
		τεθῶ			
		τεθῇς			
		τεθῇ			
		τεθῶμεν			
		τεθῆτε			
		τεθῶσι			
Infinitive					
		τεθῆναι			
Participle					
		τεθείς			

τίθημι—Perfect and Pluperfect

PERFECT		PLUPERFECT	
Active	*M/P*	*Active*	*M/P*
Indicative	**Indicative**	**Indicative**	
τέθεικα	τέθειμαι		ἐτεθείμην[36]
τέθεικας	τέθεισαι		ἐτεθείσο
τέθεικε	τέθειται		ἐτεθείτο
τεθείκαμεν	τεθείμεθα		ἐτεθείμεθα
τεθείκατε	τέθεισθε		ἐτεθείσθε
τέθεικαν	τέθεινται		ἐτεθείντο
Participle			
τεθεικώς[37]	τεθειμένος		
-------	-------		
-------	-------		

---

[36]Representing a rare example in the New Testament, συνετεθείντο, from συντίθημι (John 9:22). Periphrastically, one has ἦν δεδομένον (John 19:11) and ἦσαν παραδεδομένοι (Acts 14:26).
[37]2 Pet. 2:6.

ἵστημι—Present, Imperfect, Second Aorist

PRESENT		IMPERFECT		SECOND AORIST	
Active	*M/P*	*Active*	*M/P*	*Active*	*Middle*
Indicative		**Indicative**		**Indicative**	
ἵστημι	ἵσταμαι	ἵστην[38]	ἱστάμην	ἔστην	
ἵστης	ἵστασαι	ἵστης	ἵστασο	ἔστης	
ἵστησι	ἵσταται	ἵστη	ἵστατο	ἔστη	
ἵσταμεν	ἱστάμεθα	ἵσταμεν	ἱστάμεθα	ἔστημεν	
ἵστατε	ἵστασθε	ἵστατε	ἵστασθε	ἔστητε	
ἱστᾶσι	ἵστανται	ἵστασαν	ἵσταντο	ἔστησαν	
				Subjunctive	
				στῶ	
				στῇς	
				στῇ	
				στῶμεν	
				στῆτε	
				στῶσι	
Imperative				**Imperative**	
-------	-------			-------	
ἵσταθι[39]	ἵστασο			στῆθι (στά)	
ἱστάτω	ἱστάσθω			στήτω	
-------	-------				
ἵστατε	ἵστασθε			στῆτε	
ἱστάτωσαν	ἱστάσθωσαν			στήτωσαν	
Infinitive				**Infinitive**	
ἱστάναι[40]	ἵστασθαι			στῆναι	στάσθαι
Participle				**Participle**	
ἱστάς	ἱστάμενος			στάς	στάμενος
-------	-------			στᾶσα	σταμένη
-------	-------			στάν	στάμενον

[38]In fact, the only form in the New Testament is ἕστηκεν (John 8:44), which actually is derived from στήκω, an -ω verb form encroaching upon the use of the -μι verb form of ἵστημι.

[39]In fact, the only form in the New Testament is παριστάνετε (Rom. 6:13), which actually is derived from παριστάνω, an -ω verb form encroaching on the -μι verb form of ἵστημι.

[40]The form συνιστάνειν (2 Cor. 3:1) reflects the influence of the -ω verb form συνιστάνω.

ἵστημι—First Aorist, Future

	FIRST AORIST			FUTURE		
Active	*Middle*	*Passive*	*Active*	*Middle*	*Passive*
Indicative			**Indicative**		
ἔστησα		ἐστάθην	στήσω	στήσομαι	σταθήσομαι
ἔστησας		ἐστάθης	στήσεις	στήσῃ	σταθήσῃ
ἔστησε		ἐστάθη	στήσει	στήσεται	σταθήσεται
ἐστήσαμεν		ἐστάθημεν	στήσομεν	στησόμεθα	σταθησόμεθα
ἐστήσατε		ἐστάθητε	στήσετε	στήσεσθε	σταθήσεσθε
ἔστησαν		ἐστάθησαν	στήσουσι	στήσονται	σταθήσονται
Subjunctive					
στήσω		σταθῶ			
στήσῃς		σταθῇς			
στήσῃ		σταθῇ			
στήσωμεν		σταθῶμεν			
στήσητε		σταθῆτε			
στήσουσι		σταθῶσι			
Imperative					

στῆσον[41]					
στησάτω					

στήσατε					
στησάτωσαν					
Infinitive					
στῆσαι[42]		σταθῆναι			
Participle					
στήσας		σταθείς			
-------		-------			
-------		-------			

---

[41]Representing παραστήσατε (Rom. 6:13, 19), from παρίστημι; also, cf. κίχρημι, "I lend" as χρῆσον (Luke 11:5); κεράννυμι, "I mix," as κεράσατε (Rev. 18:6); ἐπιδείκνυμι, "I show," as ἐπιδείξατε (Matt. 22:19; Luke 17:14).

[42]Cf. σβέσαι, from σβέννυμι, "I extinguish" (Eph. 6:16); δεῖξαι, from δείκνυμι, "I show" (Rev. 1:1; 22:6); ἀπολέσαι, from ἀπόλλυμι, "I destroy."

ἵστημι—Perfect and Pluperfect

PERFECT		PLUPERFECT
Active	*M/P*	*Active*
Indicative		**Indicative**
ἕστηκα[43]		εἱστήκειν[44]
ἕστηκας		εἱστήκεις
ἕστηκε		εἱστήκει
ἑστήκαμεν		εἱστήκειμεν
ἑστήκατε		εἱστήκειτε
ἕστηκαν		εἱστήκεισαν
Infinitive		
ἑστακέναι[45]		
Participle		
ἑστηκώς[46]		
ἑστηκυῖα		
ἑστηκός		

---

[43]Periphrastically, one has εἰσὶν . . . ἑστῶτες (Acts 5:25) and ἑστώς εἰμι (Acts 25:10).

[44]Some give as ἑστήκειν, etc. Periphrastically, one has ἦν ἑστώς (Luke 5:1; 18:18, 25; Acts 16:9) and ἤμην ἐφεστώς (22:20).

[45]For the compound form ἐξεστακέναι, from ἐξίστημι (Acts 8:11). One *second* perfect active infinitive is ἑστάναι, also from ἵστημι; the ε does not show, but the reason is obscure.

[46]Alternately without the -κ, as ἑστώς, ἑστῶσα, ἑστός.

ἵημι—Present, Imperfect, Second Aorist[47]

PRESENT		IMPERFECT		SECOND AORIST	
Active	*M/P*	*Active*	*M/P*	*Active*	*Middle*
Indicative		**Indicative**			
ἵημι	ἵεμαι	ἵην[48]			
ἵης	ἵεσαι	ἵης			
ἵησι	ἵεται	ἵη			
ἵεμεν	ἱέμεθα	ἵεμεν			
ἵετε	ἵεσθε	ἵετε			
ἱεῖσι	ἵενται	ἵεσαν			
Subjunctive				**Subjunctive**	
ἱῶ				ὧ	
ἱῆς				ἧς	
ἱῆ				ᾖ	
ἱῶμεν				ὧμεν	
ἱῆτε				ἧτε	
ἱῶσι				ὧσι	
Imperative				**Imperative**	

ἵεθι				ἕς	
ἱέτω				ἕτω	

ἵετε				ἕτε	
ἱέωσαν				ἕτωσαν	
Infinitive				**Infinitive**	
ἱέναι				εἶναι	
Participle				**Participle**	
ἱείς	-------			εἵς	
-------	ἱεμένη			-------	
-------	ἱέμενον			-------	

---

[47]The verb ἵημι occurs only in compound forms in the New Testament; e.g., ἀφίημι.

[48]Alternately, ἵον, ἵες, ἵε(ν) in the singular, as if from ἀφίω; cf. ἤφιεν in Mark 1:34; 11:16.

ἵημι—First Aorist, Future

FIRST AORIST			FUTURE		
Active	Middle	Passive	Active	Middle	Passive
Indicative			**Indicative**		
ἧκα		ἕθην	ἥσω		ἐθήσομαι
ἧκας		ἕθης	ἥσεις		ἐθήσῃ
ἧκε		ἕθη	ἥσει		ἐθήσεται
ἥκαμεν		ἕθημεν	ἥσομεν		ἐθησόμεθα
ἥκατε		ἕθητε	ἥσετε		ἐθήσεσθε
ἧκαν		ἕθησαν	ἥσουσι		ἐθήσονται
Subjunctive					
		ἐθῶ			
		ἐθῇς			
		ἐθῇ			
		ἐθῶμεν			
		ἐθῆτε			
		ἐθῶσι			

ἵημι—Perfect and Pluperfect[49]

PERFECT	
Active	M/P
Indicative	
	εἷμαι [50]
	εἷσαι
	εἷται
	εἵμεθα
	εἷσθε
	εἷνται

---

[49]No pluperfect form of ἵημι compounds occurs in the New Testament.

[50]In fact, only the third person plural form appears in the New Testament, but showing up in an irregular form as ἀφέωνται (Luke 5:20, 23; 7:47, 48; John 20:23; 1 John 2:12).

εἰμί—Conjugation

PRESENT	IMPERFECT	FUTURE
Indicative	**Indicative**	**Indicative**
εἰμί	ἤμην	ἔσομαι
εἶ	ἦς (ἦσθα)	ἔσῃ
ἐστί	ἦν	ἔσται
ἐσμέν	ἦμεν (ἤμεθα)[51]	ἐσόμεθα
ἐστέ	ἦτε	ἔσεσθε
εἰσί	ἦσαν	ἔσονται
Subjunctive		
ὦ		
ᾖς		
ᾖ		
ὦμεν		
ἦτε		
ὦσι		
Imperative		

ἴσθι		
ἔστω (ἤτω)		

ἔστε		
ἔστωσαν		
Optative[52]		
εἴην		
εἴης		
εἴη		
εἴημεν		
εἴητε		
εἴησαν		
Infinitive		**Infinitive**
εἶναι		ἔσεσθαι
Participle		**Participle**
ὤν[53]		ἐσόμενος[54]
οὖσα		ἐσομένη
ὄν		ἐσόμενον

---

[51] Alternate form (Matt. 23:30; Acts 27:37; Gal. 4:3; Eph. 2:3).

[52] In fact, just the form εἴη in the New Testament, twelve times (Luke 1:29; 3:15; 8:9; 9:46; 15:26; 18:36; 22:23; John 13:24; Acts 8:20; 10:17; 20:16; 21:33).

[53] Full paradigm in Table 26.4 (*NTG*, 306).

[54] In fact, only ἐσόμενον at Luke 22:49.

Miscellaneous Verbs: (1) φημί, (2) κεῖμαι, (3) γινώσκω[55]

φημί		κεῖμαι		γινώσκω
Present	**Imperfect**	**Present**	**Imperfect**	**2nd Aorist**
Active	*Active*	*Middle*	*Middle*	*Active*
Indicative	**Indicative**	**Indicative**	**Indicative**	**Indicative**
φημί	ἔφην	κεῖμαι	ἐκείμην	ἔγνων
φής	ἔφης	κεῖσαι	ἔκεισο	ἔγνως
φησί	ἔφη	κεῖται	ἔκειτο	ἔγνω
φαμέν	ἔφαμεν	κείμεθα	ἐκείμεθα	ἔγνωμεν
φατέ	ἔφατε	κεῖσθε	ἔκεισθε	ἔγνωτε
φασί	ἔφασαν	κεῖνται	ἔκειντο	ἔγνωσαν
				Subjunctive
				γνῶ
				γνῷς
				γνῷ (γνοῖ)
				γνῶμεν
				γνῶτε
				γνῶσι
				Imperative

				γνῶθι
				γνώτω

				γνῶτε
				γνώτωσαν
				Infinitive
				γνῶναι
		Participle		**Participle**
		κείμενος		γνούς
		κειμένη		γνοῦσα
		κείμενον		γνόν

---

[55]The verb φημί, though fairly common, occurs in only four forms in the New Testament: φημί, φησί, φασί, and ἔφη. The verb κεῖμαι is a common deponent -μι verb. The -ω verb γινώσκω has an athematic second aorist on the order of ἵστημι (also, ἀναβαίνω; *NTG*, 386).

As to other forms, the verb δείκνυμι, "I show," and compounds is quite regular except for what might appear to the beginning student to be atypical participial forms: δεικνύς, δεικνῦσα, δεικνύν. Rare -μι verb forms would include: (1) ἵστημι, in the two perfect forms ἴσασι (active indicative) and ἴστε (active imperative), perhaps connected to εἴδω; (2) ἐπίσταμαι, a deponent conjugated on a ἵστημι pattern; (3) εἶμι, "I go," easily confused with εἰμί, "I am," and occurring in present (εἶμι, εἷς, εἶ, etc.), imperfect (ᾔειν, ᾔεις, ᾔει, etc.), participial (ἰών, ἰοῦσα, ἰόν), and compounded forms (ἄπειμι, εἴσειμι, ἔξειμι, ἔπειμι, σύνειμι).

PRINCIPAL PARTS

This principal parts list is given for indicative first person singular in the traditional order. A dash line indicates a part that does not occur in the New Testament; however, some parts are included for comparison. Alternate forms are indicated in parentheses. Other tenses can be derived from these principal parts (imperfect from the first principal part; future passive the sixth principal part; pluperfect, fourth and fifth principal parts).

Principal Parts	Tenses	Voices		
First Principal Part	Present	active	middle	passive
	Imperfect	active	middle	passive
Second Principal Part	Future	active	middle	
Third Principal Part	First Aorist	active	middle	
	Second Aorist	active	middle	
Fourth Principal Part	Perfect	active		
	Future Perfect	active		
	Pluperfect	active		
Fifth Principal Part	Perfect		middle	passive
	Future Perfect		middle	passive
	Pluperfect		middle	passive
Sixth Principal Part	First Aorist			passive
	First Future			passive
	Second Aorist			passive
	Second Future			passive

Volatilization patterns must be allowed for in a given person and number (such as contraction, lengthening, liquids, sigma, theta, etc.). Also, remember that moods outside the indicative do not use an augment

Bold	=	**fifty or more times** in the New Testament
Italic	=	*liquid verbs*
Asterisk	=	second aorists*

for secondary tenses. Generally, non-compounded forms are given, except for very common verbs, but the compounded forms easily can be derived from them.

First	Second	Third	Fourth	Fifth	Sixth
ἀγαλλιάω	ἀγαλλιάσομαι	ἠγαλλίασα	----------	----------	ἠγαλλιάθην
ἀγανακτέω	ἀγανακτήσω	ἠγανάκτησα	----------	----------	----------
ἀγαπάω	ἀγαπήσω	ἠγάπησα	ἠγάπηκα	ἠγάπημαι	ἠγαπήθην
ἀγγαρεύω	ἀγγαρεύσω	ἠγγάρευσα	----------	----------	----------
ἀγγέλλω	*ἀγγελῶ*	ἤγγειλα	ἤγγελκα	ἤγγελμαι	ἠγγέλθην
ἁγιάζω	ἁγιάσω	ἡγίασα	----------	ἡγίασμαι	ἡγιάσθην
ἁγνίζω	ἁγνίσω	ἥγνισα	ἥγνικα	ἥγνισμαι	ἡγνίσθην
ἀγνοέω	ἀγνοήσω	ἠγνόησα	ἠγνόηκα	ἠγνόημαι	ἠγνοήθην
ἀγοράζω	ἀγοράσω	ἠγόρασα	ἠγόρακα	ἠγόρασμαι	ἠγοράσθην
ἀγρεύω	ἀγρεύσω	ἤρευσα	----------	----------	----------
ἄγω	ἄξω	ἤγαγον *	ἦχα	ἦγμαι	ἤχθην
ἀδικέω	ἀδικήσω	ἠδίκησα	ἠδίκηκα	ἠδίκημαι	ἠδικήθην

First	Second	Third	Fourth	Fifth	Sixth
ἀθετέω	ἀθετήσω	ἠθέτησα	----------	----------	----------
αἰνέω	αἰνέσω	ᾔνεσα	ᾔνεκα	ᾔνεμαι	ᾐνέθην
αἱρέω	αἱρήσω	εἷλα εἷλον*	ᾕρηκα	ᾕρημαι	ᾑρέωην
αἴρω	ἀρῶ	ἦρα	ἦρκα	ἦρμαι	ἤρθην
αἰσθάνομαι	αἰθήσομαι	ᾐσθόμην	----------	ᾔσθημαι	----------
αἰσχύνομαι	αἰσχυνθήσομαι	---------	----------	----------	ᾐσχύνθην
αἰτέω	αἰτήσω	ᾔτησα	ᾔτηκα	ᾔτημαι	ᾐτήθην
ἀκολουθέω	ἀκολουθήσω	ἠκολούθησα	ἠκολούθηκα	ἠκολούθημαι	ἠκολουθήθην
ἀκούω	ἀκούσω	ἤκουσα	ἀκήκοα	ἤκουσμαι	ἠκούσθην
ἀλείφω	ἀλείψω	ἤλειψα	ἀλήλιφα	ἀλήλιμμαι	ἠλείφθην
ἀλάσσω	ἀλλάξω	ἤλλαξα	ἤλλαχα	ἤλλαγμαι	ἠλλάγην
ἁμαρτάνω	ἁμαρτήσω	ἡμάρτησα (ἥμαρτον)*	ἡμάρτηκα	ἡμάρτημαι	ἡμαρτήθην
ἀμελέω	ἀμελήσω	ἠμέλησα	----------	----------	----------
ἀμφιέννυμι	ἀμφιέσω	ἠμφίεσα	----------	ἠμφίεσμαι	----------
ἀναβαίνω	ἀναβήσομαι	ἀνέβην*	ἀναβέβημα	----------	----------
ἀναγκάζω	ἀναγκάσω	ἠνάγκασα	----------	----------	ἠναγκάσθην
ἀναθεματίζω	ἀναθεματίσω	ἀνεθεμάτισα	----------	----------	----------
ἀναλίσκω	ἀναλώσω	ἀνήλωσα	ἀνήλωκα	ἀνήλωμαι	ἀνηλώθην
ἀνατέλλω	ἀνατελῶ	ἀνέτειλα	ἀνατέταλκα	ἀνατέταλμαι	----------
ἀνατρέπω	ἀνατρέψω	ἀνέτρεψα	----------	----------	----------
ἀνίστημι	ἀναστήσω	ἀνέστησα	ἀνέστηκα	ἀνέστημαι	ἀνεστάθην
ἀνοίγω	ἀνοίξω	ἀνέῳξα (ἠνέῳξα, ἤνοιξα)	ἀνέῳγα	ἀνέῳγμαι (ἠνέῳγμαι)	ἀνεῴχθην (ἠνεῴχθην, ἠνοίχθην, ἠνοίγην)
ἀντλέω	ἀντλήσω	ἤντλησα	ἤντληκα	----------	----------
ἀξιόω	ἀξιώσω	ἠξίωσα	ἠξίωκα	ἠξίωμαι	ἠξιώθην
ἀπαντάω	ἀπαντήσω	ἀπήντησα	ἀπήντηκα	ἀπήντημαι	ἀπηντήθην
ἀπατάω	ἀπατήσω	ἠπάτησα	ἠπάτηκα	ἠπάτημαι	ἠπατήθην
ἀπειθέω	ἀπειθήσω	ἠπείθησα	----------	----------	----------
ἀπειλέω	ἀπειλήσω	ἠπείλησα (ἠπειλησάμην)	---------	----------	----------
ἀπέρχομαι	ἀπελεύσομαι	ἀπῆλθον*	ἀπελήλυθα	----------	----------
ἀπιστέω	ἀπιστήσω	ἠπίστησα	----------	----------	----------
ἀποθνῄσκω	ἀποθανοῦμαι	ἀπέθανον*	----------	----------	----------
ἀποκεφαλίζω	ἀπεκεφάλισα	----------	----------	----------	----------
ἀποκρίνομαι	----------	ἀπεκρινάμην	----------	----------	ἀπεκρίθην
ἀποκτείνω	ἀποκτενῶ	ἀπέκτεινα	ἀπέκτονα	----------	ἀπεκτάνθην
ἀπόλλυμι	ἀπολέσω (ἀπολῶ)	ἀπώλεσα	ἀπώλεκα (ἀπόλωλα)	ἀπολώλεσμαι	ἀπωλέσθην
ἀπολογέομαι	ἀπολογήσομαι	ἀπελογησάμην	----------	----------	ἀπελογήθην
ἀπολύω	ἀπολύσω	ἀπέλυσα	----------	ἀπολέλυμαι	ἀπελύθην

First	Second	Third	Fourth	Fifth	Sixth
ἀπορέω	ἀπορήσω	ἠπόρησα	ἠπόρηκα	ἠπόρημαι	ἠπορήθην
ἀποστεγάζω	ἀποστεγάσω	ἀπεστέγασα	----------	----------	----------
ἀποστέλλω	ἀποστελῶ	ἀπέστειλα	ἀπέσταλκα	ἀπέσταλμαι	ἀπεστάλην
ἀποστερέω	ἀποστερήσω	ἀπεστέρησα	ἀπεστέρηκα	ἀπεστέρημαι	ἀπεστερήθην
ἀποτινάσσω	----------	ἀπετίναξα	----------	----------	----------
ἅπτω	ἅψω	ἧψα (ἡψάμην)	----------	----------	----------
ἀπωθέω	ἀπωθήσομαι	ἀπωσάμην	----------	----------	----------
ἀρέσκω	ἀρέσω	ἤρεσα	----------	----------	ἠρέσθην
ἀριθμέω	ἀριθμήσω	ἠρίμησα	ἠρίμηκα	ἠρίμημαι	----------
ἀριστάω	----------	ἠρίστησα	----------	----------	----------
ἀρκέω	ἀρκέσω	ἤκεσα	----------	----------	ἠρκέσθην
ἁρμόζω	ἁρμόσω	ἥρμοσα	ἥρμοκα	ἥρμοσμαι	ἡρμόσθην
ἀρνέομαι	ἀρνήσομαι	ἠρνησάμην	----------	ἤνημαι	----------
ἁρπάζω	ἁρπάσω	ἥρπασα	ἥρπακα	ἥρπασμαι	ἡρπάσθην
ἄρχω	ἄρξω	ἦρξα	ἦρχα	ἦργμαι	ἤρχθην
ἄρχομαι	ἄρξομαι	ἠρξάμην	ἦργμαι	----------	----------
ἀσεβέω	----------	ἠσέβησα	----------	----------	----------
ἀσθενέω	ἀσθενήσω	ἠσθένησα	ἠσθένηκα	----------	----------
ἀσπάζομαι	ἀσπάσομαι	ἠσπασάμην	----------	----------	----------
ἀστοχέω	----------	ἠστόχησα	----------	----------	----------
ἀστράπτω	ἀστράψω	ἤστραψα	----------	----------	ἠστράφθην
ἀσφαλίζω	ἀσφαλίσομαι	ἠσφαλισάμην	----------	ἠσφάλισμαι	ἠσφαλίσθην
ἀτακτέω	----------	ἠτάκτησα	----------	----------	----------
ἀτενίζω	----------	ἠτένισα	----------	----------	----------
ἀτιμάζω	ἀτιμάσω	ἠτίμασα	ἠτίμακα	ἠτίμαμαι	ἠτιμάσθην
αὐγάζω	αὐγάσω	ηὔγασα	----------	----------	----------
αὐλέω	αὐλήσω	ηὔλησα	----------	----------	----------
αὐλίζομαι	----------	ηὐλισάμην	----------	----------	ηὐλίσθην
αὐξάνω	αὐξήσω	ηὔξησα	ηὔξηκα	ηὔξημαι	ηὐξήθην
ἀφίημι	ἀφήσω	ἀφῆκα	ἀφεῖκα	ἀφεῖμαι	ἀφέθην
ἀφικνέομαι	ἀφίξομαι	ἀφικόμην	----------	----------	----------
ἀφορίζω	ἀφορίσω	ἀφώρισα	ἀφώρικα	ἀφώρισμαι	ἀφωρίσθην
βάλλω	βαλῶ	ἔβαλον*	βέβληκα	βέβλημαι	ἐβλήθην
βαπτίζω	βαπτίσω	ἐβάπτισα	----------	βεβάπτισμαι	ἐβαπτίσθην
βάπτω	βάψω	ἔβαψα	----------	βέβαμμαι	ἐβάφθην
βαρέω	βαρήσω	ἐβάρησα	βεβάρηκα	βεβάρημαι	ἐβαρήθην
βασανίζω	βασανίσω	ἐβασάνισα	----------	----------	ἐβασανίσθην
βασιλεύω	βασιλεύσω	ἐβασίλευσα	----------	----------	----------
βασκαίνω	----------	ἐβάσκανα	----------	----------	----------
βαστάζω	βαστάσω	ἐβάστασα	----------	βεβάσταμμαι	ἐβαστάχθην
βδελύσσω	βδελύξω	ἐβδέλυξα	----------	ἐβδέλυγμαι	ἐβδελύχθην
βεβαιόω	βεβαιώσω	ἐβεβαίωσα	----------	----------	ἐβεβαιώθην
βιάζομαι	βιάσομαι	ἐβιασάμην	----------	βεβίασμαι	ἐβιάσθην
βιόω	βιώσομαι	ἐβίωσα	βεβίωκα	βεβίωμαι	----------

First	Second	Third	Fourth	Fifth	Sixth
βλάπτω	βλάψω	ἔβλαψα	βέβλαφα	βέβλαμμαι	ἐβλάφθην
βλαστάνω	βλαστήσω	ἐβλάστησα	βεβλάστηκα	----------	----------
βλέπω	βλέψω	ἔβλεψα	βέβλεφα	βεβλεμμαι	ἐβλέφθην
βοάω	βοήσομαι	ἐβόησα	βεβόηκα	βεβόημαι	ἐβοήθην
βοηθέω	βοηθήσω	ἐβοήθησα	βεβοήθηκα	βεβοήθημαι	ἐβοηθήθην
βολίζω	βολίσω	ἐβόλισα	----------	----------	----------
βόσκω	βοσκήσω	ἐβόσκησα	----------	----------	ἐβοσκήθην
βουλεύω	βουλεύσομαι	ἐβουλευσάμην	----------	βεβούλευμαι	----------
βούλομαι	βουλήσομαι	----------	----------	βεβούλημαι	ἐβουλήθην
βραδύνω	----------	ἐβράδυνα	----------	----------	----------
βρέχω	βρέξω	ἔβρεξα	----------	βέβρεγμαι	ἐβρέχθην
γαμέω	----------	ἔγημα (ἐγαμήσα)	γεγάμηκα	γεγάμημαι	ἐγαμήθην
γελάω	γελάσω	ἐγάλασα	----------	γεγέλαμαι	ἐγελάσθην
γεμίζω	γεμίσω	ἐγέμισα	----------	----------	ἐγεμίσθην
γεννάω	γεννήσω	ἐγέννησα	γεγέννηκα	γεγέννημαι	ἐγεννήθην
γεύομαι	γεύσομαι	ἐγευσάμην	----------	γέγευμαι	----------
γίνομαι	γενήσομαι	ἐγενόμην*	γέγονα	γεγένημαι	ἐγενήθην
γινώσκω	γνώσομαι	ἔγνων*	ἔγνωκα	ἔγνωσμαι	ἐγενώσθην
γνωρίζω	γνωρίσω	ἐγνώρισα	----------	----------	ἐγνωρίσθην
γογγύζω	γογγύσω	ἐγογγύσα	----------	----------	----------
γράφω	γράψω	ἔγραψα	γέγραφα	γέγραμμαι	ἐγράφην
γρηγορέω	γρηγορήσω	ἐγρηγόρησα	----------	----------	----------
δάκνω	δήξομαι (δήξω)	ἔδηξα	δέδηχα	δέδηγμαι	ἐδήχθην
δακρύω	δακρύσω	ἐδάκρυσα	δεδάκρυκα	δεδάκρυμαι	----------
δανείζω	δανείσω	ἐδάνεισα	δεδάνεικα	δεδανεισμαι	----------
δαπανάω	δαπανήσω	ἐδαπάνησα	δεδαπάνηκα	δεδαπανημαι	ἐδαπανήθην
δεῖ [occuring only in this impersonal, third singular form]					
δειγματίζω	δειγματίσω	ἐδειγμάτισα	----------	----------	----------
δείκνυμι (δεικνύω)	δείξω	ἔδειξα	δέδειχα	δέδειγμαι	ἐδείχθην
δειπνέω	δειπνήσω	ἐδείπνησα	δεδείπνηκα	δεδείπνημαι	----------
δεκατόω	δεκατώσω	----------	δεδεκάτωκα	δεδεκάτωμαι	----------
δέομαι	δεήσομαι	----------	----------	δεδέημαι	ἐδεήθην
δέρω	δερῶ	ἔδειρα	----------	δέδαρμαι	ἐδάρθην
δέχομαι	δέξομαι	ἐδεξάμην	----------	δέδεγμαι	ἐδέχθην
δέω	δήσω	ἔδησα	δέδεκα	δέδεμαι	ἐδέθην
δηλόω	δηλώσω	ἐδήλωσα	δεδήλωκα	δεδήλωμαι	ἐδηλώθην
διακονέω	διακονήσω	διηκόνησα	δέδεμαι	----------	----------
διανοίγω	διανοίξω	διήνοιξα	----------	----------	διηνοίχθην
διδάσκω	διδάξω	ἐδίδαξα	δεδίδαχα	δεδίδαγμαι	ἐδιδάχθην
δίδωμι	δώσω	ἔδωκα	δέδωκα	δέδομαι	ἐδόθην
δικαιόω	δικαιώσω	ἐδικαίωσα	----------	δεδικαίωμαι	ἐδικαιώθην

First	Second	Third	Fourth	Fifth	Sixth
διψάω	διψήσω	ἐδίψησα	δεδίψηκα	----------	----------
διώκω	διώξω	ἐδίωξα	δεδίωχα	δεδίωγμαι	ἐδιώχθην
δοκέω	δόξω	ἔδοξα	----------	δέδογμαι	ἐδόχθην
δοκιμάζω	δοκιμάσω	ἐδοκίμασα	----------	δεδοκίμασμαι	ἐδοκιμάσθην
δοξάζω	δοξάσω	ἐδόξασα	----------	δεδόξασμαι	ἐδοξάσθην
δουλεύω	δουλεύσω	ἐδούλευσα	δεδούλευκα	----------	----------
δουλόω	δουλώσω	ἐδούλωσα	----------	δεδούλωμαι	ἐδουλώθην
δύναμαι	δυνήσομαι	----------	----------	δεδύνημαι	ἠδυνήθην
δυναμόω	δυναμώσω	ἐδυνάμωσα	----------	----------	ἐδυναμώθην
δωρέω	δωρήσομαι	ἐδωρησάμην	----------	δεδώρημαι	ἐδωρήθην
ἐάω	ἐάσω	εἴασα	εἴακα	εἴαμαι	εἰάθην
ἐγγίζω	ἐγγιῶ	ἔγγισα	ἤγγικα	----------	----------
ἐγείρω	*ἐγερῶ*	*ἤγειρα*	*ἐγήγερκα*	*ἐγήγερμαι*	*ἠγέρθην*
ἐθίζω	ἐθίσω	εἴθισα	----------	εἴθισμαι	εἰθίσθην
εἴκω	εἴξω	εἴξα	----------	----------	----------
εἰμί	ἔσομαι	----------	----------	----------	----------
(impf. *ἤμην*)					
εἰσέρχομαι	εἰσελεύσομαι	εἰσῆλθον*	εἰσελήλυθα	----------	----------
ἐκβάλλω	*ἐκβαλῶ*	*ἐξέβαλον**	*ἐκβέβληκα*	*ἐκβέβλημαι*	*ἐξεβλήθην*
ἐκδικέω	ἐκδικήσω	ἐξεδίκησα	----------	----------	----------
ἐκέρχομαι	ἐκελεύσομαι	ἐκῆλθον*	ἐκελήλυθα	----------	----------
ἐκκεντέω	ἐκκεντήσω	ἐξεκέντησα	----------	----------	----------
ἐκχέω	*ἐκχεῶ*	ἐξέχεα	ἐκκέχυκα	ἐκκέχυμαι	ἐξεχύθην
ἐλαττόω	ἐλαττώσω	ἠλάττωσα	ἠλάττωκα	ἠλάττωμαι	ἠλαττώθην
ἐλαύνω	ἐλάσω	ἤλασα	ἐλήλακα	ἐλήλαμαι	ἠλάθην
ἐλέγχω	ἐλέγξω	ἤλεγξα	----------	ἐλήλεγμαι	ἠλέγχθην
ἐλεέω	ἐλεήσω	ἠλέησα	----------	ἠλέημαι	ἠλεήθην
ἐλευθερόω	ἐλευθερώσω	ἠλευθέρωσα	----------	----------	ἠλευθερώθην
ἐλίσσω	ἐλίξω	εἴλιξα	----------	εἴλιγμαι	εἰλίχθην
ἕλκω (ἑλκύω)	ἑλκύσω	εἵλκυσα	εἵλκυκα	εἵλκυσμαι	εἱλκύσθην
ἐλπίζω	ἐλπιῶ	ἤλπισα	ἤλπικα	----------	----------
ἐμβριμάομαι	ἐμβριμήσομαι	ἐνεβριμησάμην	-------	----------	ἐνεβριμήθην
ἐμφανίζω	ἐμφανίσω	ἐνεφάνισα	----------	----------	ἐνεφανίσθην
ἐνθυμέομαι	ἐνθύμήσομαι	----------	----------	ἐντεθύμημαι	ἐνεθυμήθην
ἐντέλλομαι	*ἐντελοῦμαι*	*ἐνετειλάμην*	----------	*ἐντέταλμαι*	----------
ἐνυπιάζομαι	----------	ἐνυπιασάμην	----------	----------	ἐνυπιάσθην
ἐξαρτίζω	ἐξαρτιῶ	ἐξήρτισα	----------	ἐξήρτισμαι	----------
ἐξέρχομαι	ἐξελεύσομαι	ἐξῆλθον*	ἐξελήλυθα	----------	----------
ἐξετάζω	ἐξετάσω	ἐξήτασα	ἐξήτακα	ἐξήτασμαι	ἐξητάσθην
ἐξουδενέω	ἐξουδενήσω	----------	----------	ἐξουδένημαι	ἐξουδενήθην
ἐξουθενέω	ἐξουθενήσω	ἐξουθένησα	----------	ἐξουθένημαι	ἐξουθενήθην
ἐπερωτάω	ἐπερωτήσω	ἐπηρώτησα	----------	----------	----------
ἐπιθυμέω	ἐπιθυμήσω	ἐπεθύμησα	----------	----------	----------
ἐπιμελέομαι	ἐπιμελήσομαι	----------	----------	ἐπιμεμέλημαι	ἐπεμελήθην

First	Second	Third	Fourth	Fifth	Sixth
ἐπιορκέω	ἐπιορκήσω	ἐπιώρκησα	ἐπιώρκηκα	----------	----------
ἐπιποθέω	ἐπιποθήσω	ἐπεπόθησα	----------	----------	----------
ἐπισκέπτομαι	ἐπισκέψομαι	ἐπεσκεψάμην	----------	----------	----------
ἐπισκιάζω	ἐπισκιάσω	ἐπεσκίασα	----------	----------	ἐπεσκιάσθην
ἐπίσταμαι	ἐπιστήσομαι	----------	----------	----------	ἠπιστήθην
ἐπιχειρέω	ἐπιχειρήσω	ἐπεχείρησα	----------	----------	----------
ἐργάζομαι	ἐργάσομαι	εἰγασάμην (ἠργασάμην)	----------	----------	εἰργάσθην
ἐρευνάω	ἐρευνήσω	ἠρεύνησα	----------	----------	----------
ἐρημόομαι	ἐρημώσομαι	----------	----------	ἠρήμωμαι	ἠρημώθην
ἑρμηνεύω	ἑρμηνεύσω	ἡρμήνευσα	ἡρμήνευκα	----------	ἡρμηνεύθην
ἔρχομαι	ἐλεύσομαι	ἦλθον*	ἐλήλυθα	----------	----------
ἐρωτάω	ἐρωτήσω	ἠρώτησα	ἠρώτηκα	----------	----------
ἐσθίω	φάγομαι	ἔφαγον*	----------	----------	----------
ἑτοιμάζω	ἑτοιμάσω	ἡτοίμασα	ἡτοίμακα	ἡτοίμασμαι	ἡτοιμάσθην
εὐαγγελίζω	εὐαγγελίσω	εὐηγγέλισα	----------	εὐηγγέλισμαι	εὐηγγελίσθην
εὐαρεστέω	εὐαρεστήσω	εὐηρέστησα	εὐηρέστηκα	----------	----------
εὐδοκέω	εὐδοκήσω	εὐδόκησα (ηὐδόκησα)			
εὐκαιρέω	εὐκαιρήσω	εὐκαίρησα	----------	----------	----------
εὐλαβέομαι	εὐλαβήσομαι	----------	----------	----------	εὐλαβήθην
εὐλογέω	εὐλογήσω	εὐλόγησα	εὐλόγηκα	εὐλόγημαι	εὐλογήθην
εὑρίσκω	εὑρήσω	εὕρησα (εὗρον)*	εὕρηκα	εὕρημαι	εὑρέθην
εὐφραίνω	εὐφρανῶ	ηὔφρανα	----------	----------	ηὐφράνθην (εὐφράνθην)
εὐχαριστέω	εὐχαριστήσω	εὐχαρίστησα	----------	----------	εὐχαριστήθην
ἔχω (impf. εἶχον)	ἕξω	ἔσχον*	ἔσχηκα	ἔσχημαι	----------
ζάω	ζήσω	ἔζησα	ἔζηκα	----------	----------
ζέω	ζέσω	ἔζεσα	----------	ἔζεσμαι	ἐζέσθην
ζηλόω	ζηλώσω	ἐζήλωσα	----------	----------	----------
ζημιόω	ζημιώσω	ἐζημίωσα	ἐζημίωκα	----------	ἐζημιώθην
ζητέω	ζητήσω	ἐζήτησα	ἐζήτηκα	----------	----------
ζυμόω	ζυμώσω	ἐζύμωσα	----------	----------	ἐζυμώθην
ζώννυμι	ζώσω	ἔζωσα	ἔζωκα	ἔζωσμαι	ἐζώσθην
ἡγέομαι	ἡγήσομαι	ἡγησάμην	----------	ἥγημαι	----------
ἥκω	ἥξω	ἧξα	ἧκα	----------	----------
ἡσυχάζω	ἡσυχάσω	ἡσύχασα	----------	----------	----------
θαμβέω	----------	----------	----------	----------	ἐθαμβήθην
θανατόω	θανατώσω	ἐθανάτωσα	τεθανάτωκα	τεθανάτωμαι	ἐθανατώθην
θάπτω	θάψω	ἔθαψα	----------	τέθαμμαι	ἐτάφην
θαυμάζω	θαυμάσω	ἐθαύμασα	τεθαύμακα	τεθαύμασμαι	ἐθαυμάσθην
θεάομαι	θεάσομαι	ἐθεασάμην	----------	τεθέαμαι	ἐθεάθην

First	Second	Third	Fourth	Fifth	Sixth
θέλω	θελήσω	ἠθέλησα	τεθέληκα	----------	----------
(impf. ἤθελον)					
θεμελιόω	θεμελιώσω	ἐθεμελίωσα	----------	τεθεμελίωμαι	----------
θεραπεύω	θεραπεύσω	ἐθεράπευσα	----------	τεθεράπευμαι	ἐθεραπεύθην
θεωρέω	θεωρήσω	ἐθεώρησα	τεθεώρηκα	----------	----------
θησαυρίζω	θησαυρίσω	ἐθησαύρισα	----------	τεθησαύριμαι	----------
θιγγάνω	θίξω	ἔθιγον*	----------	----------	----------
θλίβω	θλίψω	ἔθλιψα	τέθλιφα	τέθλιμμαι	ἐθλίφθην
θνήσκω	θανοῦμαι	ἔθανον*	τέθνηκα	----------	----------
θραύω	θραύσω	ἔθραυσα	----------	τέθραυσμαι	ἐθραύσθην
θυμόω	----------	ἐθύμωσα	----------	----------	ἐθυμώθην
θύω	θύσω	ἔθυσα	τέθυκα	τέθυμαι	ἐτύθην
ἰάομαι	ἰάσομαι	ἰασάμην	----------	ἴαμαι	ἰάθην
ἵστημι	στήσω	ἔστησα	ἕστηκα	ἕσταμαι	ἐστάθην
ἰσχύω	ἰσχύσω	ἴσχυσα	ἴσχυκα	----------	ἰσχύθην
καθαρίζω	καθαριῶ	ἐκαθάρισα	----------	κεκαθάρισμαι	ἐκαθαρίσθην
καθεύδω	καθευδήσω	ἐκαθεύδησα	κεκαθεύδηκα	----------	----------
κάθημαι	καθήσομαι	----------	----------	----------	----------
καίω	καύσω	ἔκαυσα	κέκαυκα	κέκαυμαι	ἐκαύθην
κακόω	κακώσω	ἐκάκωσα	----------	----------	----------
καλέω	καλέσω	ἐκάλεσα	κέκληκα	κέκλημαι	ἐκλήθην
καλύπτω	καλύψω	ἐκάλυψα	κεκάλυφα	κεκάλυμμαι	ἐκαλύφθην
κάμπτω	κάμψω	ἔκαμψα	----------	κέκαμμαι	ἐκάμφθην
καταβαίνω	καταβήσομαι	κατέβην*	----------	----------	----------
καταράομαι	καταράσομαι	κατηρασάμην	----------	κατήραμαι	κατηράθην
καταργέω	καταργήσω	κατήργησα	κατήργηκα	κατήργημαι	κατηργήθην
καταρτίζω	καταρτίσω	κατήρτισα	----------	κατήρτισμαι	----------
κατηγορέω	κατηγορήσω	κατηγόρησα	----------	----------	----------
καυματίζω	καυματίσω	ἐκαυμάτισα	----------	----------	ἐκαυματίσθην
καυκάομαι	καυχήσομαι	ἐκαυχησάμην	----------	κεκαύχημαι	----------
κεῖμαι	----------	----------	----------	----------	----------
κελεύω	κελεύσω	ἐκέλευσα	κεκέλευκα	κεκέλευσμαι	ἐκελεύσθην
κενόω	κενώσω	ἐκένωσα	κεκένωκα	κεκένωμαι	ἐκενώθην
κεράννυμι	κεράσω	ἐκέρασα	κεκέρακα	κεκέρασμαι	ἐκεράσθην
κερδαίνω	κερδανῶ	ἐκέρδησα	----------	κεκέρδημαι	----------
	(κερδήσω)				
κηρύσσω	κηρύξω	ἐκήρυξα	κεκήρυχα	κεκήρυγμαι	ἐκηρύχθην
κινέω	κινήσω	ἐκίνησα	κεκίνηκα	κεκίνημαι	ἐκινήθην
κίχρημι	χρήσω	ἔχρησα	κέχρηκα	κέχρημαι	----------
κλαίω	καλύσω	ἔκλαυσα	----------	κέκλαυμαι	ἐκλαύσθην
κλάω	κλάσω	ἔκλασα	----------	κέκλασμαι	ἐκλάσθην
κλείω	κλείσω	ἔκλεισα	κέκληκα	κεκλεισμαι	ἐκλείσθην
κλέπτω	κλέψω	ἔκλεψα	----------	κέκλεμμαι	ἐκλέφθην
κληρονομέω	κληρονομήσω	ἐκληρονόμησα	κεκληρονόμηκα	----------	----------

First	Second	Third	Fourth	Fifth	Sixth
κλίνω	κλινῶ	ἔκλινα	κέκλικα	κέκλιμαι	ἐκλίθην
κοιμάω	κοιμήσω	ἐκοίμησα	----------	κεκοίμημαι	ἐκοιμήθην
κοινόω	κοινώσω	ἐκοίνωσα	κεκκοίνωκα	κεκοίνωμαι	ἐκοινώθην
κοινωνέω	κοινωνήσω	ἐκοινώνησα	κεκοινώνηκα	----------	----------
κολάζω	κολάσω	ἐκόλασα	----------	κεκόλασμαι	----------
κομίζω	κομίσω	ἐκόμισα	κεκόμικα	κεκόμισμαι	ἐκομίσθην
κοπιάω	κοπιάσω	ἐκοπίασα	κεκοπίακα	----------	----------
κόπτω	κόψω	ἔκοψα	κέκοφα	κέκομμαι	ἐκόπην
κοσμέω	κοσμήσω	ἐκόσμησα	κεκόσμηκα	κεκόσμημαι	----------
κράζω	κράξω	ἔκραξα	κέκραγα	----------	----------
κρατέω	κρατήσω	ἐκράτησα	κεκράτηκα	κεκράτημαι	----------
κρίνω	κρινῶ	ἔκρινα	κέκρινα	κέκριμαι	ἐκρίθην
κρύπτω	κρύψω	ἔκρυψα	κέκρυφα	κέκρυμμαι	ἐκρύφθην
κτάομαι	κτήσομαι	ἐκτησάμην	----------	----------	----------
κτίζω	κτίσω	ἔκτισα	ἔκτικα	ἔκτισμαι	ἐκτίσθην
κυρόω	κυρώσω	ἐκύρωσα	κεκύρωκα	κεκύρωμαι	----------
κωλύω	κωλύσω	ἐκώλυσα	κεκώλυκα	κεκώλυμαι	ἐκωλύθην
λαγχάνω	λήξομαι	ἔλαχον	εἴληχα	εἴληγμαι	ἐλήχθην
λαλέω	λαλήσω	ἐλάλησα	λελάληκα	λελάλημαι	ἐλαλήθην
λαμβάνω	λήψομαι	ἔλαβον*	εἴληφα	εἴλημμαι	ἐλήφθην
	(λήμψομαι)				(ἐλήμφθην)
λάμπω	λάμψω	ἔλαμψα	λέλαμπα	----------	ἐλάμφθην
λανθάνω	λήσω	ἔλαθον*	----------	λέλησμαι	ἐλήσθην
λατρεύω	λατρεύσω	ἐλάτρευσα	----------	----------	----------
λέγω	λέξω (ἐρῶ)	ἔλεξα	(εἴρηκα)	λέλεγμαι	ἐλέγθην
		(εἶπον)*		(εἴρημαι)	(ἐρρέθην)
λείπω	λείψω	ἔλιπον*	λέλοιπα	λέλειμμαι	ἐλείφθην
λιθάζω	λιθάσω	ἐλίθασα	----------	----------	ἐλιθάσθην
λογίζομαι	λογίσομαι	ἐλογισάμην	----------	λελόγισμαι	ἐλογίσθην
λοιδορέω	λοιδορήσω	ἐλοιδόρησα	----------	----------	----------
λούω	λούσω	ἔλουσα	----------	λέλουμαι	ἐλούθην
λυπέω	λυπήσω	ἐλύπησα	λελύπηκα	λελύπημαι	ἐλυπήθην
λυτρόω	λυτρώσω	ἐλύτρωσα	----------	----------	ἐλυτρώθην
λύω	λύσω	ἔλυσα	λέλυκα	λέλυμαι	ἐλύθην
μαθητεύω	μαθητεύσω	ἐμαθήτευσα	----------	----------	ἐμαθητεύθην
μαίνομαι	μανοῦμαι	ἐμηνάμην	----------	----------	----------
μανθάνω	μαθήσομαι	ἔμαθον*	μεμάθηκα	μεμάθημαι	----------
μαραίνω	μαρανῶ	ἐμάρανα	----------	μεμάραμμαι	ἐμαράνθην
μαρτυρέω	μαρτυρήσω	ἐμαρτύρησα	μεμαρτύρηκα	μεμαρτύρημαι	ἐμαρτυρήθην
μαστιγόω	μαστιγώσω	ἐμαστίγωσα	----------	----------	----------
μάχομαι	μαχοῦμαι	ἐμαχεσάμην	----------	μεμάχημαι	----------
	(μαχήσομαι)				
μεγαλύνω	----------	----------	----------	----------	ἐμεγαλύνθην
μεθύσκω	μεθύσω	ἐμέθυσα	----------	μεμέθυσμαι	ἐμεθύσθην

First	Second	Third	Fourth	Fifth	Sixth
μελετάω	μελετήσω	ἐμελέτησα	----------	----------	----------
μέλλω	μελλήσω	ἐμέλλησα	----------	----------	----------
μέλω (impers. 3rd sg., μέλει)	----------	----------	----------	----------	----------
μέμφομαι	μέμψομαι	ἐμεμψάμην	----------	----------	ἐμέμφθην
μένω	μενῶ	ἔμεινα	μεμένηκα	----------	----------
μερίζω	μεριῶ	ἐμέρισα	μεμέρικα	μεμέρισμαι	ἐμερισθην
μεριμνάω	μεριμνήσω	ἐμερίμνησα	----------	----------	----------
μεταμέλομαι	μεταμελήσομαι	----------	----------	μεταμεμέλημαι	μετεμελήθην
μετρέω	μετρήσω	ἐμέτρησα	----------	----------	----------
μηνύω	μηνύσω	ἐμήνυσα	μεμήνυκα	μεμήνυμαι	ἐμηνύθην
μιαίνω	μιανῶ	ἐμίανα	*μεμίαγκα*	*μεμίασμαι*	*ἐμιάνθην*
μείγνυμι (μειγνύω)	μείξω	ἔμειξα	----------	μέμειγμαι	ἐμίγην
μιμνήσκω	μνήσω	ἔμνησα	----------	μέμνημαι	ἐμνήσθην
μισέω	μισήσω	ἐμίσησα	μεμίσηκα	μεμίσημαι	ἐμισήθην
μισθόω	μισθώσω	ἐμίσθωσα	μεμίσθωκα	μεμίσθωμαι	ἐμισθώθην
μνημονεύω	μνημονεύσω	ἐμνημόνευσα	ἐμνημόνευκα	ἐμνημόνευμαι	ἐμνημονεύθην
μοιχεύω	μοιχεύσω	ἐμοίχευσα	----------	----------	ἐμοιχεύθην
μολύνω	μολυνῶ	ἐμόλυνα	----------	----------	*ἐμολύνθην*
μορφόω	μορφώσω	ἐμόρφωσα	----------	----------	ἐμορφώθην
μυέω	μυήσω	ἐμύησα	μεμύηκα	μεμύημαι	ἐμυήθην
μυρίζω	μυρίσω	ἐμύρισα	----------	----------	----------
μωμάομαι	μωμήσομαι	ἐμωμησάμην	----------	----------	ἐμωμήθην
μωραίνω	*μωρανῶ*	*ἐμώρανα*	----------	----------	*ἐμωράνθην*
νεκρόω	νεκρώσω	ἐνέκρωσα	νενέκρωκα	νενέκρωμαι	ἐνεκρώθην
νέμω	*νεμῶ*	ἔνειμα	*νενέμηκα*	*νενέμημαι*	*ἐνεμήθην*
νεύω	νεύσω	ἔνευσα	νένευκα	----------	----------
νηστεύω	νηστεύσω	ἐνήστευσα	----------	----------	----------
νήφω	νήψω	ἔνηψα	----------	----------	----------
νικάω	νικήσω	ἐνίκησα	νενίκηκα	νενίκημαι	ἐνικήθην
νίπτω	νίψω	ἔνιψα	----------	νένιμμαι	ἐνίφθην
νοέω	νοήσω	ἐνόησα	νενόηκα	νενόημαι	ἐνοήθην
νομίζω	νομιῶ (νομίσω)	ἐνόμισα	νενόμικα	νενόμισμαι	ἐνομίσθην
νομοθετέω	νομοθετήσω	ἐνομοθέτησα	----------	νενομοθέτημαι	----------
νυστάζω	νυστάξω	ἐνύσταξα	----------	----------	----------
ξενίζω	ξενίσω	ἐξένισα	----------	----------	ἐξενίσθην
ξηραίνω	ξηρανῶ	ἐξήρανα	----------	ἐξήραμμαι	ἐξηράνθην
ὁδεύω	ὁδεύσω	ὥδευσα	----------	----------	----------
ὀδυνάω	ὀδυνήσω	ὠδύνησα	----------	----------	ὠδυνήθην
ὄζω	ὀζήσω	ὤζησα	ὤζηκα	----------	----------
οἶδα	εἰδήσω	ᾔδειν	----------	----------	----------
οἰκέω	οἰκήσω	ᾤκησα	ᾤκηκα	ᾤκημαι	ᾠκήθην

First	Second	Third	Fourth	Fifth	Sixth
οἰκοδομέω	οἰκοδομήσω	ᾠκοδόμησα	ᾠκοδόμηκα	ᾠκοδόμημαι	ᾠκοδομήθην
οἴομαι (οἶμαι)	οἰήσομαι	----------	----------	----------	ᾠήθην
ὀκνέω	ὀκνήσω	ὤκνησα	----------	----------	----------
ὁμιλέω	ὁμιλήσω	ὡμίλησα	----------	----------	----------
ὀμνύω (ὄμνυμι)	ὀμόσω	ὤμοσα	ὀμώμοκα	ὀμώμομαι	ὠμόθην
ὁμοιόω	ὁμοιώσω	ὡμοίωσα	----------	ὡμοίωμαι	ὡμοιώθην
ὁμολογέω	ὁμολογήσω	ὡμολόγησα	ὡμολόγηκα	ὡμολόγημαι	ὡμολογήθην
ὀνειδίζω	ὀνειδίσω	ὠνείδισα	ὠνείδικα	----------	ὠνειδίσθην
ὀνίνημι	ὀνήσω	ὤνησα (ὠνάμην)	----------	ὤνημαι	ὠνήθην
ὀνομάζω	ὀνομάσω	ὠνόμασα	ὠνόμακα	ὠνόμασμαι	ὠνομάσθην
ὁπλίζω	ὁπλίσομαι	ὥπλισα	ὥπλικα	----------	ὡπλίσθην
ὁράω	ὄψομαι	εἶδον*	ἑώρακα (ἑόρακα)	ἑώραμαι	ὤφθην
ὀργίζω	ὀργιῶ	ὤργισα	----------	ὤργισμαι	ὠργίσθην
ὀρέγω	ὀρέξω	ὤρεξα	----------	ὤρεγμαι	ὠρέχθην
ὁρίζω	ὁρίσω	ὥρισα	ὥρικα	ὥρισμαι	ὡρίσθην
ὁρμάω	ὁρμήσω	ὥρμησα	ὥρμηκα	ὥρμημαι	ὡρμήθην
ὀρύσσω	ὀρύξω	ὤρυξα	ὀρώρυχα	ὀρώρυγμαι	ὠρύχθην
ὀρχέομαι	ὀρχήσομαι	ὠρχησάμην	----------	----------	----------
ὀφείλω	ὀφειλήσω	ὠφείλησα	ὠφείληκα	----------	ὠφειλήθην
παγιδεύω	παγιδεύσω	ἐπαγίδευσα	----------	----------	----------
παιδεύω	παιδεύσω	ἐπαίδευσα	πεπαίδευκα	πεπαίδευμαι	ἐπαιδεύθην
παίζω	παίξω	ἔπαιξα	πέπαικα	πέπαισμαι	ἐπαίχθην
παίω	παίσω	ἔπαισα	πέπαικα	πέπαισμαι	ἐπαίσθην
παλαιόω	παλαιώσω	ἐπαλαίωσα	πεπαλαίωκα	----------	----------
παραδίδωμι	παραδώσω	παρέδωκα	παραδέδωκα	παραδέδομαι	παρεδόθην
παρακαλέω	παρακαλέσω	παρεκάλεσα	παρακέκληκα	παρακέκλημαι	παρεκλήθην
παραμυθέομαι	παραμυθήσομαι	⤳ παρεμυθησάμην	----------	----------	----------
παροξύνω	παροξυνῶ	παρώξυνα	----------	----------	παρωξύνθην
παρρησιάζομαι	⤳ παρρησιάσομαι	ἐπαρρησιασάμην ⤳ πεπαρρησίασμαι	----------	----------
πάσχω	πείσομαι	ἔπαθον*	πέπονθα	----------	----------
πατάσσω	πατάξω	ἐπάταξα	πεπάτηκα	----------	ἐπατήθην
παύω	παύσω	ἔπαυσα	πέπαυκα	πέπαυμαι	ἐπαύθην
πειθαρχέω	πειθαρχήσω	ἐπειθάρκησα	----------	----------	----------
πείθω	πείσω	ἔπεισα	πέποιθα	πέπεισμαι	ἐπείσθην
πεινάω	πεινάσω	ἐπείνασα	πεπείνηκα	----------	----------
πειράζω	πειράσω	ἐπείρασα	πεπείρακα	πεπείραμαι	ἐπειράθην
πέμπω	πέμψω	ἔπεμψα	πέπομφα	πέπεμμαι	ἐπέμφθην
πενθέω	πενθήσω	ἐπένθησα	πεπένθηκα	----------	----------

First	Second	Third	Fourth	Fifth	Sixth
περιπατέω	περιπατήσω	περιεπάτησα	----------	----------	περιεπατήθην
περισσεύω	περισσεύσω	ἐπερίσσευσα	----------	----------	----------
περιτέμνω	περιτεμῶ	περιέτεμον*	περιτέτμηκα	περιτέτμημαι	περιετμήθην
πετάομαι	πετήσομαι	ἐπτόμην*	----------	πεπότημαι	----------
(πέτομαι)					
πήγνυμι	πήξω	ἔπηξα	----------	πέπηγμαι	ἐπάγην
πηδάω	πηδήσομαι	ἐπήδησα	πεπήδηκα	πεπήδημαι	----------
πιάζω	----------	ἐπίασα	----------	πεπίασμαι	ἐπιάσθην
πικραίνω	πικρανῶ	ἐπίκρανα	----------	----------	ἐπικράνθην
πίμπλημι	πλήσω	ἔπλησα	πέπληκα	πέπλησμαι	ἐπλήσθην
πίνω	πίομαι	ἔπιον*	πέπωκα	πέπομαι	ἐπόθην
πιπράσκω	----------	----------	πέπρακα	πέπραμαι	ἐπράθην
πίπτω	πεσοῦμαι	ἔπεσον*	πέπτωκα	----------	----------
		(ἔπεσα)			
πιστεύω	πιστεύσω	ἐπίστευσα	πεπίστευκα	πεπίστευμαι	ἐπιστεύθην
πλανάω	πλανήσω	ἐπλάνησα	πεπλάνηκα	πεπλάνημαι	ἐπλανήθην
πλάσσω	πλάσω	ἔπλασα	πέπλακα	πέπλασμαι	ἐπλάσθην
πλεονάζω	πλεονάσω	ἐπλεόνασα	----------	----------	----------
πλεονεκτέω	πλεονεκτήσω	ἐπλεονέκτησα	----------	----------	ἐπλεονεκτήθην
πλέω	πλεύσομαι	ἔπλευσα	πέπλευκα	πέπλευσμαι	ἐπλεύσθην
πληθύνω	πληθυνῶ	ἐπλήθυνα	----------	----------	ἐπληθύνθην
πληρόω	πληρώσω	ἐπλήρωσα	πεπλήρωκα	πεπλήρωμαι	ἐπληρώθην
πλήσσω	πλήξω	ἔπληξα	πεπληγα	πέπληγμαι	ἐπλήγην
πλουτέω	πλουτήσω	ἐπλούτησα	πεπλούτηκα	----------	----------
πνέω	πνεύσω	ἔπνευσα	πέπνευκα	πέπνευσμαι	ἐπνεύσθην
πνίγω	πνίξω	ἔπνιξα	----------	πέπνιγμαι	ἐπνίχθην
ποιέω	ποιήσω	ἐποίησα	πεποίηκα	πεποίημαι	ἐποιήθην
ποιμαίνω	ποιμανῶ	ἐποίμανα	----------	----------	----------
πολεμέω	πολεμήσω	ἐπολέμησα	πεπολέμηκα	πεπολέμημαι	ἐπολεμήθην
πορεύομαι	πορεύσομαι	----------	----------	πεπόρευμαι	ἐπορεύθην
πορνεύω	πορνεύσω	ἐπόρνευσα	----------	----------	----------
ποτίζω	ποτίσω	ἐπότισα	πεπότικα	----------	ἐποτίσθην
πραγματεύομαι	⌐→	ἐπραγματευσάμην	-----	----------	----------
	πραγματεύσομαι				
πράσσω	πράξω	ἔπραξα	πέπραχα	πέπραγμαι	ἐπράχθην
προσέρχομαι	προσελεύσομαι	προσῆλθον*	προσελήλυθα	----------	----------
προσεύχομαι	προσεύξομαι	προσηυξάμην	----------	----------	----------
προσκυνέω	προσκυνήσω	προσεκύνησα	προσκεκύνηκα	----------	----------
προφητεύω	προφητεύσω	ἐπροφήτευσα	προπεφήτευκα	προπεφήτευσμαι	----------
πταίω	πταίσω	ἔπταισα	ἔπταικα	ἔπταισμαι	ἐπταίσθην
πτοέω	πτοήσω	ἐπτόησα	----------	----------	ἐπτοήθην
πτύσσω	πτύξω	ἔπτυξα	----------	ἔπτυγμαι	ἐπτύχθην
πτύω	πτύσω	ἔπτυσα	ἔπτυκα	----------	ἐπτύσθην
πυνθάνομαι	πεύσομαι	ἐπυθόμην	----------	πέπυσμαι	----------

First	Second	Third	Fourth	Fifth	Sixth
πωλέω	πωλήσω	ἐπώλησα	----------	----------	ἐπωλήθην
πωρόω	πωρώσω	ἐπώρωσα	πεπώρωκα	πεπώρωμαι	ἐπωρώθην
ῥαβδίζω	ῥαβδίσω	----------	----------	----------	ἐραβδίσθην
ῥαντίζω	ῥαντιῶ	ἐράντισα	----------	ῥερράντισμαι	----------
ῥαπίζω	ῥαπίσω	ἐράπισα	----------	ῥεράπισμαι	ἐρραπίσθην
ῥέω	ῥεύσω (ῥεύσομαι)	ἔρρευσα	ἐρρύηκα	----------	----------
ῥήγνυμι (ῥήσσω)	ῥήξω	ἔρρηξα	ἔρρηχα	ἔρρηγμαι	ἐρρήχθην (ἐράγην)
ῥιζόω	ῥιζώσω	ἐρίζωσα	----------	ἐρρίζωμαι	ἐριζώθην
ῥίπτω	ῥίψω	ἔρριψα (ἔριψα)	ἔρριφα	ἔρριμαι	ἐρρίφθην
ῥύομαι	ῥύσομαι	ἐρρυσάμην (ἐρυσάμην)	----------	----------	ἐρρύσθην (ἐρύσθην)
ῥώννυμι	ῥώσω	ἔρρωσα	----------	ἔρρωμαι	ἐρρώσθην
σαλεύω	σαλεύσω	ἐσάλευσα	----------	σεσάλευμαι	ἐσαλεύθην
σαλπίζω	σαλπίσω	ἐσάλπισα	----------	σεσάλπισμαι	----------
σβέννυμι	σβέσω	ἔσβεσα	ἔσβηκα	ἔσβεσμαι	ἐσβέσθην
σέμομαι	----------	----------	----------	----------	ἐσέφθην
σείω	σείσω	ἔσεισα	σέσεικα	σέσεισμαι	ἐσείσθην
σημαίνω	σημανῶ	ἐσήμανα	σεσημαγκα	σεσήμασμαι	ἐσημάθην
σήπω	σήψω	ἔσηψα	σέσηπα	----------	----------
σθενόω	σθενώσω	ἐσθένωσα	----------	----------	----------
σιγάω	σιγήσω	ἐσίγησα	σεσίγηκα	σεσίγημαι	ἐσιγήθην
σιωπάω	σιωπήσω	ἐσιώπησα	σεσιώπηκα	σεσιώπημαι	ἐσιωπήθην
σκανδαλίζω	σκανδαλίσω	ἐσκανδάλισα	----------	----------	ἐσκανδαλίσθην
σκάπτω	σκάψω	ἔσκαψα	ἔσκαφα	ἔσκαμμαι	ἐσκάφθην
σκευάζω	σκευάσω	ἐσκεύασα	----------	ἐσκεύασμαι	ἐσκευάσθην
σκηνόω	σκηνώσω	ἐσκήνωσα	----------	----------	----------
σκιρτάω	σκιρτήσω	ἐσκίρτησα	----------	----------	----------
σκληρύνω	σκληρυνῶ	ἐσκλήρυνα	----------	----------	ἐσκληρύνθην
σκοπέω	σκοπήσω	ἐσκόπησα	----------	ἐσκόπημαι	----------
σκορπίζω	σκορπίσω	ἐσκόρπισα	----------	ἐσκόρπισμαι	ἐσκορπίσθην
σκοτίζω	σκοτίσω	ἐσκότισα	----------	ἐσκότισμαι	ἐσκοτίσθην
σκοτόω	σκοτώσω	ἐσκότωσα	----------	ἐσκότωμαι	ἐσκοτώθην
σκύλλω	----------	----------	----------	ἔσκυλμαι	----------
σοφίζω	----------	ἐσόφισα	----------	σεσόφισμαι	ἐσοφίσθην
σπαράσσω	σπαράξω	ἐσπάραξα	----------	----------	----------
σπαργανόω	σπαργανώσω	ἐσπαργάνωσα	----------	ἐσπαργάνωμαι	----------
σπάω	σπάσω	ἔσπασα	ἔσπακα	ἔσπασμαι	ἐσπάσθην
σπείρω	σπερῶ	ἔσπειρα	ἔσπαρκα	ἔσπαρμαι	ἐσπάρην
σπένδω	σπείσω	ἔσπεισα	ἔσπεικα	ἔσπεισμαι	ἐσπείσθην
σπεύδω	σπεύσω	ἔσπευσα	ἔσπευκα	ἔσπευσμαι	----------
σπιλόω	σπιλώσω	----------	----------	ἐσπίλωμαι	----------

First	Second	Third	Fourth	Fifth	Sixth
σπλαγχνίζομαι	---------	----------	----------	----------	ἐσπλαγχνίσθην
σπουδάζω	σπουδάσω	ἐσπούδασα	ἐσπούδακα	ἐσπούδασμαι	ἐσπουδάσθην
σταυρόω	σταυρώσω	ἐσταύρωσα	ἐσταύρωκα	ἐσταύρωμαι	ἐσταυρώθην
στέλλω	στελῶ	ἔστειλα	ἔσταλκα	ἔσταλμαι	ἐστάλην
στενάζω	στενάξω	ἐστέναξα	----------	ἐστέναγμαι	----------
στερεόω	στερεώσω	ἐστερέωσα	----------	----------	ἐστερεώθην
στεφανόω	στεφανώσω	ἐστεφάνωσα	ἐστεφάνωκα	ἐστεφάνωμαι	----------
στηρίζω	στηρίξω (στηρίσω)	ἐστήριξα (ἐστήρισα)	----------	ἐστήριγμαι	ἐστηρίχθην
στοιχέω	στοιχήσω	ἐστοίχησα	----------	----------	----------
στρατεύομαι	στρατεύσομαι	ἐστρατευσάμην	--------	ἐστράτευμαι	----------
στρέφω	στρέψω	ἔστρεψα	ἔστροφα	ἔστραμμαι	ἐστράφην
στρώννυμι (στρωννύω)	στρώσω	ἔστρωσα	ἔστρωκα	ἔστρωμαι	ἐστρώθην
συγχέω (συγχύνω)	συγχεῶ	συνέχεα	συγκέχυκα	συγκέχυμαι	συνεχύθην
συλάω	συλήσω	ἐσύλησα	σεσύληκα	σεσύλημαι	ἐσυλήθην
συμπαθέω	συμπαθήσω	ἐσυμπάθησα	----------	----------	----------
συνάγω	συνάξω	συνήγαγον*	----------	σέσυρμαι	ἐσύρην
σύρω	συρῶ	ἔσυρα	σέσυρκα	σέσυρμαι	ἐσύρην
σφάζω	σφάξω	ἔσφαξα	----------	ἔσφαγμαι	ἐσφάγην
σφραγίζω	σφραγίσω	ἐσφράγισα	----------	ἐσφράγισμαι	ἐσφραγίσθην
σχίζω	σχίσω	ἔσχισα	----------	----------	ἐσχίσθην
σχολάζω	σχολάσω	ἐσχόλασα	----------	----------	----------
σῴζω (σώζω)	σώσω	ἔσωσα	σέσωκα	σέσωμαι	ἐσώθην
σωφρονέω	σωφρονήσω	ἐσωφρόνησα	----------	----------	----------
ταλαιπωρέω	ταλαιπωρήσω	ἐταλαιπώρησα	τεταλαιπώρηκα ⌐↓ τεταλαιπώρημαι		ἐταλαιπωρήθην
ταπεινόω	ταπεινώσω	ἐταπείνωσα	----------	----------	ἐταπεινώθην
ταράσσω	ταράξω	ἐτάραξα	----------	τετάραγμαι	ἐταράχθην
τάσσω	τάξω	ἔταξα	τέταχα	τέταγμαι	ἐτάχθην
τείνω	τενῶ	ἔτεινα	τέτακα	τέταμαι	ἐτάθην
τελειόω	τελειώσω	ἐτελείωσα	τετελείωκα	τετελείωμαι	ἐτελειώθην
τελευτάω	τελευτήσω	ἐτελεύτησα	τετελεύτηκα	----------	ἐτελευτήθην
τελέω	τελέσω	ἐτέλεσα	τετέλεκα	τετέλεσμαι	ἐτελέσθην
τέμνω	τεμῶ	ἔτεμον*	τέτμηκα	τέτμημαι	ἐτμήθην
τήκω	τήξω	ἔτηξα	τέτηκα	τέτηγμαι	ἐτάκην
τηρέω	τηρήσω	ἐτήρησα	τετήρηκα	τετήρημαι	ἐτηρήθην
τίθημι	θήσω	ἔθηκα	τέθεικα	τέθειμαι	ἐτέθην
τίκτω	τέξω (τέξομαι)	ἔτεκον*	τέτοχα	τέτεγμαι	ἐτέχθην
τίλλω	τιλῶ	ἔτιλα	----------	τέτιλμαι	ἐτίλθην
τιμάω	τιμήσω	ἐτίμησα	τετίμηκα	τετίμημαι	ἐτιμήθην
τιμωρέω	τιμωρήσω	----------	----------	----------	ἐτιμωρήθην

First	Second	Third	Fourth	Fifth	Sixth
τίνω	τίσω	ἔτισα	τέτικα	τέτισμαι	ἐτίσθην
τολμάω	τολμήσω	ἐτόλμησα	----------	----------	----------
τραυματίζω	τραυματίσω	ἐτραυμάτισα	----------	τετραυμάτισμαι	----------
τρέπω	τρέψω	ἔτρεψα	τέτροφα (τέτραφα)	τέτραμμαι	ἐτρέφθην (ἐτράπην)
τρέφω	θρέψω	ἔθρεψα	τετραφα (τέτροφα)	τέθραμμαι	ἐθρέφθην (ἐτράφην)
τρέχω	δραμοῦμαι	ἔδραμον*	δεδράμηκα	δεδράμμαι	----------
τρίβω	τρίψω	ἔτριψα	τέτριφα	τέτριμμαι	ἐτρίφθην (ἐτρίβην)
τυγχάνω	τεύξομαι	ἐτύχησα (ἔτυχον)*	τετύχηκα (τέτευχα, τέτυχα)	τέτευγμαι	ἐτύχθην
τύπτω	τύψω	ἔτυψα	τέτυφα	τέτυμμαι	ἐτύφθην
τυφλόω	τυφλώσω	ἐτύφλωσα	τετύφλωκα	τετύφλωμαι	ἐτυφλώθην
τυφόω	τυφώσω	ἐτύφωσα	τετύφωκα	τετυφωμαι	ἐτυφώθην
ὑβρίζω	ὑβρίσω	ὕβρισα	ὕβρικα	ὕβρισμαι	ὑβρίσθην
ὑγιαίνω	ὑγιανῶ	ὑγίανα	----------	----------	ὑγιάσθην
ὑμνέω	ὑμνήσω	ὕμνησα	----------	----------	----------
ὑπάγω	ὑπάξω	ὑπήγαγον*	----------	ὑπῆγμαι	ὑπήχθην
ὑπάρχω	ὑπάρξομαι	ὑπηρξάμην	----------	----------	----------
ὑστερέω	ὑστερήσω	ὑστέρησα	ὑστέρηκα	----------	ὑστερήθην
ὑψόω	ὑψώσω	ὕψωσα	----------	----------	ὑψώθην
φαίνω	φανῶ	ἔφηνα (ἔφανα)	πέφαγκα	πέφασμαι	ἐφάνθην (ἐφάνην)
φανερόω	φανερώσω	ἐφανέρωσα	πεφανέρωκα	πεφανέρωμαι	ἐφανερώθην
φείδομαι	φείσομαι	ἐφεισάμην	----------	πέφεισμαι	----------
φέρω	οἴσω	ἤνεγκα*	ἐνήνοχα	ἐνήνεγμαι	ἠνέχθην
φεύγω	φεύξομαι	ἔφυγον*	πέφευγα	----------	----------
φημί [three other forms in the New Testament: ἔφη (impf., act.), φησί (pre., act.), φασί (pre., act.)]
φημίζω	φημίσω (φημιῶ)	ἐφήμισα	----------	πεφήμισμαι	ἐφημίσθην
φθάνω	φθάσω	ἔφθασα (ἔφθην)	ἔφθακα	----------	ἐφθάσθην
φθέγγομαι	φθέγξομαι	ἐφθεγξάμην	----------	ἔφθεγμαι	----------
φθείρω	φθερῶ	ἔφθειρα	ἔφθαρκα	ἔφθαρμαι	ἐφθάρην
φιλέω	φιλήσω	ἐφίλησα	πεφίληκα	πεφίλημαι	ἐφιλήθην
φιλοτιμέομαι	φιλοτιμήσομαι	ἐφιλοτιμησάμην	--------	πεφιλοτίμημαι	----------
φιμόω	φιμώσω	ἐφίμωσα	πεφίμωκα	----------	ἐφιμώθην
φοβέομαι	----------	----------	----------	----------	ἐφοβήθην
φοβέω	φοβήσω	ἐφόβησα	----------	πεφόβημαι	ἐφοβήθην
φονεύω	φονεύσω	ἐφόνευσα	----------	----------	----------
φορέω	φορέσω	ἐφόρεσα	πεφόρηκα	πεφόρημαι	ἐφορήθην
φορτίζω	φορτίσω	ἐφόρτισα	----------	πεφόρτισμαι	----------

First	Second	Third	Fourth	Fifth	Sixth
φραγελλόω	φραγελλώσω	ἐφραγέλλωσα	----------	----------	----------
φράζω	φράσω	ἔφρασα	πέφρακα	πέφρασμαι	ἐφράσθην
φρίσσω	φρίξω	ἔφριξα	πέφρικα	----------	----------
φρονέω	φρονήσω	ἐφρόνισα	πέφρονικα	----------	----------
φρουρέω	φρουρήσω	ἐφρούρησα	----------	πεφρούρημαι	ἐφρουρήθην
φυλάσσω	φυλάξω	ἐφύλαξα	πεφύλαχα	πεφύλαγμαι	ἐφυλάχθην
φυτεύω	φυτεύσω	ἐφύτευσα	πεφύτευκα	πεφύτευμαι	ἐφυτεύθην
φύω	φύσω	ἔφυσα (ἔφυν)	πέφυκα	----------	ἐφύην
φωνέω	φωνήσω	ἐφώνησα	----------	----------	ἐφωνήθην
φωτίζω	φωτίσω	ἐφώτισα	----------	πεφώτισμαι	ἐφωτίσθην
χαίρω	χαρήσομαι	ἐχάρην (ἐχαίρησα)	κεχάρηκα	κεχάρημαι	ἐχάρην
χαλάω	χαλάσω	ἐχάλασα	κεχάλακα	κεχάλασμαι	ἐχαλάσθην
χαρίζομαι	χαρίσομαι	ἐχαρισάμην	----------	κεχάρισμαι	ἐχαρίσθην
χαριτόω	χαριτώσω	ἐχαρίτωσα	----------	κεχαρίτωμαι	----------
χέω	χεῶ	ἔχεα	κέχυκα	κέχυμαι	ἐχύθην
χορηγέω	χορηγήσω	ἐχορήγησα	----------	----------	----------
χορτάζω	χορτάσω	ἐχόρτασα	----------	----------	ἐχορτάσθην
χράομαι	χρήσομαι	ἐχρησάμην	----------	κέχρημαι	ἐχρήσθην
χρηματίζω	χρηματίσω	ἐχρημάτισα	----------	κεχρημάτισμαι	ἐχρηματίσθην
χρίω	χρίσω	ἔχρισα	κέχρικα	κέχρισμαι	ἐχρίσθην
χρονίζω	χρονίσω (χρονιῶ)	----------	----------	----------	----------
χρυσόω	χρυσώσω	----------	----------	κεχρύσωμαι	----------
χωρέω	χωρήσω	ἐχώρησα	κεχώρηκα	κεχώρημαι	ἐχωρήθην
χωρίζω	χωρίσω	ἐχώρισα	----------	κεχώρισμαι	ἐχωρίσθην
ψάλλω	ψαλῶ	----------	----------	----------	----------
ψεύδομαι	ψεύσομαι	ἐψευσάμην	----------	ἔψευσμαι	----------
ψηλαφάω	ψηλαφήσω	ἐψηλάφησα	----------	----------	----------
ψηφίζω	----------	ἐψήφισα	ἐψήφικα	ἐψήφισμαι	ἐψηφίσθην
ὠδίνω	ὠδινήσω (ὠδινῶ)	ὠδίνα (ὠδίνασα, ὠδίνησα)	----------	----------	----------
ὠφελέω	ὠφελήσω	ὠφέλησα	ὠφέληκα	ὠφέλημαι	ὠφελήθην

GREEK–ENGLISH VOCABULARY

Α, α

ἀγαθός, -ή, -όν, good — 6
ἀγαπάω, I love — 7
ἀγάπη, love — 5
ἀγαπητός, -ή, -όν, beloved — 6
ἄγγελος, angel — 3
ἀγγέλλω, I tell, announce — 18
ἁγιάζω, I sanctify — 27
ἅγιος, -α, -ον, holy — 12
ἀγοράζω, I buy — 25
ἀγρός, field — 10
ἄγω, I lead — 4
ἀδελφή, -ῆς, ἡ, sister — 27
ἀδελφός, brother — 3
ἀδικέω, I wrong, do wrong — 29
ἀδικία, -ας, ἡ,
  unrighteousness — 27
ἀήρ, ἀέρος, ὁ, air — 15
αἷμα, -ατος, τό, blood — 14
αἴρω, I take up, take away — 18
αἰτέω, I ask — 12
αἰών, αἰῶνος, ὁ, age, eternity — 15
αἰώνιος, -ον, eternal,
  unending — 16
ἀκάθαρτος, -ον, unclean,
  defiling — 16
ἀκήκοα (2nd perf. of ἀκούω), I
  have heard — 22
ἀκοή, -ῆς, ἡ, hearing, report — 29
ἀκολουθέω, I follow — 13
ἀκούω, I hear — 2
ἀλέκτωρ, -τορος, ὁ, rooster — 15
ἀλήθεια, truth — 5
ἀληθινός, -ά, -όν, true — 25
ἀληθής, -ές, true, truthful, real — 16
ἀλλά, but — 7
ἀλλήλοις, to one another, in

one another, etc. — 13
ἀλλήλους, one another — 13
ἀλλήλων, of one another, from
  one another — 13
ἄλλος, -η, -ο, other — 6
ἅμα, together with (adv. p.) — 9
ἁμαρτάνω, I sin — 19
ἁμαρτία, sin — 5
ἁμαρτωλός, -όν, sinful, sinner — 16
ἀμήν, truly, amen — 12
ἀμπελών, -ῶνος, ὁ, vineyard — 15
ἄν, untranslatable particle — 13
ἀνά, up; in (Ac); each one
  (Ac) — 9
ἀναβαίνω, I go up — 13
ἀναβλέπω, I look up, receive
  sight — 9
ἀναγινώσκω, I read — 9
ἀνάγω, I lead up (middle: set
  sail) — 31
ἀναιρέω, I take up, kill — 29
ἀνάστασις, -εως, ἡ,
  resurrection — 15
ἄνεμος, wind — 10
ἀνήρ, ἀνδρός, ὁ, man, husband — 15
ἄνθρωπος, man — 2
ἀνίστημι, I cause to arise
  (transitive), I arise
  (intransitive) — 34
ἀνοίγω, I open — 4
ἀντί, against; because of (Ab);
  instead of (Ab) — 9
ἄνω, up (adv.) — 8
ἄξιος, -α, -ον, worthy — 22
ἀπαγγέλλω, I announce,
  report — 21
ἅπαξ, once — 17

ἅπας, -ασα, -αν, all — 21
ἀπέρχομαι, I go away — 10
ἄπιστος, -ον, unbelieving — 16
ἀπό, away from, off; away from
  (Ab); from (Ab); by (Ab);
  because of (Ab) — 9
ἀποδίδωμι, I give back, pay
  (active), I sell (middle) — 34
ἀποθνῄσκω, I die — 12
ἀποκαλύπτω, I reveal — 27
ἀποκρίνομαι, I answer — 10
ἀποκτείνω, I kill — 18
ἀπόλλυμι, I destroy (active), I
  perish (middle) — 33
ἀπολύω, I release — 21
ἀποστέλλω, I send, send out — 12
ἀπόστολος, apostle — 3
ἅπτομαι, I touch — 22
ἄρα, so, then, as a result — 21
ἀρνέομαι, I deny — 25
ἀρνίον, τό, lamb — 25
ἄρσην, -εν, male, man — 16
ἄρτι, now, just now (adv.) — 23
ἄρτος, bread — 4
ἀρχή, ἡ, beginning — 19
ἀρχιερεύς, -έως, ὁ, chief
  priest — 15
ἄρχομαι, I begin (middle v.) — 13
ἄρχω, I rule (active voice) — 13
ἄρχων, -οντος, ὁ, ruler — 14
ἀσθένεια, -ας, ἡ, weakness — 29
ἀσθενέω, I am weak — 23
ἀσθενής, -ές, sick, weak — 16
ἀσπάζομαι, I greet — 10
ἀστήρ, ἀστέρος, ὁ, star — 15
αὐξάνω, I cause to grow — 31
αὕτη, this (cf. οὗτος) — 12
αὐτός, he, she, it (self, same) — 11
ἀφίημι, I permit, forgive — 34
ἄφρων, -ον, fool, foolish — 16

ἄχρι, *up to* (adv. p.) 9

B, β

βάλλω, *I throw* 18
βαπτίζω, *I baptize* 4
βασιλεία, *kingdom* 5
βασιλεύς, -έως, ὁ, *king* 15
βασιλικός, -ή, -όν, *royal* 6
βαστάζω, *I bear, carry* 27
βιβλίον, τό, *book* 24
βλασφημέω, *I blaspheme* 23
βλέπω, *I see* 2
βούλομαι, *I wish* 10

Γ, γ

γαμέω, *I marry* 26
γάμος, *marriage, wedding* 4
γάρ, *for* 4
γέ (enclitic), *indeed, really, even* 25
γέγονα (2nd perf. of γίνομαι), *I have become* 22
γέγραμμαι, (perf. mid. of γράφω), *I have written* 23
γέγραφα (2nd perf. of γράφω), *I have written* 22
γενεά, ἡ, *generation* 21
γεννάω, *I beget, give birth to* 7
γένος, γένους, τό, *race, descendents* 14
γῆ, γῆς, ἡ, *earth, land* 8
γίνομαι, *I am, become, take place* 10
γινώσκω, *I know* 3
γλῶσσα, *tongue* 5
γνωρίζω, *I make known* 27
γνῶσις, -εως, ἡ, *knowledge (wisdom)* 26
γράμμα, -ατος, τό, *letter* 14
γραμματεύς, -έως, ὁ, *scribe, scholar* 15
γραφείς, -εῖσα, -έν, *having been written* (second aorist passive part.) 28
γραφή, *writing, scripture* 5
γράφηθι, cf. λίπε, *be written!* 31

γράφω, *I write* 2
γρηγορέω, *I watch* 31
γυνή, γυναικός, ἡ, *woman* 14

Δ, δ

δαιμόνιον, τό, *demon* 19
δέ, *and, but, now, so* 4
δεῖ, *it is necessary, must* 25
δείκνυμι, *I show* 33
δέκα, *ten* 10, 17
δεκαέξ, *sixteen* 16, 17
δεκαπέντε, *fifteen* 15, 17
δεκατέσσαρες, -ων, *fourteen* 14, 17
δέκατος, -η, -ον, *tenth* 17
[δεκατρεῖς], *thirteen* 13, 17
δένδρον, -ου, τό, *tree* 28
δεξιός, -ά, -όν, *right* (direction) 20
δεύτερος, -α, -ον, *second* 17
δέχομαι, *I receive* 10
δέω, *I bind* 21
δηλόω, *I show* 7
διά, *through; through* (G); *through* (Ab); *because of* (Ac) 9
διάβολος, ὁ, *Devil* 23
διάβολος, -ον, *slanderous, falsely accusing* 16
διαθήκη, -ης, ἡ, *covenant* 24
διακονέω, *I serve* 23
διακονία, -ας, ἡ, *service, ministry* 25
διάκονος, ὁ, ἡ, *servant, administrator* ﹐ 25
διακόσιοι, -αι, -α, *two hundred* 17
διδάσκαλος, ὁ, *teacher* 19
διδάσκω, *I teach* 3
διδαχή, -ῆς, ἡ, *teaching* 5
δίδωμι, *I give, grant, allow* 33
διέρχομαι, *I go through* 10
δίκαιος, -α, -ον, *righteous* 6
δικαιοσύνη, *righteousness* 12
δικαιόω, *I justify* 22
δικαίως, *justly* (adv.) 8

διό, *wherefore* 20
διότι, *because, for* 29
δίς, *twice* 17
δισχίλιοι, -αι, -α, *two thousand* 17
δοκέω, *I think, seem* 19
δόξα, *glory* 5
δοξάζω, *I glorify, honor* 18
δουλεύω, *I serve* 29
δοῦλος, *slave* 4
δύναμαι, *I am able* 25
δύναμις, -εως, ἡ, *power* 15
δυνατός, -ή, -όν, *powerful, able* 24
δύο, δύσιν, *two* 2, 17
δώδεκα, *twelve* 12, 17
δῶρον, *gift* 4

E, ε

ἐάν, *if, when, although* 30
ἑαυτοῦ, -ῆς, οὗ, *himself, herself, itself* 13
ἔβαλον (2nd aor. of βάλλω), *I threw* 20
ἑβδομήκοντα, *seventy* 17
ἑβδομηκοντάκις, *seventy times* 17
ἕβδομος, -η, -ον, *seventh* 17
ἐβεβλήμην (pluperf. mid./pass. of βάλλω), *I had thrown* 24
ἐγγίζω, *I draw near* 18
ἐγγύς, *near* (adv. p.) 8, 9
ἐγεγόνειν (pluperf. act. of γίνομαι), *I had become* 24
ἐγείρω, *I raise, raise up* 18
ἐγενόμην (2nd aor. of γίνομαι), *I became, happened* 20
ἔγνων (2nd aor. of γινώσκω), *I knew* 20
ἔγνωσμαι, (perf. mid. of γινώσκω) *I have known* 23
ἐγώ, *I* 1, 11
ἔθνος, ἔθνους, τό, *nation, gentile* 14
εἰ, *if* 13
εἶδον (2nd aor. of ὁράω), *I saw*

	20
εἴη, (εἰμί, optative) *may he (she, it) be!*	32
εἴκοσι, *twenty*	17
εἰκών, εἰκόνος, ὁ, *likeness, image*	15
εἴληφα (2nd perf. of λαμβάνω), *I have received*	22
εἰμί, *I am*	6
εἶναι, *to be* (present tense)	25
εἵνεκεν (cf. ἕνεκεν), *for the sake of* (adv. p.)	9
εἶπον (2nd aor. of λέγω), *I said*	20
εἰρήκειν (pluperf. act. of εἶπον), *I had said*	24
εἰρήνη, *peace*	5
εἰς, *into; to* (Ac); *in* (Ac); *with respect to* (Ac); *for* (Ac); *resulting in* (Ac)	9
εἷς, μία, ἕν, *one*	1, 17
εἰσάγω, *I lead into*	9
εἰσέρχομαι, *I enter*	10
εἴτε, *whether*	26
ἐκ, *out of; out of* (Ab); *from* (Ab); *by* (Ab); *because of* (Ab)	9
ἑκατόν, *one hundred*	17
ἐκβάλλω, *I throw out*	9
ἐκβεβλήκειν (pluperf. act. of ἐκβάλλω), *I had thrown out*	24
ἐκεῖ, *there* (adv.)	13
ἐκεῖθεν, *from there* (adv.)	27
ἐκεῖνος, -η, -ο, *that, those*	12
ἐκκλησία, *church*	5
ἐκλεκτός, -ή, -όν, *chosen, elect*	29
ἐκπορεύομαι, *I go out*	10
ἕκτος, -η, -ον, *sixth*	17
ἔλαβον (2nd aor. of λαμβάνω), *I took, received*	20
ἐλάχιστος, -η, -ον, *least, smallest*	16
ἐλεάω (also ἐλεέω), *I have*	

mercy	26
ἐλεέω (cf. ἐλεάω), *I have mercy*	26
ἔλεος, -ους, τό, *mercy, pity*	27
ἐλεύθερος, -α, -ον, *free*	31
ἐλήλυθα (2nd perf. of ἔρχομαι), *I have gone*	22
ἐληλύθειν (pluperf. act. of ἔρχομαι), *I had come*	24
ἔλιπον (2nd aor. of λείπω), *I left*	20
Ἕλλην, -ηνος, ὁ, *Greek, gentile*	15
ἐλπίζω, *I hope*	18
ἐλπίς, ἐλπίδος, ἡ, *hope*	14
ἐμαυτοῦ, -ης, --, *myself*	13
ἐμός, -η, -ον, *my*	13
ἔμπροσθεν, *before* (adv. p.)	9
ἐν, *in; to* (D); *with respect to* (D); *among* (L); *in* (L); *at* (L); *with* (I); *because of* (I); *in, with* (I); *by* (I)	9
ἕν [cf. εἷς] *one*	17
[ἐνακόσιοι, -αι, -α], *nine hundred*	17
ἔνατος, -η, -ον, *ninth*	17
ἕνδεκα, *eleven*	11, 17
ἑνδέκατος, -η, -ον, *eleventh*	17
ἐνδύω, *I put on, clothe*	26
ἕνεκα (cf. ἕνεκεν), *for the sake of* (adv. p.)	9
ἕνεκεν (ἕνεκα, εἵνεκεν), *for the sake of* (adv. p.)	9
ἐνενήκοντα, *ninety*	17
ἐννέα, *nine*	9, 17
ἐντολή, *commandment*	5
ἐνώπιον, *before* (adv. p.)	9
ἕξ, *six*	6, 17
ἑξακόσιοι, -αι, -α, *six hundred*	17
ἐξέρχομαι, *I go out*	10
ἔξεστι(ν), *it is lawful*	25
ἑξήκοντα, *sixty*	17
ἐξουσία, *authority*	12
ἔξω, *outside* (adv. p.)	8, 9

ἑορτή, -ῆς, ἡ, *feast*	27
ἐπαγγελία, ἡ *promise*	20
ἐπάνω, *above* (adv. p.)	9
ἐπεγεγράμμην (pluperf. mid./pass. of ἐπιγράφω), *I had written on*	24
ἐπερωτάω, *I ask, question*	19
ἔπεσον (2nd aor. of πίπτω), *I fell*	20
ἐπί, *on, upon; during* (G); *on* (G); *to, for* (D); *with respect to* (D); *at* (L); *during* (L); *in* (L); *because of* (I); *on* (Ac)	9
ἐπιγινώσκω, *I know fully*	9
ἐπιθυμία, -ας, ἡ, *desire, passion*	22
ἐπικαλέω, *I call, name*	26
ἐπικαλοῦμαι, *I appeal* (middle)	26
ἔπιον (2nd aor. of πίνω), *I drank*	20
ἐπιστολή, -ῆς, ἡ, *letter*	29
ἐπιστρέφω, *I turn to, return*	23
ἐπιτίθημι, *I lay upon*	34
ἐπιτιμάω, *I rebuke, warn*	26
ἑπτά, *seven*	7, 17
[ἑπτὰ καὶ δέκα], *seventeen*	17
ἑπτάκις, *seven times*	17
ἑπτακισχίλιοι, -αι, -α, *seven thousand*	17
[ἑπτακόσιοι, -αι, -α], *seven hundred*	17
ἐργάζομαι, *I work*	10
ἔργον, *work*	4
ἔρημος, -ου, ἡ, *wilderness*	8
ἔρημος, -ον, *lonely, deserted*	16
ἔρχομαι, *I come, go*	10
ἐρωτάω, *I ask*	7
ἔσεσθαι, *to be* (future tense)	25
ἐσθίω, *I eat*	12
ἔσομαι, *I shall be*	18
ἔσχατος, -η, -ον, *last*	6
ἔσχον (2nd aor. of ἔχω), *I had*	20

ἕτερος, -α, -ον, *another* 6
ἔτι, *still, yet* (adv.) 13
ἑτοιμάζω, *I prepare* 22
ἔτος, ἔτους, τό, *year* 14
εὐαγγελίζω, *I bring good
   news* 20
εὐαγγέλιον, *gospel, good
   news* 4
εὐθέως (εὐθύς), *immediately*
   (adv.) 8
εὐλογέω, *I bless* 7
εὑρίσκω, *I find* 4
εὗρον (2nd aor. of εὑρίσκω), *I
   found* 20
εὐχαριστέω, *I give thanks* 22
ἔφαγον (2nd aor. of ἐσθίω), *I ate*
   20
ἔφυγον (2nd aor. of φεύγω), *I
   fled* 20
ἐχθρός, -ά, -όν, *hating* 25
ἔχω, *I have* 3
ἑωράκειν (pluperf. act. of ὁράω),
   I had seen 24
ἕως, *up to* (adv. p.) 9

Z, ζ

ζάω, *I live* 7
ζητέω, *I seek* 7
ζωή, *life* 5
ζῷον, -ου, τό, *living creature*
   31

Η, η

ἡ, *the* 5
ἤ, *than, or* 8
ἤ . . . ἤ, *either . . . or* 8
ἥ, *who, whom* (cf. ὅς) 12
ἤγαγον (2nd aor. of ἄγω), *I led*
   20
ἤγγελμαι, (perf. mid. of
   ἀγγέλλω), *I have announced*
   23
ἡγεμών, -μόνος, ὁ, *governor,
   ruler* 15
ἡγέομαι, *I am chief, think,
   regard* 26
ᾔδειν (pluperf. act. of οἶδα), *I

knew (defective) 24
ἤδη, *now, already* 19
ἐγνώκειν (pluperf. act. of
   γινώσκω), *I had known* 24
ἥκω, *I come, have come* 30
ἦλθον (2nd aor. of ἔρχομαι), *I
   came* 20
ἥλιος, ὁ, *sun* 25
ἥμαρτον (2nd aor. of ἁμαρτάνω),
   I sinned 20
ἡμεῖς, *we* 11
ἡμέρα, *day* 5
ἡμέτερος, -α, -ον, *our* 13
ἤμην, *I was* 12
ἤνεγκον (2nd aor. of φέρω), *I
   bore, carried* 20
ἦργμαι, (perf. mid. of ἄρχω), *I
   have ruled* 23
ἦρμαι, (perf. mid. of αἴρω), *I
   have raised up* 23

Θ, θ

θάλασσα, *sea* 5
θάνατος, *death* 4
θαυμάζω, *I marvel, wonder* 21
θεάομαι, *I behold* 30
θέλημα, -ατος, τό, *will* 14
θέλω, *I wish, will, desire* 18
θεός, *God* 1
θεραπεύω, *I heal* 21
θεωρέω, *I observe* 7
θηρίον, τό, *beast* 21
θλῖψις, θλίψεως, ἡ, *trouble,
   distress* 15
θρίξ, τριχός, ἡ, *hair* 14
θρόνος, ὁ, *throne* 19
θυγάτηρ, -τρός, ἡ, *daughter* 15
θύρα, -ας, ἡ, *door* 22
θυσία, -ας, ἡ, *sacrifice* 26
θυσιαστήριον, -ου, τό, *altar*
   32

Ι, ι

ἰάομαι, *I heal* 27
ἴδε, *lo! behold!* 31
ἴδιος, -α, -ον, *one's own* 6

ἰδού, *lo! behold!* 31
ἱερεύς, -έως, ὁ, *priest* 15
ἱερόν, *temple* 4
Ἰησοῦς, -οῦ, ὁ, *Jesus* 8
ἱκανός, -ή, -όν, *sufficient, able,
   worthy* 22
ἱμάτιον, τό, *garment* 19
ἵνα, *in order that, so that, that*
   30
ἴσθι (εἰμί, imperative), *be!* 31
ἵστημι, *I place, set, cause to
   stand* (transitive), *I stand*
   (intransitive) 33
ἰσχυρός, -ά, -όν, *strong* 21
ἰσχύς, ἰσχύος, ἡ, *strength* 15
ἰχθύς, ἰχθύος, ὁ, *fish* 15
Ἰωάννης, -ου, ὁ, *John* 8

Κ, κ

καθαρίζω, *I cleanse* 25
καθαρός, -ά, -όν, *clean, pure*
   27
κάθημαι, *I sit down* 34
καθίζω, *I seat, sit* 21
καθώς, *as, just as* (adv.) 12
καί, *and* 1
καί . . καί, *both . . and* 7
καινός, -ή, -όν, *new* 6
καιρός, *time, season* 13
κακός, -ή, -όν, *bad* 6
κακῶς, *badly* (adv.) 8
καλέω, *I call* 7
καλός, -ή, -όν, *good* 6
καλῶς, *well* (adv.) 8
καρδία, *heart* 5
καρπός, ὁ, *fruit* 19
κατά, *down; by* (G); *against*
   (Ab); *distributive idea* (Ac);
   as (Ac); *according to* (Ac) 9
καταβαίνω, *I go down* 18
καταγινώσκω, *I condemn* 9
καταλείπω, *I leave* 29
καταργέω, *I abolish, destroy*
   27
κατηγορέω, *I accuse* 32
κατοικέω, *I inhabit, dwell* 21

κεῖμαι, *I lie, am laid* 32

κεκρίκειν (pluperf. act. of
κρίνω), *I had judged* 24

κέκριμαι, (perf. mid. of κρίνω) *I
have judged* 23

κελεύω, *I order* 27

κεφαλή, ἡ, *head* 19

κηρύσσω, *I preach* 4

κλαίω, *I weep* 22

κοινωνία - ας, ἡ, *fellowship* 30

κοπιάω, *I toil* 33

κόσμος, *world* 4

κράζω, *I shout, cry out* 18

κρατέω, *I grasp, seize* 21

κρείσσων, -ον, better, greater
(also κρείττων) 16

κρείττων (cf. κρείσσων) 16

κρίμα, -ατος, τό *judgment* 26

κρίνω, *I judge, decide* 18

κρίσις, κρίσεως, ἡ, *judgment*
15

κύριος, *Lord* 2

κωλύω, *I forbid, hinder* 34

κώμη, -ης, ἡ, *village* 27

Λ, λ

λαλέω, *I speak* 7

λαμβάνω, *I take, receive* 3

λαός, *people* 12

λέγω, *I say* 2

λείπω, *I leave* 20

λελυκώς, -κυῖα, - κός, *having
loosed* (perf. act. part. of
λύω) 29

λελυμένος, -η, -ον, *having
loosed (for myself), having
been loosed* (perf. mid./pass.
part. of λύω) 29

λελύμην (pluperf. mid./pass. of
λύω), *I had loosed* 24

λευκός, -η, - ον, *white* 30

λέων, -οντος, ὁ, *lion* 14

λίθος, ὁ *stone* 23

λίπε, λιποῦ, γράφηθι, *loose!,
loose (for yourself)!, be
written!* 31

λίποιμι, λιποίμην, *may I
leave!, may I loose (for
myself)!* 32

λιποίμην, cf. λίποιμι, *may I
loose (for myself)!* 32

λιπόμενος, -η, -ον, *having left
for myself, etc.* (second aorist
middle part.) 28

λιποῦ, cf. λίπε, *loose (for
yourself)!* 31

λιπών, -οῦσα, - όν, *having left*
(second aorist active part.)
28

λίψ, λίβος, ὁ *southwest wind*
14

λογίζομαι, *I account, reckon*
10

λόγος, *word* 2

λοιπός, -ή, - όν, *remaining, rest*
19

λῦε, λύου, *loose!, loose (for
yourself)!, be loosed!* 31

λυθείην, cf. λύσαιμι, *may I be
loosed* 32

λυθείς, -θεῖσα, -θέν, *having
been loosed* (first aorist
passive part.) 28

λύθητι, cf. λῦσον, *be loosed!*
31

λύοιμι, λυοίμην, *may I loose!,
may I loose (for myself)!,
may I be loose* 32

λυοίμην, cf. λύοιμι, *may I
loose (for myself)!, may I be
loose* 32

λυομένη, cf. λυόμενος, *being
loosed* 27

λυόμενον, cf. λυόμενος, *being
loosed* 27

λυόμενος, - η, -ον, *being loosed*
(present middle participle of
λύω) 27

λῦον, cf. λύων, *loosing* 26

λύου, cf. λῦε, *loose (for
yourself)!, be loosed!* 31

λύουσα, cf. λύων, *loosing* 26

λυπέω, *I grieve* 27

λῦσαι, cf. λῦσον, *loose (for
yourself)* 31

λύσαιμι, λυσαίμην, λυθείην,
*may I loose!, may I loose (for
myself)!, may I be loose* 32

λυσαίμην, cf. λύσαιμι, *may I
loose (for myself)!* 32

λυσάμενος, - η, -ον, *having
loosed for myself, etc.,* (first
aorist middle part.) 28

λύσας, - σασα, -σαν, *having
loosed* (first aorist active
part.) 28

λῦσον, λῦσαι, λύθητι, *loose!,
loose (for yourself)!, be
loosed!* 31

λύω, *I loose* 3

λύων, λύουσα, λῦον, *loosing*
(present active participle of
λύω) 26

Μ, μ

μαθητής, -ου, ὁ, *disciple* 8

μακάριος, - α, -ον, *blessed* 6

μᾶλλον, *more, rather* 19

μανθάνω, *I learn* 29

μαρτυρέω, *I witness, testify* 12

μαρτυρία, ἡ, *testimony,
witness* 23

μάρτυς, -τυρος, ὁ, *witness* 15

μάχαιρα, -ης, ἡ, *sword* 27

μέγας, -μεγάλη, -μέγα, *large,
great* 16

μείζων, -ον, *greater* 16

μέλας, -αινα, - αν, *black, ink*
16

μέλλω, *I am about to* 18

μέλος, μέλους, τό, *part,
member* 14

μεμενήκειν (pluperf. act. of
μένω), *I had remained* 24

μὲν . . . δὲ, *on the one hand . . .
on the other hand* 8

μέποτε, *lest, otherwise* 28

μέρος, μέρους, τό, *part*
(geographical)   14
μέσον, *in the midst* (adv. p.)   9
μέσος, -η, -ον, *middle*   19
μεσσίας, -ου, ὁ, *messiah*   8
μετά, *with; with* (G); *after*
(Ac)   9
μετανοέω, *I repent*   23
μετάνοια - ας, ἡ, *repentance*   30
μέχρι(ς), *until* (adv. p.)   9
μή, *not, lest* (usually non-
indicative moods)   13
μηδέ, *but not, nor, not even*   30
μηδείς, μηδεμία, μηδέν, *no
one*   30
μήποτε, *lest, otherwise*   28
μήτε, *and not (neither, nor)*   30
μήτηρ, μητρός, ἡ, *mother*   15
μία (cf. εἷς), *one*   17
μικρός, - ά, -όν, *small*   6
μιμνήσκομαι, *I remember*   33
μισέω, *I hate*   23
μισθός, - οῦ, ὁ, *wages, reward*
26
μνᾶ, - ᾶς, ἡ, *mina* (coin)   8
μνημεῖον, τό, *tomb, monument*
23
μόνος, -η, - ον, *only, alone*   8
μύριοι, -αι, -α, *ten thousand*
17
μυστήριον, τό, *mystery*   26

Ν, ν

ναί, *yes, truly*   25
ναός, ὁ, *temple*   21
νεκρός, - ά, -όν, *dead*   6
νέος, -α, -ον, *new*   8
νεφέλη, - ης, ἡ, *cloud*   28
νικάω, *I conquer*   27
νόμος, *law*   4
νοῦς, νοός, ὁ, *mind, thought*   15
νῦν, *now* (adv.)   8
νύξ, νυκτός, ἡ, *night*   14

Ο, ο

ὁ, *the*   4
ὅ, *that* (cf. ὅς)   12

ὀγδοήκοντα, *eighty*   17
ὄγδοος, -η, -ον, *eighth*   17
ὁδός, -οῦ, ἡ, *way, road*   8
ὀδούς, - όντος, ὁ, *tooth*   14
οἶδα (2nd perf. with present
meaning), *I know*   22
οἰκία, -ας, ἡ, *house, family,
household*   13
οἰκοδομέω, *I build*   23
οἶκος, *house*   3
οἶνος, ὁ, *wine*   25
οἷος, -α, -ον, *as*   18
[ὀκτακόσιοι, - αι, -α], *eight
hundred*   17
ὀκτώ, *eight*   8, 17
ὀλίγος, - η, -ον, *little, few*   23
ὅλος, - η, -ον, *whole, complete,
all, entire*   13
ὀμνύω, *I swear, take oath*   29
ὅμοιος, -α, -ον, *like*   21
ὁμοίως, *likewise*   25
ὁμολογέω, *I confess, profess*   7
ὄν, cf. λύων, *loosing*   26
ὄνομα, -ατος, τό, *name*   14
ὀπίσω, *after, behind* (adv. p.)   9
ὅπου, *where* (adv.)   13
ὅπως, *that* (*in order that*)   20
ὁράω, *I see*   12
ὀργή, -ῆς, ἡ, *wrath, anger*   23
ὄρος, ὄρους, τό, *mountain*   14
ὅς, ἥ, ὅ, *who, whom, that*   12
ὅσος, -η, -ον, *as much as*   18
ὅστις, ἥτις, ὅτι, *who, whoever*
17
ὀσφῦς, ὀσφύος, ἡ, *waist*   15
ὅταν, *whenever*   30
ὅτε, *when*   12
ὅτι, *that, because*   7
οὐ (οὐκ before vowels; οὐχ
with rough breathing) *not*   3
οὗ, *where*   30
οὐαί, *woe! alas!*   22
οὐδέ, *and not, nor, neither*   8
οὐδὲ . . οὐδὲ, *neither . . nor*   8
οὐδείς, οὐδεμία, οὐδέν, *no

one, nothing   17
οὐκ (cf. οὐ), *not*   3
οὐκέτι, *no longer*   21
οὖν, *therefore*   8
οὔπω, *not yet*   26
οὐρανός, *heaven*   4
οὖς, ὠτός, τό, *ear*   14
οὖσα, cf. λύων, *loosing*   26
οὔτε, *and not*   10
οὔτε . . οὔτε, *neither . . nor* 10
οὗτος, αὕτη, τοῦτο, *this, these*
12
οὕτως, *thus* (adv.)   12
οὐχ (cf. οὐ), *not*   3
οὐχί, *not* (strengthened form)   19
ὀφείλω, *I owe, ought*   24
ὀφθαλμός, *eye*   13
ὄχλος, *crowd*   12

Π, π

παιδίον, τό, *child*   20
παῖς, παιδός, ὁ, ἡ, *boy, girl,
child, servant*   30
πάλιν, *again* (adv.)   8
πάντοτε, *always*   22
παρά, *beside; from* (Ab); *by*
(Ab); *with* (L); *beside* (L);
with (I); *beside* (Ac); *than*
(Ac)   9
παραβολή, *parable*   5
παραγγέλλω, *I command,
charge*   26
παραγίνομαι, *I come, arrive*
23
παραδίδωμι, *I hand over,
betray*   34
παρακαλέω, *I comfort*   7
παράκλησις, -εως, ἡ,
exhortation, consolation   26
παραλαμβάνω, *I receive*   21
πάρειμι, *I am present, have
arrived*   30
παρέρχομαι, *I pass by*   10
παρθένος, - ου, ἡ, *virgin*   8
παρίστημι, *I present, offer*
(transitive), *I am present,*

stand by (intransitive) 34

παρουσία, -ας, ἡ, presence, coming 30

παρρησία, -ας, ἡ, boldness, confidence 26

πᾶς, πᾶσα, πᾶν, every, all, whole 16

πάσχα, τό, Passover (indeclinable) 27

πάσχω, I suffer 22

πατήρ, πατρός, ὁ, father 15

πείθω, I persuade 20

πεινάω, I hunger 34

πειράζω, I test, tempt, attempt 24

πέμπτος, -η, -ον, fifth 17

πέμπω, I send 4

πεντάκις, five times 17

πεντακόσιοι, -αι, -α, five hundred 17

πεντακισχίλιοι, -αι, -α, five thousand 17

πέντε, five 5, 17

πεντεκαιδέκατος, -η, -ον, fifteenth 17

πεντήκοντα, fifty 17

πέπεισμαι, (perf. mid. of πείθω) I have persuaded 23

πεπιστεύκειν (pluperf. act. of πιστεύω), I had believed 24

πεποιήκειν (pluperf. act. of ποιέω), I had made 24

πέποιθα (2nd perf. of πείθω), I have persuaded 22

πέπομφα (2nd perf. of πέμπω), I have sent 22

πέπονα (2nd perf. of πάσχω), I have suffered 22

πέραν, beyond (adv. p.) 9

περί, around; for, concerning (G); in regard to (Ac); around (Ac) 9

περιβάλλω, I clothe, put around 32

περιπατέω, I walk 7

περισσός, -ή, -όν, abundant 32

περισσεύω, I abound, am rich 23

περιτομή, -ῆς, ἡ, circumcision 23

πέφευγα (2nd perf. of φεύγω), I have fled 22

πίνω, I drink 18

πίπτω, I fall 18

πιστεύω, I believe 4

πίστις, πίστεως, ὁ, faith, trust, belief 15

πιστός, -ή, -όν, faithful 6

πλανάω, I deceive, lead astray 23

πλείων, -ον, more than (also πλέον) 16

πλέον (cf. πλείων) 16

πλῆθος, -ους, τό, crowd, multitude 14

πλήν, except (adv. p.) 9

πλήρης, -ες, full, complete 16

πληρόω, I fulfill 7

πλησίον, near (adv. p.) 9

πλοῖον, τό, boat 19

πλούσιος, -α, -ον, rich 27

πνεῦμα, -ατος, τό, spirit, wind 14

πνευματικός, -ή, -όν, spiritual 27

πόθεν, from where? where? 26

ποιέω, I do, make 7

ποιμήν, -μένος, ὁ, shepherd 15

ποῖος, -α, -ον, what type? 18

πόλις, πόλεως, ἡ, city, town 15

πολύς, -πολλή, -πολύ, much, many 16

πονηρός, -ά, -όν, evil 19

πορεύομαι, I proceed 10

πορνεία, -ας, ἡ, fornication 28

πόσος, -η, -ον, how much? 18

ποτέ, at some time, once, ever, formerly 26

ποτήριον, τό, cup 25

πούς, ποδός, ὁ, foot 14

πράσσω, I do, practice 18

πραΰτης, πραΰτητος, ἡ, humility 14

πρεσβύτερος, -α, -ον, elder 19

πρίν (or πρὶν ἤ), before 25

πρό, before; before, from (Ab); above (Ab) 9

πρόβατον, -ου, τό, sheep 22

πρός, near, toward; at, on (L); beside (Ac); with, to (Ac); with respect to (Ac); for (Ac) 9

προσέρχομαι, I come to 10

προσευχή, -ῆς, ἡ, prayer 24

προσεύχομαι, I pray 10

προσέχω, I attend to, heed 29

προσκαλέομαι, I summon 26

προσκυνέω, I worship 19

προσφέρω, I bring to, offer 21

πρόσωπον, face 4

προφητεύω, I prophesy 27

προφήτης, -ου, ὁ, prophet 8

πρῶτος, -η, -ον, first 17

πτωχός, -ή, -όν, poor 24

πῦρ, πυρός, τό, fire 15

πῶς, how? (interrog. part.) 12

πώς, somehow, in some way 12

Ρ, ρ

ῥῆμα, -ατος, τό, word 14

Σ, σ

σάββατον, τό, sabbath 19

σάλπιγξ, σάλπιγγος, ἡ, trumpet 14

σάρξ, σαρκός, ἡ, flesh 14

σεαυτοῦ, -ης, --, yourself 13

σημεῖον, τό, sign, miracle 19

σήμερον, today 22

Σίμων, Σίμωνος, ὁ, Simon 15

σκανδαλίζω, I cause to stumble 26

σκεῦος, -ους, τό, vessel, goods 32

σκότος, -ους, τό, darkness 14

σός, -η, -ον, your (sg.) 13

σοφία, ἡ wisdom 20

σοφός, -ή, -όν, *wise* 8

σπείρω, *I sow* 21

σπέρμα, - ατος, τό, *seed, descendents* 14

σταυρός, -ου, ὁ, *cross* 27

σταυρόω, *I crucify* 7

στόμα, - ατος, τό, *mouth* 14

σύ, *you* 11

συγγενής, -ές, *relative* 16

συκῆ, ῆς, ἡ, *fig tree* 8

σύν, *with, together; with* (I) 9

συνάγω, *I bring together* 9

συναγωγή, ἡ, *synagogue* 19

συνέδριον, - ου, τό, *Sanhedrin (Council)* 29

συνείδησις, -εως, ἡ, *conscience* 26

συνέρχομαι, *I come together, gather together* 10

συνίημι, *I understand* 34

σῴζω, *I save* 4

σῶμα, - ατος, τό, *body* 14

σωτήρ, σωτῆρος, ὁ, *savior, redeemer* 15

σωτηρία, ἡ, *salvation* 21

Τ, τ

ταχέως (ταχύ), *soon* (adv.) 8

ταχύς, -εῖα, ύ, *quick, swift* 16

τέ, *and, and so, so* (particle) 12

τὲ . . . τέ (or τὲ . . . δέ) *both . . . and, not only . . . but also* 12

τέκνον, *child* 4

τελειόω, *I fulfill, finish, make complete, make perfect* 34

τελέω, *I complete, fulfill* 27

τέλος, τέλους, τό, *end* 14

τέσσαρες, τέσσαρα, *four* 4, 17

τεσσαρεσκαιδέκατος, -η, - ον, *fourteenth* 17

τεσσεράκοντα, *forty* 17

τέταρτος, -η, -ον, *fourth* 17

τετρακισχίλιοι, -αι, -α, *four thousand* 17

τετρακόσιοι, -αι, -α, *four hundred* 17

τηρέω, *I keep, observe* 19

τίθημι, *I put, place, lay* 33

τιμάω, *I honor* 7

τιμή, -ῆς, ἡ, *honor, price* 21

τίς, τίς, τί, *who?, which? what?* 17

τις, τις, τι, *someone, something* 17

τό, *the* 4

τοιοῦτος, -αύτη, -οῦτο(ν), *such* 12

τόπος, *place* 13

τοσοῦτος, -αύτη, -οῦτον, *so much, so great, so many* 18

τότε, *then, at that time, next, thereupon* (adv.) 12

τοῦτο, *this* (cf. οὗτος) 12

τρεῖς, τρία, *three* 3, 17

τριάκοντα, *thirty* 17

τριακόσιοι, -αι, -α, *three hundred* 17

τρίς, *three times* 17

τρισχίλιοι, -αι, -α, *three thousand* 17

τρίτος, -η, -ον, *third* 17

τυφλός, -ή, -όν, *blind* 21

Υ, υ

ὑγιής, -ές, *healthy, whole* 16

ὕδωρ, ὕδατος, τό, *water* 14

υἱός, *son* 4

ὑμεῖς, *you (pl.)* 11

ὑμέτερος, - α, - ον, *your* (pl.) 13

ὑπάγω, *I go, go away* 19

ὑπάρχω, *I am, exist* 10

ὑπέρ, *over, above; for* (G); *in behalf of* (G); *concerning* (G); *than* (Ac) 9

ὑπό, *under; by* (Ab); *under* (Ac) 9

ὑποκάτω, *under* (adv. p.) 9

ὑπομονή, -ῆς, ἡ, *steadfastness, patient endurance* 25

ὑποστρέφω, *I return* 23

ὑποτάσσω, *I put in subjection* 24

ὕψιστος, -η, -ον, *highest* 16

Φ, φ

φαίνω, *I shine, appear* 25

φανερόω, *I make manifest* 21

φέρω, *I bring, carry* 18

φεύγω, *I flee, run away* 18

φημί, *I say* 33

φιλέω, *I love* 7

φίλος, - η, -ον, *loving* (noun = *friend*) 26

φοβέομαι, *I fear* (deponent) 13

φόβος, *fear* 13

φρονέω, *I think* 27

φυλακή, ἡ, *guard, prison, watch* 21

φυλάσσω, *I guard, keep* 25

φυλή, - ῆς, ἡ, *tribe* 25

φωνέω, *I call* 22

φωνή, *voice, sound* 5

φῶς, φωτός, τό, *light* 14

Χ, χ

χαίρω, *I rejoice* 18

χαρά, *joy* 5

χαρίζομαι, *I give, grant, pardon, forgive* 33

χάρις, χάριτος, ἡ, *grace, favor* 14

χείρ, χειρός, ἡ, *hand* 15

χείρων, -ον, *worse* 16

χήρα, -ας, ἡ, *widow* 27

χίλιοι, -αι, -α, *one thousand* 17

χρεία, ἡ, *need* 21

Χριστός, -οῦ, ὁ *Christ, Messiah, Anointed* 4

χρόνος, ὁ *time* 20

χρυσοῦς, -ῆ, - οῦν, *golden* 16

χώρα, -ας, ἡ, *country, district* 27

χωρίς, *without* (adv. p.) 9

Ψ, ψ

ψυχή, *life, soul* 5

Ω, ω

ὧδε, *here* 19

ὤν, οὖσα, ὄν, *being* (present
participle of εἰμί) 26
ὥρα, *hour* 5

ὡς, *as, that, how, about, while,
when* (compar. particle) 12
ὥσπερ, *just as, even as* 23

ὥστε, *so that, therefore* 21

GREEK VOCABULARY BY LESSON

Lesson 1
εἷς, μία, ἕν (ἑνός, μιᾶς, ἑνός), one   1
ἐγώ, *I*   1
θεός, *God*   1
καί, *and*   1

Lesson 2
δύο, *two*   2
ἄνθρωπος, *man*   2
κύριος, *Lord*   2
λόγος, *word*   2
ἀκούω, *I hear*   2
βλέπω, *I see*   2
γράφω, *I write*   2
λέγω, *I say*   2
λύω, *I loose*   2

Lesson 3
τρεῖς, *three*   3
ἄγγελος, *angel*   3
ἀδελφός, *brother*   3
ἀπόστολος, *apostle*   3
οἶκος, *house*   3
οὐ (οὐκ, οὐχ), *not*   3
γινώσκω, *I know*   3
διδάσκω, *I teach*   3
ἔχω, *I have*   3
λαμβάνω, *I take, receive*   3

Lesson 4
τέσσαρες, *four*   4
γάρ, *for*   4
δέ, *and, but, now, so*   4
ὁ, *the*   4
τό, *the*   4
ἄρτος, *bread*   4
γάμος, *marriage*   4
δοῦλος, *slave*   4
θάνατος, *death*   4
κόσμος, *world*   4
νόμος, *law*   4
οὐρανός, *heaven*   4

υἱός, *son*   4
Χριστός, -οῦ, ὁ *Christ, Messiah, Anointed*   4
δῶρον, *gift*   4
ἔργον, *work*   4
εὐαγγέλιον, *gospel, good news*   4
ἱερόν, *temple*   4
πρόσωπον, *face*   4
τέκνον, *child*   4
ἄγω, *I lead*   4
βαπτίζω, *I baptize*   4
εὑρίσκω, *I find*   4
κηρύσσω, *I preach*   4
πέμπω, *I send*   4
πιστεύω, *I believe*   4
σῴζω, *I save*   4

Lesson 5
πέντε, *five*   5
ἡ, *the*   5
ἀλήθεια, *truth*   5
ἁμαρτία, *sin*   5
βασιλεία, *kingdom*   5
ἐκκλησία, *church*   5
ἡμέρα, *day*   5
καρδία, *heart*   5
χαρά, *joy*   5
ὥρα, *hour*   5
ἀγάπη, *love*   5
γραφή, *writing, scripture*   5
διδαχή, -ῆς, ἡ, *teaching*   5
εἰρήνη, *peace*   5
ἐντολή, *commandment*   5
ζωή, *life*   5
παραβολή, *parable*   5
φωνή, *voice, sound*   5
ψυχή, *life, soul*   5
γλῶσσα, *tongue*   5
δόξα, *glory*   5
θάλασσα, *sea*   5

Lesson 6
ἕξ, *six*   6
εἰμί, *I am*   6
ἀγαθός, -ή, -όν, *good*   6
ἀγαπητός, -ή, -όν, *beloved*   6
ἄλλος, -η, -ο, *other*   6
βασιλικός, -ή, -όν, *royal*   6
δίκαιος, -α, -ον, *righteous*   6
ἔσχατος, -η, -ον, *last*   6
ἕτερος, -η, -ον, *another*   6
ἴδιος, -α, -ον, *one's own*   6
καινός, -ή, -όν, *new*   6
κακός, -ή, -όν, *bad*   6
καλός, -ή, -όν, *good*   6
μακάριος, -α, -ον, *blessed*   6
μικρός, -ά, -όν, *small*   6
νεκρός, -ά, -όν, *dead*   6
πιστός, -ή, -όν, *faithful*   6

Lesson 7
ἑπτά, *seven*   7
ἀλλά, *but*   7
καὶ . . . καί, *both . . . and*   7
ὅτι, *because, that*   7
εὐλογέω, *I bless*   7
ζητέω, *I seek*   7
θεωρέω, *I observe*   7
καλέω, *I call*   7
λαλέω, *I speak*   7
ὁμολογέω, *I confess, profess*   7
παρακαλέω, *I comfort*   7
περιπατέω, *I walk*   7
ποιέω, *I do, make*   7
φιλέω, *I love*   7
δηλόω, *I show*   7
πληρόω, *I fulfill*   7
σταυρόω, *I crucify*   7
ἀγαπάω, *I love*   7
γεννάω, *I beget, give birth to*   7
ἐρωτάω, *I ask*   7
ζάω, *I live*   7

τιμάω, *I honor* 7 | ἐπί, *upon* 9 | ἀσπάζομαι, *I greet* 10
Lesson 8 | κατά, *down* 9 | βούλομαι, *I wish* 10
ὀκτώ, *eight* 8 | μετά, *with* 9 | γίνομαι, *I am, become, take*
ἤ, *than, or* 8 | παρά, *beside* 9 | *place* 10
ἤ . . . ἤ, *either . . . or* 8 | περί, *around* 9 | δέχομαι, *I receive* 10
μέν . . . δέ, *on the one hand . . .* | πρό, *before* 9 | ἐργάζομαι, *I work* 10
on the other hand 8 | πρός, *to, toward* 9 | ἔρχομαι, *I come, I go* 10
οὐδέ, *and not, nor, neither* 8 | σύν, *with* 9 | ἀπέρχομαι, *I go away* 10
οὐδέ . . . οὐδέ, *neither . . . nor* | ὑπέρ, *over* 9 | διέρχομαι, *I go through* 10
8 | ὑπό, *under* 9 | εἰσέρχομαι, *I enter* 10
οὖν, *therefore* 8 | ἅμα, *together with* (adv. p.) 9 | ἐξέρχομαι, *I go out* 10
ὁδός, -οῦ, ἡ, *way, road* 8 | ἄχρι, *up to* (adv. p.) 9 | παρέρχομαι, *I pass by* 10
ἔρημος, -ου, ἡ, *wilderness* 8 | ἐγγύς, *near* (adv. p.) 9 | προσέρχομαι, *I come to* 10
παρθένος, -ου, ἡ, *virgin* 8 | ἔμπροσθεν, *before* (adv. p.) 9 | συνέρχομαι, *I come together,*
Ἰησοῦς, -οῦ, ὁ, *Jesus* 8 | ἕνεκεν (ἕνεκα, εἵνεκεν), *for* | *gather together* 10
Ἰωάννης, -ου, ὁ, *John* 8 | *the sake of* (adv. p.) 9 | λογίζομαι, *I account, reckon*
μαθητής, -οῦ, ὁ, *disciple* 8 | ἐνώπιον, *before* (adv. p.) 9 | 10
μεσσίας, -ου, ὁ, *messiah* 8 | ἔξω, *outside* (adv. p.) 9 | πορεύομαι, *I proceed* 10
προφήτης, -ου, ὁ, *prophet* 8 | ἐπάνω, *above* (adv. p.) 9 | ἐκπορεύομαι, *I go out* 10
γῆ, γῆς, ἡ, *earth, land* 8 | ἕως, *up to* (adv. p.) 9 | προσεύχομαι, *I pray* 10
συκῆ, ῆς, ἡ, *fig tree* 8 | μέσον, *in the midst* (adv. p.) 9 | **Lesson 11**
μνᾶ, -ᾶς, ἡ, *mina* (coin) 8 | μέχρι(ς), *until* (adv. p.) 9 | ἕνδεκα, *eleven* 11
μόνος, -η, -ον, *only, alone* 8 | ὀπίσω, *after* (adv. p.) 9 | ἐγώ (ἡμεῖς), *I (we)* 11
νέος, -α, -ον, *new* 8 | πέραν, *beyond* (adv. p.) 9 | σύ (ὑμεῖς), *you (you—pl.)* 11
σοφός, -ή, -όν, *wise* 8 | πλήν, *except* (adv. p.) 9 | αὐτός, -ή, -ό, *he, she, it (self,*
ἄνω, *up* (adv.) 8 | πλησίον, *near* (adv. p.) 9 | *same)* 11
δικαίως, *justly* (adv.) 8 | ὑποκάτω, *under* (adv. p.) 9 | **Lesson 12**
ἐγγύς, *near* (adv.) 8 | χωρίς, *without* (adv. p.) 9 | δώδεκα, *twelve* 12
ἔξω, *outside* (adv.) 8 | ἀναβλέπω, *I look up* (*receive* | οὗτος, αὕτη, τοῦτο, *this, these*
εὐθέως (εὐθύς), *immediately* | *sight*) 9 | 12
(adv.) 8 | ἀναγινώσκω, *I read* 9 | ἐκεῖνος, -η, -ο, *that, those* 12
κακῶς, *badly* (adv.) 8 | εἰσάγω, *I lead into* 9 | τοιοῦτος, -αύτη, -οῦτο(ν),
καλῶς, *well* (adv.) 8 | ἐκβάλλω, *I throw out* 9 | *such* 12
νῦν, *now* (adv.) 8 | ἐπιγινώσκω, *I know fully* 9 | ὅς, ἥ, ὅ, *who, whom, that* 12
πάλιν, *again* (adv.) 8 | καταγινώσκω, *I condemn* 9 | καθώς, *as, just as* (adv.) 12
ταχέως (ταχύ), *soon* (adv.) 8 | συνάγω, *I gather together* 9 | οὕτως, *thus* (adv.) 12
Lesson 9 | **Lesson 10** | τότε, *then, at that time, next,*
ἐννέα, *nine* 9 | δέκα, *ten* 10 | *thereupon* (adv.) 12
ἀνά, *up* 9 | οὔτε, *and not* 10 | πῶς, *how?* (interrog. part.) 12
ἀντί, *against* 9 | οὔτε . . . οὔτε, *neither . . . nor* | πώς, *somehow, in some way* 12
ἀπό, *away from* 9 | 10 | τέ, *and, and so, so* (particle) 12
διά, *through* 9 | ἀγρός, *field* 10 | τὲ . . . τέ (or τὲ . . . δέ) *both . . .*
εἰς, *into* 9 | ἄνεμος, *wind* 10 | *and, not only . . . but also* 12
ἐκ, *out of* 9 | ὑπάρχω, *I am, exist* 10 | ὡς, *as, that, how, about, while,*
ἐν, *in* 9 | ἀποκρίνομαι, *I answer* 10 | *when* (compar. particle) 12

ἀμήν, *truly, amen* 12
ὅτε, *when* 12
δικαιοσύνη, *righteousness* 12
ἐξουσία, *authority* 12
λαός, *people* 12
ὄχλος, *crowd* 12
ἅγιος, -α, -ον, *holy* 12
αἰτέω, *I ask* 12
ἀποθνῄσκω, *I die* 12
ἀποστέλλω, *I send* 12
ἐσθίω, *I eat* 12
ἤμην, *I was* 12
μαρτυρέω, *I witness, testify* 12
ὁράω, *I see* 12

Lesson 13
δεκατρεῖς, *thirteen* 13
ἄν, untranslatable particle 13
εἰ, *if* 13
ὅλος, -η, -ον, *whole, complete,
    all, entire* 13
καιρός, *time, season* 13
οἰκία, -ας, ἡ, *house, family,
    household* 13
ὀφθαλμός, *eye* 13
τόπος, *place* 13
φόβος, *fear* 13
ἐμός, -η, -ον, *my* 13
ἡμέτερος, -α, -ον, *our* 13
σός, -η, -ον, *your* (sg.) 13
ὑμέτερος, -α, -ον, *your* (pl.) 13
ἐμαυτοῦ, -ης, --, *myself* 13
σεαυτοῦ, -ης, --, *yourself* 13
ἑαυτοῦ, -ῆς, οὗ, *himself,
    herself, itself* 13
ἀλλήλων, *of one another, from
    one another* 13
ἀλλήλοις, *to one another, in
    one another, etc.* 13
ἀλλήλους, *one another* 13
ἐκεῖ, *there* (adv.) 13
ἔτι, *still, yet* (adv.) 13
ὅπου, *where* (adv.) 13
μή, *not, lest* (non-indicative) 13
φοβέομαι, *I fear* (deponent) 13
ἀκολουθέω, *I follow* 13

ἀναβαίνω, *I go up* 13
ἀνοίγω, *I open* 13
ἄρχω, *I rule* (active voice) 13
ἄρχομαι, *I begin* (middle v.) 13

Lesson 14
δεκατέσσαρες, *fourteen* 14
λίψ, λίβος, ὁ *southwest wind*
    14
γυνή, γυναικός, ἡ, *woman* 14
θρίξ, τριχός, ἡ, *hair* 14
σάλπιγξ, σάλπιγγος, ἡ,
    trumpet 14
σάρξ, σαρκός, ἡ, *flesh* 14
ἐλπίς, ἐλπίδος, ἡ, *hope* 14
πούς, ποδός, ὁ, *foot* 14
χάρις, χάριτος, ἡ, *grace, favor*
    14
πραΰτης, πραΰτητος, ἡ,
    humility 14
αἷμα, -ατος, τό, *blood* 14
γράμμα, -ατος, τό, *letter* 14
θέλημα, -ατος, τό, *will* 14
ὄνομα, -ατος, τό, *name* 14
πνεῦμα, -ατος, τό, *spirit, wind*
    14
ῥῆμα, -ατος, τό, *word* 14
σπέρμα, -ατος, τό, *seed,
    descendents* 14
στόμα, -ατος, τό, *mouth* 14
σῶμα, -ατος, τό, *body* 14
ἄρχων, -οντος, ὁ, *ruler* 14
λέων, -οντος, ὁ, *lion* 14
ὀδούς, -όντος, ὁ, *tooth* 14
νύξ, νυκτός, ἡ, *night* 14
οὖς, ὠτός, τό, *ear* 14
ὕδωρ, ὕδατος, τό, *water* 14
φῶς, φωτός, τό, *light* 14
γένος, γένους, τό, *race,
    descendents* 14
ἔθνος, ἔθνους, τό, *nation,
    gentile* 14
ἔτος, ἔτους, τό, *year* 14
μέλος, μέλους, τό, *part,
    member* 14

μέρος, μέρους, τό, *part*
    (geographical) 14
ὄρος, ὄρους, τό, *mountain* 14
πλῆθος, -ους, τό, *crowd,
    multitude* 14
σκότος, -ους, τό, *darkness* 14
τέλος, τέλους, τό, *end* 14

Lesson 15
δεκαπέντε, *fifteen* 15
αἰών, αἰῶνος, ὁ, *age, eternity*
    15
μάρτυς, -τυρος, ὁ, *witness* 15
πῦρ, πυρός, τό, *fire* 15
σωτήρ, σωτῆρος, ὁ, *savior,
    redeemer* 15
χείρ, χειρός, ἡ, *hand* 15
Ἕλλην, -ηνος, ὁ, *Greek,
    gentile* 15
ἀμπελών, -ῶνος, ὁ, *vineyard*
    15
Σίμων, Σίμωνος, ὁ, *Simon* 15
ἀήρ, ἀέρος, ὁ, *air* 15
ἀλέκτωρ, -τορος, ὁ, *rooster* 15
ἀστήρ, ἀστέρος, ὁ, *star* 15
εἰκών, εἰκόνος, ὁ, *likeness,
    image* 15
ἡγεμών, -μόνος, ὁ, *governor,
    ruler* 15
ποιμήν, -μένος, ὁ, *shepherd* 15
ἀνήρ, ἀνδρός, ὁ, *man, husband*
    15
θυγάτηρ, -τρός, ἡ, *daughter* 15
μήτηρ, μητρός, ἡ, *mother* 15
πατήρ, πατρός, ὁ, *father* 15
πίστις, πίστεως, ὁ, *faith, trust,
    belief* 15
πόλις, πόλεως, ἡ, *city, town* 15
κρίσις, κρίσεως, ἡ, *judgment*
    15
θλῖψις, θλίψεως, ἡ, *trouble,
    distress* 15
δύναμις, -εως, ἡ, *power* 15
ἀνάστασις, -εως, ἡ,
    resurrection 15
ἰσχύς, ἰσχύος, ἡ, *strength* 15

ἰχθύς, ἰχθύος, ὁ, *fish* 15
ὀσφῦς, ὀσφύος, ἡ, *waist* 15
ἀρχιερεύς, -έως, ὁ, *chief priest* 15
βασιλεύς, -έως, ὁ, *king* 15
γραμματεύς, -έως, ὁ, *scribe, scholar* 15
ἱερεύς, -έως, ὁ, *priest* 15
νοῦς, νοός, ὁ, *mind, thought* 15

Lesson 16

δεκαέξ, *sixteen* 16
αἰώνιος, -ον, *eternal, unending* 16
ἀκάθαρτος, -ον, *unclean, defiling* 16
ἁμαρτωλός, -όν, *sinful, sinner* 16
ἄπιστος, -ον, *unbelieving* 16
διάβολος, -ον, *slanderous, falsely accusing* 16
ἔρημος, -ον, *lonely, deserted* 16
χρυσοῦς, -ῆ, -οῦν, *golden* 16
ἀληθής, -ές, *true, truthful, real* 16
ἀσθενής, -ές, *sick, weak* 16
πλήρης, -ες, *full, complete* 16
συγγενής, -ές, *relative* 16
ὑγιής, -ές, *healthy, whole* 16
ἄρσην, -εν, *male, man* 16
ἄφρων, -ον, *fool, foolish* 16
ταχύς, -εῖα, ύ, *quick, swift* 16
πᾶς, πᾶσα, πᾶν, *every, all, whole* 16
μέλας, -αινα, -αν, *black, ink* 16
μέγας, -μεγάλη, -μέγα, *large, great* 16
πολύς, -πολλή, -πολύ, *much, many* 16
κρείσσων, -ον, *better, greater* (also κρείττων) 16
μείζων, -ον, *greater* 16
πλείων, -ον, *more than* (also πλέον) 16

χείρων, -ον, *worse* 16
ἐλάχιστος, -η, -ον, *least, smallest* 16
ὕψιστος, -η, -ον, *highest* 16

Lesson 17

τίς, τίς, τί, *who?, which? what?* 17
τις, τις, τι, *someone, something* 17
ὅστις, ἥτις, ὅτι, *who, whoever* 17
οὐδείς, οὐδεμία, οὐδέν, *no one, nothing* 17
εἷς, μία, ἕν, *one* 17
δύο, δύσιν, *two* 17
τρεῖς, τρία, *three* 17
τέσσαρες, τέσσαρα, *four* 17
πέντε, *five* 17
ἕξ, *six* 17
ἑπτά, *seven* 17
ὀκτώ, *eight* 17
ἐννέα, *nine* 17
δέκα, *ten* 17
ἕνδεκα, *eleven* 17
δώδεκα, *twelve* 17
[δεκατρεῖς], *thirteen* 17
δεκατέσσαρες, -ων, *fourteen* 17
δεκαπέντε, *fifteen* 17
[δεκαέξ], *sixteen* 17
[ἑπτά καὶ δέκα], *seventeen* 17
δεκαοκτώ, *eighteen* 17
[ἐννέα καὶ δέκα], *nineteen* 17
εἴκοσι, *twenty* 17
τριάκοντα, *thirty* 17
τεσσεράκοντα, *forty* 17
πεντήκοντα, *fifty* 17
ἑξήκοντα, *sixty* 17
ἑβδομήκοντα, *seventy* 17
ὀγδοήκοντα, *eighty* 17
ἐνενήκοντα, *ninety* 17
ἑκατόν, *one hundred* 17
διακόσιοι, -αι, -α, *two hundred* 17

τριακόσιοι, -αι, -α, *three hundred* 17
τετρακόσιοι, -αι, -α, *four hundred* 17
πεντακόσιοι, -αι, -α, *five hundred* 17
ἑξακόσιοι, -αι, -α, *six hundred* 17
[ἑπτακόσιοι, -αι, -α], *seven hundred* 17
[ὀκτακόσιοι, -αι, -α], *eight hundred* 17
[ἐνακόσιοι, -αι, -α], *nine hundred* 17
χίλιοι, -αι, -α, *one thousand* 17
δισχίλιοι, -αι, -α, *two thousand* 17
τρισχίλιοι, -αι, -α, *three thousand* 17
τετρακισχίλιοι, -αι, -α, *four thousand* 17
πεντακισχίλιοι, -αι, -α, *five thousand* 17
ἑπτακισχίλιοι, -αι, -α, *seven thousand* 17
μύριοι, -αι, -α, *ten thousand* 17
πρῶτος, -η, -ον, *first* 17
δεύτερος, -α, -ον, *second* 17
τρῖτος, -η, -ον, *third* 17
τέταρτος, -η, -ον, *fourth* 17
πέμπτος, -η, -ον, *fifth* 17
ἕκτος, -η, -ον, *sixth* 17
ἕβδομος, -η, -ον, *seventh* 17
ὄγδοος, -η, -ον, *eighth* 17
ἔνατος, -η, -ον, *ninth* 17
δέκατος, -η, -ον, *tenth* 17
ἑνδέκατος, -η, -ον, *eleventh* 17
δωδέκατος, -η, -ον, *twelfth* 17
τεσσαρεσκαιδέκατος, -η, -ον, *fourteenth* 17
πεντεκαιδέκατος, -η, -ον, *fifteenth* 17
ἅπαξ, *once* 17

δίς, *twice* 17
τρίς, *three times* 17
πεντάκις, *five times* 17
ἑπτάκις, *seven times* 17
ἑβδομηκοντάκις, *seventy times* 17

Lesson 18

τοσοῦτος, -αύτη, -οῦτον, *so much, so great, so many* 18
οἷος, -α, -ον, *as* 18
ὅσος, -η, -ον, *as much as* 18
ποῖος, -α, -ον, *what type?* 18
πόσος, -η, -ον, *how much?* 18
αἴρω, *I take up, take away* 18
ἀποκτείνω, *I kill* 18
ἐγείρω, *I raise, raise up* 18
κρίνω, *I judge, decide* 18
μένω, *I remain* 18
ἀγγέλλω, *I tell, announce* 18
βάλλω, *I throw* 18
πράσσω, *I do, practice* 18
δοξάζω, *I glorify, honor* 18
ἐγγίζω, *I draw near* 18
ἐλπίζω, *I hope* 18
κράζω, *I shout, cry out* 18
ἔσομαι, *I shall be* 18
θέλω, *I wish, will, desire* 18
καταβαίνω, *I go down* 18
μέλλω, *I am about to* 18
πίνω, *I drink* 18
πίπτω, *I fall* 18
φέρω, *I bring, carry* 18
φεύγω, *I flee, run away* 18
χαίρω, *I rejoice* 18

Lesson 19

ἀρχή, ἡ, *beginning* 19
δαιμόνιον, τό, *demon* 19
διδάσκαλος, ὁ, *teacher* 19
θρόνος, ὁ, *throne* 19
ἱμάτιον, τό, *garment* 19
καρπός, ὁ, *fruit* 19
κεφαλή, ἡ, *head* 19
πλοῖον, τό, *boat* 19
σάββατον, τό, *sabbath* 19
σημεῖον, τό, *sign, miracle* 19

συναγωγή, ἡ, *synagogue* 19
λοιπός, -ή, - όν, *remaining, rest* 19
μέσος, -η, -ον, *middle* 19
πονηρός, -ά, -όν, *evil* 19
πρεσβύτερος, -α, -ον, *elder* 19
ἤδη, *now, already* 19
μᾶλλον, *more, rather* 19
οὐχί, *not* (strengthened form) 19
ὧδε, *here* 19
δοκέω, *I think, seem* 19
ἐπερωτάω, *I ask, question* 19
προσκυνέω, *I worship* 19
τηρέω, *I keep, observe* 19
ἁμαρτάνω, *I sin* 19
ὑπάγω, *I go, go away* 19

Lesson 20

διό, *wherefore* 20
ὅπως, *that* (in order that) 20
δεξιός, -ά, -όν, *right* (direction) 20
ἐπαγγελία, ἡ *promise* 20
παιδίον, τό, *child* 20
σοφία, ἡ *wisdom* 20
χρόνος, ὁ *time* 20
εὐαγγελίζω, *I bring good news* 20
λείπω, *I leave* 20
πείθω, *I persuade* 20
ἔβαλον (2nd aor. of βάλλω), *I threw* 20
ἐγενόμην (2nd aor. of γίνομαι), *I became, happened* 20
ἔγνων (2nd aor. of γινώσκω), *I knew* 20
εἶδον (2nd aor. of ὁράω), *I saw* 20
εἶπον (2nd aor. of λέγω), *I said* 20
ἔλαβον (2nd aor. of λαμβάνω), *I took, received* 20
ἔλιπον (2nd aor. of λείπω), *I left* 20
ἔπεσον (2nd aor. of πίπτω), *I fell* 20

ἔπιον (2nd aor. of πίνω), *I drank* 20
ἔσχον (2nd aor. of ἔχω), *I had* 20
εὗρον (2nd aor. of εὑρίσκω), *I found* 20
ἔφαγον (2nd aor. of ἐσθίω), *I ate* 20
ἔφυγον (2nd aor. of φεύγω), *I fled* 20
ἤγαγον (2nd aor. of ἄγω), *I led* 20
ἦλθον (2nd aor. of ἔρχομαι), *I came* 20
ἥμαρτον (2nd aor. of ἡμαρτάνω), *I sinned* 20
ἤνεγκον (2nd aor. of φέρω), *I bore, carried* 20

Lesson 21

οὐκέτι, *no longer* 21
ἄρα, *so, then, as a result* 21
ὥστε, *so that, therefore* 21
γενεά, ἡ, *generation* 21
θηρίον, τό, *beast* 21
ναός, ὁ, *temple* 21
σωτηρία, ἡ, *salvation* 21
τιμή, -ῆς, ἡ, *honor, price* 21
φυλακή, ἡ, *guard, prison, watch* 21
χρεία, ἡ, *need* 21
ἅπας, - ασα, - αν, *all* 21
ἰσχυρός, -ά, -όν, *strong* 21
ὅμοιος, -α, -ον, *like* 21
τυφλός, -ή, -όν, *blind* 21
ἀπαγγέλλω, *I announce, report* 21
ἀπολύω, *I release* 21
δέω, *I bind* 21
διώκω, *I pursue, persecute* 21
θαυμάζω, *I marvel, wonder* 21
θεραπεύω, *I heal* 21
καθίζω, *I seat, sit* 21
κατοικέω, *I inhabit, dwell* 21
κρατέω, *I grasp, seize* 21
παραλαμβάνω, *I receive* 21

ENGLISH–GREEK VOCABULARY

A

able, δυνατός	24
able, δύναμαι	25
able, ἱκανός	22
abolish, καταργέω	27
abound, περισσεύω	23
about, ὡς	12
above, ἐπάνω	9
above, ὑπέρ	9
abundant, περισσός	32
according to, κατά	9
account, λογίζομαι	10
accuse, κατηγορέω	32
administrator, διάκονος	25
after, μετά	9
after, behind, ὀπίσω	9
again, πάλιν	8
against, ἀντί, κατά	9
age, αἰών, αἰῶνος, ὁ	15
air, ἀήρ, ἀέρος, ὁ	15
alas! οὐαί	22
all, ἅπας	21
all, ὅλος	13
all, πᾶς, πᾶσα, πᾶν	16
allow, δίδωμι	33
alone, μόνος	8
already, ἤδη	19
although, ἐάν	30
altar, θυσιαστήριον	32
always, πάντοτε	22
am, εἰμί	6
am, γίνομαι	10
am, ὑπάρχω	10
am about to, μέλλω	18
am chief, ἡγέομαι	26
am present, πάρειμι	30
am weak, ἀσθενέω	23
amen, ἀμήν	12
among, ἐν	9
and, καί	1

and, δέ	4
and, τέ	12
and not, οὐδέ	8
and not, οὔτε	10
and not (neither, nor), μήτε	30
angel, ἄγγελος	3
anger, ὀργή	23
announce, ἀγγέλλω	18
announce, ἀπαγγέλλω	21
Anointed, Χριστός, -οῦ, ὁ	4
another, ἕτερος	6
answer, ἀποκρίνομαι	10
apostle, ἀπόστολος	3
appeal, ἐπικαλοῦμαι	26
appear, φαίνω	25
arise, ἀνίστημι	34
around, περί	9
arrive, παραγίνομαι	23
as, κατά	9
as, καθώς	12
as, οἷος	18
as, τοσοῦτος	18
as, ὡς	12
as a result, ἄρα	21
as much as, ὅσος	18
ask, αἰτέω	12
ask, ἐπερωτάω	19
ask, ἐρωτάω	7
at, ἐν, πρός	9
at some time, ποτέ	26
at that time, τότε	12
ate, ἔφαγον (2d aor., ἐσθίω)	20
attempt, πειράζω	24
attend to, προσέχω	29
authority, ἐξουσία	12
away from, ἀπό	9

B

bad, κακός	6
badly, κακῶς	8
baptize, βαπτίζω	4

be! ἴσθι	31
be loosed! λύου	31
be loosed! λύθητι	31
be written! γράφηθι	31
bear, βαστάζω	27
beast, θηρίον, τό	21
became, ἐγενόμην	20
because, διότι	29
because, ὅτι	7
become, γίνομαι	10
before, ἔμπροσθεν	9
before, ἐνώπιον	9
before, πρίν	25
before, πρό	9
beget, γεννάω	7
begin, ἄρχομαι	13
beginning, ἀρχή	19
behind, ὀπίσω	9
behold! ἴδε, ἰδού	31
behold, θεάομαι	30
being, ὤν, οὖσα, ὄν	26
belief, πίστις	15
believe, πιστεύω	4
beloved, ἀγαπητός	6
beside, παρά, πρός	9
betray, παραδίδωμι	34
better, κρείσσων	16
beyond, πέραν	9
bind, δέω	21
black, μέλας	16
blaspheme, βλασφημέω	23
bless, εὐλογέω	7
blessed, μακάριος	6
blind, τυφλός	21
blood, αἷμα	14
boat, πλοῖον	19
body, σῶμα	14
boldness, παρρησία	26
book, βιβλίον	24
bore, ἤνεγκον (2nd aor. of	

φέρω)	20	clothe, ἐνδύω	26	desire, ἐπιθυμία	22
both . . and, τὲ . . τέ (τὲ . . δέ)		clothe, περιβάλλω	32	desire, θέλω	18
	12	cloud, νεφέλη	28	destroy, ἀπόλλυμι	33
both . . and, καὶ . . καὶ	7	come, ἔρχομαι	10	destroy, καταργέω	27
boy, παῖς, παιδός, ὁ, ἡ	30	come, ἥκω	30	Devil, διάβολος	23
bread, ἄρτος	4	come to, προσέρχομαι	10	die, ἀποθνῄσκω	12
bring, φέρω	18	come together, συνέρχομαι	10	disciple, μαθητής, -ου, ὁ	8
bring good news, εὐαγγελίζω		come about, παραγίνομαι	23	distress, θλῖψις, θλίψεως, ἡ	15
	20	comfort, παρακαλέω	7	district, χώρα, -ας, ἡ	27
bring to, προσφέρω	21	coming, παρουσία	30	do, ποιέω	7
bring together, συνάγω	9	command, παραγγέλλω	26	do, πράσσω	18
brother, ἀδελφός	3	commandment, ἐντολή	5	do wrong, ἀδικέω	29
build, οἰκοδομέω	23	concerning, περί, ὑπέρ	9	door, θύρα, -ας, ἡ	22
but, ἀλλά	7	complete, ὅλος	13	down, κατά	9
but, δέ	4	complete, πλήρης, -ες	16	drank, ἔπιον (2nd aor. of πίνω)	
but not, μηδέ	30	complete, τελέω	27		20
buy, ἀγοράζω	25	condemn, καταγινώσκω	9	draw near, ἐγγίζω	18
by, ἐν, κατά, παρά, ὑπό	9	confess, ὁμολογέω	7	drink, πίνω	18
C		confidence, παρρησία, ἡ	26	during, ἐπί	9
call, φωνέω	22	conquer, νικάω	27	dwell, κατοικέω	21
call, καλέω	7	conscience, συνείδησις, ἡ	26	**E**	
call upon, ἐπικαλέω	26	consolation, παράκλησις, ἡ	26	ear, οὖς, ὠτός, τό	14
came, ἦλθον (2nd aor. of		Council, συνέδριον, -ου, τό	29	earth, γῆ, γῆς, ἡ	8
ἔρχομαι)	20	country, χώρα, -ας, ἡ	27	eat, ἐσθίω	12
carried, ἤνεγκον (2nd aor. of		covenant, διαθήκη	24	eight, ὀκτώ	8,17
φέρω)	20	cross, σταυρός, -ου, ὁ	27	eighth, ὄγδοος	17
carry, βαστάζω	27	crowd, ὄχλος	12	eighty, ὀγδοήκοντα	17
carry, φέρω	18	crowd, πλῆθος, -ους, τό	14	either . . . or, ἤ . . . ἤ	8
cause to arise, ἀνίστημι	34	crucify, σταυρόω	7	elder, πρεσβύτερος, -α, -ον	19
cause to grow, αὐξάνω	31	cry out, κράζω	18	elect, ἐκλεκτός	29
cause to stand, ἵστημι	33	cup, ποτήριον, τό	25	eleven, ἕνδεκα	11,17
cause to stumble, σκανδαλίζω		**D**		eleventh, ἑνδέκατος	17
	26	darkness, σκότος, -ους, τό	14	end, τέλος, τέλους, τό	14
charge, παραγγέλλω	26	daughter, θυγάτηρ, -τρός, ἡ	15	enter, εἰσέρχομαι	10
chief priest, ἀρχιερεύς	15	day, ἡμέρα	5	entire, ὅλος	13
child, παῖς, παιδός, ὁ, ἡ	30	dead, νεκρός, -ά, -όν	6	eternal, αἰώνιος	16
child, παιδίον, τό	20	death, θάνατος	4	eternity, αἰών, αἰῶνος, ὁ	15
child, τέκνον	4	deceive, πλανάω	23	even as, ὥσπερ	23
chosen, ἐκλεκτός	29	decide, κρίνω	18	even, γέ (enclitic)	25
Christ, Χριστός, -οῦ, ὁ	4	defiling, ἀκάθαρτος	16	ever, ποτέ	26
church, ἐκκλησία	5	demon, δαιμόνιον, τό	19	every, πᾶς, πᾶσα, πᾶν	16
circumcision, περιτομή	23	deny, ἀρνέομαι	25	evil, πονηρός, -ά, -όν	19
city, πόλις	15	descendents, γένος, τό	14	except, πλήν	9
clean, καθαρός	27	descendents, σπέρμα, τό	14	exhortation, παράκλησις, ἡ	26
cleanse, καθαρίζω	25	deserted, ἔρημος	16	exist, ὑπάρχω	10

eye, ὀφθαλμός	13	ἕνεκεν, ἕνεκα	9	*go away*, ἀπέρχομαι	10
F		*forbid*, κωλύω	34	*go away*, ὑπάγω	19
face, πρόσωπον	4	*forgive*, ἀφίημι	34	*go down*, καταβαίνω	18
faith, πίστις, πίστεως, ὁ	15	*forgive*, χαρίζομαι	33	*go out*, ἐκπορεύομαι	10
faithful, πιστός	6	*fornication*, πορνεία, -ας, ἡ	28	*go out*, ἐξέρχομαι	10
fall, πίπτω	18	*forty*, τεσσεράκοντα	17	*go through*, διέρχομαι	10
falsely accusing, διάβολος	23	*found*, εὗρον (2nd aor. of		*go up*, ἀναβαίνω	13
family, οἰκία, -ας, ἡ	13	εὑρίσκω)	20	*God*, θεός	1
father, πατήρ, πατρός, ὁ	15	*four hundred*, τετρακόσιοι	17	*golden*, χρυσοῦς, -ῆ, -οῦν	16
favor, χάρις, χάριτος, ἡ	14	*four thousand*,		*good news*, εὐαγγέλιον	4
fear, φοβέομαι	13	τετρακισχίλιοι,	17	*good*, ἀγαθός	6
fear, φόβος	13	*four*, τέσσαρες, τέσσαρα	4,17	*good*, καλός	6
feast, ἑορτή	27	*fourteen*, δεκατέσσαρες	14,17	*goods*, σκεῦος, -ους, το	32
fell, ἔπεσον (2nd aor. of πίπτω)		*fourteenth*,		*gospel*, εὐαγγέλιον	4
	20	τεσσαρεσκαιδέκατος	17	*governor*, ἡγεμών, ὁ	15
fellowship, κοινωνία, ἡ	30	*fourth*, τέταρτος	17	*grace*, χάρις, χάριτος, ἡ	14
few, ὀλίγος	23	*free*, ἐλεύθερος, -α, -ον	31	*grant*, χαρίζομαι	33
field, ἀγρός	10	*friend*, φίλος, -ου, ὁ (-ης, ἡ)	26	*grant*, δίδωμι	33
fifteen, δεκαπέντε	15,17	*from*, ἀπό, ἐκ, παρά	9	*grasp*, κρατέω	21
fifteenth, πεντεκαιδέκατος	17	*from one another*, ἀλλήλων	13	*great*, μέγας, μεγάλη, μέγα	16
fifth, πέμπτος	17	*from there*, ἐκεῖθεν	27	*greater*, κρείττων, κρείσσων	
fifty, πεντήκοντα	17	*from where?* πόθεν	26		16
fig tree, συκῆ	8	*fruit*, καρπός, ὁ	19	*greater*, μείζων, -ον	16
find, εὑρίσκω	4	*fulfill*, πληρόω	7	*Greek*, Ἕλλην	15
finish, τελειόω	34	*fulfill*, τελειόω	34	*greet*, ἀσπάζομαι	10
fire, πῦρ, πυρός, τό	15	*fulfill*, τελέω	27	*grieve*, λυπέω	27
first, πρῶτος	17	*full*, πλήρης, -ες	16	*guard*, φυλακή, ἡ	21
fish, ἰχθύς, ἰχθύος, ὁ	15	**G**		*guard*, φυλάσσω	25
five hundred, πεντακόσιοι	17	*garment*, ἱμάτιον, τό	19	**H**	
five thousand, πεντακισχίλιοι,		*gather together*, συνέρχομαι		*had become*, ἐγεγόνειν	
	17		10	(pluperf. act. of γίνομαι)	24
five times, πεντάκις	17	*generation*, γενεά	21	*had believed*, πεπιστεύκειν	
five, πέντε	5,17	*gentile*, Ἕλλην	15	(pluperf. act. of πιστεύω)	24
fled, ἔφυγον (2nd aor. of φεύγω)		*gentile*, ἔθνος, ἔθνους, τό	14	*had come*, ἐληλύθειν (pluperf.	
	20	*gift*, δῶρον	4	act. of ἔρχομαι)	24
flee, φεύγω	18	*girl*, παῖς, παιδός, ὁ, ἡ	30	*had judged*, κεκρίκειν (pluperf.	
flesh, σάρξ, σαρκός, ἡ	14	*give*, χαρίζομαι	33	act. of κρίνω)	24
follow, ἀκολουθέω	13	*give*, δίδωμι	33	*had known*, ἤγνώκειν (pluperf.	
fool, ἄφρων	16	*give back*, ἀποδίδωμι	34	act. of γινώσκω)	24
foolish, ἄφρων	16	*give birth to*, γεννάω	7	*had loosed*, λελύμην (pluperf.	
foot, πούς, ποδός, ὁ	14	*give thanks*, εὐχαριστέω	22	mid./pass. of λύω)	24
for, γάρ	4	*glorify*, δοξάζω	18	*had made*, πεποιήκειν (pluperf.	
for, διότι	29	*glory*, δόξα	5	act. of ποιέω)	24
for, ὑπέρ, περί, πρός	9	*go*, ἔρχομαι	10	*had remained*, μεμενήκειν	
for the sake of, εἵνεκεν,		*go*, ὑπάγω	19	(pluperf. act. of μένω)	24

had said, εἰρήρκειν (pluperf. act. of εἶπον)	24	*of* πάσχω)	22
had seen, ἑωράκειν (pluperf. act. of ὁράω)	24	*have written,* γέγραφα (2nd perf. of γράφω)	22
had thrown out, ἐκβεβλήκειν (pluperf. act. of ἐκβάλλω)	24	*have written,* γέγραμμαι, (perf. mid. of γράφω)	23
had thrown, ἐβεβλήμην (pluperf. mid./pass. of βάλλω)	24	*have,* ἔχω	3
had written on, ἐπεγεγράμμην (pluperf. mid./pass. of ἐπιγράφω)	24	*having been loosed* (first aorist passive part.), λυθείς, -θεῖσα, -θέν,	28
had, ἔσχον (2nd aor. of ἔχω)	20	*having been written,* γραφείς	28
hair, θρίξ, τριχός, ἡ	14	*having left* (second aorist active part.), λιπών, -οῦσα, -όν	28
hand over, παραδίδωμι	34	*having left for myself, etc.* (second aorist middle part.), λιπόμενος	28
hand, χείρ, χειρός, ἡ	15		
happened, ἐγενόμην	20	*having loosed* (first aorist active part.), λύσας, -σασα, -σαν	28
hate, μισέω	23		
hating, ἐχθρός	25	*having loosed (for myself), having been loosed* (perf. mid./pass. part. of λύω), λελυμένος	29
have announced, ἤγγελμαι, (perf. mid. of ἀγγέλλω)	23		
have arrived, πάρειμι	30	*having loosed* (perf. act. part. of λύω), λελυκώς, -κυῖα, -κός	29
have become, γέγονα (2nd perf. of γίνομαι)	22		
have come, ἥκω	30	*having loosed for myself, etc.,* (first aorist middle part.), λυσάμενος	28
have fled, πέφευγα (2nd perf. of φεύγω)	22		
have gone, ἐλήλυθα (2nd perf. of ἔρχομαι)	22	*he,* αὐτός	11
have judged, κέκριμαι (perf. mid. of κρίνω)	23	*head,* κεφαλή, ἡ	19
have mercy, ἐλεάω (ἐλεέω)	26	*heal,* ἰάομαι	27
have persuaded, πέπεισμαι, (perf. mid. of πείθω)	23	*heal,* θεραπεύω	21
have persuaded, πέποιθα (2nd perf. of πείθω)	22	*healthy,* ὑγιής, -ές	16
have raised up, ἦρμαι, (perf. mid. of αἴρω)	23	*hear,* ἀκούω	2
have received, εἴληφα (2nd perf. of λαμβάνω)	22	*heard,* ἀκήκοα (2nd perf. of ἀκούω)	22
have ruled, ἦργμαι, (perf. mid. of ἄρχω)	23	*hearing,* ἀκοή	29
have sent, πέπομφα (2nd perf. of πέμπω)	22	*heart,* καρδία	5
have suffered, πέπονα (2nd perf.		*heaven,* οὐρανός	4
		heed, προσέχω	29
		here, ὧδε	19
		herself, ἑαυτοῦ	13
		highest, ὕψιστος	16
		himself, ἑαυτοῦ	13
		hinder, κωλύω	34

holy, ἅγιος	12
honor, δοξάζω	18
honor, τιμάω	7
honor, τιμή, -ῆς, ἡ	21
hope, ἐλπίς, ἐλπίδος, ἡ	14
hope, ἐλπίζω	18
hour, ὥρα	5
house, οἶκος	3
house, οἰκία, -ας, ἡ	13
household, οἰκία, -ας, ἡ	13
how much? πόσος	18
how, ὡς	12
how? πῶς	12
humility, πραΰτης, ἡ	14
hunger, πεινάω	34
husband, ἀνήρ	15

I

I, ἐγώ	1, 11
if, εἰ	13
if, ἐάν	30
image, εἰκών, εἰκόνος, ὁ	15
immediately, εὐθέως (εὐθύς)	8
in, ἐν	9
in behalf of, ὑπέρ	9
in one another, ἀλλήλοις	13
in order that, ἵνα	30
in some way, πώς	12
in the midst, μέσον	9
indeed, γέ (enclitic)	25
inhabit, κατοικέω	21
ink, μέλας, -αινα, -αν	16
into, εἰς	9
it, αὐτό	11
it is lawful, ἔξεστι(ν)	25
itself, ἑαυτοῦ	13

J

Jesus, Ἰησοῦς, -οῦ, ὁ	8
John, Ἰωάννης, -ου, ὁ	8
joy, χαρά	5
judge, κρίνω	18
judgment, κρίμα, -ατος, τό	26
judgment, κρίσις, ἡ	15
just as, καθώς	12
just as, ὥσπερ	23
just now, ἄρτι	23

justify, δικαιόω	22	*light,* φῶς, φωτός, τό	14	λυοίμην, λυσαίμην	32

justify, δικαιόω 22
justly, δικαίως 8

K

keep, guard, φυλάσσω 25
keep, observe, τηρέω 19
kill, ἀναιρέω 29
kill, ἀποκτείνω 18
king, βασιλεύς 15
kingdom, βασιλεία 5
knew, ἤδειν (pluperf. act. of οἶδα) 24
knew, ἔγνων (2nd aor. of γινώσκω) 20
know, γινώσκω 3
know, οἶδα (2nd perf. with present meaning) 22
know fully, ἐπιγινώσκω 9
knowledge , γνῶσις, -εως, ἡ 26

L

lamb, ἀρνίον, τό 25
large, μέγας, μεγάλη, μέγα 16
last, ἔσχατος 6
law, νόμος 4
lay, τίθημι 33
lay upon, ἐπιτίθημι 34
lead, ἄγω 4
lead astray, πλανάω 23
lead into, εἰσάγω 9
lead up, ἀνάγω 31
learn, μανθάνω 29
least, ἐλάχιστος 16
leave, καταλείπω 29
leave, λείπω 20
leave! λίπε, λιποῦ 31
led, ἤγαγον (2nd aor. of ἄγω) 20
left, ἔλιπον (2nd aor. of λείπω) 20
lest, μή 13
lest, μέποτε 28
let go, ἀφίημι 34
letter, ἐπιστολή 29
letter, γράμμα, -ατος, τό 14
lie, κεῖμαι 32
life, ψυχή 5
life, ζωή 5

light, φῶς, φωτός, τό 14
like, ὅμοιος, -α, -ον 21
likeness, εἰκών, εἰκόνος, ὁ 15
likewise, ὁμοίως 25
lion, λέων, -οντος, ὁ 14
little, ὀλίγος 23
live, ζάω 7
living creature, ζῷον, τό 31
lo! ἴδε, ἰδού 31
lonely, ἔρημος 16
look up, ἀναβλέπω 9
loose, λύω 3
loose! λῦε, λύου 31
loose! λῦσον, λῦσαι 31
loose (for yourself)! λύου 31
loosing, λύων, λύουσα, λῦον 26

Lord, κύριος 2
love, ἀγαπάω 7
love, ἀγάπη 5
love, φιλέω 7
loving, φίλος, - η, -ον 26

M

make, ποιέω 7
make complete, τελειόω 34
make known, γνωρίζω 27
make manifest, φανερόω 21
make perfect, τελειόω 34
male, ἄρσην 16
man, ἀνήρ, ἀνδρός 15
man, ἄρσην 16
man, ἄνθρωπος 2
many, πολύς, πολλή, πολύ 16
marriage, γάμος 4
marry, γαμέω 26
marvel, θαυμάζω 21
may he (she, it) be! εἴη 32
may I be loose, λυοίμην, λυθείην 32
may I leave! λίποιμι 32
*may I leave (for myself)! λιποίμην 32
may I loose! λύοιμι, λύσαιμι 32
may I loose (for myself)!

λυοίμην, λυσαίμην 32
member, μέλος, μέλους, τό 14
mercy, ἔλεος 27
messiah, μεσσίας, - ου, ὁ 8
Messiah, Χριστός, - οῦ, ὁ 4
middle, μέσος 19
mina (coin), μνᾶ, -ᾶς, ἡ 8
mind, νοῦς, νοός, ὁ 15
ministry, διακονία 25
miracle, σημεῖον, τό 19
monument, μνημεῖον, τό 23
more, μᾶλλον 19
more than , πλείων (πλέον) 16
mother, μήτηρ, μητρός, ἡ 15
mountain, ὄρος, ὄρους, τό 14
mouth, στόμα, -ατος, τό 14
much, πολύς, πολλή, πολύ 16
multitude, πλῆθος, -ους, τό 14
must, δεῖ 25
my, ἐμός 13
myself, ἐμαυτοῦ 13
mystery, μυστήριον, τό 26

N

name, ἐπικαλέω 26
name, ὄνομα, - ατος, τό 14
nation, gentile, ἔθνος, τό 14
near, πρός 9
near, ἐγγύς 8, 9
near, πλησίον 9
necessary, δεῖ 25
need, χρεία, ἡ 21
neither, οὐδέ 8
neither . . . nor , οὐδὲ . . . οὐδὲ 8
neither . . . nor , οὔτε . . . οὔτε 10
new, καινός 6
new, νέος, -α, -ον 8
next, τότε 12
night, νύξ, νυκτός, ἡ 14
nine, ἐννέα 9,17
ninety, ἐνενήκοντα 17
ninth, ἔνατος 17
no longer, οὐκέτι 21
no one, μηδείς, μηδεμία,

μηδέν	30	**P**	
no one, οὐδείς, οὐδεμία,		*parable,* παραβολή	5
οὐδέν	17	*pardon,* χαρίζομαι	33
nor, μηδέ	30	*part* (geographical), μέρος, τό	14
nor, οὐδέ	8	*part,* μέλος, μέλους, τό	14
not, οὐχί	19	*pass by,* παρέρχομαι	10
not even, μηδέ	30	*passion,* ἐπιθυμία	22
not only . . . but also, τὲ . . . τέ		*Passover,* πάσχα, τό	27
(or τὲ . . . δέ)	12	*patient endurance,* ὑπομονή, ἡ	
not yet, οὔπω	26		25
not, οὐ (οὐκ, οὐχ)	3	*pay,* ἀποδίδωμι	34
not, μή	13	*peace,* εἰρήνη	5
nothing, οὐδείς, οὐδεμία,		*people,* λαός	12
οὐδέν	17	*perish,* ἀπόλλυμι	33
now, νῦν	8	*permit,* ἀφίημι	34
now, ἄρτι	23	*persuade,* πείθω	20
now, δέ	4	*pity,* ἔλεος	27
now, ἤδη	19	*place,* ἵστημι	33
		place, τίθημι	33
O		*place,* τόπος	13
observe, θεωρέω	7	*poor,* πτωχός	24
of one another, ἀλλήλων	13	*power,* δύναμις	15
of what sort, ὁποῖος, -α, - ον	18	*powerful,* δυνατός	24
offer, παρίστημι	34	*practice,* πράσσω	18
offer, προσφέρω	21	*pray,* προσεύχομαι	10
on the one hand . . . on the		*prayer,* προσευχή, -ῆς, ἡ	24
other hand, μὲν . . . δὲ	8	*preach,* κηρύσσω	4
on, ἐπί, πρός	9	*prepare,* ἑτοιμάζω	22
once, ἅπαξ	17	*presence,* παρουσία, -ας, ἡ	30
once, ποτέ	26	*present,* παρίστημι	34
one another, ἀλλήλους	13	*price,* τιμή, - ῆς, ἡ	21
one hundred, ἑκατόν	17	*priest,* ἱερεύς, -έως, ὁ	15
one thousand, χίλιοι	17	*prison,* φυλακή, ἡ	21
one's own, ἴδιος, -α, -ον	6	*proceed,* πορεύομαι	10
one, εἷς, μία, ἕν	1,17	*profess,* ὁμολογέω	7
only, μόνος	8	*promise,* ἐπαγγελία, ἡ	20
open, ἀνοίγω	13	*prophesy,* προφητεύω	27
order, κελεύω	27	*prophet,* προφήτης, - ου, ὁ	8
other, ἄλλος		*pure,* καθαρός, -ά, -όν	27
otherwise, μέποτε, μήποτε	28	*put,* τίθημι	33
ought, ὀφείλω	24	*put around,* περιβάλλω	32
our, ἡμέτερος	13	*put in subjection,* ὑποτάσσω	24
out of, ἐκ	9	*put on,* ἐνδύω	26
outside, ἔξω	8, 9		
over, above, ὑπέρ	9	**Q**	
owe, ὀφείλω	24	*question,* ἐπερωτάω	19

quick, ταχύς, -εῖα	16
R	
race, γένος, γένους, τό	14
raise, raise up, ἐγείρω	18
read, ἀναγινώσκω	9
real, ἀληθής	16
really, γέ (enclitic)	25
rebuke, ἐπιτιμάω	26
receive sight, ἀναβλέπω	9
receive, δέχομαι	10
receive, λαμβάνω	3
receive, παραλαμβάνω	21
received, ἔλαβον (2nd aor. of	
λαμβάνω)	20
reckon, λογίζομαι	10
redeemer, σωτήρ, ὁ	15
regard, ἡγέομαι	26
rejoice, χαίρω	18
relative, συγγενής, - ές	16
release, ἀπολύω	21
remaining, λοιπός	19
remember, μιμνήσκομαι	33
repent, μετανοέω	23
repentance, μετάνοια - ας, ἡ	30
report, ἀκοή	29
report, ἀπαγγέλλω	21
rest, λοιπός	19
resurrection, ἀνάστασις	15
return, ἐπιστρέφω	23
return, ὑποστρέφω	23
reveal, ἀποκαλύπτω	27
rich, πλούσιος, -α, - ον	27
right (direction), δεξιός	20
righteous, δίκαιος	6
righteousness, δικαιοσύνη	12
road, ὁδός	8
rooster, ἀλέκτωρ	15
royal, βασιλικός	6
rule, ἄρχω	13
ruler, ἄρχων	14
ruler, ἡγεμών, -μόνος, ὁ	15
run away, φεύγω	18
S	
sabbath, σάββατον, τό	19
sacrifice, θυσία, - ας, ἡ	26

said, εἶπον (2nd aor. of λέγω) 20	*shepherd*, ποιμήν, -μένος, ὁ 15	*star*, ἀστήρ, ἀστέρος, ὁ, 15
salvation, σωτηρία, ἡ 21	*shine*, φαίνω 25	*steadfastness*, ὑπομονή, ἡ 25
same, αὐτός 11	*shout*, κράζω 18	*still, yet*, ἔτι 13
sanctify, ἁγιάζω 27	*show*, δείκνυμι 33	*stone*, λίθος, ὁ 23
Sanhedrin, συνέδριον 29	*show*, δηλόω 7	*strength*, ἰσχύς, ἰσχύος, ἡ 15
save, σῴζω 4	*sick*, ἀσθενής 16	*strong*, ἰσχυρός, -ά, -όν 8
savior, σωτήρ, σωτῆρος, ὁ 15	*sign*, σημεῖον, τό 19	*such*, τοιοῦτος 12
saw, εἶδον (2nd aor. of ὁράω) 20	*Simon*, Σίμων, Σίμωνος, ὁ 15	*suffer*, πάσχω 22
say, φημί 33	*sin*, ἁμαρτάνω 19	*sufficient*, ἱκανός 22
say, λέγω 2	*sin*, ἁμαρτία 5	*summon*, προσκαλέομαι 26
scholar, γραμματεύς 15	*sinful*, ἁμαρτωλός 16	*sun*, ἥλιος, ὁ 25
scribe, γραμματεύς 15	*sinned*, ἥμαρτον (2nd aor. of	*swear*, ὁμνύω 29
scripture, γραφή 5	ἁμαρτάνω) 20	*swift*, ταχύς, -εῖα 16
sea, θάλασσα 5	*sinner*, ἁμαρτωλός 16	*sword*, μάχαιρα, -ης, ἡ 27
season, καιρός 13	*sister*, ἀδελφη 27	*synagogue*, συναγωγή, ἡ 19
seat, καθίζω 21	*sit down*, κάθημαι 34	**T**
second, δεύτερος ,17	*sit*, καθίζω 21	*take*, λαμβάνω 3
see, βλέπω 2	*six hundred*, ἑξακόσιοι 17	*take away*, αἴρω 18
see, ὁράω 12	*six*, ἕξ 6,17	*take oath*, ὁμνύω 29
seed, σπέρμα, -ατος, τό 14	*sixteen*, δεκαέξ 16,17	*take place*, γίνομαι 10
seek, ζητέω 7	*sixth*, ἕκτος 17	*take up*, αἴρω 18
seem, δοκέω 19	*sixty*, ἑξήκοντα 17	*take up*, ἀναιρέω 29
seize, κρατέω 21	*slanderous*, διάβολος 16	*teach*, διδάσκω 3
self, αὐτός 11	*slave*, δοῦλος 4	*teacher*, διδάσκαλος 19
sell, ἀποδίδωμι 34	*small*, μικρός, -ά, -όν 6	*teaching*, διδαχη 5
send, ἀποστέλλω 12	*smallest*, ἐλάχιστος 16	*tell*, ἀγγέλλω 18
send, πέμπω 3	*so*, δέ 4	*temple*, ἱερόν 4
send out, ἀποστέλλω 12	*so*, τέ 12	*temple*, ναός, ὁ 21
servant, διάκονος 25	*so*, ἄρα 21	*tempt*, πειράζω 24
servant, παῖς, παιδός, ὁ, ἡ 30	*so that*, ἵνα 30	*ten thousand*, μύριοι 17
serve, διακονέω 23	*so that*, ὥστε 21	*ten*, δέκα 10,17
serve, δουλεύω 29	*somehow*, πώς 12	*tenth*, δέκατος 17
service, διακονία 25	*someone*, τις, τις, τι 17	*test*, πειράζω 24
set, ἵστημι 33	*something*, τις, τις, τι 17	*testify*, μαρτυρέω 12
seven thousand,	*son*, υἱός 4	*testimony*, μαρτυρία, ἡ 23
ἑπτακισχίλιοι 17	*soon*, ταχέως (ταχύ) 8	*than, or*, ἤ 9
seven times, ἑπτάκις 17	*soul*, ψυχή 5	*than, or*, ὑπέρ 8
seven, ἑπτά 7,17	*sound*, φωνή 5	*that*, ἐκεῖνος 12
seventh, ἕβδομος 17	*southwest wind*, λίψ, ὁ 14	*that*, ἵνα 30
seventy times, ἑβδομηκοντάκις	*sow*, σπείρω 21	*that* (cf. ὅς), ὅ 12
17	*speak*, λαλέω 7	*that*, ὅπως 20
seventy, ἑβδομήκοντα 17	*spirit*, πνεῦμα, -ατος, τό 14	*that*, ὅς, ἥ, ὅ 12
shall be, ἔσομαι 18	*spiritual*, πνευματικός 27	*that*, ὅτι 7
she, αὐτή 11	*stand by*, παρίστημι 34	*that*, ὡς 12
sheep, πρόβατον, -ου, τό 22	*stand*, ἵστημι 33	*the*, ὁ, τό 4

the, ἡ	5	*tree*, δένδρον	28	*watch*, γρηγορέω	31
then, τότε	12	*tribe*, φυλή, -ῆς, ἡ	25	*water*, ὕδωρ, ὕδατος, τό	14
then, ἄρα	21	*trouble*, θλῖψις, θλίψεως, ἡ	15	*way*, ὁδός	8
there, ἐκεῖ	13	*true*, ἀληθινός	25	*we*, ἡμεῖς	11
therefore, οὖν	8	*true*, ἀληθής	16	*weak*, ἀσθενής	16
therefore, ὥστε	21	*truly*, ἀμήν	12	*weakness*, ἀσθένεια	29
thereupon, τότε	12	*truly*, ναί	25	*wedding*, γάμος	4
these, οὗτος, αὕτη, τοῦτο	12	*trumpet*, σάλπιγξ, ἡ	14	*weep*, κλαίω	22
think, δοκέω	19	*trust*, πίστις, πίστεως, ὁ	15	*well*, καλῶς	8
think, φρονέω	27	*truth*, ἀλήθεια	5	*what type?* ποῖος, -α, -ον	18
think, ἡγέομαι	26	*truthful*, ἀληθής	16	*what?* τίς, τίς, τί	17
third, τρίτος	17	*turn to*, ἐπιστρέφω	23	*when*, ὅτε, ὡς	12
thirty, τριάκοντα	17	*twelve*, δώδεκα	12,17	*when*, ἐάν	30
this, οὗτος, αὕτη, τοῦτο	12	*twenty*, εἴκοσι	17	*whenever*, ὅταν	30
those, ἐκεῖνος	12	*twice*, δίς	17	*where*, ὅπου	13
thought, νοῦς, νοός, ὁ	15	*two hundred*, διακόσιοι	17	*where*, οὗ	30
three hundred, τριακόσιοι	17	*two thousand*, δισχίλιοι	17	*where?* πόθεν	26
three thousand, τρισχίλιοι	17	*two*, δύο, δύσιν	2,17	*wherefore*, διό	20
three times, τρίς	17	**U**		*whether*, εἴτε	26
three, τρεῖς, τρία	3,17	*unbelieving*, ἄπιστος	16	*which?* τίς, τίς, τί	17
threw, ἔβαλον (2nd aor. of		*unclean*, ἀκάθαρτος	16	*while*, ὡς	12
βάλλω)	20	*under*, ὑποκάτω	9	*white*, λευκός	30
throne, θρόνος, ὁ	19	*under*, ὑπό	9	*who*, ὅς, ἥ, ὅ	12
through, διά	9	*understand*, συνίημι	34	*who?* τίς, τίς, τί	17
throw, βάλλω	18	*unending*, αἰώνιος	16	*whoever*, ὅστις, ἥτις, ὅτι	17
throw out, ἐκβάλλω	9	*unrighteousness*, ἀδικία	27	*whole*, ὅλος	13
thus, οὕτως	12	*until*, μέχρι(ς)	9	*whole*, πᾶς, πᾶσα, πᾶν	16
time, καιρός	13	[untranslatable particle] ἄν	13	*whole*, ὑγιής, -ές	16
time, χρόνος, ὁ	20	*up*, ἀνά	9	*whom*, ὅς, ἥ, ὅ	12
to, ἐν, ἐπί, πρός	9	*upon*, ἐπί	9	*widow*, χήρα, -ας, ἡ	27
to be (future tense), ἔσεσθαι	25	*up to*, ἕως, ἄχρι	9	*wilderness*, ἔρημος	8
to be (present tense), εἶναι	25	*upward*, ἄνω	8	*will*, θέλημα, -ατος, τό	14
to one another, ἀλλήλοις	13	**V**		*will*, θέλω	18
today, σήμερον	22	*vessel*, σκεῦος, -ους, το	32	*wind*, ἄνεμος	10
together, σύν	9	*village*, κώμη, - ης, ἡ	27	*wind*, πνεῦμα, - ατος, τό	14
together with, ἅμα	9	*vineyard*, ἀμπελών	15	*wine*, οἶνος, ὁ	25
toil, κοπιάω	33	*virgin*, παρθένος, - ου, ἡ	8	*wisdom*, γνῶσις	26
tomb, μνημεῖον, τό	23	*voice*, φωνή	5	*wisdom*, σοφία, η	20
tongue, γλῶσσα	5	**W**		*wise*, σοφός	8
took, ἔλαβον (2nd aor. of		*wages*, μισθός, -οῦ, ὁ	26	*wish*, βούλομαι	10
λαμβάνω)	20	*waist*, ὀσφῦς, ὀσφύος, ἡ	15	*wish*, θέλω	18
tooth, ὀδούς, -όντος, ὁ	14	*walk*, περιπατέω	7	*with*, μετά, σύν, παρά, πρός	9
touch, ἅπτομαι	22	*warn*, ἐπιτιμάω	26	*without*, χωρίς	9
toward, πρός	9	*was*, ἤμην	12	*witness*, μαρτυρέω	12
town, πόλις, πόλεως, ἡ	15	*watch*, φυλακή, ἡ	21	*witness*, μαρτυρία, ἡ	23

witness, μάρτυς, -τυρος, ὁ	15	worse, χείρων, -ον	16	**Y**			
woe! οὐαί	22	worship, προσκυνέω	19	year, ἔτος, ἔτους, τό	14		
woman, γυνή, γυναικός, ἡ	14	worthy, ἄξιος	22	yes, ναί	25		
wonder, θαυμάζω	21	worthy, ἱκανός	22	you (pl.), ὑμεῖς	11		
word, λόγος	2	wrath, ὀργή, -ῆς, ἡ	23	you (sg.), σύ	11		
word, ῥῆμα, -ατος, τό	14	write, γράφω	2	your (pl.), ὑμέτερος, -α, -ον	13		
work, ἔργον	4	writing, γραφή	5	your (sg.), σός	13		
work, ἐργάζομαι	10	wrong, ἀδικέω	29	yourself, σεαυτοῦ, -ης, --	13		
world, κόσμος	4						

INDEX OF SUBJECTS

485